System Requirements

Hardware (recommended)

Screen dimensions: 1920px x 1080px or higher (full HD or higher)

Processor speed: 2Ghz / multi-core

Broadband / Internet access requirements: 5mb download, 1mb upload (per user)

Hardware (minimum)

Screen dimensions: 1280px x 1024px

Processor speed: 1.5Ghz

Broadband / Internet access requirements: 2mb download, 256kbps upload (per user)

Operating System

Microsoft Windows XP with SP2/Vista/7/8/8.1/10

Microsoft Windows Server 2003/2008/2013

Linux Red Hat, Fedora, SUSE, Ubuntu

Apple Mac OS X

Networking

HTTPS Access (Port 443)

HTTP Access (Port 80)

Software

Oracle Java version 1.7+ (If using our Java client)

For full system requirement details, please visit the Practice Labs User Guide found under the Support tab.

CompTIA®
Network+®
Deluxe Study Guide
Fifth Edition

CompTIA®
Network+®

Deluxe Study Guide

Exam N10-008

Fifth Edition

Todd Lammle

Acknowledgments

Kim Wimpsett was the development editor of this Sybex CompTIA series as with the previous three. Thank you, Kim, for your patience and kindness and for working so hard on this book with me once again, and I look forward to any book that has Kim on the editorial board.

Kenyon Brown was the acquisitions editor for this book. Thank you, Kenyon, for making this fourth book in the series a reality.

In addition, Christine O'Connor was an excellent managing editor, and she worked hard to get the book done as quickly as possible. I have worked with Christine for well over a decade and I am always very pleased when I hear that she will be working with me on yet a new project. Barath Kumar Rajasekaran, who is a content refinement specialist, did a great job of keeping this book on track with both authors; thank you!

As with Kim and Christine, I have also worked with Judy Flynn for more than a decade. She knows my work so well she can provide some technical advice and also understands how I write and can wordsmith right along with my tone and voice. Thank you, Judy!

Troy McMillan literally hashed and rehashed each topic in this guide with me at all hours of the day and night. Thank you, Troy, yet again!

Todd Montgomery really came through when I was in a tight spot and helped me finalize Chapters 21–25 as well as a few other chapters. Thank you, Todd—you're a lifesaver!

Chris Crayton tech edited and reviewed each topic in this guide, scrutinizing the material until we both agreed it was verifiably solid. Thank you, Chris!

About the Author

Todd Lammle is the authority on CompTIA and Cisco certifications and is certified in most CompTIA and Cisco certification categories.

He is a world-renowned author, speaker, trainer, and consultant. Todd has three decades of experience working with LANs, WANs, and large enterprise licensed and unlicensed wireless networks, and lately he's been concentrating on implementing large Cisco Security networks using Snort, Firepower/FTD, ISE, and Stealthwatch.

His years of real-world experience are evident in his writing; he is not just an author but an experienced networking engineer with very practical experience from working on the largest networks in the world, at such companies as Xerox, Hughes Aircraft, Texaco, AAA, Cisco, and Toshiba, among many others.

Todd has published over 100 books, including the very popular *CCNA: Cisco Certified Network Associate Study Guide, CompTIA Network+ Study Guide, CCNA Wireless Study Guide, CCNA Data Center Study Guide, SSFIPS (Firepower), and CCNP Security*, all from Sybex.

He runs an international consulting and training company based in Colorado, where he spends his free time in the mountains playing with his golden retrievers.

You can reach Todd through his website at www.lammle.com.

About the Technical Editor

Chris Crayton is a technical consultant, trainer, author, and industry-leading technical editor. He has worked as a computer technology and networking instructor, information security director, network administrator, network engineer, and PC specialist. Chris has authored several print and online books on PC repair, CompTIA A+ exam, CompTIA Security+ exam, and Microsoft Windows. He has also served as technical editor and content contributor on numerous technical titles for several of the leading publishing companies. He holds numerous industry certifications, has been recognized with many professional and teaching awards, and has served as a state-level SkillsUSA final competition judge.

Contents at a Glance

Contents

Introduction

If you're like most of us in the networking community, you probably have one or more network certifications. If that's you, you're very wise in choosing a CompTIA Network+ (N10-008) certification to proudly add to your repertoire because this achievement will make you all the more valuable as an employee.

In these challenging economic times, keeping ahead of the competition—even standing out among your present colleagues—could make a big difference in whether you gain a promotion or possibly keep your job instead of being the one who gets laid off! Or maybe this is your first attempt at certification because you've decided to venture into a new career in information technology (IT). You've realized that getting into the IT sector is a good way to go because as the information age marches on, the demand for knowledgeable professionals in this dynamic field will only intensify dramatically.

Either way, certification is one of the best things you can do for your career if you are working in, or want to break into, the networking profession because it proves that you know what you're talking about regarding the subjects in which you're certified. It also powerfully endorses you as a professional in a way that's very similar to a physician being board-certified in a certain area of expertise.

In this book, you'll find out what the Network+ exam is all about because each chapter covers a part of the exam. I've included some great review questions at the end of each chapter to help crystallize the information you learned and solidly prepare you to ace the exam.

A really cool thing about working in IT is that it's constantly evolving, so there are always new things to learn and fresh challenges to master. Once you obtain your Network+ certification and discover that you're interested in taking it further by getting into more complex networking (and making more money), the Cisco CCNA certification is definitely your next step; you can get the skinny on that and even more in-depth certifications on my blog at www.lammle.com.

 For Network+ training with Todd Lammle, both instructor-led and online, please see www.lammle.com.

What Is the Network+ Certification?

Network+ is a certification developed by the Computing Technology Industry Association (CompTIA) that exists to provide resources and education for the computer and technology community. This is the same body that developed the A+ exam for PC technicians.

The Network+ exam was designed to test the skills of network technicians with 18 to 24 months of experience in the field. It tests areas of networking technologies such as the definition of a protocol, the Open Systems Interconnection (OSI) model and its layers, and the concepts of network design and implementation—the minimum knowledge required for working on a network and some integral prerequisites for network design and implementation.

Why Become Network+ Certified?

Because CompTIA is a well-respected developer of vendor-neutral industry certifications, becoming Network+ certified proves you're competent in the specific areas covered by the Network+ objectives.

Four major benefits are associated with becoming Network+ certified:

Proof of Professional Achievement   Networking professionals are pretty competitive when it comes to collecting more certifications than their peers. And because the Network+ certification broadly covers the entire field of networking, technicians want this certification a lot more than they want just Microsoft certifications—Network+ is a lot more prestigious and valuable. Because it's rare to gain something that's worth a lot with little effort, I'll be honest—preparing for the Network+ exam isn't exactly a lazy day at the beach. (However, beaches do happen to be really high on my personal list of great places to study!) And people in IT know that it isn't all that easy to pass the Network+ exam, so they'll definitely respect you more and know that you've achieved a certain level of expertise about vendor-independent, networking-related subjects.

Opportunity for Advancement   We all like to get ahead in our careers—advancement results in more responsibility and prestige, and it usually means a fatter paycheck, greater opportunities, and additional options. In the IT sector, a great way to make sure all that good stuff happens is by earning a lot of technology certifications, including Network+.

Fulfillment of Training Requirements   Network+, because of its wide-reaching industry support, is recognized as a baseline of networking information. Some companies actually specify the possession of a Network+ certification as a job requirement before they'll even consider hiring you, or it may be specified as a goal to be met before your next review.

Customer Confidence   As companies discover the CompTIA advantage, they will undoubtedly require qualified staff to achieve these certifications. Many companies outsource their work to consulting firms with experience working with security. Firms that have certified staff have a definite advantage over firms that don't.

How to Become Network+ Certified

As this book goes to press, Pearson VUE is the sole Network+ exam provider. The following is the necessary contact information and exam-specific details for registering. Exam pricing might vary by country or by CompTIA membership.

Vendor	Website	Phone Number
Pearson VUE	https://www.pearsonvue.com/comptia	US and Canada: 877-551-PLUS (7587)

When you schedule the exam, you'll receive instructions regarding appointment and cancellation procedures, ID requirements, and information about the testing center location. In addition, you'll receive a registration and payment confirmation letter. Exams can be scheduled up to six weeks out or as soon as the next day (or, in some cases, even the same day).

 Exam prices and codes may vary based on the country in which the exam is administered. For detailed pricing and exam registration procedures, refer to CompTIA's website at www.comptia.org.

After you've successfully passed your Network+ exam, CompTIA will award you a certification. Within four to six weeks of passing the exam, you'll receive your official CompTIA Network+ certificate and ID card. (If you don't receive these within eight weeks of taking the test, contact CompTIA directly using the information found in your registration packet.)

Tips for Taking the Network+ Exam

Here are some general tips for taking your exam successfully:

- Bring two forms of ID with you. One must be a photo ID, such as a driver's license. The other can be a major credit card or a passport. Both forms must include a signature.

- Arrive early at the exam center so you can relax and review your study materials, particularly tables and lists of exam-related information. After you are ready to enter the testing room, you will need to leave everything outside; you won't be able to bring any materials into the testing area.

- Read the questions carefully. Don't be tempted to jump to an early conclusion. Make sure you know exactly what each question is asking.

- Don't leave any unanswered questions. Unanswered questions are scored against you. There will be questions with multiple correct responses. When there is more than one correct answer, a message at the bottom of the screen will prompt you to either "choose two" or "choose all that apply." Be sure to read the messages displayed to know how many correct answers you must choose.

- When answering multiple-choice questions you're not sure about, use a process of elimination to get rid of the obviously incorrect answers first. Doing so will improve your odds if you need to make an educated guess.

- On form-based tests (nonadaptive), because the hard questions will take the most time, save them for last. You can move forward and backward through the exam.

Who Should Read This Book?

You—if want to pass the Network+ exam, and pass it confidently! This book is chock-full of the exact information you need and directly maps to Network+ exam objectives, so if you use it to study for the exam, your odds of passing shoot way up.

And in addition to including every bit of knowledge you need to learn to pass the exam, I've included some really great tips and solid wisdom to equip you even further to successfully work in the real IT world.

What Does This Book Cover?

This book covers everything you need to know to pass the CompTIA Network+ exam. But in addition to studying the book, it's a good idea to practice on an actual network if you can.
  Here's a list of the 25 chapters in this book:

Chapter 1, "Introduction to Networks"   This chapter includes an introduction to networks and an overview of the most common physical network topologies you'll find in today's networks.

Chapter 2, "The Open Systems Interconnection Specifications"   This chapter covers the OSI model, what it is, what happens at each of its layers, and how each layer works.

Chapter 3, "Networking Connectors and Wiring Standards"   This chapter covers the various networking media and topologies, plus the cable types and properties used in today's networks.

Chapter 4, "The Current Ethernet Specifications"   This chapter covers how a basic Ethernet LAN works and describes and categorizes the different Ethernet specifications.

Chapter 5, "Networking Devices"   It's important for you to understand all the various devices used in today's networks, and this chapter will describe how hubs, routers, switches, and some other devices work within a network.

Chapter 6, "Introduction to the Internet Protocol"   This is your introduction to the all-important IP protocol stack.

Chapter 7, "IP Addressing"   This chapter will take up from where Chapter 6 left off and move into IP addressing. It also contains information about public versus private addressing and DHCP.

Chapter 8, "IP Subnetting, Troubleshooting IP, and Introduction to NAT"   This chapter will continue the subject from Chapter 7 and also will tackle IP subnetting. But no worries here—I've worked hard to make this not-so-popular-yet-vital topic as painless as possible.

Chapter 9, "Introduction to IP Routing"   This is an introduction to routing that basically covers what routers do and how they do it. Along with Chapter 10 and Chapter 11, this chapter covers routing and switching in much more detail than what is necessary to meet the CompTIA Network+ objectives because this knowledge is so critical to grasp when working with today's networks.

Chapter 10, "Routing Protocols"   This chapter goes into detail describing the protocols that run on routers and that update routing tables to create a working map of the network.

Chapter 11, "Switching and Virtual LANs"   This chapter covers layer 2 switching, the Spanning Tree Protocol (STP), and virtual LANs. I went deeper than needed for the exam with the routing chapters, and in this chapter I'll cover switching and virtual LANs (which are also vital in today's corporate networks) more thoroughly as well.

Chapter 12, "Wireless Networking"   Because wireless is so important for both home and business networks today, this chapter is loaded with all the information you need to be successful at wireless networking at home and work.

Chapter 13, "Using Statistics and Sensors to Ensure Network Availability"   In this chapter you'll learn what sort of data you should be monitoring and some of the ways to do so.

Chapter 14, "Organizational Documents and Policies"   In this chapter you'll learn that plans and procedures should be developed to manage operational issues such as change management, incident response, disaster recovery, business continuity, and the system life cycle. You'll also learn the standard operating procedures that should be developed to guide each of these processes.

Chapter 15, "High Availability and Disaster Recovery"   In this chapter you will learn about redundancy concepts, fault tolerance, and the process of disaster recovery.

Chapter 16, "Common Security Concepts"   In this chapter you will learn the basic concepts, terms, and principles that all network professionals should understand to secure an enterprise network.

Chapter 17, "Common Types of Attacks"   In this chapter you will learn the common types of attacks that all network professionals should understand to secure an enterprise network.

Chapter 18, "Network Hardening Techniques"   In this chapter you'll learn best practices for hardening devices and for hardening the network environment in which these devices reside. At the end of the chapter, you'll learn about the newest challenge to secure, the Internet of Things (IoT).

Chapter 19, "Remote Access Security"   In this chapter you'll learn the importance of providing both fault tolerance and high availability. You'll also learn about VPN architectures. These include site-to-site VPNs, client-to-site VPNs, clientless VPNs, split tunnel vs. full VPN, and SSH VPNs.

Chapter 20, "Physical Security"   In this chapter you will learn the basic concepts, terms, and principles that all network professionals should understand to physically secure a network.

Chapter 21, "Data Center Architecture and Cloud Concepts"   In this chapter, I'll talk a lot about the documentation aspects of network administration. The chapter will start off discussing physical diagrams and schematics and move on to the logical form as well as configuration-management documentation. You'll learn about the importance of these diagrams as well as the simple to complex forms they can take and the tools used to create them—from pencil and paper to high-tech AutoCAD schematics. You'll also find out a great deal about creating performance baselines.

Chapter 22, "Ensuring Network Availability"   In this chapter you'll learn about network availability and some of the ways to achieve a stable network. I'll talk about how environmental parameters, CPU load, and memory utilization can cause low-performance problems.

Chapter 23, "Cable Connectivity Issues and Tools"   Specialized tasks require specialized tools, and installing network components is no exception. We use some of these tools on an everyday basis, but most of the hardware tools I'll be covering in this chapter are used mainly in the telecommunications industry.

Chapter 24, "Network Troubleshooting Methodology"   In this chapter, you'll learn about all things troubleshooting, such as how to sleuth out and solve a lot of network problems.

Chapter 25, "Network Software Tools and Commands"   This chapter introduces you to the network tools you will use to help you run your networks. Specialized tasks require specialized tools and installing network components is no exception. We use some of these tools, like network scanners, on an everyday basis, but as with the hardware tools covered in Chapter 23, most of the software tools I'll be covering in this chapter are used mainly in the telecommunications industry.

What's Included in the Book

I've included several study tools throughout the book:

Assessment Test   At the end of this introduction is an assessment test that you can use to check your readiness for the exam. Take this test before you start reading the book; it will help you determine the areas you might need to brush up on. The answers to the assessment test questions appear on a separate page after the last question of the test. Each answer includes an explanation and a note telling you the chapter in which the material appears.

Objective Map and Opening List of Objectives   Later in this introduction is an objective map showing you where each of the exam objectives is covered in this book. In addition, each chapter opens with a list of the exam objectives it covers. Use these to see exactly where each of the exam topics is covered.

Exam Essentials   Each chapter includes a number of exam essentials. These are the key topics you should take from the chapter in terms of areas to focus on when preparing for the exam.

Written Lab   Each chapter includes a written lab. These are short exercises that map to the exam objectives. The answers to these can be found in Appendix A.

Chapter Review Questions   To test your knowledge as you progress through the book, there are review questions at the end of each chapter. As you finish each chapter, answer the review questions and then check your answers—the correct answers and explanations are in Appendix B. You can go back to reread the section that deals with each question you got wrong to ensure that you answer correctly the next time you're tested on the material.

Interactive Online Learning Environment and Test Bank

The interactive online learning environment that accompanies *CompTIA Network+ Study Guide: Exam N10-008* provides a test bank with study tools to help you prepare for the certification exam and increase your chances of passing it the first time! The test bank includes the following tools:

Sample Tests   All of the questions in this book are provided, including the assessment test, which you'll find at the end of this introduction, and the chapter tests that include the review questions at the end of each chapter. In addition, there are six practice exams. Use these questions to test your knowledge of the study guide material. The online test bank runs on multiple devices.

Flashcards   Approximately 300 questions are provided in digital flashcard format (a question followed by a single correct answer). You can use the flashcards to reinforce your learning and provide last-minute test prep before the exam.

Glossary   A glossary of key terms from this book and their definitions are available as a fully searchable PDF.

NOTE

Go to www.wiley.com/go/sybextestprep to register and gain access to this interactive online learning environment and test bank with study tools.

How to Use This Book

If you want a solid foundation for the serious effort of preparing for the Network+ exam, then look no further because I've spent countless hours putting together this book with the sole intention of helping you pass it!

This book is loaded with valuable information, and you will get the most out of your study time if you understand how I put the book together. Here's a list that describes how to approach studying:

1. Take the assessment test immediately following this introduction. (The answers are at the end of the test, but no peeking!) It's okay if you don't know any of the answers—that's what this book is for. Carefully read over the explanation for any question you get wrong and make note of the chapter where that material is covered.

2. Study each chapter carefully, making sure you fully understand the information and the exam objectives listed at the beginning of each one. Again, pay extra-close attention to any chapter that includes material covered in questions you missed on the assessment test.

3. Complete the written lab at the end of each chapter. Do *not* skip these written exercises because they directly map to the CompTIA objectives and what you've got to have nailed down to meet them.

4. Answer all the review questions related to each chapter. Specifically note any questions that confuse you, and study the corresponding sections of the book again. And don't just skim these questions—make sure you understand each answer completely.

5. Try your hand at the practice exams. Before you take your test, be sure to visit my website for questions, videos, audios, and other useful information.

6. Test yourself using all the electronic flashcards. This is a brand-new and updated flashcard program to help you prepare for the latest CompTIA Network+ exam, and it is a really great study tool.

I tell you no lies—learning every bit of the material in this book is going to require applying yourself with a good measure of discipline. So try to set aside the same time period every day to study, and select a comfortable and quiet place to do so. If you work hard, you will be surprised at how quickly you learn this material.

If you follow the steps listed here and study with the review questions, practice exams, electronic flashcards, and all the written labs, you would almost have to try to fail the CompTIA Network+ exam. However, studying for the Network+ exam is like training for a marathon—if you don't go for a good run every day, you're not likely to finish very well.

N10-008 Exam Objectives

Speaking of objectives, you're probably pretty curious about those, right? CompTIA asked groups of IT professionals to fill out a survey rating the skills they felt were important in their jobs, and the results were grouped into objectives for the exam and divided into five domains.

This table gives you the extent by percentage that each domain is represented on the actual examination.

Objective	Percentage of Exam
1.0 Networking Fundamentals	24%
2.0 Network Implementations	19%
3.0 Network Operations	16%
4.0 Network Security	19%
5.0 Network Troubleshooting	22%

Objective Map

The following table shows where each objective is covered in the book.

Objective Number	Objective	Chapter
1.0	**Networking Fundamentals**	
1.1	Compare and contrast the Open Systems Interconnection (OSI) model layers and encapsulation concepts.	2, 6
1.2	Explain the characteristics of network topologies and network types.	1
1.3	Summarize the types of cables and connectors and explain which is the appropriate type for a solution.	3, 4
1.4	Given a scenario, configure a subnet and use appropriate IP addressing schemes.	7, 8
1.5	Explain common ports and protocols, their application, and encrypted alternatives.	6
1.6	Explain the use and purpose of network services.	5
1.7	Explain basic corporate and datacenter network architecture.	21
1.8	Summarize cloud concepts and connectivity options.	21

Assessment Test

1. What is the basic purpose of a local area network (LAN)?
   A. To interconnect networks in several different buildings
   B. To connect one or more computers together so they can share resources
   C. To interconnect 2 to 10 routers
   D. To make routers unnecessary

2. You need a topology that is easy to troubleshoot and scalable. Which would you use?
   A. Bus
   B. Star
   C. Mesh
   D. Ring

3. IP resides at which layer of the OSI model?
   A. Application
   B. Data Link
   C. Network
   D. Physical

4. Layer 2 of the OSI model is named _____.
   A. Application layer
   B. Network layer
   C. Transport layer
   D. Data Link layer

5. Which RG rating of coax is used for cable modems?
   A. RG-59
   B. RG-58
   C. RG-6
   D. RG-8

6. Which UTP wiring uses four twisted wire pairs (eight wires) and is rated for 250 MHz?
   A. Category 3 UTP
   B. Category 5 STP
   C. Category 5 UTP
   D. Category 6 UTP

7. If you are running half-duplex Internet, which of the following is true? (Choose all that apply.)

   A. Your digital signal cannot transmit and receive data at the same time.

   B. Hosts use the CSMA/CD protocol to detect collisions.

   C. The physical connection consists of one wire pair.

   D. None of the above.

8. You need to connect a hub to a switch. You don't like this idea because you know that it will create congestion. What type of cable do you need to use to connect the hub to the switch?

   A. EtherIP

   B. Crossover

   C. Straight-through

   D. Cable Sense, Multiple Access

9. Your boss asks you why you just put in a requisition to buy a bunch of switches. He said he just bought you a bunch of hubs five years ago! Why did you buy the switches?

   A. Because each switch port is its own collision domain.

   B. The cable connecting devices to the hub wore out, and switches were cheaper than new cable.

   C. There were too many broadcast domains, and a switch breaks up broadcast domains by default.

   D. The hubs kept repeating signals but quit recognizing frames and data structures.

10. Which device would connect network segments together, creating separate collision domains for each segment but only a single broadcast domain?

    A. Hub

    B. Router

    C. Switch

    D. Modem

11. Most Application layer protocols use only UDP or TCP at the Transport layer. Which of the following could use both?

    A. TCP

    B. Microsoft Word

    C. Telnet

    D. DNS

12. HTTP, FTP, and Telnet work at which layer of the OSI model?

    A. Application

    B. Presentation

    C. Session

    D. Transport

13. IPv6 uses multiple types of addresses. Which of the following would describe an anycast address used by an IPv6 host?

   A. Communications are routed to the most distant host that shares the same address.

   B. Packets are delivered to all interfaces identified by the address. This is also called one-to-many addressing.

   C. This address identifies multiple interfaces, and the anycast packet is only delivered to one address. This address can also be called one-to-one-of-many.

   D. Anycast is a type of broadcast.

14. Which of the following IP addresses are not allowed on the Internet? (Choose all that apply.)

   A. 11.255.255.1

   B. 10.1.1.1

   C. 172.33.255.0

   D. 192.168.0.1

15. What is the subnetwork address for a host with the IP address 200.10.5.168/28?

   A. 200.10.5.156

   B. 200.10.5.132

   C. 200.10.5.160

   D. 200.10.5.0

   E. 200.10.5.255

16. If you wanted to verify the local IP stack on your computer, what would you do?

   A. Ping 127.0.0.0

   B. Ping 127.0.0.1

   C. Telnet 1.0.0.127

   D. Ping 169.5.3.10

   E. Telnet 255.255.255.255

17. The OSI model uses an encapsulation method to describe the data as it is encapsulated at each layer. What is the encapsulation named at the Data Link layer?

   A. Bits

   B. Packets

   C. Frames

   D. Data

   E. Segments

18. Where does a Data Link layer frame have to carry a Network layer packet if the packet is destined for a remote network?

   A. Router

   B. Physical medium

   C. Switch

   D. Another host

19. Which of the following are not distance-vector routing protocols? (Choose all that apply.)

    A. OSPF

    B. RIP

    C. RIPv2

    D. IS-IS

20. Which of the following uses both distance-vector and link-state properties?

    A. IGRP

    B. OSPF

    C. RIPv1

    D. EIGRP

    E. IS-IS

21. You need to break up broadcast domains in a layer 2 switched network. What strategy will you use?

    A. Implement a loop-avoidance scheme.

    B. Create a flatter network structure using switches.

    C. Create a VLAN.

    D. Disable the spanning tree on individual ports.

22. Why do most switches run the Spanning Tree Protocol by default?

    A. It monitors how the network is functioning.

    B. It stops data from forwarding until all devices are updated.

    C. It prevents switching loops.

    D. It manages the VLAN database.

23. Which of the following describes MIMO correctly?

    A. A protocol that requires acknowledgment of each and every frame

    B. A data-transmission technique in which several frames are sent by several antennas over several paths and are then recombined by another set of antennas

    C. A modulation technique that allows more than one data rate

    D. A technique that packs smaller packets into a single unit, which improves throughput

24. Which practices help secure your wireless access points from unauthorized access? (Choose two.)

    A. Assigning a private IP address to the AP

    B. Changing the default SSID value

    C. Configuring a new administrator password

    D. Changing the mixed-mode setting to single mode

    E. Configuring traffic filtering

25. You can view top talkers on your network by using which service listed below?

A. NetFlow

B. SIEM

C. Syslog

D. SNMP

26. You want to see the normal operating capacity for your whole network. Which chart can refer to the standard level?

A. Normal

B. Target

C. Baseline

D. Utilization

27. Which of the following are device hardening techniques? (Choose three.)

A. Remove unnecessary applications.

B. Block unrequired ports.

C. Deploy an access control vestibule.

D. Disable unnecessary services.

28. You want to automatically log users out that that have been logged in for a specified period without activity, so which policy would you configure?

A. Password complexity

B. Password history

C. Password length

D. Authentication period

29. Which protocol will help you have redundancy with your physical routers?

A. FHRP

B. NAT

C. NAC

D. CMS

30. Which of the following provides a method to join multiple physical switches into a single logical switching unit?

A. Stacking

B. Daisy chaining

C. Segmenting

D. Federating

31. An attack that no one knows about has just started coming into your corporate network in real time. What is this called?

    A. RGE

    B. Right Now Attack

    C. Nothing; just escalate to a senior tech ASAP

    D. Zero-day

32. What database describes each entry of a security vulnerability in detail using a number and letter system?

    A. ISACA

    B. WHOIS

    C. CVE

    D. NIST

33. Someone calls you and asks for your mother's maiden name because a credit card company is having problems with your account. You give them this information and later find out that you were scammed. What type of attack is this?

    A. Phishing

    B. Calling scam

    C. Analog scam

    D. Trust-exploration attack

    E. On-path attack

    F. Rogue access point

34. Which of the following are types of denial of service attacks? (Choose all that apply.)

    A. Ping of Death

    B. Stacheldraht

    C. SYN flood

    D. Virus FloodSyn

35. Which of the following is NOT referred to as whitelisting? (Choose three.)

    A. Implicit allow

    B. Least privilege

    C. Implicit deny

    D. Need to know

36. You want to grant rights and permissions for a group of users. What type of access control describes granting rights and permissions required for users to perform their job?

    A. MAC

    B. RBAC

    C. DAC

    D. BBAC

37. Which of the following allow you access to the GUI through a remote connection? (Choose all that apply.)

A. RDP

B. LogMeIn

C. SSH

D. GoToMyPC

38. Split tunnel and full tunnel are examples of which type of VPN?

A. Site-to-site

B. Client-to-site

C. RDP VPN

D. Clientless VPN

39. Which of the following occurs when an illegitimate user is allowed access in a biometric system?

A. False negative

B. True negative

C. True positive

D. False positive

40. Which of the following are not considered an access control vestibule? (Choose three.)

A. Trapdoor

B. Mantrap

C. Smart door

D. Turnstile

41. You have just tested your theory of a problem to determine the cause. Based on the standard troubleshooting methodology, what is your next step?

A. Question the obvious.

B. Establish a theory of probable cause.

C. Establish a plan of action to resolve the problem and identify potential effects.

D. Verify full system functionality, and if applicable, implement preventative measures.

42. Which network performance optimization technique can delay packets that meet certain criteria to guarantee usable bandwidth for other applications?

A. Traffic shaping

B. Jitter control

C. Logical network mapping

D. Load balancing

E. Access lists

43. Which of the following is a software management application running on servers that analyzes the received information from your network and puts the information in a type of phone book of information?

A. Syslog

B. NetFlow

C. SPAN

D. SNMP

44. Which of the following is an Application layer protocol that provides a message format for agents on a variety of devices to communicate with network management stations (NMSs)?

A. Syslog

B. NetFlow

C. SPAN

D. SNMP

45. You are using a TDR. Which of the following actions can you do with this device? (Choose all that apply.)

A. Estimate cable lengths.

B. Find splice and connector locations and their associated loss amounts.

C. Display unused services.

D. Define cable-impedance characteristics.

46. Which of the following is not considered a cabling issue?

A. Crosstalk

B. Shorts

C. Open impedance mismatch

D. DNS configurations

47. What is step 7 of the seven-step troubleshooting methodology?

A. Establish a theory of probable cause.

B. Implement the solution or escalate as necessary.

C. Establish a plan of action to resolve the problem and identify potential effects.

D. Document findings, actions, outcomes, and lessons learned.

48. What is step 4 of the seven-step troubleshooting methodology?

A. Establish a theory of probable cause.

B. Implement the solution or escalate as necessary.

C. Establish a plan of action to resolve the problem and identify potential effects.

D. Document findings, actions, outcomes, and lessons learned.

49. Which two `arp` utility switches perform the same function?

   A.   –g

   B.   –Z

   C.   –d

   D.   –a

   E.   –h

   F.   –b

50. You want to see a table that tells packets a direction in which to flow. Which command will show you this table?

   A.   route print

   B.   ping

   C.   show telnet

   D.   show table direction

Answers to AssessmentTest

1. B. LANs generally have a geographic scope of a single building or smaller. They can be simple (two hosts) to complex (with thousands of hosts). See Chapter 1 for more information.

2. B. Star topologies are the easiest to troubleshoot and can easily scale to large sizes. See Chapter 1 for more information.

3. C. IP is a Network layer protocol. HTTPS is an example of an Application layer protocol, Ethernet is an example of a Data Link layer protocol, and T1 can be considered a Physical layer protocol. See Chapter 2 for more information.

4. D. Layer 2 of the OSI model is the Data Link layer, which provides the physical transmission of the data and handles error notification, network topology, and flow control. See Chapter 2 for more information.

5. C. Cable modems use RG-6 coax cables. See Chapter 3 for more information.

6. D. To get the high data-transfer speed, like 1 Gbps, you need to use a wire standard that is highly rated, such as Category 5e, 6, 7 and 8. See Chapter 3 for more information.

7. A, B, C. With half-duplex, you are using one wire pair with a digital signal either transmitting or receiving (but not both at once). Carrier Sense Multiple Access with Collision Detection (CSMA/CD) helps packets that are transmitted simultaneously from different hosts share bandwidth evenly. See Chapter 4 for more information.

8. B. To connect two switches together or a hub to a switch, you need a crossover cable. See Chapter 4 for more information.

9. A. For the most part, switches are not cheap; however, one of the biggest benefits of using switches instead of hubs in your internetwork is that each switch port is actually its own collision domain. A hub creates one large collision domain. Switches still can't break up broadcast domains (do you know which devices do?). Hubs do not recognize frames and data structures but switches do. See Chapter 5 for more information.

10. C. A switch creates separate collision domains for each port but does not break up broadcast domains by default. See Chapter 5 for more information.

11. D. DNS uses TCP for zone exchanges between servers and UDP when a client is trying to resolve a hostname to an IP address. See Chapter 6 for more information.

12. A. HTTP, FTP, and Telnet use TCP at the Transport layer; however, they are all Application layer protocols, so the Application layer is the best answer for this question. See Chapter 6 for more information.

13. C. Anycast is a newer type of communication that replaces broadcasts in IPv4. Anycast addresses identify multiple interfaces, which is the same as multicast; however, the big

difference is that the anycast packet is delivered to only one address: the first one it finds defined in terms of routing distance. This address can also be called one-to-one-of-many. See Chapter 7 for more information.

14. B, D. The addresses in the ranges 10.0.0.0 through 10.255.255.255 and 172.16.0.0 through 172.31.255.255 as well as 192.168.0.0 through 192.168.255.255 are all considered private, based on RFC 1918. Use of these addresses on the Internet is prohibited so that they can be used simultaneously in different administrative domains without concern for conflict. See Chapter 7 for more details on IP addressing and information on private IP addresses.

15. C. This is a pretty simple question. A /28 is 255.255.255.240, which means that our block size is 16 in the fourth octet. 0, 16, 32, 48, 64, 80, 96, 112, 128, 144, 160, 176, and so on. The host is in the subnet 160. See Chapter 8 for more information.

16. B. To test the local stack on your host, ping the loopback interface of 127.0.0.1. See Chapter 8 for more information.

17. C. The Data Link layer is responsible for encapsulating IP packets into frames and for providing logical network addresses. See Chapter 9 for more information.

18. A. Packets specifically have to be carried to a router in order to be routed through a network. On your local computer, the IP address of this router is displayed as the gateway address. See Chapter 9 for more information.

19. A, D. RIP and RIPv2 are distance-vector routing protocols. OSPF and IS-IS are link-state protocols. See Chapter 10 for more information.

20. D. EIGRP is called a hybrid routing protocol because it uses the characteristics of both distance-vector and link-state routing protocols. See Chapter 10 for more information.

21. C. Virtual LANs (VLANs) break up broadcast domains in layer 2 switched internetworks. See Chapter 11 for more information.

22. C. The Spanning Tree Protocol (STP) was designed to stop layer 2 loops. All enterprise model switches have STP by default. See Chapter 11 for more information.

23. B. Part of the 802.11n wireless standard, MIMO sends multiple frames by several antennas over several paths; they are then recombined by another set of antennas to optimize throughput and multipath resistance. This is called spatial multiplexing. See Chapter 12 for more information.

24. B, C. At a minimum, you need to change the default SSID value on each AP and configure new usernames and passwords on the AP. See Chapter 12 for more information.

25. A. NetFlow statistics can analyze the traffic on your network by showing the major users of the network, meaning top talkers, top listeners, top protocols, and so on. See Chapter 13 for more information.

26. C. In networking, baseline can refer to the standard level of performance of a certain device or to the normal operating capacity for your whole network. See Chapter 13 for more information.

27. A, B, D. An access control vestibule is an access control solution, not a device hardening technique. See Chapter 14 for more information.

28. D. Authentication period controls how long a user can remain logged in. If a user remains logged in for the specified period without activity, the user will be automatically logged out. See Chapter 14 for more information.

29. A. First-hop redundancy protocol (FHRP) works by giving you a way to configure more than one physical router to appear as if they were only a single logical one. This makes client configuration and communication easier because you can simply configure a single default gateway and the host machine can use its standard protocols to communicate. See Chapter 15 for more information.

30. A. Switch stacking is the process of connecting multiple switches together (usually in a stack) to be managed as a single switch. See Chapter 15 for more information.

31. D. This condition is known as a zero-day attack because it is the first day the virus has been released and therefore no known fix exists. This term may also be applied to an operating system bug that has not been corrected. This can turn into a Resume Generating Event (RGE) quickly! See Chapter 16 for more information.

32. C. A database of known vulnerabilities using this classification system is called Common Vulnerabilities and Exposures (CVE). It is maintained by the MITRE Corporation and each entry describes a vulnerability in detail, using a number and letter system to describe what it endangers, the environment it requires to be successful in, and in many cases the proper mitigation. See Chapter 16 for more information.

33. A. Social engineering, or phishing, refers to the act of attempting to illegally obtain sensitive information by pretending to be a credible source. Phishing usually takes one of two forms: an email or a phone call. See Chapter 17 for more information.

34. A, B, C. A denial of service (DoS) attack prevents users from accessing the system. All of the options are possible DoS attacks except Virus FloodSyn. See Chapter 17 for more information.

35. A, B, D. Implicit deny means that all traffic is denied unless it is specifically allowed by a rule. This is also called whitelisting or allow listing in that you are creating a whitelist or allow list of allowed traffic with the denial of all other traffic. See Chapter 18 for more information.

36. B. Role-based access control (RBAC) is commonly used in networks to simplify the process of assigning new users the permissions required to perform a job role. In this arrangement, users are organized by job role into security groups, which are then granted the rights and permissions required to perform that job. See Chapter 18 for more information.

37. A, B, D. A remote desktop connection gives one access to the desktop. SSH provides access to a command prompt. See Chapter 19 for more information.

38. B. When a client-to-site VPN is created, it is possible to do so in two ways, split tunnel and full tunnel. The difference is whether the user uses the VPN for connecting to the Internet as well as for connecting to the office. See Chapter 19 for more information.

39. D. One of the issues with biometrics is the occurrence of false positives and false negatives. A false positive is when a user that should not be allowed access is indeed allowed access. A false negative, on the other hand, is when an authorized individual is denied passage by mistake. See Chapter 20 for more information.

40. A, C, D. An access control vestibule (previously known as a mantrap) is used to control access to the vestibule of a building. It is a series of two doors with a small room between them. The user is authenticated at the first door and then allowed into the room. At that point, additional verification will occur (such as a guard visually identifying the person) and then they are allowed through the second door. See Chapter 20 for more information.

41. C. Based on the standard troubleshooting methodology, the next step would be to establish a plan of action to resolve the problem and identify potential effects. See Chapter 21 for more information.

42. A. Traffic shaping, also known as packet shaping, is a form of bandwidth optimization. See Chapter 21 for more information.

43. B. NetFlow shows which devices are talking to each other and what the traffic flows look like; adds timestamps, traffic peaks, and valleys; and produces nice charts and graphs of the data flowing through your network. See Chapter 22 for more information.

44. D. SNMP agents send messages to the NMS station, which then either reads or writes information in the database that's stored on the NMS and called a management information base (MIB). See Chapter 22 for more information.

45. A, B, D. Due to sensitivity to any variation and impedance to cabling, options A, B, and D are all reasons you'd use a time-domain reflectometer (TDR). See Chapter 23 for more information.

46. D. Because most of today's networks still consist of large amounts of copper cable, they can continue to suffer from the physical issues (the options are not a complete list) that have plagued all networks since the very beginning of networking. See Chapter 23 for more information.

47. D. The steps, in order, are as follows:

   1. Identify the problem.

   2. Establish a theory of probable cause.

   3. Test the theory to determine cause.

   4. Establish a plan of action to resolve the problem and identify potential effects.

   5. Implement the solution or escalate as necessary.

   6. Verify full system functionality, and if applicable, implement preventative measures.

   7. Document findings, actions, outcomes, and lessons learned.

   See Chapter 24 for more information.

48. C. The steps, in order, are as follows:

1. Identify the problem.

2. Establish a theory of probable cause.

3. Test the theory to determine cause.

4. Establish a plan of action to resolve the problem and identify potential effects.

5. Implement the solution or escalate as necessary.

6. Verify full system functionality, and if applicable, implement preventative measures.

7. Document findings, actions, outcomes, and lessons learned.

See Chapter 24 for more information.

49. A, D. The arp utility's –a and –g switches perform the same function. They both show the current ARP cache. See Chapter 25 for more information.

50. A. Route print will show you the routing table. See Chapter 25 for more information.

Chapter

1

Introduction to Networks

THE FOLLOWING COMPTIA NETWORK+ EXAM OBJECTIVES ARE COVERED IN THIS CHAPTER:

✓ **1.2 Explain the characteristics of network topologies and network types.**

- Mesh

- Star/hub-and-spoke

- Bus

- Ring

- Hybrid

- Network types and characteristics

    - Peer-to-peer

    - Client-server

    - Local area network (LAN)

    - Metropolitan area network (MAN)

    - Wide area network (WAN)

    - Wireless local area network (WLAN)

    - Personal area network (PAN)

    - Campus area network (CAN)

    - Storage area network (SAN)

    - Software-defined wide area network (SDWAN)

    - Multiprotocol label switching (MPLS)

    - Multipoint generic routing encapsulation (mGRE)

- Service-related entry point

    - Demarcation point

    - Smartjack

- Virtual network concepts
    - vSwitch
    - Virtual network interface card (vNIC)
    - Network function virtualization (NFV)
    - Hypervisor
- Provider links
    - Satellite
    - Digital subscriber line (DSL)
    - Cable
    - Leased line
    - Metro-optical

You'd have to work pretty hard these days to find someone who would argue when we say that our computers have become invaluable to us personally and professionally. Our society has become highly dependent on the resources they offer and on sharing them with each other. The ability to communicate with others—whether they're in the same building or in some faraway land—completely hinges on our capacity to create and maintain solid, dependable networks.

And those vitally important networks come in all shapes and sizes—ranging from small and simple to humongous and super complicated. But whatever their flavor, they all need to be maintained properly, and to do that well, you have to understand networking basics. The various types of devices and technologies that are used to create networks, as well as how they work together, is what this book is about, and I'll go through this critical information one step at a time with you. Understanding all of this will not only equip you with a rock-solid base to build on as you gain IT knowledge and grow in your career, it will also arm you with what you'll need to ace the Network+ certification exam!

To find Todd Lammle CompTIA videos and practice questions, please see www.lammle.com.

First Things First: What's a Network?

The dictionary defines the word *network* as "a group or system of interconnected people or things." Similarly, in the computer world, the term *network* means two or more connected computers that can share resources such as data and applications, office machines, an Internet connection, or some combination of these, as shown in Figure 1.1.

FIGURE 1.1   A basic network

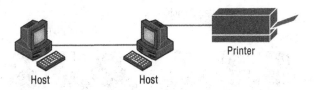

Figure 1.1 shows a really basic network made up of only two host computers connected; they share resources such as files and even a printer hooked up to one of the hosts. These two hosts "talk" to each other using a computer language called *binary code*, which consists of lots of 1s and 0s in a specific order that describes exactly what they want to "say."

Next, I'm going to tell you about local area networks, how they work, and even how we can connect LANs together. Then, later in this chapter, I'll describe how to connect remote LANs together through something known as a wide area network.

The Local Area Network

Just as the name implies, a *local area network (LAN)* is usually restricted to spanning a particular geographic location such as an office building, a single department within a corporate office, or even a home office.

Back in the day, you couldn't put more than 30 workstations on a LAN, and you had to cope with strict limitations on how far those machines could actually be from each other. Because of technological advances, all that's changed now, and we're not nearly as restricted in regard to both a LAN's size and the distance a LAN can span. Even so, it's still best to split a big LAN into smaller logical zones known as *workgroups* to make administration easier.

 The meaning of the term *workgroup* in this context is slightly differ-ent than when the term is used in contrast to domains. In that context, a workgroup is a set of devices with no security association with one another (whereas in a domain they do have that association). In this con-text, we simply mean they physically are in the same network segment.

In a typical business environment, it's a good idea to arrange your LAN's workgroups along department divisions; for instance, you would create a workgroup for Accounting, another one for Sales, and maybe another for Marketing—you get the idea. Figure 1.2 shows two separate LANs, each as its own workgroup.

FIGURE 1.2   Two separate LANs (workgroups)

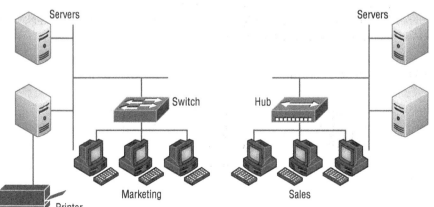

First, don't stress about the devices labeled *hub* and *switch*—these are just connectivity devices that allow hosts to physically connect to resources on an LAN. Trust me; I'll describe them to you in much more detail in Chapter 5, "Networking Devices."

Anyway, back to the figure. Notice that there's a Marketing workgroup and a Sales workgroup. These are LANs in their most basic form. Any device that connects to the Marketing LAN can access the resources of the Marketing LAN—in this case, the servers and printer.

There are two problems with this:

- You must be physically connected to a workgroup's LAN to get the resources from it.

- You can't get from one LAN to the other and use the server data and printing resources remotely.

This is a typical network issue that's easily resolved by using a cool device called a *router* to connect the two LANs, as shown in Figure 1.3.

FIGURE 1.3 A router connects LANs.

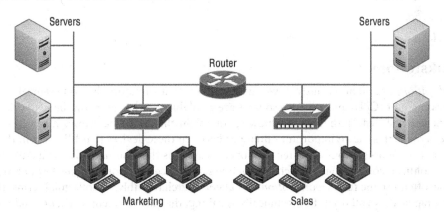

Nice—problem solved! Even though you can use routers for more than just connecting LANs, the router shown in Figure 1.3 is a great solution because the host computers from the Sales LAN can get to the resources (server data and printers) of the Marketing LAN, and vice versa.

Now, you might be thinking that we don't really need the router—that we could just physically connect the two workgroups with a type of cable that would allow the Marketing and Sales workgroups to hook up somehow. Well, we could do that, but if we did, we would have only one big, cumbersome workgroup instead of separate workgroups for Marketing and Sales, and that kind of arrangement just isn't practical for today's networks.

This is because with smaller, individual-yet-connected groups, the users on each LAN enjoy much faster response times when accessing resources, and administrative tasks are a lot easier too. Larger workgroups run more slowly because there's a legion of hosts within them that are all trying to get to the same resources simultaneously. So the router shown in Figure 1.3, which separates the workgroups while still allowing access between them, is a really great solution!

Don't focus too much on the network connectivity devices like the hubs, routers, and switches I've mentioned so far in this chapter yet. We'll thoroughly cover them all later, in Chapter 5. Right now, I really want you to prioritize your understanding of the concepts that I'm presenting here, so at this point, all you need to know is that hubs and switches are devices that connect other devices together into a network and routers connect networks together.

So let me define the other terms I've used so far: *workstations*, *servers*, and *hosts*.

Common Network Components

There are a lot of different machines, devices, and media that make up our networks. Let's talk about three of the most common:

- Workstations
- Servers
- Hosts

Workstations

Workstations are often seriously powerful computers that run more than one central processing unit (CPU) and whose resources are available to other users on the network to access when needed. With this much power, you might think I am describing a server—not quite because there is an important difference between these devices that I'll cover in the next section. Workstations are often employed as systems that end users use on a daily basis. Don't confuse workstations with client machines, which can be workstations but not always. People often use the terms *workstation* and *client* interchangeably. In colloquial terms, this isn't a big deal; we all do it. But technically speaking, they are different. A *client machine* is any device on the network that can ask for access to resources like a printer or other hosts from a server or powerful workstation.

The terms *workstation, client,* and *host* can sometimes be used interchangeably. Computers have become more and more powerful and the terms have become somewhat fuzzy because hosts can be clients, workstations, servers, and more! The term *host* is used to describe pretty much anything that takes an IP address.

Servers

Servers are also powerful computers. They get their name because they truly are "at the service" of the network and run specialized software known as the network operating system to maintain and control the network.

In a good design that optimizes the network's performance, servers are highly specialized and are there to handle one important labor-intensive job. This is not to say that a single server can't do many jobs, but more often than not, you'll get better performance if you dedicate a server to a single task. Here's a list of common dedicated servers:

File Server　Stores and dispenses files

Mail Server　The network's post office; handles email functions

Print Server　Manages printers on the network

Web Server　Manages web-based activities by running Hypertext Transfer Protocol Secure (HTTPS) for storing web content and accessing web pages

Fax Server　The "memo maker" that sends and receives paperless faxes over the network

Application Server　Manages network applications

Telephony Server　Handles the call center and call routing and can be thought of as a sophisticated network answering machine

Proxy Server　Handles tasks in the place of other machines on the network, particularly an Internet connection

See how the name of each kind of server indicates what it actually does— how it serves the network? This is an excellent way to remember them.

As I said, servers are usually dedicated to doing one specific important thing within the network. Not always, though—sometimes they have more than one job. But whether servers are designated for one job or are network multitaskers, they can maintain the network's data integrity by backing up the network's software and providing redundant hardware (for fault tolerance). And no matter what, they all serve a number of client machines.

Back in Figure 1.2, I showed you an example of two really simple LAN networks. I want to make sure you know that servers must have considerably superior CPUs, hard-drive space, and memory—a lot more than a simple client's capacity—because they serve many client machines and provide any resources they require. Because they're so important, you should always put your servers in a very secure area. My company's servers are in a locked server room because not only are they really pricey workhorses, they also store huge amounts of important and sensitive company data, so they need to be kept safe from any unauthorized access.

In Figure 1.4, you can see a network populated with both workstations and servers. Also notice that the hosts can access the servers across the network, which is pretty much the general idea of having a network in the first place!

FIGURE 1.4   A network populated with servers and workstations

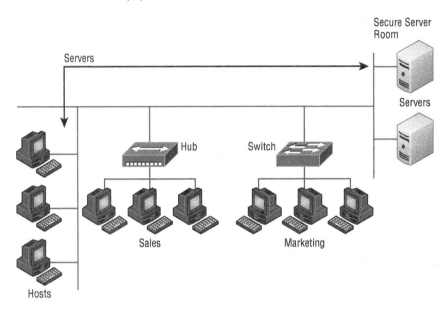

You probably picked up on the fact that there are more workstations here than servers, right? Think of why that is. If you answered that it's because one server can provide resources to what can sometimes be a huge number of individual users at the same time but workstations don't, you nailed it!

Hosts

This can be kind of confusing because when people refer to hosts, they really can be referring to almost any type of networking devices—including workstations and servers. But if you dig a bit deeper, you'll find that usually this term comes up when people are talking about resources and jobs that have to do with Transmission Control Protocol/Internet Protocol (TCP/IP). The scope of possible machines and devices is so broad because, in TCP/IP-speak, *host* means any network device with an IP address. Yes, you'll hear IT professionals throw this term around pretty loosely; for the Network+ exam, stick to the definition of hosts as being network devices, including workstations and servers, with IP addresses.

Here's a bit of background: The name *host* harks back to the Jurassic period of networking when those dinosaurs known as *mainframes* were the only intelligent devices able to roam the network. These were called *hosts* whether they had TCP/IP functionality or not. In that bygone age, everything else in the network-scape was referred to as *dumb terminals* because only mainframes—hosts—were given IP addresses. Another fossilized term from way back then is *gateways*, which was used to talk about any layer 3 machines like routers. We still use these terms today, but they've evolved a bit to refer to the many intelligent devices populating our present-day networks, each of which has an IP address. This is exactly the reason you hear *host* used so broadly.

Metropolitan Area Network

A *metropolitan area network (MAN)* is just as it sounds, a network covering a metropolitan area used to interconnect various buildings and facilities usually over a carrier provided network. Think of a MAN as a concentrated WAN and you've got it. MANs typically offer high speed interconnections using in-ground fiber optics and can be very cost effective for high-speed interconnects.

Wide Area Network

There are legions of people who, if asked to define a *wide area network (WAN)*, just couldn't do it. Yet most of them use the big dog of all WANs—the Internet—every day! With that in mind, you can imagine that WAN networks are what we use to span large geographic areas and truly go the distance. Like the Internet, WANs usually employ both routers and public links, so that's generally the criteria used to define them.

Here's a list of some of the important ways that WANs are different from LANs:

- WANs usually need a router port or ports.
- WANs span larger geographic areas and/or can link disparate locations.
- WANs are usually slower.
- We can choose when and how long we connect to a WAN. A LAN is all or nothing—our workstation is connected to it either permanently or not at all, although most of us have dedicated WAN links now.
- WANs can utilize either private or public data transport media such as phone lines.

We get the word *Internet* from the term *internetwork*. An internetwork is a type of LAN and/or WAN that connects a bunch of networks, or *intranets*. In an internetwork, hosts still use hardware addresses to communicate with other hosts on the LAN. However, they use logical addresses (IP addresses) to communicate with hosts on a different LAN (on the other side of the router).

And *routers* are the devices that make this possible. Each connection into a router is a different logical network. Figure 1.5 demonstrates how routers are employed to create an internetwork and how they enable our LANs to access WAN resources.

The Internet is a prime example of what's known as a *distributed WAN*—an internetwork that's made up of a lot of interconnected computers located in a lot of different places. There's another kind of WAN, referred to as *centralized*, that's composed of a main, centrally located computer or location that remote computers and devices can connect to. A good example is remote offices that connect to a main corporate office, as shown in Figure 1.5.

FIGURE 1.5   An internetwork

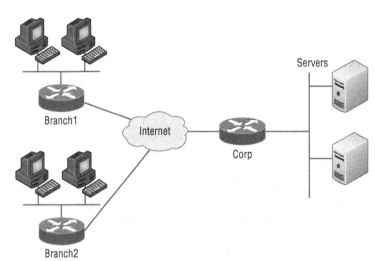

Personal Area Network

For close proximity connections there are *PANs*, or *personal area networks*. These are seen with smartphones and laptops in a conference room where local connections are used to collaborate and send data between devices. While a PAN can use a wired connection such as Ethernet or USB, it is more common that short distance wireless connections are used such as Bluetooth, infrared, or ZigBee.

PANs are intended for close proximity between devices such as connecting to a projector, printer, or a coworker's computer, and they extend usually only a few meters.

Campus Area Network

A *CAN*, or *campus area network*, covers a limited geographical network such as a college or corporate campus. The CAN typically interconnects LANs in various buildings and offers a Wi-Fi component for roaming users.

A campus area network is between a LAN and WAN in scope. They are larger than a local area network (LAN) but smaller than a metropolitan area network (MAN) or wide area network (WAN).

Most CANs offer Internet connectivity as well as access to data center resources.

Storage Area Network

A *storage area network (SAN)* is designed for, and used exclusively by, storage systems. SANs interconnect servers to storage arrays containing centralized banks of hard drive or similar storage media. SANs are usually only found in data centers and do not mix traffic with other LANs. The protocols are designed specifically for storage with Fibre Channel being the most prevalent along with iSCSI. The network hardware is different from LAN switches and routers and are designed specifically to carry storage traffic.

Software-Defined Wide Area Network

A *software-defined wide area network (SDWAN)* is a virtual WAN architecture that uses software to manage connectivity, devices, and services and can make changes in the network based on current operations.

SDWANs integrate any type of transport architectures such as MPLS, LTE, and broadband Internet services to securely connect users to applications. The SDWAN controller can make changes in real time to add or remove bandwidth or to route around failed circuits. SDWANs can simplify wide area networking management and operations by decoupling the networking hardware from its control mechanism.

Multiprotocol Label Switching

The term *Multiprotocol Label Switching (MPLS)*, as used in this chapter, will define the actual layout of what is one of the most popular WAN protocols in use today. MPLS has become one of the most innovative and flexible networking technologies on the market, and it has some key advantages over other WAN technologies:

- Physical layout flexibility
- Prioritizing of data
- Redundancy in case of link failure
- One-to-many connection

MPLS is a switching mechanism that imposes labels (numbers) to data and then uses those labels to forward data when it arrives at the MPLS network, as shown in Figure 1.6.

FIGURE 1.6   Multiprotocol Label Switching layout

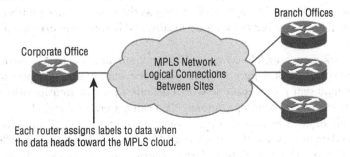

The labels are assigned on the edge of the MPLS network, and forwarding inside the MPLS network (cloud) is done solely based on labels through virtual links instead of physical links. Prioritizing data is a huge advantage; for example, voice data could have priority over basic data based on the labels. And since there are multiple paths for the data to be forwarded through the MPLS cloud, there's even some redundancy provided as well.

Multipoint Generic Routing Encapsulation

The *Multipoint Generic Routing Encapsulation (mGRE)* protocol refers to a carrier or service provider offering that dynamically creates and terminates connections to nodes on a network. mGRE is used in Dynamic Multipoint VPN deployments. The protocol enables dynamic connections without having to pre-configure static tunnel endpoints.

The protocol encapsulates user data, creates a VPN connection to one or many nodes, and when completed, tears down the connection.

Network Architecture: Peer-to-Peer or Client-Server?

We've developed networking as a way to share resources and information, and how that's achieved directly maps to the particular architecture of the network operating system software. There are two main network types you need to know about: peer-to-peer and client-server. And by the way, it's really tough to tell the difference just by looking at a diagram or even by checking out live video of the network humming along. But the differences between peer-to-peer and client-server architectures are pretty major. They're not just physical; they're logical differences. You'll see what I mean in a bit.

Peer-to-Peer Networks

Computers connected together in *peer-to-peer networks* do not have any central, or special, authority—they're all *peers*, meaning that when it comes to authority, they're all equals. The authority to perform a security check for proper access rights lies with the computer that has the desired resource being requested from it.

It also means that the computers coexisting in a peer-to-peer network can be client machines that access resources and server machines and provide those resources to other computers. This actually works pretty well as long as there isn't a huge number of users on the network, if each user backs things up locally, and if your network doesn't require much security.

If your network is running Windows, macOS, or Linux in a local LAN workgroup, you have a peer-to-peer network. Figure 1.7 gives you a snapshot of a typical peer-to-peer network. Keep in mind that peer-to-peer networks definitely present security-oriented challenges; for instance, just backing up company data can get pretty sketchy!

Since it should be clear by now that peer-to-peer networks aren't all sunshine, backing up all your critical data may be tough, but it's vital! Haven't all of us forgotten where we've put an important file? And then there's that glaring security issue to tangle with. Because security is not centrally governed, each and every user has to remember and maintain a list of users

FIGURE 1.7   A peer-to-peer network

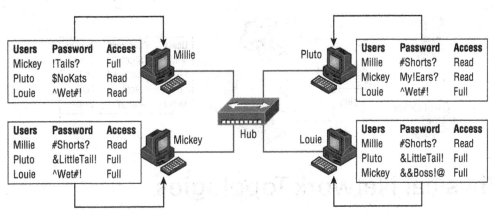

and passwords on each and every machine. Worse, some of those all-important passwords for the same users change on different machines—even for accessing different resources. What a mess!

Client-Server Networks

Client-server networks are pretty much the polar opposite of peer-to-peer networks because in them, a single server uses a network operating system for managing the whole network. Here's how it works: A client machine's request for a resource goes to the main server, which responds by handling security and directing the client to the desired resource. This happens instead of the request going directly to the machine with the desired resource, and it has some serious advantages. First, because the network is much better organized and doesn't depend on users remembering where needed resources are, it's a whole lot easier to find the files you need because everything is stored in one spot—on that special server. Your security also gets a lot tighter because all usernames and passwords are on that specific server, which is never ever used as a workstation. You even gain scalability—client-server networks can have legions of workstations on them. And surprisingly, with all those demands, the network's performance is actually optimized—nice!

Check out Figure 1.8, which shows a client-server network with a server that has a database of access rights, user accounts, and passwords.

Many of today's networks are hopefully a healthy blend of peer-to-peer and client-server architectures, with carefully specified servers that permit the simultaneous sharing of resources from devices running workstation operating systems. Even though the supporting machines can't handle as many inbound connections at a time, they still run the server service reasonably well. And if this type of mixed environment is designed well, most networks benefit greatly by having the capacity to take advantage of the positive aspects of both worlds.

FIGURE 1.8   A client-server network

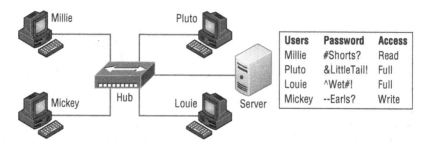

Physical Network Topologies

Just as a topographical map is a type of map that shows the shape of the terrain, the *physical topology* of a network is also a type of map. It defines the specific characteristics of a network, such as where all the workstations and other devices are located and the precise arrangement of all the physical media such as cables. On the other hand, the *logical topologies* we covered earlier delineate exactly how data moves through the network. Now, even though these two topologies are usually a lot alike, a particular network can actually have physical and logical topologies that are very different. Basically, what you want to remember is that a network's physical topology gives you the lay of the land and the logical topology shows how a digital signal or data navigates through that layout.

Here's a list of the topologies you're most likely to run into these days:

- Bus
- Star/hub-and-spoke
- Ring
- Mesh
- Point-to-point
- Point-to-multipoint
- Hybrid

Bus Topology

This type of topology is the most basic one of the bunch, and it really does sort of resemble a bus, but more like one that's been in a wreck! Anyway, the *bus topology* consists of two distinct and terminated ends, with each of its computers connecting to one unbroken cable running its entire length. Back in the day, we used to attach computers to that main cable with wire taps, but this didn't work all that well so we began using drop cables in their place. If we were dealing with 10Base2 Ethernet, we would slip a "T" into the main cable anywhere we wanted to connect a device to it instead of using drop cables.

Figure 1.9 depicts what a typical bus network's physical topology looks like.

FIGURE 1.9   A typical bus network's physical topology

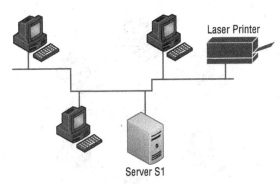

Laser Printer

Server S1

Even though all the computers on this kind of network see all the data flowing through the cable, only the one computer, which the data is specifically addressed to, actually *gets* the data. Some of the benefits of using a bus topology are that it's easy to install and it's not very expensive, partly because it doesn't require as much cable as the other types of physical topologies. But it also has some drawbacks: For instance, it's hard to troubleshoot, change, or move, and it really doesn't offer much in the way of fault tolerance because everything is connected to that single cable. This means that any fault in the cable would basically bring the whole network down!

> By the way, *fault tolerance* is the capability of a computer or a network system to respond to a condition automatically, often resolving it, which reduces the impact on the system. If fault-tolerance measures have been implemented correctly on a network, it's highly unlikely that any of that network's users will know that a problem ever existed at all.

Star Topology

A star (*hub-and-spoke*) topology's computers are connected to a central point with their own individual cables or wireless connections. You'll often find that central spot inhabited by a device like a hub, a switch, or an access point.

Star topology offers a lot of advantages over bus topology, making it more widely used even though it obviously requires more physical media. One of its best features is that because each computer or network segment is connected to the central device individually, if the cable fails, it only brings down the machine or network segment related to the point of failure. This makes the network much more fault tolerant as well as a lot easier to troubleshoot. Another great thing about a star topology is that it's a lot more scalable—all you have to do if you want to add to it is run a new cable and connect to the machine at the core of the star. In Figure 1.10, you'll find a great example of a typical star topology.

FIGURE 1.10   Typical star topology with a hub

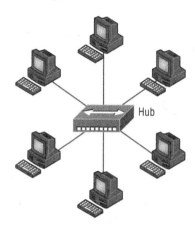

Although it is called a *star* (hub-and-spoke) topology, it also looks a lot like a bike wheel with spokes connecting to the hub in the middle of the wheel and extending outward to connect to the rim. And just as with that bike wheel, it's the hub device at the center of a star topology network that can give you the most grief if something goes wrong with it. If that central hub happens to fail, down comes the whole network, so it's a very good thing hubs don't fail often!

Just as it is with pretty much everything, a star topology has its pros and cons. But the good news far outweighs the bad, which is why people often opt for star topology. And here's a list of benefits you gain by going with it:

- New stations can be added or moved easily and quickly.
- A single cable failure won't bring down the entire network.
- It's relatively easy to troubleshoot.

And here are the disadvantages to using a star topology:

- The total installation cost can be higher because of the larger number of cables, even though prices are becoming more competitive.
- It has a single point of failure—the hub or other central device.

There are two more sophisticated implementations of a star topology. The first is called a *point-to-point link*, where you have not only the device in the center of the spoke acting as a hub but also the device on the other end, which extends the network. This is still a star-wired topology, but as I'm sure you can imagine, it gives you a lot more scalability!

Another refined version is the wireless version, but to understand this variety well, you've got to have a solid grasp of all the capabilities and features of any devices populating the wireless star topology. No worries, though—I'll be covering wireless access points later on in Chapter 12, "Wireless Networking." For now, it's good enough for you to know that access points are pretty much just wireless hubs or switches that behave like their wired counterparts. Basically, they create a point-by-point connection to endpoints and other wireless access points.

Ring Topology

In this type of topology, each computer is directly connected to other computers within the same network. Looking at Figure 1.11, you can see that the network's data flows from computer to computer back to the source, with the network's primary cable forming a ring. The problem is, the *ring topology* has a lot in common with the bus topology because if you want to add to the network, you have no choice but to break the cable ring, which is likely to bring down the entire network!

FIGURE 1.11   A typical ring topology

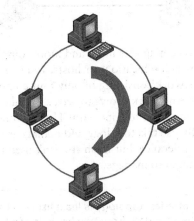

This is one big reason that ring topology isn't very popular—you just won't run into it a lot as I did in the 1980s and early 1990s. It's also pricey because you need several cables to connect each computer, it's really hard to reconfigure, and as you've probably guessed, it's not fault tolerant.

But even with all that being said, if you work at an ISP, you may still find a physical ring topology in use for a technology called SONET or some other WAN technology. However, you just won't find any LANs in physical rings anymore.

Mesh Topology

In this type of topology, you'll find that there's a path from every machine to every other one in the network. That's a lot of connections—in fact, the *mesh topology* wins the prize for "most physical connections per device"! You won't find it used in LANs very often, if ever, these days, but you will find a modified version of it known as a *hybrid mesh* used in a restrained manner on WANs, including the Internet.

Often, hybrid mesh topology networks will have quite a few connections between certain places to create redundancy (backup). And other types of topologies can sometimes be found in the mix too, which is another reason it's dubbed *hybrid*. Just remember that it isn't a full-on mesh topology if there isn't a connection between all devices in the network. And understand that it's fairly complicated. Figure 1.12 gives you a great picture of just how much only four connections can complicate things!

FIGURE 1.12   A typical mesh topology

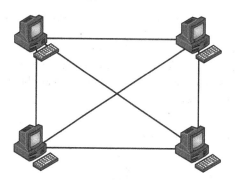

You can clearly see that everything gets more and more complex as both the wiring and the connections multiply. For each *n* locations or hosts, you end up with *n*(*n*–1)/2 connections. This means that in a network consisting of only four computers, you have 4(4–1)/2, or 6 connections. And if that little network grows to, say, a population of 10 computers, you'll then have a whopping 45 connections to cope with! That's a huge amount of overhead, so only small networks can really use this topology and manage it well. On the bright side, you get a really nice level of fault tolerance, but mesh still isn't used in corporate LANs anymore because they were so complicated to manage.

A full mesh physical topology is least likely to have a collision, which happens when the data from two hosts trying to communicate simultaneously "collides" and gets lost.

This is also the reason you'll usually find the hybrid version in today's WANs. In fact, the mesh topology is actually pretty rare now, but it's still used because of the robust fault tolerance it offers. Because you have a multitude of connections, if one goes on the blink, computers and other network devices can simply switch to one of the many redundant connections that are up and running. And clearly, all that cabling in the mesh topology makes it a very pricey implementation. Plus, you can make your network management much less insane than it is with mesh by using what's known as a *partial mesh topology* solution instead, so why not go that way? You may lose a little fault tolerance, but if you go the partial mesh route, you still get to use the same technology between all the network's devices. Just remember that with partial mesh, not all devices will be interconnected, so it's very important to choose the ones that will be very wisely.

Point-to-Point Topology

As its name implies, in a *point-to-point* topology you have a direct connection between two routers or switches, giving you one communication path. The routers in a point-to-point topology can be linked by a serial cable, making it a physical network, or if they're located far apart and connected only via a circuit within a Frame Relay or MPLS network, it's a logical network instead.

Figure 1.13 illustrates three examples of a typical T1, or WAN, point-to-point connection.

FIGURE 1.13   Three point-to-point connections

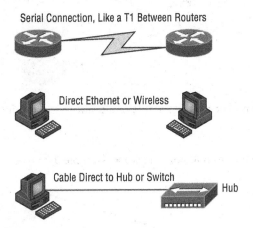

What you see here is a lightning bolt and a couple of round things with a bunch of arrows projecting from them, right? Well, the two round things radiating arrows represent our network's two routers, and that lightning bolt represents a WAN link. These symbols are industry standard, and I'll be using them throughout this book, so it's a good idea to get used to them!

Okay—so part two of the diagram shows two computers connected by a cable—a point-to-point link. By the way, this should remind you of something we just went over. Remember peer-to-peer networks? Good! I hope you also remember that a big drawback to peer-to-peer network sharing is that it's not very scalable. With this in mind, you probably won't be all that surprised that even if both machines have a wireless point-to-point connection, this network still won't be very scalable.

You'll usually find point-to-point networks within many of today's WANs, and as you can see in part three of Figure 1.13, a link from a computer to a hub or switch is also a valid point-to-point connection. A common version of this setup consists of a direct wireless link between two wireless bridges that's used to connect computers in two different buildings together.

Point-to-Multipoint Topology

Again, as the name suggests, a *point-to-multipoint* topology consists of a succession of connections between an interface on one router and multiple destination routers—one point of connection to multiple points of connection. Each of the routers and every one of their interfaces involved in the point-to-multipoint connection are part of the same network.

Figure 1.14 shows a WAN and demonstrates a point-to-multipoint network. You can clearly see a single, corporate router connecting to multiple branches.

FIGURE 1.14   A point-to-multipoint network, example 1

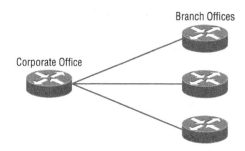

Figure 1.15 shows another prime example of a point-to-multipoint network: a college or corporate campus.

FIGURE 1.15   A point-to-multipoint network, example 2

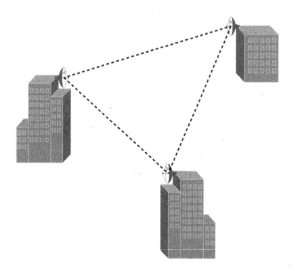

Hybrid Topology

I know I just talked about the hybrid network topology in the section about mesh topology, but I didn't give you a mental picture of it in the form of a figure. I also want to point out that *hybrid topology* means just that—a combination of two or more types of physical or logical network topologies working together within the same network.

Figure 1.16 depicts a simple hybrid network topology; it shows a LAN switch or hub in a star topology configuration that connects to its hosts via a bus topology.

FIGURE 1.16   A simple hybrid network

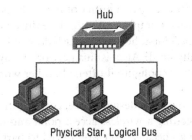

Hub

Physical Star, Logical Bus

Topology Selection, Backbones, and Segments

Now that you're familiar with many different types of network topologies, you're ready for some tips on selecting the right one for your particular network. You also need to know about backbones and segments, which I'll cover in the very last part of this chapter.

They're Just Cables, Right?

Wrong! Regardless of the type of network you build, you need to start thinking about quality at the bottom and work up.

Think of it as if you were at an electronics store buying the cables for your home theater system. You've already spent a bunch of time and money getting the right components to meet your needs. Because you've probably parted with a hefty chunk of change, you might be tempted to cut corners, but why would you stop now and connect all your high-quality devices together with the cable equivalent of twine? No, you're smarter than that—you know that the exact cables that will maximize the sound and picture quality of your specific components can also protect them!

It's the same thing when you're faced with selecting the physical media for a specific network. You just don't want to cut corners here because this is the backbone of the network and you definitely don't want to be faced with going through the costly pain of replacing this infrastructure once it's been installed. Doing that will cost you a lot more than taking the time to wisely choose the right cables and spending the money it takes to get them in the first place. The network downtime alone can cost a company a bundle! Another reason for choosing the network's physical media well is that it's going to be there for a good 5 to 10 years. This means two things: It better be solid quality, and it better be scalable because that network is going to grow and change over the years.

Selecting the Right Topology

As you now know, not only do you have a buffet of network topologies to choose from, but each one also has pros and cons to implementing it. It really comes down to that well-known adage "Ask the right questions." First, how much cash do you have? How much fault tolerance and security do you really need? Also, is this network likely to grow like a weed—will you need to quickly and easily reconfigure it often? In other words, how scalable does your network need to be?

For instance, if your challenge is to design a nice, cost-effective solution that involves only a few computers in a room, getting a wireless access point and some wireless network cards is definitely your best way to go because you won't need to part with the cash for a bunch of cabling and it's super easy to set up. Alternatively, if you're faced with coming up with a solid design for a growing company's already-large network, you're probably good to go with using a wired star topology because it will nicely allow for future changes. Remember, a star topology really shines when it comes to making additions to the network, moving things around, and making any kind of changes happen quickly, efficiently, and cost effectively.

If, say, you're hired to design a network for an ISP that needs to be up and running 99.9 percent of the time with no more than eight hours a year allowed downtime, well, you need Godzilla-strength fault tolerance. Do you remember which topology gives that up the best? (Hint: Internet.) Your primo solution is to go with either a hybrid or a partial mesh topology. Remember that partial mesh leaves you with a subset of $n(n-1)/2$ connections to maintain—a number that could very well blow a big hole in your maintenance budget!

Here's a list of things to keep in mind when you're faced with coming up with the right topology for the right network:

- Cost
- Ease of installation
- Ease of maintenance
- Fault-tolerance requirement
- Security requirement

The Network Backbone

Today's networks can get pretty complicated, so we need to have a standard way of communicating with each other intelligibly about exactly which part of the network we're referencing. This is the reason we divide networks into different parts called *backbones* and *segments*.

Figure 1.17 illustrates a network and shows which part is the backbone and which parts are segments.

You can see that the network backbone works similar to how a human backbone does. It's what all the network segments and servers connect to and what gives the network its structure. As you can imagine, being such an important nerve center, the backbone must use some kind of seriously fast, robust technology—often Gigabit Ethernet. And to optimize network performance—its speed and efficiency—it follows that you would want to connect all of the network's servers and segments directly to the network's backbone.

FIGURE 1.17   Backbone and segments on a network

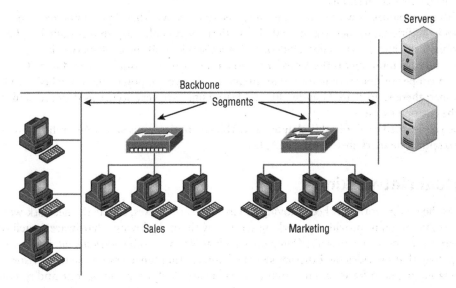

Network Segments

When we refer to a segment, we can mean any small section of the network that may be connected to, but isn't actually a piece of, the backbone. The network's workstations and servers organized into segments connect to the network backbone, which is the common connecting point for all segments; you can see this by taking another look at Figure 1.17, which displays four segments.

Service-Related Entry Points

In the networking world, there are clearly defined boundaries where one entity hands off a connection to another. These are common when connecting to a service provider's or carrier's WAN circuit. The service entry point defines the point of responsibility. The common term used is the *demarcation point*, or *demarc* for short. A carrier will usually terminate with a piece of equipment called a *smart jack* that allows them to run diagnostics up to the physical point where the customer's network connects.

Service Provider Links

Service providers are Internet service providers and cable and telephone companies that provide networking services. There are many different technologies used to provide these services such as satellite links for earth station to satellite connections.

Traditional telephone companies may have extensive copper connections to homes and businesses that use Digital Subscriber Lines, or DSL, to provide last hop high speed digital services. DSL used to be a popular method to connect to the Internet and a solid alternative to cable or fiber connections.

Cable companies now offer data and Internet services over their hybrid fiber/coax networks in additional to their traditional video offerings. A cable modem is installed at the customer's site and provides data, video, and voice services off the cable network.

Another common link is the *leased line*. When the provider installs a leased line, it is either a copper or fiber termination that interconnects two endpoints and is exclusive to the customer; there is no shared bandwidth and leased lines are very secure as they are dedicated for the customer's use.

As you learned earlier in this chapter, a MAN uses optical; it is sometimes referred to as *metro optical network* instead of a MAN.

Virtual Networking

Just as the server world has been moving to virtualized processes, so has the network world. It is now common to provide networking services without deploying a hardware switch or router; it is all done in software! Companies such as VMware offer *virtual switch (vSwitch)* technology that provides the Ethernet switched and routing functions on the hypervisor, eliminating the need for external networking hardware. A vSwitch can operate and be configured the same as an external hardware appliance; just remember, a vSwitch is similar to software virtualization.

Virtualized servers do not have the means for inserting a hardware network interface card since they only exist in software. A *virtual network interface card (vNIC)* is installed to connect the virtual device to the hypervisor, and from there, out to the LAN.

Network function virtualization (NFV) is the process of taking networking functions such as routers, switches, firewalls, load balancers, and controllers and virtualizing them. This process allows all of these functions to run on a single device.

The magic behind all of the virtual networking popularity is the hypervisor. The hypervisor is software that is installed directly on a bare metal server and allows for many virtual machines (VMs) to run thinking they are using the server's hardware directly. This allows for many servers and virtual network devices to run a on a single piece of computing hardware.

Summary

This chapter created a solid foundation for you to build your networking knowledge on as you go through this book.

In it, you learned what, exactly, a network is, and you got an introduction to some of the components involved in building one—routers, switches, and hubs—as well as the jobs they do in a network.

You also learned that the components required to build a network aren't all you need. Understanding the various types of network connection methods, like peer-to-peer and client-server, is also vital.

Further, you learned about the various types of logical and physical network topologies and the features and drawbacks of each. I wrapped up the chapter with a discussion about network virtualization and equipped you with the right questions to ask yourself to ensure that you come up with the right network topology for your networking needs.

Exam Essentials

Know your network topologies.   Know the names and descriptions of the topologies. Be aware of the difference between physical networks (what humans see) and logical networks (what the equipment "sees").

Know the advantages and disadvantages of the topologies.   It is important to know what each topology brings to the table. Knowing the various characteristics of each topology comes in handy during troubleshooting.

Understand the terms *LAN* and *WAN*.   You need to understand when you would use a LAN and when you would use a WAN. A LAN is used to connect a group of hosts together, and a WAN is used to connect various LANs together.

Written Lab

You can find the answers to the written labs in Appendix A.

1. What are the three basic LAN topologies?

2. What common WAN topology often results in multiple connections to a single site (leading to a high degree of fault tolerance) and has one-to-many connections?

3. What is the term for a device that shares its resources with other network devices?

4. What network model draws a clear distinction between devices that share their resources and devices that do not?

5. Which network topology or connection type can be implemented with only two endpoints?

6. What device is generally implemented as a star topology?

7. What does MPLS stand for?

8. What does WAN stand for?

9. Will a computer that shares no resources most likely be connected to the backbone or to a segment?

10. Which LAN topology is characterized by all devices being daisy-chained together with the devices at each end being connected to only one other device?

Review Questions

You can find the answers to the review questions in Appendix B.

1. You need a network that provides centralized authentication for your users. Which of the following logical topologies should you use?

   A. VLANs

   B. Peer-to-peer

   C. Client-server

   D. Mesh

2. You need a topology that is scalable to use in your network. Which of the following will you install?

   A. Bus

   B. Ring

   C. Star

   D. Mesh

3. Which of the following physical topologies has the most connections and is the least popular for LANs?

   A. Bus

   B. Star

   C. Ring

   D. Mesh

4. In a physical star topology, what happens when a workstation loses its physical connection to another device?

   A. The ring is broken, so no devices can communicate.

   B. Only that workstation loses its ability to communicate.

   C. That workstation and the device it's connected to lose communication with the rest of the network.

   D. No devices can communicate because there are now two unterminated network segments.

5. Which type of WAN technology uses labels, which enables priority of voice through the network?

   A. VPN

   B. T1

   C. MPLS

   D. LAN

   E. Bus

6. What is a logical grouping of network users and resources called?

  A. WAN

  B. LAN

  C. MPLS

  D. Host

7. Which of the following is a concern when using peer-to-peer networks?

  A. Where to place the server

  B. Whose computer is least busy and can act as the server

  C. The security associated with such a network

  D. Having enough peers to support creating such a network

8. Which of the following is an example of when a point-to-multipoint network is called for?

  A. When a centralized office needs to communicate with many branch offices

  B. When a full mesh of WAN links is in place

  C. When multiple offices are daisy-chained to one another in a line

  D. When there are only two nodes in the network to be connected

9. Which of the following is an example of a LAN?

  A. Ten buildings interconnected by Ethernet connections over fiber-optic cabling

  B. Ten routers interconnected by Frame Relay circuits

  C. Two routers interconnected with a T1 circuit

  D. A computer connected to another computer so they can share resources

10. Which of the following is a disadvantage of the star topology?

  A. When a single port on the central concentrating device fails, the entire network loses connectivity.

  B. When the central concentrating device experiences a complete failure, all attached devices lose connectivity to the rest of the network.

  C. In a star topology, a more expensive type of host must be used compared to the host used when implementing a physical bus.

  D. It is more difficult to add stations and troubleshoot than with other topologies.

11. What is a difference between a LAN and a WAN?

  A. WANs require a router.

  B. WANs cover larger geographical areas.

  C. WANs can utilize either private or public data transport.

  D. All of the above.

12. Which of the following provides the most physical layout flexibility in a very large, geographically dispersed enterprise network?

A. Bus topology

B. LAN switch

C. Star topology

D. MPLS cloud network

13. In what type of network are all computers considered equal and do not share any central authority?

A. Peer-to-peer

B. Client-server

C. Physical topology

D. None of the above

14. What advantage does the client-server architecture have over peer-to-peer?

A. Easier maintenance

B. Greater organization

C. Tighter security

D. All of the above

15. Which of the following is an example of a hybrid network?

A. Ethernet switch

B. Ring topology

C. Bus topology

D. Star topology

16. You have a network with multiple LANs and want to keep them separate but still connect them together so they can all get to the Internet. Which of the following is the best solution?

A. Use static IP addresses.

B. Add more hubs.

C. Implement more switches.

D. Install a router.

17. Which type of topology has the greatest number of physical connections?

A. Point-to-multipoint

B. Star

C. Point-to-point

D. Mesh

18. What type of topology gives you a direct connection between two routers so that there is one communication path?

    A. Point-to-point

    B. Star

    C. Bus

    D. Straight

19. Which network topology is a combination of two or more types of physical or two or more types of logical topologies?

    A. Point-to-multipoint

    B. Hybrid

    C. Bus

    D. Star

20. When designing a network and deciding which type of network topology to use, which item(s) should be considered? (Choose all that apply.)

    A. Cost

    B. Ease of installation

    C. Ease of maintenance

    D. Fault-tolerance requirements

Chapter

2

The Open Systems Interconnection Specifications

THE FOLLOWING COMPTIA NETWORK+ EXAM OBJECTIVES ARE COVERED IN THIS CHAPTER:

✓ **1.1 Compare and contrast the Open Systems Interconnection (OSI) model layers and encapsulation concepts**

- OSI Model
    - Layer 1 – Physical
    - Layer 2 – Data link
    - Layer 3 – Network
    - Layer 4 – Transport
    - Layer 5 – Session
    - Layer 6 – Presentation
    - Layer 7 – Application
- Data encapsulation and decapsulation within the OSI model context

✓ **1.5 Explain common ports and protocols, their application, and encrypted alternatives**

- Connectionless vs. Connection-oriented

In this chapter, we're going to analyze the Open Systems Interconnection (OSI) model. I'll thoroughly describe each part to
you in detail because it's imperative for you to grasp the OSI
model's key concepts. Once solidly equipped with this vital foundation, you'll be set to move
on and build your own personal storehouse of networking knowledge.

The OSI model has seven hierarchical layers that were developed to enable different
networks to communicate reliably between disparate systems.

Because this book is centering upon all things Network+, it's crucial for you to understand the OSI model as CompTIA sees it, so I'll present each of its seven layers in that light.

I'll also provide you with an introduction to *encapsulation*, which is the process of encoding data as it goes down the OSI stack.

To find Todd Lammle CompTIA videos and questions, please see
www.lammle.com.

Internetworking Models

In the very first networks, the computers involved could communicate only with other computers made by the same manufacturer. For example, companies ran either a complete DEC-
net solution or an IBM solution—not both together. In the late 1970s, the *Open Systems
Interconnection (OSI) reference model* was created by the International Organization for
Standardization (ISO) to break through this barrier.

The OSI model was meant to help vendors create interoperable network devices and
software in the form of protocols, or standards, so that different vendors' networks could
become compatible and work together. Like world peace, it'll probably never happen completely, but it's still a great goal.

The OSI model is the primary architectural model for networks. It describes how data
and network information are communicated from an application on one computer through
the network media to an application on another computer. The OSI reference model breaks
this approach into layers.

Let's move on and explore this layered approach as well as how you can utilize its key
concepts to troubleshoot internetworks.

The Layered Approach

Basically, a *reference model* is a conceptual blueprint of how communications should take place. It addresses all the processes required for effective communication and divides these processes into logical groupings called *layers*. When a communication system is designed in this manner, it's known as *layered architecture*.

Think of it like this: Say you and some friends want to start a company. One of the first things you'll do is sit down and think through what tasks must be done, who will do them, the order in which they will be done, and how they relate to each other. Ultimately, you might group these tasks into departments. Let's say you decide to have a customer service department, an inventory department, and a shipping department. Each of your departments has its own unique tasks, keeping its staff members busy and requiring them to focus only on their own duties.

In this scenario, I'm using departments as a metaphor for the layers in a communication system. For things to run smoothly, the staff of each department has to trust and rely heavily on the others to do their jobs and competently handle their unique responsibilities. During your planning sessions, you'll probably take notes, recording the entire process to facilitate later discussions about standards of operation that will serve as your business blueprint or reference model.

Once your business is launched, each department leader will need to develop practical methods to implement their assigned tasks using the specific part of the business model's blueprint that relates to their branch. These practical methods, or protocols, must be compiled into a standard operating procedures manual and followed closely. The procedures in your manual will have been included for different reasons and have varying degrees of importance and implementation. If you form a partnership or acquire another company, it will be crucial for its business protocols to either match or be compatible with yours.

Similarly, software developers can use a reference model to understand computer communication processes and see exactly what must be accomplished on any one layer and how. In other words, if I need to develop a protocol for a certain layer, I only need to focus on that specific layer's functions. I don't need to be concerned with those of any other layer because different protocols will be in place to meet the different layers' needs. The technical term for this idea is *binding*. The communication processes that are related to each other are bound, or grouped together, at a particular layer.

Advantages of Reference Models

The OSI model is hierarchical, and I'd like to point out that the same beneficial characteristics can actually apply to any layered model, such as the TCP/IP model. Understand that the central purpose of the OSI model, and all networking models, is to allow different vendors' networks to interoperate smoothly.

This short list depicts some of the most important advantages we gain by using the OSI layered model:

- The OSI model divides network communication processes into smaller and simpler components, thus aiding component development, design, and troubleshooting.

- It allows multiple-vendor development through the standardization of network components.

- It encourages industry standardization by defining the specific functions that occur at each layer of the model.

- It allows various types of network hardware and software to communicate.

- It prevents changes in one layer from affecting other layers, facilitating development and making application programming much easier.

The OSI Reference Model

One of the greatest functions of the OSI specifications is to assist in data transfer between disparate hosts regardless of whether they're Unix/Linux, Windows, or macOS based.

But keep in mind that the OSI model isn't a physical model; it's a conceptual and comprehensive yet fluid set of guidelines, which application developers utilize to create and implement applications that run on a network. It also provides a framework for creating and implementing networking standards, devices, and internetworking schemes. The OSI model has seven layers:

- Application (layer 7)
- Presentation (layer 6)
- Session (layer 5)
- Transport (layer 4)
- Network (layer 3)
- Data Link (layer 2)
- Physical (layer 1)

Figure 2.1 summarizes the functions that occur at each layer of the OSI model.

With this in mind, you're ready to delve into what takes place at each layer in detail.

Some people like to use the mnemonic Please Do Not Throw Sausage Pizza Away to remember the seven layers (starting at layer 1 and moving up to layer 7). I didn't make that up!

FIGURE 2.1   Layer functions

Application	• File, print, message, database, and application services
Presentation	• Data encryption, compression, and translation services
Session	• Dialog control
Transport	• End-to-end connection
Network	• Routing
Data Link	• Framing
Physical	• Physical topology

The OSI's seven layers are divided into two groups. The top three layers define the rules of how the applications working within host machines communicate with each other as well as with end users. The bottom four layers define how the actual data is transmitted from end to end. Figure 2.2 shows the top three layers and their functions, and Figure 2.3 shows the four lower layers and their functions.

FIGURE 2.2   The upper layers

Application	• Provides a user interface
Presentation	• Presents data • Handles processing such as encryption
Session	• Keeps different applications' data separate

FIGURE 2.3   The lower layers

Transport	• Provides reliable or unreliable delivery • Performs error correction before retransmit
Network	• Provides logical addressing, which routers use for path determination
Data Link	• Combines packets into bytes and bytes into frames • Provides access to media using MAC address • Performs error detection, not correction
Physical	• Moves bits between devices • Specifies voltage, wire speed, and pin-out of cables

Looking at Figure 2.2, it's clear that actual users interact with the computer at the Application layer. It's also apparent that the upper layers are responsible for applications communicating between hosts. Remember that none of the upper layers "know" anything about networking or network addresses. That's the responsibility of the four bottom layers.

Figure 2.3 illustrates that the four bottom layers define how data is transferred through physical media, switches, and routers. These bottom layers also determine how to rebuild a data stream from a transmitting host to a destination host's application.

Okay—so let's start at the Application layer and work our way down the stack.

The Application Layer

The *Application layer* of the OSI model marks the spot where users actually communicate or interact with the computer. Technically, users communicate with the network stack through application processes, interfaces, or application programming interfaces (APIs) that connect the application in use to the operating system of the computer. The Application layer chooses and determines the availability of communicating partners along with the resources necessary to make their required connections. It coordinates partnering applications and forms a consensus on procedures for controlling data integrity and error recovery. The Application layer comes into play only when it's apparent that access to the network will be needed soon. Take the case of Chrome or Firefox. You could uninstall every trace of networking components from a system, such as TCP/IP, the network card, and so on, and you could still use Chrome to view a local HTML document without a problem. But things would definitely get messy if you tried to do something like view an HTML document that had to be retrieved using HTTP or nab a file with FTP or TFTP because Chrome or Firefox responds to requests like those by attempting to access the Application layer. So what's happening is that the Application layer acts as an interface between the application program—which isn't part of the layered structure—and the next layer down by providing ways for the application to send information down through the protocol stack. In other words, browsers don't reside within the Application layer—it interfaces with Application layer protocols when it needs to deal with remote resources.

The Application layer is also responsible for identifying and establishing the availability of the intended communication partner and determining whether sufficient resources for the requested communication exist.

These tasks are important because computer applications sometimes require more than just desktop resources. Often, they unite communicating components from more than one network application. Prime examples are file transfers and email as well as enabling remote access, network-management activities, and client-server processes like printing and information location. Many network applications provide services for communication over enterprise networks, but for present and future internetworking, the need is fast developing to reach beyond the limitations of current physical networking.

It's important to remember that the Application layer acts as an interface between application programs. For instance, Microsoft Word doesn't *reside* at the Application layer, it *interfaces* with the Application layer protocols. Later, in Chapter 6, "Introduction to the Internet Protocol," I'll tell you all about key programs or processes that actually do reside at the Application layer, like FTP and TFTP.

The Presentation Layer

The *Presentation layer* gets its name from its purpose: it presents data to the Application layer and is responsible for data translation and code formatting.

A successful data-transfer technique is to adapt the data into a standard format before transmission. Computers are configured to receive this generically formatted data and then convert it back into its native format for reading—for example, from EBCDIC to ASCII. By providing translation services, the Presentation layer ensures that the data transferred from one system's Application layer can be read and understood by the Application layer on another system.

The OSI has protocol standards that define how standard data should be formatted. Tasks like data compression, decompression, encryption, and decryption are all associated with this layer. Some Presentation layer standards are even involved in multimedia operations.

The Session Layer

The *Session layer* is responsible for setting up, managing, and then tearing down sessions between Presentation layer entities. This layer also provides dialog control between devices, or nodes. It coordinates communication between systems and serves to organize their communication by offering three different modes: one direction (*simplex*), both directions, but only one direction at a time (*half-duplex*), and bi-directional (*full-duplex*). To sum up, the Session layer basically keeps an application's data separate from other applications' data. For a good example, the Session layer allows multiple web browser sessions on your desktop at the same time.

The Transport Layer

The *Transport layer* segments and reassembles data into a data stream. Services located in the Transport layer handle data from upper-layer applications and unite it onto the same data stream. They provide end-to-end data transport services and can establish a logical connection between the sending host and destination host on an internetwork.

The Transport layer is responsible for providing the mechanisms for multiplexing upper-layer applications, establishing virtual connections, and tearing down virtual circuits. It also hides the many and sundry details of any network-dependent information from the higher layers, facilitating data transfer.

We'll cover Transmission Control Protocol (TCP) and User Datagram Protocol (UDP) thoroughly in Chapter 6, but if you're already familiar with them, you know that they both work at the Transport layer. You also know that TCP is a reliable service and UDP is not. These two protocols give application developers more options because they have a choice between them when they're working with TCP/IP protocols.

> The term *reliable networking* relates to the Transport layer and means that acknowledgments, sequencing, and flow control will be used.

The Transport layer can be connectionless or connection-oriented, but it's especially important for you to really understand the connection-oriented portion of the Transport layer. So let's take some time to delve into the connection-oriented (reliable) protocol of the Transport layer now.

Connection-Oriented Communication

Before a transmitting host starts to send segments down the model, the sender's TCP process contacts the destination's TCP process to establish a connection. The resulting creation is known as a *virtual circuit*. This type of communication is called *connection-oriented*. During this initial *handshake*, the two TCP processes also agree on the amount of information that will be sent in either direction before the respective recipient's TCP sends back an acknowledgment. With everything agreed on in advance, the path is paved for reliable communication to take place.

Figure 2.4 depicts a typical reliable session taking place between sending and receiving systems. Both of the hosts' application programs begin by notifying their individual operating systems that a connection is about to be initiated.

FIGURE 2.4   Establishing a connection-oriented session

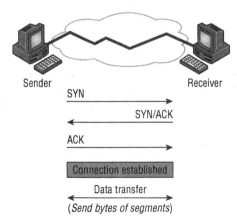

The two operating systems communicate by sending messages over the network confirming that the transfer is approved and that both sides are ready for it to take place. After all of this required synchronization occurs, a connection is fully established and the data transfer begins. This virtual circuit setup is called *overhead*.

While the information is being transferred between hosts, the two machines periodically check in with each other, communicating through their protocol software to ensure that all is going well and that data is being received properly.

Let me sum up the steps in the connection-oriented session—the TCP three-way handshake—pictured in Figure 2.4:

1. The first "connection agreement" segment is a request for synchronization.

2. The next segments acknowledge the request and establish connection parameters—the rules—between hosts. These segments request that the receiver's sequencing is synchronized here as well so that a bidirectional connection is formed.

3. The final segment is also an acknowledgment. It notifies the destination host that the connection agreement has been accepted and that the connection has been established. Data transfer can now begin.

I know I went into a lot of detail about this connection setup, and I did that so you would have a really clear picture of how it works. You can refer to this entire process as "the three-way handshake" I already mentioned, known as SYN, SYN/ACK, ACK or synchronize, synchronize-acknowledgment, acknowledgment.

That sounds pretty simple, but things don't always flow so well. Sometimes congestion can occur during a transfer because a high-speed computer is generating data traffic a lot faster than the network can handle transferring it. A bunch of computers simultaneously sending datagrams through a single gateway or to a destination can also clog things up. In the latter case, a gateway or destination can become congested even though no single source caused the problem. Either way, the problem is like a freeway bottleneck—too much traffic for too small a capacity. It's not usually one car that's the problem; it's that there are just too many cars on that particular route.

Flow Control

Data integrity is ensured at the Transport layer by maintaining *flow control* and by allowing users to request reliable data transport between systems. Flow control provides a means for the receiver to govern the amount of data sent by the sender. It prevents a sending host on one side of the connection from overflowing the buffers in the receiving host—an event that can result in lost data. Reliable data transport employs a connection-oriented communications session between systems, and the protocols involved ensure that the following will be achieved:

1. The segments delivered are acknowledged back to the sender upon their reception.

2. Any segments not acknowledged are retransmitted.

3. Segments are sequenced back into their proper order upon arrival at their destination.

4. A manageable data flow is maintained in order to avoid congestion, overloading, and data loss.

Okay, so what happens when a machine receives a flood of datagrams too quickly for it to process? It stores them in a memory section called a *buffer*. But this buffering tactic can only solve the problem if the datagrams are part of a small burst. If not, and the datagram deluge continues, a device's memory will eventually be exhausted, its flood capacity will be exceeded, and it will react by discarding any additional datagrams that arrive like a dam spilling over!

This sounds pretty bad, and it would be if it weren't for the transport function of network flood-control that actually works really well. But how? Well, instead of just dumping resources and allowing data to be lost, the transport can issue a "not ready" indicator to the sender, or source, of the flood, as shown in Figure 2.5.

FIGURE 2.5   Transmitting segments with flow control

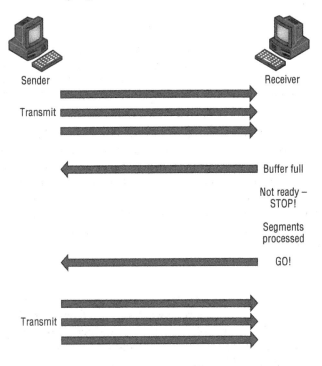

This mechanism is similar to a stoplight, signaling the sending device to stop transmitting segment traffic to its overwhelmed peer. After the peer machine's receiver processes the segments abounding in its memory reservoir (its buffer), it sends out a "ready" transport indicator. When the machine waiting to transmit the rest of its datagrams receives this "go" indictor, it resumes its transmission.

During fundamental, reliable, connection-oriented data transfer, datagrams are delivered to the receiving host in exactly the same sequence they're transmitted. So, if any data segments are lost, duplicated, or damaged along the way, a failure notice is transmitted. This error is corrected by making sure the receiving host acknowledges it has received each and every data segment, and in the correct order.

To summarize, a service is considered connection-oriented if it has the following characteristics:

- A virtual circuit is set up (such as a three-way handshake).
- It uses sequencing.
- It uses acknowledgments.
- It uses flow control.

Windowing

Ideally, data throughput happens quickly and efficiently. And as you can imagine, it would be slow if the transmitting machine had to wait for an acknowledgment after sending each segment. But because time is available *after* the sender transmits the data segment and *before* it finishes processing acknowledgments from the receiving machine, the sender uses the break as an opportunity to transmit more data. The quantity of data segments (measured in bytes) that the transmitting machine is allowed to send without receiving an acknowledgment is represented by something called a *window*.

Windows are used to control the amount of outstanding, unacknowledged data segments.

It's important to understand that the size of the window controls how much information is transferred from one end to the other. Although some protocols quantify information by observing the number of packets, TCP/IP measures it by counting the number of bytes.

Figure 2.6 illustrates two window sizes—one set to 1 and one set to 3. In this simplified example, both the sending and receiving machines are workstations.

When you've configured a window size of 1, the sending machine waits for an acknowledgment for each data segment it transmits before transmitting another. If you've configured a window size of 3, the sending machine is allowed to transmit three data segments before an acknowledgment is received. In reality, the window size actually delimits the amount of bytes that can be sent at a time.

If a receiving host fails to receive all the segments that it should acknowledge, the host can improve the communication session by decreasing the window size.

FIGURE 2.6   Windowing

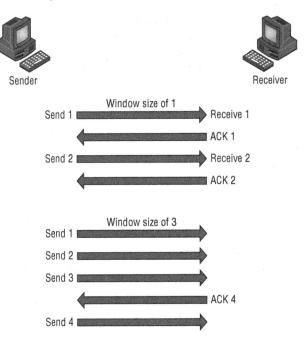

Acknowledgments

Reliable data delivery ensures the integrity of a data stream being sent from one machine to the other through a fully functional data link. It guarantees that the data won't be duplicated or lost. This is achieved through something called *positive acknowledgment with retransmission*—a technique that requires a receiving machine to communicate with the transmitting source by sending an acknowledgment message back to the sender when it receives data. The sender documents each segment it sends and waits for this acknowledgment before sending the next segment. When it sends a segment, the transmitting machine starts a timer and retransmits if it expires before an acknowledgment is returned from the receiving end.

In Figure 2.7, the sending machine transmits segments 1, 2, and 3. The receiving node acknowledges it has received them by requesting segment 4. When it receives the acknowledgment, the sender then transmits segments 4, 5, and 6. If segment 5 doesn't make it to the destination, the receiving node acknowledges that event with a request for the segment to be resent. The sending machine will then resend the lost segment and wait for an acknowledgment, which it must receive in order to move on to the transmission of segment 7.

The Transport layer doesn't need to use a connection-oriented service. That choice is up to the application developer. It's safe to say that if you're connection-oriented, meaning that you've created a virtual circuit, you're using TCP. If you aren't setting up a virtual circuit, then you're using UDP and are considered connectionless.

FIGURE 2.7   Transport layer reliable delivery

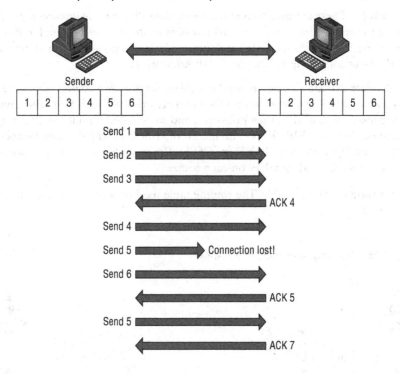

 Transmission Control Protocol (TCP) and User Datagram Protocol (UDP) are protocols that work at the Transport layer and will be covered in detail in Chapter 6.

The Network Layer

The *Network layer* manages logical device addressing, tracks the location of devices on the network, and determines the best way to move data. This means that the Network layer must transport traffic between devices that aren't locally attached. Routers are layer 3 devices that are specified at the Network layer and provide the routing services within an internetwork.

It happens like this: First, when a packet is received on a router interface, the destination IP address is checked. If the packet isn't destined for that particular router, the router looks up the destination network address in the routing table. Once the router chooses an exit interface, the packet is sent to that interface to be framed and sent out on the local network. If the router can't find an entry for the packet's destination network in the routing table, the router drops the packet.

Two types of packets are used at the Network layer:

Data Packets These are used to transport user data through the internetwork. Protocols used to support data traffic are called *routed protocols*. Two examples of routed protocols are Internet Protocol (IP) and Internet Protocol version 6 (IPv6), which you'll learn all about coming up in Chapter 7, "IP Addressing."

Route-Update Packets These are used to update neighboring routers about the networks connected to all routers within the internetwork. Protocols that send route-update packets are called routing protocols, and some common ones are Routing Information Protocol (RIP), RIPv2, Enhanced Interior Gateway Routing Protocol (EIGRP), and Open Shortest Path First (OSPF). Route-update packets are used to help build and maintain routing tables on each router.

Figure 2.8 shows a routing table. The routing table used by a router includes the following information:

FIGURE 2.8 Routing table used in a router

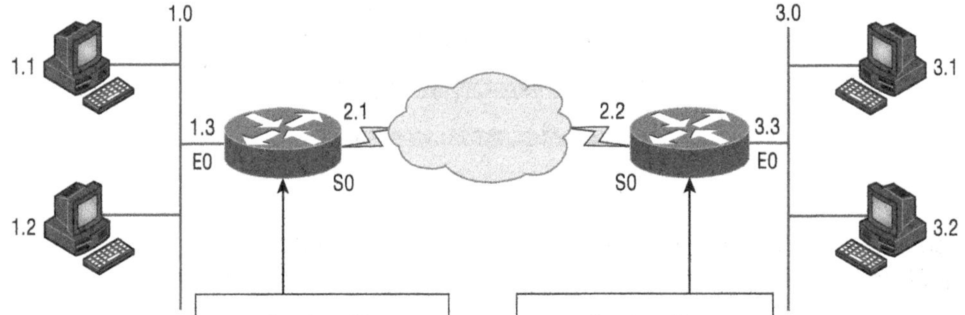

Routing table		
NET	INT	Metric
1	E0	0
2	S0	0
3	S0	1

Routing table		
NET	INT	Metric
1	S0	1
2	S0	0
3	E0	0

Network Addresses These are protocol-specific network addresses. A router must maintain a routing table for individual routing protocols because each routing protocol keeps track of a network that includes different addressing schemes, like IP and IPv6. Think of it as a street sign in each of the different languages spoken by the residents who live on a particular street. If there were American, Spanish, and French folks on a street named Cat, the sign would read Cat/Gato/Chat.

Interface   This is the exit interface a packet will take when destined for a specific network.

Metric   This value equals the distance to the remote network. Different routing protocols use different ways of computing this distance. I'll cover routing protocols in Chapter 9, "Introduction to IP Routing." For now, just know that some routing protocols, namely RIP, use something called a *hop count*—the number of routers a packet passes through en route to a remote network. Other routing protocols alternatively use bandwidth, delay of the line, and even something known as a tick count, which equals 1/18 of a second, to make routing decisions.

Routers break up broadcast domains, which means that broadcasts by default aren't forwarded through a router. This is a good thing because it reduces traffic on the network. Routers also break up collision domains, but this can be accomplished using layer 2 (Data Link layer) switches as well.

> Broadcast and collision domains will be covered in detail in Chapter 5. For now, just remember that routers break up broadcast domains and switches break up collision domains.

Because each interface in a router represents a separate network, it must be assigned unique network identification numbers, and each host on the network connected to that router must use the same network number.

Figure 2.9 demonstrates how a router works within an internetwork.

FIGURE 2.9   A router in an internetwork

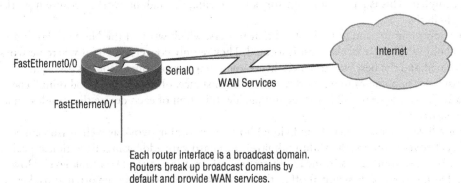

Each router interface is a broadcast domain. Routers break up broadcast domains by default and provide WAN services.

Here are some key points about routers that you really should commit to memory:

- Routers, by default, won't forward any broadcast or multicast packets.
- Routers use the logical address in a Network layer header to determine the next-hop router to forward the packet to.

- Routers can use access lists, created by an administrator, to control security on the types of packets that are allowed to enter or exit an interface.

- Routers can provide layer 2 bridging functions if needed and can simultaneously route through the same interface.

- Layer 3 devices (routers, in this case) provide connections between virtual LANs (VLANs).

- Routers can provide quality of service (QoS) for specific types of network traffic.

 A router can also be referred to as a layer 3 switch. These terms are interchangeable.

The Data Link Layer

The *Data Link layer* provides the physical transmission of the data and handles error notification, network topology, and flow control. This means the Data Link layer ensures that messages are delivered to the proper device on a LAN using hardware (MAC) addresses and translates messages from the Network layer into bits for the Physical layer to transmit.

The Data Link layer formats the message into pieces, each called a *data frame*, and adds a customized header containing the destination and source hardware addresses. This added information forms a sort of capsule that surrounds the original message in much the same way that engines, navigational devices, and other tools were attached to the lunar modules of the Apollo project. These various pieces of equipment were useful only during certain stages of flight and were stripped off the module and discarded when their designated stage was complete. This is a great analogy for data traveling through networks because it works very similarly.

It's important for you to understand that routers, which work at the Network layer, don't care about where a particular host is located. They're only concerned about where networks are located and the best way to reach them—including remote ones. Routers are totally obsessive when it comes to networks, and in this instance, obsession is a good thing! The Data Link layer is responsible for the unique identification of each device that resides on a local network.

For a host to send packets to individual hosts on a local network as well as transmit packets between routers, the Data Link layer uses hardware addressing. Each time a packet is sent between routers, it's framed with control information at the Data Link layer. However, that information is stripped off at the receiving router, and only the original packet is left completely intact. This framing of the packet continues for each hop until the packet is finally delivered to the correct receiving host. It's important to understand that the packet itself is never altered along the route; it's only encapsulated with the type of control information required for it to be properly passed on to the different media types.

Figure 2.10 shows the Data Link layer with the Ethernet and Institute of Electrical and Electronics Engineers (IEEE) specifications.

FIGURE 2.10   Data Link layer

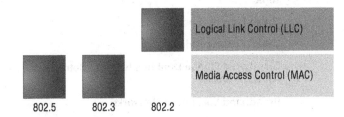

When you check it out, notice that the IEEE 802.2 standard is not only used in conjunction with the other IEEE standards, it also adds functionality to those standards.

The IEEE Ethernet Data Link layer has two sublayers:

Media Access Control (MAC)   Defines how packets are placed on the media. Contention media access is "first come, first served" access, where everyone shares the same bandwidth—hence the name. Physical addressing is defined here, as are logical topologies. What's a logical topology? It's the signal path through a physical topology. Line discipline, error notification (not correction), ordered delivery of frames, and optional flow control can also be used at this sublayer.

Logical Link Control (LLC)   Responsible for identifying Network layer protocols and then encapsulating them, an LLC header tells the Data Link layer what to do with a packet once a frame is received. It works like this: A host receives a frame and looks in the LLC header to find out where the packet is destined—say, the IP protocol at the Network layer. The LLC can also provide flow control and sequencing of control bits.

Project 802

One of the major components of the Data Link layer is the result of the IEEE's 802 subcommittees and their work on standards for local area and metropolitan area networks (LANs/MANs). The committee met in February 1980, so they used the 80 from 1980 and the 2 from the second month to create the name Project 802. The designation for an 802 standard always includes a dot (.) followed by either a single or a double digit. These numeric digits specify particular categories within the 802 standard. These standards are listed in the following table.

Standard	Topic
802.1	LAN/MAN Management (and Media Access Control Bridges)
802.2	Logical Link Control
802.3	CSMA/CD (Ethernet)

continues

continued

Standard	Topic
802.4	Token Passing Bus
802.5	Token Passing Ring
802.6	Distributed Queue Dual Bus (DQDB) Metropolitan Area Network (MAN)
802.7	Broadband Local Area Networks
802.8	Fiber-Optic LANs and MANs
802.9	Isochronous LANs
802.10	LAN/MAN Security
802.11	Wireless LAN
802.12	Demand Priority Access Method
802.15	Wireless Personal Area Network
802.16	Wireless Metropolitan Area Network (also called WiMAX)
802.17	Resilient Packet Ring

Note that 802.1, 802.3, 802.11, and 802.15 are the only Active 802 standards. The others are either Disbanded or Hibernating.

From this sidebar, you just need to remember that 802.3 calls out anything having to do with Ethernet, and 802.11 is anything wireless.

The Physical Layer

Finally, we're hitting bottom. Well, not in a bad way—we've now arrived at the *Physical layer*, which does two important things: it sends bits and receives bits. Bits come only in values of 1 or 0—a Morse code with numerical values. The Physical layer communicates directly with the various types of actual communication media. Different kinds of media represent these bit values in different ways. Some use audio tones, and others employ *state transitions*—changes in voltage from high to low and low to high. Specific protocols are needed for each type of media to describe the proper bit patterns to be used, how data is encoded into media signals, and the various qualities of the physical media's attachment interface.

The Physical layer specifies the electrical, mechanical, procedural, and functional requirements for activating, maintaining, and deactivating a physical link between end systems. This layer is also where you identify the interface between the *data terminal equipment (DTE)* and the *data communication equipment (DCE)*. (Some older phone company employees still call DCE data circuit-terminating equipment.) The DCE is usually located at the customer, whereas the DTE is the attached device. The services available to the DTE are most often accessed via the DCE device, which is a modem or *channel service unit/data service unit (CSU/DSU)*.

The Physical layer's connectors and different physical topologies are defined by the standards, allowing disparate systems to communicate.

Finally, the Physical layer specifies the layout of the transmission media, otherwise known as its topology. A physical topology describes the way the cabling is physically laid out, as opposed to the logical topology that we just talked about in the section "The Data Link Layer." The various physical topologies include bus, star, ring, and mesh and were described in Chapter 1, "Introduction to Networks."

Introduction to Encapsulation

When a host transmits data across a network to another device, the data goes through *encapsulation*: It's wrapped with protocol information at each layer of the OSI model. Each layer communicates only with its peer layer on the receiving device.

To communicate and exchange information, each layer uses *protocol data units (PDUs)*. These hold the control information attached to the data at each layer of the model. They're usually attached to the header in front of the data field but can also be in the trailer, or end, of it.

At a transmitting device, the data-encapsulation method works like this:

1. User information is converted to data for transmission on the network.

2. Data is converted to segments, and a reliable connection is set up between the transmitting and receiving hosts.

3. Segments are converted to packets or datagrams, and a logical address is placed in the header so each packet can be routed through an internetwork. A packet carries a segment of data.

4. Packets or datagrams are converted to frames for transmission on the local network. Hardware (Ethernet) addresses are used to uniquely identify hosts on a local network segment. Frames carry packets.

5. Frames are converted to bits, and a digital encoding and clocking scheme is used.

Figure 2.11 shows how user data is encapsulated at a transmitting host.

Before we move onto the next chapter, how does step 5 work when frames are converted to bits and an encoding and clocking scheme is used? This is called a modulation technique and we'll end the chapter on this discussion.

FIGURE 2.11   Data encapsulation

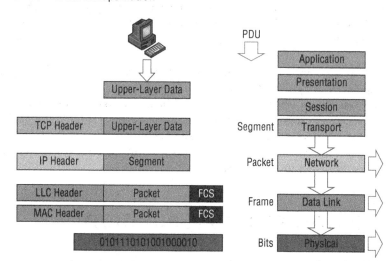

Modulation Techniques

In networks, modulation is the process of varying one or more properties of a waveform, called the *carrier signal*, with a signal that typically contains information to be transmitted.

Modulation of a waveform transforms a baseband (Ethernet or wireless) message signal into a passband signal (a passband, also known as a bandpass filtered signal, is the range of frequencies or wavelengths that can pass through a filter without being attenuated). In current networks, modulation takes a digital or analog signal and puts it in another signal that can be physically transmitted.

A modulator is a device that performs modulation of a signal and a demodulator is a device that performs demodulation, the inverse of modulation. We typically just call these modems (from modulator–demodulator), which can perform both operations.

The purpose of digital modulation is to transfer a digital bit stream over an analog bandpass channel. (A good example would be data transmitting over the public switched telephone network, where a bandpass filter limits the frequency range to 300–3400 Hz, or over a limited radio frequency band.) The purpose of an analog modulation is to transfer an analog baseband (or lowpass) signal (for example, an audio signal, wireless network, or TV signal) over an analog bandpass channel at a different frequency.

Analog and digital modulation use something called frequency-division multiplexing (FDM), where several low-pass information signals are transferred simultaneously over the same shared physical network, using separate passband channels (several different frequencies).

The digital baseband modulation methods found in our Ethernet networks, and also known as line coding, are used to transfer a digital bit stream over a baseband channel. Baseband means that the signal being modulated used the complete available bandwidth.

Time-division multiplexing (TDM) is a method of transmitting and receiving many independent signals over a common signal path by means of synchronized network devices at each end of the transmission line so that each signal appears on the line only a fraction of time in an alternating pattern. The receiving end demultiplexes the signal back to its original form.

After you learn more foundational material about networking in the next few chapters, I'll come back to the encapsulation method and discuss it further in Chapter 6.

Summary

You're now armed with a ton of fundamental information. You're set to build on it and are well on your way to certification.

Let's take a minute to go over what you've learned in this chapter. We started by discussing internetworking models and the advantages of having them. I then discussed the OSI model—the seven-layer model used to help application developers design applications that can run on any type of system or network. Each layer has its special jobs and select responsibilities within the model to ensure that solid, effective communications do, in fact, occur. I provided you with complete details of each layer and discussed how you need to view the specifications of the OSI model.

I also discussed the encapsulation method used in networking. Encapsulation is a highly important concept to understand, and I'll continue to discuss it throughout this book.

This chapter finished with a brief introduction to modulation of digital and analog signals.

Exam Essentials

Remember the OSI layers.   You absolutely must remember and understand the seven layers of the OSI model as well as what function each layer provides. The Application, Presentation, and Session layers are upper layers and are responsible for communicating from a user interface to an application. The Transport layer provides segmentation, sequencing, and virtual circuits. The Network layer provides logical network addressing and routing through an internetwork. The Data Link layer provides framing and placing of data on the network medium. The Physical layer is responsible for taking 1s and 0s and encoding them into a digital signal for transmission on the network segment.

Know the sublayers of the Data Link layer.   In addition to the OSI layers, knowing that this is the only layer that has sublayers and the functions of those sublayers is extremely important. The Data Link layer has two sublayers: LLC and MAC. The LLC sublayer is responsible primarily for the multiplexing of Network layer protocols. The MAC sublayer is responsible for physical addressing and determining the appropriate time to place data on the network.

Know the devices that operate at each layer of the OSI model.   Hubs and repeaters see only bits, making them layer 1 devices. Because all networking devices have physical connectivity to the network, they all operate at layer 1, but hubs and repeaters operate only at this layer, whereas other devices also work in higher layers. Nevertheless, we generally consider that a device operates at the highest layer it supports; that layer's functionality is the main reason we implement the device on the network. For example, switches and bridges are considered layer 2 devices because they understand and make decisions based on layer 2 addresses. Routers are layer 3 devices for a similar reason; they deal with layer 3 addresses. Networking devices, such as workstations that run applications, are said to operate at the Application layer (or you may hear that they operate at all layers) because they must include Application layer protocols that offer services to networked applications.

Written Lab

You can find the answers to the written labs in Appendix A.

1.   Which layer chooses and determines the availability of communicating partners along with the resources necessary to make the connection, coordinates partnering applications, and forms a consensus on procedures for controlling data integrity and error recovery?

2.   Which layer is responsible for converting frames from the Data Link layer into electrical signals?

3.   At which layer is routing implemented, enabling connections and path selection between two end systems?

4.   Which layer defines how data is formatted, presented, encoded, and converted?

5.   Which layer is responsible for creating, managing, and terminating sessions between applications?

6.   Which layer manages the transmission of data across a physical link and is primarily concerned with physical addressing and the ordered delivery of frames?

7.   Which layer is used for reliable communication between end nodes over the network and provides mechanisms for establishing, maintaining, and terminating virtual circuits as well as controlling the flow of information?

8.   Which layer provides logical addressing that routers use for path determination?

9.   Which layer specifies voltage, wire speed, and connector pin-outs and moves bits between devices?

10.   Which layer combines bits into bytes and bytes into frames and uses MAC addressing?

Review Questions

You can find the answers to the review questions in Appendix B.

1. Host 1 sent a SYN packet to Host 2. What will Host 2 send in response?

   A. ACK

   B. NAK

   C. SYN/ACK

   D. SYN/NAK

   E. SYN

2. TCP and UDP reside at which layer of the OSI model?

   A. 1

   B. 2

   C. 3

   D. 4

3. Which layer of the OSI model provides an entry point for programs to access the network infrastructure?

   A. Application

   B. Transport

   C. Network

   D. Physical

4. You are connected to a server on the Internet and you click a link on the server and receive a time-out message. What layer could be the source of this message?

   A. Application

   B. Transport

   C. Network

   D. Physical

5. Which layer of the OSI model is responsible for code and character-set conversion as well as recognizing data formats?

   A. Application

   B. Presentation

   C. Session

   D. Network

6. At which layers of the OSI model do bridges, hubs, and routers primarily operate, respectively?

   A. Physical, Physical, Data Link

   B. Data Link, Data Link, Network

   C. Data Link, Physical, Network

   D. Physical, Data Link, Network

7. Which layer of the OSI model is responsible for converting data into signals appropriate for the transmission medium?

   A. Application

   B. Network

   C. Data Link

   D. Physical

8. A receiving host has failed to receive all the segments that it should acknowledge. What can the host do to improve the reliability of this communication session?

   A. Send a different source port number.

   B. Restart the virtual circuit.

   C. Decrease the sequence number.

   D. Decrease the window size.

9. Which layer 1 devices can be used to enlarge the area covered by a single LAN segment? (Choose two.)

   A. Firewall

   B. NIC

   C. Hub

   D. Repeater

   E. RJ-45 transceiver

10. Segmentation of a data stream happens at which layer of the OSI model?

   A. Physical

   B. Data Link

   C. Network

   D. Transport

11. When data is encapsulated, which is the correct order?

   A. Data, frame, packet, segment, bits

   B. Segment, data, packet, frame, bits

   C. Data, segment, packet, frame, bits

   D. Data, segment, frame, packet, bits

12. What are two purposes for segmentation with a bridge? (Choose two.)

    A. To add more broadcast domains

    B. To create more collision domains

    C. To add more bandwidth for users

    D. To allow more broadcasts for users

13. Acknowledgments, sequencing, and flow control are characteristic of which OSI layer?

    A. Layer 2

    B. Layer 3

    C. Layer 4

    D. Layer 7

14. Which of the following is true regarding sequencing and acknowledgments? (Choose all that apply.)

    A. The segments delivered are acknowledged back to the sender upon their reception.

    B. If a segment is not received, the virtual circuit must be restarted from the beginning at a slower transmit interval.

    C. Any segments not acknowledged are retransmitted.

    D. Segments are sequenced back into their proper order upon arrival at their destination.

    E. All segments are retransmitted on time slot intervals.

15. What is the purpose of flow control?

    A. To ensure that data is retransmitted if an acknowledgment is not received

    B. To reassemble segments in the correct order at the destination device

    C. To provide a means for the receiver to govern the amount of data sent by the sender

    D. To regulate the size of each segment

16. At which layer of the OSI model would you find IP?

    A. Transport

    B. Network

    C. Data Link

    D. Physical

17. Of the following, which is the highest layer in the OSI model?

    A. Transport

    B. Session

    C. Network

    D. Presentation

18. Routers perform routing at which OSI layer?

   A. Physical

   B. Data Link

   C. Network

   D. Transport

   E. Application

19. Which of the following mnemonic devices can you use to remember the first letter of the name of each layer of the OSI model in the proper order?

   A. All People Seem To Need Processed Data.

   B. Always Should People Never Threaten Dog Police.

   C. Please Do Not Throw Sausage Pizza Away.

   D. All Day People Should Try New Professions.

20. Which IEEE standard specifies the protocol for CSMA/CD?

   A. 802.2

   B. 802.3

   C. 802.5

   D. 802.11

Chapter

3

Networking Connectors and Wiring Standards

THE FOLLOWING COMPTIA NETWORK+ EXAM OBJECTIVES ARE COVERED IN THIS CHAPTER:

✓ **1.3 Summarize the types of cables and connectors and explain which is the appropriate type for a solution.**

- Copper
  - Twisted pair
  - Cat 5
  - Cat 5e
  - Cat 6
  - Cat 6a
  - Cat 7
  - Cat 8
  - Coaxial/RG-6
  - Twinaxial
  - Termination standards
  - TIA/EIA-568A
  - TIA/EIA-568B
- Fiber
  - Single-mode
  - Multimode
- Connector types
  - Local connector (LC)

- straight tip (ST)
- subscriber connector (SC)
- mechanical transfer (MT)
- registered jack (RJ)
- Angled physical contact (APC)
- Ultra-physical contact (UPC)
- RJ11
- RJ45
- F-type connector
- Transceivers/media converters
- Transceiver type, Small form-factor pluggable (SFP), Enhanced form-factor pluggable (SFP+), Quad small form-factor pluggable (QSFP), Enhanced quad small form-factor pluggable (QSFP+)
- Cable management
  - Patch panel/patch bay
  - Fiber distribution panel
  - Punchdown block
  - 66
  - 110
  - Krone
  - Bix

The idea of connecting a bunch of computers together hasn't changed a whole lot since the mid-1980s, but how we go about doing that certainly has. Like everything else, the technologies and devices we create our networks with have evolved dramatically and will continue to do so in order to keep up with the ever-quickening pace of life and the way we do business.

When you connect computers together to form a network, you want error-free, blazingly fast communication, right? Although "error-free" and reality don't exactly walk hand in hand, keeping lapses in communication to a minimum and making that communication happen really fast is definitely possible. But it isn't easy, and understanding the types of media and network topologies used in networking today will go far in equipping you to reach these goals; so will being really knowledgeable about the array of components and devices used to control network traffic.

All of these networking ingredients are going to be the focus of this chapter. In it, I'll cover different types of networking media, discuss common topologies and devices, and compare the features that they all bring into designing a solid network that's as problem free and turbo charged as possible.

To find Todd Lammle CompTIA videos and practice questions, please see www.lammle.com.

Physical Media

A lot of us rely on wireless networking methods that work using technologies like radio frequency and infrared, but even wireless depends on a physical media backbone in place somewhere. And the majority of installed LANs today communicate via some kind of cabling, so let's take a look at the three types of popular cables used in modern networking designs:

- Coaxial
- Twisted-pair
- Fiber optic

Coaxial Cable

Coaxial cable, referred to as *coax*, contains a center conductor made of copper that's surrounded by a plastic jacket with a braided shield over it. A plastic such as polyvinyl chloride (PVC) or fluoroethylenepropylene (FEP, commonly known as Teflon) covers this metal shield. The Teflon-type covering is frequently referred to as a *plenum-rated coating*, and it's definitely expensive but often mandated by local or municipal fire code when cable is hidden in walls and ceilings. Plenum rating applies to all types of cabling and is an approved replacement for all other compositions of cable sheathing and insulation like PVC-based assemblies.

The difference between plenum and non-plenum cable comes down to how each is constructed and where you can use it. Many large multistory buildings are designed to circulate air through the spaces between the ceiling of one story and the floor of the next; this space between floors is referred to as the *plenum*. And it just happens to be a perfect spot to run all the cables that connect the legions of computers that live in the building. Unless there's a fire—if that happens, the non-plenum cable becomes a serious hazard because its insulation gives off poisonous smoke that gets circulated throughout the whole building. Plus, non-plenum cables can actually become "wicks" for the fire, helping it quickly spread from room to room and floor to floor—yikes!

Because the goal is to prevent towering infernos, the National Fire Protection Association (NFPA) demands that cables run within the plenum have been tested and guaranteed as safe. They must be fire retardant and create little or no smoke and poisonous gas when burned. This means you absolutely can't use a non-plenum-type cable in the plenum, but it doesn't mean you can't use it in other places where it's safe. And because it's a lot cheaper, you definitely want to use it where you can.

Thin Ethernet, also referred to as *thinnet* or 10Base2, is a thin coaxial cable. It is basically the same as thick coaxial cable except it's only about 5 mm, or 2/10″, diameter coaxial cable. Thin Ethernet coaxial cable is Radio Grade 58, or just RG-58. Figure 3.1 shows an example of thinnet. This connector resembles the coaxial connector used for cable TV, which is called an *F-type connector*.

FIGURE 3.1 A stripped-back thinnet cable

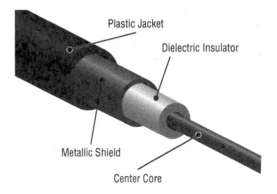

Plastic Jacket

Dielectric Insulator

Metallic Shield

Center Core

Oh, by the way, if you use thinnet cable, you've got to use *BNC* connectors to attach stations to the network, as shown in Figure 3.2, and you have to use 50 ohm terminating resistors at each end of the cable in order to achieve the proper performance.

FIGURE 3.2   Male and female BNC connectors

 You don't have to know much about most coax cable types in networks anymore, especially the thinnet and thicknet types of coaxial cable. Thicknet was known as RG-8 and was about 1/2" in diameter, also requiring 50 ohm terminating resistors on each end of the cable. Nowadays, we use 75-ohm coax for cable TV; using coax in the Ethernet LAN world is pretty much a thing of the past, but we do use them for high-bandwidth runs in our data centers. RG-6, or CATV coax, is used in our broadband world.

You can attach a BNC connector to the cable with a crimper that looks like a weird pair of pliers and has a die to crimp the connector. A simple squeeze crimps the connector to the cable. You can also use a screw-on connector, but I avoid doing that because it's not very reliable.

You can use a BNC coupler to connect two male connectors together or two female connectors together.

Table 3.1 lists some specifications for the different types of coaxial cable, but understand that we use only RG-59 and RG-6 in today's world.

F-type

The F connector, or F-type connector, is a form of coaxial connector that is used for cable TV. It has an end that screws to tighten the connector to the interface. It resembles the RG-58 mentioned earlier in this section.

TABLE 3.1   Coaxial cable specifications

RG Rating	Popular Name	Ethernet Implementation	Type of Cable
RG-58 U	N/A	None	Solid copper
RG-58 A/U	Thinnet	10Base2	Stranded copper
RG-8	Thicknet	10Base5	Solid copper
RG-59	Cable television Low cost, short distance	N/A	Solid copper
RG-6	Cable television, cable modems Longer distances than RG-59; some power implementations	N/A	Solid copper
RG-62	ARCnet (obsolete)	N/A	Solid/stranded

An advantage of using coax cable is the braided shielding that provides resistance to electronic pollution like *electromagnetic interference (EMI)*, *radio frequency interference (RFI)*, and other types of stray electronic signals that can make their way onto a network cable and cause communication problems.

Twisted-Pair Cable

Twisted-pair cable consists of multiple individually insulated wires that are twisted together in pairs. Sometimes a metallic shield is placed around them, hence the name *shielded twisted-pair (STP)*. Cable without outer shielding is called *unshielded twisted-pair (UTP)*, and it's used in twisted-pair Ethernet (10BaseT, 100BaseTX, 1000BaseTX, and 10GBaseT) networks.

Twinaxial Cable

Twinaxial cabling is used for short-distance high-speed connections such as 10G Ethernet connections in a data center. The advantage of using Twinax is that there is a significant cost savings over fiber-optic cabling since Twinaxial cables are copper based.

Ethernet Cable Descriptions

Ethernet cable types are described using a code that follows this format: *N* *<Signaling>* *X*. The *N* refers to the signaling rate in megabits per second. *<Signaling>* stands for the signaling type—either baseband or broadband—and the X is a unique identifier for a specific Ethernet cabling scheme.

Here's a common example: 100BaseX. The 100 tells us that the transmission speed is 100 Mb, or 100 megabits. The X value can mean several different things; for example, a T is short for *twisted-pair*. This is the standard for running 100-megabit Ethernet over two pairs (four wires) of Category 5, 5e, 6, 6a, 7, and 8 UTP.

So why are the wires in this cable type twisted? Because when electromagnetic signals are conducted on copper wires in close proximity—like inside a cable—it causes interference called *crosstalk*. Twisting two wires together as a pair minimizes interference and even protects against interference from outside sources. This cable type is the most common today for the following reasons:

- It's cheaper than other types of cabling.

- It's easy to work with.

- It allows transmission rates that were impossible 10 years ago.

UTP cable is rated in these categories:

Category 1   Two twisted wire pairs (four wires). It's the oldest type and is only voice grade—it isn't rated for data communication. People refer to it as plain old telephone service (POTS). Before 1983, this was the standard cable used throughout the North American telephone system. POTS cable still exists in parts of the public switched telephone network (PSTN) and supports signals limited to the 1 MHz frequency range.

Category is often shortened to *Cat*. Today, any cable installed should be a minimum of Cat 5e because some cable is now certified to carry bandwidth signals of 350 MHz or beyond. This allows unshielded twisted-pair cables to exceed speeds of 1 Gbps—fast enough to carry broadcast-quality video over a network.

Category 2   Four twisted wire pairs (eight wires). It handles up to 4 Mbps, with a frequency limitation of 10 MHz, and is now obsolete.

Category 3   Four twisted wire pairs (eight wires) with three twists per foot. This type can handle transmissions up to 16 MHz. It was popular in the mid-1980s for up to 10 Mbps Ethernet, but it's now limited to telecommunication equipment and, again, is obsolete for networks.

Category 4   Four twisted wire pairs (eight wires), rated for 20 MHz; also obsolete.

Category 5   Four twisted wire pairs (eight wires), used for 100BaseTX (two pair wiring) and rated for 100 MHz. But why use Cat 5 when you can use Cat 5e for the same price? I am not sure you can even buy plain Cat 5 anymore! Using Cat 6 is an option but it's slightly harder to install due to its size compared to 5e.

Category 5e (Enhanced) Four twisted wire pairs (eight wires), recommended for 1000BaseT (four pair wiring) and rated for 100 MHz but capable of handling the disturbance on each pair that's caused by transmitting on all four pairs at the same time—a feature that's needed for Gigabit Ethernet. Any category below 5e shouldn't be used in today's network environments.

Figure 3.3 shows a basic Cat 5e cable with the four wire pairs twisted to reduce crosstalk.

FIGURE 3.3   Cat 5e UTP cable

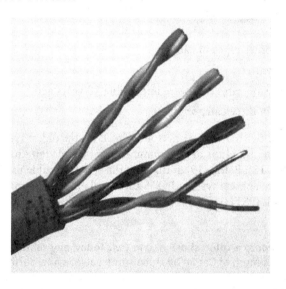

Category 6 Four twisted wire pairs (eight wires), used for 1000BaseTX (two pair wiring) and rated for 250 MHz. Cat 6 became a standard back in June 2002. You would generally use it as riser cable to connect floors together. If you're installing a new network in a new building, there's no reason to use anything but Category 6 UTP cabling as well as using fiber runs between floors.

Category 6A (Augmented) Basic Category 6 cable has a reduced maximum length when used for 10GBaseT; however, Category 6A cable, or Augmented Category 6, is characterized to 500 MHz and has improved crosstalk characteristics, which allows 10GBaseT to be run for up to 100 meters. The most important point is a performance difference between Electronic Industries Alliance and Telecommunications Industry Association (EIA/TIA) component specifications for the NEXT (near-end crosstalk) transmission parameter. Running at a frequency of 500 MHz, an ISO/IEC Cat 6A connector provides double the power (3db) of a Cat 6A connector that conforms with the EIA/TIA specification. Note that 3 dB equals a 100 percent increase of a near-end crosstalk noise reduction.

Category 7   Category 7 cable, Cat 7, allows 10 Gigabit Ethernet over 100 meters of copper cabling. The cable contains four twisted copper wire pairs, just like the earlier standards.

Category 8   Cat 8 cable was developed to address the ever-increasing speed of Ethernet and added support for 25G and 40G transmission with a distance of 30 meters, which is perfect for data center deployments.

Connecting UTP

BNC connectors won't fit very well on UTP cable, so you need to use a *registered jack (RJ)* connector, which you're familiar with because most telephones connect with them. The connector used with UTP cable is called RJ-11 for phones that use four wires; RJ-45 has four pairs (eight wires), as shown in Figure 3.4.

FIGURE 3.4   RJ-11 and RJ-45 connectors

Figure 3.5 shows the pin-outs used in a typical RJ-45 connector.

FIGURE 3.5   The pin-outs in an RJ-45 connector, T568B standard

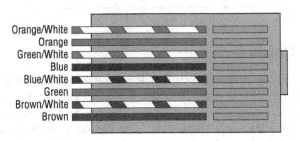

Most of the time, UTP uses RJ connectors, and you use a crimper to attach them to a cable, just as you would with BNC connectors. The only difference is that the die that holds the connector is a different shape. Higher-quality crimping tools have interchangeable dies for both types of cables. We don't use RJ-11 for local area networks (LANs), but we do use them for our home Digital Subscriber Line (DSL) connections.

RJ-11 uses two wire pairs, and RJ-45 uses four wire pairs.

There's one other type of copper connector, called the RJ-48c, which looks exactly like an RJ-45 connector. This plug is very similar to the RJ-45 in that it has four wire pairs, but they are wired differently and used for different circumstances.

RJ-45 is mainly used in LANs with short distances (typically up to 100 meters), where the RJ-48c wiring type would be used with a T1 connection, which is a long-distance wide area network (WAN). In addition, to protect the signal in an RJ-48c, the wires are typically shielded, whereas the RJ-45 uses unshielded wiring.

Category 5e Cabling Tips

Since you want data rates faster than 10 Mbps over UTP, ensure that all components are rated to deliver this and be really careful when handling all components. If you yank on Cat 5e cable, it will stretch the number of twists inside the jacket, rendering the Cat 5e label on the outside of the cable invalid. Also, be certain to connect and test all four pairs of wire. Although today's wiring generally uses only two pairs (four wires), the standard for Gigabit Ethernet over UTP requires that all four pairs (eight wires) be in good condition.

Also be aware that a true Cat 5e cabling system uses rated components from end to end, patch cables from workstation to wall panel, cable from wall panel to patch panel, and patch cables from patch panel to hub. So, if any components are missing, or if the lengths don't match the Category 5e specification, you just don't have a Category 5e cabling installation. And certify that the entire installation is Category 5e compliant. I've got to warn you that doing this requires some pretty pricey test equipment to make the appropriate measurements!

Fiber-Optic Cable

Because fiber-optic cable transmits digital signals using light impulses rather than electricity, it's immune to EMI and RFI. Anyone who's seen a network's UTP cable run down an elevator shaft would definitely appreciate this fiber feature. Fiber cable allows light impulses to be carried on either a glass or a plastic core. Glass can carry the signal a greater distance, but plastic costs less. Whichever the type of core, it's surrounded by a glass or plastic cladding with a different refraction index that reflects the light back into the core. Around this is a layer of flexible plastic buffer that can be wrapped in an armor coating that's usually Kevlar, which is then sheathed in PVC or plenum.

The cable itself comes in either single-mode fiber (SMF) or multimode fiber (MMF); the difference between them is in the number of light rays (the number of signals) they can carry. Multimode fiber is most often used for shorter-distance applications and single-mode fiber for spanning longer distances.

Although fiber-optic cable may sound like the solution to many problems, it has its pros and cons just like the other cable types.

Here are the pros:

- It's completely immune to EMI and RFI.
- It can transmit up to 40 kilometers (about 25 miles).

And here are the cons:

- It's difficult to install.
- It's more expensive than twisted-pair.
- Troubleshooting equipment is more expensive than twisted-pair test equipment.
- It's harder to troubleshoot.

Single-Mode Fiber

Single-mode fiber-optic cable (SMF) is a very high-speed, long-distance media that consists of a single strand—sometimes two strands—of glass fiber that carries the signals. Light-emitting diodes (LEDs) and laser are the light sources used with SMF. The light source is transmitted from end to end and pulsed to create communication. This is the type of fiber cable employed to span really long distances because it can transmit data 50 times farther than multimode fiber at a faster rate.

Clearly, because the transmission media is glass, the installation of SMF can be a bit tricky. Yes, there are outer layers protecting the glass core, but the cable still shouldn't be crimped or pinched around any tight corners.

Multimode Fiber

Multimode fiber-optic cable (MMF) also uses light to communicate a signal, but with it, the light is dispersed on numerous paths as it travels through the core and is reflected back. A special material called *cladding* is used to line the core and focus the light back onto it. MMF provides high bandwidth at high speeds over medium distances (up to about 3,000 feet), but beyond that it can be really inconsistent. This is why MMF is most often used within a smaller area of one building; SMF can be used between buildings.

MMF is available in glass or in a plastic version that makes installation a lot easier and increases the installation's flexibility. Fiber specifications are covered in great detail in Chapter 4.

APC vs. UPC

The choice between *angled physical contact (APC)* and *ultra physical contact (UPC)* can make a pretty big difference on how your network will perform.

The ultra-polished connector looks like what you'd expect to find in a fiber-optic end. The cut is perfectly straight, as shown on the right in Figure 3.6.

The angle-polished connector looks like the one on the left in Figure 3.6. Notice the perfectly cut angle, which seems odd, but there is a reason for this and it's a good one!

With the UPC, the light is reflected back down to the core of the fiber cable, which causes a loss of dB called a return loss because the angled connector causes the light to reflect back into the cladding—the thick sides of the glass instead of the core. But the APC doesn't cause nearly as much dB loss when using this type of connector. Very cool design indeed!

FIGURE 3.6   APC and UPC connectors

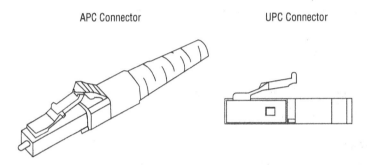

APC Connector   UPC Connector

Fiber-Optic Connectors

A whole bunch of different types of connectors are available to use with fiber-optic cables, but the two most popular are the *straight tip (ST)* and the *subscriber (or square) connector (SC)*. The ST fiber-optic connector (developed by AT&T) is one of the most widely used fiber-optic connectors; it uses a BNC attachment mechanism similar to thinnet's that makes connections and disconnections fairly frustration free. In fact, this is the feature that makes this connector so popular. Figure 3.7 shows an example of an ST connector. Notice the BNC attachment mechanism.

FIGURE 3.7   An example of an ST connector

The SC connector is another type of fiber-optic connector. As you can see in Figure 3.8, SC connectors are *latched*—a mechanism holds the connector in securely and prevents it from falling out.

FIGURE 3.8   A sample SC connector

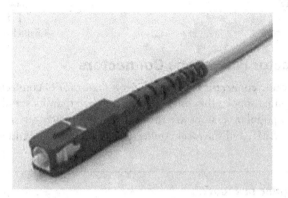

SC connectors work with both single-mode and multimode optical fibers and will last for around 1,000 mattings. They're being used more now but still aren't nearly as popular as ST connectors for LAN connections.

Another type of connector I want to mention is the FC connector (although not covered in the exam objectives, it's important to know for foundation), or field assembly connector, also called the ferrule connector, which isn't very popular. It's still used in telecommunications and measurement equipment with single-mode lasers, but the SC is a way more popular fiber end. These look identical to ST connectors.

You can also get a fiber coupler in order to connect an ST to an SC connector, for example, but you will lose a lot of your power (dB) if you do so.

Fiber Distribution Panel

Fiber distribution panels (FDPs) are termination and distribution systems for fiber-optic cable facilities. They consist of a cable management tray and a splice drawer. They are designed for central offices, remote offices, and LANs using fiber-optic facilities.

Fiber-Optic Transceivers

Fiber-optic transceivers can be either unidirectional (simplex) or bidirectional (duplex).

Bidirectional   Bidirectional communication is possible if the cable used is following the EEE 802.3ah 1000BASE-BX10-D and 1000BASE-BX10-U standards. The communication over a single strand of fiber is achieved by separating the transmission wavelength of the two devices, as depicted in Figure 3.9.

FIGURE 3.9   Bidirectional communication

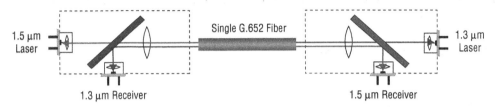

Small Form Factor Fiber-Optic Connectors

Another cool fiber-optic connector is the *small form factor (SFF)* connector, which allows more fiber-optic terminations in the same amount of space than its standard-sized counterparts. The two most popular versions are the *mechanical transfer registered jack (MT-RJ or MTRJ)*, designed by AMP, and the *local connector (LC)*, designed by Lucent.

Should I Use Copper or Fiber?

If your data runs are measured in miles, fiber optic is your cable of choice because copper just can't give you more than about 1,500 feet without electronics regenerating the signal. The standards limit UTP to a pathetic 328 feet.

Another good reason to opt for fiber is if you require high security because it doesn't create a readable magnetic field. Although fiber-optic technology was initially super expensive and nasty to work with, it's now commonly used for Gigabit, 10 GB, or 40 GB Internet backbones.

Ethernet running at 10 Mbps over fiber-optic cable to the desktop is designated 10BaseFL; the 100 Mbps version of this implementation is 100BaseFX. The *L* in the 10 Mbps version stands for *link*. Other designations are *B* for *backbone* and *P* for *passive*.

The MT-RJ fiber-optic connector was the first small form factor fiber-optic connector to be widely used, and it's only one-third the size of the SC and ST connectors it most often replaces. It offers these benefits:

- Small size
- TX and RX strands in one connector
- Keyed for single polarity
- Pre-terminated ends that require no polishing or epoxy
- Easy to use

Figure 3.10 shows an example of an MT-RJ fiber-optic connector.

FIGURE 3.10   A sample MT-RJ fiber-optic connector

LC is a newer style of SFF fiber-optic connector that's pulling ahead of the MT-RJ. It's especially popular for use with Fibre-Channel adapters (FCs) and is a standard used for fast storage area networks and Gigabit Ethernet adapters. Figure 3.11 depicts an example of the LC connector.

FIGURE 3.11   A sample LC fiber-optic connector

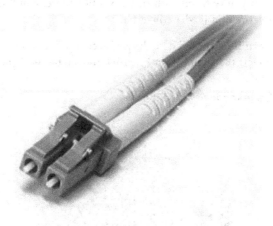

It has similar advantages to MT-RJ and other SFF-type connectors but it's easier to terminate. It uses a ceramic insert just as standard-sized fiber-optic connectors do.

Transceivers

A transceiver is a device made up of both a transmitter and a receiver, which are combined and share common circuitry or a single housing. The term applies to wireless communications devices such as cellular telephones, cordless telephone sets, handheld two-way radios, and mobile two-way radios. Occasionally, the term is used in reference to transmitter and receiver devices in cable or optical fiber systems.

SFP+   The *small form-factor pluggable (SFP)* is a compact pluggable optical module transceiver used for both telecommunication and data communications applications. The *enhanced small form-factor pluggable (SFP+)* transceiver is an enhanced version of the SFP that supports data rates up to 16 Gbit/s.

QSFP   The *quad small form-factor pluggable (QSFP)* is another compact, hot-pluggable transceiver used for data communications applications. It interfaces networking hardware (such as servers and switches) to a fiber-optic cable or active or passive electrical copper connection. It allows data rates from 4x1 Gb/s for QSFP and 4x10 Gbit/s for QSFP+ to the highest rate of 4x28 Gbit/s known as QSFP28 used for 100 Gbit/s links.

Media Converters

Sometimes, you'll need to convert from one media type to another. Maybe you need to go from one mode of fiber to another mode, or in an even more extreme case, you need to go from fiber to Ethernet. If you're faced with situations like these, you'll need to be familiar with some of the more common media converters:

Single-Mode Fiber to Ethernet   These devices accept a fiber connector and an Ethernet connector and convert the signal from Ethernet and single-mode fiber (see Figure 3.12).

FIGURE 3.12   Single-mode fiber to Ethernet

Multimode Fiber to Ethernet   These devices accept a fiber connector and an Ethernet connector and convert the signal from Ethernet and multimode fiber (see Figure 3.13).

FIGURE 3.13   Multimode fiber to Ethernet

Fiber to Coaxial   These devices accept a fiber connector and a coaxial connector and convert digital signals from optical to coax (see Figure 3.14).

FIGURE 3.14   Fiber to coaxial

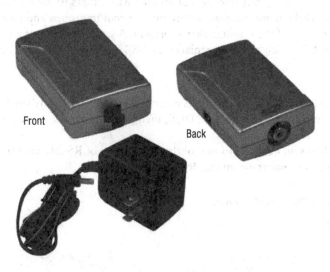

Single-Mode to Multimode Fiber   These devices accept a single-mode fiber connector and a multimode fiber connector and convert the signals between the two (see Figure 3.15).

FIGURE 3.15   Single-mode to multimode fiber

Serial Cables

Except for multimode fiber, all the cable varieties I've talked about so far are considered serial cable types. In network communications, *serial* means that one bit after another is sent out onto the wire or fiber and interpreted by a network card or other type of interface on the other end.

Each 1 or 0 is read separately and then combined with others to form data. This is very different from parallel communication, where bits are sent in groups and have to be read together to make sense of the message they represent. A good example of a parallel cable is an old printer cable—which has been replaced by USB, as I'll get to in a minute.

RS-232

Recommended Standard 232 (RS-232) was a cable standard commonly used for serial data signals connecting the DTE and the DCE, such as a computer's serial port to an external modem.

Figure 3.16 shows an example of one of the many types of RS-232 cables. These cables normally connect to a connector on the device called a *DB-9*.

FIGURE 3.16   RS-232 cable ends

Because laptops don't even come with these types of connectors anymore, they've pretty much been replaced by things like USB and USB-C.

DB-25

Now here's a connector that has been around for a while! The D series of connectors was invented by ITT Cannon in 1952, and the *D* was followed by *A*, *B*, *C*, *D*, or *E*, which described the shell size, and then the numbers of pins or sockets. DB-25 tells us we have 25 pins in a "B" size shell. RS-232 devices generally used the DB-25 connector, but today we don't use RS-232 or DB-25, and we rarely use a DB-9, which was used for Cisco console cables but has mostly been replaced by USB.

Universal Serial Bus

Universal Serial Bus (USB) is now the built-in serial bus used on most motherboards. You usually get a maximum of 4 external USB interfaces, but add-on adapters can take that up to as many as 16 serial interfaces. USB can actually connect a maximum of 127 external devices, and it's a much more flexible peripheral bus than either serial or parallel.

We use USB to connect printers, scanners, and a host of other input devices like keyboards, joysticks, and mice. When connecting USB peripherals, you've got to connect them either directly to one of the USB ports on the PC or to a USB hub that is connected to one of those USB ports. You can get a picture of this in Figure 3.17.

FIGURE 3.17   A USB port

Hubs can be chained together to provide multiple USB connections, but even though you can connect up to 127 devices, it's really not practical to go there. Each device has a USB plug, shown in Figure 3.18.

FIGURE 3.18   A USB plug

Cable Properties

The reason we use so many different types of cables in a network is that each type has its own set of properties that specifically make it the best to use for a particular area or purpose. Different types vary in transmission speeds, distance, duplex, noise immunity, and frequency, and I'll cover each of these next.

Transmission Speeds

Based on the type of cable or fiber you choose and the network that it's installed in, network administrators can control the speed of a network to meet the network's traffic demands. Admins usually permit, or would like to have, transmission speeds of up to 10 Gbps or higher on the core areas of their networks that connect various network segments. In the distribution and access areas, where users connect to switches, it's typically 100 Mbps per connection, but transmission speeds are creeping up because the traffic demand is getting higher.

Distance

Deciding factors used in choosing what cable type to use often come down to the topology of a network and the distance between its components. Some network technologies can run much farther than others without communication errors, but all network communication technologies are prone to *attenuation*—the degradation of a signal due to the medium itself and the distance signals have to travel. Some cable types suffer from attenuation more than others. For instance, any network using twisted-pair cable should have a maximum segment length of only 328 feet (100 meters).

Duplex

All communications are either half-duplex or full-duplex. The difference is whether the communicating devices can "talk" and "listen" at the same time.

During half-duplex communication, a device can either send communication or receive communication, but not both at the same time. Think walkie-talkie—when you press the button on the walkie-talkie, you turn the speaker off and you can't hear anything the other side is saying.

In full-duplex communication, both devices can send and receive communication at the same time. This means that the effective throughput is doubled and communication is much more efficient. Full duplex is typical in most of today's switched networks. I'll discuss both full- and half-duplex in more detail in Chapter 4, "The Current Ethernet Specifications."

Noise Immunity (Security, EMI)

Anytime electrons are pushed through two wires next to each other, a magnetic current is created. And we can create a current in the wires. This is good because without *magnetic flux*, we wouldn't be using computers—the power that surges through them is a result of it. The bad news is that it also creates two communications issues.

First, because the wire is creating a current based on the 1s and 0s coursing through it, with the right tools in hand, people can read the message in the wire without cutting it or even removing the insulation. You've heard of this—it's called *tapping* the wire, and it's clearly a valid security concern. In ancient history, high-security installations like the Pentagon actually encased communication wires in lead shielding to prevent them from being tapped. STP wires make tapping a little harder, but not hard enough.

The best way to solve the magnetic-flux problem caused by electricity is to not use these wires at all. As I said, fiber-optic cables carry the signal as light on a glass or a really pure plastic strand, and light is not susceptible to magnetic flux, making fiber optics a whole lot harder to tap. It's still not impossible—you can do it at the equipment level, but you have to actually cut and then repair the cable to do that, which isn't likely to go unnoticed.

The second magnetic-flux issue comes from the outside in instead of from the inside out. Because wires can take on additional current if they're near any source of magnetism, you've got to be really careful where you run your cables. You can avoid EMI by keeping copper cables away from all powerful magnetic sources like electric motors, speakers, amplifiers, fluorescent light ballasts, and so on. Just keep them away from anything that can generate a magnetic field!

Frequency

Each cable type has a specified maximum frequency that gives you the transmission bandwidth it can handle. Cat 5e cable is tested to 100 MHz maximum frequency and can run 1 Gbps signals for relatively short distances. That's maxing it out, but it's still good for connecting desktop hosts at high speeds. On the other hand, Cat 6 is a 250 MHz cable that can handle 1 Gbps data flow all day long with ease. Cat 6 has a lot more twists and thicker cables, so it's best used when connecting floors of a building; however, be sure to check out Cat 7 and 8, which is more of our future cabling.

Although a signal is measured as bandwidth, the capacity to carry the signal in a cable is measured as frequency.

Wiring Standards

Ethernet cabling is an important thing to understand, especially if you're planning to work on any type of LAN. There are different types of wiring standards available:

- T568A
- T568B
- Straight-through
- Crossover
- Rolled/rollover

We will look into each one of these, and then I'll end this discussion with some examples for you.

T568A vs. T568B

If you look inside a network cable, you'll find four pairs of wires twisted together to prevent crosstalk; they're also twisted like this to help prevent EMI and tapping. The same pins have to be used on the same colors throughout a network to receive and transmit, but how do you decide which color wire goes with which pin? The good news is that you don't have to decide—at least not completely.

Two wiring standards have surfaced that have been agreed on by over 60 vendors, including AT&T, 3Com, and Cisco, although there isn't 100 percent agreement. In other words, over the years, some network jacks have been pinned with the T568A standard and some have used the T568B standard, which can cause a bit of confusion if you don't know what you're looking at in your network.

T568A   By looking at Figure 3.19, you can see that the green pair is used for pins 1 and 2 but the orange pair is split to pins 3 and 6, separated by the blue pair.

T568B   Now take a look at Figure 3.20. The orange pair is pins 1 and 2 and the green pair is pins 3 and 6, again separated by the blue pair.

FIGURE 3.19   T568A wired standard

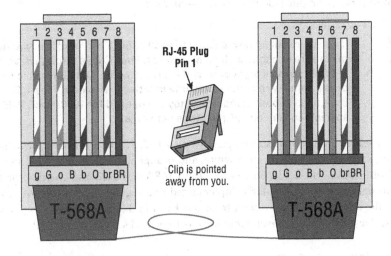

FIGURE 3.20   T568B wired standard

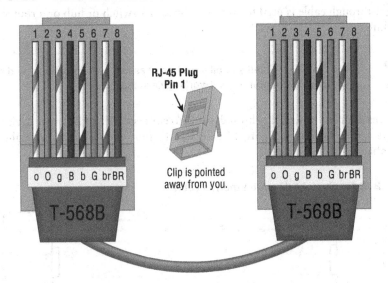

 Note that the only difference between T568A and T568B is that pairs 2 and 3 (orange and green) are swapped. Also, you can use a UTP coupler in order to connect two RJ-45 connectors together to lengthen a cable or in order to make a straight-through cable into a crossover, and vice versa.

If you're thinking, "What's the difference, and why does it matter?," the answer is the position of four wires on one side of the cable—that's it!

If you're installing new cabling to each cubicle and/or office, you need to make sure to connect all eight pins—and use Cat 5e through 8. Voice over IP (VoIP) uses all eight pins, and it's really common to have voice and data on the same wire at the same time in today's networks. Pins 4, 5, 7, and 8 are used in both standards. They are needed for 1000BaseT, PoE, and specialized versions of 100 Mbps networks.

This only leaves the wire pairs to connect to pins 1, 2, 3, and 6 for data. Remember, if we connect the green-white, green, orange-white, and orange wires to pins 1, 2, 3, and 6, respectively, on both sides of the cable, we're using the T568A standard and creating the kind of straight-through cable that's regularly implemented as a regular *patch cable* for most networks. On the other hand, if we switch from pin 1 to pin 3 and from pin 2 to pin 6 on one side only, we've created a *crossover cable* for most networks. Let's take a look.

Straight-Through Cable

The straight-through cable is used to connect a host to a switch or hub or a router to a switch or hub.

No worries—I'll tell you all about devices like switches, hubs, and routers in detail in Chapter 5, "Networking Devices."

Four wires are used in straight-through cable to connect 10/100 Ethernet devices. It's really pretty simple to do this; Figure 3.21 depicts the four wires used in a straight-through Ethernet cable.

FIGURE 3.21   Straight-through Ethernet cable

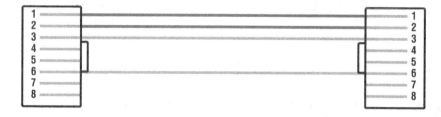

Notice that only pins 1, 2, 3, and 6 are used. Connect 1 to 1, 2 to 2, 3 to 3, and 6 to 6 and you'll be up and networking in no time. Just remember that this would be a 10/100 Ethernet-only cable, so it wouldn't work with 1000 Mbps or greater Ethernet.

Crossover Cable

The same four wires are used in this cable, and just as with the straight-through cable, you simply connect the different pins together. Crossover cables can be used to connect these devices:

- Switch to switch
- Hub to hub
- Host to host
- Hub to switch
- Router direct to host

Take a look at Figure 3.22, which demonstrates how each of the four wires is used in a crossover Ethernet cable.

FIGURE 3.22   Crossover Ethernet cable

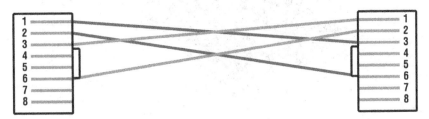

Okay—did you notice that instead of connecting 1 to 1, 2 to 2, and so on, we connected pins 1 to 3 and 2 to 6 on each side of the cable? A crossover cable is typically used to connect two switches together, but it can also be used to test communications between two workstations directly, bypassing the switch.

A crossover cable is used only in Ethernet UTP installations. You can connect two workstation NICs or a workstation and a server NIC directly with it.

If you are trying to match the straight-through and crossover cables with the T568A and T568B standard, here is how it would look:

T568A+T568A = straight-through

T568B+T568B = straight-through

T568A+T568B = crossover

You're going to find out a lot more about how important it is to label basically everything. But for now, make sure to label a crossover cable as what it is so that no one tries to use it as a workstation patch cable. If they do that, the workstation won't be able to communicate with the hub and the rest of the network!

It's really cool that you can carry a crossover cable with you in your tool bag along with your laptop—then, if you want to ensure that a server's NIC is functioning correctly, you can just connect your laptop directly to the server's NIC using your handy crossover cable. You should be able to log in to the server if both NICs are configured correctly.

Use a cable tester to make sure that what you're dealing with is in fact a crossover cable. The tester can also tell you if there's a problem with the cable. Figure 3.23 shows an inexpensive cable tester for UTP.

FIGURE 3.23   An inexpensive cable tester

This cost-effective little tool will tell you beyond a shadow of a doubt if you have a straight-through or crossover cable—or even if there's a problem with the cable.

UTP Gigabit Wiring (1000BaseT)

In the previous examples of 10BaseT and 100BaseT UTP wiring, only two wire pairs were used, but that's just not good enough for Gigabit UTP transmission.

1000BaseT UTP wiring (Figure 3.24) requires four wire pairs and uses more advanced electronics so that each and every pair in the cable can transmit simultaneously. Even so, Gigabit wiring is almost identical to my earlier 10/100 example, except that we'll use the other two pairs in the cable.

For a straight-through cable it's still 1 to 1, 2 to 2, and so on up to pin 8.

FIGURE 3.24   UTP gigabit crossover Ethernet cable

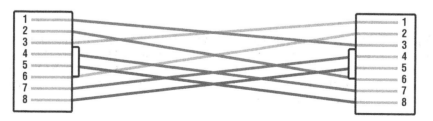

Rolled/Rollover Cable

Although *rolled cable* isn't used to connect any Ethernet connections together, you can use a rolled Ethernet cable to connect a host EIA-TIA 232 interface to a router console serial communication (COM) port.

If you have a Cisco router or switch, you would use this cable to connect your PC, Mac, or a device like a tablet to the Cisco hardware. Eight wires are used in this cable to connect serial devices, although not all eight are used to send information, just as in Ethernet networking. Figure 3.25 shows the eight wires used in a rolled cable.

FIGURE 3.25   Rolled Ethernet cable

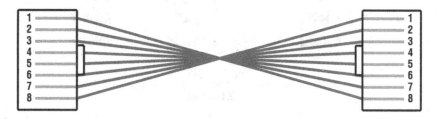

These are probably the easiest cables to make because you just cut the end off on one side of a straight-through cable, turn it over, and put it back on—with a new connector, of course!

T1 Crossover Cable

There is an old device called a CSU/DSU, which used to be all-so-important. This old device may still be your connection to the Internet for the enterprise if you have serial WANs. The type of cable you use to connect to this device from your router depends on the interface types that are available on the router.

The router may connect with several types of serial cables if a T1 connection is not built into it. If a T1 connection is built into the router, you will use an Ethernet cable. Figure 3.26 shows a T1 crossover cable connected to an RJ-45 connector.

In rare instances you may need to run a cable between two CSU/DSUs. In that case you would need a T1 crossover cable. A T1 cable uses pairs 1 and 2, so to connect two T1 CSU/DSU devices back-to-back requires a crossover cable that swaps these pairs. Specifically, pins 1, 2, 4, and 5 are connected to 4, 5, 1, and 2, respectively.

FIGURE 3.26   T1 crossover cable

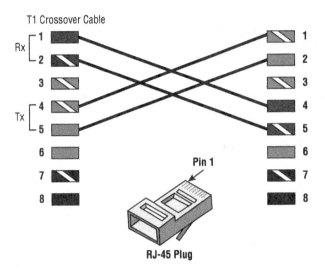

Test Your Cable Understanding

You've taken a look at the various RJ-45 UTP cables. With that in mind, what cable is used between the switches in the following image?

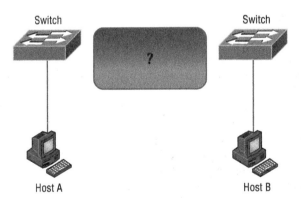

For host A to ping host B, you need a crossover cable to connect the two switches together. But what types of cables are used in the network shown in the following image?

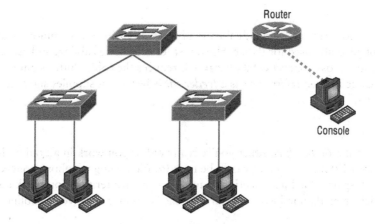

In the second example, there are a variety of cables in use. For the connection between the switches, we'd clearly use a crossover cable like the one you saw in the earlier example. The trouble is, here we have a console connection that uses a rolled cable. Plus, the connection from the router to the switch is a straight-through cable, which is also what's running between the hosts to the switches.

Installing Wiring Distributions

By now, you're probably getting the idea that there are a lot more components in the average computer networks than meets the eye, right? If this isn't exactly a news bulletin to you, then you either already are, or have been, involved in the initial installation of a network. If this describes you, you probably will be, or already are, involved in the purchase and installation of the components that will connect the computers throughout your organization's building. And it may also be up to you to verify that all of the network components have been installed properly and tested. So, let's go over each of these components and the process of verifying their proper installation.

MDF/IDF

The *main distribution frame (MDF)* is a wiring point that's generally used as a reference point for telephone lines. It's also considered the WAN termination point. It's installed in the building as part of the prewiring, and the internal lines are connected to it. After that, all that's left is to connect the external (telephone company) lines to the other side to complete the circuit. Often, another wire frame called an *intermediate distribution frame (IDF)* is located in an equipment or telecommunications room. It's connected to the MDF and is used to provide greater flexibility for the distribution of all the communications lines to the building. It's typically a sturdy metal rack designed to hold the bulk of cables coming from all over the building!

25 Pair

A *25-pair cable* consists of 25 individual pairs of wires all inside one common insulating jacket. It's not generally used for data cabling, just for telephone cabling, and especially for backbone and cross-connect cables because it reduces the cable clutter significantly. This type of cable is often referred to as a *feeder cable* because it supplies signal to many connected pairs.

66 Block

If you know what a *66 block* is, either you're really old or you work in an old building since they came out in 1962 and can really only be used for old analog telephone connections. This uses the 25-pair cable I just mentioned and is a standard termination block containing 50 rows, which created an industry standard for easy termination of voice cabling.

110 Block

A newer type of wiring distribution point called a *110 block* has replaced most telephone wire installations and is also used for computer networking. On one side, wires are punched down; the other side has RJ-11 (for phone) or RJ-45 (for network) connections.

You'll find 110 blocks in sizes from 25 to more than 500 wire pairs, and some are capable of carrying 1 Gbps connections when used with Category 6 or greater cables. The hitch is that using Cat 6 with the 110 block is really difficult because of the size of the Cat 6 wiring. Figure 3.27 shows a 110 block and describes each section used in the 110 block.

There is a proprietary European variant of the 110 block called a Krone block. The *Krone* block is compatible with the 110 block and can be used interchangeably.

FIGURE 3.27   A 110 block

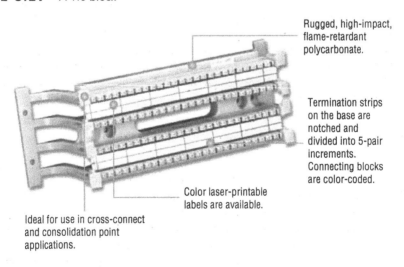

Rugged, high-impact, flame-retardant polycarbonate.

Termination strips on the base are notched and divided into 5-pair increments. Connecting blocks are color-coded.

Color laser-printable labels are available.

Ideal for use in cross-connect and consolidation point applications.

BIX Block

Another type of punch-down block is the *BIX* block. A BIX block can terminate up to 25 cable pairs and have a slip-in fitting that does not require the wires to be pre-stripped.

Demarc/Demarc Extension

The *demarc* (short for demarcation) is the last point of responsibility for the service provider. It's often at the MDF in your building connection, especially if your building is large, but it's usually just an RJ-45 jack that your channel service unit/data service unit (CSU/DSU) connects from your router to wide area network (WAN) connections.

When troubleshooting, network admins often test for connectivity on both sides of the demarc to determine if the problem is internal or external. The length of copper or fiber that begins after the demarc but still doesn't reach all the way up to your office is referred to as a *demarc extension*.

Smart Jack

A *smart jack*, also called a network interface device (NID) or network interface unit (NIU), is owned by the PSTN and is a special network interface that's often used between the service provider's network and the internal network. You can't physically test to an actual demarc because it's just an RJ-45 jack, but the service provider may install an NID that has power and can be looped for testing purposes.

The smart jack device may also provide for code and protocol conversion, making the signal from the service provider usable by the devices on the internal network like the CSU/DSU.

Summary

I know getting through this chapter probably wasn't the most fun you've had recently. But understanding all those types of wires and cabling, along with their unique capacities, their associated standards, and the right connectors to use with them plus where to place them, is integral to having a solid, foundational understanding of the things that make a great network run quickly and reliably.

It's critical for you to grasp the basics of networking. Having the facts about how a good network is designed and implemented and what goes into that process will make you an effective and efficient technician—and maybe, some day, a highly paid system administrator.

Exam Essentials

Understand the various types of cables used in today's networks. Coaxial (other than for cable modems) is rarely used, but twisted-pair and fiber-optic cable are very common in today's networks.

Understand the various types of ends that are used on each type of cable. Coax uses BNC; twisted-pair uses RJ-11 for voice and RJ-45 for data; and fiber uses various ends, depending on its use.

Describe the various types of media converters that are available. These include single-mode fiber to Ethernet, multimode fiber to Ethernet, fiber to coaxial, and single-mode to multimode fiber.

Understand what a T568A to T568A cable is. A T568A to T568A cable is also known as an Ethernet straight-through cable and is used to connect hosts to switches, for example.

Understand what a T568A to T568B cable is. A T568A to T568B cable is also known as an Ethernet crossover cable and is used to connect switches to switches, for example.

Define the function of a T1 crossover cable. In rare instances, you may have the need to run a cable between two CSU/DSUs. In that case, you will need a T1 crossover cable. A T1 cable uses pairs 1 and 2, so to connect two T1 CSU/DSU devices back-to-back requires a crossover cable that swaps these pairs. Specifically, pins 1, 2, 4, and 5 are connected to 4, 5, 1, and 2, respectively.

Written Lab

You can find the answers to the written labs in Appendix A.

1. Which UTP wiring uses four twisted wire pairs (eight wires) and is rated for 250 MHz?

2. The point at which the operational control or ownership changes from your company to a service provider is referred to as what?

3. Which type of cable will you use to connect two switches to each other?

4. Which RG rating of coax is used for cable modems?

5. Which UTP uses four twisted wire pairs (eight wires), is rated for 100 MHz, and is capable of handling the disturbance on each pair caused by transmitting on all four pairs at the same time?

6. You want to connect a host to a switch port. What type of Ethernet cable will you use?

7. In what instance would you use T1 crossover cable?

8. T568A uses which pins to make a connection?

9. A crossover uses which pins to make a connection?

10. What are two advantages of fiber-optic cabling?

Review Questions

You can find the answers to the review questions in Appendix B.

1. Why would a network administrator use plenum-rated cable during an installation? (Choose two.)
   A. Low combustion temperature
   B. High combustion temperature
   C. Reduces toxic gas released during a fire
   D. Is not susceptible to any interference

2. Which of the following Ethernet unshielded twisted-pair cabling types is/are commonly used?
   A. 10BaseT
   B. 100BaseTX
   C. 1000BaseTX
   D. All of the above

3. In which of the following categories is UTP cable not rated?
   A. Category 2
   B. Category 3
   C. Category 5e
   D. Category 9

4. What type of connector does UTP cable typically use?
   A. BNC
   B. ST
   C. RJ-45

5. Which of the following provides the longest cable run distance?
   A. Single-mode fiber
   B. Multimode fiber
   C. Category 3 UTP
   D. Coax

6. You need to crimp on a connector using an RJ-45 connector. Which pin-out configuration would you use to connect a host to a switch?
   A. UTP
   B. Straight-through
   C. Crossover
   D. Rolled

7. Why is fiber-optic cable immune to electromagnetic interference (EMI) and radio frequency interference (RFI)?

    A. Because it transmits analog signals using electricity

    B. Because it transmits analog signals using light impulses

    C. Because it transmits digital signals using light impulses

    D. Because it transmits digital signals using electricity

8. What type of cable transmits lights from end to end?

    A. Coax

    B. Fiber-optic

    C. UTP

    D. Category 2

9. What is the main difference between single-mode fiber (SMF) and multimode fiber (MMF)?

    A. Electrical signals

    B. Number of light rays

    C. Number of digital signals

    D. That signal-mode can be run a shorter distance

10. What type of cable should be used if you need to make a cable run longer than 100 meters?

    A. Category 5e

    B. Category 6

    C. Fiber-optic

    D. Coaxial

11. Which of the following are fiber-optic connectors? (Choose three.)

    A. BNC

    B. ST

    C. RJ-11

    D. SC

    E. LC

    F. RJ-45

12. You need to connect two devices on a network and they need to send voice traffic. Which of the following cables will you use?

    A. Cat 3

    B. Cat 5

    C. CSU/DSU

    D. Rolled

13. How many hosts on a half-duplex segment can talk at one time?

    A. Zero

    B. One

    C. Two

    D. Unlimited

14. On which type of cable does EMI have the least effect?

    A. Coax

    B. Fiber-optic

    C. UTP

    D. STP

15. How many devices can be connected to a full-duplex segment?

    A. Zero

    B. One

    C. Two

    D. Four

16. How many wires are used in a 100BaseTX UTP transmission?

    A. Two

    B. Four

    C. Six

    D. Eight

17. A crossover cable is used to connect all of the following except _____.

    A. Switch to switch

    B. Host to host

    C. Hub to switch

    D. Host to switch

18. How is a T1 crossover cable wired?

    A. Pins 1, 2, 4, and 5 are connected to 4, 5, 1, and 2.

    B. Pins 2, 3, 4, and 5 are connected to 4, 5, 1, and 2.

    C. Pins 1, 2, 4, and 5 are connected to 3, 4, 5, and 6.

    D. Pins 4, 5, 6, and 7 are connected to 4, 5, 1, and 2.

19. The purpose of the demarcation point is to separate the customer from whom?

    A. The branch office

    B. Headquarters

    C. The data center

    D. The service provider

20. You need to make a T568B cable for a Fast Ethernet link. How many pairs will you use?

   A.   One

   B.   Two

   C.   Three

   D.   Four

The Current Ethernet Specifications

THE FOLLOWING COMPTIA NETWORK+ EXAM OBJECTIVES ARE COVERED IN THIS CHAPTER:

✓ **1.3 Summarize the types of cables and connectors and explain which is the appropriate type for a solution.**

- Ethernet standards
  - Copper
  - 10BASE-T
  - 100BASE-TX
  - 1000BASE-T
  - 10GBASE-T
  - 40GBASE-T
  - Fiber
  - 100BASE-FX
  - 100BASE-SX
  - 1000BASE-SX
  - 1000BASE-LX
  - 10GBASE-SR
  - 10GBASE-LR
  - Coarse wavelength division multiplexing (CWDM)
  - Dense wavelength division multiplexing (DWDM)
  - Bidirectional wavelength division multiplexing (WDM)

Before we dive into the complex worlds of networking devices, the TCP/IP and DoD models, IP addressing, subnetting, and routing in the upcoming chapters, you have to understand the big picture of LANs and learn the answer to these key questions: How is Ethernet used in today's networks? What are Media Access Control (MAC) addresses, and how are these identifiers utilized in networking?

This chapter will answer those questions and more. I'll not only discuss the basics of Ethernet and the way MAC addresses are used on an Ethernet LAN, I'll also cover the protocols used with Ethernet at the Data Link layer. You'll also learn about the various Ethernet specifications.

So now, let's get started with the fundamentals of connecting two hosts together.

To find Todd Lammle CompTIA videos and questions, please see www.lammle.com.

Network Basics

Networks and networking have grown exponentially over the last 20 years—understandably so. They've had to evolve at light speed just to keep up with huge increases in basic mission-critical user needs ranging from sharing data and printers to more advanced demands like videoconferencing. Unless everyone who needs to share network resources is located in the same office area (an increasingly uncommon situation), the challenge is to connect the sometimes large number of relevant networks together so all users can share the networks' wealth.

Let's take a look at how communication happens on a basic local area network (LAN), which I started to discuss in Chapter 1, "Introduction to Networks." Starting with Figure 4.1, you get a picture of a basic LAN network that's connected together using an Ethernet connection to a hub. This network is actually one collision domain and one broadcast domain, but don't stress if you have no idea what this means as I'll start to cover those terms in this chapter; however, I'm going to talk about both collision and broadcast domains in depth in Chapter 5, "Networking Devices."

FIGURE 4.1   The basic network

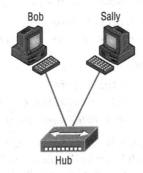

Okay, about Figure 4.1; how would you say the PC named Bob communicates with the PC named Sally? Well, they're both on the same LAN connected with a multiport repeater (a hub). So does Bob just send out a data message, "Hey Sally, you there?" or does Bob use Sally's IP address and put things more like, "Hey 192.168.0.2, are you there?" I hope you picked the IP address option, but even if you did, the news is still bad—both answers are wrong! Why? Because Bob is actually going to use Sally's MAC address (known as a *hardware address*), which is burned right into the network card of Sally's PC, to get a hold of her.

This is all good, but how does Bob get Sally's MAC address when Bob knows only Sally's name and doesn't even have her IP address? Bob is going to start by using name resolution (hostname–to–IP address resolution), something that's usually accomplished using Domain Name Service (DNS). And note that if these two hosts are on the same LAN, Bob can just broadcast to Sally asking her for the information (no DNS needed)—welcome to Microsoft Windows!

Here's the output from a network analyzer depicting a simple name-resolution process from Bob to Sally:

```
Time      Source    Destination  Protocol  Info
53.892794 192.168.0.2 192.168.0.255 NBNS    Name query NB SALLY<00>
```

As I already mentioned, because the two hosts are on a local LAN, Windows (Bob) will broadcast to resolve the name Sally (notice the destination 192.168.0.255 is a broadcast address). Let's take a look at the second part of the information:

```
EthernetII,Src:192.168.0.2(00:14:22:be:18:3b),Dst:Broadcast(ff:ff:ff:ff:ff:ff)
```

This output shows that Bob knows his own MAC address and source IP address but not Sally's IP address or MAC address. So, Bob sent a Data Link layer broadcast address of all Fs and an IP LAN broadcast to 192.168.0.255. Again, no worries—you're going to learn all about broadcasts in Chapter 6, "Introduction to the Internet Protocol."

After the name is resolved, the next thing Bob has to do is broadcast on the LAN to get Sally's MAC address so he can communicate to her PC:

```
Time    Source    Destination Protocol Info
5.153054 192.168.0.2 Broadcast  ARP Who has 192.168.0.3? Tell 192.168.0.2
```

Next, check out Sally's response:

```
Time     Source    Destination Protocol Info
5.153403  192.168.0.3 192.168.0.2 ARP 192.168.0.3 is 00:0b:db:99:d3:5e
5.53.89317 192.168.0.3 192.168.0.2 NBNS Name query response NB 192.168.0.3
```

Okay, sweet—Bob now has both Sally's IP address and her MAC address (00:0b:db:99:d3:5e). These are both listed as the source address at this point because this information was sent from Sally back to Bob. So, *finally*, Bob has all the goods he needs to communicate with Sally. And just so you know, I'm also going to tell you all about Address Resolution Protocol (ARP) and show you exactly how Sally's IP address was resolved to a MAC address a little later, in Chapter 6.

Importantly, I want you to understand that Sally still had to go through the same resolution processes to communicate back to Bob—sounds crazy, huh? Consider this a welcome to IPv4 and basic networking with Windows—and we haven't even added a router yet!

Ethernet Basics

Ethernet is a contention media-access method that allows all hosts on a network to share the same bandwidth of a link. Ethernet is popular because it's readily scalable, meaning that it's comparatively easy to integrate new technologies, such as Fast Ethernet and Gigabit Ethernet, into an existing network infrastructure. It's also relatively simple to implement in the first place, and with it, troubleshooting is reasonably straightforward.

Ethernet uses both Data Link and Physical layer specifications, and this part of the chapter will give you both the Data Link layer and Physical layer information you need to effectively implement, troubleshoot, and maintain an Ethernet network.

In the following sections, I'll also cover some basic terms used in networking with Ethernet technologies. Let's start with collision domains.

Collision Domain

The term *collision domain* is an Ethernet term that refers to a particular network scenario wherein one device sends a packet out on a network segment and thereby forces every other device on that same physical network segment to pay attention to it. This is bad because if two devices on one physical segment transmit at the same time, a *collision event*—a situation where each device's digital signals interfere with another on the wire—occurs and forces the devices to retransmit later. Collisions have a dramatically negative effect on network performance, so they're definitely something we want to avoid!

The situation I just described is typically found in a hub environment where each host segment connects to a hub that represents only one collision domain and one broadcast domain. This begs the question, "What's a broadcast domain?".

Broadcast Domain

Here's that answer: A *broadcast domain* refers to the set of all devices on a network segment that hear all the broadcasts sent on that segment.

Even though a broadcast domain is typically a boundary delimited by physical media like switches and repeaters, it can also reference a logical division of a network segment where all hosts can reach each other via a Data Link layer (hardware address) broadcast.

That's the basic story, but rest assured, I'll be delving deeper into the collision and broadcast domains a bit later, in Chapter 5.

CSMA/CD

Ethernet networking uses *carrier sense multiple access with collision detection (CSMA/CD)*, a media access control contention method that helps devices share the bandwidth evenly without having two devices transmit at the same time on the network medium. CSMA/CD was created to overcome the problem of those collisions that occur when packets are transmitted simultaneously from different hosts. And trust me—good collision management is crucial because when a host transmits in a CSMA/CD network, all the other hosts on the network receive and examine that transmission. Only bridges, switches, and routers, but not hubs, can effectively prevent a transmission from propagating throughout the entire network.

So, how does the CSMA/CD protocol work? Let's start by taking a look at Figure 4.2, where a collision has occurred in the network.

When a host wants to transmit over the network, it first checks for the presence of a digital signal on the wire. If all is clear, meaning that no other host is transmitting, the host will then proceed with its transmission. But it doesn't stop there. The transmitting host constantly monitors the wire to make sure no other hosts begin transmitting. If the host detects another signal on the wire, it sends out an extended jam signal that causes all hosts on the segment to stop sending data (think busy signal). The hosts respond to that jam signal by waiting a while before attempting to transmit again. Backoff algorithms, represented by the clocks counting down on either side of the jammed devices, determine when the colliding stations can retransmit. If collisions keep occurring after 15 tries, the hosts attempting to transmit will then time out. Pretty clean!

When a collision occurs on an Ethernet LAN, the following things happen:

- A jam signal informs all devices that a collision occurred.

- The collision invokes a random backoff algorithm.

- Each device on the Ethernet segment stops transmitting for a short time until the timers expire.

- All hosts have equal priority to transmit after the timers have expired.

FIGURE 4.2   CSMA/CD

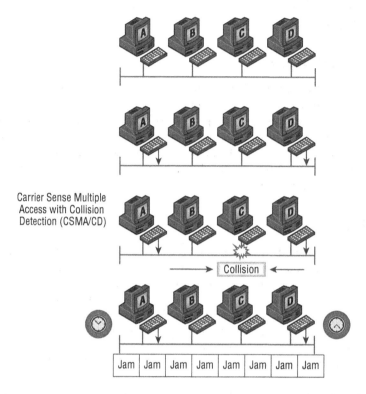

Carrier Sense Multiple
Access with Collision
Detection (CSMA/CD)

And following are the effects of having a CSMA/CD network that has sustained heavy collisions:

- Delay
- Low throughput
- Congestion

NOTE   Backoff on an 802.3 Ethernet network is the retransmission delay that's enforced when a collision occurs. When a collision occurs, a host will resume transmission after the forced time delay has expired. After this backoff delay period has expired, all stations have equal priority to transmit data.

Broadband/Baseband

We have two ways to send analog and digital signals down a wire: broadband and baseband.

We hear the term *broadband* a lot these days because that is pretty much what everyone uses at home. It allows us to have both our analog voice and digital data carried on the same network cable or physical medium. Broadband allows us to send multiple frequencies of different signals down the same wire at the same time (called frequency-division multiplexing) and to send both analog and digital signals.

Baseband is what all LANs use. This is where all the bandwidth of the physical media is used by only one signal. For example, Ethernet uses only one digital signal at a time, and it requires all the available bandwidth. If multiple signals are sent from different hosts at the same time, we get collisions; same with wireless, except that uses only analog signaling.

Bit Rates vs. Baud Rate

Bit rate is a measure of the number of data bits (0s and 1s) transmitted in one second in either a digital or analog signal. A figure of 56,000 bits per second (bps) means 56,000 0s or 1s can be transmitted in one second, which we simply refer to as bps.

In the 1970s and 1980s, we used the term *baud rate* a lot, but that was replaced by *bps* because it was more accurate. *Baud* was a term of measurement named after a French engineer, Jean-Maurice-Émile Baudot, because he used it to measure the speed of telegraph transmissions.

One baud is one electronic state change per second—for example, from 0.2 volts to 3 volts or from binary 0 to 1. However, since a single state change can involve more than a single bit of data, the bps unit of measurement has replaced it as a more accurate definition of how much data you're transmitting or receiving.

Wavelength

Has anyone ever told you that they were on the same wavelength as you? That means they thought you were basically thinking the same way they were. The same is true of the inverse—if they say, "You're not on the same wavelength." With electromagnetic radiation, radio waves, light waves, or even infrared (heat) waves make characteristic patterns as they travel through space. Some patterns can be the same, and some can be different, as shown in Figure 4.3.

Each wave pattern has a certain shape and length. The distance between peaks (high points) is called wavelength. If two wave patterns are different, we would say they're not on the same wavelength and that is the way we tell different kinds of electromagnetic energy apart. We can use this to our advantage in electronics by sending traffic on different wavelengths at the same time.

FIGURE 4.3   Shorter and longer wavelengths

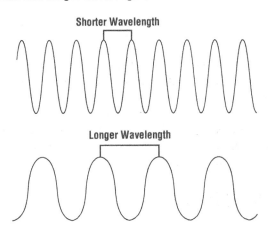

In the following sections, I'm going to cover Ethernet in detail at both the Data Link layer (layer 2) and the Physical layer (layer 1).

Half- and Full-Duplex Ethernet

Just so you know, half-duplex Ethernet is defined in the original 802.3 Ethernet specification. Basically, when you run half-duplex, you're using only one wire pair with a digital signal either transmitting or receiving. This really isn't all that different from full-duplex because you can both transmit and receive—you just don't get to do that at the same time running half-duplex as you can if you're running full-duplex.

Here's how it works: If a host hears a digital signal, it uses the CSMA/CD protocol to help prevent collisions and to permit retransmitting if a collision does occur. Half-duplex Ethernet—typically 10BaseT—is only about 30 to 40 percent efficient because a large 10BaseT network will usually provide only 3 Mbps to 4 Mbps at most. Although it's true that 100 Mbps Ethernet can and sometimes does run half-duplex, it's just not very common to find that happening anymore.

In contrast, full-duplex Ethernet uses two pairs of wires at the same time instead of one measly wire pair like half-duplex employs. Plus, full-duplex uses a point-to-point connection between the transmitter of the sending device and the receiver of the receiving device (in most cases the switch). This means that with full-duplex data transfer, you not only get faster data-transfer speeds, but you get collision prevention too—sweet!

You don't need to worry about collisions because now it's like a freeway with multiple lanes instead of the single-lane road provided by half-duplex. Full-duplex Ethernet is supposed to offer 100 percent efficiency in both directions—for example, you can get 20 Mbps with a 10 Mbps Ethernet running full-duplex, 200 Mbps for Fast Ethernet, or even 2000 Mbps for Gigabit Ethernet. But this rate is something known as an *aggregate rate*, which translates as "you're supposed to get" 100 percent efficiency. No guarantees, in networking as in life.

Full-duplex Ethernet can be used in many situations; here are some examples:

- With a connection from a switch to a host
- With a connection from a switch to a switch
- With a connection from a host to a host using a crossover cable

You can run full-duplex with just about any device except a hub.

You may be wondering: If it's capable of all that speed, why wouldn't it deliver? Well, when a full-duplex Ethernet port is powered on, it first connects to the remote end and then negotiates with the other end of the Fast Ethernet link. This is called an *auto-detect mechanism*. This mechanism first decides on the exchange capability, which means it checks to see if it can run at 10, 100, or even 1000 Mbps. It then checks to see if it can run full-duplex, and if it can't, it will run half-duplex instead.

Hosts usually auto-detect both the Mbps and the duplex type available (the default setting), but you can manually set both the speed and duplex type on the network interface card (NIC), as shown in Figure 4.4.

FIGURE 4.4   Manually adding the speed and duplex type

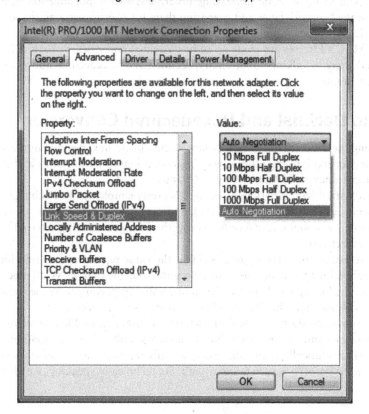

Today, it's pretty rare to go into a NIC configuration on a host and change these settings, but this example demonstrates that you can do that if you want.

 Remember that half-duplex Ethernet shares a collision domain and provides a lower effective throughput than full-duplex Ethernet, which typically has a private collision domain and a higher effective throughput.

Lastly, remember these important points:

- There are no collisions in full-duplex mode.
- A dedicated switch port is required for each full-duplex host.
- The host network card and the switch port must be capable of operating in full-duplex mode.

Now let's take a look at how Ethernet works at the Data Link layer.

Ethernet at the Data Link Layer

Ethernet at the Data Link layer is responsible for Ethernet addressing, commonly referred to as *hardware addressing* or *MAC addressing*. Ethernet is also responsible for framing packets received from the Network layer and preparing them for transmission on the local network through the Ethernet contention media-access method known as CSMA/CD.

Ethernet MAC addresses are made up of hexadecimal addresses. So, before I discuss MAC addresses, let's start by talking about binary, decimal, and hexadecimal addresses and how to convert one to another.

Binary to Decimal and Hexadecimal Conversion

Understanding the differences between binary, decimal, and hexadecimal numbers and how to convert one format into the other is very important before we move on to discussing the TCP/IP protocol stack and IP addressing in Chapters 6 and 7.

So let's get started with binary numbering. It's pretty simple, really. Each digit used is limited to being either a 1 (one) or a 0 (zero), and each digit is called 1 bit (short for *bi*nary digi*t*). Typically, you count either 4 or 8 bits together, with these being referred to as a *nibble* and a *byte*, respectively.

What's interesting about binary numbering is the value represented in a decimal format—the typical decimal format being the base-10 number scheme that we've all used since kindergarten. The binary numbers are placed in a value spot, starting at the right and moving left, with each spot having double the value of the previous spot.

Table 4.1 shows the decimal values of each bit location in a nibble and a byte. Remember, a nibble is four bits and a byte is eight bits. In network addressing, we often refer to a byte as an *octet*. Mathematically, octal addressing actually refers to base 8, which is completely different from the base 10 we are familiar with. So, technically speaking, we are using the term incorrectly, but it's the common usage anyway. When we get to Chapter 8, "IP Subnetting, Troubleshooting IP, and Introduction to NAT," you'll see that I'll use *byte* and *octet* interchangeably when discussing IP addressing.

TABLE 4.1 Binary values

Nibble Values	Byte Values
8 4 2 1	128 64 32 16 8 4 2 1

What all this means is that if a one digit (1) is placed in a value spot, then the nibble or byte takes on that decimal value and adds it to any other value spots that have a 1. And if a zero (0) is placed in a bit spot, you don't count that value.

Let me clarify things for you—if we have a 1 placed in each spot of our nibble, we then add up 8 + 4 + 2 + 1 to give us a maximum value of 15. Another example for our nibble values is 1010, which means that the 8 bit and the 2 bit are turned on and equal a decimal value of 10. If we have a nibble binary value of 0110, then our decimal value is 6 because the 4 and 2 bits are turned on.

But the byte values can add up to a value that's significantly higher than 15. This is how—if we count every bit as a 1, then the byte binary value looks like this (remember, 8 bits equal a byte):

11111111

We then count up every bit spot because each is turned on. It looks like this, which demonstrates the maximum value of a byte:

128 + 64 + 32 + 16 + 8 + 4 + 2 + 1 = 255

A binary number can equal plenty of other decimal values. Let's work through a few examples:

10010110

Which bits are on? The 128, 16, 4, and 2 bits are on, so we'll just add them up: 128 + 16 + 4 + 2 = 150.

01101100

Which bits are on? The 64, 32, 8, and 4 bits are on, so we add them up: 64 + 32 + 8 + 4 = 108.

11101000

Which bits are on? The 128, 64, 32, and 8 bits are on, so we add the values:

128 + 64 + 32 + 8 = 232.

You should memorize Table 4.2 before braving the IP sections in Chapter 6 and Chapter 7 since this lists all available subnet masks.

TABLE 4.2 Binary-to-decimal memorization chart

Binary Value	Decimal Value
10000000	128
11000000	192
11100000	224
11110000	240
11111000	248
11111100	252
11111110	254
11111111	255

Hexadecimal addressing is completely different than binary or decimal—it's converted by reading nibbles, not bytes. By using a nibble, we can convert these bits to hex pretty simply. First, understand that the hexadecimal addressing scheme uses only the numbers 0 through 9. And because the numbers 10, 11, 12, and so on can't be used (because they are two-digit numbers), the letters *A, B, C, D, E,* and *F* are used to represent 10, 11, 12, 13, 14, and 15, respectively.

Table 4.3 shows both the binary value and the decimal value for each hexadecimal digit.

TABLE 4.3 Hex-to-binary-to-decimal chart

Hexadecimal Value	Binary Value	Decimal Value
0	0000	0
1	0001	1
2	0010	2
3	0011	3
4	0100	4

Hexadecimal Value	Binary Value	Decimal Value
5	0101	5
6	0110	6
7	0111	7
8	1000	8
9	1001	9
A	1010	10
B	1011	11
C	1100	12
D	1101	13
E	1110	14
F	1111	15

Did you notice that the first 10 hexadecimal digits (0–9) are the same values as the decimal values? If not, look again. This handy fact makes those values super easy to convert.

So suppose you have something like this: 0x6A. (Some manufacturers put *0x* in front of characters so you know that they're a hex value, while others just give you an *h*. It doesn't have any other special meaning.) What are the binary and decimal values? To correctly answer that question, all you have to remember is that each hex character is one nibble and two hex characters together make a byte. To figure out the binary value, first put the hex characters into two nibbles and then put them together into a byte. 6 = 0110 and A (which is 10 in decimal) = 1010, so the complete byte is 01101010.

To convert from binary to hex, just take the byte and break it into nibbles.

Here's how you do that: Say you have the binary number 01010101. First, break it into nibbles—0101 and 0101—with the value of each nibble being 5 because the 1 and 4 bits are on. This makes the hex answer 0x55. And in decimal format, the binary number is 01010101, which converts to 64 + 16 + 4 + 1 = 85.

Okay, now try another binary number:

11001100

Our answer is 1100 = 12 and 1100 = 12 (therefore, it's converted to CC in hex). The decimal conversion answer is 128 + 64 + 8 + 4 = 204.

One more example, and then we need to get working on the Physical layer. Suppose we're given the following binary number:

10110101

The hex answer is 0xB5 because 1011 converts to B and 0101 converts to 5 in hex value. The decimal equivalent is $128 + 32 + 16 + 4 + 1 = 181$.

See the written lab at the end of this chapter for more practice with binary/hex/decimal conversion.

Ethernet Addressing

Now that you've got binary-to-decimal and hexadecimal address conversion down, we can get into how Ethernet addressing works. It uses the *Media Access Control (MAC) address* burned into each and every Ethernet NIC. The MAC, or hardware, address is a 48-bit (6-byte) address written in a hexadecimal format.

Figure 4.5 shows the 48-bit MAC addresses and how the bits are divided.

FIGURE 4.5   Ethernet addressing using MAC addresses

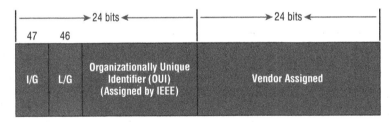

The *organizationally unique identifier (OUI)* is assigned by the Institute of Electrical and Electronics Engineers (IEEE) to an organization. It's composed of 24 bits, or 3 bytes. The organization, in turn, assigns a globally administered address (24 bits, or 3 bytes) that is unique to each and every adapter it manufactures. Look closely at the figure. The Individual/Group (I/G) address bit is used to signify if the destination MAC address is a unicast or a multicast/broadcast Layer 2 address. If the bit is set to 0, then it is an Individual MAC address and is a unicast address. If the bit is set to 1, it is a Group address and is a multicast/broadcast address.

The next bit is the Local/Global bit (L/G). This bit is used to tell if the MAC address is the burned-in-address (BIA) or a MAC address that has been changed locally. You'll see this happen when we get to IPv6 addressing. The low-order 24 bits of an Ethernet address represent a locally administered or manufacturer-assigned code. This portion commonly starts with 24 0s for the first card made and continues in order until there are 24 1s for the last

(16,777,216th) card made. You'll find that many manufacturers use these same six hex digits as the last six characters of their serial number on the same card.

Ethernet Frames

The Data Link layer is responsible for combining bits into bytes and bytes into frames. Frames are used at the Data Link layer to encapsulate packets handed down from the Network layer for transmission on a type of physical media access.

The function of Ethernet stations is to pass data frames between each other using a group of bits known as a MAC frame format. This provides error detection from a cyclic redundancy check (CRC). But remember—this is error detection, not error correction. The 802.3 frames and Ethernet frame are shown in Figure 4.6.

FIGURE 4.6   802.3 and Ethernet frame formats in bytes

Ethernet_II

Preamble 7	SOF 1	Destination 6	Source 6	Type 2	Data and Pad 46 – 1500	FCS 4

802.3_Ethernet

Preamble 7	SOF 1	Destination 6	Source 6	Length 2	Data and Pad 46 – 1500	FCS 4

Encapsulating a frame within a different type of frame is called *tunneling*.

The following information regarding frame headings and the various types of Ethernet frames are beyond the scope of the CompTIA Network+ objectives. Throughout the rest of this book, I'll show you screen shots from a network analyzer. It's always good to understand what you are looking at, so I put this information in to help you understand a frame structure.

Following are the details of the different fields in the 802.3 and Ethernet frame types:

Preamble   An alternating 1,0 pattern provides a clock at the start of each packet, which allows the receiving devices to lock the incoming bit stream.

Start of Frame Delimiter (SOF)/Synch   The preamble is seven octets, and the start of a frame (SOF) is one octet (synch). The SOF is 10101011, where the last pair of 1s allows the receiver to come into the alternating 1,0 pattern somewhere in the middle and still sync up and detect the beginning of the data.

Destination Address (DA)   This transmits a 48-bit value using the least significant bit (LSB) first. The DA is used by receiving stations to determine whether an incoming packet is addressed to a particular host and can be an individual address or a broadcast or multicast MAC address. Remember that a broadcast is all 1s (or Fs in hex) and is sent to all devices, but a multicast is sent only to a similar subset of hosts on a network.

Source Address (SA)   The SA is a 48-bit MAC address used to identify the transmitting device, and it uses the LSB first. Broadcast and multicast address formats are illegal within the SA field.

Length or Type   802.3 uses a Length field, but the Ethernet frame uses a Type field to identify the Network layer protocol. 802.3 by itself cannot identify the upper-layer routed protocol and must be used with a proprietary LAN protocol—Internetwork Packet Exchange (IPX), for example.

Data   This is a packet sent down to the Data Link layer from the Network layer. The size can vary from 64 to 1,500 bytes.

Frame Check Sequence (FCS)   FCS is a field that is at the end of the frame and is used to store the CRC.

Okay—let's take a minute to look at some frames caught on our trusty network analyzer. You can see that the following frame has only three fields: Destination, Source, and Type, displayed as Protocol Type on this analyzer:

Destination: 00:60:f5:00:1f:27
Source: 00:60:f5:00:1f:2c

Protocol Type: 08-00 IP   This is an Ethernet_II frame. Notice that the Type field is IP, or 08-00 (mostly just referred to as 0x800) in hexadecimal.

The next frame has the same fields, so it must be an Ethernet_II frame too:

Destination: ff:ff:ff:ff:ff:ff Ethernet Broadcast
Source: 02:07:01:22:de:a4

Protocol Type: 08-00 IP   Did you notice that this frame was a broadcast? You can tell because the destination hardware address is all 1s in binary, or all Fs in hexadecimal.

Let's take a look at one more Ethernet_II frame. You can see that the Ethernet frame is the same Ethernet_II frame we use with the IPv4 routed protocol. The difference is that the Type field has 0x86dd when we are carrying IPv6 data, and when we have IPv4 data, we use 0x0800 in the Protocol field:

Destination: IPv6-Neighbor-Discovery_00:01:00:03 (33:33:00:01:00:03)
Source: Aopen_3e:7f:dd (00:01:80:3e:7f:dd)

Type: IPv6 (0x86dd)   This is the beauty of the Ethernet_II frame. Because of the Protocol field, we can run any Network layer routed protocol and it will carry the data because it can identify that particular Network layer protocol!

Ethernet at the Physical Layer

Ethernet was first implemented by a group called DIX (Digital, Intel, and Xerox). They created and implemented the first Ethernet LAN specification, which the IEEE used to create the IEEE 802.3 Committee. This was a 10 Mbps network that ran on coax, then on twisted-pair, and finally on fiber physical media.

The IEEE extended the 802.3 Committee to three new committees known as 802.3u (Fast Ethernet), 802.3ab (Gigabit Ethernet on Category 5+), and then finally to 802.3ae (10 Gbps over fiber and coax).

Figure 4.7 shows the IEEE 802.3 and original Ethernet Physical layer specifications.

FIGURE 4.7   Ethernet Physical layer specifications

Data Link (MAC Layer)	Ethernet	802.3						
Physical		10Base2	10Base5	10BaseT	10BaseF	100BaseTX	100BaseFX	100BaseT4

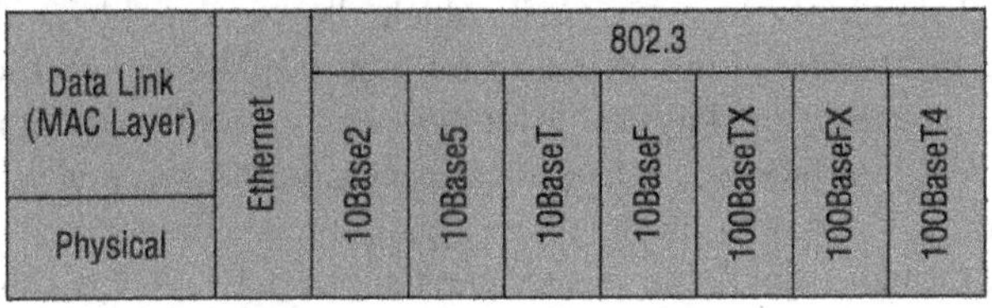

When designing your LAN, it's really important to understand the different types of Ethernet media available to you. Sure, it would be great to run Gigabit Ethernet to each desktop and 10 Gbps between switches, as well as to servers. Although this is just starting to happen, justifying the cost of that network today for most companies would be a pretty hard sell. But if you mix and match the different types of Ethernet media methods currently available instead, you can come up with a cost-effective network solution that works great!

The Electronic Industries Association and the newer Telecommunications Industry Alliance (EIA/TIA) together form the standards body that creates the Physical layer specifications for Ethernet. The EIA/TIA specifies that Ethernet use a *registered jack (RJ) connector* on *unshielded twisted-pair (UTP)* cabling (RJ-45). However, the industry is calling this just an 8-pin modular connector.

Each Ethernet cable type that is specified by the EIA/TIA has something known as *inherent attenuation*, which is defined as the loss of signal strength as it travels the length of a cable and is measured in decibels (dB). The cabling used in corporate and home markets is measured in categories. A higher-quality cable will have a higher-rated category and lower attenuation. For example, Category 5 is better than Category 3 because Category 5 cables have more wire twists per foot and therefore less crosstalk. *Crosstalk* is the unwanted signal interference from adjacent pairs in the cable.

Here are the original IEEE 802.3 standards:

10Base2   This is also known as *thinnet* and can support up to 30 workstations on a single segment. It uses 10 Mbps of baseband technology, coax up to 185 meters in length, and a physical and logical bus with Attachment Unit Interface (AUI) connectors. The 10 means 10 Mbps, and *Base* means baseband technology—a signaling method for communication on the network—and the 2 means almost 200 meters. 10Base2 Ethernet cards use BNC (British Naval Connector, Bayonet Neill-Concelman, or Bayonet Nut Connector) and T-connectors to connect to a network.

10Base5   Also known as *thicknet*, 10Base5 uses a physical and logical bus with AUI connectors, 10 Mbps baseband technology, and coax up to 500 meters in length. You can go up to 2,500 meters with repeaters and 1,024 users for all segments.

10BaseT   This is 10 Mbps using Category 3 UTP wiring. Unlike on 10Base2 and 10Base5 networks, each device must connect into a hub or switch, and you can have only one host per segment or wire. It uses an RJ-45 connector (8-pin modular connector) with a physical star topology and a logical bus.

Each of the 802.3 standards defines an AUI, which allows a one-bit-at-a-time transfer to the Physical layer from the Data Link media-access method. This allows the MAC address to remain constant but means the Physical layer can support both existing and new technologies. The original AUI interface was a 15-pin connector, which allowed a transceiver (transmitter/receiver) that provided a 15-pin-to-twisted-pair conversion.

There's an issue, though—the AUI interface can't support 100 Mbps Ethernet because of the high frequencies involved. So basically, 100BaseT needed a new interface, and the 802.3u specifications created one called the Media Independent Interface (MII) that provides 100 Mbps throughput. The MII uses a nibble, which you of course remember is defined as 4 bits. Gigabit Ethernet uses a Gigabit Media Independent Interface (GMII) and transmits 8 bits at a time.

802.3u (Fast Ethernet) is compatible with 802.3 Ethernet because they share the same physical characteristics. Fast Ethernet and Ethernet use the same maximum transmission unit (MTU) and the same MAC mechanisms, and they both preserve the frame format that is used by 10BaseT Ethernet. Basically, Fast Ethernet is just based on an extension to the IEEE 802.3 specification, and because of that, it offers us a speed increase of 10 times 10BaseT.

Here are the expanded IEEE Ethernet 802.3 standards, starting with Fast Ethernet:

100BaseTX (IEEE 802.3u)   100BaseTX, most commonly known as Fast Ethernet, uses EIA/TIA Category 5 or 5e or 6 and UTP two-pair wiring. It allows for one user per segment up to 100 meters long (328 feet) and uses an RJ-45 connector with a physical star topology and a logical bus.

100BaseT and 100BaseTX: What's the difference? 100BaseT is the name of a group of standards for Fast Ethernet that includes 100BaseTX. Also included are 100BaseT4 and 100BaseT2. The same can be said about 1000BaseT and 1000BaseX.

100BaseFX (IEEE 802.3u)   Uses 62.5/125-micron multimode fiber cabling up to 412 meters long and point-to-point topology. It uses ST and SC connectors, which are media-interface connectors.

Ethernet's implementation over fiber can sometimes be referred to as 100BaseTF even though this isn't an actual standard. It just means that Ethernet technologies are being run over fiber cable.

1000BaseCX (IEEE 802.3z)   Copper twisted-pair called twinax (a balanced coaxial pair) that can run only up to 25 meters and uses a special 9-pin connector known as the High-Speed Serial Data Connector (HSSDC).

1000BaseT (IEEE 802.3ab)   Category 5, four-pair UTP wiring, and up to 100 meters long (328 feet).

1000BaseTX   Category 5, two-pair UTP wiring up to 100 meters long (328 feet). Not used, and has been replaced by Category 6 cabling.

1000BaseSX (IEEE 802.3z)   The implementation of Gigabit Ethernet runs over multimode fiber-optic cable instead of copper twisted-pair cable and uses short wavelength laser. Multimode fiber (MMF), using a 62.5- and 50-micron core, utilizes an 850 nanometer (nm) laser and can go up to 220 meters with 62.5-micron; 550 meters with 50-micron.

1000BaseLX (IEEE 802.3z)   Single-mode fiber that uses a 9-micron core, 1,300 nm laser, and can go from 3 km up to 10 km.

10GBaseT   10GBaseT is a standard created by the IEEE 802.3an committee to provide 10 Gbps connections over conventional UTP cables (Category 5e, 6, 6A, or 7 cables). 10GBaseT allows the conventional RJ-45 used for Ethernet LANs. It can support signal transmission at the full 100-meter distance specified for LAN wiring. If you need to implement a 10 Gbps link, this is the most economical way to go!

10GBaseSR   An implementation of 10 Gigabit Ethernet that uses short-wavelength lasers at 850 nm over multimode fiber. It has a maximum transmission distance of between 2 and 300 meters (990 feet), depending on the size and quality of the fiber.

10GBaseLR   An implementation of 10 Gigabit Ethernet that uses long-wavelength lasers at 1,310 nm over single-mode fiber. It also has a maximum transmission distance between 2 meters and 10 km, or 6 miles, depending on the size and quality of the fiber.

10GBaseER   An implementation of 10 Gigabit Ethernet running over single-mode fiber that uses extra-long-wavelength lasers at 1,550 nm. It has the longest transmission distances possible of all the 10 Gigabit technologies: anywhere from 2 meters up to 40 km, again depending on the size and quality of the fiber used.

10GBaseSW   10GBaseSW, as defined by IEEE 802.3ae, is a mode of 10GBaseS for MMF with an 850 nm laser transceiver and a bandwidth of 10 Gbps. It can support up to 300 meters of cable length. This media type is designed to connect to SONET equipment.

10GBaseLW   10GBaseLW is a mode of 10GBaseL supporting a link length of 10 km on standard single-mode fiber (SMF) (G.652). This media type is also designed to connect to SONET equipment.

10GBaseEW   10GBaseEW is a mode of 10GBaseE supporting a link length of up to 40 km on SMF based on G.652 using optical-wavelength 1,550 nm. This is another media type designed to connect to SONET equipment.

40GBaseT   40GBaseT is a standard created by the IEEE 802.3bq committee and supports Ethernet speeds up to 40G and is also used for 25G Ethernet connections commonly found in server NICs. There is less distance than the slower Ethernet types with 40GBaseT limited to 30 meters. This is usually sufficient for data center cabling. Category 8 cabling is required to support the high data rates of 25GBaseT and 40GBaseT.

If you want to implement a network medium that is not susceptible to electromagnetic interference (EMI), fiber-optic cable provides a more secure, long-distance cable that is not susceptible to EMI at high speeds as UTP is.

Table 4.4 summarizes the cable types.

TABLE 4.4   Common Ethernet cable types

Ethernet Name	Cable Type	Maximum Speed	Maximum Transmission Distance	Notes
10Base5	Coax	10 Mbps	500 meters per segment	Also called thicknet, this cable type uses vampire taps to connect devices to cable.
10Base2	Coax	10 Mbps	185 meters per segment	Also called thinnet, a very popular implementation of Ethernet over coax.

Ethernet Name	Cable Type	Maximum Speed	Maximum Transmission Distance	Notes
10BaseT	UTP	10 Mbps	100 meters per segment	One of the most popular network cabling schemes.
100BaseTX	UTP, STP	100 Mbps	100 meters per segment	Two pairs of Category 5 UTP.
10BaseFL	Fiber	10 Mbps	Varies (ranges from 500 meters to 2,000 meters)	Ethernet over fiber optics to the desktop.
100BaseFX	MMF	100 Mbps	2,000 meters	100 Mbps Ethernet over fiber optics.
1000BaseT	UTP	1000 Mbps	100 meters	Four pairs of Category 5 or higher.
1000BaseTX	UTP	1000 Mbps	100 meters	Two pairs of Category 6 or higher.
1000BaseSX	MMF	1000 Mbps	550 meters	Uses SC fiber connectors. Max length depends on fiber size.
1000BaseCX	Balanced, shielded copper	1000 Mbps	25 meters	Uses a special connector, the HSSDC.
1000BaseLX	MMF and SMF	1000 Mbps	550 meters multi-mode/2,000 meters single mode	Uses longer wavelength laser than 1000BaseSX. Uses SC and LC connectors.
10GBaseT	UTP	10 Gbps	100 meters	Connects to the network like a Fast Ethernet link using UTP.
10GBaseSR	MMF	10 Gbps	300 meters	850 nm laser. Max length depends on fiber size and quality.
10GBaseLR	SMF	10 Gbps	10 kilometers	1,310 nm laser. Max length depends on fiber size and quality.

(continues)

TABLE 4.4 Common Ethernet cable types *(continued)*

Ethernet Name	Cable Type	Maximum Speed	Maximum Transmission Distance	Notes
10GBaseER	SMF	10 Gbps	40 kilometers	1,550 nm laser. Max length depends on fiber size and quality.
10GBaseSW	MMF	10 Gbps	400 meters	850 nm laser transceiver.
10GBaseLW	SMF	10 Gbps	10 kilometers	Typically used with SONET.
10GBaseEW	SMF	10 Gbps	40 kilometers	1,550 nm optical wavelength.
40GBaseT	UTP Category 8	40G	30 Meters	Connects to the network like a Fast Ethernet link using UTP.

An advantage of 100BaseFX over 100BaseTX is longer cable runs, but 100BaseTX is easier to install.

I know there's a lot of information to remember about the various Ethernet and fiber types used in today's networks, but for the CompTIA Network+ exam, you really need to know them. Trust me, I haven't inundated you with unnecessary information!

Real World Scenario

Deploy the Appropriate Wired Connectivity Standard

You have been tasked with installing wiring to handle the new networking technologies of 1000 Mbps to the desktop and Voice over IP (VoIP), with 10 Gbps between the access switches and the core switches. What cabling do you consider installing in order to accomplish this in a cost-effective manner?

First, you need to verify your distances. Since this will not include any wireless stations, you need to double-check the distances to each station and make sure the phone is within 100 meters (or closer) for connectivity to your access switches.

Once you have your distances verified at 100 meters or less, you can use UTP wiring to the stations and phones and possibly even connect the stations into the back of the phones.

Most phones have switches included, so this means you only need to run one Category 5 or better 1000BaseT four-pair cable to each cubicle or office.

For your connections from your access switches to your core switches, you can use 10GBaseT if your runs are 100 meters or less, or you can use 10GBaseSR, which allows runs up to 400 meters using multimode fiber.

Ethernet over Other Standards (IEEE 1905.1-2013)

IEEE 1905.1-2013 is an IEEE standard that defines a convergent digital home network for both wireless and wireline technologies. The technologies include IEEE 802.11 (Wi-Fi), IEEE 1901 (HomePlug, HD-PLC) powerline networking, IEEE 802.3 Ethernet, and Multimedia over Coax (MoCA). The 1905.1-2013 was published in April 2013. The IEEE 1905.1 Standard Working Group is sponsored by the IEEE Power Line Communication Standards Committee (PLCSC). The idea behind the 1905.1 technology standards is simple setup, configuration, and operation of home networking devices using both wired and wireless technologies. This will take advantage of the performance, coverage, and mobility benefits of multiple interfaces (Ethernet, Wi-Fi, Powerline, and MoCA), which enables better coverage and throughput in every room for both wireless and fixed devices.

We'll discuss the following:

- Ethernet over Power Line
- Ethernet over HDMI

Ethernet over Power Line

In February 2011, the IEEE finally published a standard for Broadband over Power Line (BPL) called IEEE 1901, also referred to as Power Line Communication (PLC) or even Power Line Digital Subscriber Line (PDSL). Although this technology has been available for decades in theory, without an IEEE standard it was just not adopted as an alternative to other high-speed media.

However, it is highly likely that this technology will really start to see some traction, especially from the power companies who will be able to gather data from every device in your house and specifically tell you how much power is being used by your refrigerator, washers and dryers, and especially your computer and televisions, among all the other devices plugged into a wall power outlet.

In the future, BPL will allow you to just plug a computer into a wall power socket and have more than 500 Mbps for up to 1,500 meters.

Near my home in Boulder, Colorado, Xcel Energy is using BPL in combination with radio links for its SmartGridCity pilot project, which will send data from power meters, hot water heaters, thermostats, and more.

An example of an adapter is shown in Figure 4.8.

FIGURE 4.8   Powerline adapter sets

This technology can be used to deliver Internet access to the home as well. For a computer (or any other device), you would simply need to plug a BPL modem into any outlet in an equipped building to have high-speed Internet access. The basic BPL installation is shown in Figure 4.9.

FIGURE 4.9   Basic BPL installation

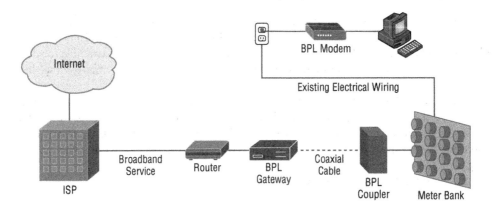

After the gateway is connected through the coupler to the meter bank for the building, any electrical outlet can be used with the BPL modem to receive the ISP connection to the Internet. The following challenges still exist:

- The fact that power lines are typically noisy.
- The frequency at which the information is transmitted is used by shortwave, and the unshielded power lines can act as antennas, thereby interfering with shortwave communications.

Ethernet over HDMI

HDMI Ethernet Channel technology consolidates video, audio, and data streams into a single HDMI cable, combining the signal quality of HDMI connectivity with the power and flexibility of home entertainment networking.

Figure 4.10 shows how a possible home entertainment network will look before and after Ethernet over HDMI is implemented.

It incorporates a dedicated data channel into the HDMI link, enabling high-speed, bidirectional networking at up to 100 Mbps.

Bidirectional Wavelength-Division Multiplexing (WDM)

Modern optical networks can support multiple optical wavelengths down a single fiber-optical cable. This reduces the number of fiber cables required to interconnect locations.

By implementing wavelength-division multiplexing, optical networks can support multiple optical wavelengths down a single fiber-optical cable.

Optical multiplexing is used in carrier and service provider networks to maximize the use of buried fiber. (WDM) is a technology that multiplexes a number of optical carrier signals onto a single optical fiber by using different wavelengths (i.e., colors) of laser light.

Course Wavelength-Division Multiplexing (CWDM)

CWDM allows up to 18 channels to be transported over a single dark fiber. Wavelengths are commonly 1310 nm and 1550 nm. CWDM can support distances of up to 70 km.

Dense Wavelength-Division Multiplexing (DWDM)

With DWDM, more than 80 individual wavelengths can share a single fiber. DWDM can handle higher speeds than CWDM, with up to 400 Gbps per channel. Each channel is 0.8 nm apart instead of the 20 nm you would find in a CWDM system.

Dense wavelength-division multiplexing is a very similar technology to CWDM but has a higher channel capacity. It can also be amplified to support much longer distances than CWDM but with DWDM achieving 1000 m using amplification.

FIGURE 4.10   Ethernet over HDMI

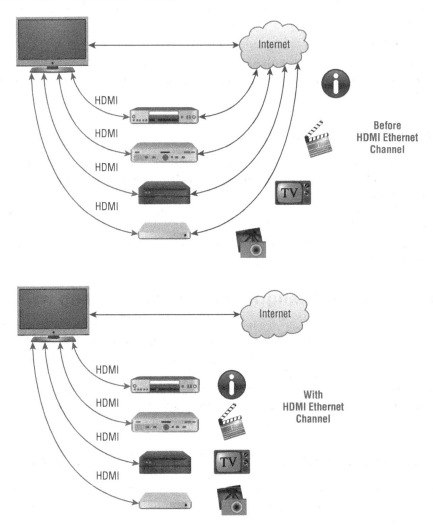

Armed with the basics covered in the chapter, you're equipped to go to the next level and put Ethernet to work using various network devices. But to ensure that you're really ready, read the summary, go over the exam essentials, and do the written lab and review questions for this chapter!

Summary

In this chapter, you learned the fundamentals of Ethernet networking, how hosts communicate on a network, and how CSMA/CD works in an Ethernet half-duplex network.

I also showed you the differences between half- and full-duplex modes.

I finished the chapter with a description of the common Ethernet cable types and standards used in today's networks. And by the way, you'd be wise to study that section really well!

Exam Essentials

Understand basic Ethernet communication.   Know how hosts use hardware addresses to communicate on an Ethernet LAN.

Understand Ethernet addressing.   Know the hexadecimal addressing scheme used to create an Ethernet address.

Understand binary, decimal, and hexadecimal addressing.   Know the different addressing types, and also use the written lab to practice your conversions.

Know the various Ethernet standards.   This includes understanding the various copper and fiber-based standards.

Written Lab

In this section, you will write in the answers to the following conversion tables. You can find the answers in Appendix A.

1. Convert from decimal IP address to binary format.

    Complete the following table to express 192.168.10.15 in binary format.

128	64	32	16	8	4	2	1	Binary

2. Complete the following table to express 172.16.20.55 in binary format.

128	64	32	16	8	4	2	1	Binary

3. Complete the following table to express 10.11.12.99 in binary format.

128	64	32	16	8	4	2	1	Binary

4. Convert the following from binary format to decimal IP address.

Complete the following table to express 11001100.00110011.10101010.01010101 in decimal IP address format.

128	64	32	16	8	4	2	1	Binary

128	64	32	16	8	4	2	1	Binary

5. Complete the following table to express 11000110.11010011.00111001.11010001 in decimal IP address format.

128	64	32	16	8	4	2	1	Binary

6. Complete the following table to express 10000100.11010010.10111000.10100110 in decimal IP address format.

128	64	32	16	8	4	2	1	Binary

128	64	32	16	8	4	2	1	Binary

7. Convert the following from binary format to hexadecimal.

Complete the following table to express 11011000.00011011.00111101.01110110 in hexadecimal.

128	64	32	16	8	4	2	1	Hexadecimal

8. Complete the following table to express 11001010.11110101.10000011.11101011 in hexadecimal.

128	64	32	16	8	4	2	1	Hexadecimal

128	64	32	16	8	4	2	1	Hexadecimal

9. Complete the following table to express 10000100.11010010.01000011.10110011 in hexadecimal.

128	64	32	16	8	4	2	1	Hexadecimal

Review Questions

You can find the answers to the review questions in Appendix B.

1. On an Ethernet switched network, what address does one host computer use to communicate with another?

    A. IP address

    B. MAC address

    C. Street address

    D. HUB address

2. Which of the following can run full-duplex and achieve 200 Mbps with Cat 5e cable?

    A. 100BaseF

    B. 100BaseTX

    C. 1000BaseF

    D. 1000BaseT

3. How many devices in a collision domain have to listen when a single host talks?

    A. Two

    B. Three

    C. One

    D. All

4. If you are using a cable medium called 10Base2, what does this mean?

    A. That you are running Ethernet over HDMI

    B. That you are running Ethernet over fiber

    C. That you are running Ethernet over thicknet

    D. That you are bundling multiple connections

    E. That you are really old and using thinnet coax for your LAN medium

5. What network access control method helps devices share the bandwidth evenly without having two devices transmit at the same time on the network medium? (Choose two.)

    A. TCP/IP

    B. CSMA/CD

    C. HTTPS

    D. TFTP

    E. CSMA/CA

6. What is the maximum distance of 10GBaseSR?

    A. 100 meters (328 feet)

    B. 302 meters (990 feet)

    C. 305 meters (1,000 feet)

    D. 1,593 km (990 miles)

7. How many wire pairs are used with half-duplex?

    A. Two

    B. One

    C. Four

    D. None of the above

8. How many wire pairs are used with 100BaseTX full-duplex?

    A. Two

    B. One

    C. Four

    D. A or C

9. What is the maximum distance of 10GBaseLR?

    A. 1 mile

    B. 3 miles

    C. 6 miles

    D. 25 miles

10. What is the effective total throughput increase with a full-duplex connection?

    A. None

    B. Twice as much

    C. Four times as much

    D. Ten times as much

11. What device can you not use full-duplex communication with?

    A. Host

    B. Hub

    C. Switch

    D. Router

12. What is the decimal equivalent of this binary number:
11000000.10101000.00110000.11110000?

    A. 192.168.48.192

    B. 192.168.48.240

    C. 192.168.64.224

    D. 192.168.32.248

13. Which IEEE standard is used for Ethernet over power lines?

    A. 802.3p

    B. 1901

    C. 802.16

    D. 1918

14. How is the decimal value 10 represented in binary?

    A. 1000

    B. 1001

    C. 1010

    D. 1011

15. What is the decimal value for the binary number 11101000?

    A. 128

    B. 194

    C. 224

    D. 232

16. What is the decimal number 10 in hexadecimal?

    A. 9

    B. A

    C. C

    D. B

17. How many bits is a MAC address?

    A. 16

    B. 32

    C. 48

    D. 64

18. What is the maximum distance of 1000BaseT?

   A. 100 meters (328 feet)

   B. 128 meters (420 feet)

   C. 1,000 meters (3280 feet)

   D. 1,024 meters (3360 feet)

19. What is the purpose of the frame check sequence (FCS) in an Ethernet frame?

   A. Error correction

   B. Error detection

   C. Error recovery

   D. Creating errors

20. What does the *Base* mean in 100BaseTX?

   A. Broadband

   B. 100 Mbps

   C. Baseband

   D. Twisted-pair at 100 Mbps

Chapter 5

Networking Devices

THE FOLLOWING COMPTIA NETWORK+ EXAM OBJECTIVES ARE COVERED IN THIS CHAPTER:

✓ **1.6 Explain the use and purpose of network services.**

- DHCP
  - Scope
  - Exclusion ranges
  - Reservation
  - Dynamic assignment
  - Static assignment
  - Lease time
  - Scope options
  - Available leases
  - DHCP relay
  - IP helper/UDP forwarding

- DNS
  - Record types
  - Address (A)
  - Canonical name (CNAME)
  - Mail exchange (MX)
  - Authentication, authorization, accounting, auditing (AAAA)
  - Start of authority (SOA)
  - Pointer (PTR)
  - Text (TXT)
  - Service (SRV)
  - Name server (NS)

- Global hierarchy
- Root DNS servers
- Internal vs. external
- Zone transfers
- Authoritative name servers
- Time to live (TTL)
- DNS caching
- Reverse DNS/reverse lookup/forward lookup
- Recursive lookup/iterative lookup
- NTP
  - Stratum
  - Clients
  - Servers

✓ **2.1 Compare and contrast various devices, their features, and their appropriate placement on the network.**

- Networking devices
  - Layer 2 switch
  - Layer 3 capable switch
  - Router
  - Hub
  - Access point
  - Bridge
  - Wireless LAN controller
  - Load balancer
  - Proxy server
  - Cable modem
  - DSL modem
  - Repeater
  - Voice gateway

- Media converter
- Intrusion prevention system (IPS)/intrusion detection system (IDS) device
- Firewall
- VPN headend
- Networked devices
  - Voice over Internet Protocol (VoIP) phone
  - Printer
  - Physical access control devices
  - Cameras
  - Heating, ventilation, and air conditioning (HVAC) sensors
  - Internet of Things (IoT)
  - Refrigerator
  - Smart speakers
  - Smart thermostats
  - Smart doorbells
  - Industrial control systems/supervisory control and data acquisition (SCADA)

In this chapter, I'll tell you all about the networking devices I've introduced so far. I'll go into much greater detail about each device, and yes—I'm going to present even more of them to you! Because all the components that you'll learn about shortly are typically found in today's networks and internetworks, it's very important that you be familiar with them.

We'll start by covering the more common network devices that you would be most likely to come across and then move on to discuss some of the more specialized devices that you may or may not always find running in a network.

I'll finish the chapter by using examples to discuss how routers, hubs, and switches work within internetworks today.

To find Todd Lammle CompTIA videos and practice questions, please see www.lammle.com.

Common Network Connectivity Devices

By now, you should be fairly savvy regarding the various types of network media and connections, so it's time to learn about some of the devices they hook up to that are commonly found on today's networks.

First, I'll define the basic terms; then, later in this chapter, I'll show you how these devices actually work within a network. At that time, I'll give you more detailed descriptions of these devices and the terminology associated with them.

Because these devices connect network entities, they're known as *connectivity devices*. Here's a list of the devices and related concepts I'll be covering in this chapter:

- Network interface card (NIC)
- Hub
- Bridge
- Basic switch
- Basic router
- Basic firewall
- IDS/IPS/HIDS

- Access point
- Wireless range extender
- Contention methods
- Dynamic Host Configuration Protocol (DHCP) server
- Load balancer
- Proxy server
- Cable modem
- DSL modem
- Repeater
- Voice gateway
- Media converter
- VPN headend
- Voice over Internet Protocol (VoIP) phone
- Printer
- Physical access control devices
- Cameras
- Heating, ventilation, and air conditioning (HVAC) sensors
- Internet of Things (IoT)
- Refrigerator
- Smart speakers
- Smart thermostats
- Smart doorbells
- Industrial control systems/supervisory control and data acquisition (SCADA)

Network Interface Card

Those of you who aren't familiar with NICs probably want to be, at this point, so here goes: a *network interface card (NIC)* is installed in your computer to connect, or interface, your computer to the network. It provides the physical, electrical, and electronic connections to the network media. The NIC is called a layer 2 device because the information it uses for communication, the MAC address, resides on the Data Link layer.

A NIC either is an expansion card or is built right into the computer's motherboard. Today, almost all NICs are built into the computer motherboard, providing 10, 100, and 1000 megabits per second (Mbps), but there was a time when all NICs were expansion cards that plugged into motherboard expansion slots. In some notebook computers, NIC adapters can be connected to the USB port or through a PC card slot. Ethernet speeds have been steadily increasing, especially in server chassis with 25, 40 and 100 G NICs now quite common.

Figure 5.1 shows a typical 1 Gbps Ethernet NIC.

FIGURE 5.1   Network interface card

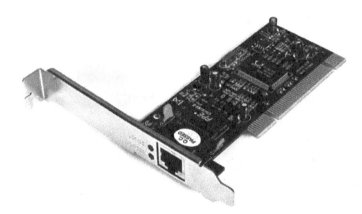

Nowadays, most PCs and laptops of all types come with an Ethernet and wireless connector built into the motherboard, so you usually don't need a separate card. It's rare to find a laptop today without a built-in wireless network card, but you can buy external wireless cards for desktops and laptops if you've got legacy equipment that needs them.

NICs today usually have one, two, or more LEDs; one, usually green, is called a link light, indicating that an Ethernet connection has been established with the device on the other end of the cable, and it flickers when traffic is being passed back or forth. The other, or others, usually indicates the speed of the connection: 10, 100, or 1000 Mbps. There's no universal standard for NIC LEDs, so check the manual to familiarize yourself with the ones you are working with. But it's not always that cut-and-dried that a blinking LED can mean the NIC is receiving a proper signal from the hub or switch; it can also indicate connectivity to and detection of a carrier on a segment. Another possibility is that it's found connectivity with a router or other end device using a crossover cable.

The other LED is aptly named the activity LED, and it tends to flicker constantly. That activity indicates the intermittent transmission and reception of frames arriving at the network or leaving it.

The first LED you should verify is the link LED because if it's not illuminated, the activity LED simply cannot illuminate.

Hub

As you learned earlier, a *hub* is the device that connects all the segments of the network together in a star topology Ethernet network. As a hub has no intelligence, it is a layer 1 device. Each device in the network connects directly to the hub through a single cable and is used to connect multiple devices without segmenting a network. Any transmission received on one port will be sent out to all the other ports in the hub, including the receiving pair for the transmitting device, so that Carrier Sense Multiple Access with Collision Detection (CSMA/CD) on the transmitter can monitor for collisions.

So, basically, this means that if one station sends a broadcast, all the others will receive it; yet based on the addressing found in the frame, only the intended recipient will actually listen and process it. This arrangement simulates the physical bus that the CSMA/CD standard was based on, and it's why we call the use of a hub in an Ethernet environment a physical star/logical bus topology.

Figure 5.2 depicts a typical hub as you might find it employed within a small network. Since there are only two users, there isn't a problem in using a hub here. However, if there were 20 users, everyone would see Bob's request to send a packet to Sally. Most of the time, hubs really aren't recommended for corporate networks because of their limitations.

FIGURE 5.2   A typical hub

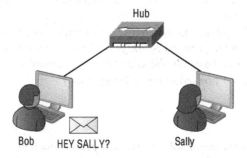

It's important to note that hubs are nothing more than glorified repeaters that are incapable of recognizing frames and data structures—the reason they act with such a lack of intelligence. A broadcast sent out by any device on the hub will be propagated to all devices connected to it. And just as in a physical bus topology configuration, any two or more of those connected devices have the potential of causing a collision with each other, which means that this hardware device will create a LAN with the most network traffic collisions. Hubs are not suggested for use in today's corporate network for this reason.

Bridge

A *bridge*—specifically, a transparent bridge—is a network device that connects two similar network segments together. Its primary function is to keep traffic separated on either side of the bridge, breaking up collision domains, as pictured in Figure 5.3.

FIGURE 5.3   Bridges break up collision domains.

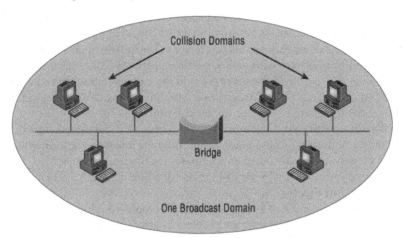

What we can see here is that traffic is allowed to pass through the bridge only if the transmission is intended for a station on the opposite side. The main reasons you would place a bridge in your network would be to connect two segments together or to divide a busy network into two segments. As bridges use MAC addresses to make forwarding decisions, they are considered layer 2 devices.

Bridges are software based, so, interestingly, you can think of a switch as a hardware-based, multiport bridge. In fact, the terms *bridge* and *switch* are often used interchangeably because the two devices used basically the same bridging technologies. The past tense is there for a reason—you'd be hard-pressed to buy a bridge today.

Switch

Switches connect multiple segments of a network together much like hubs do, but with three significant differences—a switch recognizes frames and pays attention to the source and destination MAC address of the incoming frame as well as the port on which it was received. A switch makes each of its ports a unique, singular collision domain. Hubs don't do those things. They simply send anything they receive on one port out to all the others. As switches use MAC addresses to make forwarding decisions, they are considered layer 2 devices.

So, if a switch determines that a frame's final destination happens to be on a segment that's connected via a different port than the one on which the frame was received, the switch will only forward the frame out from the specific port on which its destination is located. If the switch can't figure out the location of the frame's destination, it will flood the frame out of every port except the one on which the frame port was received.

Figure 5.4 shows a typical low-cost Ethernet switch. It looks a lot like a hub. However, switches can come in very large, expensive sizes. Switches that can perform the basic switching process and do not allow you to configure more advanced features—like adding an

IP address for telnetting to the device or adding VLANs—are called unmanaged switches. Others, like Cisco switches that do allow an IP address to be configured for management with such applications as simple network management protocol (SNMP) and do allow special ports to be configured (as in VoIP), are called managed switches.

FIGURE 5.4   Typical Ethernet switch

That's as far as we're going with switches right now. I'll bring them up later on in this chapter and cover them in much greater detail in Chapter 11, "Switching and Virtual LANs." For now, you can think of a switch as a faster, smarter bridge that has more ports.

Switches are layer 2 devices, which means they segment the network with MAC addresses. If you see the term *layer 3 switch*, that means you are talking about a router, not a layer 2 switch. The terms *router* and *layer 3 switch* are interchangeable.

Router

A *router* is a network device used to connect many, sometimes disparate, network segments together, combining them into what we call an *internetwork*. A well-configured router can make intelligent decisions about the best way to get network data to its destination. It gathers the information it needs to make these decisions based on a network's particular performance data. As routers use IP addresses to make forwarding decisions, they are considered layer 3 devices.

Figure 5.5 shows a small office, home office (SOHO) router that provides wired and wireless access for hosts and connects them to the Internet without any necessary configuration. But know that I certainly don't recommend leaving a router with the default configuration! No worries, though—I'll go over the configuration process with you in Chapter 10, "Routing Protocols."

Routers can be multifaceted devices that behave like computers unto themselves with their own complex operating systems—for example, Cisco's IOS. You can even think of them as CPUs that are totally dedicated to the process of routing packets. And due to their complexity and flexibility, you can configure them to actually perform the functions of other types of network devices (like firewalls, for example) by simply implementing a specific feature within the router's software.

FIGURE 5.5   Router connected to the Internet, providing access for hosts

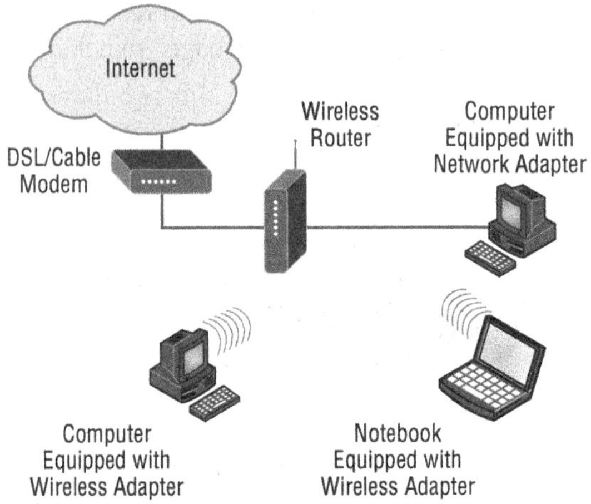

Routers can have many different names: *layer 3 switch* and *multilayer switch* are the most common, besides the name *router*, of course. Remember, if you hear just the word *switch*, that means a layer 2 device. Routers, layer 3 switches, and multilayer switches are all layer 3 devices.

Interface Configurations

When configuring interfaces on a router or switch, unless you're doing complex configurations such as connecting up a Voice over IP (VoIP) network, the interface configurations are pretty straightforward.

There is a major difference between a router interface and a switch interface configuration, however. On a switch, you do not add an IP address since they only read to layer 2, and most of the time, you never even need to configure a switch interface. First, they are enabled by default, and second, they are very good at auto-detecting the speed, duplex, and, in newer switches, even the Ethernet cable type (crossover or straight-through). A router is much different and an IP address is expected on each interface; they are not enabled by default, and a good layer 3 network design must be considered before installing a router.

Let's start by taking a look at a basic Cisco switch configuration. First, notice by the output shown that there is no configuration on the interfaces, yet you can plug this switch into your network and it would work. This is because all ports are enabled and there are some very basic configurations that allow the switch to run without any configuration—they can be considered plug-and-play in a small or home network:

```
Switch#sh running-config
[Some output cut for brevity]
!
```

```
interface FastEthernet0/1
!
interface FastEthernet0/2
!
interface FastEthernet0/3
!
interface FastEthernet0/4
!
interface FastEthernet0/5
!
interface FastEthernet0/6
!
interface FastEthernet0/7
!
interface FastEthernet0/8
!
```

Let's take a look at a configuration of a simple switch interface. First, we'll notice the duplex options:

```
Switch(config-if)#duplex ?
  auto  Enable AUTO duplex configuration
  full  Force full duplex operation
  half  Force half-duplex operation
```

All switch ports are set to duplex auto by default, and usually you can just leave this configuration alone. However, be aware that if your network interface card is set to half-duplex and the switch port is configured for full-duplex, the port will receive errors and you'll eventually get a call from the user. This is why it is advised to just leave the defaults on your hosts and switch ports, but it is a troubleshooting spot to check when a problem is reported from a single user.

The next configuration and/or troubleshooting spot you may need to consider is the speed of the port:

```
Switch(config-if)#speed ?
  10    Force 10 Mbps operation
  100   Force 100 Mbps operation
  1000  Force 1000 Mbps operation
  auto  Enable AUTO speed configuration
```

Again, this is set to auto, but you may want to force the port to be 1000 and full-duplex. Typically, the NIC will run this without a problem and you'll be sure you're getting the most bang for your buck on your switch port.

Let's take a look at a router interface. We're pretty much going to configure (or not configure) the same parameters. However, you should be very aware that a router interface and a switch interface perform different functions. A router interface will break up collision domains just as a switch interface does, but the purpose of a router interface is to create and maintain broadcast domains and connectivity of WAN services. Basic layer 2 switches cannot provide these services. As I mentioned, you must have a layer 3 design before you can implement a router, meaning you must have your subnet design laid out on your network diagram, and your IP addressing scheme must be completely understood. You cannot start configuring router interfaces randomly; there must be a design and it needs to be correct.

Unlike switches, router interfaces do not just work when you plug them into the network—they must be configured and enabled. All ports are shut down by default, and why shouldn't they be? Unless you have a network design and understand IP addressing, what good is a router to your network?

Let's take a look:

```
Router(config-if)#duplex ?
  auto  Enable AUTO duplex configuration
  full  Force full duplex operation
  half  Force half-duplex operation


Router(config-if)#speed ?
  10    Force 10 Mbps operation
  100   Force 100 Mbps operation
  1000  Force 1000 Mbps operation
  auto  Enable AUTO speed configuration


Router(config-if)#ip address ?
  A.B.C.D  IP address
  dhcp     IP Address negotiated via DHCP
  pool     IP Address autoconfigured from a local DHCP pool
```

First, we can see that the basics are there, duplex and speed, but also, to make a router interface useful at all we must add an IP address. Notice that the options allow you to configure a specific IP address or allow the interface to receive the address from a DHCP server. You would only use this option if you had an IP address reservation for the router interface on your DHCP server because having your router get a random IP address from a DHCP server would be hard to manage. Let's finish the basics:

```
Router(config-if)#ip address 1.1.1.1 255.0.0.0
Router(config-if)#no shutdown
Router(config-if)#
*Oct  5 17:26:46.522: %LINK-3-UPDOWN: Interface FastEthernet0/0,
changed state to up
*Oct  5 17:26:47.522: %LINEPROTO-5-UPDOWN: Line protocol on
Interface FastEthernet0/0, changed state to up
```

The interface can now be connected to a layer 2 switch and the hosts connected to the same broadcast domain must set their default gateway address to 1.1.1.1, and voilà, they can now send packets to the router.

Firewall

So what exactly is a *firewall*? Basically, firewalls are your network's security guards, and to be real, they're probably the most important thing to implement on your network. That's because today's networks are almost always connected to the Internet—a situation that makes security crucial! A firewall protects your LAN resources from invaders that prowl the Internet for unprotected networks while simultaneously preventing all or some of your LAN's computers from accessing certain services on the Internet. You can employ them to filter packets based on rules that you or the network administrator create and configure to strictly delimit the type of information allowed to flow in and out of the network's Internet connection. Firewalls operate at multiple layers of the OSI model. Some firewalls can operate up to the Application layer.

A firewall can be either a stand-alone "black box" or a software implementation placed on a server or router. Either way, the firewall will have at least two network connections: one to the Internet (known as the *public* side) and one to the network (known as the *private* side). Sometimes, there is a second firewall, as shown in Figure 5.6. This firewall is used to connect servers and equipment that can be considered both public and private (like web and email servers). This intermediary network is known as a screened subnet or, as it is often called, a *demilitarized zone (DMZ)*.

FIGURE 5.6   Example of firewalls with a screened subnet or DMZ

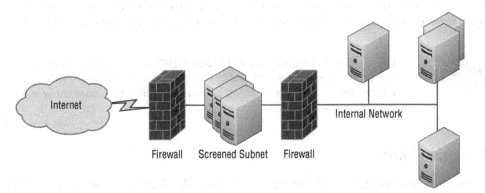

Firewalls are the first line of defense for an Internet-connected network. Without them in place, any network that's connected to the Internet is essentially wide open to anyone who is a little tech-savvy and seeks to exploit LAN resources or access your network's sensitive information.

In network security, a *screened subnet* refers to the use of one or more logical screening routers as a first defense on your network.

A typical firewall design can define three separate networks, or zones, to separate the external (untrusted) zone to a trusted (internal and DMZ) zone, also referred to as a perimeter network. Now, CompTIA likes to call this perimeter network a screened subnet or demilitarized zone (DMZ), where your DNS server and possibly HTTPS servers are.

IDS/IPS

Intrusion detection systems (IDSs) and *intrusion prevention systems (IPSs)* are very important in today's networks. They are network security appliances that monitor networks and packets for malicious activity. An IDS is considered to be monitor mode and just records problems and tells you about them, whereas an IPS can work in real time to stop threats as they occur.

The main difference between them is that an IPS works inline to actively prevent and block intrusions that are detected based on the rules you set up. IPSs can send an alarm, create correlation rules and remediation, drop malicious packets, provide malware protection, and reset the connection of offending source hosts.

HIDS

In a *host-based IDS (HIDS)*, software runs on one computer to detect abnormalities on that system alone by monitoring applications, system logs, and event logs—not by directly monitoring network traffic.

Systems like these are typically implemented on servers because they're a bear to manage if spread across several client computers on a network. Plus, if the IDS database is on the local computer and its data becomes compromised by an attack, the IDS data could be corrupted, too.

 Other types of IDSs are protocol based (PIDS), which monitor traffic for one protocol on one server, and application protocol based (APIDS), which monitor traffic for a group of servers running the same application (such as SQL).

Access Point

I'll be covering access points (APs) in depth in Chapter 12, "Wireless Networking," but I'll introduce them here. Understand that an AP is just a hub that accepts wireless clients via an analog wireless signal. APs operate at layer 2.

It's no secret that wireless is the key to all networks in the world today, and wireless networks will be even more prevalent in the future when all our home appliances have IP addresses and communicate wirelessly to our networks, for example. The ease of communicating on a network using an AP instead of having to use an Ethernet cable has changed our world forever.

Figure 5.7 shows how an AP would look in a small network, such as a home.

FIGURE 5.7   Example of an AP in a network

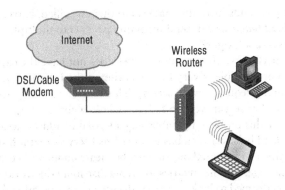

The wireless client modulates a digital signal to an analog signal, which the AP can read and demodulate back to a digital signal. The AP creates one collision domain and can only run half-duplex, which is why you can describe an AP as being like a hub. However, even though there are some standards that provide some full-duplex-type connectivity, a wireless host will never achieve the same type of throughput, security, and consistency that a wired Ethernet network would, but does that matter? Wireless is here to stay.

Wireless Range Extender

In some cases, you need the WLAN to extend further than the technology in use is designed to deliver. In that case, you can deploy what is called an extender. These are radios and antennas that operate in the same frequency or channel and receive the signal as a station would and then transmit it in the direction you desire to clients that are out of reach of the original AP.

These devices should be placed so there is at least 15 percent overlap of the coverage areas of the AP and the extender.

Wireless LAN Controller

In larger wireless networks it becomes an administrative burden to manage dozens, hundreds, or even thousands of wireless access points. This led to the design and deployment of a centralized Wi-Fi configuration controller known as a WLC, or *wireless LAN controllers*. The WLC lets you configure the complete network on a single device and push the configurations out to the Wi-Fi access points. The access points also tunnel the user data back to the controller, which then forwards the traffic onto the local area network (LAN).

WLCs greatly reduce the amount of administrative overhead required to manage large enterprise wireless networks.

Load Balancer

Your average router just sends incoming packets to their specified, correlative IP address on the network, but a *load balancer* can send incoming packets to multiple machines hidden behind one IP address—cool, right?

In large and busy networks, often a single server does not have the capabilities to serve all requested traffic. For example, a very busy website on the Internet could have hundreds of thousands of incoming requests every second. This if often too large for a single server to accommodate. Also, if that server were to fail, the whole website could go offline.

Load balancers solve this problem by publishing a virtual IP address to a domain to receive incoming traffic. The load balancer then has a pool of real servers that it distributes the connections to. The distribution can be based on round-robin, least number of connections, response time, a weighted percentage, or other metrics to evenly distribute the workload to the servers.

Health checks are performed to make sure that the servers are operational. If one does not respond, it can be automatically taken offline with the site still operating on the remaining servers.

Capacity can be dynamically added or removed using load balancers by using either manual or automatic scaling based on the current servers' workloads. New servers can dynamically be added and removed from the pool to scale the service up or down.

Today's load-balancing routers follow various rules to determine specifically how they will route network traffic. Depending on your needs, you can set rules based on the least load, fault tolerance, the fastest response times, or just dividing up (balancing) outbound requests for smooth network operations.

In fact, the fault tolerance, or redundancy, as well as the scalability so vital to large networking environments and e-commerce are some of the great benefits we gain using load balancers.

Think about this scenario: Say you have a website where people are placing orders for the stuff you've got for sale. Obviously, the orders placed vary in size, and the rate at which they come in varies; you definitely wouldn't want your servers becoming so overloaded that they hose up and crash your site, causing you to lose lots of money, now would you? That's where balancing the load of traffic between a group of servers comes to the rescue, because even if one of them freezes, your customers will still be able to access your site and place orders.

Contention Methods

In both wireless and wired environments that are shared mediums, meaning devices share a collision domain, such as when connected to a hub or when connected to a wireless access point, there is potential for frames from multiple devices colliding, destroying both packets. Both wired and wireless environments use a *contention method* to arbitrate access to the medium to help prevent collisions or at the least to recover from them when they occur. In the following sections, we'll look at the method used in each environment.

CSMA/CA

When the device sending the frame is transmitting onto a wireless network, the *Carrier Sense Multiple Access with Collision Avoidance (CSMA/CA)* contention method is used.

The method starts with a check of the medium (in this case, a check of the radio frequency) for activity called *physical carrier sense*.

The frame will go to the AP. The AP will acknowledge reception of the frame. If the frame is destined for another wireless station located on this wireless LAN, the frame will be forwarded to it by the AP. When this occurs, the AP will follow the same CSMA/CA contention method to get the frame onto the wireless medium.

If the frame is destined for a station on the wired LAN, the AP will drop the 802.11 MAC header (which is structured differently from an Ethernet MAC header) and build a new Ethernet MAC header by using its MAC address as the source address and the MAC address of the default gateway as the destination. The LAN router will receive the frame, and normal LAN routing to the destination will continue from there, using the CSMA/CD contention mechanism (covered a bit later) to place the frame in the wire at each step. If frames are returned to the station, the AP will receive them, drop the Ethernet MAC header, build an 802.11 MAC header, and return the frame to the wireless station. When this occurs, the AP will follow the same CSMA/CA contention method to get the frame onto the wireless medium.

Describing CSMA/CA Operation

Because it is impossible for wireless stations to detect collisions, the CSMA/CA contention method is required to arbitrate access to the network. It requires a more involved process of checking for existing wireless traffic before a frame can be transmitted wirelessly. The stations (including the AP) must also acknowledge all frames. The steps in the process are as follows:

1. Laptop A has a frame to send to laptop B. Before sending, laptop A must check for traffic in two ways. First, it performs carrier sense, which means it listens to see whether any radio waves are being received on its transmitter.

2. If the channel is *not* clear (traffic is being transmitted), laptop A will decrement an internal countdown mechanism called the *random back-off algorithm*. This counter will have started counting down after the last time this station was allowed to transmit. All stations will be counting down their own individual timers. When a station's timer expires, it is allowed to send.

3. If laptop A checks for carrier sense and there is no traffic and its timer hits zero, it will send the frame.

4. The frame goes to the AP.

5. The AP sends an acknowledgment back to laptop A. Until that acknowledgment is received by laptop A, all other stations must remain silent. The AP will cache the frame, where it already may have other cached frames that need to be relayed to other stations. Each frame that the AP needs to relay must wait its turn to send the frame using the same mechanism as the stations.

6. When the frame's turn comes up in the cache queue, the frame from laptop A will be relayed to laptop B.

7. Laptop B sends an acknowledgment back to the AP. Until that acknowledgment is received by the AP, all other stations must remain silent.

When you consider that this process has to occur for every single frame and that there are many other frame types used by the AP to manage other functions of the network that also create competition for air time, it is no wonder that actual throughput on a wireless LAN is at best about half the advertised rate.

For example, if two wireless stations were the only wireless clients and they were using 802.11g, which is capable of 56 Mbps, the *very best* throughput experienced would be about 25 to 28 Mbps. Moreover, as soon as a third station arrives, throughput will go down again because the stations are dividing the air time by 3 instead of 2. Add a fourth, and it gets even worse! Such is the challenge of achieving throughput on a wireless LAN.

CSMA/CD

When the device sending the frame is transmitting onto a wired network, the *Carrier Sense Multiple Access with Collision Detection (CSMA/CD)* contention method is used. This method is somewhat more efficient because it is possible for wired computers to detect collisions while wireless stations cannot. When a host's or router's interface needs to send a frame, it checks the wire, and if no traffic is detected, it sends without checking a random back-off timer.

However, it continues to listen, and if it detects that a collision has occurred, it sends out a jam signal that requires all stations to stop transmitting. Then the two computers that were involved in the collision will both wait a random amount of time (that each arrives at independently) and will resend. So instead of using a random break-off algorithm every time a transmission occurs, Ethernet uses its ability to detect collisions and uses this timer only when required, which makes the process more efficient.

Describing CSMA/CD Operation

CSMA/CD has mechanisms that help minimize but not eliminate collisions. Its operation is as follows:

1. When a device needs to transmit, it checks the wire. If a transmission is already under way, the device can tell. This is called *carrier sense*.

2. If the wire is clear, the device will transmit. Even as it is transmitting, it is performing carrier sense.

3. If another host is sending simultaneously, there will be a collision. The collision is detected by both devices through carrier sense.

4. Both devices will issue a jam signal to all the other devices, which indicates to them to *not* transmit.

5. Then both devices will increment a retransmission counter. This is a cumulative total of the number of times this frame has been transmitted and a collision has occurred. There is a maximum number at which the device aborts the transmission of the frame.

6. Both devices will calculate a random amount of time and will wait that amount of time before transmitting again. This calculation is called a *random back-off*.

7. In most cases, because both devices choose random amounts of time to wait, another collision will not occur.

Dynamic Host Configuration Protocol Server

Even though I'm going to discuss the finer points of DHCP soon, in Chapter 6, "Introduction to the Internet Protocol," I want to give you some basic insight into this server service here.

In essence, DHCP servers assign IP addresses to hosts. This protocol gives us a much easier way to administer—by automatically providing IP information—than the alternative and tedious method known as static IP addressing or *static assignment*, where we have to address each host manually. It works well in any network environment, from tiny to huge, and allows all types of hardware to be employed as a DHCP server, including routers.

It works like this: A DHCP server receives a request for IP information from a DHCP client using a broadcast (as Chapter 6 will show you in detail). The DHCP server is configured by the administrator with what is called a pool of addresses that it uses for this purpose. When the administrator configures this pool, they can also set some addresses in the pool as "off limits." These are called IP exclusions or *exclusion ranges*. It means that these addresses cannot be assigned. An example might be the address of the router interface.

The only hitch is that if the DHCP server isn't on the same segment as the DHCP client, the broadcast won't be received by the server because by default, routers won't forward broadcasts, as shown in Figure 5.8.

FIGURE 5.8   DHCP client sends broadcasts looking for a DHCP server.

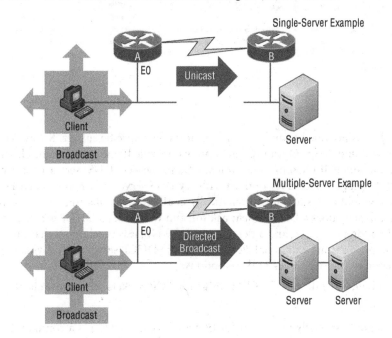

In Figure 5.8, Router A is configured with the IP helper address command on interface E0 of the router. Whenever interface E0 receives a broadcast request, Router A will forward that request as a unicast (meaning instead of a broadcast, the packet now has the destination IP address of the DHCP server).

So, as shown in the figure, you can configure Router A to forward these requests and even use multiple DHCP servers for redundancy, if needed. This works because the router has been configured to forward the request to a single server using a unicast or by sending the request to multiple servers via a directed broadcast.

Personally, most of the time I use a Windows server to act as the DHCP server for my entire internetwork and have my routers forward client requests. It is possible to have a DHCP server on every network segment, but that is not necessary because of the routers' forwarding ability.

Figure 5.9 shows a Windows server with something called scope options.

FIGURE 5.9   A Windows DHCP server's scope options

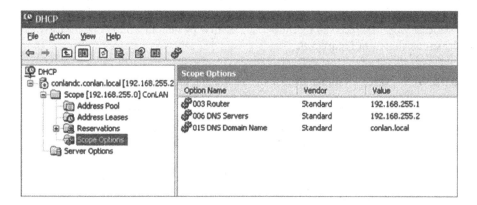

Scope options provide IP configuration for hosts on a specific subnet. Below Scope Options, you'll find Server Options; these options provide IP information for all scopes configured on the server. If I had just one Domain Name Service (DNS) server for the entire network, I'd configure the server options with my DNS server information; that DNS server information would then show up automatically in all scopes configured on my server.

So, what exactly does a DHCP client ask for, and what does a DHCP server provide? Is it just an IP address, a mask, and a default gateway? No, it is much more than that. Scope options comprise the informational elements that the DHCP server can provide to the DHCP clients. Here are some examples of these options:

- TTL (provides the default TCP TTL value for TCP packets sent by the client)

- DNS server

- TFTP server (especially important for IP phones that need to get a configuration for a TFTP server)

Let's take a look at a DHCP client request on an analyzer. Figure 5.10 shows the options that the client is requesting from the DHCP server.

FIGURE 5.10   DHCP client request to a DHCP server

```
⊞ Frame 33 (344 bytes on wire, 344 bytes captured)
⊞ Ethernet II, Src: Usi_d0:e9:35 (00:1e:37:d0:e9:35), Dst: Broadcast (ff:ff:ff:ff:ff:ff)
⊞ Internet Protocol, Src: 0.0.0.0 (0.0.0.0), Dst: 255.255.255.255 (255.255.255.255)
⊞ User Datagram Protocol, Src Port: bootpc (68), Dst Port: bootps (67)
⊟ Bootstrap Protocol
     Message type: Boot Request (1)
     Hardware type: Ethernet
     Hardware address length: 6
     Hops: 0
     Transaction ID: 0xb16f1532
     Seconds elapsed: 0
   ⊞ Bootp flags: 0x8000 (Broadcast)
     Client IP address: 0.0.0.0 (0.0.0.0)
     Your (client) IP address: 0.0.0.0 (0.0.0.0)
     Next server IP address: 0.0.0.0 (0.0.0.0)
     Relay agent IP address: 0.0.0.0 (0.0.0.0)
     Client MAC address: Usi_d0:e9:35 (00:1e:37:d0:e9:35)
     Server host name not given
     Boot file name not given
     Magic cookie: (OK)
   ⊞ Option: (t=53,l=1) DHCP Message Type = DHCP Discover
   ⊞ Option: (t=116,l=1) DHCP Auto-Configuration
   ⊞ Option: (t=61,l=7) Client identifier
   ⊞ Option: (t=50,l=4) Requested IP Address = 10.100.36.38
   ⊞ Option: (t=12,l=14) Host Name = "globalnet-todd"
   ⊞ Option: (t=60,l=8) Vendor class identifier = "MSFT 5.0"
   ⊞ Option: (t=55,l=12) Parameter Request List
     End Option
```

First, you can see that the DHCP service runs on top of the BootP protocol (port 68) and that the DHCP client is looking for a BootP server (port 67). The client IP address is 0.0.0.0, and the client doesn't know the DHCP server address either because this is a broadcast to 255.255.255.255 (the Data Link layer broadcast shows ff:ff:ff:ff:ff:ff). Basically, all the DHCP client knows for sure is its own MAC address. The client is "requesting" a certain IP address because this is the IP address it received from the server the last time it requested an IP address.

The DHCP client Parameter Request List option shown at the bottom of Figure 5.10 has been expanded and is shown in Figure 5.11. Notice all the parameter information that can be sent to a DHCP client from the server.

That is quite a request list! The DHCP server will respond with the options that it has configured and are available to provide to a DHCP client. Let's take a look and see what the server responds with. Figure 5.12 shows the DHCP server response.

The client is going to get the IP address that it asked for (10.100.36.38), a subnet mask of 255.255.255.224, a lease time of 23 hours (the amount of time before the IP address and other DHCP information expires on the client), the IP address of the DHCP server, the default gateway (router), the DNS server IP address (it gets two), the domain name used by DNS, and some NetBIOS information (used by Windows for name resolution).

FIGURE 5.11 DHCP client parameter request list

```
⊟ Option: (t=55,l=12) Parameter Request List
    Option: (55) Parameter Request List
    Length: 12
    Value: 010F03062C2E2F1F2179F92B
    1 = Subnet Mask
    15 = Domain Name
    3 = Router
    6 = Domain Name Server
    44 = NetBIOS over TCP/IP Name Server
    46 = NetBIOS over TCP/IP Node Type
    47 = NetBIOS over TCP/IP Scope
    31 = Perform Router Discover
    33 = Static Route
    121 = Classless Static Route
    249 = Classless Static Route (Microsoft)
    43 = Vendor-Specific Information
  End Option
```

FIGURE 5.12 DHCP server response

```
⊞ Frame 34 (359 bytes on wire, 359 bytes captured)
⊞ Ethernet II, Src: Cisco_90:ed:80 (00:0b:5f:90:ed:80), Dst: Broadcast (ff:ff:ff:ff:ff:ff)
⊞ Internet Protocol, Src: 10.100.36.33 (10.100.36.33), Dst: 255.255.255.255 (255.255.255.255)
⊞ User Datagram Protocol, Src Port: bootps (67), Dst Port: bootpc (68)
⊟ Bootstrap Protocol
    Message type: Boot Reply (2)
    Hardware type: Ethernet
    Hardware address length: 6
    Hops: 0
    Transaction ID: 0xb16f1532
    Seconds elapsed: 0
  ⊞ Bootp flags: 0x8000 (Broadcast)
    Client IP address: 0.0.0.0 (0.0.0.0)
    Your (client) IP address: 10.100.36.38 (10.100.36.38)
    Next server IP address: 10.100.36.12 (10.100.36.12)
    Relay agent IP address: 10.100.36.33 (10.100.36.33)
    Client MAC address: Usi_d0:e9:35 (00:1e:37:d0:e9:35)
    Server host name not given
    Boot file name not given
    Magic cookie: (OK)
  ⊞ Option: (t=53,l=1) DHCP Message Type = DHCP Offer
  ⊞ Option: (t=1,l=4) Subnet Mask = 255.255.255.224
  ⊞ Option: (t=58,l=4) Renewal Time Value = 11 hours, 30 minutes
  ⊞ Option: (t=59,l=4) Rebinding Time Value = 20 hours, 7 minutes, 30 seconds
  ⊞ Option: (t=51,l=4) IP Address Lease Time = 23 hours
  ⊞ Option: (t=54,l=4) Server Identifier = 10.100.36.12
  ⊞ Option: (t=15,l=16) Domain Name = "globalnet.local"
  ⊞ Option: (t=3,l=4) Router = 10.100.36.33
  ⊞ Option: (t=6,l=8) Domain Name Server
  ⊞ Option: (t=44,l=4) NetBIOS over TCP/IP Name Server = 10.100.36.13
  ⊞ Option: (t=46,l=1) NetBIOS over TCP/IP Node Type = H-node
    End Option
```

The *lease time* is important and can even be used to tell you if you have a DHCP problem or, more specifically, that the DHCP server is no longer handing out IP addresses to hosts. If hosts start failing to get onto the network one at a time as they try to get a new IP address as their lease time expires, you need to check your server settings.

Here is another example of a possible DHCP problem: You arrive at work after a weekend and find that some hosts were left on and some were shut down. The hosts that were left running and not shut down are still working, but the hosts that were shut down and were restarted on Monday morning do not get a new IP address. This is a good indication that you need to head over to your DHCP server and take a look at what is going on.

A DHCP server can also be configured with a reservation list so that a host always receives the same IP address. When this is done, the reservation is made on the basis of the router interface MAC address. Therefore, it is sometimes called a MAC reservation. You would use this reservation list for routers or servers if they were not statically assigned. However, you can use reservation lists for any host on your network as well.

DHCP is an Application layer protocol. While the DORA (Discover, Offer, Request, Acknowledgment) components operate at layer 2, the protocol is managed and responds to the Application layer. DHCP uses UDP ports 67 and 68.

DHCP Relay

If you need to provide addresses from a DHCP server to hosts that aren't on the same LAN as the DHCP server, you can configure your router interface to relay or forward the DHCP client requests, as shown in Figure 5.13. This is referred to as a *DHCP relay*. If we don't provide this service, our router would receive the DHCP client broadcast, promptly discard it, and the remote host would never receive an address—unless we added a DHCP server on every broadcast domain! Let's take a look at how we would typically configure DHCP service in today's networks.

FIGURE 5.13 Configuring a DHCP relay

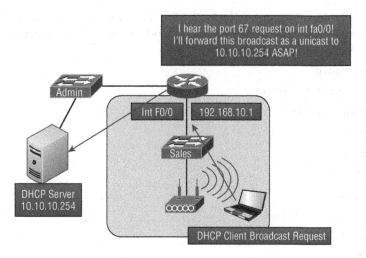

So we know that because the hosts off the router don't have access to a DHCP server, the router will simply drop their client request broadcast messages by default. To solve this problem, we can configure the F0/0 interface of the router to accept the DHCP client requests and forward them to the DHCP server like this:

```
Router#config t
Router(config)#interface fa0/0
Router(config-if)#ip helper-address 10.10.10.254
```

Now I know that was a pretty simple example, and there are definitely other ways to configure the relay, but rest assured that I've covered the objectives for you. Also, I want you to know that ip helper-address forwards more than just DHCP client requests, so be sure to research this command before you implement it!

IPAM

IP address management (IPAM) tools are software products that integrate the management of DHCP and DNS. They are used to plan, track, and manage the IP addresses. With the integration of DNS ad DHCP, each process is kept abreast of changes made to the other service. Many products offer additional functionality as well, such as tracking of information such as which IP addresses are in use and the time, user, and devices for which an IP is assigned.

Other Specialized Devices

In addition to the network connectivity devices I've discussed, there are several devices that, while they may not be directly connected to a network, do actively participate in moving network data. Here's a list of them:

- Multilayer switch
- Domain Name Service server
- Network Time Protocol
- Proxy server
- Encryption devices
- Analog modem
- Packet shaper
- VPN concentrator headend
- Media converter
- VoIP PBX
- VoIP endpoint
- NGFW/layer 7 firewall
- VoIP gateway

- Cable modem
- DSL modem

Multilayer Switch

A *multilayer switch (MLS)* is a computer networking device that switches on Open Systems Interconnection (OSI) layer 2 like an ordinary network switch but provides routing. A 24-port MLS gives you the best of both worlds. It operates at layer 3 (routing) while still providing 24 collision domains, which a router could not do.

The major difference between the packet-switching operation of a router and that of a layer 3 or multilayer switch lies in the physical implementation. In routers, packet switching takes place using a microprocessor, whereas a layer 3 switch handles this by using application-specific integrated circuit (ASIC) hardware. I'd show you a picture of a layer 3 switch, but they look just like regular layer 2 switches and you already know what those look like. The differences are the hardware inside and the operating system.

Domain Name Service Server

A *Domain Name Service (DNS) server* is one of the most important servers in your network and on the Internet as well. Why? Because without a DNS server, you would have to type `https://206.123.114.186` instead of simply entering `www.lammle.com`. So it follows that you can pretty much think of the DNS system as the phone book of the Internet.

A hostname is typically the name of a device that has a specific IP address; on the Internet, it is part of what is known as a fully qualified domain name (FQDN). An FQDN consists of a hostname and a domain name.

The process of finding the IP address for any given hostname is known as *name resolution,* and it can be performed in several ways: a hosts file (meaning you statically type in all names and IP addresses on each and every host), a request broadcast on the local network (Microsoft's favorite—why ask a server when you can just broadcast, right?), DNS, and Microsoft's Windows Internet Naming Service (WINS). DNS is the most popular today and is the resolution method you really need to know.

On the Internet, domains are arranged in a hierarchical tree structure. The following list includes some of the root or top-level domains currently in use:

`.com`   A commercial organization. Most companies end up as part of this domain.

`.edu`   An educational establishment, such as a university.

`.gov`   A branch of the US government.

`.int`   An international organization, such as NATO or the United Nations.

`.mil`   A branch of the US military.

`.net`   A network organization.

`.org`   A nonprofit organization.

Your local ISP is probably a member of the .net domain, and your company is probably part of the .com domain. The .gov and .mil domains are reserved strictly for use by the government and the military within the United States. In other parts of the world, the final part of a domain name represents the country in which the server is located (.ca for Canada, .jp for Japan, .uk for Great Britain, and .ru for Russia, for example). Well over 130 countries are represented on the Internet.

The .com domain is by far the largest, followed by the .edu domain. Some new domain names are becoming popular, however, because of the increasing number of domain-name requests. These include .firm for businesses and companies, .store for businesses selling goods rather than services, .arts for cultural and entertainment organizations, and .info for informational services. The domains .cc, .biz, .travel, and .post are also in use on the Internet.

Figure 5.14 shows how, when you type in a domain name, the DNS server resolves it, allowing the host to send the HTTPS packets to the server.

FIGURE 5.14   DNS resolution example

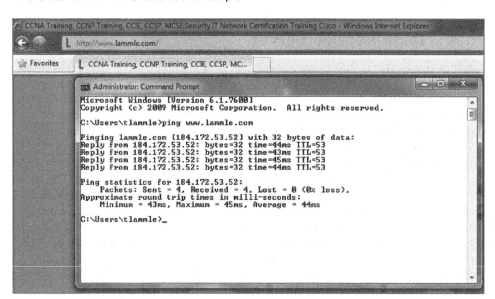

This Command Prompt screen shows how the DNS server can resolve the human name to the IP address of the Lammle.com server when I ping the server by the name instead of the IP address.

It should be easy to imagine how hard life would be without DNS translating human names to IP addresses, routing your packet through the Internet or internetwork to get to your servers. Figure 5.15 gives you an example of a Windows server configured as a DNS server.

To complete unqualified Domain Name Service (DNS) names that will be used to search and submit DNS queries at the client for resolution, you must have a list of DNS suffixes that can be appended to these DNS names. For DHCP clients, this can be set by assigning the DNS

FIGURE 5.15   A Windows DNS server

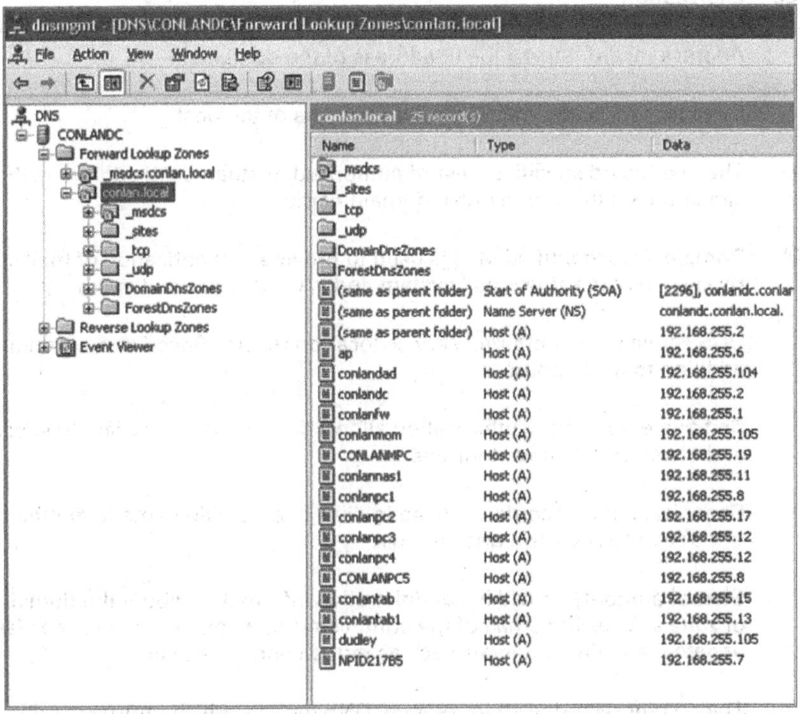

domain name option (option 15) and providing a single DNS suffix for the client to append and use in searches. For example, if you just wanted to ping todd instead of pinging todd .lammle.com, you can configure the DHCP server option 15 to provide the suffix for you.

Now the hosts can receive the IP address of this DNS server, and then this server will resolve hostnames to correct IP addresses. This is a mission-critical service in today's networks, don't you think? As shown in Figure 5.15, if I ping from a host to conlanpc1, the host will send the name-resolution request to the DNS server and translate this name to IP address 192.168.255.8.

Host (A) is called an A record or *address (A)* record and is what gives you the IP address of a domain or host. In IPv6, it's called a quad-A or AAAA record. In Figure 5.15, you can see that each name has an A record, which is associated to an IP address. So, A records resolve hostnames to IP addresses, but what happens if you know the IP address and want to know the hostname? There is a record for this, too! It's called the *pointer record (PTR)*.

Another typical type of record found on DNS servers is the *mail exchanger (MX) record*, which is used to translate mail records. The MX record points to the mail exchanger for a particular host. DNS is structured so that you can actually specify several mail exchangers for one host. This feature provides a higher probability that email will arrive at its intended destination. The mail exchangers are listed in order in the record, with a priority code that indicates the order in which they should be accessed by other mail-delivery systems.

There are many types of records the DNS server keeps as, shown in Table 5.1.

TABLE 5.1 Additional DNS record types

Record Type	Explanation
A	Address record returns the IP address of the domain.
AAAA	Used to map hostnames to an IPv6 address of the host.
TXT (SPF)	The text record specifies a list of authorized hostnames/IP addresses that mail can originate from for a given domain name.
TXT (DKIM)	Domain Keys Identified Mail is used to provide authentication of mail sent and received by the same email system and is used to prevent spam.
SRV	DNS service or generalized service location record. Specifies a port number in addition to the IP address.
CAA	Certificate Authority Authorization allows domain name owners to specify authorized certificate authorities.
CNAME	Canonical name records are used to alias one domain name to another such as toddlammle.com to Lammle.com.
SOA	Start of authority provides administrative information about the domain or zone such as the email of the administrator, when the domain was last updated, and time intervals such as refresh and time to live.
PTR	The pointer record used for reverse DNS lookup, which returns the domain name when given the IP address.
MX	Mail exchanger record specifies how email messages should be routed.
NS	Name server represents the authoritative DNS server for the domain.

If the first-priority mail exchanger doesn't respond in a given amount of time, the mail-delivery system tries the second one, and so on. Here are some sample mail-exchange records:

```
hostname.company.com.    IN    MX    10 mail.company.com.
hostname.company.com.    IN    MX    20 mail2.company.com.
hostname.company.com.    IN    MX    30 mail3.company.com.
```

In this example, if the first mail exchanger, mail.company.com, does not respond, the second one, mail2.company.com, is tried, and so on.

Another important record type on a DNS server is the *canonical name (CNAME) record*. This is also commonly known as the *alias record*, and it allows hosts to have more than one name. For example, suppose your web server has the hostname www and you want that machine to also have the name ftp so that users can use FTP to access a different portion of the file system as an FTP root. You can accomplish this with a CNAME record. Given that you already have an address record established for the hostname www, a CNAME record that adds `ftp` as a hostname would look something like this:

```
www.company.com.        IN    A      204.176.47.2
ftp.company.com.        IN    CNAME  www.company.com.
```

When you put all these record types together in a zone file, or DNS table, it might look like this:

```
mail.company.com.       IN    A      204.176.47.9
mail2.company.com.      IN    A      204.176.47.21
mail3.company.com.      IN    A      204.176.47.89
yourhost.company.com.   IN    MX     10 mail.company.com.
yourhost.company.com.   IN    MX     20 mail2.company.com.
yourhost.company.com.   IN    MX     30 mail3.company.com.
www.company.com.        IN    A      204.176.47.2
ftp.company.com.        IN    CNAME  www.company.com.
```

DNS uses zone transfers from the primary DNS server for a zone to update standby servers, this allows us to have some redundancy in our DNS deployments and distribute the workload across multiple DNS servers.

When a client gets a DNS reply from a query, it will store it locally (cached) for a period of time to reduce the number of lookups on the DNS servers. In each DNS reply there is a field called TTL, or time to live. This instructs the client how long to store the replay before requesting again. This allows us to reduce the network workload and keep the DNS data fresh on the client. All devices use a cache system that stores the requests locally for a period of time and the *time to live (TTL)* value tells the client how long that should be.

What if you know the IP address but want to know what the domain name is? DNS can perform reverse lookup to query the server with the IP address and it will return the domain name. Other lookup types include recursive and iterative. When a DNS system uses a recursive lookup, one DNS server will query other DNS servers instead of the client performing all of the operations. The other option is to have the client communicate with multiple DNS servers during the name resolution process and it's referred to as an iterative DNS query.

Finally, there are other record types you should know about such as AAAA (for authentication IPV6 host addresses), PTR (pointer) records, and SOA (start of authority) records. PTR records are IP address–to–name mapping records rather than name–to–IP address mapping records. They reside in what is called a *reverse lookup zone* (or table) in the server and are used when an IP address is known but not a name. The start of authority (SOA) record stores information about the DNS domain or zone such as how to contact the administrator, when the domain was last updated, and how long the server should wait between refreshes.

Let's take a better look at how resolution takes place between a host and a DNS server. Figure 5.16 shows a DNS query from my host to `www.lammle.com` from a browser.

FIGURE 5.16   A DNS query to www.lammle.com

```
⊞ Frame 775: 74 bytes on wire (592 bits), 74 bytes captured (592 bits) on interface 0
⊞ Ethernet II, Src: Vmware_3e:06:c4 (00:0c:29:3e:06:c4), Dst: Vmware_fb:70:bb (00:50:56:fb:70:bb)
⊞ Internet Protocol Version 4, Src: 192.168.133.147 (192.168.133.147), Dst: 192.168.133.2 (192.168.133.2)
⊞ User Datagram Protocol, Src Port: 53870 (53870), Dst Port: domain (53)
⊟ Domain Name System (query)
     [Response In: 826]
     Transaction ID: 0xb8e0
  ⊞ Flags: 0x0100 Standard query
     Questions: 1
     Answer RRs: 0
     Authority RRs: 0
     Additional RRs: 0
  ⊟ Queries
     ⊟ www.lammle.com: type A, class IN
        Name: www.lammle.com
        Type: A (Host address)
        Class: IN (0x0001)
```

This figure shows that DNS uses User Datagram Protocol (UDP) at the Transport layer (it uses Transport Control Protocol [TCP] if it is updating its phone book pages—we call these *zone updates*), and this query is asking destination port 53 (the DNS service) on host 192.168.133.2 who the heck www.lammle.com is.

Let's take a look at the server's response. Figure 5.17 shows the DNS answer to our query for www.lammle.com.

FIGURE 5.17   The DNS answer to our query

```
⊟ Frame 826: 104 bytes on wire (832 bits), 104 bytes captured (832 bits) on interface 0
⊞ Ethernet II, Src: Vmware_fb:70:bb (00:50:56:fb:70:bb), Dst: Vmware_3e:06:c4 (00:0c:29:3e:06:c4)
⊞ Internet Protocol Version 4, Src: 192.168.133.2 (192.168.133.2), Dst: 192.168.133.147 (192.168.133.147)
⊞ User Datagram Protocol, Src Port: domain (53), Dst Port: 53870 (53870)
⊟ Domain Name System (response)
     [Request In: 775]
     [Time: 0.916685000 seconds]
     Transaction ID: 0xb8e0
  ⊞ Flags: 0x8180 Standard query response, No error
     Questions: 1
     Answer RRs: 2
     Authority RRs: 0
     Additional RRs: 0
  ⊟ Queries
     ⊟ www.lammle.com: type A, class IN
        Name: www.lammle.com
        Type: A (Host address)
        Class: IN (0x0001)
  ⊟ Answers
     ⊟ www.lammle.com: type CNAME, class IN, cname lammle.com
        Name: www.lammle.com
        Type: CNAME (Canonical name for an alias)
        Class: IN (0x0001)
        Time to live: 5 seconds
        Data length: 2
        Primaryname: lammle.com
     ⊟ lammle.com: type A, class IN, addr 184.172.53.52
        Name: lammle.com
        Type: A (Host address)
        Class: IN (0x0001)
        Time to live: 5 seconds
        Data length: 4
        Addr: 184.172.53.52 (184.172.53.52)
```

Port 53 answered from server 192.168.133.147 with a CNAME and an A record with the IP address of 184.172.53.52. My host can now go to that server requesting HTTP pages using the IP address.

DNS is an Application layer protocol. DNS queries are made on UDP port 53.

Dynamic DNS

At one time all DNS records had to be manually entered into the DNS server and edited manually when changes occurred. Today, DNS is dynamic. It uses *dynamic assignment* and works in concert with the DHCP function. Hosts register their names with the DNS server as they receive their IP address configuration from the DHCP server. Some older operating systems are not capable of self-registration, but the DHCP server can even be configured to perform registration on behalf of these clients with the DNS server.

This doesn't mean that manual records cannot be created if desired. In fact, some of the record types we have discussed can only be created manually. These include MX and CNAME records.

Internal and External DNS

DNS servers can be located in the screened subnet (or DMZ) or inside the intranet, as shown in Figure 5.18.

FIGURE 5.18   Internal and external DNS

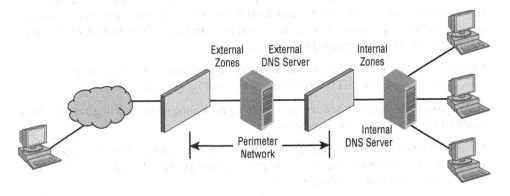

When located in the DMZ, the DNS server should only contain the records of the devices that are placed in the DMZ. Implementing separate internal and external DNS servers might require you to include external resource records in the internal DNS zone. You need to do this when the Active Directory forest root uses the same DNS domain name as the external network or when you want to reference the externally accessible resources by their true IP addresses in the perimeter network rather than using the addresses published to the Internet by the firewall protecting the perimeter network.

Third-Party/Cloud-Hosted DNS

Some smaller organizations find that it makes more sense to outsource the DNS function. Rather than hire and train staff to set up, configure, and maintain the infrastructure required to keep name resolution up and secure, they might find it more cost effective to utilize a third party who make it their business to provide this service. There is no shortage of cloud providers falling all over themselves to provide you with cloud-based storage, and these same vendors stand ready to provide you with DNS as a service, and they'll probably do a better job at it than you will.

Network Time Protocol

The *Network Time Protocol (NTP)* provides the time synchronization of the clocks on networking devices and computers on a network. This is used for distributed tasks that require accurate time to make sure tasks are processed in the correct sequence and recorded properly. NTP is needed for security and log tracking across many devices to correlate and trace events based on time. Many network management applications rely on timestamps for performance measurements and troubleshooting. If all of the devices in a network did not have the same time provided by syncing to a master clock using NTP, these would not be possible.

Stratum   The *stratum* level indicates how accurate the time source is. If the primary reference clock is a master time source such as a nuclear clock or a satellite navigation array, it is considered to be stratum level 0. Stratum 1 takes its time source from a stratum 0 clock and stratum 2 syncs from stratum 1 and so on. The accuracy is less the further you are from a stratum 0 time source.

Clients   Clients use the NTP protocol to query NTP servers to set their clocks. If every device in a network uses NTP, then all the clocks will be synchronized.

Once a client has synchronized its clock from an NTP time server, it will generally check every 10 minutes to keep its time updated.

Servers   NTP servers can be specialized hardware on your network that sync to stratum 0 devices or on the Internet. The site at `https://tf.nist.gov/tf-cgi/servers.cgi` lists servers available for public use.

Proxy Server

A *proxy server* is basically a type of server that handles its client-machine requests by forwarding them on to other servers while allowing granular control over the traffic between the local LAN and the Internet. When it receives a request, the proxy will then connect to the specific server that can fulfill the request for the client that wants it. A proxy server operates at the Application layer.

Sometimes the proxy modifies the client's request or a server's response to it—or even handles the client's request itself. It will actually cache, or "remember," the specific server that would have normally been contacted for the request in case it's needed another time. This behavior really speeds up the network's function, thereby optimizing its performance. However, proxy servers can also limit the availability of the types of sites that users on a LAN have access to, which is a benefit for an administrator of the network if users are constantly connected to non-work sites and using all the WAN bandwidth.

Figure 5.19 shows where a proxy server would be typically found in a small-to-medium network.

FIGURE 5.19   A proxy server

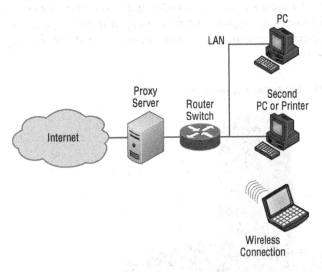

There are two main types of proxy servers you'll typically find working in present-day networks:

Web Proxy Server   A web proxy server is usually used to create a web cache. You experience this when you google a site you've visited before. The web proxy "remembers" you, and the site not only loads faster, it sometimes even recalls your personal information by automatically filling in your username—or even your billing/shipping information when you place another order.

Caching Proxy Server   A caching proxy server speeds up the network's service requests by recovering information from a client's earlier request. Caching proxies keep local copies of the resources requested often, which really helps minimize the upstream use of bandwidth. These servers can greatly enhance network performance.

I want to mention one more thing before we move on from proxies, and this is reverse proxies. Unlike a forward proxy, a reverse proxy takes requests from the Internet and forwards them to servers in an internal network, whereas the forward proxy we discussed in this section takes client requests and sends them to the Internet.

Encryption and Content Filtering

Although a number of the devices we have discussed earlier can perform encryption services, there are dedicated appliances that can perform encryption as well. The advantage of using these devices is that they normally provide more choice of encryption methods and stronger encryption options. They also offload the process from other devices like routers and servers, which is a good thing since the encryption/decryption process is very processor intensive and interferes with other functions that those routers and servers might be performing.

Sometimes these devices are called encryption gateways. They can either sit in line with a server or a local network, encrypting and decrypting all traffic, or function as an application server, encrypting any file sent to them within a network. Examples of encryption appliances are shown in Figure 5.20.

FIGURE 5.20   Encryption appliances

While an encryption appliance is dedicated to encryption, a content filtering appliance scans the content of what goes through it and filters out specific content or content types. Dedicating a device to this process offloads the work from servers or routers that could do this but at a cost of greatly slowing the devices. Also, there is usually more functionality and granular control available with a dedicated appliance.

Email is a good example of what you might run through one of these devices to filter out spam and objectionable content before the email is delivered. Another example of the use of a content filter might be to block websites based on the content of the web pages rather than on the basis of the URL or IP address. An example of a dedicated content/URL filtering appliance from SecPoint is shown in Figure 5.21.

FIGURE 5.21   Content filtering appliance

Analog Modem

A modem (modulator-demodulator) is a device that modulates an analog carrier signal to encode digital information and demodulates the signal to decode the transmitted information. I gave you an example of this when I explained APs earlier in the chapter because an AP modulates and demodulates a signal just like a modem. Figure 5.22 shows a current analog modem that can be used in today's networks, albeit with slow throughput.

FIGURE 5.22   Analog modem

The goal is to produce a signal that can be transmitted easily and decoded to reproduce the original digital data. These signals are transmitted over telephone lines and demodulated by another modem at the receiver side in order to read the digital data.

Because modems connect to phone lines, the location and installation of these devices is fairly cut-and-dried. It will have to be near a phone line, with one end connected to the phone line and another to a computer or modem bank. The analog modem operates at layer 1, like a repeater.

Packet Shaper

Packet shaping (also known as traffic shaping, it's a form of rate limiting) is an Internetworking traffic management technique that delays some or all packets to bring them into compliance with your or your company's traffic profile. Figure 5.23 shows a dedicated packet shaper appliance from Blue Coat.

FIGURE 5.23   Packet shaper

This process is used to optimize or guarantee performance, improve latency, and/or increase usable bandwidth for some kinds of packets by delaying other kinds, decided on by you.

VPN Concentrator/Headend

A VPN concentrator, or as it is often called, a headend, is a device that accepts multiple VPN connections from remote locations. Although this function can be performed by a router or server, as with the encryption gateways and content filtering devices discussed earlier, the same performance benefits can be derived from dedicating a device to this. Moreover, additional functionality usually comes with these devices, one of which is shown in Figure 5.24.

FIGURE 5.24   VPN headend

A headend device is a central control device required by some networks (for example, LANs or MANs). A headend device can also refer to a central control device within CATV systems that provides centralized functions such as re-modulation.

Media Converter

Media converters are used when you need to convert from one type of cabling to another type. This might be required to convert from one type of fiber to another or from Ethernet to fiber, for example. Figure 5.25 shows an Ethernet-to-fiber conversion box. Obviously, the location of these devices depends on where the conversion needs to take place. Media converters operate at layer 1.

FIGURE 5.25   Media converter

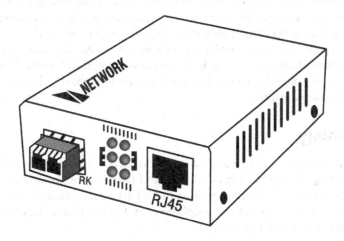

VoIP PBX

A private branch exchange (PBX) is a private telephone switch that resides on the customer premises. It has a direct connection to the telecommunication provider's switch. It performs call routing within the internal phone system. This is how a company can have two "outside" lines but 50 internal phones. The call comes in on one of the two outside lines, and the PBX routes it to the proper extension. Sometimes the system converts analog to digital but not always.

A VoIP PBX is one that switches calls between VoIP (Voice over Internet Protocol, or IP) users on local lines while allowing all users to share a certain number of external phone lines. The typical IP PBX can also switch calls between a VoIP user and a traditional telephone user or between two traditional telephone users in the same way that a conventional PBX does.

VoIP Endpoint

VoIP endpoints are desktop phone systems or wireless phone systems that are part of the converged networks where data and voice traffic are now combined in today's networks. These endpoints may also be implemented as conferencing systems in meeting rooms. There is more flexibility and freedom in the location and installation of these systems as more wireless modes of connectivity are introduced for these devices.

NGFW/Layer 7 Firewall

Next-generation firewalls (NGFWs) are a category of devices that attempt to address traffic inspection and application awareness shortcomings of a traditional stateful firewall without hampering the performance. Although unified threat management (UTM) devices also attempt to address these issues, they tend to use separate internal engines to perform individual security functions. This means a packet may be examined several times by different engines to determine whether it should be allowed into the network.

NGFWs are application aware, which means they can distinguish between specific applications instead of allowing all traffic coming in via typical web ports. Moreover, they examine packets only once during the deep packet inspection phase (which is required to detect malware and anomalies).

VoIP Gateway

A VoIP gateway (Voice over IP gateway) is a network device that helps to convert voice and fax calls between an IP network and public switched telephone network (PSTN) in real time. A VoIP gateway can typically support at least two T1/E1 digital channels. Most VoIP gateways feature at least one Ethernet and telephone port. Various protocols, such as MGCP, SIP, and LTP, can help to control a gateway.

Cable Modem

The cable modem allows for voice, video, and data (usually Internet) to connect from a home or small business to a cable provider's network. The cable modem is installed at the customer site and connects to the coax (coaxial) cable network. The Data Over Cable Service Interface Specifications (DOCSIS) standard allows both voice and data to share the cable with the standard video TV offerings provided by the local cable company.

DSL Modem

Digital Subscriber Line (DSL) modems are commonly deployed by traditional phone companies that have twisted-pair copper as the local connection to homes and businesses. DSL modems allow for voice, video, and data (usually Internet) to piggyback on the local copper line as a high-frequency carrier above the standard voice frequencies.

Networked Devices

The field of networking is constantly evolving and moving forward. In the good old days networks usually only connected desktop computers to servers and printers. In today's world, almost everything is being networked. As a network engineer you must be aware of these devices and their requirements.

VoIP Phones

As you learned earlier in this chapter, phones have migrated from the older analog style to digital Ethernet. While they tend to be low bandwidth, they are sensitive to delay and jitter so some form of quality of service (QoS) is usually required on the network to make sure the voice quality is acceptable.

Printers

Instead of having a printer connected to each desktop, they can be shared on the network with NIC cards installed directly in the printer or by using a print server that connects to the Ethernet network and to the printer using a serial or parallel connection.

Physical Access Control Devices

In modern office buildings and industrial sites, access control systems are installed at key points such as a door or a gate. These devices are connected to an authorization server on the network, which can connect back to directory services such as Microsoft Active Directory. When a user scans their badge, a lookup is performed by the server and a response is sent back to the access control device to either unlock the door or prevent the person from entering.

Cameras

Cameras have moved from the analog world to digital and are now very common in today's networks. They operate off TCP/IP and send video feeds back to a central server for processing and recording. Advanced features may include Pan/Tilt/Zoom (PTZ) to remotely control the camera and detection capabilities such as facial recognition are now common. Some cameras have heat and metal sensing capabilities.

Heating, Ventilation, and Air Conditioning (HVAC) Sensors

Modern office buildings and industrial sites have intelligent HVAC systems that use sensors to monitor and control air conditioning and heating systems. This allows them to either manually or automatically adjust the environmental controls and has the added advantage of cost saving by changing the temperature values after hours when no one is in the facility.

Internet of Things (IoT)

The number of devices connected to the Internet has exploded in the past few years and only shows signs of increasing to numbers in the billions of devices.

Wearable devices such as watches, fitness analyzers, and medical sensors are driving this growth. At home we now have digital assistants such as Siri and Alexa that connect to digital doorbells, refrigerators, thermostats, lights, cameras, televisions, and speakers.

This is collectively known as the *Internet of Things (IoT)* and the number and types of things is constantly increasing as new products and applications are introduced.

We see IoT devices everywhere, including weather monitoring stations, traffic control devices, security devices, and devices for an almost infinite number of other uses. They connect to the network using what connectivity options are available at their locations. Common network connections include Ethernet, Wi-Fi, Bluetooth, and cellular. IoT devices connect to centralized server applications and usually consume very little network bandwidth. However, if there are a very large number of IoT devices, the additive bandwidth may become significant.

Industrial Control Systems

The *industrial control systems (ICS)* technology space uses sensors for monitoring and control of everything from power grids to machines on the factory floor. By monitoring machinery, companies can proactively detect problems and flag the device for maintenance, potentially saving money on repairs and downtime. Other uses are to monitor assembly line workflows and dynamically change them based on workload.

The *supervisory control and data acquisition (SCADA)* architecture is an industry standard for monitoring and collecting industrial data such as a power grid or water utility.

SCADA systems consist of an architecture that includes computers, sensors, and networks that collect and display the status of the monitored systems in a graphical format. SCADA systems are used to monitor electrical or water systems, industrial plants, and machinery. The monitored systems use programmable logic controllers (PLCs) or other types of sensors such as flow or electrical meters to interface with the machinery or systems.

Planning and Implementing a Basic SOHO Network Using Network Segmentation

It's likely that at some point you'll have to break up one large network into a bunch of smaller ones because user response will have dwindled to a slow crawl as the network grew and grew. With all that growth, your LAN's traffic congestion will have reached epic proportions.

Determining Requirements

When implementing a SOHO network, the first thing is to identify the requirements of the network and the constraints around which you must operate. This should drive your design and device choices. An example set of requirements and constraints might be as follows:

- A small number of computers are needed.

- There is a high need for Internet access.

- Resources need to be shared.

- Wired hosts and wireless hosts will need to communicate with each other.

- Security is very important.

With these constraints in mind, you might find that you'll need more than just a switch and some Ethernet cabling for this project. There is a need for a router, an AP, and a firewall in this case. In addition, you need to think about compatibility between equipment and the types and brands of equipment to buy as well as environmental issues or limitations.

> Wireless and security constraints are covered in Chapter 12 and Chapter 20, respectively. Chapter 12 is "Wireless Networking," and Chapter 20 is "Physical Security."

One of the most important considerations you must take very seriously when building a basic network is LAN traffic congestion, which can be lessened with network segmentation and is directly related to device types and compatibility requirements as well as equipment limitations. Let's look at how to use the segmentation devices I have defined so far in this chapter.

Here's a list of some of the nasty things that commonly cause LAN traffic congestion:

- Too many hosts in a broadcast domain

- Broadcast storms

- Multicasting

- Low bandwidth

- Adding hubs for connectivity to the network

The answer to fixing a huge but slow network is to break it up into a number of smaller networks—something called *network segmentation*. You do this by using devices like routers and switches, which are sometimes still referred to as bridges because switches still use bridging technologies. Figure 5.26 displays a network that's been segmented with a switch so each network segment connected to the switch is now a separate collision domain. But make note of the fact that this network is actually still one *broadcast domain*—the set of all devices on a network segment that hear all the broadcasts sent on that segment.

FIGURE 5.26   A switch can replace the hub, breaking up collision domains.

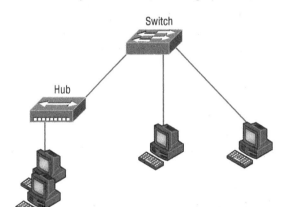

And keep in mind that the hub used in Figure 5.26 just extended the one collision domain from the switch port.

Routers are used to connect networks together and route packets of data from one network to another. (Cisco has become the de facto standard for routers because of its high-quality router products, great selection, and fantastic service.) Routers, by default, break up a broadcast domain. Figure 5.27 shows a router in our little network that creates an internetwork and breaks up broadcast domains.

FIGURE 5.27   Routers create an internetwork.

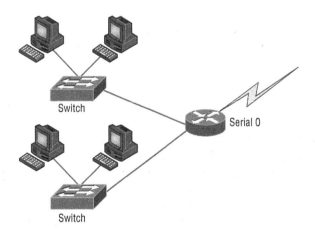

The network in Figure 5.27 is pretty cool. Each host is connected to its own collision domain, and the router has created two broadcast domains. And don't forget that the router provides connections to WAN services as well. The router uses something called a serial interface for WAN connections: specifically, a V.35 physical interface.

Breaking up a broadcast domain is important because when a host or server sends a network broadcast, every device on the network must read and process that broadcast—unless you've got a router. When the router's interface receives this broadcast, it can respond by basically saying, "Thanks, but no thanks," and discard the broadcast without forwarding it on to other networks. Even though routers are known for breaking up broadcast domains by default, it's important to remember that they break up collision domains as well.

There are two advantages of using routers in your network:

- They don't forward broadcasts by default.

- They can filter the network based on layer 3 (Network layer) information (such as an IP address).

Four router functions in your network can be listed as follows:

- Packet switching

- Packet filtering

- Internetwork communication

- Path selection

Remember that routers are really switches; they're actually what we call layer 3 switches. Unlike layer 2 switches, which forward or filter frames, routers (layer 3 switches) use logical addressing and provide what is called *packet switching*. Routers can also provide packet filtering by using access lists, and when routers connect two or more networks together and use logical addressing (IP or IPv6), this is called an *internetwork*. Last, routers use a *routing table* (map of the internetwork) to make path selections and to forward packets to remote networks.

Conversely, switches aren't used to create internetworks (they do not break up broadcast domains by default); they're employed to add functionality to a network LAN. The main purpose of a switch is to make a LAN work better—to optimize its performance—providing more bandwidth for the LAN's users. And switches don't forward packets to other networks as routers do. Instead, they only "switch" frames from one port to another within the switched network.

By default, switches break up collision domains, as mentioned in Chapter 4, "The Current Ethernet Specifications." *Collision domain* is an Ethernet term used to describe a network scenario wherein one particular device sends a packet on a network segment, forcing every other device on that same segment to pay attention to it. At the same time, a different device tries to transmit, leading to a collision, after which both devices must retransmit, one at a time. Not very efficient! This situation is typically found in a hub environment where each host segment connects to a hub that represents only one collision domain and only one broadcast domain. By contrast, each and every port on a switch represents its own collision domain.

 Switches create separate collision domains but a single broadcast domain. Routers provide a separate broadcast domain for each interface.

The term *bridging* was introduced before routers and hubs were implemented, so it's pretty common to hear people referring to bridges as switches. That's because bridges and switches basically do the same thing—break up collision domains on a LAN. (In reality, you cannot buy a physical bridge these days, only LAN switches, but these switches use bridging technologies.)

So this means a switch is basically just a multiple-port bridge with more brainpower, right? Well, pretty much, but there are differences. Switches do provide this function, but they do so with greatly enhanced management ability and features. Plus, most of the time, bridges only had two or four ports. Yes, you could get your hands on a bridge with up to 16 ports, but that's nothing compared to the hundreds available on some switches.

> You would use a bridge in a network to reduce collisions within broadcast domains and to increase the number of collision domains in your network. Doing this provides more bandwidth for users. And keep in mind that using hubs in your network can contribute to congestion on your Ethernet network. As always, plan your network design carefully!

Figure 5.28 shows how a network would look with all these internetwork devices in place. Remember that the router will not only break up broadcast domains for every LAN interface but also break up collision domains.

FIGURE 5.28   Internetworking devices

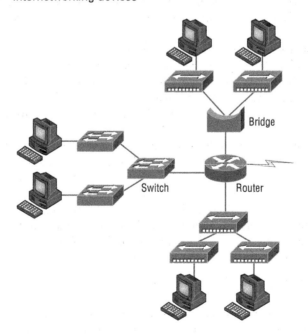

When you look at Figure 5.28, do you see the router at center stage and see how it connects each physical network together? We have to use this layout because of the older technologies involved—bridges and hubs.

On the top internetwork in Figure 5.28, you'll notice that a bridge is used to connect the hubs to a router. The bridge breaks up collision domains, but all the hosts connected to both hubs are still crammed into the same broadcast domain. Also, the bridge creates only two collision domains, so each device connected to a hub is in the same collision domain as every other device connected to that same hub. This is actually pretty lame, but it's still better than having one collision domain for all hosts.

Notice something else: The three hubs at the bottom that are connected also connect to the router, creating one collision domain and one broadcast domain. This makes the bridged network look much better indeed.

 Although bridges/switches are used to segment networks, they will not isolate broadcast or multicast packets.

The best network connected to the router is the LAN switch network on the left. Why? Because each port on that switch breaks up collision domains. But it's not all good—all devices are still in the same broadcast domain. Do you remember why this can be a really bad thing? Because all devices must listen to all broadcasts transmitted, that's why. And if your broadcast domains are too large, the users have less bandwidth and are required to process more broadcasts, and network response time will slow to a level that could cause office riots.

Once we have only switches in our network, things change a lot. Figure 5.29 shows the network that is typically found today.

FIGURE 5.29   Switched networks creating an internetwork

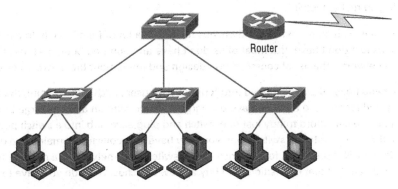

Router

Here I've placed the LAN switches at the center of the network world so the router is connecting only logical networks together. If I implement this kind of setup, I've created virtual LANs (VLANs), something I'm going to tell you about in Chapter 11, "Switching and Virtual LANs". So don't stress. But it is really important to understand that even though you have a switched network, you still need a router to provide your inter-VLAN communication, or internetworking. Don't forget that.

Obviously, the best network is one that's correctly configured to meet the business requirements of the company it serves. LAN switches with routers, correctly placed in the network, are the best network design. This book will help you understand the basics of routers and switches so you can make tight, informed decisions on a case-by-case basis.

Let's go back to Figure 5.28 again. Looking at the figure, how many collision domains and broadcast domains are in this internetwork? I hope you answered nine collision domains and three broadcast domains.

The broadcast domains are definitely the easiest to see because only routers break up broadcast domains by default. And because there are three connections, that gives you three broadcast domains. But do you see the nine collision domains? Just in case that's a no, I'll explain. The all-hub network is one collision domain; the bridge network equals three collision domains. Add in the switch network of five collision domains—one for each switch port—and you've got a total of nine.

Now, in Figure 5.29, each port on the switch is a separate collision domain and each VLAN is a separate broadcast domain. But you still need a router for routing between VLANs. How many collision domains do you see here? I'm counting 10—remember that connections between the switches are considered collision domains.

 Real World Scenario

Should I Replace All My Hubs with Switches?

You're a network administrator at a large company in San Jose. The boss comes to you and says that he got your requisition to buy a switch and is not sure about approving the expense; do you really need it?

Well, if you can have it, sure—why not? Switches really add a lot of functionality to a network that hubs just don't have. But most of us don't have an unlimited budget. Hubs still can create a nice network—that is, of course, if you design and implement the network correctly.

Let's say that you have 40 users plugged into four hubs, 10 users each. At this point, the hubs are all connected together so that you have one large collision domain and one large broadcast domain. If you can afford to buy just one switch and plug each hub into a switch port, as well as plug the servers into the switch, then you now have four collision domains and one broadcast domain. Not great; but for the price of one switch, your network is a much better thing. So, go ahead! Put that requisition in to buy all new switches. What do you have to lose?

So now that you've gotten an introduction to internetworking and the various devices that live in an internetwork, it's time to head into internetworking models.

As I mentioned earlier, routers break up broadcast domains, which means that by default, broadcasts aren't forwarded through a router. Do you remember why this is a good thing? Routers break up collision domains, but you can also do that using layer 2 (Data Link layer) switches. Because each interface in a router represents a separate network, it must be assigned unique network identification numbers, and each host on the network connected to that router must use the same network number. Figure 5.30 shows how a router works in an internetwork.

FIGURE 5.30   A router in an internetwork

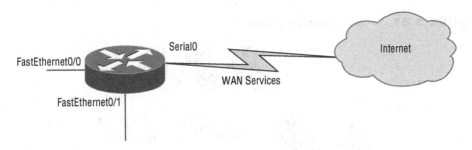

Here are some points about routers that you should commit to memory:

- Routers, by default, will not forward any broadcast or multicast packets.

- Routers use the logical address in a Network layer header to determine the next hop router to forward the packet to.

- Routers can use access lists, created by an administrator, to control security on the types of packets that are allowed to enter or exit an interface.

- Routers can provide layer 2 bridging functions if needed and can simultaneously route through the same interface.

- Layer 3 devices (routers, in this case) provide connections between virtual LANs (VLANs).

- Routers can provide quality of service (QoS) for specific types of network traffic.

Switching and VLANs are covered in Chapter 11.

Switches and Bridges at the Data Link Layer

Layer 2 switching is considered hardware-based bridging because it uses specialized hardware called an *application-specific integrated circuit (ASIC)*. ASICs can run up to multi-gigabit speeds with very low latency rates.

Latency is the time measured from when a frame enters a port to when it exits.

Bridges and switches read each frame as it passes through the network. The layer 2 device then puts the source hardware address in a filter table and keeps track of which port the frame was received on. This information (logged in the bridge's or switch's filter table) is what helps the machine determine the location of the specific sending device. Figure 5.31 shows a switch in an internetwork.

FIGURE 5.31   A switch in an internetwork

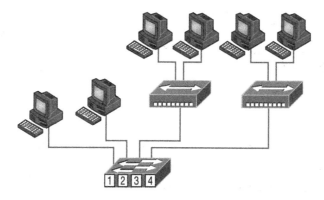

Each segment has its own collision domain.
All segments are in the same broadcast domain.

The real estate business is all about location, location, location, and it's the same way for both layer 2 and layer 3 devices. Although both need to be able to negotiate the network, it's crucial to remember that they're concerned with very different parts of it. Primarily, layer 3 machines (such as routers) need to locate specific networks, whereas layer 2 machines (switches and bridges) need to eventually locate specific devices. So, networks are to routers as individual devices are to switches and bridges. And routing tables that "map" the internetwork are for routers as filter tables that "map" individual devices are for switches and bridges.

After a filter table is built on the layer 2 device, it will forward frames only to the segment where the destination hardware address is located. If the destination device is on the same segment as the frame, the layer 2 device will block the frame from going to any other segments. If the destination is on a different segment, the frame can be transmitted only to that segment. This is called *transparent bridging*.

When a switch interface receives a frame with a destination hardware address that isn't found in the device's filter table, it will forward the frame to all connected segments. If the unknown device that was sent the "mystery frame" replies to this forwarding action, the switch updates its filter table regarding that device's location. But in the event that the destination address of the transmitting frame is a broadcast address, the switch will forward all broadcasts to every connected segment by default.

All devices that the broadcast is forwarded to are considered to be in the same broadcast domain. This can be a problem. Layer 2 devices propagate layer 2 broadcast storms that choke performance, and the only way to stop a broadcast storm from propagating through an internetwork is with a layer 3 device—a router.

The biggest benefit of using switches instead of hubs in your internetwork is that each switch port is actually its own collision domain. (Conversely, a hub creates one large collision domain.) But even armed with a switch, you still can't break up broadcast domains. Neither switches nor bridges will do that. They'll typically simply forward all broadcasts instead.

Another benefit of LAN switching over hub-centered implementations is that each device on every segment plugged into a switch can transmit simultaneously—at least they can as long as there is only one host on each port and a hub isn't plugged into a switch port. As you might have guessed, hubs allow only one device per network segment to communicate at a time.

Hubs at the Physical Layer

As you know, a hub is really a multiple-port repeater. A repeater receives a digital signal, reamplifies or regenerates that signal, and then forwards the digital signal out all active ports without looking at any data. An active hub does the same thing. Any digital signal received from a segment on a hub port is regenerated or reamplified and transmitted out all ports on the hub. This means all devices plugged into a hub are in the same collision domain as well as in the same broadcast domain. Figure 5.32 shows a hub in a network.

FIGURE 5.32   A hub in a network

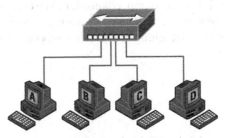

All devices are in the same collision domain.
All devices are in the same broadcast domain.
Devices share the same bandwidth.

Hubs, like repeaters, don't examine any of the traffic as it enters and is then transmitted out to the other parts of the physical media. Every device connected to the hub, or hubs, must listen if a device transmits. A physical star network—where the hub is a central device and cables extend in all directions out from it—is the type of topology a hub creates. Visually, the design really does resemble a star, whereas Ethernet networks run a logical bus topology, meaning that the signal has to run through the network from end to end.

 Hubs and repeaters can be used to enlarge the area covered by a single LAN segment, although I do not recommend this. LAN switches and/or wireless APs are affordable for almost every situation.

Environmental Considerations

All of the equipment discussed in this chapter—switches, routers, hubs, and so on—require proper environmental conditions to operate correctly. These devices have the same needs as any computing device. The environmental concerns can be categorized as follows:

Temperature   Like any device with a CPU, infrastructure devices such as routers, switches, and specialty appliances must have a cool area to operate. When temperatures rise, servers start rebooting and appliance CPUs start overworking as well. The room(s) where these devices are located should be provided with heavy-duty HVAC systems and ample ventilation. It may even be advisable to dedicate a suite for this purpose and put the entire system on a UPS with a backup generator in the case of a loss of power.

Modern data centers use the architecture of hot and cold isles. This maximizes the cooling of the equipment racks by forcing cold air in one row of racks and the exhaust of the hot air exiting into the next row.

Humidity   The air around these systems can be neither too damp nor too dry; it must be "just right." If it is too dry, static electricity will build up in the air, making the situation ripe for damaging a system. It takes very little static electricity to fry some electrical components. If it is too damp, connections start corroding and shorts begin to occur. A humidifying system should be used to maintain the level above 50 percent. The air conditioning should keep it within acceptable levels on the upper end.

Summary

Whew, this chapter covered quite a bit of information. You learned the difference between a router, a switch (bridge), and a hub and when to use each one. I also covered some devices that you might find in a network today, but not as often, such as VPN concentrators and content filters.

The information I discussed about DNS and DHCP is critical to your success on the Network + exam, and I highly suggest that you reread those sections. I covered how both the DNS and DHCP services work on a network.

In addition to the most common devices, I discussed the specialized network devices mentioned in the Network + objectives. I finished the chapter by discussing environmental conditions.

All of the information in this chapter is fundamental, and you must understand it before moving on to the other chapters in this book.

Exam Essentials

Understand how DHCP works and its purpose.   Dynamic Host Configuration Protocol (DHCP) provides IP configuration information to hosts. It is important to know how a DHCP client requests information from a server, how a server receives this information, and also how the server responds to the client and with what type of information.

Understand how DNS works and its purpose.   Domain Name Service (DNS) is used to resolve human names to IP addresses. Understanding how DNS resolves these names is critical, as is understanding how a DNS query is sent and how a DNS server responds. Know the different types of DNS records and what they are used for.

Understand the difference between a hub, a switch (bridge), and a router   A hub just connects network segments together. A switch/bridge segments the network using MAC addresses, and a router segments the network using logical addressing (IP and IPv6). Switches break up collision domains, and routers break up broadcast domains by default.

Remember the different names for a router.   A router is a layer 3 hardware device, but it can also be called a layer 3 switch or a multilayer switch.

Remember the various devices used on networks today and when you would use each one and how.   Understand the differences and how each device works: routers, switches, hubs, DNS servers, and DHCP servers.

Identify the purpose, benefits, and characteristics of using a proxy service.   A proxy server keeps a LAN somewhat separated from the Internet. Doing so increases security and filtering control and has the tendency to speed up Internet access through caching of recently used web pages.

Describe the proper use of network segmentation when planning and implementing a basic SOHO network.   Understand and apply the concepts of proper network segmentation when planning the use of various devices in the design of a SOHO network.

Describe the benefits of using a network load balancer   Network load balancers allow incoming connections to be spread out across multiple servers for scalability and resiliency. Understand the architecture of how load balancers are inserted into a network

Describe the benefits of using dedicated appliances for certain services.   Using appliances to offload functions such as encryption, content filtering, and VPN concentrators can decrease the workload of other systems and add functionality that may be present in these dedicated devices.

Also, wireless LAN controllers let you configure the complete network on a single device and push the configurations out to the Wi-Fi access points. The access points also tunnel the user data back to the controller, which then forwards the traffic onto the Local Area Network (LAN).

Lastly, NTP servers provide accurate date and time information to servers and networking equipment.

Identify the environmental requirements of infrastructure devices.   A cool temperature, ample ventilation, and the proper humidity level are all key to maintaining the operation of devices like routers, switches, and appliances.

Written Lab

Complete the table by filling in the appropriate layer of the OSI or hub, switch, or router device. You can find the answers in Appendix A.

Description	Device or OSI layer
This device sends and receives information about the Network layer.	
This layer creates a virtual circuit before transmitting between two end stations.	
A layer 3 switch or multilayer switch.	
This device uses hardware addresses to filter a network.	
Ethernet is defined at these layers.	
This layer supports flow control and sequencing.	
This device can measure the distance to a remote network.	
Logical addressing is used at this layer.	
Hardware addresses are defined at this layer.	
This device creates one big collision domain and one large broadcast domain.	
This device creates many smaller collision domains, but the network is still one large broadcast domain.	
This device can never run full-duplex.	
This device breaks up collision domains and broadcast domains.	

Review Questions

You can find the answers to the review questions in Appendix B.

1. Which of the following is not a term used when making SOHO Internet connections?
   A. Hub
   B. Router
   C. NIC
   D. Switch
   E. IDS/IPS

2. What advantage does a switch have over a hub?
   A. It discards frames.
   B. Transmissions received on one port will be sent out all the other ports.
   C. It recognizes frame boundaries and destination MAC addresses of incoming frames.
   D. Any two or more devices the switch connects are capable of causing a collision with each other.

3. Which device is used to segment a network?
   A. Hub
   B. Switch
   C. Repeater
   D. All of the above

4. What is the primary function of a bridge?
   A. Breaks up collision domains
   B. Allows a NIC or other networking device to connect to a different type of media than it was designed for
   C. Allows mobile users to connect to a wired network wirelessly
   D. None of the above

5. A network device that is used to connect multiple devices together without segmenting a network is a _____.
   A. Hub
   B. Wireless access point
   C. Switch
   D. Router

6. Which of the following is among the benefits of a switch?

    A. Protects LAN resources from attackers on the Internet

    B. Provides extra bandwidth

    C. Reduces throughput

    D. Allows access to all computers on a LAN

7. Which of the following devices can work at both layers 2 and 3 of the OSI model?

    A. Hub

    B. Switch

    C. Multilayer switch

    D. Bridge

8. What is an advantage of using DHCP in a network environment?

    A. More difficult administration of the network

    B. Static IP addressing

    C. Can send an operating system for the PC to boot from

    D. Assigns IP address to hosts

9. What is a benefit of a multilayer switch (MLS) over a layer 2 switch?

    A. Less bandwidth

    B. Routing functions

    C. Fewer features

    D. Fewer ports

10. Which device should be used if you need to send incoming packets to one or more machines that are hidden behind a single IP address?

    A. Switch

    B. Load balancer

    C. Hub

    D. Repeater

11. What role does the A record in a Domain Name Service (DNS) server have in your network?

    A. Translates human name to IP address

    B. Translates IP address to human name

    C. Enables printing, copying, and faxing from one device

    D. Controls network packets to optimize performance

12. Which device does not aid in network segmentation?

    A. Router

    B. Switch

    C. Hub

    D. Bridge

13. What is the most common use for a web proxy?

   A. Web cache

   B. Throughput increase

   C. DHCP services

   D. Support for user authentication

14. Which is not an advantage of network segmentation?

   A. Reducing congestion

   B. Improving security

   C. Containing network problems

   D. Preventing broadcast storms

15. Users arrive at the office after a weekend and the hosts that were shut down over the weekend are restarted but cannot access the LAN or Internet. Hosts that were not shut down are working fine. Where can the problem be?

   A. The DNS server

   B. The DHCP server

   C. The proxy server

   D. The firewall

16. You need a device that can prevent your users from accessing certain websites. Which device should you install?

   A. Firewall

   B. IDS

   C. IPS

   D. Proxy server

17. Which device creates separate collision domains and a single broadcast domain?

   A. Hub

   B. Router

   C. Switch

   D. Modem

18. Which of the following is *not* an advantage of using appliances to offload services like encryption and content filtering?

   A. Less expensive

   B. Reduced load on other devices

   C. Additional functionality

   D. Better performance

19. Which type of server in your network uses pointer and A records?

 A. NAT translation server

 B. IDS/IPS server

 C. DNS server

 D. Proxy server

20. Users on your network are saturating your bandwidth because they are using too many non-work-related sites. What device would limit the availability of the types of sites that users on a LAN have access to while providing granular control over the traffic between the local LAN and the Internet?

 A. Switch

 B. DHCP server

 C. DNS server

 D. Proxy server

Chapter

6

Introduction to the Internet Protocol

THE FOLLOWING COMPTIA NETWORK+ EXAM OBJECTIVES ARE COVERED IN THIS CHAPTER:

✓ **1.1 Compare and contrast the Open Systems Interconnection (OSI) model layers and encapsulation concepts.**

- OSI model

    - Layer 1 – Physical

    - Layer 2 – Data link

    - Layer 3 – Network

    - Layer 4 –Transport

    - Layer 5 – Session

    - Layer 6 – Presentation

    - Layer 7 – Application

- Data Encapsulation and decapsulation within the OSI model context

    - Ethernet header

    - Internet Protocol (IP) header

    - Transmission Control Protocol (TCP)/User Datagram Protocol (UDP) headers

    - TCP flags

    - Payload

    - Maximum transmission unit (MTU)

✓ **1.5 Explain common ports and protocols, their application, and encrypted alternatives.**

- Protocols Ports

    - File Transfer Protocol (FTP) 20/21

    - Secure Shell (SSH) 22

- Secure File Transfer Protocol (SFTP) 22
- Telnet 23
- Simple Mail Transfer Protocol (SMTP) 25
- Domain Name System (DNS) 53
- Dynamic Host Configuration Protocol (DHCP) 67/68
- Trivial File Transfer Protocol (TFTP) 69
- Hypertext Transfer Protocol (HTTP) 80
- Post Office Protocol v3 (POP3) 110
- Network Time Protocol (NTP) 123
- Internet Message Access Protocol (IMAP) 143
- Simple Network Management Protocol (SNMP) 161/162
- Lightweight Directory Access Protocol (LDAP) 389
- Hypertext Transfer Protocol Secure (HTTPS) [Secure Sockets Layer (SSL)] 443
- HTTPS [Transport Layer Security (TLS)] 443
- Server Message Block (SMB) 445
- Syslog 514
- SMTP TLS 587
- Lightweight Directory Access Protocol (over SSL) (LDAPS) 636
- IMAP over SSL 993
- POP3 over SSL 995
- Structured Query Language (SQL) Server 1433
- SQLnet 1521
- MySQL 3306
- Remote Desktop Protocol (RDP) 3389
- Session Initiation Protocol (SIP) 5060/5061

- IP protocol types
  - Internet Control Message Protocol (ICMP)
  - TCP
  - UDP
  - Generic Routing Encapsulation (GRE)
  - Internet Protocol Security (IPSec)
  - Authentication Header (AH)/Encapsulating Security Payload (ESP)

The *Transmission Control Protocol/Internet Protocol (TCP/IP)* suite was created by the Department of Defense (DoD) to ensure and preserve data integrity as well as to maintain communications in the event of catastrophic war.

So it follows that if designed and implemented correctly, a TCP/IP network can truly be a solid, dependable, and resilient network solution. In this chapter, I'll cover the protocols of TCP/IP.

I'll begin by covering the DoD's version of TCP/IP and then compare this version and its protocols with the OSI reference model discussed in Chapter 2, "The Open Systems Interconnection Specifications."

After going over the various protocols found at each layer of the DoD model, I'll finish the chapter by adding more detail to the explanation of data encapsulation that I started in Chapter 2.

To find Todd Lammle CompTIA videos and practice questions, please see www.lammle.com.

Introducing TCP/IP

Because TCP/IP is so central to working with the Internet and intranets, it's essential for you to understand it in detail. I'll begin by giving you some background on TCP/IP and how it came about and then move on to describe the important technical goals defined by the original designers. After that, you'll find out how TCP/IP compares to a theoretical model—the Open Systems Interconnection (OSI) model.

A Brief History of TCP/IP

The very first Request for Comments (RFC) was published in April 1969, which paved the way for today's Internet and its protocols. Each of these protocols is specified in the multitude of RFCs, which are observed, maintained, sanctioned, filed, and stored by the Internet Engineering Task Force (IETF).

TCP first came on the scene in 1974. In 1978, it was divided into two distinct protocols, TCP and IP, and finally documented into an RFC in 1980. Then, in 1983, TCP/IP replaced the Network Control Protocol (NCP) and was authorized as the official means of data transport for anything connecting to ARPAnet. ARPAnet was the Internet's ancestor, created by ARPA, the DoD's Advanced Research Projects Agency, again, way back in 1969 in reaction to the Soviets' launching of *Sputnik*. ARPA was soon redubbed DARPA, and it was divided into ARPAnet and MILNET (also in 1983); both were finally dissolved in 1990.

But contrary to what you might think, most of the development work on TCP/IP happened at UC Berkeley in Northern California, where a group of scientists were simultaneously working on the Berkeley version of Unix, which soon became known as the BSD, or the Berkeley Software Distribution series of Unix versions. Of course, because TCP/IP worked so well, it was packaged into subsequent releases of BSD Unix and offered to other universities and institutions if they bought the distribution tape. Basically, BSD Unix bundled with TCP/IP began as shareware in the world of academia and, as a result, became the basis of the huge success and exponential growth of today's Internet as well as smaller private and corporate intranets.

As usual, what may have started as a small group of TCP/IP aficionados evolved, and as it did, the US government created a program to test any new published standards and make sure they passed certain criteria. This was to protect TCP/IP's integrity and to ensure that no developer changed anything too dramatically or added any proprietary features. It's this very quality—this open-systems approach to the TCP/IP family of protocols—that pretty much sealed its popularity because it guarantees a solid connection between myriad hardware and software platforms with no strings attached.

TCP/IP and the DoD Model

The DoD model is basically a condensed version of the OSI model; it's composed of four, instead of seven, layers:

- Process/Application layer
- Host-to-Host layer
- Internet layer
- Network Access layer

Figure 6.1 shows a comparison of the DoD model and the OSI reference model. As you can see, the two are similar in concept, but each has a different number of layers with different names.

When the different protocols in the IP stack are discussed, two layers of the OSI and DoD models are interchangeable. In other words, the Internet layer and the Network layer describe the same thing, as do the Host-to-Host layer and the Transport layer. The other two layers of the DoD model, Process/Application and Network Access, are composed of multiple layers of the OSI model.

A vast array of protocols operate at the DoD model's *Process/Application layer* to integrate the various activities and duties spanning the focus of the OSI's corresponding top three layers (Application, Presentation, and Session). We'll be looking closely at those protocols in the next part of this chapter. The Process/Application layer defines protocols for node-to-node application communication and also controls user-interface specifications.

FIGURE 6.1   The DoD and OSI models

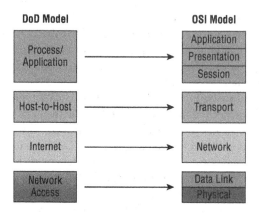

The *Host-to-Host layer* parallels the functions of the OSI's Transport layer, defining protocols for setting up the level of transmission service for applications. It tackles issues such as creating reliable end-to-end communication and ensuring the error-free delivery of data. It handles packet sequencing and maintains data integrity.

The *Internet layer* corresponds to the OSI's Network layer, designating the protocols relating to the logical transmission of packets over the entire network. It takes care of the logical addressing of hosts by giving them an IP address, and it handles the routing of packets among multiple networks.

At the bottom of the DoD model, the *Network Access layer* monitors the data exchange between the host and the network. The equivalent of the Data Link and Physical layers of the OSI model, the Network Access layer oversees hardware addressing and defines protocols for the physical transmission of data.

The DoD and OSI models are alike in design and concept and have similar functions in similar layers. Figure 6.2 shows the TCP/IP protocol suite and how its protocols relate to the DoD model layers.

FIGURE 6.2   The TCP/IP protocol suite

DoD Model

| Process/
Application | Telnet | FTP | LPD | SNMP |
| | TFTP | SMTP | NFS | X Window |

| Host-to-Host | TCP | | UDP | |

| Internet | ICMP | ARP | | RARP |
| | IP | | | |

| Network
Access | Ethernet | Fast
Ethernet | Gigabit
Ethernet | Wireless
/802.11 |

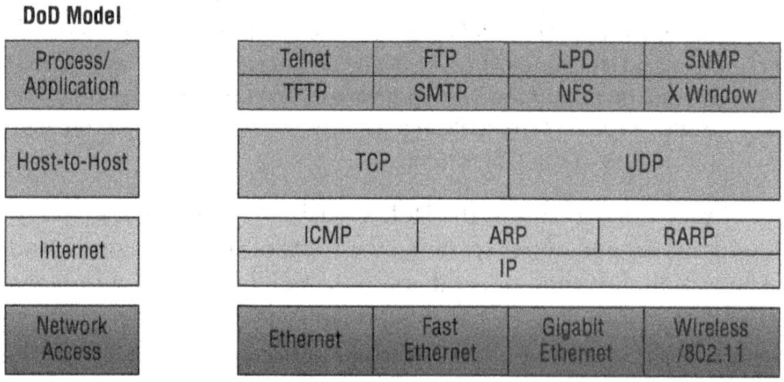

We'll now look at the different protocols in more detail, starting with the Process/Application layer protocols.

The Process/Application Layer Protocols

In the following sections, I'll describe the different applications and services typically used in IP networks and list their associated port numbers as well, which are discussed in detail in this chapter.

File Transfer Protocol (TCP 20, 21)

File Transfer Protocol (FTP) is the protocol that actually lets you transfer files across an IP network, and it can accomplish this between any two machines that are using it. But FTP isn't just a protocol; it's also a program. Operating as a protocol, FTP is used by applications. As a program, it's employed by users to perform file tasks by hand. FTP also allows for access to both directories and files and can accomplish certain types of directory operations, such as relocating files into different directories. Figure 6.3 shows an FTP example.

FIGURE 6.3   File Transfer Protocol

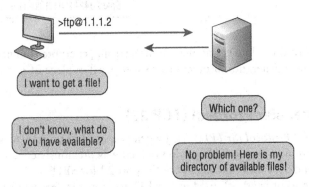

Accessing a host through FTP is only the first step, though. Users must then be subjected to an authentication login that's probably secured with passwords and usernames implemented by system administrators to restrict access. You can get around this somewhat by adopting the username *anonymous*—although what you'll gain access to will be limited.

Even when employed by users manually as a program, FTP's functions are limited to listing and manipulating directories, typing file contents, and copying files between hosts. It can't execute remote files as programs. The problem with FTP is that all data is sent in clear text, just as with Telnet. If you need to make sure your FTP transfers are secure, then you'll use SFTP, which is covered after the next section.

Secure Shell (TCP 22)

The *Secure Shell (SSH)* protocol sets up a secure Telnet session over a standard TCP/IP connection and is employed for doing things like logging into other systems, running programs on remote systems, and moving files from one system to another. Figure 6.4 shows an SSH example.

FIGURE 6.4   SSH

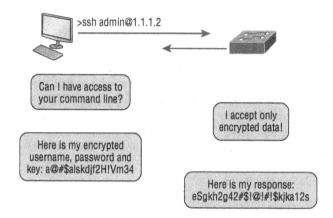

And it does all of this while maintaining a nice, strong, encrypted connection. You can think of it as the new-generation protocol that's now used in place of `rsh` and `rlogin`—even Telnet.

Secure File Transfer Protocol (TCP 22)

Secure File Transfer Protocol (SFTP) is used when you need to transfer files over an encrypted connection. It uses an SSH session (which was previously covered), which encrypts the connection, and SSH uses port 22, hence the port 22 for SFTP.

Apart from the secure part, it's used just as FTP is—for transferring files between computers on an IP network, such as the Internet.

Telnet (TCP 23)

Telnet is the chameleon of protocols—its specialty is terminal emulation. It allows a user on a remote client machine, called the Telnet client, to access the resources of another machine, the Telnet server. Telnet achieves this by pulling a fast one on the Telnet server and making the client machine appear as though it were a terminal directly attached to the local network. This projection is actually a software shell—a virtual terminal that can interact with the chosen remote host. Figure 6.5 shows a Telnet example.

These emulated terminals are of the text-mode type and can execute refined procedures such as displaying menus that give users the opportunity to choose options and access the applications on the duped server. Users begin a Telnet session by running the Telnet client software and then logging into the Telnet server.

FIGURE 6.5   Telnet

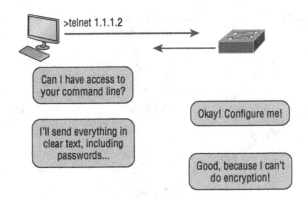

Telnet offers no security or encryption and is replaced by Secure Shell (SSH) when security across the remote-configuration session is needed or desired.

Simple Mail Transfer Protocol (TCP 25)

Simple Mail Transfer Protocol (SMTP), answering our ubiquitous call to email, uses a spooled, or queued, method of mail delivery. Once a message has been sent to a destination, the message is spooled to a device—usually a disk. The server software at the destination posts a vigil, regularly checking the queue for messages. When it detects them, it proceeds to deliver them to their destination. SMTP is used to send mail; POP3 is used to receive mail.

Domain Name Service (TCP and UDP 53)

Domain Name Service (DNS) resolves hostnames—specifically, Internet names, such as www.lammle.com—to their corresponding IP addresses.

You don't have to use DNS; you can just type in the IP address of any device you want to communicate with. An IP address identifies hosts on a network and the Internet as well. However, DNS was designed to make our lives easier. Think about this: What would happen if you wanted to move your web page to a different service provider? The IP address would change, and no one would know what the new one was. DNS allows you to use a domain name to specify an IP address. You can change the IP address as often as you want and no one will know the difference. Figure 6.6 shows a DNS example.

DNS is used to resolve a *fully qualified domain name (FQDN)*—for example, www.lammle.com or todd.lammle.com—to an IP address. An FQDN, or DNS namespace, is a hierarchy that can logically locate a system based on its domain identifier.

If you want to resolve the name *todd*, you must either type in the FQDN of todd.lammle.com or have a device, such as a PC or router, add the suffix for you. For example, on a Cisco router, you can use the command ip domain-name lammle.com to append each request with the lammle.com domain. If you don't do that, you'll have to type in the FQDN to get DNS to resolve the name.

FIGURE 6.6 Domain Name Service

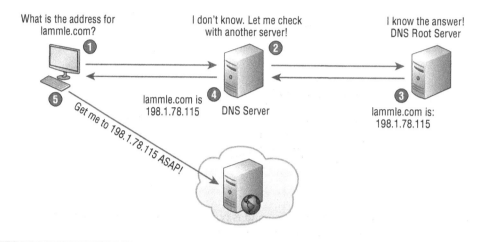

 An important thing to remember about DNS is that if you can ping a device with an IP address but can't use its FQDN, you might have some type of DNS configuration failure.

Dynamic Host Configuration Protocol/Bootstrap Protocol (UDP 67/68)

Dynamic Host Configuration Protocol (DHCP) assigns IP addresses to hosts with information provided by a server. It allows easier administration and works well in small to even very large network environments. Many types of hardware can be used as a DHCP server, including routers.

DHCP differs from Bootstrap Protocol (BootP) in that BootP assigns an IP address to a host but the host's hardware address must be entered manually in a BootP table. You can think of DHCP as a dynamic BootP. But remember that BootP is also used to send an operating system that a host can boot from. DHCP can't do that.

 Please also read the sections on DHCP and DNS servers in Chapter 5, "Networking Devices," if you have not done so; both figure largely in the exam objectives.

But there is a lot of information a DHCP server can provide to a host when the host is requesting an IP address from the DHCP server. Here's a partial list of the information a DHCP server can provide:

- IP address
- Subnet mask
- Domain name

- Default gateway (routers)

- DNS

- Windows Internet Naming Service (WINS) information

A DHCP server can give even more information than this, but the items in the list are the most common.

A client that sends out a DHCP Discover message in order to receive an IP address sends out a broadcast at both layer 2 and layer 3. The layer 2 broadcast is all *F*s in hex, which looks like this: FF:FF:FF:FF:FF:FF. The Layer 3 broadcast is 255.255.255.255, which means all networks and all hosts. DHCP is connectionless, which means it uses User Datagram Protocol (UDP) at the Transport layer, also known as the Host-to-Host layer, which we'll talk about later.

In case you don't believe me, here's an example of output from my trusty analyzer:

```
Ethernet II,Src:192.168.0.3(00:0b:db:99:d3:5e),Dst:Broadcast(ff:ff:ff:ff:ff:ff)
Internet Protocol,Src:0.0.0.0(0.0.0.0),Dst:255.255.255.255(255.255.255.255).
```

The Data Link and Network layers are both sending out "all hands" broadcasts saying, "Help! I don't know my IP address!"

Figure 6.7 shows the process of a client-server relationship using a DHCP connection.

FIGURE 6.7   DHCP client four-step process

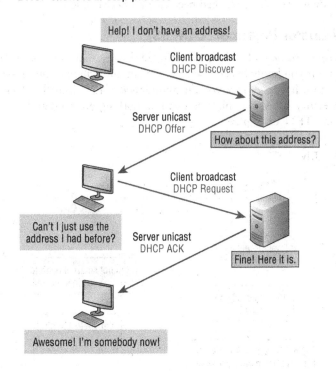

The following is the four-step process (sometimes known as the DORA process) a client takes to receive an IP address from a DHCP server:

1. The DHCP client broadcasts a DHCP Discover message looking for a DHCP server (port 67).

2. The DHCP server that received the DHCP Discover message sends a unicast DHCP Offer message back to the host.

3. The client then broadcasts to the server a DHCP Request message asking for the offered IP address and possibly other information.

4. The server finalizes the exchange with a unicast DHCP Acknowledgment message.

What happens if you have a few hosts connected together with a switch or hub and you don't have a DHCP server? You can add IP information by hand (this is called *static IP addressing*), or Windows provides what is called Automatic Private IP Addressing (APIPA), a feature of later Windows operating systems. With APIPA, clients can automatically self-configure an IP address and subnet mask (basic IP information that hosts use to communicate, which is covered in detail in Chapter 7, "IP Addressing," and Chapter 8, "IP Subnetting, Troubleshooting IP, and Introduction to NAT") when a DHCP server isn't available. The IP address range for APIPA is 169.254.0.1 through 169.254.255.254. The client also configures itself with a default Class B subnet mask of 255.255.0.0. If you have a DHCP server and your host is using this IP address, this means your DHCP client on your host is not working or the server is down or can't be reached because of a network issue.

Trivial File Transfer Protocol (UDP 69)

Trivial File Transfer Protocol (TFTP) is the stripped-down, stock version of FTP, but it's the protocol of choice if you know exactly what you want and where to find it—plus it's easy to use, and it's fast, too! It doesn't give you the abundance of functions that FTP does, though. TFTP has no directory-browsing abilities; it can do nothing but send and receive files. Figure 6.8 shows a TFTP example.

FIGURE 6.8   Trivial FTP

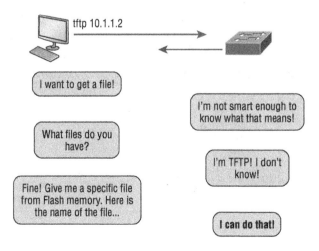

This compact little protocol also skimps in the data department, sending much smaller blocks of data than FTP, and there's no authentication as with FTP, so it's insecure. Few sites support it because of the inherent security risks.

 Real World Scenario

When Should You Use FTP?

The folks at your San Francisco office need a 50 MB file emailed to them right away. What do you do? Most email servers would reject the email because they have size limits. Even if there's no size limit on the server, it would still take a while to send this big file. FTP to the rescue! Most ISPs don't allow files larger than 10 MB to be emailed, so FTP is an option you should consider if you need to send and receive.

If you need to give someone a large file or you need to get a large file from someone, FTP is a nice choice. Smaller files (smaller than 10 MB) can be sent via email if you have the bandwidth (who doesn't these days?), even if they're compressed. To use FTP, you'll need to set up an FTP server on the Internet so that the files can be shared.

Besides, FTP is faster than email, which is another reason to use FTP for sending or receiving large files. In addition, because it uses TCP and is connection-oriented, if the session dies, FTP can sometimes start up where it left off. Try that with your email client!

Hypertext Transfer Protocol (TCP 80)

All those snappy websites comprising a mélange of graphics, text, links, and so on—the *Hypertext Transfer Protocol (HTTP)* is making it all possible. Figure 6.9 shows an HTTP example.

FIGURE 6.9   HTTP

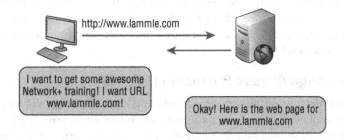

HTTP is used to manage communications between web browsers and web servers, and it opens the right resource when you click a link, wherever that resource may actually reside. See the section on HTTPS for what we normally use today for this type of data transfer.

Post Office Protocol v3 (TCP 110)

Post Office Protocol (POP) gives us a storage facility for incoming mail, and the latest version is called POP3 (sound familiar?). Basically, how this protocol works is when a client device connects to a POP3 server, messages addressed to that client are released for downloading. It doesn't allow messages to be downloaded selectively, but once they are, the client-server interaction ends and you can delete and tweak your messages locally at will. A newer standard, IMAP, is being used more and more in place of POP3 because of security.

Network Time Protocol (UDP 123)

Kudos to Professor David Mills of the University of Delaware for coming up with this handy protocol that's used to synchronize the clocks on our computers to one standard time source (typically, an atomic clock). *Network Time Protocol (NTP)* works in conjunction with other synchronization utilities to ensure that all computers on a given network agree on the time. See Figure 6.10.

FIGURE 6.10   Network Time Protocol

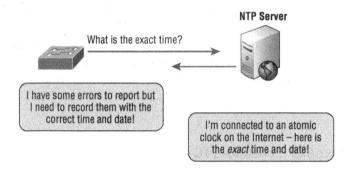

This may sound pretty simple, but it's very important because so many of the transactions done today are time- and date-stamped. Think about your precious databases, for one. It can mess up a server pretty badly if it's out of sync with the machines connected to it, even by mere seconds (think crash!). You can't have a transaction entered by a machine at, say, 1:50 a.m. when the server records that transaction as having occurred at 1:45 a.m. So basically, NTP works to prevent "back to the future sans DeLorean" from bringing down the network—very important indeed!

Internet Message Access Protocol (TCP 143)

Because *Internet Message Access Protocol (IMAP)* makes it so you get control over how you download your mail, with it, you also gain some much-needed security. It lets you peek at the message header or download just a part of a message—you can now just nibble at the bait instead of swallowing it whole and then choking on the hook hidden inside!

With it, you can choose to store messages on the email server hierarchically and link to documents and user groups too. IMAP even gives you search commands to use to hunt for messages based on their subject, header, or content. As you can imagine, it has some serious authentication features—it actually supports the Kerberos authentication scheme that MIT developed. And yes, IMAP4 is the current version.

Simple Network Management Protocol (UDP 161/162)

Simple Network Management Protocol (SNMP) collects and manipulates valuable network information. It gathers data by polling the devices on the network from a management station at fixed or random intervals, requiring them to disclose certain information. When all is well, SNMP receives something called a *baseline*—a report delimiting the operational traits of a healthy network. This protocol can also stand as a watchdog over the network, quickly notifying managers of any sudden turn of events. The network watchdogs are called *agents,* and when aberrations occur, agents send an alert called a *trap* to the management station. The Network Management System (NMS) polls the agents through a Management Information Base (MIB). The MIB is basically a database with a set of predefined questions the NMS can ask the agents regarding the health of the device or network. Figure 6.11 shows an NMS station at work.

FIGURE 6.11   Network Management Station

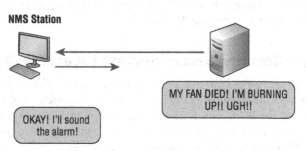

In addition, SNMP can help simplify the process of setting up a network as well as the administration of your entire internetwork.

SNMP Versions 1, 2, and 3

SNMP versions 1 and 2 are pretty much obsolete. This doesn't mean you won't see them in a network at some time, but v1 is super old and, well, outdated. SNMPv2 provided improvements, especially in performance. But one of the best additions was GETBULK, which allowed a host to retrieve a large amount of data at once. However, v2 never really caught on in the networking world. SNMPv3 is now the standard and uses both TCP and UDP, unlike v1, which used only UDP. Version 3 added even more security and message integrity, authentication, and encryption. So, be careful when running SNMPv1 and v2 because they are susceptible to a packet sniffer reading the data.

Lightweight Directory Access Protocol (TCP 389)

If you're the system administrator of any decent-sized network, odds are you have a type of directory in place that keeps track of all your network resources, such as devices and users. But how do you access those directories? Through the *Lightweight Directory Access Protocol (LDAP)*, that's how. LDAP is a protocol used to access and query directory services systems such as Microsoft Active Directory. And there is a secure version of LDAP called LDAPS that uses port 636, which I'll cover a bit later.

This protocol standardizes how you access directories, and its first and second inceptions are described in RFCs 1487 and 1777, respectively. There were a few glitches in those two earlier versions, so a third version—the one most commonly used today—was created to address those issues and is described in RFC 3377.

Hypertext Transfer Protocol Secure (TCP 443)

Hypertext Transfer Protocol Secure (HTTPS) is a secure version of HTTP that arms you with a whole bunch of security tools for keeping transactions secure between a web browser and a server. It's what your browser needs to fill out forms, sign in, authenticate, and encrypt an HTTP message when you make a reservation or buy something online.

    Both SSH (port 22) and HTTPS (port 443) are used to encrypt packets over your intranet and the Internet.

Transport Layer Security/Secure Sockets Layer (TCP 995/465)

Both *Transport Layer Security (TLS)* and its forerunner, Secure Sockets Layer (SSL), are cryptographic protocols that come in really handy for enabling secure online data-transfer activities like browsing the Web, instant messaging, Internet faxing, and so on. They're so similar that it's not within the scope of this book to detail the differences between them. They both use X.509 certificates and asymmetric cryptography to authenticate to the host they are communicating with and to exchange a key. This key is then used to encrypt data flowing between the hosts. This allows for data/message confidentiality, message integrity, and message authentication.

Even though I listed TLS/SSL as using ports 995 and 465, which is true if you're using Gmail, TLS/SSL isn't tied down to any certain ports and can use various different ones.

Server Message Block (TCP 445)

Server Message Block (SMB) is used for sharing access to files and printers and other communications between hosts on a Microsoft Windows network. SMB runs mostly on TCP port 445 now, but SMB can also run on UDP port 137 and 138 and on TCP port 137 and 139 using NetBIOS.

Syslog (UDP 514)

Reading system messages from a switch's or router's internal buffer is the most popular and efficient method of seeing what's going on with your network at a particular time. But the best way is to log messages to a *syslog* server, which stores messages from you and can even time-stamp and sequence them for you, and it's easy to set up and configure!

Syslog allows you to display, sort, and even search messages, all of which makes it a really great troubleshooting tool. The search feature is especially powerful because you can use keywords and even severity levels. Plus, the server can email admins based on the severity level of the message.

Network devices can be configured to generate a syslog message and forward it to various destinations. These four examples are popular ways to gather messages from Cisco devices:

- Logging buffer (on by default)
- Console line (on by default)
- Terminal lines (using the `terminal monitor` command)
- Syslog server

The severity levels, from the most severe level to the least severe, are explained in Table 6.1. Information is the default and will result in all messages being sent to the buffers and console.

TABLE 6.1   Severity levels

Severity Level	Explanation
Emergency (severity 0)	System is unusable.
Alert (severity 1)	Immediate action is needed.
Critical (severity 2)	Critical condition.
Error (severity 3)	Error condition.
Warning (severity 4)	Warning condition.
Notification (severity 5)	Normal but significant condition.
Information (severity 6)	Normal information message.
Debugging (severity 7)	Debugging message.

SMTP TLS (TCP 587)

As discussed previously, Simple Mail Transfer Protocol (SMTP), answers our ubiquitous call to email, uses a spooled, or queued, method of mail delivery using TCP port 25. However, this email is sent in clear text and some email servers can still use this.

SMTP TLS encrypts email when it is sent, and most email servers use or can use port 587 to send email now, some even demand it. This port, coupled with TLS encryption, will ensure that email is securely sent, following the guidelines set out by the IETF of course.

Lightweight Directory Access Protocol over SSL (TCP 636)

Building on our discussion earlier on TCP 389 LDAP, understand that this traffic is transmitted unsecured. Bring in LDAP over SSL TCP 636, which is the suggested use of LDAP in today's networks. To make this function correctly, you just need to install a proper certificate from a Microsoft certification authority (CA) or other type of CA.

IMAP over SSL (TCP 993)

Because Internet Message Access Protocol (IMAP) ensures that you get control over how you download your mail, with it, you also gain some much-needed security. However, IMAP over SSL means that IMAP traffic travels over a security socket to a security port, using TCP port 993 usually.

POP3 over SSL (TCP 995)

As discussed previously, Post Office Protocol (POP) gives us a storage facility for incoming mail, and the latest version of POP is called POP3. You can probably guess that this email is downloaded in clear text. Either POP3 over SSL or IMAP over SSL is more commonly used to encrypt emails being download from servers today.

Structured Query Language (SQL) Server (TCP 1433)

Microsoft SQL Server has grown from a simple relational database engine to a multipurpose enterprise-level data platform. TCP port 1433 is the default port for SQL Server, and it's also the official Internet Assigned Number Authority (IANA) socket number for SQL Server. Client systems use TCP 1433 to connect to the database engine.

SQLnet (TCP 1521)

SQLnet (also referred to as SQL*Net and Net8) is Oracle's networking software that allows remote data access between programs using Oracles Database. Applications and databases are shared with different machines and continue to communicate as if they were local.

SQLnet is based on Oracle's Transparent Network Substrate (TNS), a network technology that provides a generic interface to all network protocols; however, you can guess this is no longer needed today since we have TCP/IP.

SQL*Net is used by both client and server to communicate with one another. Without the Net8 layer acting as the interpreter, the client process and the server process are unable to interconnect (noticed how I used all three names in this section—all define the same thing).

MySQL (TCP 3306)

MySQL is a relational database management system based on Structured Query Language (SQL). This is used within companies for data warehousing, e-commerce, logging applications, and more. The most common use for MySQL is for the purpose of a cloud-based database.

Remote Desktop Protocol (TCP 3389)

Remote Desktop Protocol (RDP) is a proprietary protocol developed by Microsoft. It allows you to connect to another computer and run programs. RDP operates somewhat like Telnet, except instead of getting a command-line prompt as you do with Telnet, you get the actual graphical user interface (GUI) of the remote computer. Clients exist for most versions of Windows, and Macs now come with a preinstalled RDP client.

Microsoft currently calls its official RDP server software Remote Desktop Services; it was called Terminal Services for a while. Microsoft's official client software is currently referred to as Remote Desktop Connection (RDC), which was called Terminal Services Client in the past.

RDP is an excellent tool for remote clients, allowing users to connect to their work computer from home, for example, and get their email or perform work on other applications without running or installing any of the software on their home computer.

SIP (VoIP) (TCP or UDP 5060/TCP 5061)

Session Initiation Protocol (SIP) is a hugely popular signaling protocol used to construct and deconstruct multimedia communication sessions for many things like voice and video calls, videoconferencing, streaming multimedia distributions, instant messaging, presence information, and online games over the Internet.

RTP (VoIP) (UDP 5004/TCP 5005)

Real-time Transport Protocol (RTP) describes a packet-formatting standard for delivering audio and video over the Internet. Although initially designed as a multicast protocol, it's now used for unicast applications too. It's commonly employed for streaming media, video-conferencing, and push-to-talk systems—all things that make it a de facto standard in Voice over IP (VoIP) industries.

MGCP (Multimedia) (TCP 2427/2727)

Media Gateway Control Protocol (MGCP) is a standard protocol for handling the signaling and session management needed during a multimedia conference.

The protocol defines a means of communication between a media gateway, which converts data from the format required for a circuit-switched network to that required for a packet-switched network, and the media gateway controller.

MGCP can be used to set up, maintain, and terminate calls between multiple endpoints.

H.323 (Video) (TCP 1720)

H.323 is a protocol that provides a standard for video on an IP network that defines how real-time audio, video, and data information is transmitted. This standard provides signaling, multimedia, and bandwidth control mechanisms. H.323 uses the RTP standard for communication.

Internet Group Management Protocol

Internet Group Management Protocol (IGMP) is the TCP/IP protocol used for managing IP multicast sessions. It accomplishes this by sending out unique IGMP messages over the network to reveal the multicast-group landscape and to find out which hosts belong to which multicast group. The host machines in an IP network also use IGMP messages to become members of a group and to quit the group too. IGMP messages come in seriously handy for tracking group memberships as well as active multicast streams. IGMP works at the Network layer and doesn't use port numbers.

NetBIOS (TCP and UDP 137–139)

Network Basic Input/Output System works only in the upper layers of the OSI model and allows for an interface on separate computers to communicate over a network.

It was first created in the early 1980s to work on an IBM LAN and was proprietary. Microsoft and Novell both created a NetBIOS implementation to allow their hosts to communicate to their servers, but Microsoft's version became the de facto version.

The Host-to-Host Layer Protocols

The main purpose of the Host-to-Host layer is to shield the upper-layer applications from the complexities of the network. This layer says to the upper layer, "Just give me your data stream, with any instructions, and I'll begin the process of getting your information ready to send."

The following sections describe the two protocols at this layer:

- Transmission Control Protocol (TCP)
- User Datagram Protocol (UDP)

In addition, we'll look at some of the key host-to-host protocol concepts as well as the port numbers.

Transmission Control Protocol

Transmission Control Protocol (TCP) takes large blocks of information from an application and breaks them into segments. It numbers and sequences each segment so that the destination's TCP process can put the segments back into the order the application intended. After these segments are sent, TCP (on the transmitting host) waits for an acknowledgment from the receiving end's TCP process, retransmitting those segments that aren't acknowledged.

Remember that in a reliable transport operation, a device that wants to transmit sets up a connection-oriented communication with a remote device by creating a session. The transmitting device first establishes a connection-oriented session with its peer system; that session is called a *call setup* or a *three-way handshake*. Data is then transferred, and when the transfer is complete, a call termination takes place to tear down the virtual circuit.

TCP is a full-duplex, connection-oriented, reliable, and accurate protocol, but establishing all these terms and conditions, in addition to error checking, is no small task. TCP is very complicated, and so not surprisingly, it's costly in terms of network overhead. And since today's networks are much more reliable than those of yore, this added reliability is often unnecessary. Most programmers use TCP because it removes a lot of programming work, but for real-time video and VoIP, *User Datagram Protocol (UDP)* is often better because using it results in less overhead.

TCP Segment Format

Because the upper layers just send a data stream to the protocols in the Transport layers, I'll use Figure 6.12 to demonstrate how TCP segments a data stream and prepares it for the Internet layer. When the Internet layer receives the data stream, it routes the segments as packets through an internetwork. The segments are handed to the receiving host's Host-to-Host layer protocol, which rebuilds the data stream for the upper-layer applications or protocols.

The TCP header is 24 bytes long, or up to 60 bytes with options. Figure 6.12 shows the TCP segment format and the different fields within the TCP header.

FIGURE 6.12   TCP segment format

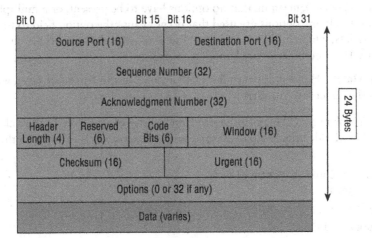

Again, it's good to understand what each field in the TCP segment is in order to build a strong educational foundation:

Source Port   This is the port number of the application on the host sending the data, which I'll talk about more thoroughly a little later in the Port Numbers section.

Destination Port   This is the port number of the application requested on the destination host.

Sequence Number   A number used by TCP that puts the data back in the correct order or retransmits missing or damaged data during a process called sequencing.

Acknowledgment Number   The value is the TCP octet that is expected next.

Header Length   The number of 32-bit words in the TCP header, which indicates where the data begins. The TCP header (even one including options) is an integral number of 32 bits in length.

Reserved   Always set to zero.

Code Bits/TCP Flags   Controls functions used to set up and terminate a session.

Window   The window size the sender is willing to accept, in octets.

Checksum   The cyclic redundancy check (CRC), used because TCP doesn't trust the lower layers and checks everything. The CRC checks the header and data fields.

Urgent   A valid field only if the Urgent pointer in the code bits is set. If so, this value indicates the offset from the current sequence number, in octets, where the segment of non-urgent data begins.

Options   May be 0, meaning that no options have to be present, or a multiple of 32 bits. However, if any options are used that do not cause the option field to total a multiple of 32 bits, padding of 0s must be used to make sure the data begins on a 32-bit boundary. These boundaries are known as words.

Payload (Data)   Handed down to the TCP protocol at the Transport layer, which includes the upper-layer headers.

Let's take a look at a TCP segment copied from a network analyzer. In the following output, I have bolded the Payload (data) area that the packet is carrying to the destination host:

```
TCP - Transport Control Protocol
Source Port: 5973
Destination Port: 23
Sequence Number: 1456389907
Ack Number: 1242056456
Offset: 5
Reserved: %000000
```

```
Code: %011000
Ack is valid
Push Request
Window: 61320
Checksum: 0x61a6
Urgent Pointer: 0
No TCP Options
```
TCP Data Area:
vL.5.+.5.+.5.+.5 76 4c 19 35 11 2b 19 35 11 2b 19 35 11
2b 19 35 +. 11 2b 19
Frame Check Sequence: 0x0d00000f

Did you notice that everything I talked about earlier is in the segment? As you can see from the number of fields in the header, TCP creates a lot of overhead. Again, this is why application developers may opt for efficiency over reliability to save overhead and go with UDP instead. It's also defined at the Transport layer as an alternative to TCP.

User Datagram Protocol

If you were to compare *User Datagram Protocol (UDP)* with TCP, the former is basically the scaled-down economy model that's sometimes referred to as a *thin protocol*. Like a thin person on a park bench, a thin protocol doesn't take up a lot of room—or in this case, much bandwidth on a network.

UDP doesn't offer all the bells and whistles of TCP either, but it does do a fabulous job of transporting information that doesn't require reliable delivery—and it does so using far fewer network resources.

There are some situations in which it would definitely be wise for developers to opt for UDP rather than TCP. Remember the watchdog SNMP up there at the Process/Application layer? SNMP monitors the network, sending intermittent messages and a fairly steady flow of status updates and alerts, especially when running on a large network. The cost in overhead to establish, maintain, and close a TCP connection for each one of those little messages would reduce what would be an otherwise healthy, efficient network to a dammed-up bog in no time!

Another circumstance calling for UDP over TCP is when reliability is already handled at the Process/Application layer. DNS handles its own reliability issues, making the use of TCP both impractical and redundant. But ultimately, it's up to the application developer to decide whether to use UDP or TCP, not the user who wants to transfer data faster.

UDP does *not* sequence the segments and doesn't care in which order the segments arrive at the destination. But after that, UDP sends the segments off and forgets about them. It doesn't follow through, check up on them, or even allow for an acknowledgment of safe arrival—complete abandonment. Because of this, it's referred to as an *unreliable* protocol. This doesn't mean that UDP is ineffective, only that it doesn't handle issues of reliability. Because UDP assumes that the application will use its own reliability method, it doesn't use any. This gives an application developer a choice when running the IP stack: TCP for reliability or UDP for faster transfers.

Further, UDP doesn't create a virtual circuit, nor does it contact the destination before delivering information to it. Because of this, it's also considered a *connectionless* protocol.

Figure 6.13 clearly illustrates UDP's markedly low overhead as compared to TCP's hungry usage. Look at the figure carefully—can you see that UDP doesn't use windowing or provide for acknowledgments in the UDP header?

FIGURE 6.13   UDP segment

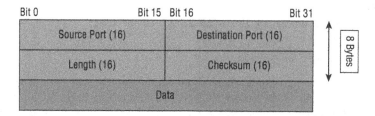

 For more detailed information regarding the UDP header, which is beyond the scope of the CompTIA Network+ exam objectives, please see my book *CCNA: Cisco Certified Network Associate Study Guide (Sybex 2019)*.

Key Concepts of Host-to-Host Protocols

Now that you've seen both a connection-oriented (TCP) and connectionless (UDP) protocol in action, it would be good to summarize the two here. Table 6.2 highlights some of the key concepts that you should keep in mind regarding these two protocols. You should memorize this table.

TABLE 6.2   Key features of TCP and UDP

TCP	UDP
Sequenced	Unsequenced
Reliable	Unreliable
Connection-oriented	Connectionless
Virtual circuit	Low overhead
Acknowledgments	No acknowledgment
Windowing flow control	No windowing or flow control of any type

A telephone analogy could really help you understand how TCP works. Most of us know that before you speak to someone on a phone, you must first establish a connection with that person—wherever they are. This is like a virtual circuit with TCP. If you were giving someone important information during your conversation, you might say, "You know?" or ask, "Did you get that?" Saying something like this is a lot like a TCP acknowledgment—it's designed to get your verification. From time to time (especially on cell phones), people also ask, "Are you still there?" They end their conversations with a "Good-bye" of some kind, putting closure on the phone call. TCP also performs these types of functions.

Alternatively, using UDP is like sending a postcard. To do that, you don't need to contact the other party first. You simply write your message, address the postcard, and mail it. This is analogous to UDP's connectionless orientation. Because the message on the postcard is probably not a matter of life or death, you don't need an acknowledgment of its receipt. Similarly, UDP doesn't involve acknowledgments.

Port Numbers

TCP and UDP must use *port numbers* to communicate with the upper layers because they're what keeps track of different simultaneous conversations originated or accepted by the local host. Originating source port numbers are dynamically assigned by the source host and will usually have a value of 1024 or higher. Ports 1023 and below are defined in RFC 3232, which discusses what are called *well-known port numbers*.

Virtual circuits that don't use an application with a well-known port number are assigned port numbers randomly from a specific range instead. These port numbers identify the source and destination application or process in the TCP segment.

Figure 6.14 illustrates how both TCP and UDP use port numbers.

FIGURE 6.14   Port numbers for TCP and UDP

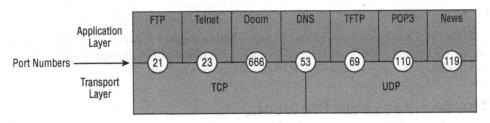

You just need to remember that numbers below 1024 are considered well-known port numbers and are defined in RFC 3232. Numbers 1024 and above are used by the upper layers to set up sessions with other hosts and by TCP as source and destination identifiers in the TCP segment.

Table 6.3 gives you a list of the typical applications used in the TCP/IP suite, their well-known port numbers, and the Transport layer protocols used by each application or process. It's important that you study and memorize this table for the CompTIA Network+ exam.

TABLE 6.3   Key protocols that use TCP and UDP

TCP	UDP
Telnet 23	SNMPv1/2 161
SMTP 25	TFTP 69
HTTP 80	DNS 53
FTP 20, 21	BOOTPS/DHCP 67,68
SFTP 22	NTP 123
DNS 53	
HTTPS 443	
SSH 22	
SMB 445	
POP3 110	
IMAP4 143	
RDP 3389	
SNMPv3 161	

Notice that DNS uses both TCP and UDP. Whether it opts for one or the other depends on what it's trying to do. Even though it's not the only application that can use both protocols, it's certainly one that you should remember in your studies.

The Internet Layer Protocols

In the DoD model, there are two main reasons for the Internet layer's existence: routing and providing a single network interface to the upper layers.

None of the other upper- or lower-layer protocols have any functions relating to routing—that complex and important task belongs entirely to the Internet layer. The Internet layer's second duty is to provide a single network interface to the upper-layer protocols. Without this layer, application programmers would need to write what are called *hooks* into every one of their applications for each different Network Access protocol. This would not only be a pain in the neck, it would also lead to different versions of each application—one for Ethernet, another one for Token Ring, and so on. To prevent this, IP provides one single network interface for the upper-layer protocols. That accomplished, it's then the job of IP and the various Network Access protocols to get along and work together.

All network roads don't lead to Rome—they lead to IP. And all the other protocols at this layer, as well as all those at the upper layers, use it. Never forget that. All paths through the DoD model go through IP. The following sections describe the protocols at the Internet layer:

- Internet Protocol (IP)
- Internet Control Message Protocol (ICMP)
- Address Resolution Protocol (ARP)
- Reverse Address Resolution Protocol (RARP)
- GRE/IPSec

Internet Protocol

Internet Protocol (IP) is essentially the Internet layer. The other protocols found here merely exist to support it. IP holds the big picture and could be said to "see all" in that it's aware of all the interconnected networks. It can do this because all the machines on the network have a software, or logical, address called an IP address, which I'll cover more thoroughly in the next chapter.

IP looks at each packet's destination address. Then, using a routing table, it decides where a packet is to be sent next, choosing the best path. The protocols of the Network Access layer at the bottom of the DoD model don't possess IP's enlightened scope of the entire network; they deal only with physical links (local networks).

Identifying devices on networks requires answering these two questions: Which network is it on? And what is its ID on that network? The answer to the first question is the *software address*, or *logical address* (the correct street). The answer to the second question is the *hardware address* (the correct mailbox). All hosts on a network have a logical ID called an IP address. This is the software, or logical, address and contains valuable encoded information, greatly simplifying the complex task of routing. (IP is discussed in RFC 791.)

IP receives segments from the Host-to-Host layer and fragments them into packets if necessary. IP then reassembles packets back into segments on the receiving side. Each packet is assigned the IP address of the sender and of the recipient. Each router (Layer 3 device) that receives a packet makes routing decisions based on the packet's destination IP address.

Figure 6.15 shows an IPv4 header. This will give you an idea of what IP has to go through every time user data is sent from the upper layers to a remote network.

The following fields make up the IP header:

Version   IP version number.

Header Length   Header length (HLEN) in 32-bit words.

Priority and Type of Service   Type of Service tells how the datagram should be handled. The first 3 bits are the priority bits, now called the differentiated services bits.

Total Length   Length of the packet, including header and data.

FIGURE 6.15   IPv4 header

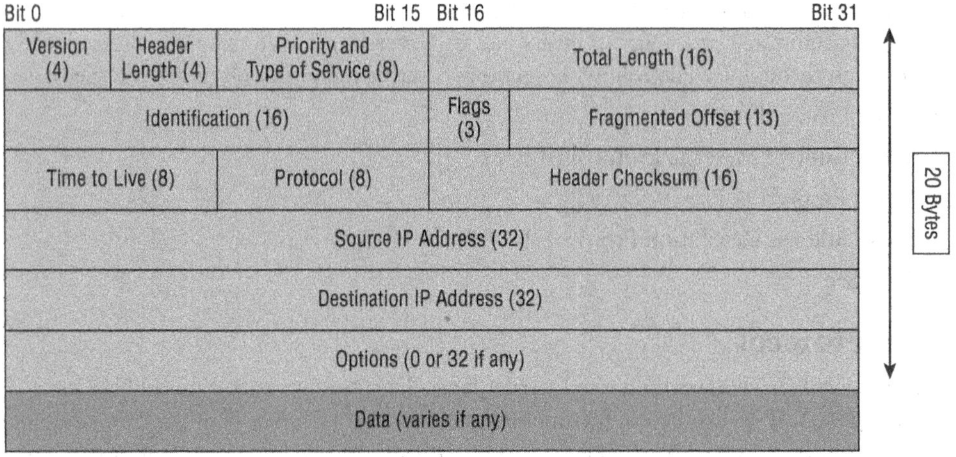

Version (4)	Header Length (4)	Priority and Type of Service (8)	Total Length (16)		
Identification (16)			Flags (3)	Fragmented Offset (13)	
Time to Live (8)		Protocol (8)	Header Checksum (16)		
Source IP Address (32)					
Destination IP Address (32)					
Options (0 or 32 if any)					
Data (varies if any)					

Bit 0 ... Bit 15 Bit 16 ... Bit 31

20 Bytes

Identification   Unique IP-packet value used to differentiate fragmented packets from different datagrams.

Flags   This one field specifies whether fragmentation of the packet should occur.

Fragment Offset   Provides fragmentation and reassembly if the packet is too large to put in a frame. It also allows different maximum transmission units (MTUs define the size of packets) on the Internet.

Time To Live   The time to live (TTL) is set into a packet when it is originally generated. If it doesn't get to where it's supposed to go before the TTL expires, boom—it's gone. This stops IP packets from continuously circling the network looking for a home.

Protocol   Port of upper-layer protocol; for example, TCP is port 6 or UDP is port 17. Also supports Network layer protocols, like ARP and ICMP, and can be referred to as the Type field in some analyzers. We'll talk about this field more in a minute.

Header Checksum   Cyclic redundancy check (CRC) on header only.

Source IP Address   32-bit IP address of sending station.

Destination IP Address   32-bit IP address of the station this packet is destined for.

Options   Used for network testing, debugging, security, and more.

Data   After the IP option field, will be the upper-layer data.

Here's a snapshot of an IP packet caught on a network analyzer. Notice that all the header information discussed previously appears here:

```
IP Header - Internet Protocol Datagram
Version: 4
Header Length: 5
Precedence: 0
Type of Service: %000
Unused: %00
Total Length: 187
Identifier: 22486
Fragmentation Flags: %010 Do Not Fragment
Fragment Offset: 0
Time To Live: 60
IP Type: 0x06 TCP
Header Checksum: 0xd031
Source IP Address: 10.7.1.30
Dest. IP Address: 10.7.1.10
No Internet Datagram Options
```

The Type field is typically a Protocol field, but this analyzer sees it as an IP Type field. This is important. If the header didn't carry the protocol information for the next layer, IP wouldn't know what to do with the data carried in the packet. The preceding example clearly tells IP to hand the segment to TCP.

Figure 6.16 demonstrates how the Network layer sees the protocols at the Transport layer when it needs to hand a packet up to the upper-layer protocols.

FIGURE 6.16   The Protocol field in an IP header

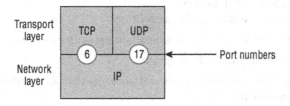

In this example, the Protocol field tells IP to send the data to either TCP port 6 or UDP port 17. But it will be UDP or TCP only if the data is part of a data stream headed for an upper-layer service or application. It could just as easily be destined for Internet Control Message Protocol (ICMP), Address Resolution Protocol (ARP), or some other type of Network layer protocol.

Table 6.4 is a list of some other popular protocols that can be specified in the Protocol field.

TABLE 6.4   Possible protocols found in the Protocol field of an IP header

Protocol	Protocol Number
ICMP	1
IP in IP (tunneling)	4
TCP	6
UDP	17
EIGRP	88
OSPF	89
IPv6	41
GRE	47
Layer 2 tunnel (L2TP)	115

You can find a complete list of Protocol field numbers at https://www
.iana.org/assignments/protocol-numbers.

Internet Control Message Protocol

Internet Control Message Protocol (ICMP) works at the Network layer and is used by IP for many different services. ICMP is a management protocol and messaging service provider for IP. Its messages are carried as IP packets.

ICMP packets have the following characteristics:

- They can provide hosts with information about network problems.
- They are encapsulated within IP datagrams.

The following are some common events and messages that ICMP relates to, and the two most popular programs that use ICMP:

Destination Unreachable   If a router can't send an IP datagram any further, it uses ICMP to send a message back to the sender, advising it of the situation. For example, take a look at Figure 6.17, which shows that the Ethernet interface of the Lab B router is down.

FIGURE 6.17   ICMP error message is sent to the sending host from the remote router

e0 on Lab B is down. Host A is trying to communicate to Host B. What happens?

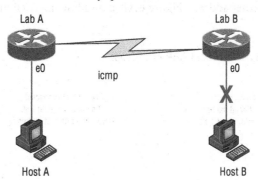

When Host A sends a packet destined for Host B, the Lab B router will send an ICMP Destination Unreachable message back to the sending device (directly to Host A, in this example).

Buffer Full   If a router's memory buffer for receiving incoming datagrams is full, it will use ICMP to send out this message until the congestion abates.

Hops   Each IP datagram is allotted a certain number of routers, called *hops*, to pass through. If a datagram reaches its limit of hops before arriving at its destination, the last router to receive it deletes it. The executioner router then uses ICMP to send an obituary message, informing the sending machine of the demise of its datagram.

Ping   Ping uses ICMP echo request and reply messages to check the physical and logical connectivity of machines on an internetwork.

Traceroute   Traceroute uses IP packet time to live time-outs to discover the path a packet takes as it traverses an internetwork.

Both Ping and Traceroute (also just called Trace, and Microsoft Windows uses tracert) allow you to verify address configurations in your internetwork.

Address Resolution Protocol

Address Resolution Protocol (ARP) finds the hardware address of a host from a known IP address. Here's how it works: When IP has a datagram to send, it must inform a Network Access protocol, such as Ethernet or Token Ring, of the destination's hardware address on the local network. (It has already been informed by upper-layer protocols of the destination's IP address.) If IP doesn't find the destination host's hardware address in the ARP cache, it uses ARP to find this information.

As IP's detective, ARP interrogates the local network by sending out a broadcast asking the machine with the specified IP address to reply with its hardware address. So basically, ARP translates the software (IP) address into a hardware address—for example, the destination machine's Ethernet address. Figure 6.18 shows how an ARP broadcast looks to a local network.

FIGURE 6.18   Local ARP broadcast

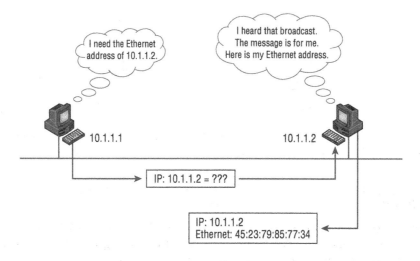

   ARP resolves IP addresses to Ethernet (MAC) addresses.

The following trace shows an ARP broadcast—notice that the destination hardware address is unknown and is all 0s in the ARP header. In the Ethernet header, a destination of all *F*s in hex (all 1s in binary), a hardware-address broadcast, is used to make sure all devices on the local link receive the ARP request:

```
Flags:         0x00
Status:        0x00
Packet Length: 64
Timestamp:     09:17:29.574000 12/06/21
Ethernet Header
 Destination:  FF:FF:FF:FF:FF:FF Ethernet Broadcast
 Source:       00:A0:24:48:60:A5
 Protocol Type: 0x0806 IP ARP
ARP - Address Resolution Protocol
 Hardware:              1 Ethernet (10Mb)
```

```
Protocol:                 0x0800 IP
Hardware Address Length: 6
Protocol Address Length: 4
Operation:                1 ARP Request
Sender Hardware Address: 00:A0:24:48:60:A5
Sender Internet Address: 172.16.10.3
Target Hardware Address: 00:00:00:00:00:00 (ignored)
Target Internet Address: 172.16.10.10
Extra bytes (Padding):
............... 0A 0A 0A 0A 0A 0A 0A 0A 0A 0A 0A 0A 0A
 0A 0A 0A 0A 0A
Frame Check Sequence: 0x00000000
```

Reverse Address Resolution Protocol (RARP)

When an IP machine happens to be a diskless machine, it has no way of initially knowing its IP address. But it does know its MAC address. *Reverse Address Resolution Protocol (RARP)* discovers the identity of the IP address for diskless machines by sending out a packet that includes its MAC address and a request for the IP address assigned to that MAC address. A designated machine, called a *RARP server*, responds with the answer, and the identity crisis is over. RARP uses the information it does know about the machine's MAC address to learn its IP address and complete the machine's ID portrait.

Figure 6.19 shows a diskless workstation asking for its IP address with a RARP broadcast.

FIGURE 6.19   RARP broadcast example

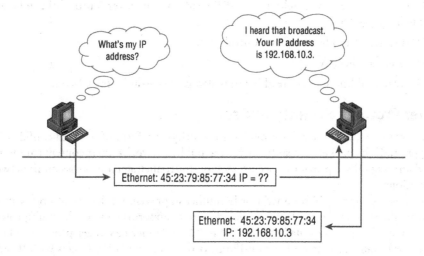

Generic Routing Encapsulation (GRE)

Generic Routing Encapsulation (GRE) is a tunneling protocol that can encapsulate many protocols inside IP tunnels. Some examples would be routing protocols such as EIGRP and OSPF and the routed protocol IPv6. Figure 6.20 shows the different pieces of a GRE header.

FIGURE 6.20   Generic Routing Encapsulation (GRE) tunnel structure

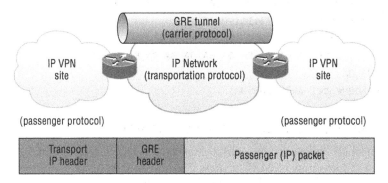

A GRE tunnel interface supports a header for each of the following:

- A passenger protocol or encapsulated protocols like IP or IPv6, which is the protocol being encapsulated by GRE
- GRE encapsulation protocol
- A transport delivery protocol, typically IP

GRE tunnels have the following characteristics:

- GRE uses a protocol-type field in the GRE header so any layer 3 protocol can be used through the tunnel.
- GRE is stateless and has no flow control.
- GRE offers no security.
- GRE creates additional overhead for tunneled packets—at least 24 bytes.

Internet Protocol Security (IPSec)

As I just mentioned, GRE by itself provides no security—no form of payload confidentiality or encryption. If the packets are sniffed over the public networks, their contents are in plaintext, and although IPsec provides a secure method for tunneling data across an IP network, it has limitations.

IPSec does not support IP broadcast or IP multicast, preventing the use of protocols that need them, like routing protocols. IPSec also does not support the use of the multiprotocol traffic. GRE is a protocol that can be used to "carry" other passenger protocols like IP broadcast or IP multicast, as well as non-IP protocols. So using GRE tunnels with IPSec allows you to run a routing protocol, IP multicast, as well as multiprotocol traffic across your network.

With a generic hub-and-spoke topology (Corp to Branch for example), you can implement static tunnels, typically GRE over IPSec, between the corporate office and branch offices. When you want to add a new spoke to the network, all you need to do is configure it on the hub router. The traffic between spokes has to traverse the hub, where it must exit one tunnel and enter another. Static tunnels can be an appropriate solution for small networks, but this solution actually becomes an unacceptable problem as the number of spokes grows larger and larger!

Authentication Header (AH)/Encapsulating Security Payload (ESP)

The two primary security protocols used by IPSec are *Authentication Header (AH)* and *Encapsulating Security Payload (ESP)*.

Authentication Header (AH)

The AH protocol provides authentication for the data and the IP header of a packet using a one-way hash for packet authentication. It works like this: The sender generates a one-way hash; then the receiver generates the same one-way hash. If the packet has changed in any way, it won't be authenticated and will be dropped. So basically, IPsec relies upon AH to guarantee authenticity. AH checks the entire packet, but it doesn't offer any encryption services.

This is unlike ESP, which only provides an integrity check on the data of a packet.

Encapsulating Security Payload (ESP)

It won't tell you when or how the NASDAQ's gonna bounce up and down like a superball, but ESP will provide confidentiality, data origin authentication, connectionless integrity, anti-replay service, and limited traffic-flow confidentiality by defeating traffic flow analysis—which is almost as good! Anyway, there are five components of ESP:

Confidentiality (Encryption)   This allows the sending device to encrypt the packets before transmitting in order to prevent eavesdropping. Confidentiality is provided through the use of symmetric encryption algorithms. Confidentiality can be selected separately from all other services, but the confidentiality selected must be the same on both endpoints of your VPN. The following cryptographic algorithms are defined for use with IPSec:

- HMAC-SHA1/SHA2 for integrity protection and authenticity
- TripleDES-CBC for confidentiality
- AES-CBC and AES-CBC for confidentiality
- AES-GCM AND ChaCha20-Poly1305 providing confidentiality and authentication together efficiently

Data Integrity   Data integrity allows the receiver to verify that the data received was not altered in any way along the way. IPSec uses checksums as a simple check of the data.

Authentication   Authentication ensures that the connection is made with the correct partner. The receiver can authenticate the source of the packet by guaranteeing and certifying the source of the information.

Anti-Replay Service   Anti-replay election is based upon the receiver, meaning the service is effective only if the receiver checks the sequence number. In case you were wondering, a replay attack is when a hacker nicks a copy of an authenticated packet and later transmits it to the intended destination. When the duplicate, authenticated IP packet gets to the destination, it can disrupt services and generally wreak havoc. The *Sequence Number* field is designed to foil this type of attack.

Traffic Flow   For traffic flow confidentiality to work, you have to have at least tunnel mode selected. It's most effective if it's implemented at a security gateway where tons of traffic amasses because it's precisely the kind of environment that can mask the true source-destination patterns to bad guys who are trying to breach your network's security.

Data Encapsulation

I started to discuss data encapsulation in Chapter 2, but I could only provide an overview at that point in the book because you needed to have a firm understanding of how ports work in a virtual circuit. With the last five chapters of foundational material under your belt, you're ready to get more into the details of encapsulation.

When a host transmits data across a network to another device, the data goes through *encapsulation*: It's wrapped with protocol information at each layer of the OSI model. Each layer communicates only with its peer layer on the receiving device.

To communicate and exchange information, each layer uses *protocol data units (PDUs)*. These hold the control information attached to the data at each layer of the model. They're usually attached to the header in front of the data field but can also be in the trailer, or end, of it.

Each PDU attaches to the data by encapsulating it at each layer of the OSI model, and each has a specific name depending on the information provided in each header. This PDU information is read only by the peer layer on the receiving device. After it's read, it's stripped off, and the data is then handed to the next layer up.

Figure 6.21 shows the PDUs and how they attach control information to each layer. This figure demonstrates how the upper-layer user data is converted for transmission on the network.

The data stream is then handed down to the Transport layer, which sets up a virtual circuit to the receiving device by sending over a synch packet. Next, the data stream is broken up into smaller pieces, and a Transport layer header (a PDU) is created and attached to the header of the data field; now the piece of data is called a *segment*. Each segment is sequenced so the data stream can be put back together on the receiving side exactly as it was transmitted.

FIGURE 6.21   Data encapsulation

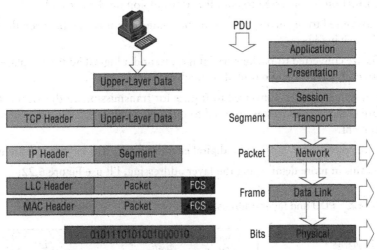

Each segment is then handed to the Network layer for network addressing and routing through the internetwork. Logical addressing (for example, IP) is used to get each segment to the correct network. The Network layer protocol adds a control header to the segment handed down from the Transport layer, and what we have now is called a *packet* or *datagram*. Remember that the Transport and Network layers work together to rebuild a data stream on a receiving host, but it's not part of their work to place their PDUs on a local network segment—which is the only way to get the information to a router or host.

It's the Data Link layer that's responsible for taking packets from the Network layer and placing them on the network medium (cable or wireless). The Data Link layer encapsulates each packet in a *frame*, and the frame's header carries the hardware address of the source and destination hosts. If the destination device is on a remote network, then the frame is sent to a router to be routed through an internetwork. Once it gets to the destination network, a new frame is used to get the packet to the destination host.

To put this frame on the network, it must first be put into a digital signal. Because a frame is really a logical group of 1s and 0s, the Physical layer is responsible for encoding these digits into a digital signal, which is read by devices on the same local network. The receiving devices will synchronize on the digital signal and extract (decode) the 1s and 0s from the digital signal. At this point, the devices build the frames, run a cyclic redundancy check (CRC), and then check their answer against the answer in the frame's Frame Check Sequence (FCS) field. If it matches, the packet is pulled from the frame and what's left of the frame is discarded. This process is called *de-encapsulation*. The packet is handed to the Network layer, where the address is checked. If the address matches, the segment is pulled from the packet and what's left of the packet is discarded. The segment is processed at the Transport layer, which rebuilds the data stream and acknowledges to the transmitting station that it received each piece. It then happily hands the data stream to the upper-layer application.

In summary, at a transmitting device, the data-encapsulation method works like this:

1. User information is converted to data for transmission on the network.

2. Data is converted to segments, and a reliable connection is set up between the transmitting and receiving hosts.

3. Segments are converted to packets or datagrams, and a logical address is placed in the header so each packet can be routed through an internetwork.

4. Packets or datagrams are converted to frames for transmission on the local network. Hardware (Ethernet) addresses are used to uniquely identify hosts on a local network segment.

5. Frames are converted to bits, and a digital encoding and clocking scheme are used.

To explain this in more detail using the layer addressing, I'll use Figure 6.22.

FIGURE 6.22   PDU and layer addressing

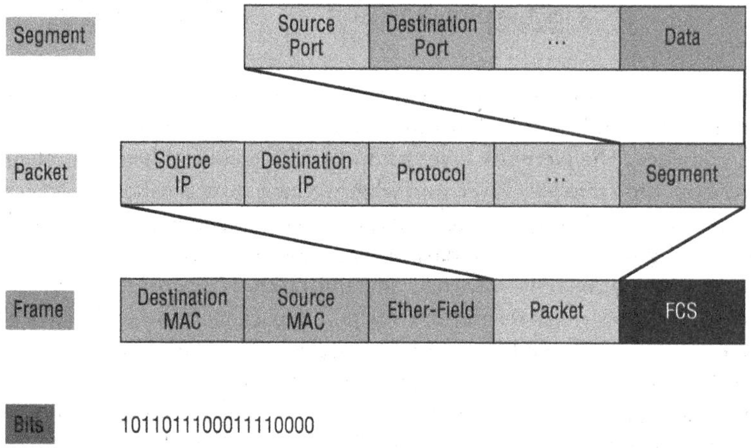

Remember that a data stream is handed down from the upper layer to the Transport layer. As technicians, we really don't care who the data stream comes from because that's a programmer's problem. Our job is to rebuild the data stream reliably and hand it to the upper layers on the receiving device.

Before we go further in our discussion of Figure 6.22, let's review port numbers and make sure you understand them. The Transport layer uses port numbers to define both the virtual circuit and the upper-layer process, as you can see from Figure 6.23.

The Transport layer takes the data stream, makes segments out of it, and establishes a reliable session by creating a virtual circuit. It then sequences (numbers) each segment and uses acknowledgments and flow control. If you're using TCP, the virtual circuit is defined by the source port number. Remember, the host just makes this up starting at port number 1024 (0 through 1023 are reserved for well-known port numbers). The destination port number defines the upper-layer process (application) that the data stream is handed to when the data stream is reliably rebuilt on the receiving host.

FIGURE 6.23   Port numbers at the Transport layer

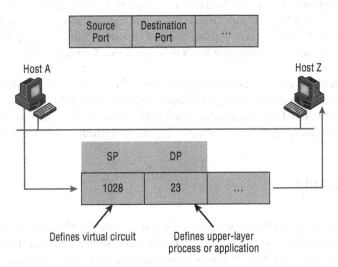

Now that you understand port numbers and how they're used at the Transport layer, let's go back to Figure 6.22. Once the Transport layer header information is added to the piece of data, it becomes a segment and is handed down to the Network layer along with the destination IP address. (The destination IP address was handed down from the upper layers to the Transport layer with the data stream, and it was discovered through a name resolution method at the upper layers—probably DNS.)

The Network layer adds a header and also the logical addressing (IP addresses) to the front of each segment. Once the header is added to the segment, the PDU is called a *packet*. The packet has a protocol field that describes where the segment came from (either UDP or TCP) so it can hand the segment to the correct protocol at the Transport layer when it reaches the receiving host.

The Network layer is responsible for finding the destination hardware address that dictates where the packet should be sent on the local network. It does this by using ARP. IP at the Network layer looks at the destination IP address and compares that address to its own source IP address and subnet mask. If it turns out to be a local network request, the hardware address of the local host is requested via an ARP request. If the packet is destined for a remote host, IP will look for the IP address of the default gateway from its configuration information, then ARP for the hardware address of the default gateway (router) instead.

The packet, along with the destination hardware address of either the local host or default gateway, is then handed down to the Data Link layer. The Data Link layer will add a header to the front of the packet, and the piece of data then becomes a *frame*. (We call it a frame because both a header and a trailer are added to the packet, which makes the data resemble bookends or a frame, if you will.) This is shown in Figure 6.22. The frame uses an Ether-Type field to describe which protocol the packet came from at the Network layer. Now a CRC is run on the frame, and the answer to the CRC is placed in the FCS field found in the trailer of the frame.

The frame is now ready to be handed down, one bit at a time, to the Physical layer, which will use bit-timing rules to encode the data into a digital signal. Every device on the network segment will synchronize with the clock, extract the 1s and 0s from the digital signal, and build a frame. After the frame is rebuilt, a CRC is run to make sure the frame is okay. If everything turns out to be good, the hosts will check the destination address to see if the frame is for them.

If all this is making your eyes cross and your brain freeze, don't freak—things will become much clearer as we go through the book—really! Soon, I'll be going over exactly how data is encapsulated and routed through an internetwork in even more detail, in an easy-to-understand, step-by-step manner, in Chapter 9, "Introduction to IP Routing."

Summary

Protocols, protocols everywhere—so many different reasons for them, and so many jobs they do for us! And sometimes they even work in conjunction with each other. This can seem like way too much information, but no worries—as you become familiar with the various layers and their functions, I promise it will soon become clear that this hierarchical structure is a seriously tight, robust networking foundation.

Similarly, as you understand the TCP/IP big picture, the reason why all these protocols exist and are necessary will also become much easier to understand. They're really like a team that works jointly, from layer to layer, to make our TCP/IP networks the wonderful, great tools they are.

Exam Essentials

Remember the Process/Application layer protocols.   Telnet is a terminal-emulation program that allows you to log into a remote host and run programs. File Transfer Protocol (FTP) is a connection-oriented service that allows you to transfer files. Trivial FTP (TFTP) is a connectionless file transfer program. Simple Mail Transfer Protocol (SMTP) is a sendmail program.

Understand data encapsulation and decapsulation within the OSI model context.   This includes Ethernet header and the Internet Protocol (IP) header, Transmission Control Protocol (TCP)/User Datagram Protocol (UDP) headers, TCP flags, Payload, and Maximum transmission unit (MTU).

Be able to explain common ports and protocols, their application, and encrypted alternatives.   Know all the protocol ports listed in the objectives for FTP, SSH, SFTP, and more.

Be able to identify and define protocol types.   This includes Internet Control Message Protocol (ICMP), TCP, UDP, Generic Routing Encapsulation (GRE), Internet Protocol Security (IPSec), Authentication Header (AH)/Encapsulating Security Payload (ESP).

Remember the Host-to-Host layer protocols.   Transmission Control Protocol (TCP) is a connection-oriented protocol that provides reliable network service by using acknowledgments and flow control. User Datagram Protocol (UDP) is a connectionless protocol that provides low overhead and is considered unreliable.

Remember the Internet layer protocols.   Internet Protocol (IP) is a connectionless protocol that provides logical network addressing and routing through an internetwork. Address Resolution Protocol (ARP) finds a hardware address from a known IP address. Internet Control Message Protocol (ICMP) provides diagnostics and Destination Unreachable messages.

Written Lab

Provide the answers to the following questions. You can find the answers in Appendix A.

1. What would an ARP destination MAC address appear as?

2. Name the protocol that uses both TCP ports 20 and 21.

3. What Transport layer protocol does a DNS server use?

4. Which protocol dynamically reports errors to source hosts by using IP directly to build packets?

5. What could cause a server that you can ping to not provide the particular TCP/IP service, such as FTP, HTTP, and so on, that you expect it to offer?

6. What is the well-known port number for RDP?

7. Which ports does the protocol MGCP use?

8. What protocol is at the heart of the `ping` and `tracert` commands in a Windows operating system?

9. Which destination Transport layer protocol and port number does a TFTP client use to transfer files over the network?

10. What well-known port numbers do SMTP, POP3, RDP, and IMAP4 servers use?

Review Questions

You can find the answers to the review questions in Appendix B.

1. The OSI model has seven layers and the DoD has four. At which layer does SMTP work in both models?

   A. Network

   B. Transport

   C. Session

   D. Application

   E. Internet

2. You need to have secure communications using HTTPS. What port number is used by default?

   A. 69

   B. 23

   C. 21

   D. 443

3. You want to implement a mechanism that automates the IP configuration, including IP address, subnet mask, default gateway, and DNS information. Which protocol will you use to accomplish this?

   A. SMTP

   B. SNMP

   C. DHCP

   D. ARP

4. What protocol is used to find the hardware address of a local device?

   A. RARP

   B. ARP

   C. IP

   D. ICMP

   E. BootP

5. You need to log in to a Unix/Linux server across a network that is not secure. Which of the following protocols will allow you to remotely administer this server securely?

   A. Telnet

   B. SSH

   C. SFTP

   D. HTTP

6. If you can ping by IP address but not by hostname, or FQDN, which of the following port numbers is related to the server process that is involved?

   A. 21

   B. 23

   C. 53

   D. 69

   E. 80

7. Which of the following describe the DHCP Discover message? (Choose two.)

   A. It uses FF:FF:FF:FF:FF:FF as a layer 2 broadcast.

   B. It uses UDP as the Transport layer protocol.

   C. It uses TCP as the Transport layer protocol.

   D. It does not use a layer 2 destination address.

8. What layer 4 protocol is used for a Telnet connection, and what is the default port number?

   A. IP, 6

   B. TCP, 21

   C. UDP, 23

   D. ICMP, 21

   E. TCP, 23

9. Which statements are true regarding ICMP packets? (Choose two.)

   A. They acknowledge receipt of a TCP segment.

   B. They guarantee datagram delivery.

   C. They can provide hosts with information about network problems.

   D. They are encapsulated within IP datagrams.

   E. They are encapsulated within UDP datagrams.

10. Which of the following services use TCP? (Choose four.)

   A. DHCP

   B. SMTP

   C. SNMP

   D. FTP

   E. HTTP

   F. TFTP

11. Which of the following services use UDP? (Choose three.)

    A. DHCP

    B. SMTP

    C. SNMP

    D. FTP

    E. HTTP

    F. TFTP

12. Which of the following TCP/IP protocols are used at the Application layer of the OSI model? (Choose three.)

    A. IP

    B. TCP

    C. Telnet

    D. FTP

    E. TFTP

13. Which of the following protocols is used by email servers to exchange messages with one another?

    A. POP3

    B. IMAP

    C. SMTP

    D. HTTP

14. You need to have a connection to run applications that are installed on only your desktop computer at your office. Which protocol will provide a GUI interface to your work computer?

    A. Telnet

    B. FTP

    C. RDP

    D. IMAP

    E. SMTP

15. Which of the following protocols can use TCP and UDP, permits authentication and secure polling of network devices, and allows for automated alerts and reports on network devices?

    A. DNS

    B. SNMP

    C. SMTP

    D. TCP

16. You need to transfer files between two hosts. Which protocol can you use?

   A. SNMP

   B. RIP

   C. NTP

   D. FTP

17. What layer in the IP stack is equivalent to the Transport layer of the OSI model?

   A. Application

   B. Host-to-Host

   C. Internet

   D. Network Access

18. You need to make sure that the time is consistent across all your network devices. What protocol do you need to run on your network?

   A. FTP

   B. SCP

   C. NTP

   D. RTP

19. Which of the following allows a server to distinguish among different simultaneous requests from the same host?

   A. They use different port numbers.

   B. A NAT server changes the IP address for subsequent requests.

   C. A server is unable to accept multiple simultaneous sessions from the same host. One session must end before another can begin.

   D. The MAC address for each one is unique.

20. Which of the following uses both TCP and UDP?

   A. FTP

   B. SMTP

   C. Telnet

   D. DNS

Chapter

7

IP Addressing

THE FOLLOWING COMPTIA NETWORK+ EXAM OBJECTIVES ARE COVERED IN THIS CHAPTER:

✓ **1.4 Given a scenario, configure a subnet and use appropriate IP addressing schemes.**

- Public vs. private
    - RFC1918
    - Network address translation (NAT)
- IPv4 vs. IPv6
    - Automatic Private IP Addressing (APIPA)
    - Extended unique identifier (EUI-64)
    - Multicast
    - Unicast
    - Anycast
    - Broadcast
    - Link local
    - Loopback
    - Default gateway
- IPv4 subnetting
    - Classless (variable-length subnet mask)
    - Classful
        - A
        - B
        - C

- D
- E
- Classless Inter-Domain Routing (CIDR) notation
- IPv6 concepts
  - Tunneling
  - Dual stack
  - Shorthand notation
  - Router advertisement
  - Stateless address autoconfiguration (SLAAC)
- Virtual IP (VIP)
- Subinterfaces

One of the most important topics in any discussion of TCP/IP is IP addressing. An IP address is a numeric identifier assigned to each machine on an IP network. It designates the specific location of a device on the network.

An IP address is a logical address, not a hardware address—the latter is hard-coded on a network interface card (NIC) and used for finding hosts on a local network. IP addressing was designed to allow hosts on one network to communicate with a host on a different network regardless of the type of LANs the hosts are participating in.

Before we get into the more complicated aspects of IP addressing, you need to understand some of the basics. First, I'm going to explain some of the fundamentals of IP addressing and its terminology. Then you'll learn about the hierarchical IP addressing scheme and private IP addresses.

I'll define unicast, multicast, and broadcast addresses and then finish the chapter with a discussion on IPv6. And I promise to make it all as painless as possible.

The reason that we would even discuss IPv6 (besides to cover the objectives, of course) is the lack of IPv4 addresses available for use in future networks, which we need to keep our corporate and private networks and even the Internet running. Basically, we're running out of addresses for all our new hosts! IPv6 will fix this for us.

To find Todd Lammle CompTIA videos and practice questions, please see www.lammle.com.

IP Terminology

Throughout this chapter, you'll learn several important terms vital to your understanding of the Internet Protocol. Here are a few to get you started:

Bit A *bit* is one binary digit, either a 1 or a 0.

Byte A *byte* is 7 or 8 bits, depending on whether parity is used. For the rest of this chapter, always assume a byte is 8 bits.

Octet An octet, made up of 8 bits, is just an ordinary 8-bit binary number. In this chapter, the terms *byte* and *octet* are completely interchangeable, and they are typically displayed in decimal up to 255.

Network Address   This is the designation used in routing to send packets to a remote network—for example, 10.0.0.0, 172.16.0.0, and 192.168.10.0.

IP Address   A logical address used to define a single host; however, IP addresses can be used to reference many or all hosts as well. If you see something written as just IP, it is referring to IPv4. IPv6 will always be written as IPv6.

Broadcast Address   The *broadcast address* is used by applications and hosts to send information to all hosts on a network. Examples include 255.255.255.255, which designates all networks and all hosts; 172.16.255.255, which specifies all subnets and hosts on network 172.16.0.0; and 10.255.255.255, which broadcasts to all subnets and hosts on network 10.0.0.0.

The Hierarchical IP Addressing Scheme

An IP address consists of 32 bits of information. These bits are divided into four sections, referred to as octets or bytes, and four octets sum up to 32 bits ($8 \times 4 = 32$). You can depict an IP address using one of three methods:

- Dotted-decimal, as in 172.16.30.56

- Binary, as in 10101100.00010000.00011110.00111000

- Hexadecimal, as in AC.10.1E.38

Each of these examples validly represents the same IP address. Hexadecimal is used with IPv6, and IP addressing uses dotted-decimal or binary, but you still might find an IP address stored in hexadecimal in some programs. Windows is a good example of a program that stores a machine's IP address in hex. Windows 10 (and all other Windows versions) store the IP addresses in hexadecimal subkeys in HKEY_LOCAL_MACHINE\SYSTEM\Current-ControlSet\Services\ Tcpip\Parameters\Interfaces.

The 32-bit IP address is known as a structured, or hierarchical, address as opposed to a flat, or nonhierarchical, address. Although either type of addressing scheme can be used, *hierarchical addressing* has been chosen for a very important reason. The major advantage of this scheme is that it can handle a large number of addresses, namely, 4.3 billion (a 32-bit address space with two possible values for each position—either 0 or 1—gives you 2^{32}, or 4,294,967,296). The disadvantage of the flat-addressing scheme, and the reason it's not used for IP addressing, relates to routing. If every address were unique, all routers on the Internet would need to store the address of each and every machine on the Internet. This would make efficient routing impossible, even if only a fraction of all possible addresses were used.

The solution to this problem is to use a two- or three-level hierarchical addressing scheme that is structured by network and host or by network, subnet, and host.

This two- or three-level scheme is comparable to a telephone number. The first section, the area code, designates a very large area. The second section, the prefix, narrows the scope to a local calling area. The final segment, the customer number, zooms in on the specific connection. IP addresses use the same type of layered structure. Rather than all 32 bits being treated as a unique identifier, as in flat addressing, a part of the address is designated as the network address and the other part is designated as either the subnet and host or just the host address.

Next, I'm going to cover IP network addressing and the different classes of addresses used for our networks.

Network Addressing

The *network address*—also called the network number—uniquely identifies each network. Every machine on the same network shares that network address as part of its IP address. In the IP address 172.16.30.56, for example, 172.16 is the network address (and in just a minute I'll show you how this is true).

The *host address* is assigned to and uniquely identifies each machine on a network. This part of the address must be unique because it identifies a particular machine—an individual—as opposed to a network, which is a group. So in the sample IP address 172.16.30.56, the 30.56 is the host address.

The designers of the Internet decided to create classes of networks based on network size. For the small number of networks possessing a very large number of hosts, they created the rank *Class A network*. At the other extreme is the *Class C network*, which is reserved for the numerous networks with a small number of hosts. The class distinction for networks between very large and very small is predictably the *Class B network*.

Subdividing an IP address into a network and host address is determined by the class designation of your network. Figure 7.1 summarizes the classes of networks—a subject I'll explain in greater detail throughout this chapter.

FIGURE 7.1   Summary of the three classes of networks

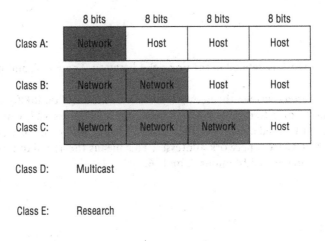

To ensure efficient routing, Internet designers defined a mandate for the leading-bits section of the address for each different network class. For example, since a router knows that a Class A network address always starts with a 0, the router might be able to speed a packet on its way after reading only the first bit of its address. This is where the address schemes define the difference between a Class A, a Class B, and a Class C address. Coming up, I'll discuss the differences between these three classes followed by a discussion of the Class D and Class E addresses. For now, know that Classes A, B, and C are the only ranges that are used to address hosts in our networks.

Class A Addresses

In a Class A network address, the first byte is assigned to the network address, and the three remaining bytes are used for the host addresses. The Class A format is as follows:

`network.host.host.host`

For example, in the IP address 49.22.102.70, the 49 is the network address and 22.102.70 is the host address. Every machine on this particular network would begin with the distinctive network address of 49.

Class A network addresses are 1 byte long, with the first bit of that byte reserved and the 7 remaining bits available for manipulation or addressing. As a result, the theoretical maximum number of Class A networks that can be created is 128. Why? Well, each of the 7-bit positions can be either a 0 or a 1 and 2^7 gives you 128.

The designers of the IP address scheme said that the first bit of the first byte in a Class A network address must always be off, or 0. This means a Class A address must be between 0 and 127 in the first byte, inclusive.

Consider the following network address:

`0xxxxxxx`

If we turn the other 7 bits all off and then turn them all on, we'll find the Class A range of network addresses:

```
00000000 = 0
01111111 = 127
```

So, a Class A network is defined in the first octet between 0 and 127, and it can't be less or more.

To complicate matters further, the network address of all 0s (0000 0000) is reserved to designate the default route (see Table 7.1). Additionally, the address 127, which is reserved for diagnostics, can't be used either. This means that you can really only use the numbers 1 to 126 to designate Class A network addresses. This means the actual number of usable Class A network addresses is 128 minus 2, or 126.

TABLE 7.1   Reserved IP addresses

Address	Function
Network address of all 0s	Interpreted to mean "this network or segment."
Network address of all 1s	Interpreted to mean "all networks."
Network 127.0.0.1	Reserved for loopback tests. Designates the local host and allows that host to send a test packet to itself without generating network traffic.
Host address of all 0s	Interpreted to mean "network address" or any host on specified network.
Host address of all 1s	Interpreted to mean "all hosts" on the specified network; for example, 126.255.255.255 means "all hosts" on network 126 (Class A address).
Entire IP address set to all 0s	Used by Cisco routers to designate the default route. Could also mean "any network."
Entire IP address set to all 1s (same as 255.255.255.255)	Broadcast to all hosts on the current network; sometimes called an "all 1s broadcast" or limited broadcast.

Each Class A address has 3 bytes (24 bit positions) for the host address of a machine. This means there are 2^{24}—or 16,777,216—unique combinations and, therefore, precisely that many potential unique host addresses for each Class A network. Because host addresses with the two patterns of all 0s and all 1s are reserved, the actual maximum usable number of hosts for a Class A network is 2^{24} minus 2, which equals 16,777,214. Either way, you can see that's a seriously huge number of hosts to have on a network segment!

Here's an example of how to figure out the valid host IDs in a Class A network address:

- All host bits off is the network address: 10.0.0.0.
- All host bits on is the broadcast address: 10.255.255.255.

The valid hosts are the numbers in between the network address and the broadcast address: 10.0.0.1 through 10.255.255.254. Notice that 0s and 255s can be valid host IDs. All you need to remember when trying to find valid host addresses is that the host bits can't ever be all turned off or all turned on at the same time.

Class B Addresses

In a Class B network address, the first 2 bytes are assigned to the network address and the remaining 2 bytes are used for host addresses. The format is as follows:

`network.network.host.host`

For example, in the IP address 172.16.30.56, the network address is 172.16 and the host address is 30.56.

With a network address being 2 bytes (8 bits each), we're left with 2^{16} unique combinations. But the Internet designers decided that all Class B network addresses should start with the binary digit 1, then 0. This leaves 14 bit positions available to manipulate, so in reality, we get 16,384 (that is, 2^{14}) unique Class B network addresses.

In a Class B network, the Request For Comments (RFCs) state that the first bit of the first byte must always be turned on but the second bit must always be turned off. If we turn the other 6 bits all off and then all on, we will find the range for a Class B network:

```
10000000 = 128
10111111 = 191
```

As you can see, a Class B network is defined when the first byte is configured from 128 to 191.

A Class B address uses 2 bytes for host addresses. This is 2^{16} minus the two reserved patterns (all 0s and all 1s), for a total of 65,534 possible host addresses for each Class B network.

Here's an example of how to find the valid hosts in a Class B network:

- All host bits turned off is the network address: 172.16.0.0.
- All host bits turned on is the broadcast address: 172.16.255.255.

The valid hosts would be the numbers in between the network address and the broadcast address: 172.16.0.1 through 172.16.255.254.

Class C Addresses

The first 3 bytes of a Class C network address are dedicated to the network portion of the address, with only 1 measly byte remaining for the host address. Here's the format:

`network.network.network.host`

Using the example IP address 192.168.100.102, the network address is 192.168.100 and the host address is 102.

In a Class C network address, the first 3 bit positions are always the binary 110. The calculation is as follows: 3 bytes, or 24 bits, minus 3 reserved positions leaves 21 positions. Hence, there are 2^{21}, or 2,097,152, possible Class C networks.

For Class C networks, the RFCs define the first 2 bits of the first octet as always turned on, but the third bit can never be on. Following the same process as the previous classes, convert from binary to decimal to find the range. Here's the range for a Class C network:

```
11000000 = 192
11011111 = 223
```

So, if you see an IP address with a range from 192 up to 223, you'll know it's a Class C IP address.

Each unique Class C network has 1 byte to use for host addresses. This gets us to 2^8, or 256, minus the two reserved patterns of all 0s and all 1s for a total of 254 available host addresses for each Class C network.

Here's an example of how to find a valid host ID in a Class C network:

- All host bits turned off is the network ID: 192.168.100.0.

- All host bits turned on is the broadcast address: 192.168.100.255.

The valid hosts would be the numbers in between the network address and the broadcast address: 192.168.100.1 through 192.168.100.254.

Class D and E Addresses

Addresses with the first octet of 224 to 255 are reserved for Class D and E networks. Class D (224–239) is used for multicast addresses and Class E (240–255) for scientific purposes. You do need to remember that the multicast range is from 224.0.0.0 through 239.255.255.255. Multicasts will be covered later in this chapter.

Special Purposes of Network Addresses

Some IP addresses are reserved for special purposes, so network administrators can't ever assign them to hosts. Table 7.1 listed the members of this exclusive little club and the reasons they're included in it.

Private IP Addresses (RFC 1918)

The people who created the IP addressing scheme also created what we call *private IP addresses*. These addresses can be used on a private network, but they're not routable through the Internet. This is designed for the purpose of creating a measure of much-needed security, but it also conveniently saves valuable IP address space.

If every host on every network had to have real routable IP addresses, we would have run out of available IP addresses to hand out years ago. But by using private IP addresses, ISPs, corporations, and home users need only a relatively tiny group of bona fide IP addresses to connect their networks to the Internet. This is economical because they can use private IP addresses on their inside networks and get along just fine.

To accomplish this task, the ISP and the corporation—the end users, no matter who they are—need to use something called network address translation (NAT), which basically takes a private IP address and converts it for use on the Internet. NAT provides security in that these IP addresses cannot be seen by external users. External users will only be able to see the public IP address to which the private IP address has been mapped. Moreover, multiple devices in the same private network can use the same, real IP address to transmit out onto the Internet. Doing things this way saves megatons of address space—a very good thing for us all!

Table 7.2 lists the RFC 1918 reserved private addresses.

TABLE 7.2   Reserved RFC 1918 IP address space

Address Class	Reserved Address Space
Class A	10.0.0.0 through 10.255.255.255 (prefix /8)
Class B	172.16.0.0 through 172.31.255.255 (prefix /12)
Class C	192.168.0.0 through 192.168.255.255 (prefix /16)

 Real World Scenario

So, What Private IP Address Should I Use?

That's a really great question: Should you use Class A, Class B, or even Class C private addressing when setting up your network? Let's take Acme Corporation in San Francisco as an example. This company is moving into a new building and needs a whole new network (what a treat this is!). It has 14 departments, with about 70 users in each. You could probably squeeze three or four Class C addresses to use, or maybe you could use a Class B, or even a Class A just for fun.

The rule of thumb in the consulting world is that when you're setting up a corporate network—regardless of how small it is—you should use a Class A network address because it gives you the most flexibility and growth options. For example, if you used the 10.0.0.0 network address with a /24 mask, then you'd have 65,536 networks, each with 254 hosts. Lots of room for growth with this network design! You would then subnet this network address space using Classless Inter-Domain Routing (CIDR, also referred to as variable-length subnet mask, or VLSM), which provides only the needed number of hosts to each department or building without wasting IP addresses. (A /24 tells you that a subnet mask has 24 bits out of 32 bits turned on for subnetting a network. This will be covered, as well as CIDR, in more detail in Chapter 8.)

But if you're setting up a home network, you'd opt for a Class C address because it is the easiest for people to understand and configure. Using the default Class C mask gives you one network with 254 hosts—plenty for a home network.

With the Acme Corporation, a nice 10.1.x.0 with a /24 mask (the x is the subnet for each department) makes this easy to design, install, and troubleshoot.

Virtual IP (VIP)

When a public IP address is substituted for the actual private IP address that has been assigned to the network interface of the device, the public IP address becomes an example of what is called a *virtual IP address*. This means it doesn't correspond to an actual physical network interface. A well-used example is a subinterface configured on a physical router interface, which allows you to create multiple IPs or subnets on one interface.

There are other examples of such virtual IP addresses. For example, when a web proxy server substitutes its IP address for the sender's IP address before sending a packet to the Internet, it is another example of creating a virtual IP address.

APIPA

I discussed this in Chapter 6, "Introduction to the Internet Protocol," but it is worth repeating here. What happens if you have a few hosts connected together with a switch or hub and you don't have a DHCP server? You can add static IP information to a host or you can use what is called Automatic Private IP Addressing (APIPA). I don't recommend this, but APIPA is a "feature," so you do need to remember it, hence mentioning it two chapters in a row!

With APIPA, clients can automatically self-configure an IP address and subnet mask, which is the minimum information needed for hosts to communicate when a DHCP server isn't available. In this way, it could be thought of as a DHCP failover scheme. If all of the hosts set themselves with an APIPA address, they could communicate with one another but unfortunately not with any addresses that were statically configured, such as default gateways!

The IP address range for APIPA is 169.254.0.1 through 169.254.255.254. The client also configures itself with a default Class B subnet mask of 255.255.0.0.

However, when you're in your corporate network and you're running a DHCP server and your host displays that it is using this IP address range, this means that either your DHCP client on the host is not working or the DHCP server is down or can't be reached because of a network issue. For example, if you plug a DHCP client into a port that is disabled, the host will receive an APIPA address. I don't know anyone who has seen a host in the APIPA address range and been happy about it! If users cannot connect to the Internet and their IP addresses fall into the APIPA address range, the DHCP server is most likely the problem.

IPv4 Address Types

Most people use *broadcast* as a generic term, and most of the time, we understand what they mean. But not always. For example, you might say, "The host broadcasted through a router to a DHCP server," but, well, it's pretty unlikely that this would ever really happen.

What you probably mean—using the correct technical jargon—is, "The DHCP client broadcasted for an IP address; a router then forwarded this as a unicast packet to the DHCP server." Oh, and remember that with IPv4, broadcasts are pretty important, but with IPv6, there aren't any broadcasts sent at all—as you'll see in a bit!

Okay, I've referred to broadcast addresses throughout earlier chapters, and even showed you some examples of various IP addresses. But I really haven't gone into the different terms and uses associated with them yet, and it's about time I did. So here are the four IPv4 address types that I'd like to define for you:

Layer 2 Broadcasts   These are sent to all nodes on a LAN.

Broadcasts (Layer 3)   These are sent to all nodes on the network.

Unicast   This is an address for a single interface, and these are used to send packets to a single destination host.

Multicast   These are packets sent from a single source and transmitted to many devices on different networks. This is referred to as *one-to-many*.

Layer 2 Broadcasts

First, understand that layer 2 broadcasts are also known as hardware broadcasts—they only go out on a LAN, and they don't go past the LAN boundary (router).

The typical hardware address is 6 bytes (48 bits) and looks something like 0c.43.a4.f3.12.c2. The broadcast would be all 1s in binary, which would be all *F*s in hexadecimal, as in FF.FF.FF.FF.FF.FF.

Layer 3 Broadcasts

Then there are the plain old broadcast addresses at layer 3. Broadcast messages are meant to reach all hosts on a broadcast domain. These are the network broadcasts that have all host bits on.

Here's an example that you're already familiar with: The network address of 172.16.0.0 would have a broadcast address of 172.16.255.255—all host bits on. Broadcasts can also be "any network and all hosts," as indicated by 255.255.255.255.

A good example of a broadcast message is an Address Resolution Protocol (ARP) request. When a host has a packet, it knows the logical address (IP) of the destination. To get the packet to the destination, the host needs to forward the packet to a default gateway if the destination resides on a different IP network. If the destination is on the local network, the source will forward the packet directly to the destination. Because the source doesn't have the MAC address to which it needs to forward the frame, it sends out a broadcast, something that every device in the local broadcast domain will listen to. This broadcast says, in essence, "If you are the owner of IP address 192.168.2.3, please forward your MAC address to me," with the source giving the appropriate information.

Unicast Address

A unicast address is assigned to a single interface, and this term is used in both IPv4 and IPv6 to describe your host interface IP address.

Multicast Address (Class D)

Multicast is a different beast entirely. At first glance, it appears to be a hybrid of unicast and broadcast communication, but that isn't quite the case. Multicast does allow point-to-multipoint communication, which is similar to broadcasts, but it happens in a different manner. The crux of *multicast* is that it enables multiple recipients to receive messages without flooding the messages to all hosts on a broadcast domain. However, this is not the default behavior—it's what we can do with multicasting if it's configured correctly!

Multicast works by sending messages or data to IP multicast group addresses. Routers then forward copies (unlike broadcasts, which are not forwarded) of the packet out to every interface that has hosts subscribed to a particular group address. This is where multicast differs from broadcast messages—with multicast communication, copies of packets, in theory, are sent only to subscribed hosts. When I say in theory, this means that the hosts will receive, for example, a multicast packet destined for 224.0.0.10 (this is an EIGRP packet and only a router running the EIGRP protocol will read it). All hosts on the broadcast LAN (Ethernet is a broadcast multi-access LAN technology) will pick up the frame, read the destination address, and immediately discard the frame, unless they are in the multicast group. This saves PC processing, not LAN bandwidth. Multicasting can cause severe LAN congestion, in some instances, if not implemented carefully.

There are several different groups that users or applications can subscribe to. The range of multicast addresses starts with 224.0.0.0 and goes through 239.255.255.255. As you can see, this range of addresses falls within IP Class D address space based on classful IP assignment.

Internet Protocol Version 6 (IPv6)

People refer to IPv6 as "the next-generation Internet protocol," and it was originally created as the answer to IPv4's inevitable, looming address-exhaustion crisis. Though you've probably heard a thing or two about IPv6 already, it has been improved even further in the quest to bring us the flexibility, efficiency, capability, and optimized functionality that can truly meet our ever-increasing needs. The capacity of its predecessor, IPv4, pales in comparison—and that's the reason it will eventually fade into history completely.

The IPv6 header and address structure has been completely overhauled, and many of the features that were basically just afterthoughts and addendums in IPv4 are now included as full-blown standards in IPv6. It's well equipped, poised, and ready to manage the mind-blowing demands of the Internet to come.

Why Do We Need IPv6?

Well, the short answer is because we need to communicate and our current system isn't really cutting it anymore—kind of like how the Pony Express couldn't compete with airmail. Just look at how much time and effort we've invested in coming up with slick new ways to conserve bandwidth and IP addresses.

It's reality: the number of people and devices that connect to networks increases each and every day. That's not a bad thing at all—we're finding new and exciting ways to communicate with more people all the time, something that's become integral to our culture today. In fact, it's now pretty much a basic human need. But the forecast isn't exactly blue skies and sunshine because, as I alluded to in this chapter's introduction, IPv4, upon which our ability to communicate is presently dependent, is going to run out of addresses for us to use. IPv4 has only about 4.3 billion addresses available—in theory—and we know that we don't even get to use all of those. There really are only about 250 million addresses that can be assigned to devices. Sure, the use of Classless Inter-Domain Routing (CIDR, also referred to as variable-length subnet mask, or VLSM) and NAT/PAT has helped to delay the inevitable dearth of addresses, but the truth is we will run out of them, and it's going to happen within a few years. China is barely online, compared to their huge population, and corporations there surely want to be. There are a lot of reports that give us all kinds of numbers, but all you really need to think about to convince yourself that I'm not just being an alarmist is the fact that there are about 7.8 billion people in the world today, and it's estimated that just over 59 percent of the population is connected to the Internet—wow! IPv6 to the rescue!

That statistic is basically screaming at us the ugly truth that, based on IPv4's capacity, every person can't have a single computer with an IP address—let alone all the other devices we use with them. I have more than one computer, and it's pretty likely you do, too. And I'm not even including in the mix phones, laptops, game consoles, fax machines, routers, switches, and a mother lode of other devices we use every day! So I think I've made it pretty clear that we've got to do something before we run out of addresses and lose the ability to connect with each other as we know it. And that "something" just happens to be implementing IPv6.

The Benefits of and Uses for IPv6

What's so fabulous about IPv6? Is it really the answer to our coming dilemma? Is it really worth it to upgrade from IPv4? All good questions—you may even think of a few more. Of course, there's going to be that group of people with the time-tested and well-known "resistance-to-change syndrome," but don't listen to them. If we had done that years ago, we'd still be waiting weeks, even months for our mail to arrive via horseback. Instead, just know that the answer is a resounding YES! Not only does IPv6 give us lots of addresses $(3.4 \times 10^{38} = \text{definitely enough})$, but there are many other features built into this version that make it well worth the cost, time, and effort required to migrate to it.

Today's networks, as well as the Internet, have a ton of unforeseen requirements that simply were not considerations when IPv4 was created. We've tried to compensate with a collection of add-ons that can actually make implementing them more difficult than mandating them by a standard. By default, IPv6 has improved upon and included many of those features as standard and mandatory. One of these sweet new standards is IPSec—a feature that provides end-to-end security. Another little beauty is known as *mobility*, and as its name suggests, it allows a device to roam from one network to another without dropping connections.

But it's the efficiency features that are really going to rock the house! For starters, the header in an IPv6 packet has half the fields, and they are aligned to 64 bits, which gives us some seriously souped-up processing speed—compared to IPv4, lookups happen at light speed. Most of the information that used to be bound into the IPv4 header was taken out, and now you can choose to put it, or parts of it, back into the header in the form of optional extension headers that follow the basic header fields.

And of course there's that whole new universe of addresses (3.4×10^{38}) we talked about already. But where did we get them? Did that *Criss Angel Mindfreak* dude just show up and, blammo, they all materialized? The obvious answer is no, but that huge proliferation of addresses had to come from somewhere, right? Well, it just so happens that IPv6 gives us a substantially larger address space, meaning the address is a whole lot bigger—four times bigger, as a matter of fact! An IPv6 address is actually 128 bits in length, and no worries— I'm going to break down the address piece by piece and show you exactly what it looks like coming up in the next section, "IPv6 Addressing and Expressions." For now, let me just say that all that additional room permits more levels of hierarchy inside the address space and a more flexible address architecture. It also makes routing much more efficient and scalable because the addresses can be aggregated a lot more effectively. And IPv6 also allows multiple addresses for hosts and networks. Plus, the new version of IP now includes an expanded use of multicast communication (one device sending to many hosts or to a select group), which will also join in to boost efficiency on networks because communications will be more specific.

IPv4 uses broadcasts very prolifically, causing a bunch of problems, the worst of which is, of course, the dreaded broadcast storm—an uncontrolled deluge of forwarded broadcast traffic that can bring an entire network to its knees and devour every last bit of bandwidth. Another nasty thing about broadcast traffic is that it interrupts each and every device on the network. When a broadcast is sent out, every machine has to stop what it's doing and analyze the traffic, whether the broadcast is meant for it or not.

But smile, everyone: There is no such thing as a broadcast in IPv6 because it uses multicast traffic instead. And there are two other types of communication as well: unicast, which is the same as it is in IPv4, and a new type called *anycast*. Anycast communication allows the same address to be placed on more than one device so that when traffic is sent to one device addressed in this way, it is routed to the nearest host that shares the same address. This is just the beginning—we'll get more into the various types of communication later in this chapter in the section "Address Types."

IPv6 Addressing and Expressions

Just as understanding how IP addresses are structured and used is critical with IPv4 addressing, it's also vital when it comes to IPv6. You've already read about the fact that at 128 bits, an IPv6 address is much larger than an IPv4 address. Because of this, as well as because of the new ways the addresses can be used, you've probably guessed that IPv6 will be more complicated to manage. But no worries! As I said, I'll break it down into the basics and show you what the address looks like, how you can write it, and what many of its common uses are. It's going to be a little weird at first, but before you know it, you'll have it nailed.

So let's take a look at Figure 7.2, which has a sample IPv6 address broken down into sections.

FIGURE 7.2   IPv6 address example

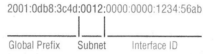

As you can now see, the address is truly much larger—but what else is different? Well, first, notice that it has eight groups of numbers instead of four, and also that those groups are separated by colons instead of periods. And hey, wait a second. . .there are letters in that address! Yep, the address is expressed in hexadecimal just like a MAC address is, so you could say this address has eight 16-bit hexadecimal colon-delimited blocks. That's already quite a mouthful, and you probably haven't even tried to say the address out loud yet.

One other thing I want to point out is for when you set up your test network to play with IPv6, because I know you're going to want to do that. When you use a web browser to make an HTTPS connection to an IPv6 device, you have to type the address into the browser with brackets around the literal address. Why? Well, a colon is already being used by the browser for specifying a port number. So basically, if you don't enclose the address in brackets, the browser will have no way to identify the information.

Here's an example of how this looks:

`https://[2001:0db8:3c4d:0012:0000:0000:1234:56ab]/default.html`

Now obviously, if you could, you would rather use names to specify a destination (like `www.lammle.com`); but even though it's definitely going to be a pain in the rear, you just have to accept the fact that sometimes you have to bite the bullet and type in the address number. It should be pretty clear that DNS is extremely important when implementing IPv6.

Shortened Expression

The good news is there are a few tricks to help rescue you when you're writing these monster addresses. For one thing, you can actually leave out parts of the address to abbreviate it, but to get away with doing that you have to follow a couple of rules. First, you can drop any leading zeros in each of the individual blocks. After you do that, the sample address from earlier would then look like this:

`2001:db8:3c4d:12:0:0:1234:56ab`

That's a definite improvement—at least you don't have to write all of those extra zeros! But what about whole blocks that don't have anything in them except zeros? Well, you can kind of lose those, too—at least some of them. Again, referring to our sample address, you can remove the two blocks of zeros by replacing them with double colons, like this:

`2001:db8:3c4d:12::1234:56ab`

Cool—you replaced the blocks of all zeros with double colons. The rule you have to follow to get away with this is that you can only replace one contiguous block of zeros in an address. So if my address has four blocks of zeros and each of them is separated, I don't get to replace them all. Check out this example:

`2001:0000:0000:0012:0000:0000:1234:56ab`

And just know that you *can't* use double colons twice, like this:

`2001::12::1234:56ab`

Instead, this is the best that you can do:

`2001::12:0:0:1234:56ab`

The reason why this example is your best shot is that if you remove two sets of zeros, the device looking at the address will have no way of knowing where the zeros go back in. Basically, the router would look at the incorrect address and say, "Well, do I place two blocks into the first set of double colons and two into the second set, or do I place three blocks into the first set and one block into the second set?" And on and on it would go because the information the router needs just isn't there.

Address Types

We're all familiar with IPv4's unicast, broadcast, and multicast addresses, which basically define who or at least how many other devices we're talking to. But as I mentioned, IPv6 introduces the anycast address type. Broadcasts, as we know them, have been eliminated in IPv6 because of their cumbersome inefficiency.

Since a single interface can have multiple types of IPv6 addresses assigned for various purposes, let's find out what each of these types of IPv6 addresses are and the communication methods of each:

Unicast   Packets addressed to a unicast address are delivered to a single interface, same as in IPv4. For load balancing, multiple interfaces can use the same address.

Global Unicast Addresses   These are your typical publicly routable addresses, and they're used the same way globally unique addresses are in IPv4.

Link-Local Addresses   These are like the APIPA addresses in IPv4 in that they're not meant to be routed and are unique for each link (LAN). Think of them as a handy tool that gives you the ability to throw a temporary LAN together for meetings or for creating a small LAN that's not going to be routed but still needs to share and access files and services locally. However, link-local is used on every LAN that connects to a router interface as well.

Unique Local Addresses   These addresses are also intended for nonrouting purposes, but they are nearly globally unique, so it's unlikely you'll ever have one of them overlap with any other address. Unique local addresses were designed to replace site-local addresses, so they basically do almost exactly what IPv4 private addresses do—allow communication throughout a site while being routable to multiple local networks. The difference between link-local and unique local is that unique local can be routed within your organization or company.

Multicast   Again, as in IPv4, packets addressed to a multicast address are delivered to all interfaces identified by the multicast address. Sometimes people call them *one-to-many addresses*. It's really easy to spot multicast addresses in IPv6 because they always start with *FF*.

Anycast   Like multicast addresses, an anycast address identifies multiple interfaces, but there's a big difference: The anycast packet is delivered to only one address—actually, to the first IPv6 address it finds defined in terms of routing distance. And again, this address is special because you can apply a single address to more than one interface. You could call them one-to-one-of-many addresses, but just saying anycast is a lot easier. This is also referred to as one-to-nearest addressing.

You're probably wondering if there are any special, reserved addresses in IPv6 because you know they're there in IPv4. Well, there are—plenty of them! Let's go over them now.

Special Addresses

I'm going to list some of the addresses and address ranges that you should definitely make a point to remember in Table 7.3 because you'll eventually use them. They're all special or reserved for specific use, but unlike IPv4, IPv6 gives us a galaxy of addresses, so reserving a few here and there doesn't hurt a thing.

TABLE 7.3   Special IPv6 addresses

Address	Meaning
0:0:0:0:0:0:0:0	Equals ::. This is the equivalent of IPv4's 0.0.0.0 and is typically the source address of a host before the host receives an IP address when you're using DHCP-driven stateful configuration.
0:0:0:0:0:0:0:1	Equals ::1. The equivalent of 127.0.0.1 in IPv4.
0::FFFF:192.168.100.1	This is how an IPv4 address would be written in a mixed IPv6/IPv4 network environment.

Address	Meaning
2000::/3	The global unicast address range allocated for Internet access.
FC00::/7	The unique local unicast range.
FE80::/10	The link-local unicast range.
FF00::/8	The multicast range.
3FFF:FFFF::/32	Reserved for examples and documentation.
2001:0DB8::/32	Also reserved for examples and documentation.
2002::/16	Used with 6to4 tunneling, which is an IPv4-to-IPv6 transition system. The structure allows IPv6 packets to be transmitted over an IPv4 network without the need to configure explicit tunnels.

Stateless Address Autoconfiguration (SLAAC)

Autoconfiguration is an especially useful solution because it allows devices on a network to address themselves with a link-local unicast address as well as with a global unicast address. This process happens through first learning the prefix information from the router and then appending the device's own interface address as the interface ID. But where does it get that interface ID? Well, you know every device on an Ethernet network has a physical MAC address, which is exactly what's used for the interface ID. But since the interface ID in an IPv6 address is 64 bits in length and a MAC address is only 48 bits, where do the extra 16 bits come from? The MAC address is padded in the middle with the extra bits—it's padded with FF:FE.

For example, let's say I have a device with a MAC address that looks like this: 0060:d673:1987. After it's been padded, it would look like this: 0260:d6FF:FE73:1987. Figure 7.3 illustrates what an EUI-64 address looks like.

FIGURE 7.3 EUI-64 interface ID assignment

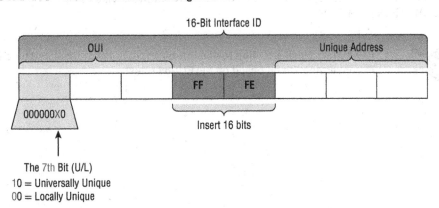

So where did that 2 in the beginning of the address come from? Another good question. You see that part of the process of padding, called modified EUI-64 format, changes the Universal/Local (U/L) bit to specify if the address is locally unique or globally unique. And the bit that gets changed is the 7th bit in the address.

The reason for modifying the U/L bit is that, when using manually assigned addresses on an interface, you can simply assign the address 2001:db8:1:9::1/64 instead of the much longer 2001:db8:1:9:0200::1/64. Also, if you are going to manually assign link-local addresses, you can assign the short address fe80::1 instead of the long fe80::0200:0:0:1 or fe80:0:0:0:0200::1. So, even though at first glance it seems the IETF made this harder for you to simply understand IPv6 addressing by flipping the 7th bit, in reality this made addressing much simpler. Also, since most people don't typically override the burned-in address, the U/L bit is by default a 0, which means that you'll see this inverted to a 1 most of the time. But because you're studying the exam objectives, you'll need to look at inverting it both ways.

Here are a few examples:

- MAC address 0090:2716:fd0f

- IPv6 EUI-64 address: 2001:0db8:0:1:0290:27ff:fe16:fd0f

That one was easy! Too easy for the exam objectives, so let's do another:

- MAC address aa12:bcbc:1234

- IPv6 EUI-64 address: 2001:0db8:0:1:a812:bcff:febc:1234

10101010 represents the first 8 bits of the MAC address (aa), which when inverting the 7th bit becomes 10101000. The answer becomes a8. I can't tell you how important this is for you to understand, so bear with me and work through a couple more!

- MAC address 0c0c:dede:1234

- IPv6 EUI-64 address: 2001:0db8:0:1:0e0c:deff:fede:1234

0c is 00001100 in the first 8 bits of the MAC address, which then becomes 00001110 when flipping the 7th bit. The answer is then 0e. Let's practice one more:

- MAC address 0b34:ba12:1234

- IPv6 EUI-64 address: 2001:0db8:0:1:0934:baff:fe12:1234

0b in binary is 00001011, the first 8 bits of the MAC address, which then becomes 00001001. The answer is 09.

Pay extra-special attention to this EUI-64 address assignment and be able to convert the 7th bit based on the EUI-64 rules!

DHCPv6 (Stateful)

DHCPv6 works pretty much the same way DHCP does in v4, with the obvious difference that it supports IPv6's new addressing scheme. And it might come as a surprise, but there are a couple of other options that DHCP still provides for us that autoconfiguration doesn't. And no, I'm not kidding—in autoconfiguration, there's absolutely no mention of DNS servers, domain names, or many of the other options that DHCP has always generously provided for us via IPv4. This is a big reason that the odds favor DHCP's continued use in IPv6 into the future at least partially—maybe even most of the time!

This means that you're definitely going to need another server around to supply and dispense all the additional, required information—maybe to even manage the address assignment, if needed!

Migrating to IPv6

We certainly have talked a lot about how IPv6 works and how we can configure it to work on our networks, but what is doing that going to cost us? And how much work is it really going to take? Good questions for sure, but the answers to them won't be the same for everyone. This is because how much you are going to end up having to pony up is highly dependent upon what you've got going on already in terms of your infrastructure. Obviously, if you've been making your really old routers and switches "last" and therefore have to upgrade every one of them so that they're IPv6 compliant, that could very well turn out to be a good-sized chunk of change! Oh, and that sum doesn't even include server and computer operating systems (OSs) and the blood, sweat, and maybe even tears spent on making all your applications compliant. So, my friend, it could cost you quite a bit! The good news is that unless you've really let things go, many OSs and network devices have been IPv6 compliant for a few years—we just haven't been using all their features until now.

Then there's that other question about the amount of work and time. Straight up—this one could still be pretty intense. No matter what, it's going to take you some time to get all of your systems moved over and make sure that things are working correctly. And if you're talking about a huge network with tons of devices, well, it could take a really long time! But don't panic—that's why migration strategies have been created, to allow for a gradual integration. I'm going to show you three of the primary transition strategies available to us. The first is called dual stacking, which allows a device to have both the IPv4 and IPv6 protocol stacks running so it's capable of continuing on with its existing communications and simultaneously running newer IPv6 communications as they're implemented. The next strategy is the 6to4 tunneling approach; this is your choice if you have an all-IPv6 network that must communicate over an IPv4 network to reach another IPv6 network. I'll surprise you with the third one just for fun!

Dual Stacking

This is the most common type of migration strategy because, well, it's the easiest on us—it allows our devices to communicate using either IPv4 or IPv6. Dual stacking lets you upgrade your devices and applications on the network one at a time. As more and more hosts and devices on the network are upgraded, more of your communication will happen over IPv6. Once your migration is complete, everything's running on IPv6 and you get to remove all the old IPv4 protocol stacks you no longer need.

6to4 Tunneling

6to4 tunneling is really useful for carrying IPv6 packets over a network that's still running IPv4. It's quite possible that you'll have IPv6 subnets or other portions of your network that are all IPv6, and those networks will have to communicate with each other. Not so complicated, but when you consider that you might find this happening over a WAN or some other network that you don't control, well, that could be a bit ugly. So what do we do about this if we don't control the whole tamale? Create a tunnel that will carry the IPv6 traffic for us across the IPv4 network, that's what.

The whole idea of tunneling isn't a difficult concept, and creating tunnels really isn't as hard as you might think. All it really comes down to is snatching the IPv6 packet that's happily traveling across the network and sticking an IPv4 header onto the front of it. This is kind of like catch-and-release fishing, except for the fish doesn't get something plastered on its face before being thrown back into the stream.

To get a picture of this, take a look at Figure 7.4.

FIGURE 7.4   A 6to4 tunnel

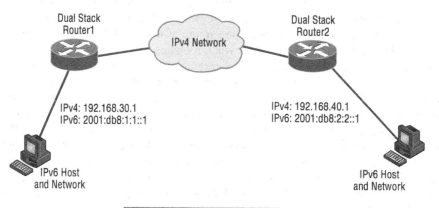

IPv6 packet encapsulated in an IPv4 packet

Nice—but to make this happen, we're going to need a couple of dual-stacked routers, which I just demonstrated for you, so you should be good to go. Now we have to add a little configuration to place a tunnel between those routers. Tunnels are pretty simple—we just have to tell each router where the tunnel begins and where we want it to end up. The opposite of this would be a *4to6 tunnel*, which is rare to find because this means your whole business network is IPv4 (okay, this sounds normal so far) but you're traversing an IPv6-only Internet to get to another IPv4 network. That's not so common at the time of this writing.

One important note here—if the IPv4 network that you're traversing in this 6to4 situation has a NAT translation point, it would absolutely break the tunnel encapsulation we've just created! Over the years, NAT/PAT has been upgraded a lot so that it can handle specific protocols and dynamic connections, and without one of these upgrades, NAT likes to demolish most connections. And since this transition strategy isn't present in most NAT implementations, that means trouble.

But there is a way around this little problem (the third strategy I told you about), and it's called *Teredo*, which allows all your tunnel traffic to be placed in UDP packets. NAT doesn't blast away at UDP packets, so they won't get broken as other protocol packets do. So with Teredo in place and your packets disguised under their UDP cloak, the packets will easily slip by NAT alive and well!

Miredo is a tunneling technique used on native IPv6 Linux and BSD Unix machines to communicate on the IPv4 Internet directly without a dual-stack router or 6to4 tunnel. This is rarely used.

Summary

In this chapter, I covered the very basics of both IPv4 and IPv6 and how they work in an internetwork (remember that if the acronym *IP* is used alone, it is referring to just IPv4). As you now know by reading this chapter, even when discussing and configuring the basics, there is a lot to understand—and we just scratched the surface. We also covered RFC 1918, APIPA addresses, address Classes A-D, NAT, EUI-64, tunneling, dual-stack and virtual IP addressing. But trust me when I say this—you now know more than you'll need to meet the Network+ objectives.

I discussed in detail the difference between each class of address and how to find a network address, broadcast address, and valid host range.

I explained why we need IPv6 and the benefits associated with it. I followed that up by covering addressing with IPv6 as well as how to use the shortened expressions. And during the discussion on addressing with IPv6, I showed you the different address types, plus the special addresses reserved in IPv6.

The next chapter is very important, but it's one that some people find rather challenging, so take a break and get ready for a really fun but long chapter on IP subnetting. I promise not to torture you too much!

Exam Essentials

Remember the Class A range.   The IP range for a Class A network is 1 through 126. This provides 8 bits of network addressing and 24 bits of host addressing by default.

Remember the Class B range.   The IP range for a Class B network is 128 through 191. Class B addressing provides 16 bits of network addressing and 16 bits of host addressing by default.

Remember the Class C range.   The IP range for a Class C network is 192 through 223. Class C addressing provides 24 bits of network addressing and 8 bits of host addressing by default.

Remember the private IP ranges.   The Class A private address range is 10.0.0.0 through 10.255.255.255.

The Class B private address range is 172.16.0.0 through 172.31.255.255.

The Class C private address range is 192.168.0.0 through 192.168.255.255.

Remember the APIPA range.   The IP address range for APIPA is 169.254.0.1 through 169.254.255.254. The client also configures itself with a default Class B subnet mask of 255.255.0.0.

Understand why we need IPv6.   Without IPv6, the world would soon be depleted of IP addresses.

Understand link-local.   Link-local addresses are like an IPv4 APIPA IP address, but they can't be routed at all, not even in your organization.

Understand unique local.   Similar to link-local, this is like a private IP address in IPv4 and cannot be routed to the Internet. However, the difference between link-local and unique local is that unique local can be routed within your organization or company.

Remember IPv6 addressing.   IPv6 addressing is not like IPv4 addressing. IPv6 addressing has much more address space and the address is 128 bits long, represented in hexadecimal, unlike an IPv4 address, which is only 32 bits long and represented in decimal.

Understand and be able to read an EUI-64 address with the 7th bit inverted.   Hosts can use autoconfiguration to obtain an IPv6 address, and one of the ways is through what is called EUI-64. This takes the unique MAC address of a host and inserts FF:FE in the middle of the address to change a 48-bit MAC address to a 64-bit interface ID. In addition to the 16 bits being inserted into the interface ID, the 7th bit of the first byte is inverted, typically from a 0 to a 1.

Written Labs

You can find the answers to the written labs in Appendix A.

Written Lab 7.1

Provide the answers to the following questions:

1. What is the valid range used for a Class C private IP address?

2. Name some of the benefits of IPv6 over IPv4.

3. What is the term for the autoconfiguration technology responsible for addresses that start with 169.254?

4. What defines a unicast address?

5. What defines a multicast address?

6. What is the name for a 48-bit (6-byte) numerical address physically assigned to a network interface, such as a NIC?

7. IPv6 has how many more bits, compared to addresses in IPv4?

8. What is the private address range for Class B networks?

9. What is the Class C range of values for the first octet in decimal and in binary?

10. What is the 127.0.0.1 address used for?

Written Lab 7.2

In this lab, write the answers to the following IPv6 questions:

1. Which type of packet is addressed and delivered to only a single interface?

2. Which type of address is used just like a regular public routable address in IPv4?

3. Which type of address is not meant to be routed?

4. Which type of address is not meant to be routed to the Internet but is still globally unique?

5. Which type of address is meant to be delivered to multiple interfaces?

6. Which type of address identifies multiple interfaces, but packets are delivered only to the first address it finds?

7. Which addressing type is also referred to as one-to-nearest?

8. IPv4 had a loopback address of 127.0.0.1. What is the IPv6 loopback address?

9. What does a link-local address always start with?

10. What does a unique local unicast range start with?

Review Questions

You can find the answers to the review questions in Appendix B.

1. Which of the following addresses is not allowed on the Internet?
   A. 191.192.168.1
   B. 191.168.169.254
   C. 172.32.255.0
   D. 172.31.12.251

2. A host automatically configured with an address from which of the following ranges indicates an inability to contact a DHCP server?
   A. 169.254.0.x with a mask of 255.255.255.0
   B. 169.254.x.x with a mask of 255.255.0.0
   C. 169.254.x.x with a mask of 255.255.255.0
   D. 169.255.x.x with a mask of 255.255.0.0

3. Which statement regarding private IP addresses is most accurate?
   A. Private addresses cannot be used in intranets that require routing.
   B. Private addresses must be assigned by a registrar or ISP.
   C. A remote host across the Internet cannot ping your host if it has a private address.
   D. Private addresses can only be used by a single administrative domain.

4. Which of the following is a valid Class A address?
   A. 191.10.0.1
   B. 127.10.0.1
   C. 128.10.0.1
   D. 126.10.0.1

5. Which of the following is a valid Class B address?
   A. 10.1.1.1
   B. 126.1.1.1
   C. 129.1.1.1
   D. 192.168.1.1

6. Which of the following describes a broadcast address?
   A. All network bits are on (1s).
   B. All host bits are on (1s).
   C. All network bits are off (0s).
   D. All host bits are off (0s).

7. Which of the following is a layer 2 broadcast?

   A. FF.FF.FF.EE.EE.EE

   B. FF.FF.FF.FF.FF.FF

   C. 255.255.255.255

   D. 255.0.0.0

8. In a Class C IP address, how long is the network address?

   A. 8 bits

   B. 16 bits

   C. 24 bits

   D. 32 bits

9. Which of the following is true when describing a unicast address?

   A. Packets addressed to a unicast address are delivered to a single interface.

   B. These are your typical publicly routable addresses, just like regular publicly routable addresses in IPv4.

   C. These are like private addresses in IPv4 in that they are not meant to be routed.

   D. These addresses are meant for nonrouting purposes, but they are almost globally unique, so it is unlikely they will have an address overlap.

10. A host is rebooted and you view the IP address that it was assigned. The address is 169.123.13.34. Which of the following happened?

   A. The host received an APIPA address.

   B. The host received a multicast address.

   C. The host received a public address.

   D. The host received a private address.

11. An IPv4 address uses 32 bits. How many bits is an IPv6 address?

   A. 64

   B. 128

   C. 192

   D. 255

12. Which of the following is true when describing a multicast address?

   A. Packets addressed to a unicast address from a multicast address are delivered to a single interface.

   B. Packets are delivered to all interfaces identified by the address. This is also called a one-to-many address.

   C. It identifies multiple interfaces and is delivered to only one address. This address can also be called one-to-one-of-many.

   D. These addresses are meant for nonrouting purposes, but they are almost globally unique so it is unlikely they will have an address overlap.

13. Which of the following is true when describing an anycast address?

    A. Packets addressed to a unicast address from an anycast address are delivered to a single interface.

    B. Packets are delivered to all interfaces identified by the address. This is also called a one-to-many address.

    C. This address identifies multiple interfaces, and the anycast packet is delivered to only one address: the closest one. This address can also be called one-to-nearest.

    D. These addresses are meant for nonrouting purposes, but they are almost globally unique so it is unlikely they will have an address overlap.

14. You want to ping the loopback address of your local host. Which two addresses could you type? (Choose two.)

    A. `ping 127.0.0.1`

    B. `ping 0.0.0.0`

    C. `ping ::1`

    D. `trace 0.0.::1`

15. What two statements about IPv6 addresses are true? (Choose two.)

    A. Leading zeros are required.

    B. Two colons (::) are used to represent successive hexadecimal fields of zeros.

    C. Two colons (::) are used to separate fields.

    D. A single interface will have multiple IPv6 addresses of different types.

16. What two statements about IPv4 and IPv6 addresses are true? (Choose two.)

    A. An IPv6 address is 32 bits long, represented in hexadecimal.

    B. An IPv6 address is 128 bits long, represented in decimal.

    C. An IPv4 address is 32 bits long, represented in decimal.

    D. An IPv6 address is 128 bits long, represented in hexadecimal.

17. Which of the following is a Class C network address?

    A. 10.10.10.0

    B. 127.0.0.1

    C. 128.0.0.0

    D. 192.255.254.0

18. Which of the following are private IP addresses? (Choose two.)

    A. 12.0.0.1

    B. 168.172.19.39

    C. 172.20.14.36

    D. 172.33.194.30

    E. 192.168.24.43

19. IPv6 unicast routing is running on the Corp router. Which of the following addresses would be used as the EUI-64 address?

```
Corp#sh int f0/0
FastEthernet0/0 is up, line protocol is up
Hardware is AmdFE, address is 000d.bd3b.0d80 (bia 000d.bd3b.0d80)
[output cut]
```

   A. FF02::3c3d:0d:bdff:fe3b:0d80

   B. FE80::3c3d:2d:bdff:fe3b:0d80

   C. FE80::3c3d:0d:bdff:fe3b:0d80

   D. FE80::3c3d:2d:ffbd:3bfe:0d80

20. Which of the following is an invalid IP address for a host?

   A. 10.0.0.1

   B. 128.0.0.1

   C. 224.0.0.1

   D. 172.0.0.1

IP Subnetting, Troubleshooting IP, and Introduction to NAT

THE FOLLOWING COMPTIA NETWORK+ EXAM OBJECTIVES ARE COVERED IN THIS CHAPTER:

✓ **1.4 Given a scenario, configure a subnet and use appropriate IP addressing schemes.**

- Public vs. private
    - RFC1918
    - Network address translation (NAT)
    - Port address translation (PAT)
- IPv4 vs. IPv6
    - Automatic Private IP Addressing (APIPA)
    - Extended unique identifier (EUI-64)
    - Multicast
    - Unicast
    - Anycast
    - Broadcast
    - Link local
    - Loopback
    - Default gateway
- IPv4 subnetting
    - Classless (variable-length subnet mask)

- Classful
  - A
  - B
  - C
  - D
  - E
- Classless Inter-Domain Routing (CIDR) notation

This chapter's focus will really zoom in on IP addressing to ensure that you have it nailed down tight. This is an integral aspect of networking, and it's important for your success on the exams and as a professional, too!

We'll start with subnetting an IP network. You're going to have to really apply yourself because it takes time and practice in order to do subnetting correctly and quickly. So be patient and do whatever it takes to get this stuff dialed in. This chapter truly is important—possibly the most important chapter in this book for you to understand. Make it part of you!

I'll thoroughly cover IP subnetting from the very beginning. I know this might sound weird to you, but I think you'll be much better off if you can try to forget everything you've learned about subnetting before reading this chapter—especially if you've been to a Microsoft class!

I'll also walk you through IP address troubleshooting and each of the recommended steps for troubleshooting an IP network. Finally, I'll finish up with an introduction to Network Address Translation (NAT)—there are various types of NAT, and you need to know when you would use each one.

So get psyched—you're about to go for quite a ride! This chapter will truly help you understand IP addressing and networking, so don't get discouraged or give up. If you stick with it, I promise that one day you'll look back on this and be really glad you decided to stay the course. It's one of those things that after you understand it, you'll laugh at that time, way back when, when you thought this was hard. So, are you ready now? Let's go!

To find Todd Lammle CompTIA videos and practice questions, please see www.lammle.com.

Subnetting Basics

In Chapter 7, "IP Addressing," you learned how to define and find the valid host ranges used in a Class A, Class B, or Class C network address by turning the host bits all off and then all on. This is very good, but here's the catch: You were defining only one network. What would happen if you wanted to take one network address range and create six networks from it? You would have to do something called *subnetting*, because that's what allows you to take one larger network and break it into a bunch of smaller networks.

There are loads of reasons in favor of subnetting, including the following benefits:

Reduced Network Traffic   We all appreciate less traffic of any kind. With networks, it's no different. Without trusty routers, packet traffic could grind the entire network down to a near standstill. With routers, most traffic will stay on the local network; only packets destined for other networks will pass through the router. Routers create broadcast domains. The more broadcast domains you create, the smaller the broadcast domains and the less network traffic on each network segment.

Optimized Network Performance   This is the very cool reward you get when you reduce network traffic!

Simplified Management   It's easier to identify and isolate network problems in a group of smaller connected networks than within one gigantic network.

Facilitated Spanning of Large Geographical Distances   Because WAN links are considerably slower and more expensive than LAN links, a single large network that spans long distances can create problems in every area previously listed. Connecting multiple smaller networks makes the system more efficient.

Next, we're going to move on to subnetting a network address. This is the good part—ready?

How to Create Subnets

To create subnetworks, you take bits from the host portion of the IP address and reserve them to define the subnet address. This means fewer bits for hosts, so the more subnets, the fewer bits are left available for defining hosts.

Soon, I'll show you how to create subnets, starting with Class C addresses. But before you actually implement subnetting, you really need to determine your current requirements as well as plan for future conditions.

Follow these steps—they're your recipe for solid design:

1. Determine the number of required network IDs:

   - One for each subnet

   - One for each wide area network (WAN) connection

2. Determine the number of required host IDs per subnet:

   - One for each TCP/IP host

   - One for each router interface

3. Based on the previous requirements, create the following:

   - One subnet mask for your entire network

   - A unique subnet ID for each physical segment

   - A range of host IDs for each subnet

Understanding the Powers of 2

By the way, powers of 2 are really important to memorize for use with IP subnetting. To review powers of 2, remember that when you see a number with another number to its upper right (an exponent), this means you should multiply the number by itself as many times as the upper number specifies. For example, 2^3 is $2 \times 2 \times 2$, which equals 8. Here's a list of powers of 2 that you should commit to memory:

$2^1 = 2$

$2^2 = 4$

$2^3 = 8$

$2^4 = 16$

$2^5 = 32$

$2^6 = 64$

$2^7 = 128$

$2^8 = 256$

$2^9 = 512$

$2^{10} = 1,024$

$2^{11} = 2,048$

$2^{12} = 4,096$

$2^{13} = 8,192$

$2^{14} = 16,384$

If you hate math, don't get stressed out about knowing all these exponents—it's helpful to know them, but it's not absolutely necessary. Here's a little trick, because you're working with 2s: Each successive power of 2 is double the previous one.

For example, all you have to do to remember the value of 2^9 is to first know that $2^8 = 256$. Why? Because when you double 2 to the eighth power (256), you get 2^9 (or 512). To determine the value of 2^{10}, simply start at $2^8 = 256$, and then double it twice.

You can go the other way as well. If you needed to know what 2^6 is, for example, you just cut 256 in half two times: once to reach 2^7 and then one more time to reach 2^6. Not bad, right?

Subnet Masks

For the subnet address scheme to work, every machine on the network must know which part of the host address will be used as the subnet address. This is accomplished by assigning a *subnet mask* to each machine. A subnet mask is a 32-bit value that allows the recipient of IP packets to distinguish the network ID portion of the IP address from the host ID portion of the IP address.

The network administrator creates a 32-bit subnet mask composed of 1s and 0s. The 1s in the subnet mask represent the positions that refer to the network, or subnet, addresses.

Not all networks need subnets, meaning they use the default subnet mask. This is basically the same as saying that a network doesn't have a subnet address.

Table 8.1 shows the default subnet masks for Classes A, B, and C. These default masks cannot and do not change. In other words, you can't make a Class B subnet mask read 255.0.0.0. If you try, the host will read that address as invalid and usually won't even let you type it in. For a Class A network, you can't change the first byte in a subnet mask; it must read 255.0.0.0 at a minimum. Similarly, you cannot assign 255.255.255.255, because this is all 1s—a broadcast address. A Class B address must start with 255.255.0.0, and a Class C has to start with 255.255.255.0. Check out Table 8.1.

TABLE 8.1   Default subnet masks

Class	Format	Default subnet mask
A	*network.host.host.host*	255.0.0.0
B	*network.network.host.host*	255.255.0.0
C	*network.network.network.host*	255.255.255.0

In Chapter 7 we discussed the addresses with the first octet of 224 to 255 are reserved for Class D and E networks. Class D (224–239) is used for multicast addresses and Class E (240–255) for scientific purposes. But they're really beyond the scope of this book, so I'm not going to go into detail about them here. But you do need to remember that the multicast range is from 224.0.0.0 through 239.255.255.255.

Classless Inter-Domain Routing (CIDR)

Another term you need to know is *Classless Inter-Domain Routing (CIDR)*. It's basically the method that Internet service providers (ISPs) use to allocate a number of addresses to a company or a home connection. They provide addresses in a certain block size; I'll be going into that in greater detail later in this chapter. Another term for the use of different length subnet masks in the network is *variable-length subnet masking (VLSM)*.

When you receive a block of addresses from an ISP, what you get will look something like this: 192.168.10.32/28. This is telling you what your subnet mask is. The slash notation (/) means how many bits are turned on (1s). Obviously, the maximum could only be /32 because a byte is 8 bits and there are 4 bytes in an IP address: 4 × 8 = 32. But keep in mind that the largest subnet mask available (regardless of the class of address) can only be a /30 because you have to keep at least 2 bits for host bits.

Take, for example, a Class A default subnet mask, which is 255.0.0.0. This means that the first byte of the subnet mask is all ones (1s), or 11111111. When referring to a slash notation, you need to count all the 1s bits to figure out your mask. The 255.0.0.0 is considered a /8 because it has 8 bits that are 1s—that is, 8 bits that are turned on.

A Class B default mask would be 255.255.0.0, which is a /16 because 16 bits are (1s): 11111111.11111111.00000000.00000000.

Table 8.2 offers a listing of every available subnet mask and its equivalent CIDR slash notation.

TABLE 8.2   CIDR values

Subnet Mask	CIDR Value
255.0.0.0	/8
255.128.0.0	/9
255.192.0.0	/10
255.224.0.0	/11
255.240.0.0	/12
255.248.0.0	/13
255.252.0.0	/14
255.254.0.0	/15
255.255.0.0	/16
255.255.128.0	/17
255.255.192.0	/18
255.255.224.0	/19
255.255.240.0	/20
255.255.248.0	/21
255.255.252.0	/22
255.255.254.0	/23
255.255.255.0	/24

(continues)

TABLE 8.2   CIDR values *(continued)*

Subnet Mask	CIDR Value
255.255.255.128	/25
255.255.255.192	/26
255.255.255.224	/27
255.255.255.240	/28
255.255.255.248	/29
255.255.255.252	/30

Although according to RFC 1518, any device or software that claims to be CIDR com-pliant will allow supernetting, meaning a traditional Class C address can be used with a /23 subnet mask, in almost all cases. The /8 through /15 can be used only with Class A network addresses; /16 through /23 can be used by Class A and B network addresses; /24 through /30 can be used by Class A, B, and C network addresses. This is a big reason most companies use Class A network addresses. By being allowed the use of all subnet masks, they gain the valuable benefit of maximum flexibility for their network design.

Subnetting Class C Addresses

There are many different ways to subnet a network. The right way is the way that works best for you. In a Class C address, only 8 bits are available for defining the hosts. Remember that subnet bits start at the left and go to the right, without skipping bits. This means that the only Class C subnet masks can be those listed here:

Binary	Decimal	CIDR
00000000	0	/24
10000000	128	/25
11000000	192	/26
11100000	224	/27
11110000	240	/28
11111000	248	/29
11111100	252	/30

We can't use a /31 or /32 because, remember, we have to leave at least 2 host bits for assigning IP addresses to hosts.

Get ready for something special. I'm going to teach you an alternate method of subnetting that makes it a whole lot easier to subnet larger numbers in no time. And trust me, you really do need to be able to subnet fast!

Subnetting a Class C Address: The Fast Way!

When you've chosen a possible subnet mask for your network and need to determine the number of subnets, valid hosts, and broadcast addresses of a subnet that the mask provides, all you need to do is answer five simple questions:

- How many subnets does the chosen subnet mask produce?
- How many valid hosts per subnet are available?
- What are the valid subnets?
- What's the broadcast address of each subnet?
- What are the valid hosts in each subnet?

At this point, it's important that you both understand and have memorized your powers of 2. Please refer to the sidebar "Understanding the Powers of 2" earlier in this chapter if you need some help. Here's how you get the answers to those five big questions:

- *How many subnets?* 2^x = number of subnets. x is the number of masked bits, or the 1s. For example, in 11000000, the number of 1s gives us 2^2 subnets. In this example, there are 4 subnets.

- *How many hosts per subnet?* $2^y - 2$ = number of hosts per subnet. y is the number of unmasked bits, or the 0s. For example, in 11000000, the number of 0s gives us $2^6 - 2$ hosts. In this example, there are 62 hosts per subnet. You need to subtract 2 for the subnet address and the broadcast address, which are not valid hosts.

- *What are the valid subnets?* 256 – subnet mask = block size, or increment number. An example would be 256 – 192 = 64. The block size of a 192 mask is always 64. Start counting at zero in blocks of 64 until you reach the subnet mask value, and these are your subnets. 0, 64, 128, 192. Easy, huh?

- *What's the broadcast address for each subnet?* Now here's the really easy part. Because we counted our subnets in the last section as 0, 64, 128, and 192, the broadcast address is always the number right before the next subnet. For example, the 0 subnet has a broadcast address of 63 because the next subnet is 64. The 64 subnet has a broadcast address of 127 because the next subnet is 128. And so on. And remember, the broadcast address of the last subnet is always 255.

- *What are the valid hosts?* Valid hosts are the numbers between the subnets, omitting all the 0s and all the 1s. For example, if 64 is the subnet number and 127 is the broadcast address, then 65–126 is the valid host range—it's *always* the numbers between the subnet address and the broadcast address.

I know this can truly seem confusing. But it really isn't as hard as it seems to be at first—just hang in there! Why not try a few and see for yourself?

Subnetting Practice Examples: Class C Addresses

Here's your opportunity to practice subnetting Class C addresses using the method I just described. Exciting, isn't it? We're going to start with the first Class C subnet mask and work through every subnet that we can using a Class C address. When we're done, I'll show you how easy this is with Class B networks too!

Practice Example #1C: 255.255.255.128 (/25)

Because 128 is 10000000 in binary, there is only 1 bit for subnetting, and there are 7 bits for hosts. We're going to subnet the Class C network address 192.168.10.0.

192.168.10.0 = Network address

255.255.255.128 = Subnet mask

Now, let's answer the big five:

- *How many subnets?* Because 128 is 1 bit on (**10000000**), the answer is $2^1 = 2$.

- *How many hosts per subnet?* We have 7 host bits off (**10000000**), so the equation is $2^7 - 2 = 126$ hosts.

- *What are the valid subnets?* 256 − 128 = 128. Remember, we'll start at zero and count in our block size, so our subnets are 0, 128.

- *What's the broadcast address for each subnet?* The number right before the value of the next subnet is all host bits turned on and equals the broadcast address. For the 0 subnet, the next subnet is 128, so the broadcast address of the 0 subnet is 127.

- *What are the valid hosts?* These are the numbers between the subnet and broadcast address. The easiest way to find the hosts is to write out the subnet address and the broadcast address. This way, the valid hosts are obvious. The following table shows the 0 and 128 subnets, the valid host ranges of each, and the broadcast address of both subnets:

Subnet	0	128
First host	1	129
Last host	126	254
Broadcast	127	255

Before moving on to the next example, take a look at Figure 8.1. Okay, looking at a Class C /25, it's pretty clear there are two subnets. But so what—why is this significant? Well actually, it's not, but that's not the right question. What you really want to know is what you would do with this information!

FIGURE 8.1   Implementing a Class C /25 logical network

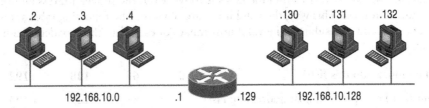

```
Router#show ip route
[output cut]
C 192.168.10.0 is directly connected to Ethernet 0.
C 192.168.10.128 is directly connected to Ethernet 1.
```

The key to understanding subnetting is to understand the very reason you need to do it. And I'm going to demonstrate this by going through the process of building a physical network—and let's add a router. (We now have an internetwork, as I truly hope you already know!) Because we added that router, in order for the hosts on our internetwork to communicate, they must now have a logical network addressing scheme. We could use IPv6, but IPv4 is still the most popular, and it also just happens to be what we're studying at the moment, so that's what we're going with.

Now take a look back at Figure 8.1. By the way, the output you see below the diagram is the routing table of the router, which was displayed by executing the show ip route command on the router. There are two physical networks, so we're going to implement a logical addressing scheme that allows for two logical networks. As always, it's a really good idea to look ahead and consider any likely growth scenarios—both short and long term, but for this example, a /25 will do the trick.

Practice Example #2C: 255.255.255.192 (/26)

In this second example, we're going to subnet the network address 192.168.10.0 using the subnet mask 255.255.255.192.

192.168.10.0 = Network address

255.255.255.192 = Subnet mask

It's time to answer the big five:

- *How many subnets?* Because 192 is 2 bits on (**11**000000), the answer is $2^2 = 4$ subnets.

- *How many hosts per subnet?* We have 6 host bits off (11**000000**), so the equation is $2^6 - 2 = 62$ hosts.

- *What are the valid subnets?* 256 − 192 = 64. Remember, we start at zero and count in our block size, so our subnets are 0, 64, 128, and 192.

- *What's the broadcast address for each subnet?* The number right before the value of the next subnet is all host bits turned on and equals the broadcast address. For the 0 subnet, the next subnet is 64, so the broadcast address for the 0 subnet is 63.

- *What are the valid hosts?* These are the numbers between the subnet and broadcast address. The easiest way to find the hosts is to write out the subnet address and the broadcast address. This way, the valid hosts are obvious. The following table shows the 0, 64, 128, and 192 subnets, the valid host ranges of each, and the broadcast address of each subnet:

	0	64	128	192
The subnets (do this first)	0	64	128	192
Our first host (perform host addressing last)	1	65	129	193
Our last host	62	126	190	254
The broadcast address (do this second)	63	127	191	255

Again, before getting into the next example, you can see that we can now subnet a /26. And what are you going to do with this fascinating information? Implement it! We'll use Figure 8.2 to practice a /26 network implementation.

FIGURE 8.2   Implementing a Class C /26 logical network

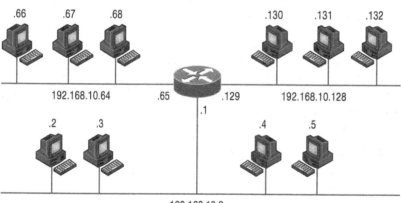

```
Router#show ip route
[output cut]
C 192.168.10.0 is directly connected to Ethernet 0
C 192.168.10.64 is directly connected to Ethernet 1
C 192.168.10.128 is directly connected to Ethernet 2
```

The /26 mask provides four subnetworks, and we need a subnet for each router interface. With this mask, in this example, we actually have room to add another router interface.

Practice Example #3C: 255.255.255.224 (/27)

This time, we'll subnet the network address 192.168.10.0 and subnet mask 255.255.255.224.

192.168.10.0 = Network address

255.255.255.224 = Subnet mask

- *How many subnets?* 224 is 11100000, so our equation is $2^3 = 8$.
- *How many hosts?* $2^5 - 2 = 30$.
- *What are the valid subnets?* $256 - 224 = 32$. We just start at zero and count to the subnet mask value in blocks (increments) of 32: 0, 32, 64, 96, 128, 160, 192, and 224.
- *What's the broadcast address for each subnet (always the number right before the next subnet)?*
- *What are the valid hosts (the numbers between the subnet number and the broadcast address)?*

To answer the last two questions, first just write out the subnets, and then write out the broadcast address—the number right before the next subnet. Last, fill in the host address. The following table gives you all the subnets for the 255.255.255.224 Class C subnet mask:

The subnet address	0	32	64	96	128	160	192	224
The first valid host	1	33	65	97	129	161	193	225
The last valid host	30	62	94	126	158	190	222	254
The broadcast address	31	63	95	127	159	191	223	255

Practice Example #4C: 255.255.255.240 (/28)

Let's practice on another one:

192.168.10.0 = Network address

255.255.255.240 = Subnet mask

- *Subnets?* 240 is 11110000 in binary. $2^4 = 16$.
- *Hosts?* 4 host bits, or $2^4 - 2 = 14$.
- *Valid subnets?* $256 - 240 = 16$. 0, 16, 32, 48, 64, 80, 96, 112, 128, 144, 160, 176, 192, 208, 224, 240.
- *Broadcast address for each subnet?*
- *Valid hosts?*

To answer the last two questions, check out the following table. It gives you the subnets, valid hosts, and broadcast address for each subnet. First, find the address of each subnet using the block size (increment). Second, find the broadcast address of each subnet increment (it's always the number right before the next valid subnet); then, just fill in the host address. The following table shows the available subnets, hosts, and broadcast address provided by a Class C network 255.255.255.240 mask:

Subnet	0	16	32	48	64	80	96	112	128	144	160	176	192	208	224	240
First host	1	17	33	49	65	81	97	113	129	145	161	177	193	209	225	241
Last host	14	30	46	62	78	94	110	126	142	158	174	190	206	222	238	254
Broad-cast	15	31	47	63	79	95	111	127	143	159	175	191	207	223	239	255

Practice Example #5C: 255.255.255.248 (/29)

Let's keep practicing:

192.168.10.0 = Network address

255.255.255.248 = Subnet mask

- *Subnets?* 248 in binary = 11111000. 2^5 = 32.
- *Hosts?* $2^3 - 2 = 6$.
- *Valid subnets?* 256 − 248 = 8, start at zero: 0, 8, 16, 24, 32, 40, 48, 56, 64, 72, 80, 88, 96, 104, 112, 120, 128, 136, 144, 152, 160, 168, 176, 184, 192, 200, 208, 216, 224, 232, 240, and 248.
- *Broadcast address for each subnet?*
- *Valid hosts?*

Take a look at the following table. It shows some of the subnets (first four and last four only), valid hosts, and broadcast address for the Class C 255.255.255.248 mask:

Subnet	0	8	16	24	...	224	232	240	248
First host	1	9	17	25	...	225	233	241	249
Last host	6	14	22	30	...	230	238	246	254
Broadcast	7	15	23	31	...	231	239	247	255

Practice Example #6C: 255.255.255.252 (/30)

I know, I know—but just one more:

192.168.10.0 = Network address

255.255.255.252 = Subnet mask

- *Subnets?* 64.
- *Hosts?* 2.
- *Valid subnets?* 0, 4, 8, 12, and so on, all the way to 252.

- *Broadcast address for each subnet (always the number right before the next subnet)?*
- *Valid hosts (the numbers between the subnet number and the broadcast address)?*

The following table shows you the subnet, valid host, and broadcast address of the first four and last four subnets in the 255.255.255.252 Class C subnet:

Subnet	0	4	8	12	...	240	244	248	252
First host	1	5	9	13	...	241	245	249	253
Last host	2	6	10	14	...	242	246	250	254
Broad-cast	3	7	11	15	...	243	247	251	255

Subnetting in Your Head: Class C Addresses

It really is possible to subnet in your head by looking at a valid IP address and subnet mask. This is extremely important for IP addressing and troubleshooting. Even if you don't believe me that you can subnet in your head, I'll show you how. And it's not all that hard either—take the following example: What is the subnet, broadcast address, and valid host range that this host IP address is a part of?

192.168.10.33 = Host address

255.255.255.224 = Subnet mask

Should We Really Use This Mask That Provides Only Two Hosts?

Imagine you are the network administrator for Acme Corporation in San Francisco, with dozens of WAN links connecting to your corporate office. Right now your network is a classful network, which means that the same subnet mask is on each host and router interface. You've read about classless routing where you can have different size masks, but you don't know what to use on your point-to-point WAN links. Is 255.255.255.252 (/30) a helpful mask in this situation?

Yes, this is a very helpful mask in wide area networks.

If you use the 255.255.255.0 mask, then each network will have 254 hosts, but you only use two addresses with a WAN link! That is a waste of 252 hosts per subnet. If you use the 255.255.255.252 mask, then each subnet has only 2 hosts, and you don't waste precious addresses.

First, determine the subnet and broadcast address of this IP address. You can do this by answering question 3 of the big five questions: 256 − 224 = 32. Start at zero: 0, 32,

64. The address of 33 falls between the two subnets of 32 and 64 and must be part of the 192.168.10.32 subnet. The next subnet is 64, so the broadcast address of the 32 subnet is 63. (Remember that the broadcast address of a subnet is always the number right before the next subnet.) The valid host range is 33–62 (the numbers between the subnet and broadcast address). I told you this is easy!

Okay, let's try another one. What is the subnet, broadcast address, and valid host range that this host IP address is a part of?

192.168.10.33 = Host address

255.255.255.240 = Subnet mask

256 – 240 = 16. Start at zero and count till you pass the valid host in the problem: 0, 16, 32, 48. Bingo—the host address is between the 32 and 48 subnets. The subnet is 192.168.10.32, and the broadcast address is 47 (the next subnet is 48). The valid host range is 33–46 (the numbers between the subnet number and the broadcast address).

We need to do more, just to make sure you have this down.

You have a host address of 192.168.10.174 with a mask of 255.255.255.240. What is the subnet, broadcast address, and valid host range that this host IP address is a part of?

The mask is 240, so we need our block size: 256 – 240 = 16. Just keep adding 16 until we pass the host address of 174, starting at zero, of course: 0, 16, 32, 48, 64, 80, 96, 112, 128, 144, 160, 176. The host address of 174 is between 160 and 176, so the subnet is 160. The broadcast address is 175; the valid host range is 161–174. That was a tough one.

Let's do one more just for fun. Of all Class C subnetting, this is the easiest:

192.168.10.17 = Host address

255.255.255.252 = Subnet mask

What subnet and broadcast address is this IP address a part of? 256 – 252 = 4. Start at zero (always start at zero unless told otherwise): 0, 4, 8, 12, 16, 20, and so on. You've got it! The host address is between the 16 and 20 subnets. The subnet is 192.168.10.16, and the broadcast address is 19. The valid host range is 17–18.

Now that you're all over Class C subnetting, let's move on to Class B subnetting. But before we do, let's do a quick review.

So What Do You Know Now?

Here's where you can really apply what you've learned so far and begin committing it all to memory. This is a very cool section that I've been using in my classes for years. It will really help you nail down subnetting!

When you see a subnet mask or slash notation (CIDR), you should know the following when working with Class C networks:

/25

What do you know about a /25?

- 128 mask
- 1 bit on and 7 bits off (10000000)
- Block size of 128
- 2 subnets, each with 126 hosts

/26

And what do you know about a /26?

- 192 mask
- 2 bits on and 6 bits off (11000000)
- Block size of 64
- 4 subnets, each with 62 hosts

/27

What about a /27?

- 224 mask
- 3 bits on and 5 bits off (11100000)
- Block size of 32
- 8 subnets, each with 30 hosts

/28

And what about a /28?

- 240 mask
- 4 bits on and 4 bits off
- Block size of 16
- 16 subnets, each with 14 hosts

/29

What do you know about a /29?

- 248 mask
- 5 bits on and 3 bits off
- Block size of 8
- 32 subnets, each with 6 hosts

/30

And last, what about a /30?

- 252 mask
- 6 bits on and 2 bits off
- Block size of 4
- 64 subnets, each with 2 hosts

Regardless of whether you have a Class A, Class B, or Class C address, the /30 mask will provide you with only two hosts, ever. This mask is suited almost exclusively for use on point-to-point links.

If you can memorize this "So What Do You Know Now?" section, you'll be much better off in your day-to-day job and in your studies. Try saying it out loud, which helps you memorize things—yes, your significant other and/or coworkers will think you've lost it, but they probably already do if you're in the networking field. And if you're not yet in the networking field but are studying all this to break into it, you might as well have people start thinking you're a little "different" now because they will eventually anyway.

It's also helpful to write these on some type of flashcards and have people test your skill. You'd be amazed at how fast you can get subnetting down if you memorize block sizes as well as this "So What Do You Know Now?" section.

Subnetting Class B Addresses

Before we dive into this, let's look at all the possible Class B subnet masks. Notice that we have a lot more possible subnet masks than we do with a Class C network address:

255.255.0.0	(/16)
255.255.128.0	(/17)
255.255.192.0	(/18)
255.255.224.0	(/19)
255.255.240.0	(/20)
255.255.248.0	(/21)
255.255.252.0	(/22)
255.255.254.0	(/23)
255.255.255.0	(/24)
255.255.255.128	(/25)
255.255.255.192	(/26)
255.255.255.224	(/27)

255.255.255.240	(/28)
255.255.255.248	(/29)
255.255.255.252	(/30)

We know the Class B network address has 16 bits available for host addressing. This means we can use up to 14 bits for subnetting (because we have to leave at least 2 bits for host addressing). Using a /16 means you are not subnetting with Class B, but it is a mask you can use.

By the way, do you notice anything interesting about that list of subnet values—a pattern, maybe? Ah-ha! That's exactly why I had you memorize the binary-to-decimal numbers earlier in this chapter. Because subnet mask bits start on the left and move to the right and bits can't be skipped, the numbers are always the same regardless of the class of address. Memorize this pattern.

The process of subnetting a Class B network is pretty much the same as it is for a Class C, except that you have more host bits and you start in the third octet.

Use the same subnet numbers for the third octet with Class B that you used for the fourth octet with Class C, but add a 0 to the network portion and a 255 to the broadcast section in the fourth octet. The following table shows you an example host range of two subnets used in a Class B 240 (/20) subnet mask:

First Subnet	Second Subnet
16.0	32.0
31.255	47.255

Notice that these are the same numbers we used in the fourth octet with a /28 mask, but we moved them to the third octet and added a .0 and .255 at the end. Just add the valid hosts between the numbers, and you're set!

Subnetting Practice Examples: Class B Addresses

The following sections will give you an opportunity to practice subnetting Class B addresses. Again, I have to mention that this is the same as subnetting with Class C, except we start in the third octet—with the exact same numbers!

Practice Example #1B: 255.255.128.0 (/17)

Let's take a look at our first example:

172.16.0.0 = Network address

255.255.128.0 = Subnet mask

- *Subnets?* $2^1 = 2$ (same as Class C).
- *Hosts?* $2^{15} - 2 = 32,766$ (7 bits in the third octet, and 8 in the fourth).
- *Valid subnets?* 256 – 128 = 128. 0, 128. Remember that subnetting in Class B starts in the third octet, so the subnet numbers are really 0.0 and 128.0, as shown in the next table. These are the exact numbers we used with Class C; we use them in the third octet and add a 0 in the fourth octet for the network address.
- *Broadcast address for each subnet?*

The following table shows the two subnets available, the valid host range, and the broadcast address of each:

Subnet	0.0	128.0
First host	0.1	128.1
Last host	127.254	255.254
Broadcast	127.255	255.255

Notice that we just added the fourth octet's lowest and highest values and came up with the answers. And again, it's done exactly the same way as for a Class C subnet. We just use the same numbers in the third octet and added 0 and 255 in the fourth octet—pretty simple, huh? I really can't say this enough: It's not hard. The numbers never change. We just use them in different octets!

Practice Example #2B: 255.255.192.0 (/18)

Let's take a look at a second example with Class B.

   172.16.0.0 = Network address

   255.255.192.0 = Subnet mask

- *Subnets?* $2^2 = 4$.
- *Hosts?* $2^{14} - 2 = 16,382$ (6 bits in the third octet, and 8 in the fourth).
- *Valid subnets?* 256 – 192 = 64. 0, 64, 128, 192. Remember that we're in the third octet, so the subnet numbers are really 0.0, 64.0, 128.0, and 192.0, as shown in the next table.
- *Broadcast address for each subnet?*
- *Valid hosts?*

The following table shows the four subnets available, the valid host range, and the broadcast address of each:

Subnet	0.0	64.0	128.0	192.0
First host	0.1	64.1	128.1	192.1
Last host	63.254	127.254	191.254	255.254

Subnet	0.0	64.0	128.0	192.0
Broadcast	63.255	127.255	191.255	255.255

Again, it's pretty much the same as it is for a Class C subnet—we just added 0 and 255 in the fourth octet for each subnet in the third octet.

Practice Example #3B: 255.255.240.0 (/20)

Let's take a look:

172.16.0.0 = Network address

255.255.240.0 = Subnet mask

- *Subnets?* $2^4 = 16$.
- *Hosts?* $2^{12} - 2 = 4{,}094$.
- *Valid subnets?* 256 – 240 = 16, but we start at 0 always. 0, 16, 32, 48, and so on, up to 240. Notice that these are the same numbers as a Class C 240 mask—we just put them in the third octet and add a 0 and 255 in the fourth octet.
- *Broadcast address for each subnet?*
- *Valid hosts?*

The following table shows the first four subnets, valid hosts, and broadcast address in a Class B 255.255.240.0 mask:

Subnet	0.0	16.0	32.0	48.0
First host	0.1	16.1	32.1	48.1
Last host	15.254	31.254	47.254	63.254
Broadcast	15.255	31.255	47.255	63.255

Practice Example #4B: 255.255.254.0 (/23)

Let's take a look:

172.16.0.0 = Network address

255.255.254.0 = Subnet mask

- *Subnets?* $2^7 = 128$.
- *Hosts?* $2^9 - 2 = 510$.
- *Valid subnets?* 256 – 254 = 0, 2, 4, 6, 8, and so on, up to 254.
- *Broadcast address for each subnet?*
- *Valid hosts?*

The following table shows the first five subnets, valid hosts, and broadcast address in a Class B 255.255.254.0 mask:

Subnet	0.0	2.0	4.0	6.0	8.0
First host	0.1	2.1	4.1	6.1	8.1
Last host	1.254	3.254	5.254	7.254	9.254
Broadcast	1.255	3.255	5.255	7.255	9.255

Practice Example #5B: 255.255.255.0 (/24)

Contrary to popular belief, 255.255.255.0 used with a Class B network address is not called a Class B network with a Class C subnet mask. It's amazing how many people see this mask used in a Class B network and think it's a Class C subnet mask. This is a Class B subnet mask with 8 bits of subnetting—it's considerably different from a Class C mask. Subnetting this address is fairly simple:

172.16.0.0 = Network address

255.255.255.0 = Subnet mask

- *Subnets?* 2^8 = 256.
- *Hosts?* $2^8 - 2$ = 254.
- *Valid subnets?* 256 − 255 = 1. 0, 1, 2, 3, and so on, all the way to 255.
- *Broadcast address for each subnet?*
- *Valid hosts?*

The following table shows the first four and last two subnets, the valid hosts, and the broadcast address in a Class B 255.255.255.0 mask:

Subnet	0.0	1.0	2.0	3.0	. . .	254.0	255.0
First host	0.1	1.1	2.1	3.1	. . .	254.1	255.1
Last host	0.254	1.254	2.254	3.254	. . .	254.254	255.254
Broadcast	0.255	1.255	2.255	3.255	. . .	254.255	255.255

Practice Example #6B: 255.255.255.128 (/25)

This is one of the hardest subnet masks you can play with. And worse, it actually is a really good subnet to use in production because it creates over 500 subnets with a whopping 126 hosts for each subnet—a nice mixture. So, don't skip over it!

172.16.0.0 = Network address

255.255.255.128 = Subnet mask

- *Subnets?* $2^9 = 512$.

- *Hosts?* $2^7 - 2 = 126$.

- *Valid subnets?* Now for the tricky part. $256 - 255 = 1$. 0, 1, 2, 3, and so on for the third octet. But you can't forget the one subnet bit used in the fourth octet. Remember when I showed you how to figure one subnet bit with a Class C mask? You figure this out the same way. (Now you know why I showed you the 1-bit subnet mask in the Class C section—to make this part easier.) You actually get two subnets for each third octet value, hence the 512 subnets. For example, if the third octet is showing subnet 3, the two subnets would actually be 3.0 and 3.128.

- *Broadcast address for each subnet?*

- *Valid hosts?*

The following table shows how you can create subnets, valid hosts, and broadcast addresses using the Class B 255.255.255.128 subnet mask (the first eight subnets are shown, and then the last two subnets):

Subnet	0.0	0.128	1.0	1.128	2.0	2.128	3.0	3.128	...	255.0	255.128
First host	0.1	0.129	1.1	1.129	2.1	2.129	3.1	3.129	...	255.1	255.129
Last host	0.126	0.254	1.126	1.254	2.126	2.254	3.126	3.254	...	255.126	255.254
Broadcast	0.127	0.255	1.127	1.255	2.127	2.255	3.127	3.255	...	255.127	255.255

Practice Example #7B: 255.255.255.192 (/26)

Now, this is where Class B subnetting gets easy. Because the third octet has a 255 in the mask section, whatever number is listed in the third octet is a subnet number. However, now that we have a subnet number in the fourth octet, we can subnet this octet just as we did with Class C subnetting. Let's try it:

172.16.0.0 = Network address

255.255.255.192 = Subnet mask

- *Subnets?* $2^{10} = 1024$.

- *Hosts?* $2^6 - 2 = 62$.

- *Valid subnets?* $256 - 192 = 64$. The subnets are shown in the following table. Do these numbers look familiar?

- *Broadcast address for each subnet?*

- *Valid hosts?*

The following table shows the first eight subnet ranges, valid hosts, and broadcast address:

Subnet	0.0	0.64	0.128	0.192	1.0	1.64	1.128	1.192
First host	0.1	0.65	0.129	0.193	1.1	1.65	1.129	1.193
Last host	0.62	0.126	0.190	0.254	1.62	1.126	1.190	1.254
Broadcast	0.63	0.127	0.191	0.255	1.63	1.127	1.191	1.255

Notice that for each subnet value in the third octet, you get subnets 0, 64, 128, and 192 in the fourth octet.

Practice Example #8B: 255.255.255.224 (/27)

This is done the same way as the preceding subnet mask, except that we have more subnets and fewer hosts per subnet available.

172.16.0.0 = Network address

255.255.255.224 = Subnet mask

- *Subnets?* 2^{11} = 2048.
- *Hosts?* $2^5 - 2$ = 30.
- *Valid subnets?* 256 – 224 = 32. 0, 32, 64, 96, 128, 160, 192, 224.
- *Broadcast address for each subnet?*
- *Valid hosts?*

The following table shows the first eight subnets:

Subnet	0.0	0.32	0.64	0.96	0.128	0.160	0.192	0.224
First host	0.1	0.33	0.65	0.97	0.129	0.161	0.193	0.225
Last host	0.30	0.62	0.94	0.126	0.158	0.190	0.222	0.254
Broadcast	0.31	0.63	0.95	0.127	0.159	0.191	0.223	0.255

This next table shows the last eight subnets:

Subnet	255.0	255.32	255.64	255.96	255.128	255.160	255.192	255.224
First host	255.1	255.33	255.65	255.97	255.129	255.161	255.193	255.225
Last host	255.30	255.62	255.94	255.126	255.158	255.190	255.222	255.254
Broadcast	255.31	255.63	255.95	255.127	255.159	255.191	255.223	255.255

Subnetting in Your Head: Class B Addresses

Are you nuts? Subnet Class B addresses in our heads? It's actually easier than writing it out—I'm not kidding! Let me show you the steps:

1. What subnet and broadcast address is the IP address 172.16.10.33 255.255.255.224 (/27) a member of?

    The interesting octet is the fourth octet. 256 − 224 = 32. 32 + 32 = 64. Bingo: 33 is between 32 and 64. However, remember that the third octet is considered part of the subnet, so the answer is the 10.32 subnet. The broadcast is 10.63 because 10.64 is the next subnet. That was a pretty easy one.

2. What subnet and broadcast address is the IP address 172.16.66.10 255.255.192.0 (/18) a member of?

    The interesting octet is the third octet instead of the fourth octet. 256 − 192 = 64. 0, 64, 128. The subnet is 172.16.64.0. The broadcast must be 172.16.127.255 because 128.0 is the next subnet.

> Notice in the last example I started counting at zero. This is called *ip subnet-zero*. It is a command that if executed on a router, allows us to use the zero subnet as our first subnet. This may or may not be enabled on your router. If it is not enabled, then you cannot start counting subnets at zero. Most routers, if not all routers these days, support ip subnet-zero.

3. What subnet and broadcast address is the IP address 172.16.50.10 255.255.224.0 (/19) a member of?

    256 − 224 = 0, 32, 64 (remember, we always start counting at zero). The subnet is 172.16.32.0, and the broadcast must be 172.16.63.255 because 64.0 is the next subnet.

4. What subnet and broadcast address is the IP address 172.16.46.255 255.255.240.0 (/20) a member of?

    256 − 240 = 16. The third octet is interesting to us. 0, 16, 32, 48. This subnet address must be in the 172.16.32.0 subnet, and the broadcast must be 172.16.47.255 because 48.0 is the next subnet. So, yes, 172.16.46.255 is a valid host.

5. What subnet and broadcast address is the IP address 172.16.45.14 255.255.255.252 (/30) a member of?

    Where is the interesting octet? 256 − 252 = 0, 4, 8, 12, 16 (in the fourth octet). The subnet is 172.16.45.12, with a broadcast of 172.16.45.15 because the next subnet is 172.16.45.16.

6. What is the subnet and broadcast address of the host 172.16.88.255/20?

    What is a /20? If you can't answer this, you can't answer this question, can you? A /20 is 255.255.240.0, which gives us a block size of 16 in the third octet, and because no subnet bits are on in the fourth octet, the answer is always 0 and 255 in the fourth octet. 0, 16, 32, 48, 64, 80, 96. Bingo: 88 is between 80 and 96, so the subnet is 80.0 and the broadcast address is 95.255.

7. A router receives a packet on an interface with a destination address of 172.16.46.191/26. What will the router do with this packet?

Discard it. Do you know why? 172.16.46.191/26 is a 255.255.255.192 mask, which gives us a block size of 64. Our subnets are then 0, 64, 128, 192. 191 is the broadcast address of the 128 subnet, so a router, by default, will discard any broadcast packets.

Troubleshooting IP Addressing

Troubleshooting IP addressing is obviously an important skill because running into trouble somewhere along the way is pretty much a sure thing, and it's going to happen to you. No— I'm not a pessimist; I'm just keeping it real. Because of this nasty fact, it will be great when you can save the day because you can both figure out (diagnose) the problem and fix it on an IP network whether you're at work or at home!

Let's use Figure 8.3 as an example of your basic IP trouble—poor Sally can't log in to the Windows server. Do you deal with this by calling the Microsoft team to tell them their server is a pile of junk and causing all your problems? Tempting, but probably not such a great idea—let's first double-check our network instead. Check out Figure 8.3.

FIGURE 8.3 Basic IP troubleshooting

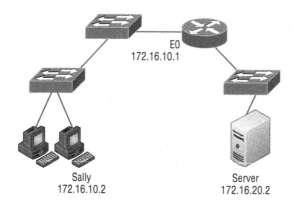

Sally
172.16.10.2

EO
172.16.10.1

Server
172.16.20.2

Let's get started by going over the basic troubleshooting steps. They're pretty simple, but important nonetheless. Pretend you're at Sally's host and she's complaining that she can't communicate to a server that just happens to be on a remote network:

1. Open a command prompt window on Sally's host, and ping 127.0.0.1.

```
C:\>ping 127.0.0.1
Pinging 127.0.0.1 with 32 bytes of data:
Reply from 127.0.0.1: bytes=32 time<1ms TTL=128
```

```
Reply from 127.0.0.1: bytes=32 time<1ms TTL=128
Reply from 127.0.0.1: bytes=32 time<1ms TTL=128
Reply from 127.0.0.1: bytes=32 time<1ms TTL=128
Ping statistics for 127.0.0.1:
    Packets: Sent = 4, Received = 4, Lost = 0 (0% loss),
Approximate round trip times in milli-seconds:
    Minimum = 0ms, Maximum = 0ms, Average = 0ms
```

This is the diagnostic, or IPv4 loopback address, and if you get a successful ping, your IP stack is considered to be initialized. If it fails, then you have an IP stack failure and need to reinstall TCP/IP on the host.

> **NOTE** If you ping the loopback address and receive an "unable to contact IP driver, error code 2" message, you need to reinstall the TCP/IP protocol suite on the host.

2. Now, from the same command prompt window, ping the IP address of the local host.

```
C:\>ping 172.16.10.2
Pinging 172.16.10.2 with 32 bytes of data:
Reply from 172.16.10.2: bytes=32 time<1ms TTL=128
Reply from 172.16.10.2: bytes=32 time<1ms TTL=128
Reply from 172.16.10.2: bytes=32 time<1ms TTL=128
Reply from 172.16.10.2: bytes=32 time<1ms TTL=128
Ping statistics for 172.16.10.2:
    Packets: Sent = 4, Received = 4, Lost = 0 (0% loss),
Approximate round trip times in milli-seconds:
    Minimum = 0ms, Maximum = 0ms, Average = 0ms
```

If that's successful, your network interface card (NIC) is functioning. If it fails, there is a problem with the NIC. Success here doesn't mean that a cable is plugged into the NIC, only that the IP protocol stack on the host can communicate to the NIC (via the LAN driver).

3. From the command prompt window, ping the default gateway (router).

```
C:\>ping 172.16.10.1
Pinging 172.16.10.1 with 32 bytes of data:
Reply from 172.16.10.1: bytes=32 time<1ms TTL=128
Reply from 172.16.10.1: bytes=32 time<1ms TTL=128
Reply from 172.16.10.1: bytes=32 time<1ms TTL=128
Reply from 172.16.10.1: bytes=32 time<1ms TTL=128
Ping statistics for 172.16.10.1:
```

```
     Packets: Sent = 4, Received = 4, Lost = 0 (0% loss),
Approximate round trip times in milli-seconds:
     Minimum = 0ms, Maximum = 0ms, Average = 0ms
```

If the ping works, it means that the NIC is plugged into the network and can communicate on the local network. If it fails, you have a local physical network problem that could be anywhere from the NIC to the router.

4. If steps 1 through 3 were successful, try to ping the remote server.

```
C:\>ping 172.16.20.2
Pinging 172.16.20.2 with 32 bytes of data:
Reply from 172.16.20.2: bytes=32 time<1ms TTL=128
Reply from 172.16.20.2: bytes=32 time<1ms TTL=128
Reply from 172.16.20.2: bytes=32 time<1ms TTL=128
Reply from 172.16.20.2: bytes=32 time<1ms TTL=128
Ping statistics for 172.16.20.2:
     Packets: Sent = 4, Received = 4, Lost = 0 (0% loss),
Approximate round trip times in milli-seconds:
     Minimum = 0ms, Maximum = 0ms, Average = 0ms
```

If that works, then you know that you have IP communication between the local host and the remote server. You also know that the remote physical network is working.

If the user still can't communicate with the server after steps 1 through 4 are successful, you probably have some type of name resolution problem and need to check your Domain Name System (DNS) settings. But if the ping to the remote server fails, then you know you have some type of remote physical network problem and need to go to the server and work through steps 1 to 3 until you find the snag.

Before we move on to determining IP address problems and how to fix them, I just want to mention some basic yet handy command-line tools that you can use to help troubleshoot your network from both a PC and a Cisco router (the commands might do the same thing, but they are implemented differently):

Packet InterNet Groper (ping)   Uses an Internet Control Message Protocol (ICMP) echo request and replies to test if a host IP stack is initialized and alive on the network.

Traceroute   Displays the list of routers on a path to a network destination by using time to live (TTL) time-outs and ICMP error messages. This command will work on a router, MAC, or Linux box, but not from a Windows command prompt.

Tracert   Same command as traceroute, but it's a Microsoft Windows command and will not work on other devices, like a Cisco router or macOS or Linux box.

arp -a   Displays IP–to–MAC-address mappings on a Windows PC.

ipconfig /all   Used only from a command prompt. Shows you the PC network configuration.

Once you've gone through all these steps and used the appropriate command-line tools, if necessary, what do you do if you find a problem? How do you go about fixing an IP address configuration error? That's exactly what you're going to learn about next—how to determine specific IP address problems and what you can do to fix them.

Determining IP Address Problems

It's common for a host, router, or other network device to be configured with the wrong IP address, subnet mask, or default gateway. Because this happens way too often, I'm going to teach you how to both determine and fix IP address configuration errors.

Once you've worked through the four basic steps of troubleshooting and determined there's a problem, you obviously then need to find and fix it. It really helps to draw out the network and IP addressing scheme. If it's already done, consider yourself lucky and go buy a lottery ticket because although it should be done, it rarely is. And if it is, it's usually outdated or inaccurate anyway. Typically, it is not done, and you'll probably just have to bite the bullet and start from scratch.

Once you have your network accurately drawn out, including the IP addressing scheme, you need to verify each host's IP address, mask, and default gateway address to determine the problem. (I'm assuming that you don't have a physical problem or that if you did, you've already fixed it.)

Let's check out the example illustrated in Figure 8.4. A user in the sales department calls and tells you that she can't get to ServerA in the marketing department. You ask her if she can get to ServerB in the marketing department, but she doesn't know because she doesn't have rights to log on to that server. What do you do?

FIGURE 8.4   IP address problem 1

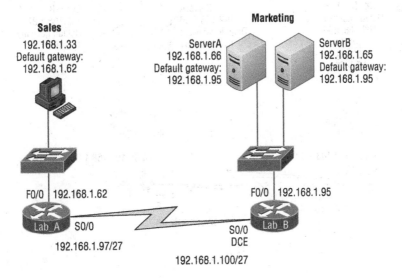

You ask the client to go through the four troubleshooting steps that you learned about in the preceding section. Steps 1 through 3 work, but step 4 fails. By looking at the figure, can you determine the problem? Look for clues in the network drawing. First, the WAN link between the Lab_A router and the Lab_B router shows the mask as a /27. You should already know that this mask is 255.255.255.224 and then determine that all networks are using this mask. The network address is 192.168.1.0. What are our valid subnets and hosts? 256 − 224 = 32, so this makes our subnets 0, 32, 64, 96, 128, and so on. So, by looking at the figure, you can see that subnet 32 is being used by the sales department, the WAN link is using subnet 96, and the marketing department is using subnet 64.

Now you have to determine what the valid host ranges are for each subnet. From what you learned at the beginning of this chapter, you should now be able to easily determine the subnet address, broadcast addresses, and valid host ranges. The valid hosts for the Sales LAN are 33 through 62—the broadcast address is 63 because the next subnet is 64, right? For the Marketing LAN, the valid hosts are 65 through 94 (broadcast 95), and for the WAN link, 97 through 126 (broadcast 127).

By looking at the figure, you can determine that the default gateway on the Lab_B router is incorrect. That address is the broadcast address of the 64 subnet, so there's no way it could be a valid host.

Did you get all that? Maybe we should try another one, just to make sure. Figure 8.5 shows a network problem. A user in the Sales LAN can't get to ServerB. You have the user run through the four basic troubleshooting steps and find that the host can communicate to the local network but not to the remote network. Find and define the IP addressing problem.

FIGURE 8.5   IP address problem 2

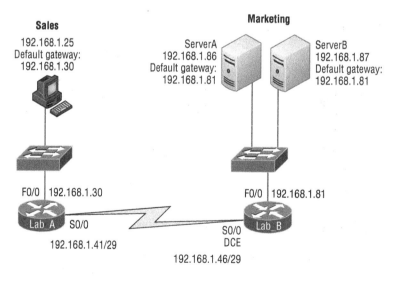

If you use the same steps used to solve the last problem, you can see first that the WAN link again provides the subnet mask to use— /29, or 255.255.255.248. You need to determine what the valid subnets, broadcast addresses, and valid host ranges are to solve this problem.

The 248 mask is a block size of 8 (256 – 248 = 8), so the subnets both start and increment in multiples of 8. By looking at the figure, you see that the Sales LAN is in the 24 subnet, the WAN is in the 40 subnet, and the Marketing LAN is in the 80 subnet. Can you see the problem yet? The valid host range for the Sales LAN is 25–30, and the configuration appears correct. The valid host range for the WAN link is 41–46, and this also appears correct. The valid host range for the 80 subnet is 81–86, with a broadcast address of 87 because the next subnet is 88. ServerB has been configured with the broadcast address of the subnet.

Now that you can figure out misconfigured IP addresses on hosts, what do you do if a host doesn't have an IP address and you need to assign one? What you need to do is look at other hosts on the LAN and figure out the network, mask, and default gateway. Let's take a look at a couple of examples of how to find and apply valid IP addresses to hosts.

You need to assign a server and router IP addresses on a LAN. The subnet assigned on that segment is 192.168.20.24/29, and the router needs to be assigned the first usable address and the server the last valid host ID. What are the IP address, mask, and default gateway assigned to the server?

To answer this, you must know that a /29 is a 255.255.255.248 mask, which provides a block size of 8. The subnet is known as 24, the next subnet in a block of 8 is 32, so the broadcast address of the 24 subnet is 31, which makes the valid host range 25–30:

Server IP address: 192.168.20.30

Server mask: 255.255.255.248

Default gateway: 192.168.20.25 (router's IP address)

As another example, let's take a look at Figure 8.6 and solve this problem.

FIGURE 8.6   Find the valid host.

RouterA

E0: 192.168.10.33/27

HostA

Look at the router's IP address on Ethernet0. What IP address, subnet mask, and valid host range could be assigned to the host?

The IP address of the router's Ethernet0 is 192.168.10.33/27. As you already know, a /27 is a 224 mask with a block size of 32. The router's interface is in the 32 subnet. The next subnet is 64, so that makes the broadcast address of the 32 subnet 63 and the valid host range 33–62:

Host IP address: 192.168.10.34–62 (any address in the range except for 33, which is assigned to the router)

Mask: 255.255.255.224

Default gateway: 192.168.10.33

Figure 8.7 shows two routers with Ethernet configurations already assigned. What are the host addresses and subnet masks of hosts A and B?

FIGURE 8.7   Find the valid host #2.

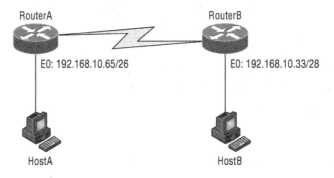

RouterA has an IP address of 192.168.10.65/26 and RouterB has an IP address of 192.168.10.33/28. What are the host configurations? RouterA Ethernet0 is in the 192.168.10.64 subnet, and RouterB Ethernet0 is in the 192.168.10.32 network:

HostA IP address: 192.168.10.66–126

HostA mask: 255.255.255.192

HostA default gateway: 192.168.10.65

HostB IP address: 192.168.10.34–46

HostB mask: 255.255.255.240

HostB default gateway: 192.168.10.33

Just a couple more examples, and then this section is history. Hang in there!

Figure 8.8 shows two routers; you need to configure the S0/0 interface on RouterA. The network assigned to the serial link is 172.16.16.0/22. What IP address can be assigned?

FIGURE 8.8   Find the valid host address #3.

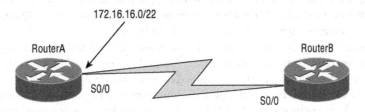

First, you must know that a /22 CIDR is 255.255.252.0, which makes a block size of 4 in the third octet. Because 16 is listed, the available range is 16.1 through 19.254; so, for example, the IP address S0/0 could be 172.16.18.255 because that's within the range.

Okay, last one! You have one Class C network ID, and you need to provide one usable subnet per city while allowing enough usable host addresses for each city specified in Figure 8.9. What is your mask?

FIGURE 8.9   Find the valid subnet mask.

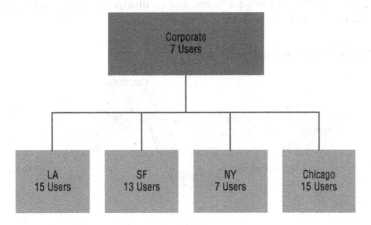

Actually, this is probably the easiest thing you've done all day! I count 5 subnets needed, and the Chicago office needs 15 users (always look for the network that needs the most hosts). What block size is needed for the Chicago office? 32. (Remember, you cannot use a block size of 16 because you always have to subtract 2!) What mask provides you with a block size of 32? 224. Bingo! This provides 8 subnets, each with 30 hosts.

Introduction to Network Address Translation (NAT)

Similar to Classless Inter-Domain Routing (CIDR), the original intention for NAT was to slow the depletion of available IP address space by allowing many private IP addresses to be represented by some smaller number of public IP addresses.

Since then, it's been discovered that NAT is also a useful tool for network migrations and mergers, server load sharing, and creating "virtual servers." So I'm going to describe the basics of NAT functionality and the terminology common to NAT.

At times, NAT really decreases the overwhelming amount of public IP addresses required in your networking environment. And NAT comes in very handy when two companies that have duplicate internal addressing schemes merge. NAT is also great to have around when an organization changes its ISP and the networking manager doesn't want the hassle of changing the internal address scheme.

Here's a list of situations in which it's best to have NAT on your side:

- You need to connect to the Internet and your hosts don't have globally unique IP addresses.
- You change to a new ISP that requires you to renumber your network.
- You need to merge two intranets with duplicate addresses.

You typically use NAT on a border router. For an illustration of this, see Figure 8.10, where NAT would be configured on the Corporate router.

FIGURE 8.10   Where to configure NAT

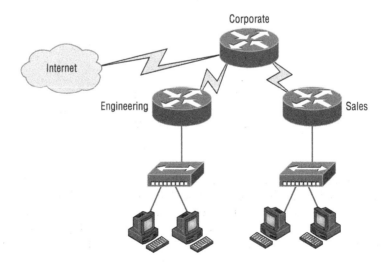

Now you may be thinking, "NAT's totally cool. It's the grooviest, greatest network gadget, and I just gotta have it." Well, hang on a minute. There are truly some serious snags related to NAT use. Oh, don't get me wrong: It really can save you sometimes, but there's a dark side you need to know about too. For a visual of the pros and cons linked to using NAT, check out Table 8.3.

TABLE 8.3   Advantages and disadvantages of implementing NAT

Advantages	Disadvantages
Conserves legally registered addresses.	Translation introduces switching path delays.
Reduces address overlap occurrences.	Loss of end-to-end IP traceability.
Increases flexibility when connecting to the Internet.	Certain applications will not function with NAT enabled.
Eliminates address renumbering as the network changes.	

Types of Network Address Translation

In this section, I'm going to go over the three types of NAT with you:

Static NAT (SNAT)   This type of NAT is designed to allow one-to-one mapping between local and global addresses. Keep in mind that the static version requires you to have one real Internet IP address for every host on your network.

Dynamic NAT (DNAT)   This version gives you the ability to map an unregistered IP address to a registered IP address from a pool of registered IP addresses. You don't have to statically configure your router to map an inside-to-an-outside address as you would using static NAT, but you do have to have enough real, bona fide IP addresses for everyone who's going to be sending packets to and receiving them from the Internet.

Overloading   This is the most popular type of NAT configuration. Understand that overloading really is a form of dynamic NAT that maps multiple unregistered IP addresses to a single registered IP address—many-to-one—by using different ports. Now, why is this so special? Well, because it's also known as port address translation (PAT). And by using PAT (NAT Overload), you get to have thousands of users connect to the Internet using only one real global IP address—pretty slick, yeah? Seriously, NAT Overload is the real reason we haven't run out of valid IP address on the Internet. Really—I'm not joking.

NAT Names

The names we use to describe the addresses used with NAT are pretty simple. Addresses used after NAT translations are called *global* addresses. These are usually the public addresses used on the Internet, but remember, you don't need public addresses if you aren't going on the Internet.

Local addresses are the ones we use before network translation. So, the inside local address is actually the private address of the sending host that's trying to get to the Internet, while the outside local address is the address of the destination host. The latter is usually a public address (web address, mail server, and so on) and is how the packet begins its journey.

After translation, the inside local address is then called the *inside global address*, and the outside global address then becomes the name of the destination host. Check out Table 8.4, which lists all this terminology, for a clear picture of the various names used with NAT.

TABLE 8.4   NAT terms

Name	Meaning
Inside local	Name of the inside source address before translation
Outside local	Name of the destination host before translation
Inside global	Name of the inside host after translation
Outside global	Name of the outside destination host after translation

How NAT Works

Now it's time to look at how this whole NAT thing works. I'm going to start by using Figure 8.11 to describe the basic translation of NAT.

FIGURE 8.11   Basic NAT translation

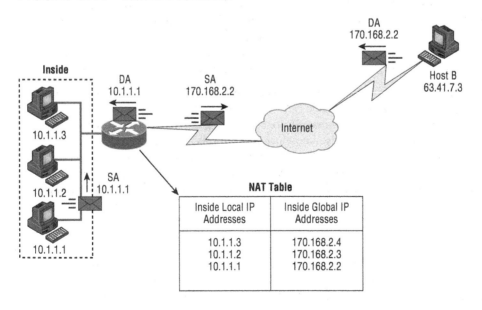

In the example shown in Figure 8.11, host 10.1.1.1 sends an outbound packet to the border router configured with NAT. The router identifies the IP address as an inside local IP address destined for an outside network, translates the address, and documents the translation in the NAT table.

The packet is sent to the outside interface with the new translated source address. The external host returns the packet to the destination host, and the NAT router translates the inside global IP address back to the inside local IP address using the NAT table. This is as simple as it gets.

Let's take a look at a more complex configuration using overloading, or what is also referred to as PAT. I'll use Figure 8.12 to demonstrate how PAT works.

With overloading, all inside hosts get translated to one single IP address, hence the term *overloading*. Again, the reason we have not run out of available IP addresses on the Internet is because of overloading (PAT).

Take a look at the NAT table in Figure 8.12 again. In addition to the inside local IP address and outside global IP address, we now have port numbers. These port numbers help the router identify which host should receive the return traffic.

FIGURE 8.12   NAT overloading example (PAT)

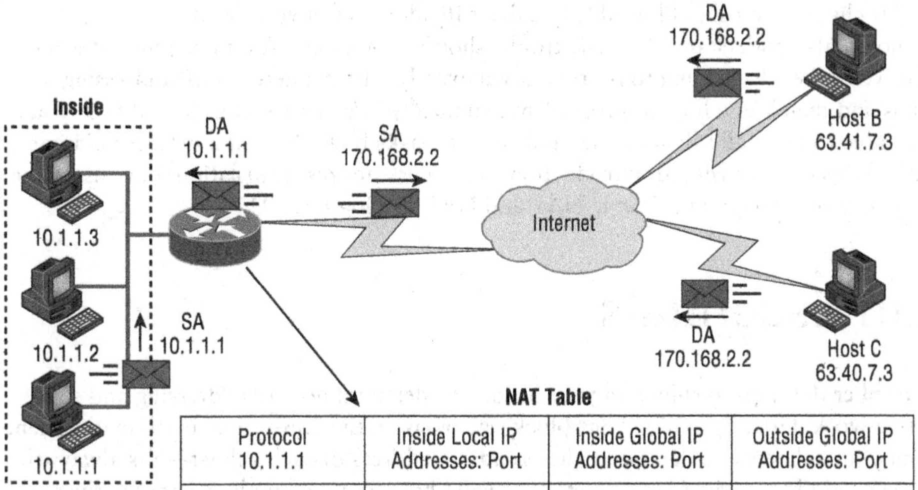

Protocol 10.1.1.1	Inside Local IP Addresses: Port	Inside Global IP Addresses: Port	Outside Global IP Addresses: Port
TCP	10.1.1.3:1492	170.168.2.2:1492	63.41.7.3:23
TCP	10.1.1.2:1723	170.168.2.2:1723	63.41.7.3:23
TCP	10.1.1.1:1024	170.168.2.2:1024	63.40.7.3:23

Port numbers are used at the Transport layer to identify the local host in this example. If we had to use IP addresses to identify the source hosts, that would be called *static NAT*, and we would run out of addresses. PAT allows us to use the Transport layer to identify the hosts, which in turn allows us to use (theoretically) up to 65,000 hosts with one real IP address.

One last thing: We've been discussing translating IP addresses using some type of network address translation. However, using a router or firewall, you can also perform port forwarding, which is translating the port number of a packet to a new destination. The destination may be a predetermined network port (using any IP protocol, but typically TCP or UDP ports) on a host within a private network behind a NAT router. Based on the received port number, a remote host can communicate to servers behind the NAT gateway to the local network.

You're done, the diva has sung, the chicken has crossed the road . . . whew! Take a good break, and then come back and go through the written lab and review questions.

Summary

Did you read Chapter 7 and this chapter and understand everything on the first pass? If so, that is fantastic—congratulations! The thing is, you probably got lost a couple of times—and as I told you, that's what usually happens, so don't stress. Don't feel bad if you have to read each chapter more than once, or even 10 times, before you're truly good to go.

This chapter provided you with an important understanding of IP subnetting. After reading this chapter, you should be able to subnet IP addresses in your head.

You should also understand the basic troubleshooting methods. You must remember the four steps you take when trying to narrow down exactly where a network/IP addressing problem is and then know how to proceed systematically in order to fix it. In addition, you should be able to find valid IP addresses and subnet masks by looking at a network diagram.

I finished this chapter with an introduction to network address translation. I discussed the difference between static and dynamic NAT and NAT overloading (PAT).

Exam Essentials

Remember the steps to subnet in your head.   Understand how IP addressing and subnetting work. First, determine your block size by using the 256-subnet mask math. Then, count your subnets and determine the broadcast address of each subnet—it is always the number right before the next subnet. Your valid hosts are the numbers between the subnet address and the broadcast address.

Understand the various block sizes.   This is an important part of understanding IP addressing and subnetting. The valid block sizes are always 4, 8, 16, 32, 64, 128, and so on. You can determine your block size by using the 256-subnet mask math.

Remember the four diagnostic steps.   The four simple steps for troubleshooting are ping the loopback address, ping the NIC, ping the default gateway, and ping the remote device.

You must be able to find and fix an IP addressing problem. Once you go through the four troubleshooting steps, you should be able to determine the IP addressing problem by drawing out the network and finding the valid and invalid hosts addressed in your network.

Understand basic NAT terminology. You want to know the difference between inside local and inside global. Inside local is before translation, and inside global is after translation. Inside global is defined as a registered address that represents an inside host to an outside network. You should also understand PAT and how it works by using different port numbers to map multiple private IP addresses to a single registered IP address.

Written Lab

You can find the answers to the written labs in Appendix A.

Write the subnet mask, subnet address, broadcast address, and valid host range for question 1 through question 6:

1. 192.168.100.25/30

2. 192.168.100.37/28

3. 192.168.100.66/27

4. 192.168.100.17/29

5. 192.168.100.99/26

6. 192.168.100.99/25

7. You have a Class B network and need 29 subnets. What is your mask?

8. What is the broadcast address of 192.168.192.10/29?

9. How many hosts are available with a Class C /29 mask?

10. What is the subnet for host ID 172.16.3.65/23?

Review Questions

You can find the answers to the review questions in Appendix B.

1. What is the maximum number of IP addresses that can be assigned to hosts on a local subnet that uses the 255.255.255.224 subnet mask?
   A. 14
   B. 15
   C. 16
   D. 30
   E. 31
   F. 62

2. You have a Class A host of 10.0.0.110/25. It needs to communicate to a host with an IP address of 10.0.0.210/25. Which of the following devices do you need to use in order for these hosts to communicate?
   A. A layer 2 switch
   B. Router
   C. DNS server
   D. Hub

3. What is the subnetwork address for a host with the IP address 200.10.5.68/28?
   A. 200.10.5.56
   B. 200.10.5.32
   C. 200.10.5.64
   D. 200.10.5.0

4. The network address of 172.16.0.0/19 provides how many subnets and hosts?
   A. 7 subnets, 30 hosts each
   B. 7 subnets, 2,046 hosts each
   C. 7 subnets, 8,190 hosts each
   D. 8 subnets, 30 hosts each
   E. 8 subnets, 2,046 hosts each
   F. 8 subnets, 8,190 hosts each

5. You receive a call from a user who is complaining that they cannot get on the Internet. You have them verify their IP address, mask, and default gateway. The IP address is 10.0.37.144, with a subnet mask of 255.255.254.0. The default gateway is 10.0.38.1. What is the problem?
   A. Incorrect DNS server address
   B. Invalid subnet mask
   C. Incorrect gateway IP
   D. IP address and mask not compatible

6. If a host on a network has the address 172.16.45.14/30, what is the subnetwork this host belongs to?

    A. 172.16.45.0

    B. 172.16.45.4

    C. 172.16.45.8

    D. 172.16.45.12

    E. 172.16.45.16

7. On a network, which mask should you use on point-to-point WAN links in order to reduce the waste of IP addresses?

    A. /27

    B. /28

    C. /29

    D. /30

    E. /31

8. On which of the following devices are you most likely to be able to implement NAT?

    A. Hub

    B. Ethernet switch

    C. Router

    D. Bridge

9. You have an interface on a router with the IP address of 192.168.192.10/29. Including the router interface, how many hosts can have IP addresses on the LAN attached to the router interface?

    A. 6

    B. 8

    C. 30

    D. 62

    E. 126

10. When configuring the IP settings on a computer on one subnet to ensure that it can communicate with a computer on another subnet, which of the following is desirable?

    A. Configure the computer with the same default gateway as the other computer.

    B. Configure the computer with the same subnet mask as the other computer.

    C. Configure the computer with a default gateway that matches the IP address of the interface of the router that is attached to the same subnet as the computer.

    D. Configure the computer with a subnet mask that matches the IP address of the interface of the router that is attached to the same subnet as the computer.

11. You have an interface on a router with the IP address of 192.168.192.10/29. What is the broadcast address the hosts will use on this LAN?

   A. 192.168.192.15

   B. 192.168.192.31

   C. 192.168.192.63

   D. 192.168.192.127

   E. 192.168.192.255

12. What is the highest usable address on the 172.16.1.0/24 network?

   A. 172.16.1.255

   B. 172.16.1.254

   C. 172.16.1.253

   D. 172.16.1.23

13. A network administrator is connecting two hosts directly through their Ethernet interfaces, as shown in the illustration. Ping attempts between the hosts are unsuccessful. What can be done to provide connectivity between the hosts? (Choose two.)

 Crossover Cable

IP Address: 192.168.1.20   IP Address: 192.168.1.201
Mask: 255.255.255.240   Mask: 255.255.255.240

   A. A crossover cable should be used in place of the straight-through cable.

   B. A rollover cable should be used in place of the straight-through cable.

   C. The subnet masks should be set to 255.255.255.192.

   D. A default gateway needs to be set on each host.

   E. The subnet masks should be set to 255.255.255.0.

14. If an Ethernet port on a router was assigned an IP address of 172.16.112.1/25, what would be the subnet address of this host?

   A. 172.16.112.0

   B. 172.16.0.0

   C. 172.16.96.0

   D. 172.16.255.0

   E. 172.16.128.0

15. Using the following illustration, what would be the IP address of E0 if you were using the eighth subnet? The network ID is 192.168.10.0/28, and you need to use the last available IP address in the range. The 0 subnet should not be considered valid for this question.

   A. 192.168.10.142

   B. 192.168.10.66

   C. 192.168.100.254

   D. 192.168.10.143

   E. 192.168.10.126

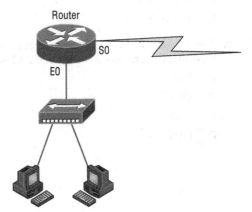

16. Using the illustration in question 15, what would be the IP address of E0 if you were using the first subnet? The network ID is 192.168.10.0/28, and you need to use the last available IP address in the range. Again, the 0 subnet should not be considered valid for this question.

   A. 192.168.10.24

   B. 192.168.10.62

   C. 192.168.10.30

   D. 192.168.10.127

17. If you are forced to replace a router that has failed to the point that you are unable to access its current configuration to aid in setting up interface addresses on the new router, which of the following can you reference for assistance?

   A. The default gateway settings on computers from each subnet that the old router interconnected.

   B. The router's configuration that was periodically cached on the DHCP server.

   C. The router's configuration that was periodically cached on the DNS server.

   D. The new router will auto-configure itself with the correct settings.

18. You have a network with a subnet of 172.16.17.0/22. Which of the following is a valid host address?

   A. 172.16.17.1 255.255.255.252

   B. 172.16.0.1 255.255.240.0

   C. 172.16.20.1 255.255.254.0

   D. 172.16.16.1 255.255.255.240

   E. 172.16.18.255 255.255.252.0

   F. 172.16.0.1 255.255.255.0

19. Your router has the following IP address on Ethernet0: 172.16.2.1/23. Which of the following can be valid host IDs on the LAN interface attached to the router? (Choose two.)

    A. 172.16.0.5

    B. 172.16.1.100

    C. 172.16.1.198

    D. 172.16.2.255

    E. 172.16.3.0

    F. 172.16.3.255

20. You have one IP address provided from your ISP with a /30 mask. However, you have 300 users that need to access the Internet. What technology will you use to implement a solution?

    A. PAT

    B. VPN

    C. DNS

    D. LANs

Chapter

9

Introduction to IP Routing

THE FOLLOWING COMPTIA NETWORK+ EXAM OBJECTIVES ARE COVERED IN THIS CHAPTER:

✓ **2.2 Compare and contrast routing technologies and bandwidth management concepts.**

- Dynamic routing
    - Routing Information Protocol (RIP), Open Shortest
    - Path First (OSPF), Enhanced
    - Interior Gateway Routing Protocol
    - (EIGRP), Border Gateway Protocol (BGP)
- Link state vs. distance vector vs. hybrid
    - Static routing
    - Default route
    - Administrative distance
    - Exterior vs. interior
    - Time to live

IP routing is the process of moving packets from one network to another network using routers. The IP routing process is a super-important subject to understand because it pertains to all routers and configurations that use IP.

Before you read this chapter, you need to understand the difference between a routing protocol and a routed protocol. A *routing protocol* is a tool used by routers to dynamically find all the networks in the internetwork as well as to ensure that all routers have the same routing table. Basically, a routing protocol determines the path of a packet through an internetwork. Examples of routing protocols are Routing Information Protocol (RIP), Routing Information Protocol version 2 (RIPv2), Enhanced Interior Gateway Routing Protocol (EIGRP), Open Shortest Path First (OSPF), and Broder Gateway Protocol (BGP).

Once all routers know about all networks, a *routed protocol* can be used to send user data (packets) through the established internetwork. Routed protocols are assigned to an interface and determine the method of packet delivery. Examples of routed protocols are Internet Protocol (IP) and Internet Protocol version 6 (IPv6).

In this chapter, I'm going to describe IP routing with routers. I will explain, in a step-by-step fashion, the IP routing process. I will also explain static and dynamic routing on a conceptual level, with more details about dynamic routing in Chapter 10, "Routing Protocols."

To find Todd Lammle CompTIA videos and practice questions, please see www.lammle.com.

Routing Basics

Once you create an internetwork by connecting your wide area networks (WANs) and local area networks (LANs) to a router, you need to configure logical network addresses, such as IP addresses, to all hosts on the internetwork so that they can communicate via routers across that internetwork.

In IT, routing essentially refers to the process of taking a packet from one device and sending it through the network to another device on a different network. Routers don't really care about hosts—they care only about networks and the best path to each network. The logical network address of the destination host is used to get packets to a network through a routed network, and then the hardware address of the host is used to deliver the packet from a router to the correct destination host.

If your network has no routers, then it should be apparent that, well, you are not routing. But if you do have them, they're there to route traffic to all the networks in your internetwork. To be capable of routing packets, a router must know at least the following information:

- Destination network address
- Neighbor routers from which it can learn about remote networks
- Possible routes to all remote networks
- The best route to each remote network
- How to maintain and verify routing information

The router learns about remote networks from neighbor routers or from an administrator. The router then builds a *routing table* (a map of the internetwork) that describes how to find the remote networks. If a network is directly connected, then the router already knows how to get to it.

If a network isn't directly connected to the router, the router must use one of two ways to learn how to get to it. One way is called *static routing*, which can be a ton of work because it requires someone to hand-type all network locations into the routing table. The other way is dynamic routing.

In *dynamic routing*, a protocol on one router communicates with the same protocol running on neighbor routers. The routers then update each other about all the networks they know and place this information into the routing table. If a change occurs in the network, the dynamic routing protocols automatically inform all routers about the event. If static routing is used, the administrator is responsible for updating all changes by hand into all routers. Understandably, in a large network, it's common to find that a combination of both dynamic and static routing is being used.

Before we jump into the IP routing process, let's take a look at a simple example that demonstrates how a router uses the routing table to route packets out of an interface. We'll be going into a more detailed study of this process in a minute.

Figure 9.1 shows a simple two-router network. Lab_A has one serial interface and three LAN interfaces.

Looking at Figure 9.1, can you figure out which interface Lab_A will use to forward an IP datagram to a host with an IP address of 10.10.10.10?

By using the Cisco IOS command `show ip route`, we can see the routing table (map of the internetwork) that router Lab_A will use to make all forwarding decisions:

```
Router_A#show ip route
[output cut]
Gateway of last resort is not set
C    10.10.10.0/24 is directly connected, FastEthernet0/0
C    10.10.20.0/24 is directly connected, FastEthernet0/1
C    10.10.30.0/24 is directly connected, FastEthernet0/2
C    10.10.40.0/24 is directly connected, Serial 0/0
```

FIGURE 9.1   A simple routing example

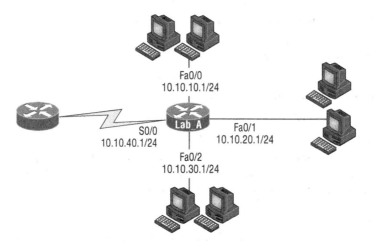

The C in the routing table output means that the networks listed are "directly connected," and until we add a routing protocol—something like RIP, EIGRP, and so on—to the routers in our internetwork, or use static routes, we'll have only directly connected networks in our routing table.

So, let's get back to the original question: By looking at the figure and the output of the routing table, can you tell what Lab_A will do with a received packet that has a destination IP address of 10.10.10.10? If you answered, "The router will packet-switch the packet to interface FastEthernet 0/0, and this interface will then frame the packet and send it out on the network segment," you're right.

Just because we can, let's look at a different example. Based on the output of the next routing table, which interface will a packet with a destination address of 10.10.10.14 be forwarded to?

```
Router_A#sh ip route
[output cut]
Gateway of last resort is not set
C       10.10.10.16/28 is directly connected, FastEthernet0/0
C       10.10.10.8/29 is directly connected, FastEthernet0/1
C       10.10.10.4/30 is directly connected, FastEthernet0/2
C       10.10.10.0/30 is directly connected, Serial 0/0
```

First, you can see that the network is subnetted and that each interface has a different mask. And I have to tell you, you positively can't answer this question if you can't subnet—no way! Here's the answer: 10.10.10.14 would be a host in the 10.10.10.8/29 subnet connected to the FastEthernet 0/1 interface. Don't freak if this one left you staring vacantly. Instead, if you're struggling, go back and reread Chapter 8, "IP Subnetting, Troubleshooting IP, and Introduction to NAT," until you get it. This should then make perfect sense to you.

When the routing tables of all routers in the network are complete (because they include information about all the networks in the inter-network), they are considered *converged*, or in a steady state. This is covered in more detail in Chapter 10.

Now, let's get into this process in more detail.

The IP Routing Process

The IP routing process is actually pretty simple, and it doesn't change, regardless of the size of your network. I'm going to use Figure 9.2 to give you a picture of this step-by-step process. The question I'm asking is this: What happens when Host_A wants to communicate with Host_B on a different network? I'll go through how to answer that question by breaking down the process with headings to make it easier to understand. First, check out Figure 9.2.

FIGURE 9.2   IP routing example using two hosts and one router

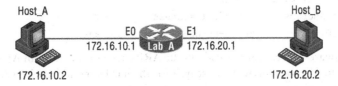

Suppose that a user on Host_A pings Host_B's IP address. Routing doesn't get any simpler than this, but it still involves a lot of steps. Let's work through them.

A packet is created on the host:

1. Internet Control Message Protocol (ICMP) creates an echo request payload (which is just the alphabet in the data field).

2. ICMP hands that payload to IP, which then creates a packet. At a minimum, this packet contains an IP source address, an IP destination address, and a Protocol field with 01h. (Remember that Cisco likes to use *0x* in front of hex characters, so this could look like 0x01.) All of that tells the receiving host whom it should hand the payload to when the destination is reached. In this example, it's ICMP.

The packet is forwarded:

3. After the packet is created, IP determines whether the destination IP address is on the local network or a remote one.

4. Because IP has discovered that this is a remote request, the packet needs to be sent to the default gateway so the packet can be routed to the correct remote network. The Registry in Windows is parsed to find the configured default gateway.

5. The default gateway of host 172.16.10.2 (Host_A) is configured to 172.16.10.1. For this packet to be sent to the default gateway, the hardware address of the router's interface Ethernet 0 (configured with the IP address of 172.16.10.1) must be known. Why? So the packet can be handed down to the Data Link layer, framed, and sent to the router's interface that's connected to the 172.16.10.0 network. Because hosts only communicate via hardware addresses on the local LAN, it's important to recognize that for Host_A to communicate to Host_B, it has to send packets to the Media Access Control (MAC) address of the default gateway on the local network.

 MAC addresses are always local on the LAN and never go through and past a router.

6. The Address Resolution Protocol (ARP) cache of the host is checked to see whether the IP address of the default gateway has already been resolved to a hardware address. If it has, the packet is then free to be handed to the Data Link layer for framing. (The hardware-destination address is also handed down with that packet.) To view the ARP cache on your host, use the following command:

```
C:\>arp -a
Interface: 172.16.10.2 --- 0x3
  Internet Address      Physical Address      Type
  172.16.10.1           00-15-05-06-31-b0     dynamic
```

If the hardware address isn't already in the ARP cache of the host, an ARP broadcast is sent out onto the local network to search for the hardware address of 172.16.10.1. The router responds to that request and provides the hardware address of Ethernet 0, and the host caches this address.

7. After the packet and destination hardware address have been handed to the Data Link layer, the LAN driver is used to provide media access via the type of LAN being used (in this example, it's Ethernet). A frame is then generated, encapsulating the packet with control information. Within that frame are the hardware-destination and source addresses plus, in this case, an Ether-Type field that describes the Network layer protocol that handed the packet to the Data Link layer—in this instance, IP. At the end of the frame is something called a Frame Check Sequence (FCS) field that houses the result of the cyclic redundancy check (CRC). The frame would look something like what I've detailed in Figure 9.3. It contains Host_A's hardware (MAC) address and the hardware-destination address of the default gateway. It does not include the remote host's MAC address—remember that because it's important!

FIGURE 9.3 Frame used from Host_A to the Lab_A router when Host_B is pinged

Destination MAC (Router's E0 MAC Address)	Source MAC (Host_A MAC Address)	Ether-Type field	Packet	FCS (CRC)

8. When the frame is completed, it's handed down to the Physical layer to be placed onto the physical medium one bit at a time. In this example, the physical medium is twisted-pair wire.

The router receives the packet:

9. Every device within the collision domain receives these bits and builds the frame. They each run a CRC and check the answer in the FCS field. If the answers don't match, the frame is discarded. But if the CRC matches, then the hardware-destination address is checked to see if it matches, too (in this example, it's the router's interface, Ethernet 0). If it's a match, then the Ether-Type field is checked to find the protocol used at the Network layer.

10. The packet is pulled from the frame, and what is left of the frame is discarded. The packet is then handed to the protocol listed in the Ether-Type field—it's given to IP.

The router routes the packet:

11. IP receives the packet and checks the IP destination address. Because the packet's destination address doesn't match any of the addresses configured on the receiving router's interfaces, the router will look up the destination IP network address in its routing table.

12. The routing table must have an entry for the network 172.16.20.0 or the packet will be discarded immediately and an ICMP message will be sent back to the originating device with a Destination Unreachable message.

13. If the router does find an entry for the destination network in its table, the packet is switched to the exit interface—in this example, interface Ethernet 1. The following output displays the Lab_A router's routing table. The C means "directly connected." No routing protocols are needed in this network because all networks (all two of them) are directly connected:

```
Lab_A>sh ip route
Codes:C - connected,S - static,I - IGRP,R - RIP,M - mobile,B -
   BGP, D - EIGRP,EX - EIGRP external,O - OSPF,IA - OSPF inter
   area, N1 - OSPF NSSA external type 1, N2 - OSPF NSSA external
type 2, E1 - OSPF external type 1, E2 - OSPF external type 2,
E - EGP,i - IS-IS, L1 - IS-IS level-1, L2 - IS-IS level-2, ia
   - IS-IS intearea * - candidate default, U - per-user static
   route, o - ODR P - periodic downloaded static route


Gateway of last resort is not set

     172.16.0.0/24 is subnetted, 2 subnets
C       172.16.10.0 is directly connected, Ethernet0
C       172.16.20.0 is directly connected, Ethernet1
```

14. The router packet-switches the packet to the Ethernet 1 buffer.

15. Now that the packet is in the Ethernet 1 buffer, IP needs to know the hardware address of the destination host and first checks the ARP cache. If the hardware address of Host_B has already been resolved and is in the router's ARP cache, then the packet and the hardware address are handed down to the Data Link layer to be framed. Let's take a look at the ARP cache on the Lab_A router by using the show ip arp command:

```
Lab_A#sh ip arp
Protocol  Address       Age(min)  Hardware Addr   Type   Interface
Internet  172.16.20.1   -         00d0.58ad.05f4  ARPA   Ethernet1
Internet  172.16.20.2   3         0030.9492.a5dd  ARPA   Ethernet1
Internet  172.16.10.1   -         0015.0506.31b0  ARPA   Ethernet0
Internet  172.16.10.2   12        0030.9492.a4ac  ARPA   Ethernet0
```

The dash (-) means that this is the physical interface on the router. From this output, we can see that the router knows the 172.16.10.2 (Host_A) and 172.16.20.2 (Host_B) hardware addresses. Cisco routers will keep an entry in the ARP table for four hours. But if the hardware address hasn't already been resolved, the router then sends an ARP request out E1 looking for the hardware address of 172.16.20.2. Host_B responds with its hardware address, and the packet and hardware-destination address are both sent to the Data Link layer for framing.

16. The Data Link layer creates a frame with the destination and source hardware address, Ether-Type field, and FCS field at the end. The frame is handed to the Physical layer to be sent out on the physical medium one bit at a time.

Finally, the remote host receives the packet:

17. Host_B receives the frame and immediately runs a CRC. If the result matches what's in the FCS field, the hardware-destination address is then checked. If the host finds a match, the Ether-Type field is then checked to determine the protocol that the packet should be handed to at the Network layer—IP, in this example.

18. At the Network layer, IP receives the packet and checks the IP destination address. Because there's finally a match made, the Protocol field is checked to find out whom the payload should be given to.

19. The payload is handed to ICMP, which understands that this is an echo request. ICMP responds to this by immediately discarding the packet and generating a new payload as an echo reply.

The destination host becomes a source host:

20. A packet is created, including the source and destination IP addresses, Protocol field, and payload. The destination device is now Host_A.

21. IP checks to see whether the destination IP address is a device on the local LAN or on a remote network. Because the destination device is on a remote network, the packet needs to be sent to the default gateway.

22. The default gateway IP address is found in the Registry of the Windows device, and the ARP cache is checked to see whether the hardware address has already been resolved from an IP address.

23. After the hardware address of the default gateway is found, the packet and destination hardware addresses are handed down to the Data Link layer for framing.

24. The Data Link layer frames the packet of information and includes the following in the header:

    - The destination and source hardware addresses
    - The Ether-Type field with 0x0800 (IP) in it
    - The FCS field with the CRC result in tow

25. The frame is now handed down to the Physical layer to be sent out over the network medium one bit at a time.

    Time for the router to route another packet:

26. The router's Ethernet 1 interface receives the bits and builds a frame. The CRC is run, and the FCS field is checked to make sure the answers match.

27. When the CRC is found to be okay, the hardware-destination address is checked. Because the router's interface is a match, the packet is pulled from the frame, and the Ether-Type field is checked to see which protocol at the Network layer the packet should be delivered to.

28. The protocol is determined to be IP, so it gets the packet. IP runs a CRC check on the IP header first and then checks the destination IP address.

> IP does not run a complete CRC the way the Data Link layer does—it only checks the header for errors.

Because the IP destination address doesn't match any of the router's interfaces, the routing table is checked to see whether it has a route to 172.16.10.0. If it doesn't have a route over to the destination network, the packet will be discarded immediately. (This is the source point of confusion for a lot of administrators—when a ping fails, most people think the packet never reached the destination host. But as we see here, that's not *always* the case. All it takes is just one of the remote routers to be lacking a route back to the originating host's network and—*poof!*—the packet is dropped on the *return trip*, not on its way to the host.)

> Just a quick note to mention that when (if) the packet is lost on the way back to the originating host, you will typically see a Request Timed Out message because it is an unknown error. If the error occurs because of a known issue, such as a route that is not in the routing table on the way to the destination device, you will see a Destination Unreachable message. This should help you determine if the problem occurred on the way to the destination or on the way back.

29. In this case, the router does know how to get to network 172.16.10.0—the exit interface is Ethernet 0—so the packet is switched to interface Ethernet 0.

30. The router checks the ARP cache to determine whether the hardware address for 172.16.10.2 has already been resolved.

31. Because the hardware address to 172.16.10.2 is already cached from the originating trip to Host_B, the hardware address and packet are handed to the Data Link layer.

32. The Data Link layer builds a frame with the destination and source hardware addresses and then puts IP in the Ether-Type field. A CRC is run on the frame, and the result is placed in the FCS field.

33. The frame is then handed to the Physical layer to be sent out onto the local network one bit at a time.

The original source host, now the destination host, receives the reply packet:

34. The destination host receives the frame, runs a CRC, checks the hardware destination address, and looks in the Ether-Type field to find out whom to hand the packet to.

35. IP is the designated receiver, and after the packet is handed to IP at the Network layer, IP checks the Protocol field for further direction. IP finds instructions to give the payload to ICMP, and ICMP determines the packet to be an ICMP echo reply.

36. ICMP acknowledges that it has received the reply by sending an exclamation point (!) to the user interface. ICMP then attempts to send four more echo requests to the destination host.

You've just been introduced to "Todd's 36 easy steps to understanding IP routing." The key point to understand here is that if you had a much larger network, the process would be the *same*. In a really big internetwork, the packet just goes through more hops before it finds the destination host.

It's super important to remember that when Host_A sends a packet to Host_B, the destination hardware address used is the default gateway's Ethernet interface. Why? Because frames can't be placed on remote networks—only local networks. So packets destined for remote networks must go through the default gateway.

Let's take a look at Host_A's ARP cache now by using the arp -a command from the DOS prompt:

```
C:\ >arp -a
Interface: 172.16.10.2 --- 0x3
  Internet Address      Physical Address        Type
  172.16.10.1           00-15-05-06-31-b0       dynamic
  172.16.20.1           00-15-05-06-31-b0       dynamic
```

Did you notice that the hardware (MAC) address that Host_A uses to get to Host_B is the Lab_A E0 interface?

Hardware addresses are *always* local, and they never pass a router's interface. Understanding this process is as important to internetworking as breathing air is to you, so carve this into your memory!

Testing Your IP Routing Understanding

I want to make sure you understand IP routing because it's really that important. So, I'm going to use this section to test your understanding of the IP routing process by having you look at a couple of figures and answer some very basic IP routing questions.

Figure 9.4 shows a LAN connected to RouterA, which is, in turn, connected via a WAN link to RouterB. RouterB has a LAN connected with an HTTP server attached. Take a look.

FIGURE 9.4 IP routing example 1

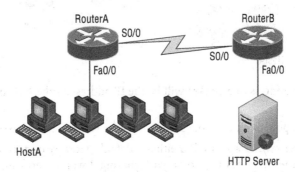

The critical information you need to glean from this figure is exactly how IP routing will occur in this example. Okay—we'll cheat a bit. I'll give you the answer, but then you should go back over the figure and see if you can answer example 2 without looking at my answers:

1. The destination address of a frame, from HostA, will be the MAC address of the Fa0/0 interface of the RouterA router.

2. The destination address of a packet will be the IP address of the network interface card (NIC) of the HTTP server.

3. The destination port number in the segment header will have a value of 80.

That example was a pretty simple one, and it was also very to the point. One thing to remember is that if multiple hosts are communicating to the server using HTTP, they must all use a different source port number. That is how the server keeps the data separated at the Transport layer.

Let's mix it up a little and add another internetworking device into the network and then see if you can find the answers. Figure 9.5 shows a network with only one router but two switches.

What you want to understand about the IP routing process here is what happens when HostA sends data to the HTTPS server:

1. The destination address of a frame from HostA will be the MAC address of the Fa0/0 interface of the RouterA router.

FIGURE 9.5   IP routing example 2

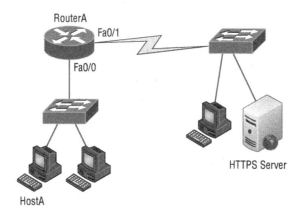

2.   The destination address of a packet will be the IP address of the NIC of the HTTPS server.

3.   The destination port number in the segment header will have a value of 443.

Notice that neither switch was used as either a default gateway or another destination. That's because switches have nothing to do with routing. I wonder how many of you chose the switch as the default gateway (destination) MAC address for HostA. If you did, don't feel bad—just take another look with that fact in mind. It's very important to remember that the destination MAC address will always be the router's interface—if your packets are destined for outside the LAN, as they were in these last two examples.

Static and Dynamic Routing

How does a router send packets to remote networks when the only way it can send them is by looking at the routing table to find out how to get to the remote networks? And what happens when a router receives a packet for a network that isn't listed in the routing table? It doesn't send a broadcast looking for the remote network—the router just discards the packet.

There are several ways to configure the routing tables to include all the networks so that packets will be forwarded. Understand that what's best for one network isn't necessarily what's best for another. Knowing about and being able to recognize the different types of routing will really help you come up with the best solution for your specific environment and business requirements.

Routing convergence is the time required by the routing protocols to update the routing tables (forwarding tables) on all routers in the network.

Looking at Figure 9.6, you can see that we can configure a router with either static or dynamic routing. If we choose static routing, then we have to go to each router and type in each network and the path that IP will use to send packets. However, static routing does not scale well in large networks, but dynamic routing does because network routes are automatically added to the routing table via the routing protocol.

FIGURE 9.6   Routing options

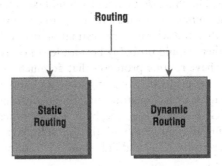

Dynamic routing protocols break up into many different categories or types of protocols, as shown in Figure 9.7. The first split in the dynamic protocol branch is the division of interior gateway protocols (IGPs) and exterior gateway protocols (EGPs). We are going to talk about each protocol and category, but for now the difference between IGP and EGP is interior or exterior routing of an autonomous system (AS).

FIGURE 9.7   Dynamic routing options

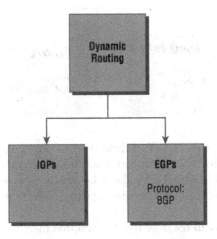

An *autonomous system* is a collection of networks or subnets that are in the same administrative domain. This is another way of saying an administrative domain is within your company's network, and you control or administer all the subnets that are within it.

You control and set the policy for what happens in the network or autonomous system. I hope you can now see that an IGP operates and routes within an AS and an EGP works outside or between more than one AS.

The most popular protocol for an EGP is Border Gateway Protocol (BGP), which is typically used by ISPs or really large corporations. As an administrator of a small to medium network, you'll probably never use BGP. (BGP will be discussed in Chapter 10.)

Now that we have that out of the way, let's talk about all the great things that dynamic routing protocols do for us. The thing that comes to mind first is the amount of time and energy we save configuring routers. We won't have to go to every single router and define for it, with a static route, what and where every destination network is. If that were the only way to configure routing, there would probably be a lot fewer of us interested in doing this for a living. Thankfully, we have routing protocols that do much of the work for us. We still have to know what the routing protocols are going to do and how they will do it, but the protocols will take care of most of the updating and sending information to each other.

That is the end of the EGP branch of the tree, but the IGP branch continues to split out as we go down further. Looking at Figure 9.8, with the IGP split, you can see that there are two primary categories: distance-vector (DV) and link-state (LS) routing protocols.

FIGURE 9.8   DV and LS routing protocols

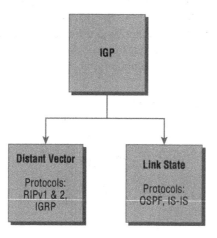

No worries—I'm going to discuss all of these types of protocols in Chapter 10, "Routing Protocols." But in the distance-vector category, for example, we have RIP and Interior Gateway Routing Protocol (IGRP). Under the link-state category are the nonproprietary OSPF and Intermediate System-to-Intermediate System (IS-IS) that were designed to work in larger internetworks.

Now, in Figure 9.9, you can see from the diagram that there is a third category: the hybrid protocol category.

FIGURE 9.9 Hybrid routing

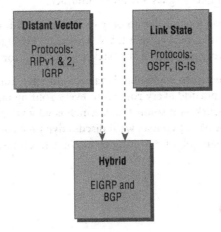

The only protocols under this category are EIGRP and BGP. It is Cisco proprietary (or used to be, but people mostly just run this with Cisco gear) and uses the features of both DV and LS. Now that we have a handle on IP routing, let's move on to Chapter 10 and discuss the IGP routing protocols introduced in this chapter.

Summary

This chapter covered the IP routing process in detail. It's extremely important that you really understand the basics we covered in this chapter because everything that's done on a router typically will have some type of IP routing configured and running.

You learned in this chapter how IP routing uses frames to transport packets between routers and to the destination host. Understanding the process of how packets and frames traverse a network is critical to your fundamental understanding of IP routing.

After I covered the basics of IP routing, I went through some examples to test your understanding and to emphasize the importance of the IP routing fundamentals that you need. I finished the chapter with an introduction to static and dynamic routing and explained IGP and EGP as well as the difference between distance-vector and link-state routing protocols. In the next chapter, we'll continue with dynamic routing by discussing the various dynamic routing protocols.

Exam Essentials

Understand the basic IP routing process.   You need to remember that the frame changes at each hop but that the packet is never changed or manipulated in any way until it reaches the destination device.

Understand that MAC addresses are always local.   A MAC (hardware) address will only be used on a local LAN. It will never pass a router's interface.

Understand that a frame carries a packet to only two places.   A frame uses MAC (hardware) addresses to send a packet on a LAN. The frame will take the packet to either a host on the LAN or a router's interface if the packet is destined for a remote network.

Remember the difference between static and dynamic routing.   Static routing is where you, as the administrator, by hand, add every route into every routing table on every router on the network. This is as much work as it sounds like, which is why we use dynamic routing protocols that do the work for us. Of course, we'll discuss dynamic routing protocols more in the next chapter, but the main job of a routing protocol is to update routing tables.

Written Lab

You can find the answers to the written labs in Appendix A. Write the answers to the following questions:

1.   True/False: RIPv2 is a hybrid routing protocol.

2.   True/False: RIPv1 is a link state routing protocol.

3.   True/False: EIGRP was created by the ISO.

4.   What defines a collection of networks or subnets that are in the same administrative domain?

5.   You need a routing protocol that can be run in a very large network with routers from multiple vendors. What routing protocol would be your best choice?

6.   Which type of routing are you performing if you have to go to each router and type in each network and the path that IP will use to send packets?

7.   You are trying to reach a server on another subnet. What will be the destination hardware address of a frame sent from your host?

8.   You are trying to reach a server on another subnet. What will be the destination IP address of a packet sent from your host?

9.   A server has received a frame from your remote host. What will be the source hardware address of the frame?

10.   A server has received a packet from your remote host. What will be the destination IP address of the packet?

Review Questions

You can find the answers to the review questions in Appendix B.

1. Which is not a routing protocol?
   A. RIP
   B. RIPv2
   C. RIPv3
   D. EIGRP

2. Which of these best describes dynamic routing?
   A. All network addresses must be hand-typed into the routing table.
   B. Only a portion of the network address must be hand-typed into the routing table.
   C. Routing tables are updated automatically when changes occur in the network.
   D. A and B.

3. Which is true regarding dynamic routing?
   A. Static routes are best in large networks and thus better to use than dynamic routing protocols.
   B. Static routes are automatically added to the routing table but dynamic routes must be added by hand.
   C. You must use a DNS and WINS server when configuring dynamic routing.
   D. Dynamic routes are automatically added to the routing table.

4. Which of the following is true for MAC addresses?
   A. MAC addresses are never local on the LAN and always pass through a router.
   B. MAC addresses are always local on the LAN and never go through or past a router.
   C. MAC addresses will always be the IP address of the Fa0/0 interface.
   D. None of the above.

5. What is it called when protocols update their forwarding tables after changes have occurred?
   A. Name resolution
   B. Routing
   C. Convergence
   D. ARP resolution

6. What command would be used to view the ARP cache on your host?
   A. `C:\ >show ip route`
   B. `C:\ >show ip arp`
   C. `C:\ >show protocols`
   D. `C:\ >arp -a`

7. What happens when a router receives a packet for a network that isn't listed in the routing table?

A. It forwards the packet to the next available router.

B. It holds the packet until the address is updated in the routing table.

C. The router will use RIP to inform the host that it can't send the packet.

D. None of the above.

8. Which of the following is not a distance-vector protocol?

A. RIPv1

B. RIPv2

C. OSPF

D. IGRP

9. Which two of the following are link-state protocols?

A. RIPv1

B. RIPv2

C. OSPF

D. IS-IS

E. IGRP

10. Which of the following is a hybrid routing protocol?

A. RIPv2

B. EIGRP

C. IS-IS

D. IGRP

11. What does the acronym EIGRP stand for?

A. Enhanced Interior Gateway Routing Protocol

B. Enhanced Inside Gateway Redundancy Protocol

C. Enhanced Interior Group Reliability Protocol

D. Enhanced Interior Gateway Redundancy Protocol

12. What EGP protocol is used on the Internet?

A. GGP

B. EGP

C. BGP

D. IGP

13. What are the two categories of IGP protocols? (Choose two.)

    A. Link state

    B. Static

    C. Distance vector

    D. EGP

14. What two pieces of information does a router require to make a routing decision? (Choose two.)

    A. Destination network (address)

    B. Destination MAC address

    C. Application layer protocol

    D. Neighbor router

15. Where does a frame have to carry a packet to if it is destined for a remote network?

    A. Default gateway

    B. Neighbor host

    C. Switch

    D. Hub

16. Where along the IP routing process does a packet get changed?

    A. Router

    B. Host A

    C. Destination device

    D. Host B

17. When all routers in a network agree about the path from one point to another, the network is said to be what?

    A. Dynamic

    B. Static

    C. Happy

    D. Converged

18. What type of request must a client send if it does not know the destination MAC address?

    A. ARP broadcast

    B. Multicast

    C. ICMP redirect

    D. Reverse ARP

19. You need to perform maintenance on a router in your corporate office. It is important that the network does not go down. What can you do to accomplish your goal?

   A. Configure BGP on the router.

   B. Implement NAT on the router.

   C. Configure on the router a static route that temporarily reroutes traffic through another office.

   D. Implement convergence on the router.

20. When are you most likely to see a Request Timed Out message?

   A. When an unknown error has occurred

   B. When you have used the `arp -a` command incorrectly

   C. When a known error has occurred

   D. When you are using a hybrid routing protocol

Chapter

10

Routing Protocols

THE FOLLOWING COMPTIA NETWORK+ EXAM OBJECTIVES ARE COVERED IN THIS CHAPTER:

✓ **2.1 Compare and contrast various devises, their features and their appropriate placement on the network.**

- Layer 3 capable switch
- Router

✓ **2.2 Compare and contrast routing technologies and bandwidth management concepts.**

- Dynamic routing
    - Routing Information Protocol (RIP), Open Shortest Path First (OSPF), Enhanced Interior Gateway Routing Protocol (EIGRP), Border Gateway Protocol (BGP)
- Link state vs. distance vector vs. hybrid
    - Static routing
    - Default route
    - Administrative distance
    - Exterior vs. interior
    - Time to live
- IPv6 concepts
    - Tunneling
    - Dual stack
    - Shorthand notation
    - Router advertisement
    - Stateless address autoconfiguration (SLAAC)

✓ **2.3 Given a scenario, configure and deploy common Ethernet switching features.**

- Neighbor Discovery Protocol

Routing protocols are critical to a network's design. This chapter focuses on dynamic routing protocols. Dynamic routing protocols run only on routers that use them in order to discover networks and update their routing tables. Using dynamic routing is easier on you, the system administrator, than using the labor-intensive, manually achieved static routing method, but it'll cost you in terms of router CPU processes and bandwidth on the network links.

The source of the increased bandwidth usage and CPU cycles is the operation of the dynamic routing protocol itself. A router running a dynamic routing protocol shares routing information with its neighboring routers, and it requires additional CPU cycles and additional bandwidth to accomplish that.

In this chapter, I'll give you all the basic information you need to know about routing protocols so you can choose the correct one for each network you work on or design.

To find Todd Lammle CompTIA videos and practice questions, please see www.lammle.com.

Routing Protocol Basics

Because getting a solid visual can really help people learn, I'll get you started by combining the last few figures used in Chapter 9, "Introduction to IP Routing." This way, you can get the big picture and really understand how routing works. Figure 10.1 shows the complete routing tree that I broke up piece by piece at the end of Chapter 9.

As I touched on in Chapter 9, two types of routing protocols are used in internetworks: interior gateway protocols (IGPs) and exterior gateway protocols (EGPs). IGPs are used to exchange routing information with routers in the same *autonomous system (AS)*. An AS is a collection of networks under a common administrative domain, which simply means that all routers sharing the same routing table information are in the same AS. EGPs are used to communicate between multiple ASs. A nice example of an EGP would be Border Gateway Protocol (BGP).

There are a few key points about routing protocols that I think it would be a good idea to talk over before getting deeper into the specifics of each one. First on the list is something known as an administrative distance.

FIGURE 10.1   Routing flow tree

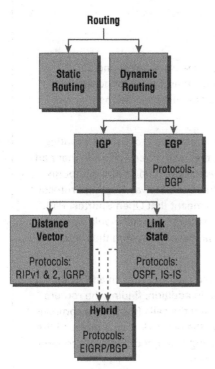

Administrative Distances

The *administrative distance (AD)* is used to rate the trustworthiness of routing information received on one router from its neighboring router. An AD is represented as an integer from 0 to 255, where 0 equals the most trusted route and 255 the least. A value of 255 essentially means, "No traffic is allowed to be passed via this route."

If a router receives two updates listing the same remote network, the first thing the router checks is the AD. If one of the advertised routes has a lower AD than the other, the route with the lower AD is the one that will get placed in the routing table.

If both advertised routes to the same network have the same AD, then routing protocol metrics like *hop count* or the amount of bandwidth on the lines will be used to find the best path to the remote network. And as it was with the AD, the advertised route with the lowest metric will be placed in the routing table. But if both advertised routes have the same AD as well as the same metrics, then the routing protocol will *load-balance* to the remote network. To perform load balancing, a router will send packets down each link to test for the best one.

Real World Scenario

Why Not Just Turn On All Routing Protocols?

Many customers have hired me because all their employees were complaining about a slow, intermittent network that had a lot of latency. Many times, I have found that the administrators did not truly understand routing protocols and just enabled them all on every router.

This may sound laughable, but it is true. When an administrator tried to disable a routing protocol, such as the Routing Information Protocol (RIP), they would receive a call that part of the network was not working. First, understand that because of default ADs, although every routing protocol was enabled, only the Enhanced Interior Gateway Routing Protocol (EIGRP) would show up in most of the routing tables. This meant that Open Shortest Path First (OSPF), Intermediate System-to-Intermediate System (IS-IS), and RIP would be running in the background but just using up bandwidth and CPU processes, slowing the routers almost to a crawl.

Disabling all the routing protocols except EIGRP (this would only work on an all-Cisco router network) improved the network at least 30 percent. In addition, finding the routers that were configured only for RIP and enabling EIGRP solved the calls from users complaining that the network was down when RIP was disabled on the network. Last, I replaced the core routers with better routers with more memory, enabling faster, more efficient routing and raising the network response time to a total of 50 percent.

Table 10.1 shows the default ADs that a router uses to decide which route to take to a remote network.

Understand that if a network is directly connected, the router will always use the interface connected to that network. Also good to know is that if you configure a static route, the router will believe that route to be the preferred one over any other routes it learns about dynamically. You can change the ADs of static routes, but by default, they have an AD of 1. That's only one place above zero, so you can see why a static route's default AD will always be considered the best by the router.

This means that if you have a static route, a RIP-advertised route, and an EIGRP-advertised route listing the same network, then by default, the router will always use the static route unless you change the AD of the static route.

TABLE 10.1   Default administrative distances

Route Source	Default AD
Connected interface	0
Static route	1
External BGP	20
Internal EIGRP	90
IGRP	100
OSPF	110
IS-IS	115
RIP	120
External EIGRP	170
Internal BGP	200
Unknown	255 (this route will never be used)

Classes of Routing Protocols

The three classes of routing protocols introduced in Chapter 9, and shown in Figure 10.1, are as follows:

Distance Vector   The *distance-vector protocols* find the best path to a remote network by judging—you guessed it—distance. Each time a packet goes through a router, it equals something we call a *hop*, and the route with the fewest hops to the destination network will be chosen as the best path to it. The vector indicates the direction to the remote network. RIP, RIPv2, and Interior Gateway Routing Protocol (IGRP) are distance-vector routing protocols. These protocols send the entire routing table to all directly connected neighbors.

Link State   Using *link-state protocols*, also called *shortest path first protocols*, the routers each create three separate tables. One of these tables keeps track of directly attached neighbors, one determines the topology of the entire internetwork, and one is used as the actual routing table. Link-state routers know more about the internetwork than any distance-vector routing protocol. OSPF and IS-IS are IP routing protocols that are completely link state. Link-state protocols send updates containing the state of their own links to all other routers on the network.

Hybrid   A *hybrid protocol* uses aspects of both distance vector and link state, and formerly, EIGRP was the only one you needed to understand to meet the Network+ objectives. But now, BGP is also listed as a hybrid routing protocol because of its capability to work as an EGP and be used in supersized internetworks internally. When deployed in this way, it's called internal BGP, or iBGP, but understand that it's still most commonly utilized as an EGP.

I also want you to understand that there's no one set way of configuring routing protocols for use in every situation because this really needs to be done on a case-by-case basis. Even though all of this might seem a little intimidating, if you understand how each of the different routing protocols works, I promise you'll be capable of making good, solid decisions that will truly meet the individual needs of any business!

Distance-Vector Routing Protocols

Okay, the distance-vector routing algorithm passes its complete routing table contents to neighboring routers, which then combine the received routing table entries with their own routing tables to complete and update their individual routing tables. This is called *routing by rumor* because a router receiving an update from a neighbor router believes the information about remote networks without verifying for itself if the news is actually correct.

It's possible to have a network that has multiple links to the same remote network, and if that's the case, the AD of each received update is checked first. As I said, if the AD is the same, the protocol will then have to use other metrics to determine the best path to use to get to that remote network.

Distance vector uses only hop count to determine the best path to a network. If a router finds more than one link with the same hop count to the same remote network, it will automatically perform what's known as *round-robin load balancing*.

It's important to understand what a distance-vector routing protocol does when it starts up. In Figure 10.2, the four routers start off with only their directly connected networks in their routing table. After a distance-vector routing protocol is started on each router, the routing tables are then updated with all route information gathered from neighbor routers.

As you can see in Figure 10.2, each router only has the directly connected networks in its routing table. Also notice that their hop count is zero in every case. Each router sends its complete routing table, which includes the network number, exit interface, and hop count to the network, out to each active interface.

Now, in Figure 10.3, the routing tables are complete because they include information about all the networks in the internetwork. They are considered *converged*. The hop count for every directly connected network remains zero, but notice that the hop count is incremented by one each time the path completely passes through a router. So, for router 2621A, the path to the 172.16.10.0 network still has a hop count of zero, but the hop count for the path to network 172.16.20.0 is one. The hop count to networks 172.16.30.0 and 172.16.40.0 increases to two, and so on. Usually, data transmission will cease while routers are converging—a good reason in favor of fast convergence time! In fact, one of the main problems with RIP is its slow convergence time.

FIGURE 10.2   The internetwork with distance-vector routing

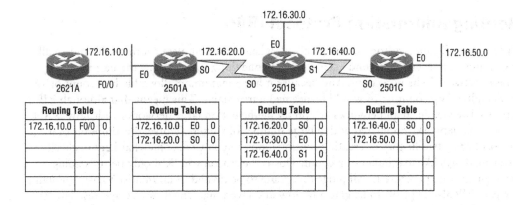

Routing Table		
172.16.10.0	F0/0	0

Routing Table		
172.16.10.0	E0	0
172.16.20.0	S0	0

Routing Table		
172.16.20.0	S0	0
172.16.30.0	E0	0
172.16.40.0	S1	0

Routing Table		
172.16.40.0	S0	0
172.16.50.0	E0	0

FIGURE 10.3   Converged routing tables

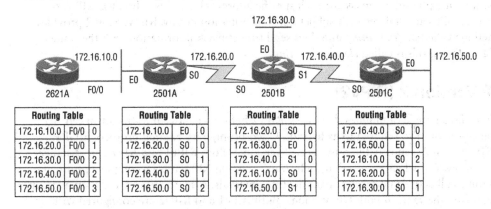

Routing Table		
172.16.10.0	F0/0	0
172.16.20.0	F0/0	1
172.16.30.0	F0/0	2
172.16.40.0	F0/0	2
172.16.50.0	F0/0	3

Routing Table		
172.16.10.0	E0	0
172.16.20.0	S0	0
172.16.30.0	S0	1
172.16.40.0	S0	1
172.16.50.0	S0	2

Routing Table		
172.16.20.0	S0	0
172.16.30.0	E0	0
172.16.40.0	S1	0
172.16.10.0	S0	1
172.16.50.0	S1	1

Routing Table		
172.16.40.0	S0	0
172.16.50.0	E0	0
172.16.10.0	S0	2
172.16.20.0	S0	1
172.16.30.0	S0	1

As you can see in Figure 10.3, once all the routers have converged, the routing table in each router keeps information about three important things:

- The remote network number
- The interface that the router will use to send packets to reach that particular network
- The hop count, or metric, to the network

Remember! Routing convergence time is the time required by protocols to update their forwarding tables after changes have occurred.

Let's start discussing dynamic routing protocols with one of the oldest routing protocols that is still in existence today.

Routing Information Protocol (RIP)

RIP is a true distance-vector routing protocol. It sends the complete routing table out to all active interfaces every 30 seconds. RIP uses only one thing to determine the best way to a remote network—the hop count. And because it has a maximum allowable hop count of 15 by default, a hop count of 16 would be deemed unreachable. This means that although RIP works fairly well in small networks, it's pretty inefficient on large networks with slow WAN links or on networks populated with a large number of routers. Worse, this dinosaur of a protocol has a bad history of creating routing loops, which were somewhat kept in check by using things like maximum hop count. This is the reason why RIP only permits going through 15 routers before it will judge that route to be invalid. If all that isn't nasty enough for you, RIP also happens to be glacially slow at converging, which can easily cause latency in your network!

RIP version 1 uses only *classful routing*, which means that all devices in the network must use the same subnet mask for each specific address class. This is because RIP version 1 doesn't send updates with subnet mask information in tow. RIP version 2 provides something called *prefix routing* and does send subnet mask information with the route updates. Doing this is called *classless routing*.

RIP Version 2 (RIPv2)

Let's spend a couple of minutes discussing RIPv2 before we move into the advanced distance-vector (also referred to as hybrid), Cisco-proprietary routing protocol EIGRP.

RIP version 2 is mostly the same as RIP version 1. Both RIPv1 and RIPv2 are distance-vector protocols, which means that each router running RIP sends its complete routing tables out to all active interfaces at periodic time intervals. Also, the timers and loop avoidance schemes are the same in both RIP versions. Both RIPv1 and RIPv2 are configured with classful addressing (but RIPv2 is considered classless because subnet information is sent with each route update), and both have the same AD (120).

But there are some important differences that make RIPv2 more scalable than RIPv1. And I've got to add a word of advice here before we move on: I'm definitely not advocating using RIP of either version in your network. But because RIP is an open standard, you can use RIP with any brand of router. You can also use OSPF because OSPF is an open standard as well.

Table 10.2 discusses the differences between RIPv1 and RIPv2.

RIPv2, unlike RIPv1, is a classless routing protocol (even though it is configured as classful, like RIPv1), which means that it sends subnet mask information along with the route updates. By sending the subnet mask information with the updates, RIPv2 can support variable-length subnet masks (VLSMs), which are described in the next section; in addition, network boundaries are summarized.

TABLE 10.2   RIPv1 vs. RIPv2

RIPv1	RIPv2
Distance vector	Distance vector
Maximum hop count of 15	Maximum hop count of 15
Classful	Classless
Broadcast based	Uses multicast 224.0.0.9
No support for VLSM	Supports VLSM networks
No authentication	Allows for MD5 authentication
No support for discontiguous networks	Supports discontiguous networks (covered in the next section, "VLSM and Discontiguous Networks")

VLSMs and Discontiguous Networks

VLSMs allow classless routing, meaning that the routing protocol sends subnet-mask information with the route updates. The reason it's good to do this is to save address space. If we didn't use a routing protocol that supports VLSMs, then every router interface, every node (PC, printer, server, and so on), would have to use the same subnet mask.

As the name suggests, with VLSMs we can have different subnet masks for different router interfaces. Check out Figure 10.4 to see an example of why classful network designs are inefficient.

Looking at this figure, you'll notice that we have two routers, each with two LANs and connected together with a WAN serial link. In a typical classful network design example (RIP or RIPv2 routing protocol), you could subnet a network like this:

192.168.10.0 = Network

255.255.255.240 (/28) = Mask

Our subnets would be (you know this part, right?) 0, 16, 32, 48, 64, 80, and so on. This allows us to assign 16 subnets to our internetwork. But how many hosts would be available on each network? Well, as you probably know by now, each subnet provides only 14 hosts. This means that with a /28 mask, each LAN can support 14 valid hosts—one LAN requires 25 addresses, so a /28 mask doesn't provide enough addresses for the hosts in that LAN! Moreover, the point-to-point WAN link also would consume 14 addresses when only 2 are required. It's too bad we can't just nick some valid hosts from that WAN link and give them to our LANs.

FIGURE 10.4   Typical classful network

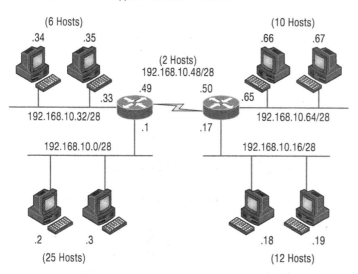

All hosts and router interfaces have the same subnet mask—again, this is called classful routing. And if we want this network to be more efficient, we definitely need to add different masks to each router interface.

But there's still another problem—the link between the two routers will never use more than two valid hosts! This wastes valuable IP address space, and it's the big reason I'm talking to you about VLSM networking.

Now let's take Figure 10.4 and use a classless design, which will become the new network shown in Figure 10.5. In the previous example, we wasted address space—one LAN didn't have enough addresses because every router interface and host used the same subnet mask. Not so good.

What would be good is to provide only the needed number of hosts on each router interface, meaning VLSMs. Remember that if a "classful routed network" requires that all subnet masks be the same length, then it follows that a "classless routed network" would allow us to use variable-length subnet masks (VLSMs).

So, if we use a /30 on our WAN links and a /27, /28, and /29 on our LANs, we'll get 2 hosts per WAN interface and 30, 14, and 6 hosts per LAN interface—nice! This makes a huge difference—not only can we get just the right number of hosts on each LAN, we still have room to add more WANs and LANs using this same network.

Remember, in order to implement a VLSM design on your network, you need to have a routing protocol that sends subnet-mask information with the route updates. This would be RIPv2, EIGRP, or OSPF. RIPv1 and IGRP will not work in classless networks and are considered classful routing protocols.

FIGURE 10.5 Classless network design

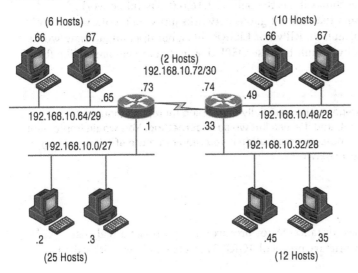

By using a VLSM design, you do not necessarily make your network run better, but you can save a lot of IP addresses.

Now, what's a discontiguous network? It's one that has two or more subnetworks of a classful network connected together by different classful networks. Figure 10.6 displays a typical discontiguous network.

FIGURE 10.6 A discontiguous network

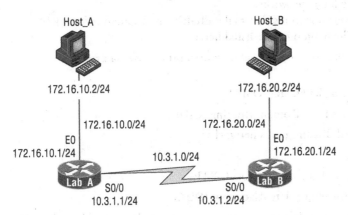

The subnets 172.16.10.0 and 172.16.20.0 are connected together with a 10.3.1.0 network. By default, each router thinks it has the only 172.16.0.0 classful network.

It's important to understand that discontiguous networks just won't work with RIPv1 at all. They don't work by default on RIPv2 or EIGRP either, but discontiguous networks do work on OSPF networks by default because OSPF does not auto-summarize like RIPv2 and EIGRP.

Route aggregation is essentially combining multiple subnets into one larger subnet, and it's also known as supernetting. You would implement this type of route summarization if you required more efficient routing tables in large networks.

EIGRP

EIGRP is a classless, enhanced distance-vector protocol that possesses a real edge over another older Cisco proprietary protocol, IGRP. That's basically why it's called Enhanced IGRP.

EIGRP uses the concept of an autonomous system to describe the set of contiguous routers that run the same routing protocol and share routing information. But unlike IGRP, EIGRP includes the subnet mask in its route updates. And as you now know, the advertisement of subnet information allows us to use VLSMs when designing our networks.

EIGRP is referred to as a *hybrid routing protocol* because it has characteristics of both distance-vector and link-state protocols. For example, EIGRP doesn't send link-state packets as OSPF does; instead, it sends traditional distance-vector updates containing information about networks plus the cost of reaching them from the perspective of the advertising router. But EIGRP has link-state characteristics as well—it synchronizes routing tables between neighbors at startup and then sends specific updates only when topology changes occur. This makes EIGRP suitable for very large networks.

There are a number of powerful features that make EIGRP a real standout from RIP, RIPv2, and other protocols. The main ones are listed here:

- Support for IP and IPv6 (and some other useless routed protocols) via protocol-dependent modules

- Considered classless (same as RIPv2 and OSPF)

- Support for VLSM/Classless Inter-Domain Routing (CIDR)

- Support for summaries and discontiguous networks

- Efficient neighbor discovery

- Communication via Reliable Transport Protocol (RTP)

- Best path selection via Diffusing Update Algorithm (DUAL)

Another great feature of EIGRP is that it's simple to configure and turn on like a distance-vector protocol, but it keeps track of more information than a distance vector does. It creates and maintains additional tables instead of just one table as distance-vector routing protocols do. To determine the best path to each network, EIGRP uses bandwidth and delay of the line as well as sending reliability, load, and the MTU information between routers, but it only uses bandwidth and delay by default.

These tables are called the neighbor table, *topology table*, and routing table, as shown in Figure 10.7.

FIGURE 10.7   EIGRP tables

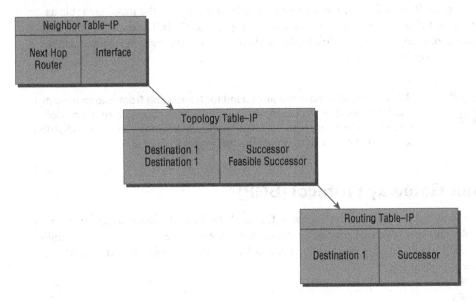

Neighbor Table   Each router keeps state information about adjacent neighbors. When a newly discovered neighbor is learned on a router interface, the address and interface of that neighbor are recorded, and the information is held in the neighbor table and stored in RAM. Sequence numbers are used to match acknowledgments with update packets. The last sequence number received from the neighbor is recorded so that out-of-order packets can be detected.

Topology Table   The topology table is populated by the neighbor table, and the best path to each remote network is found by running Diffusing Update Algorithm (DUAL). The topology table contains all destinations advertised by neighboring routers, holding each destination address and a list of neighbors that have advertised the destination. For each neighbor, the advertised metric, which comes only from the neighbor's routing table, is recorded. If the neighbor is advertising this destination, it must be using the route to forward packets.

Successor (Routes in a Routing Table)   A successor route (think successful!) is the best route to a remote network. A successor route is used by EIGRP to forward traffic to a destination and is stored in the routing table. It is backed up by a feasible successor route that is stored in the topology table—if one is available.

Feasible Successor (Backup Routes)   A *feasible successor* is a path considered a backup route. EIGRP will keep up to six feasible successors in the topology table. Only the one with the best metric (the successor) is copied and placed in the routing table.

By using the feasible distance and having feasible successors in the topology table as backup links, EIGRP allows the network to converge instantly and updates to any neighbor only consist of traffic sent from EIGRP. All of these things make for a very fast, scalable, fault-tolerant routing protocol.

Route redistribution is the term used for translating from one routing protocol into another. An example would be where you have an old router running RIP but you have an EIGRP network. You can run route redistribution on one router to translate the RIP routes into EIGRP.

Border Gateway Protocol (BGP)

In a way, you can think of Border Gateway Protocol (BGP) as the heavyweight of routing protocols. This is an external routing protocol (used between autonomous systems, unlike RIP or OSPF, which are internal routing protocols) that uses a sophisticated algorithm to determine the best route.

Even though BGP is an EGP by default, it can be used within an AS, which is one of the reasons the objectives are calling this a hybrid routing protocol. Another reason they call it a hybrid is because it's often known as a path-vector protocol instead of a distance-vector like RIP.

In fact, it just happens to be the core routing protocol of the Internet. And it's not exactly breaking news that the Internet has become a vital resource in so many organizations, is it? No—but this growing dependence has resulted in redundant connections to many different ISPs.

This is where BGP comes in. The sheer onslaught of multiple connections would totally overwhelm other routing protocols like OSPF, which I am going to talk about shortly. BGP is essentially an alternative to using default routes for controlling path selections. *Default routes* are configured on routers to control packets that have a destination IP address that is not found in the routing table.

Because the Internet's growth rate shows no signs of slowing, ISPs use BGP for its ability to make classless routing and summarization possible. These capabilities help to keep routing tables smaller and more efficient at the ISP core.

BGP is used for IGPs to connect ASs together in larger networks, if needed, as shown in Figure 10.8.

FIGURE 10.8 Border Gateway Protocol (BGP)

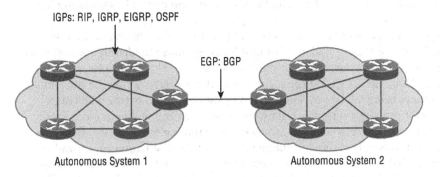

IGPs: RIP, IGRP, EIGRP, OSPF

EGP: BGP

Autonomous System 1   Autonomous System 2

An autonomous system is a collection of networks under a common administrative domain. IGPs operate within an autonomous system, and EGPs connect different autonomous systems together.

So yes, very large private IP networks can make use of BGP. Let's say you wanted to join a number of large OSPF networks together. Because OSPF just couldn't scale up enough to handle such a huge load, you would go with BGP instead to connect the ASs together. Another situation in which BGP would come in really handy would be if you wanted to multi-home a network for better redundancy, either to a multiple access point of a single ISP or to multiple ISPs.

Internal routing protocols are employed to advertise all available networks, including the metric necessary to get to each of them. BGP is a personal favorite of mine because its routers exchange path vectors that give you detailed information on the BGP AS numbers, hop by hop (called an AS path), required to reach a specific destination network. Also good to know is that BGP doesn't broadcast its entire routing table like RIP does; it updates a lot more like OSPF, which is a huge advantage. Also, the routing table with BGP is called a Routing Information Base (RIB).

And BGP also tells you about any/all networks reachable at the end of the path. These factors are the biggest differences you need to remember about BGP. Unlike IGPs that simply tell you how to get to a specific network, BGP gives you the big picture on exactly what's involved in getting to an AS, including the networks located in that AS itself.

And there's more to that "BGP big picture"—this protocol carries information like the network prefixes found in the AS and includes the IP address needed to get to the next AS (the next-hop attribute). It even gives you the history on how the networks at the end of the path were introduced into BGP in the first place, known as the origin code attribute.

All of these traits are what makes BGP so useful for constructing a graph of loop-free autonomous systems, for identifying routing policies, and for enabling us to create and enforce restrictions on routing behavior based upon the AS path—sweet!

Link-State Routing Protocols

Link-state protocols also fall into the classless category of routing protocols, and they work within packet-switched networks. OSPF and IS-IS are two examples of link-state routing protocols.

Remember, for a protocol to be a classless routing protocol, the subnet-mask information must be carried with the routing update. This enables every router to identify the best route to each and every network, even those that don't use class-defined default subnet masks (i.e., 8, 16, or 24 bits), such as VLSM networks. All neighbor routers know the cost of the network route that's being advertised. One of the biggest differences between link-state and distance-vector protocols is that link-state protocols learn and maintain much more information about the internetwork than distance-vector routing protocols do. Distance-vector routing protocols only maintain routing tables with the destination routes and vector costs (like hop counts) in them. Link-state routing protocols maintain two additional tables with more detailed information, with the first of these being the neighbor table. The neighbor table is maintained through the use of *Hello packets* that are exchanged by all routers to determine which other routers are available to exchange routing data with. All routers that can share routing data are stored in the neighbor table.

The second table maintained is the topology table, which is built and sustained through the use of link-state advertisements or packets (LSAs or LSPs). In the topology table, you'll find a listing for every destination network plus every neighbor (route) through which it can be reached. Essentially, it's a map of the entire internetwork.

Once all of that raw data is shared and each one of the routers has the data in its topology table, the routing protocol runs the Shortest Path First (SPF) algorithm to compare it all and determine the best paths to each of the destination networks.

Open Shortest Path First (OSPF)

Open Shortest Path First (OSPF) is an open-standard routing protocol that's been implemented by a wide variety of network vendors, including Cisco. OSPF works by using the *Dijkstra algorithm*. First, a shortest-path tree is constructed, and then the routing table is populated with the resulting best paths. OSPF converges quickly (although not as fast as EIGRP), and it supports multiple, equal-cost routes to the same destination. Like EIGRP, it supports both IP and IPv6 routed protocols, but OSPF must maintain a separate database and routing table for each, meaning you're basically running two routing protocols if you are using IP and IPv6 with OSPF.

OSPF provides the following features:

- Consists of areas and autonomous systems
- Minimizes routing update traffic
- Allows scalability
- Supports VLSM/CIDR

- Has unlimited hop count
- Allows multivendor deployment (open standard)
- Uses a loopback (logical) interface to keep the network stable

OSPF is the first link-state routing protocol that most people are introduced to, so it's good to see how it compares to more traditional distance-vector protocols like RIPv2 and RIPv1. Table 10.3 gives you a comparison of these three protocols.

TABLE 10.3 OSPF and RIP comparison

Characteristic	OSPF	RIPv2	RIPv1
Type of protocol	Link state	Distance vector	Distance vector
Classless support	Yes	Yes	No
VLSM support	Yes	Yes	No
Auto-summarization	No	Yes	Yes
Manual summari-zation	Yes	No	No
Discontiguous support	Yes	Yes	No
Route propagation	Multicast on change	Periodic multicast	Periodic broadcast
Path metric	Bandwidth	Hops	Hops
Hop-count limit	None	15	15
Convergence	Fast	Slow	Slow
Peer authentication	Yes	Yes	No
Hierarchical network	Yes (using areas)	No (flat only)	No (flat only)
Updates	Event triggered	Route table updates time intervals	Route table updates
Route computation	Dijkstra	Bellman-Ford	Bellman-Ford

OSPF has many features beyond the few I've listed in Table 10.3, and all of them contribute to a fast, scalable, and robust protocol that can be actively deployed in thousands of production networks. One of OSPF's most noteworthy features is that after a network change, such as when a link changes to up or down, OSPF converges with serious speed! In fact, it's the fastest of any of the interior routing protocols we'll be covering. Just to make sure you're clear, convergence refers to when all routers have been successfully updated with the change.

OSPF is supposed to be designed in a hierarchical fashion, which basically means that you can separate the larger internetwork into smaller internetworks called *areas*. This is definitely the best design for OSPF.

The following are reasons you really want to create OSPF in a hierarchical design:

- To decrease routing overhead
- To speed up convergence
- To confine network instability to single areas of the network

Pretty sweet benefits! But you have to earn them—OSPF is more elaborate and difficult to configure in this manner.

Figure 10.9 shows a typical OSPF simple design. Notice how each router connects to the backbone—called area 0, or the backbone area. OSPF must have an area 0, and all other areas should connect to this area. Routers that connect other areas to the backbone area within an AS are called area border routers (ABRs). Still, at least one interface of the ABR must be in area 0.

FIGURE 10.9   OSPF design example

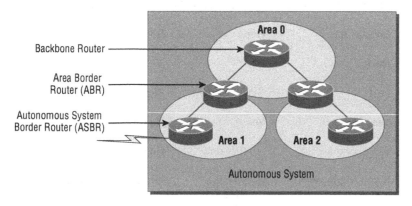

OSPF runs inside an autonomous system, but it can also connect multiple autonomous systems together. The router that connects these ASs is called an *autonomous system border router (ASBR)*. Typically, in today's networks, BGP is used to connect between ASs, not OSPF.

Ideally, you would create other areas of networks to help keep route updates to a minimum and to keep problems from propagating throughout the network. But that's beyond the scope of this chapter. Just make note of it for your future networking studies.

Intermediate System-to-Intermediate System (IS-IS)

IS-IS is an IGP, meaning that it's intended for use within an administrative domain or network, not for routing between ASs. That would be a job that an EGP (such as BGP, which we covered earlier) would handle instead.

IS-IS is a link-state routing protocol, meaning it operates by reliably flooding topology information throughout a network of routers. Each router then independently builds a picture of the network's topology, just as they do with OSPF. Packets or datagrams are forwarded based on the best topological path through the network to the destination.

Figure 10.10 shows an IS-IS network and the terminology used with IS-IS.

Here are the definitions for the terms used in the IS-IS network shown in Figure 10.10:

L1   Level 1 intermediate systems route within an area. When the destination is outside an area, they route toward a Level 2 system.

L2   Level 2 intermediate systems route between areas and toward other ASs.

The similarity between IS-IS and OSPF is that both employ the Dijkstra algorithm to discover the shortest path through the network to a destination network. The difference between IS-IS and OSPF is that IS-IS uses Connectionless Network Service (CLNS) to provide connectionless delivery of data packets between routers, and it also doesn't require an area 0 like OSPF does. OSPF uses IP to communicate between routers instead.

FIGURE 10.10   IS-IS network terminology

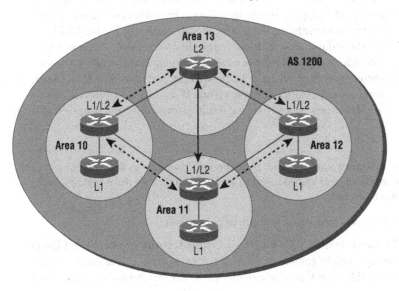

An advantage to having CLNS around is that it can easily send information about multiple routed protocols (IP and IPv6), and as I already mentioned, OSPF must maintain a completely different routing database for IP and IPv6, respectively, for it to be able to send updates for both protocols.

IS-IS supports the most important characteristics of OSPF and EIGRP because it supports VLSM and also because it converges quickly. Each of these three protocols has advantages and disadvantages, but it's these two shared features that make any of them scalable and appropriate for supporting the large-scale networks of today.

One last thing—even though it's not as common, IS-IS, although comparable to OSPF, is actually preferred by ISPs because of its ability to run IP and IPv6 without creating a separate database for each protocol as OSPF does. That single feature makes it more efficient in very large networks.

High Availability

First-hop redundancy protocols (FHRPs) work by giving you a way to configure more than one physical router to appear as if they were only a single logical one. This makes client configuration and communication easier because you can simply configure a single default gateway and the host machine can use its standard protocols to communicate. *First hop* is a reference to the default router being the first router, or first router hop, through which a packet must pass.

So how does a redundancy protocol accomplish this? The protocols I'm going to describe to you do this basically by presenting a virtual router to all of the clients. The virtual router has its own IP and MAC addresses. The virtual IP address is the address that's configured on each of the host machines as the default gateway. The virtual MAC address is the address that will be returned when an ARP request is sent by a host. The hosts don't know or care which physical router is actually forwarding the traffic, as you can see in Figure 10.11.

It's the responsibility of the redundancy protocol to decide which physical router will actively forward traffic and which one will be placed in standby in case the active router fails. Even if the active router fails, the transition to the standby router will be transparent to the hosts because the virtual router, identified by the virtual IP and MAC addresses, is now used by the standby router. The hosts never change default gateway information, so traffic keeps flowing.

Fault-tolerant solutions provide continued operation in the event of a device failure, and load-balancing solutions distribute the workload over multiple devices.

Next we'll explore these two important redundancy protocols:

Hot Standby Router Protocol (HSRP)   This is by far Cisco's favorite protocol ever! Don't buy just one router; buy up to eight routers to provide the same service, and keep seven as backup in case of failure! HSRP is a Cisco proprietary protocol that provides a redundant gateway for hosts on a local subnet, but this isn't a load-balanced solution. HSRP allows you to configure two or more routers into a standby group that shares an IP address and MAC address and provides a default gateway. When the IP and MAC addresses are independent from the routers' physical addresses (on a virtual interface, not tied to a specific interface), they can swap control of an address if the current forwarding and active router fails. But there is actually a way you can sort of achieve load balancing with HSRP—by using multiple VLANs and designating a specific router for one VLAN, then an alternate router as active for VLAN via trunking.

Virtual Router Redundancy Protocol (VRRP)   This also provides a redundant—but again, not load-balanced—gateway for hosts on a local subnet. It's an open standard protocol that functions almost identically to HSRP. I'll comb through the fine differences that exist between these protocols.

FIGURE 10.11   FHRPs use a virtual router with a virtual IP address and virtual MAC address.

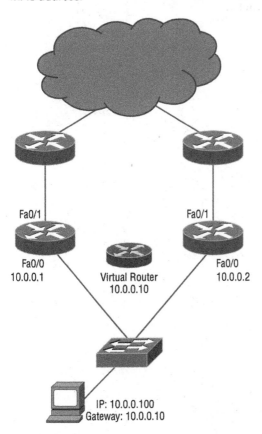

Hot Standby Router Protocol (HSRP)

Hot Standby Router Protocol (HSRP) is a Cisco proprietary protocol that can be run on most, but not all, of Cisco's router and multilayer switch models. It defines a standby group, and each standby group that you define includes the following routers:

- Active router
- Standby router
- Virtual router
- Any other routers that may be attached to the subnet

The problem with HSRP is that with it, only one router is active and two or more routers just sit there in standby mode and won't be used unless a failure occurs—not very cost effective or efficient! Figure 10.12 shows how only one router is used at a time in an HSRP group.

FIGURE 10.12   HSRP active and standby routers

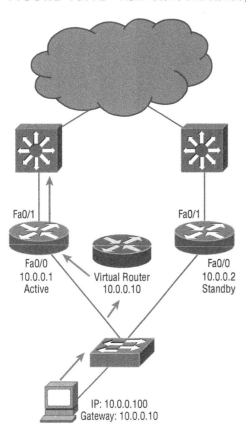

The standby group will always have at least two routers participating in it. The primary players in the group are the one active router and one standby router that communicate to each other using multicast Hello messages. The Hello messages provide all of the required communication for the routers. The Hellos contain the information required to accomplish the election that determines the active and standby router positions. They also hold the key to the failover process. If the standby router stops receiving Hello packets from the active router, it then takes over the active router role, as shown in Figure 10.13.

FIGURE 10.13   Example of HSRP active and standby routers swapping interfaces

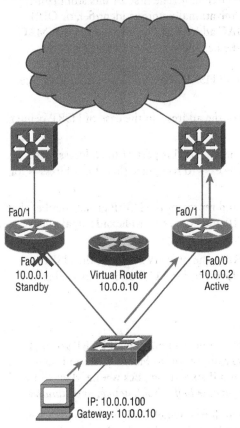

As soon as the active router stops responding to Hellos, the standby router automatically becomes the active router and starts responding to host requests.

Virtual MAC Address

A virtual router in an HSRP group has a virtual IP address and a virtual MAC address. So where does that virtual MAC come from? The virtual IP address isn't that hard to figure out; it just has to be a unique IP address on the same subnet as the hosts defined in the configuration. But MAC addresses are a little different, right? Or are they? The answer is yes—sort of. With HSRP, you create a totally new, made-up MAC address in addition to the IP address.

The HSRP MAC address has only one variable piece in it. The first 24 bits still identify the vendor who manufactured the device (the organizationally unique identifier, or OUI). The next 16 bits in the address tells us that the MAC address is a well-known HSRP MAC address. Finally, the last 8 bits of the address are the hexadecimal representation of the HSRP group number.

Let me clarify all this with an example of what an HSRP MAC address would look like: 0000.0c07.ac0a

- The first 24 bits (0000.0c) are the vendor ID of the address; in the case of HSRP being a Cisco protocol, the ID is assigned to Cisco.

- The next 16 bits (07.ac) are the well-known HSRP ID. This part of the address was assigned by Cisco in the protocol, so it's always easy to recognize that this address is for use with HSRP.

- The last 8 bits (0a) are the only variable bits and represent the HSRP group number that you assign. In this case, the group number is 10 and converted to hexadecimal when placed in the MAC address, where it becomes the 0a that you see.

You can see this MAC address added to the ARP cache of every router in the HSRP group. There will be the translation from the IP address to the MAC address as well as the interface on which it's located.

HSRP Timers

Before we get deeper into the roles that each of the routers can have in an HSRP group, I want to define the HSRP timers. The timers are very important to HSRP function because they ensure communication between the routers, and if something goes wrong, they allow the standby router to take over. The HSRP timers include *hello*, *hold*, *active*, and *standby*.

Hello Timer The hello timer is the defined interval during which each of the routers sends out Hello messages. Their default interval is 3 seconds, and they identify the state that each router is in. This is important because the particular state determines the specific role of each router and, as a result, the actions each will take within the group. Figure 10.14 shows the Hello messages being sent, and the router uses the hello timer to keep network traffic flowing in case of a failure.

This timer can be changed, and people used to avoid doing so because it was thought that lowering the hello value would place an unnecessary load on the routers. That isn't true with most of the routers today; in fact, you can configure the timers in milliseconds, meaning the

FIGURE 10.14 HSRP Hellos

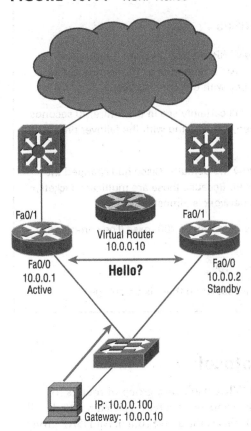

failover time can be in milliseconds! Still, keep in mind that increasing the value will make the standby router wait longer before taking over for the active router when it fails or can't communicate.

Hold Timer   The hold timer specifies the interval the standby router uses to determine whether the active router is offline or out of communication. By default, the hold timer is 10 seconds, roughly three times the default for the hello timer. If one timer is changed for some reason, I recommend using this multiplier to adjust the other timers too. By setting the hold timer at three times the hello timer, you ensure that the standby router doesn't take over the active role every time there's a short break in communication.

Active Timer   The active timer monitors the state of the active router. The timer resets each time a router in the standby group receives a Hello packet from the active router. This timer expires based on the hold time value that's set in the corresponding field of the HSRP Hello message.

Standby Timer   The standby timer is used to monitor the state of the standby router. The timer resets anytime a router in the standby group receives a Hello packet from the standby router and expires based on the hold time value that's set in the respective Hello packet.

🌐 **Real World Scenario**

Large Enterprise Network Outages with FHRPs

Years ago when HSRP was all the rage, and before VRRP, enterprises used hundreds of HSRP groups. With the hello timer set to 3 seconds and a hold time of 10 seconds, these timers worked just fine and we had great redundancy with our core routers.

However, as we've seen in the last few years, and will certainly see in the future, 10 seconds is now a lifetime! Some of my customers have been complaining with the failover time and loss of connectivity to their virtual server farms.

So lately I've been changing the timers to well below the defaults. Cisco had changed the timers so you could use subsecond times for failover. Because these are multicast packets, the overhead that is seen on a current high-speed network is almost nothing.

The hello timer is typically set to 200 msec and the hold time is 700 msec. The command is as follows:

```
(config-if)#Standby 1 timers msec 200 msec 700
```

This almost ensures that not even a single packet is lost when there is an outage.

Virtual Router Redundancy Protocol

Like HSRP, Virtual Router Redundancy Protocol (VRRP) allows a group of routers to form a single virtual router. In an HSRP or VRRP group, one router is elected to handle all requests sent to the virtual IP address. With HSRP, this is the active router. An HSRP group has only one active router, at least one standby router, and many listening routers. A VRRP group has one master router and one or more backup routers and is the open standard implementation of HSRP.

Comparing VRRP and HSRP

The LAN workstations are configured with the address of the virtual router as their default gateway, just as they are with HSRP, but VRRP differs from HSRP in these important ways:

- VRRP is an IEEE standard (RFC 2338) for router redundancy; HSRP is a Cisco proprietary protocol.

- The virtual router that represents a group of routers is known as a VRRP group.

- The active router is referred to as the master virtual router.

- The master virtual router may have the same IP address as the virtual router group.

- Multiple routers can function as backup routers.
- VRRP is supported on Ethernet, Fast Ethernet, and Gigabit Ethernet interfaces as well as on Multiprotocol Label Switching (MPLS), virtual private networks (VPNs), and VLANs.

VRRP Redundancy Characteristics

VRRP has some unique features:

- VRRP provides redundancy for the real IP address of a router or for a virtual IP address shared among the VRRP group members.
- If a real IP address is used, the router with that address becomes the master.
- If a virtual IP address is used, the master is the router with the highest priority.
- A VRRP group has one master router and one or more backup routers.
- The master router uses VRRP messages to inform group members of its status.
- VRRP allows load sharing across more than one virtual router.

Advanced IPv6 Concepts

Before we jump into the coverage of IPv6 routing protocols, we need to discuss some of the operations that are performed differently in IPv6 than in IPv4 and that includes several operations that are radically different. We'll also discuss in the following sections some of the methods that have been developed over the past few years to ease the pain of transitioning to an IPv6 environment from one that is IPv4.

Router Advertisement

A router advertisement is part of a new system configuration option in IPv6. This is a packet sent by routers to give the host a network ID (called a prefix in IPv6) so that the host can generate its own IPv6 address derived from its MAC address.

To perform autoconfiguration, a host goes through a basic three-step process:

1. First, the host needs the prefix information, similar to the network portion of an IPv4 address, to configure its interface, so it sends a router solicitation (RS) request for it. This RS is then sent out as a multicast to all routers (FF02::2). The actual information being sent is a type of ICMP message, and like everything in networking, this ICMP message has a number that identifies it. The RS message is ICMP type 133.

2. The router answers back with the required prefix information via a router advertisement (RA). An RA message also happens to be a multicast packet that's sent to the all-nodes multicast address (FF02::1) and is ICMP type 134. RA messages are sent on a periodic basis, but the host sends the RS for an immediate response so it doesn't have to wait until the next scheduled RA to get what it needs.

3. Upon receipt, the host will generate an IPv6 address. The exact process used (stateless or stateful autoconfiguration or by DHCPv6) is determined by instructions within the RA.

The first two steps are shown in Figure 10.15.

FIGURE 10.15 First two steps to IPv6 autoconfiguration

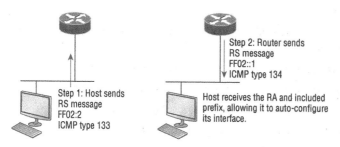

By the way, when the host generates an IPV6 address using the prefix and its MAC address, the process is called stateless autoconfiguration because it doesn't contact or connect to and receive any further information from the other device.

Take a look at Figure 10.16. In this figure, the Branch router needs to be configured, but I just don't feel like typing in an IPv6 address on the interface connecting to the Corp router. I also don't feel like typing in any routing commands, but I need more than a link-local address on that interface, so I'm going to have to do something! So basically, I want to have the Branch router work with IPv6 on the internetwork with the least amount of effort from me. Let's see if I can get away with that.

Aha—there is an easy way! I love IPv6 because it allows me to be relatively lazy when dealing with some parts of my network, yet it still works really well. When I use the command ipv6 address autoconfig, the interface will listen for RAs and then, via the EUI-64 format, it will assign itself a global address—sweet!

FIGURE 10.16 IPv6 autoconfiguration example

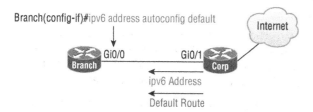

Neighbor Discovery Protocol

The Neighbor Discovery Protocol (NDP) is a protocol in the Internet protocol suite used with Internet Protocol version 6 (IPv6). It operates at the link layer of the Internet model and is responsible for gathering various information required for Internet communication, including the configuration of local connections and the domain name servers and gateways used to communicate with more distant systems.

One of the big changes in IPv6 is the discontinuation of the use of all broadcasts, including the ARP broadcast. Devices use a new process to send to one another within a subnet. They send to one another's *link-local address* rather than the MAC addresses. Even devices that have been assigned an IPv6 address manually will still generate a link-local address. These addresses are generated using the MAC address as is done in stateless auto-configuration; the prefix is *not* learned from the router. A link-local address always adopts a prefix of FE80::/64.

That means that rather than needing to learn a MAC address to send locally, the host needs to learn the link-local addresses of all of the other hosts in its subnet. This is done using a process called neighbor discovery. This is done using neighbor solicitation messages and neighbor advertisement messages. These are both sent to IPv6 multicast addresses that have been standardized for this process.

Neighbor solicitation messages are sent on the local link when a host needs the link-layer address of another node (see Figure 10.17). The source address in a neighbor solicitation message is the IPv6 address of the node sending the neighbor solicitation message. The destination address in the neighbor solicitation message is the solicited-node multicast address that corresponds to the IPv6 address of the destination node. The neighbor solicitation message also includes the link-layer address of the source node.

FIGURE 10.17   IPv6 neighbor discovery: neighbor solicitation message

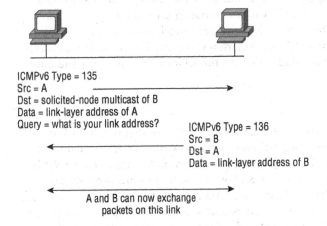

ICMPv6 Type = 135
Src = A
Dst = solicited-node multicast of B
Data = link-layer address of A
Query = what is your link address?

ICMPv6 Type = 136
Src = B
Dst = A
Data = link-layer address of B

A and B can now exchange
packets on this link

The destination node replies by sending a neighbor advertisement message, which has a value of 136 in the Type field of the ICMP packet header, on the local link. The data portion of the neighbor advertisement message includes the link-layer address of the node sending the neighbor advertisement message. After the source node receives the neighbor advertisement, the source node and destination node can communicate.

Tunneling

When tunneling is used as a transition mechanism to IPv6, it involves encapsulating one type of protocol in another type of protocol for the purpose of transmitting it across a network that supports the packet type or protocol. At the tunnel endpoint, the packet is de-encapsulated and the contents are then processed in its native form.

Overlay tunneling encapsulates IPv6 packets in IPv4 packets for delivery across an IPv4 network. Overlay tunnels can be configured between border routers or between a border router and a host capable of supporting both IPv6 and IPv4. Cisco IOS supports the following tunnel types:

- Manual
- Routing encapsulation (GRE)
- 6to4
- ISATAP

Some of the more significant methods are covered in the following sections.

GRE Tunnels

Although not used as an IPv6 transition mechanism, Generic Routing Encapsulation (GRE) tunnels are worth discussing while talking about tunneling. GRE is a general-purpose encapsulation that allows for transporting packets from one network through another network through a VPN. One of its benefits is its ability to use a routing protocol. It also can carry non-IP traffic, and when implemented as a GRE over IPSec tunnel, it supports encryption. When this type of tunnel is built, the GRE encapsulation will occur before the IPSec encryption process. One key thing to keep in mind is that the tunnel interfaces on either end must be in the same subnet.

6to4 Tunneling

6to4 tunneling is super useful for carrying IPv6 data over a network that is still IPv4. In some cases, you will have IPv6 subnets or portions of your network that are all IPv6, and those networks will have to communicate with each other. This could happen over a WAN or some other network that you do not control. So how do we fix this problem? By creating a tunnel that will carry the IPv6 traffic for you across the IPv4 network. Now having a tunnel is not that hard, and it isn't difficult to understand. It is really taking the IPv6 packet that would normally be traveling across the network, grabbing it up, and placing an IPv4 header on the front of it that specifies an IPv4 protocol type of 41.

When you're configuring either a manual or automatic tunnel (covered in the next two sections), three key pieces must be configured:

- The tunnel mode
- The IPv4 tunnel source
- A 6to4 IPv6 address that lies within 2002 ::/16

Manual IPv6 Tunneling

In order to make this happen we are going to have a couple of dual-stacked routers. We just have to add a little configuration to place a tunnel between the routers. Tunnels are very simple. We just have to tell each router where the tunnel is starting and where it has to end up. Let's take a look. The following configuration creates what is known as a manual IPv6 tunnel.

```
Router1(config)#int tunnel 0
Router1(config-if)#ipv6 address 2001:db8:1:1::1/64
Router1(config-if)#tunnel source 192.168.30.1
Router1(config-if)#tunnel destination 192.168.40.1
Router1(config-if)#tunnel mode ipv6ip

Router2(config)#int tunnel 0
Router2(config-if)#ipv6 address 2001:db8:2:2::1/64
Router2(config-if)#tunnel source 192.168.40.1
Router2(config-if)#tunnel destination 192.168.30.1
Router2(config-if)#tunnel mode ipv6ip
```

This will allow our IPv6 networks to communicate over the IPv4 network. Now this is not meant to be a permanent configuration. The end goal should be to have an all-IPv6 network end to end.

6to4 (Automatic)

The following configuration uses what is known as automatic 6to4 tunneling. This allows for the endpoints to auto-configure an IPv6 address where a site-specific /48 bit prefix is dynamically constructed by prepending the prefix 2002 to an IPv4 address assigned to the site. This means the first 2 bytes of the IPv6 address will be 0x2002 and the next 4 bytes will be the hexadecimal equivalent of the IPv4 address. Therefore, in this case 192.168.99.1 translates to 2002:c0a8:6301:: /48. Tunnel interface 0 is configured without an IPv4 or IPv6 address because the IPv4 or IPv6 addresses on Ethernet interface 0 are used to construct a tunnel source address. A tunnel destination address is not specified because the destination address is automatically constructed. It is also possible for each tunnel to have multiple destinations, which is not possible when creating a manual IPv6 tunnel.

```
Router(config)# interface ethernet 0
Router(config-if)# ip address 192.168.99.1 255.255.255.0
Router(config-if)# ipv6 address 2002:c0a8:6301::/48 eui-64
```

```
Router(config-if)# exit
Router(config)# interface tunnel 0
Router(config-if)# no ip address
Router(config-if)# ipv6 unnumbered ethernet 0
Router(config-if)# tunnel source ethernet 0
Router(config-if)# tunnel mode ipv6ip 6to4
Router(config-if)# exit
```

When using automatic 6to4 tunnels, in many cases you will need to reference the tunnel endpoint when creating the neighbor statement (for example, in BGP). When doing so, you can refer to the auto-configured address in the preceding example in three ways in the neighbor command.

```
:: c0a8:6301
:: 192.168.99.1
0:0:0:0:0:0:192.168.99.1
```

To configure a static route to a network that needs to cross a 6to4 tunnel, use the ipv6 route command. When you do so, the least significant 32 bits of the address referenced by the command will correspond to the IPv4 address assigned to the tunnel source. For example, in the following command, the final 32 bits will be the IPv4 address of the tunnel 0 interface.

```
Ipv6 route 2002::/16 tunnel 0
```

ISATAP Tunneling

Intra-Site Automatic Tunnel Addressing Protocol is another mechanism for transmitting IPv6 packets over an IPv4 network. The word *automatic* means that once an ISATAP server/router has been set up, only the clients must be configured to connect to it. A sample configuration is shown here.

```
R1(config)#ipv6 unicast-routing
R1(config)#interface tunnel 1
R1(config-if)# tunnel source ethernet 0
R1(config-if)# tunnel mode ipv6ip isatap
R1(config-if)#  ipv6 address 2001:DB8::/64 eui-64
```

One other thing that may be noteworthy: if the IPv4 network that you are traversing in this situation has a NAT translation point, it will break the tunnel encapsulation that we have created. In the following section, a solution is discussed.

Teredo

Teredo gives full IPv6 connectivity for IPv6 hosts that are on an IPv4 network but have no direct native connection to an IPv6 network. Its distinguishing feature is that it is able to perform its function even from behind network address translation (NAT) devices such as home routers.

The Teredo protocol performs several functions:

- Diagnoses UDP over IPv4 (UDPv4) connectivity and discovers the kind of NAT present (using a simplified replacement to the STUN protocol)

- Assigns a globally routable unique IPv6 address to each host

- Encapsulates IPv6 packets inside UDPv4 datagrams for transmission over an IPv4 network (this includes NAT traversal)

- Routes traffic between Teredo hosts and native (or otherwise non-Teredo) IPv6 hosts

There are several components that can make up the Teredo infrastructure:

Teredo Client   A host that has IPv4 connectivity to the Internet from behind a NAT device and uses the Teredo tunneling protocol to access the IPv6 Internet.

Teredo Server   A well-known host that is used for initial configuration of a Teredo.

Teredo Relay   The remote end of a Teredo tunnel. A Teredo relay must forward all of the data on behalf of the Teredo clients it serves, with the exception of direct Teredo client to Teredo client exchanges.

Teredo Host-Specific Relay   A Teredo relay whose range of service is limited to the very host it runs on.

Dual Stack

This is the most common type of migration strategy. It allows the devices to communicate using either IPv4 or IPv6. This technique allows for one-by-one upgrade of applications and devices on the network. As more and more things on the network are upgraded, more of your communication will occur over IPv6. Eventually all devices and software will be upgraded and the IPv4 protocol stacks can be removed. The configuration of dual stacking on a Cisco router is very easy. It requires nothing more than enabling IPv6 forwarding and applying an address to the interfaces that are already configured with IPv4. It will look something like this.

```
Corp(config)#ipv6 unicast-routing
Corp(config)#interface fastethernet 0/0
Corp(config-if)#ipv6 address 2001:db8:3c4d:1::/64 eui-64
Corp(config-if)#ip address 192.168.255.1 255.255.255.0
```

IPv6 Routing Protocols

Most of the routing protocols we've already discussed have been upgraded for use in IPv6 networks. Also, many of the functions and configurations that we've already learned will be used in almost the same way as they're used now. Knowing that broadcasts have been eliminated in IPv6, it follows that any protocols that use entirely broadcast traffic will go the way of the dodo—but unlike the dodo, it'll be good to say good-bye to these bandwidth-hogging, performance-annihilating little gremlins!

The routing protocols that we'll still use in version 6 got a new name and a face-lift. Let's talk about a few of them now.

First on the list is RIPng (next generation). Those of you who have been in IT for a while know that RIP has worked very well for us on smaller networks, which happens to be the reason it didn't get whacked and will still be around in IPv6. And we still have EIGRPv6 because it already had protocol-dependent modules and all we had to do was add a new one to it for the IPv6 protocol. Rounding out our group of protocol survivors is OSPFv3—that's not a typo; it really is version 3. OSPF for IPv4 was actually version 2, so when it got its upgrade to IPv6, it became OSPFv3.

RIPng

To be honest, the primary features of RIPng are the same as they were with RIPv2. It still is a distance-vector protocol, has a max hop count of 15, has the same loop avoidance mechanisms and uses UDP port 521.

And it still uses multicast to send its updates too, but in IPv6, it uses FF02::9 for the transport address. This is actually kind of cool because in RIPv2, the multicast address was 224.0.0.9, so the address still has a 9 at the end in the new IPv6 multicast range. In fact, most routing protocols got to keep a little bit of their IPv4 identities like that.

But of course there are differences in the new version or it wouldn't be a new version, would it? We know that routers keep the next-hop addresses of their neighbor routers for every destination network in their routing table. The difference is that with RIPng, the router keeps track of this next-hop address using the link-local address, not a global address. So just remember that RIPng will pretty much work the same way as with IPv4.

EIGRPv6

As with RIPng, EIGRPv6 works much the same as its IPv4 predecessor does—most of the features that EIGRP provided before EIGRPv6 will still be available.

EIGRPv6 is still an advanced distance-vector protocol that has some link-state features. The neighbor-discovery process using Hellos still happens, and it still provides reliable communication with a reliable transport protocol that gives us loop-free fast convergence using DUAL.

Hello packets and updates are sent using multicast transmission, and as with RIPng, EIGRPv6's multicast address stayed almost the same. In IPv4 it was 224.0.0.10; in IPv6, it's FF02::A (A = 10 in hexadecimal notation).

Last to check out in our group is what OSPF looks like in the IPv6 routing protocol.

OSPFv3

The new version of OSPF continues the trend of the routing protocols having many similarities with their IPv4 versions.

The foundation of OSPF remains the same—it is still a link-state routing protocol that divides an entire internetwork or autonomous system into areas, making a hierarchy.

Adjacencies (neighbor routers running OSPF) and next-hop attributes now use link-local addresses, and OSPFv3 still uses multicast traffic to send its updates and acknowledgments, with the addresses FF02::5 for OSPF routers and FF02::6 for OSPF-designated routers, which provide topological updates (route information) to other routers. These new addresses are the replacements for 224.0.0.5 and 224.0.0.6, respectively, which were used in OSPFv2.

With all this routing information behind you, it's time to go through some review questions and then move on to learning all about switching in the next chapter.

Shortest Path Bridging (SPB), specified in the IEEE 802.1aq standard, is a computer networking technology intended to simplify the creation and configuration of networks and replace the older 802.1d/802.1w protocols while enabling multipath routing.

Summary

This chapter covered the basic routing protocols that you may find on a network today. Probably the most common routing protocols you'll run into are RIP, OSPF, and EIGRP.

I covered RIP, RIPv2, and the differences between the two RIP protocols as well as EIGRP, and BGP in the sections on distance-vector protocols. We also covered IPv6 routing protocols and some advanced IPv6 operations, including transitional mechanisms such as dual stacking and tunneling.

I finished by discussing OSPF and IS-IS and when you would possibly see each one in a network.

Exam Essentials

Understand the various dynamic routing protocols including RIP, OSPF, EIGRP, and BGP.   RIP is a distance-vector routing protocol. It sends the complete routing table out to all active interfaces every 30 seconds. RIP uses hop count to determine the best path to a remote network. EIGRP is also a distant-vector protocol that uses link-state characteristics to determine the best path to a remote network. BGP is an external protocol that uses a path vector protocol between autonomous systems. OSPF is an open-standard and link-state protocol that uses the Dijkstra algorithm for best path selection.

Be able to distinguish between link state versus distance vector versus hybrid   Link-state protocols use an algorithm to learn more information about the internetwork. Distance-vector protocols use a hop count to determine neighbors. Hybrid protocols will use a combination of distance vector and link state to determine the best path selection.

Know what the Neighborhood Discovery Protocol (NDP) is used for   NDP is used in an IPv6 network to discover various information from neighboring devices.

Remember the differences between RIPv1 and RIPv2.   RIPv1 sends broadcasts every 30 seconds and has an AD of 120. RIPv2 sends multicasts (224.0.0.9) every 30 seconds and also has an AD of 120. RIPv2 sends subnet mask information with the route updates, which allows it to support classless networks and discontiguous networks. RIPv2 also supports authentication between routers, and RIPv1 does not.

Compare OSPF and RIPv1.   OSPF is a link-state protocol that supports VLSM and classless routing; RIPv1 is a distance-vector protocol that does not support VLSM and supports only classful routing.

Written Lab

You can find the answers to the written labs in Appendix A.

1. The default administrative distance of RIP is _____.

2. The default administrative distance of EIGRP is _____.

3. The default administrative distance of RIPv2 is _____.

4. What is the default administrative distance of a static route?

5. What is the version or name of RIP that is used with IPv6?

6. What is the version or name of OSPF that is used with IPv6?

7. What is the version or name of EIGRP that is used with IPv6?

8. When would you use BGP?

9. When could you use EIGRP?

10. Is BGP considered a link-state or distance-vector routing protocol?

Review Questions

You can find the answers to the review questions in Appendix B.

1. Which of the following protocols support VLSM, summarization, and discontiguous networking? (Choose three.)

   A. RIPv1

   B. IGRP

   C. EIGRP

   D. OSPF

   E. BGP

   F. RIPv2

2. Which of the following are considered distance-vector routing protocols? (Choose two.)

   A. OSPF

   B. RIP

   C. RIPv2

   D. IS-IS

3. Which of the following are considered link-state routing protocols? (Choose two.)

   A. OSPF

   B. RIP

   C. RIPv2

   D. IS-IS

4. Which of the following are considered hybrid routing protocols? (Choose two.)

   A. OSPF

   B. BGP

   C. RIPv2

   D. IS-IS

   E. EIGRP

5. Why would you want to use a dynamic routing protocol instead of using static routes?

   A. There is less overhead on the router.

   B. Dynamic routing is more secure.

   C. Dynamic routing scales to larger networks.

   D. The network runs faster.

6. Which of the following is a vendor-specific FHRP protocol?

    A. STP

    B. OSPF

    C. RIPv1

    D. EIGRP

    E. IS-IS

    F. HSRP

7. RIP has a long convergence time and users have been complaining of response time when a router goes down and RIP has to reconverge. Which can you implement to improve convergence time on the network?

    A. Replace RIP with static routes.

    B. Update RIP to RIPv2.

    C. Update RIP to OSPF using link state.

    D. Replace RIP with BGP as an exterior gateway protocol.

8. What is the administrative distance of OSPF?

    A. 90

    B. 100

    C. 110

    D. 120

9. Which of the following protocols will advertise routed IPv6 networks?

    A. RIP

    B. RIPng

    C. OSPFv2

    D. EIGRPv3

10. What is the difference between static and dynamic routing?

    A. You use static routing in large, scalable networks.

    B. Dynamic routing is used by a DNS server.

    C. Dynamic routes are added automatically.

    D. Static routes are added automatically.

11. Which routing protocol has a maximum hop count of 15?

    A. RIPv1

    B. IGRP

    C. EIGRP

    D. OSPF

12. Which of the following describes routing convergence time?

    A. The time it takes for your VPN to connect

    B. The time required by protocols to update their forwarding tables after changes have occurred

    C. The time required for IDS to detect an attack

    D. The time required by switches to update their link status and go into forwarding state

13. What routing protocol is typically used to connect ASs on the Internet?

    A. IGRP

    B. RIPv2

    C. BGP

    D. OSPF

14. RIPv2 sends out its routing table every 30 seconds just like RIPv1, but it does so more efficiently. What type of transmission does RIPv2 use to accomplish this task?

    A. Broadcasts

    B. Multicasts

    C. Telecast

    D. None of the above

15. Which routing protocols have an administrative distance of 120? (Choose two.)

    A. RIPv1

    B. RIPv2

    C. EIGRP

    D. OSPF

16. Which of the following routing protocols uses AS path as one of the methods to build the routing tables?

    A. OSPF

    B. IS-IS

    C. BGP

    D. RIP

    E. EIGRP

17. Which IPv6 routing protocol uses UDP port 521?

    A. RIPng

    B. EIGRPv6

    C. OSPFv3

    D. IS-IS

18. What EIGRP information is held in RAM and maintained through the usage of Hello and update packets? (Select all that apply.)

    A. DUAL table

    B. Neighbor table

    C. Topology table

    D. Successor route

19. Which is true regarding EIGRP successor routes?

    A. Successor routes are saved in the neighbor table.

    B. Successor routes are stored in the DUAL table.

    C. Successor routes are used only if the primary route fails.

    D. A successor route is used by EIGRP to forward traffic to a destination.

20. Which of the following uses only hop count as a metric to find the best path to a remote network?

    A. RIP

    B. EIGRP

    C. OSPF

    D. BGP

Chapter 11

Switching and Virtual LANs

THE FOLLOWING COMPTIA NETWORK+ EXAM OBJECTIVES ARE COVERED IN THIS CHAPTER:

✓ **2.1 Compare and contrast various devices, their features, and their appropriate placement on the network.**

- Layer 2 switch
- Bridge

✓ **2.3 Given a scenario, configure and deploy common Ethernet switching features.**

- Data virtual local area network (VLAN)
- Voice VLAN
- Port configurations
    - Port tagging/802.1Q
    - Port aggregation
    - Link Aggregation Control Protocol (LACP)
- Duplex
- Speed
- Flow control
- Port mirroring
- Port security
- Jumbo frames
- Auto-medium-dependent interface crossover (MDI-X)
- Media access control (MAC) address tables
- Power over Ethernet (PoE)/Power over Ethernet plus (PoE+)
- Spanning Tree Protocol
- Carrier-sense multiple access with collision detection (CSMA/CD)

✓ **5.5 Given a scenario, troubleshoot general networking issues.**

- Considerations
    - Device configuration review
    - VLAN assignment
    - Network performance baselines
- Common issues
    - Collisions
    - Broadcast storm
    - Switching loops
    - Incorrect VLAN

Layer 2 switching is the process of using the hardware addresses of devices on a LAN to segment a network. Because you've got the basic ideas down, I'm now going to focus on the more in-depth particulars of layer 2 switching and how it works.

You already know that switching breaks up large collision domains into smaller ones and that a collision domain is a network segment with two or more devices sharing the same bandwidth. A hub network is a typical example of this type of technology. But because each port on a switch is actually its own collision domain, you can create a much better Ethernet LAN by simply replacing your hubs with switches!

Switches truly have changed the way networks are designed and implemented. If a pure switched design is properly implemented, it will result in a clean, cost-effective, and resilient internetwork. In this chapter, we'll examine and compare how networks were designed before and after switching technologies were introduced.

Routing protocols like RIP, which you learned about in Chapter 10, "Routing Protocols," employ processes for preventing network loops from occurring at the Network layer. This is all good, but if you have redundant physical links between your switches, routing protocols won't do a thing to stop loops from occurring at the Data Link layer. That's exactly the reason Spanning Tree Protocol was developed—to put a stop to loops taking place within a layer 2 switched network. The essentials of this vital protocol, as well as how it works within a switched network, are some of the important subjects that we'll cover thoroughly in this chapter.

And to finish up this chapter, you're going to learn exactly what a VLAN is and how VLAN memberships are used in a switched network as well as how trunking is used to send information from all VLANs across a single link. Good stuff!

To find Todd Lammle CompTIA videos and practice questions, please see www.lammle.com.

Networking Before Layer 2 Switching

Because knowing the history of something really helps with understanding why things are the way they are today, I'm going to go back in time a bit and talk about the condition of networks before switches and the part switches have played in the evolution of corporate LANs by helping to segment them. For a visual of how a typical network design looked before LAN switching, check out the network in Figure 11.1.

FIGURE 11.1   A network before switching

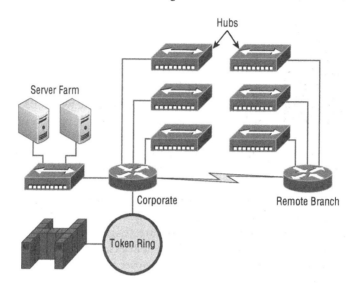

The design in Figure 11.1 was called a *collapsed backbone* because all the hosts involved had to go to the corporate backbone in order to reach any network services—both LAN and mainframe.

Going back even further, before networks like the one shown in Figure 11.1 had physical segmentation devices such as routers and hubs, there was the mainframe network. This type of network comprised mainframe controllers made by IBM, Honeywell, Sperry, DEC, and so on and dumb terminals that connected into the controller(s). Any remote sites were connected to the mainframe with bridges.

And then the PC began its rise to stardom, and the mainframe was connected to an Ethernet or Token Ring LAN where the servers were installed. These servers were usually OS/2 or LAN Manager because this was "pre-NT." Each floor of a building ran either coax or twisted-pair wiring to the corporate backbone, which was then connected to a router. PCs ran an emulating software program that allowed them to connect to mainframe services, giving those PCs the ability to access services from the mainframe and LAN simultaneously. Eventually, the PC became robust enough to allow application developers to port applications more effectively than they ever could before—an advance that markedly reduced networking prices and enabled businesses to grow at a much faster rate.

Moving forward to when Novell rose to popularity in the late 1980s and early 1990s, OS/2 and LAN Manager servers were by and large replaced with NetWare servers. This made the Ethernet network even more popular because that's what Novell 3.*x* servers used to communicate with client-server software.

So basically, that's the story about how the network in Figure 11.1 came into being. But soon a big problem arose with this configuration. As the corporate backbone grew and grew, network services became slower and slower. A big reason for this was that at the same time this huge burst in growth was taking place, LAN services began to require even faster response times. This resulted in networks becoming totally saturated and overwhelmed. Everyone was dumping the dumb terminals used to access mainframe services in favor of those slick new PCs so they could more easily connect to the corporate backbone and network services.

And all this was taking place before the Internet's momentous popularity, so everyone in the company needed to access the corporate network's own, internal services. Without the Internet, all network services were internal, meaning that they were exclusive to the company network. As you can imagine, this situation created a screaming need to segment that single, humongous, and now plodding corporate network, which was connected together with sluggish old routers.

How was this issue addressed? Well, at first, Cisco responded by simply creating faster routers (no doubt about that), but still more segmentation was needed, especially on the Ethernet LANs. The invention of Fast Ethernet was a very good and helpful thing, yet it too fell short of solving that network segmentation need. But devices called *bridges* did provide relief, and they were first used in the networking environment to break up collision domains.

Sounds good, but only so much—bridges were sorely limited by the number of ports and other network services they could provide, and that's when layer 2 switches came to the rescue. These switches saved the day by breaking up collision domains on each and every port—like a bridge—but switches could provide hundreds of ports! This early, switched LAN looked like the network pictured in Figure 11.2.

FIGURE 11.2   The first switched LAN

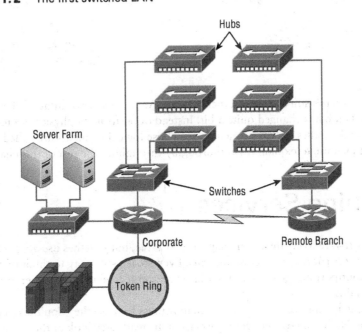

As you can see here, each hub was placed into a switch port—an innovation that vastly improved the network. So now, instead of each building being crammed into the same collision domain, each hub became its own separate collision domain. Yet still, as is too often the case, there was a catch—switch ports were still very new and, therefore, super expensive. Because switches were so cost prohibitive, simply adding a switch into each floor of the building just wasn't going to happen—at least not yet. But thanks to whomever you choose to thank for these things, the switch price tag has dropped dramatically; now, having every one of your users plugged into a switch port is a really good solution, and cost effective too!

So there it is—if you're going to create a network design and implement it, including switching services is a must.

A typical, contemporary, and complete switched network design/implementation would look something like Figure 11.3.

FIGURE 11.3   The typical switched network design

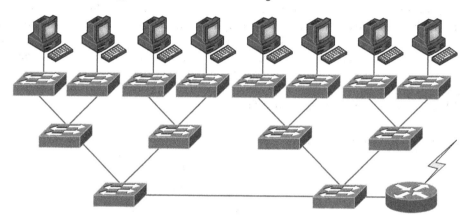

"But wait—there's still a router in there!" you say. Yes, it's not a mirage—there *is* a router in there. But its job has changed quite a bit. Instead of performing physical segmentation, it now creates and handles logical segmentation. Those logical segments are called VLANs, and no worries, I promise to explain them thoroughly throughout the rest of this chapter.

Switching Services

Bridges use software to create and manage a filter table, but switches use *application-specific integrated circuits (ASICs)* to accomplish this. Even so, it's still okay to think of a layer 2 switch as a multiport bridge because their basic reason for being is the same: to break up collision domains.

Layer 2 switches and bridges are faster than routers because they don't take up time looking at the Network layer header information. Instead, they look at the frame's hardware addresses before deciding to forward, flood, or drop the frame.

Switches create private, dedicated collision domains and provide independent bandwidth on each port, unlike hubs. Figure 11.4 shows five hosts connected to a switch—all running 100 Mbps full duplex to the server. Unlike with a hub, each host has full-duplex, 100 Mbps of dedicated communication to the server. Common switchports today can pass traffic at 10/100/1000 Mbps depending on the connected device. By default, the switchports are set to auto-configure.

FIGURE 11.4   Switches create private domains.

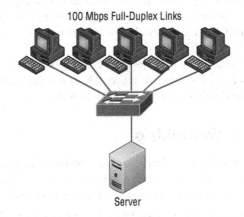

100 Mbps Full-Duplex Links

Server

Layer 2 switching provides the following benefits:

- Hardware-based bridging (ASIC)
- Wire speed
- Low latency
- Low cost

What makes layer 2 switching so efficient is that no modification to the data packet takes place. The device reads only the frame encapsulating the packet, which makes the switching process considerably faster and less error prone than routing processes.

And if you use layer 2 switching for both workgroup connectivity and network segmentation (breaking up collision domains), you can create a flatter network design with more network segments than you can with traditional routed networks.

Plus, layer 2 switching increases bandwidth for each user because, again, each connection (interface) into the switch is its own collision domain. This feature makes it possible for you to connect multiple devices to each interface—very cool.

Coming up, we'll dive deeper into the layer 2 switching technology.

Limitations of Layer 2 Switching

Because people usually toss layer 2 switching into the same category as bridged networks, we also tend to think it has the same hang-ups and issues that bridged networks do. Keep in mind that bridges are good and helpful things if we design the network correctly, keeping our devices' features as well as their limitations in mind. To end up with a solid design that includes bridges, there are two really important things to consider:

- You absolutely have to break up the collision domains properly.

- A well-oiled, functional bridged network is one whose users spend 80 percent of their time on the local segment.

So, bridged networks break up collision domains, but remember that network is really still just one big broadcast domain. Neither layer 2 switches nor bridges break up broadcast domains by default—something that not only limits your network's size and growth potential but can also reduce its overall performance!

Broadcasts and multicasts, along with the slow convergence time of spanning trees, can give you some major grief as your network grows. These are the big reasons layer 2 switches and bridges just can't completely replace routers (layer 3 devices) in the internetwork.

Bridging vs. LAN Switching

It's true—layer 2 switches really are pretty much just bridges that give us a lot more ports. But the comparison doesn't end there. Here's a list of some significant differences and similarities between bridges and switches that you need to keep in mind:

- Bridges are software based, whereas switches are hardware based because they use ASIC chips to help make filtering decisions.

- A switch can be viewed as a multiport bridge.

- There can be only one spanning-tree instance per bridge, whereas switches can have many. (I'm going to tell you all about spanning trees in a bit.)

- Switches have a higher number of ports than most bridges.

- Both bridges and switches forward layer 2 broadcasts.

- Bridges and switches learn MAC addresses by examining the source address of each frame received.

- Both bridges and switches make forwarding decisions based on layer 2 addresses.

Three Switch Functions at Layer 2

There are three distinct functions of layer 2 switching—you need to know these! They are as follows:

- Address learning

- Forward/filter decisions

- Loop avoidance

The next three sections cover these functions in detail.

Address Learning

Layer 2 switches and bridges are capable of *address learning*; that is, they remember the source hardware address of each frame received on an interface and enter this information into a MAC database known as a *forward/filter table*. But first things first—when a switch is initially powered on, the MAC forward/filter table is empty, as shown in Figure 11.5.

FIGURE 11.5 Empty forward/filter table on a switch

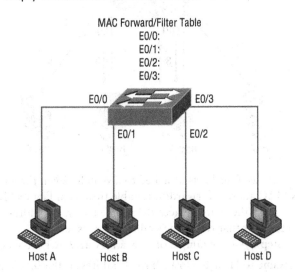

When a device transmits and an interface receives a frame, the switch places the frame's source address in the MAC forward/filter table, which allows it to remember the interface on which the sending device is located. The switch then has no choice but to flood the network with this frame out of every port except the source port because it has no idea where the destination device is actually located.

If a device answers this flooded frame and sends a frame back, then the switch will take the source address from that frame and place that MAC address in its database as well, thereby associating the newly discovered address with the interface that received the frame. Because the switch now has both of the relevant MAC addresses in its filtering table, the two devices can make a point-to-point connection. The switch doesn't need to flood the frame as it did the first time because now the frames can and will be forwarded only between the two devices recorded in the table. This is exactly the thing that makes layer 2 switches better than hubs, because in a hub network, all frames are forwarded out all ports every time—no matter what. This is because hubs just aren't equipped to collect, store, and draw upon data in a table as a switch is. Figure 11.6 shows the processes involved in building a MAC database.

FIGURE 11.6 How switches learn hosts' locations

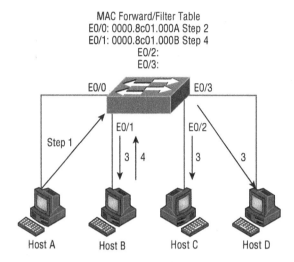

In this figure, you can see four hosts attached to a switch. When the switch is powered on, it has nothing in its MAC address forward/filter table (just as in Figure 11.5). But when the hosts start communicating, the switch places the source hardware address of each frame in the table along with the port that the frame's address corresponds to.

Let me give you a step-by-step example of how a forward/filter table becomes populated:

1. Host A sends a frame to Host B. Host A's MAC address is 0000.8c01.000A, and Host B's MAC address is 0000.8c01.000B.

2. The switch receives the frame on the E0/0 interface and places the source address in the MAC address table, associating it with the port it came in on.

3. Because the destination address is not in the MAC database, the frame is forwarded (*flooded*) out of all interfaces—except the source port.

4. Host B receives the frame and responds to Host A. The switch receives this frame on interface E0/1 and places the source hardware address in the MAC database, associating it with the port it came in on.

5. Host A and Host B can now make a point-to-point connection, and only the two devices will receive the frames. Hosts C and D will not see the frames, nor are their MAC addresses found in the database, because they haven't yet sent a frame to the switch.

Oh, by the way, it's important to know that if Host A and Host B don't communicate to the switch again within a certain amount of time, the switch will flush their entries from the database to keep it as current as possible.

Forward/Filter Decisions

When a frame arrives at a switch interface, the destination hardware address is compared to the forward/filter MAC database and the switch makes a *forward/filter decision*. In other words, if the destination hardware address is known (listed in the database), the frame is only sent out the specified exit interface. The switch will not transmit the frame out any interface except the destination interface. Not transmitting the frame preserves bandwidth on the other network segments and is called *frame filtering*.

But as I mentioned earlier, if the destination hardware address isn't listed in the MAC database, then the frame is flooded out of all active interfaces except the interface on which the frame was received. If a device answers the flooded frame, the MAC database is updated with the device's location—its particular interface.

So by default, if a host or server sends a broadcast on the LAN, the switch will flood the frame out of all active ports except the source port. Remember, the switch creates smaller collision domains, but it's still one large broadcast domain by default.

In Figure 11.7, you can see Host A sending a data frame to Host D. What will the switch do when it receives the frame from Host A?

FIGURE 11.7 Forward/filter table

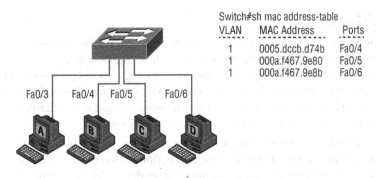

If you answered that because Host A's MAC address is not in the forward/filter table, the switch will add the source address and port to the MAC address table and then forward the frame to Host D, you're halfway there. If you also came back with, "If Host D's MAC address was not in the forward/filter table, the switch would have flooded the frame out of all ports except for port Fa0/3," then congratulations—you nailed it!

Let's take a look at the output of a `show mac address-table` command as seen from a Cisco Catalyst switch (the MAC address table works pretty much exactly the same on all brands of switches):

```
Switch#sh mac address-table
Vlan    Mac Address       Type      Ports
----    --------------    -------   -----
   1    0005.dccb.d74b    DYNAMIC   Fa0/1
   1    000a.f467.9e80    DYNAMIC   Fa0/3
```

1	000a.f467.9e8b	DYNAMIC	Fa0/4
1	000a.f467.9e8c	DYNAMIC	Fa0/3
1	0010.7b7f.c2b0	DYNAMIC	Fa0/3
1	0030.80dc.460b	DYNAMIC	Fa0/3
1	0030.9492.a5dd	DYNAMIC	Fa0/1
1	00d0.58ad.05f4	DYNAMIC	Fa0/1

Now suppose the preceding switch received a frame with the following MAC addresses:

Source MAC: 0005.dccb.d74b

Destination MAC: 000a.f467.9e8c

How will the switch handle this frame? The right answer is that the destination MAC address will be found in the MAC address table and the frame will be forwarded out Fa0/3 only. Remember that if the destination MAC address is not found in the forward/filter table, it will forward the frame out all ports of the switch looking for the destination device.

Now that you can see the MAC address table and how switches add hosts' addresses to the forward filter table, how do you stop switching loops if you have multiple links between switches? Let's talk about this possible problem in more detail.

Loop Avoidance

Redundant links between switches can be a wise thing to implement because they help prevent complete network failures in the event that one link stops working.

But it seems like there's always a downside—even though redundant links can be extremely helpful, they often cause more problems than they solve. This is because frames can be flooded down all redundant links simultaneously, creating network loops as well as other evils. Here are a few of the problems you can be faced with:

- If no loop avoidance schemes are put in place, the switches will flood broadcasts endlessly throughout the internetwork. This is sometimes referred to as a broadcast storm. (In real life, it's often referred to in less polite ways that we're not permitted to repeat in print!) Figure 11.8 illustrates how a broadcast can be propagated throughout the

FIGURE 11.8   Broadcast storm

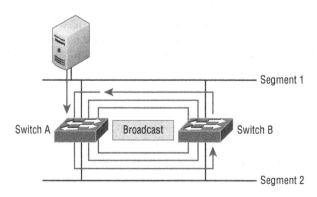

network. Pay special attention to how a frame is continually being flooded through the internetwork's physical network media. One way to test the loop avoidance operations of your switch network is to plug one end of a cable into one port and the other end of the same cable into another port. If loop avoidance is not operational, this should cause a big broadcast storm!

- What you see in Figure 11.8 is that a device can receive multiple copies of the same frame because that frame can arrive from different segments at the same time. Figure 11.9 demonstrates how a whole bunch of frames can arrive from multiple segments simultaneously. The server in the figure sends a unicast frame to another device connected to Segment 1. Because it's a unicast frame, Switch A receives and forwards the frame, and Switch B provides the same service—it forwards the unicast. This is bad because it means that the destination device on Segment 1 receives that unicast frame twice, causing additional overhead on the network.

FIGURE 11.9   Multiple frame copies

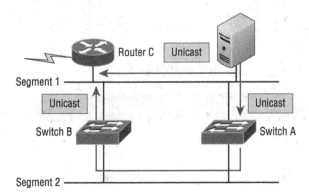

- You may have thought of this one: The MAC address filter table could be totally confused about the device's location because the switch can receive the frame from more than one link. Worse, the bewildered switch could get so caught up in constantly updating the MAC filter table with source hardware address locations that it might fail to forward a frame! This is called *thrashing* the MAC table.

- One of the nastiest things that can happen is having multiple loops propagating throughout a network. This means you end up with loops occurring within other loops, and if a broadcast storm happened at the same time, the network wouldn't be able to perform frame switching at all—it's toast!

All of these problems spell disaster (or something like it) and are decidedly ugly situations that just must be avoided or at least fixed somehow. That's where the Spanning Tree Protocol comes into the game. It was developed to solve each and every one of the problems I just told you about.

Distributed Switching

In a virtual environment such as you might find in many of today's data centers, not only are virtual servers used in the place of physical servers, but virtual switches (software based) are used to provide connectivity between the virtual systems. These virtual servers reside on physical devices that are called hosts. The virtual switches can be connected to a physical switch to enable access to the virtual servers from the outside world.

One of the unique features of these virtual switches is the ability of the switches to span multiple physical hosts. When this is done, the switch is called a distributed switch. This provides connectivity between virtual servers that are located on different hosts, as shown in Figure 11.10.

FIGURE 11.10   Distributed switching

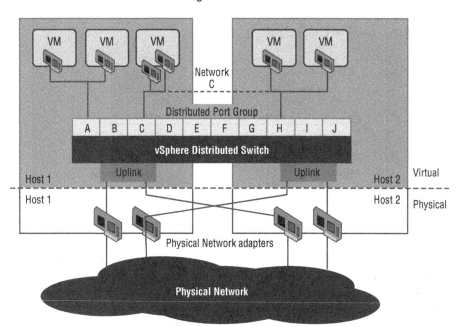

Spanning Tree Protocol

Once upon a time, a company called Digital Equipment Corporation (DEC) was purchased and renamed Compaq. But before that happened, DEC created the original version of *Spanning Tree Protocol (STP)*. The IEEE later created its own version of STP called 802.1D. Yet again, it's not all clear skies—by default, most switches run the IEEE 802.1D version of STP, which isn't compatible with the DEC version. The good news is that there is a newer industry standard called 802.1w, which is faster but not enabled by default on any switches.

To begin with, STP's main task is to stop network loops from occurring on your layer 2 network (bridges or switches). It achieves this feat by vigilantly monitoring the network to find all links and making sure that no loops occur by shutting down any redundant ones. STP uses the *Spanning Tree Algorithm (STA)* to first create a topology database and then search out and destroy redundant links. With STP running, frames will be forwarded only on the premium, STP-picked links. Switches transmit Bridge Protocol Data Units (BPDUs) out all ports so that all links between switches can be found.

STP is a layer 2 protocol that is used to maintain a loop-free switched network.

STP is necessary in networks such as the one shown in Figure 11.11.

FIGURE 11.11 A switched network with switching loops

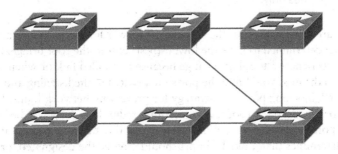

In Figure 11.11, you see a switched network with a redundant topology (switching loops). Without some type of layer 2 mechanism to stop network loops, we would fall victim to the problems I discussed previously: broadcast storms and multiple frame copies.

Understand that the network in Figure 11.11 would actually sort of work, albeit extremely slowly. This clearly demonstrates the danger of switching loops. And to make matters worse, it can be super hard to find this problem once it starts!

Spanning Tree Port States

The ports on a bridge or switch running STP can transition through five different states:

Blocking A blocked port won't forward frames; it just listens to BPDUs and will drop all other frames. The purpose of the blocking state is to prevent the use of looped paths. All ports are in a blocking state by default when the switch is powered up.

Listening   The port listens to BPDUs to make sure no loops occur on the network before passing data frames. A port in listening state prepares to forward data frames without populating the MAC address table.

Learning   The switch port listens to BPDUs and learns all the paths in the switched network. A port in learning state populates the MAC address table but doesn't forward data frames. Forward delay is the time it takes to transition a port from listening to learning mode. It's set to 15 seconds by default.

Forwarding   The port sends and receives all data frames on the bridged port. If the port is still a designated or root port at the end of the learning state, it enters the forwarding state.

Disabled   A port in the disabled state (administratively) does not participate in the frame forwarding or STP. A port in the disabled state is virtually nonoperational.

Switches populate the MAC address table in learning and forwarding modes only.

Switch ports are usually in either the blocking or forwarding state. A forwarding port is one that has been determined to have the lowest (best) cost to the root bridge. But when and if the network experiences a topology change because of a failed link or when someone adds a new switch into the mix, you'll find the ports on a switch in the listening and learning states.

As I mentioned, blocking ports is a strategy for preventing network loops. Once a switch determines the best path to the root bridge, all other redundant ports will be in blocking mode. Blocked ports can still receive BPDUs—they just don't send out any frames.

If a switch determines that a blocked port should now be the designated, or root, port, say because of a topology change, the port will respond by going into listening mode and checking all the BPDUs it receives to ensure that it won't create a loop once the port goes back into forwarding mode.

STP Convergence

Convergence is what happens when all the ports on bridges and switches have transitioned to either forwarding or blocking modes. During this phase, no data will be forwarded until the convergence event is complete. Plus, before data can begin being forwarded again, all devices must be updated. Yes—you read that right: When STP is converging, all host data stops transmitting! So if you want to remain on speaking terms with your network's users (or remain employed for any length of time), you positively must make sure that your switched network is physically designed really well so that STP can converge quickly and painlessly.

Figure 11.12 demonstrates a really great way to design and implement your switched network so that STP converges efficiently.

FIGURE 11.12   An optimal hierarchical switch design

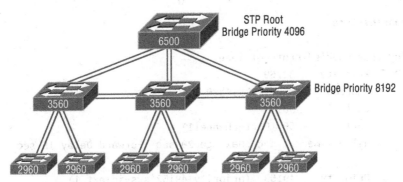

Create core switch as STP root for fastest STP convergence

Convergence is truly important because it ensures that all devices are in either the forwarding mode or the blocking mode. But as you've learned, it does cost you some time. It usually takes 50 seconds to go from blocking to forwarding mode, and I don't recommend changing the default STP timers. (You can adjust those timers if you really have to.) By creating your physical switch design in a hierarchical manner, as shown in Figure 11.12, you can make your core switch the STP root. This makes everyone happy because it makes STP convergence happen fast.

Because the typical spanning-tree topology's time to convergence from blocking to forwarding on a switch port is 50 seconds, it can create time-out problems on your servers or hosts—like when you reboot them. To address this hitch, you can disable spanning tree on individual ports.

Rapid Spanning Tree Protocol 802.1w

How would you like to have a good STP configuration running on your switched network (regardless of the brand of switches) but instead of taking 50 seconds to converge, the switched network can converge in about 5 seconds, or maybe even less? How does that sound? Absolutely—yes, we want this! Well then, welcome to the world of *Rapid Spanning Tree Protocol (RSTP)*.

RSTP was not designed to be a "brand-new" protocol but more of an evolution of the 802.1D standard, with faster convergence time when a topology change occurs. Backward compatibility was a must when 802.1w was created.

The 802.1w is defined in these different port states (compared to 802.1D):

- Disabled = discarding
- Blocking = discarding
- Listening = discarding
- Learning = learning
- Forwarding = forwarding

To verify the spanning-tree type running on your Cisco switch, use the following command:

```
S1#sh spanning-tree
VLAN0001
  Spanning tree enabled protocol ieee
  Root ID    Priority    32769
             Address     000d.29bd.4b80
             Cost        3012
             Port        56 (Port-channel1)
             Hello Time   2 sec  Max Age 20 sec  Forward Delay 15 sec

  Bridge ID  Priority    49153  (priority 49152 sys-id-ext 1)
             Address     001b.2b55.7500
             Hello Time   2 sec  Max Age 20 sec  Forward Delay 15 sec
             Aging Time 15
  Uplinkfast enabled
Interface        Role Sts Cost      Prio.Nbr Type
---------------- ---- --- --------- -------- ----------
Fa0/3            Desg FWD 3100      128.3    Edge Shr
Fa0/4            Desg FWD 3019      128.4    Edge P2p
Fa0/8            Desg FWD 3019      128.8    P2p
Po1              Root FWD 3012      128.56   P2p
```

Since the type output shows `Spanning tree enabled protocol ieee`, we know we are running the 802.1D protocol. If the output shows RSTP, then you know your switch is running the 802.1w protocol.

Virtual LANs

I know I keep telling you this, but I've got to be sure you never forget it, so here I go one last time: By default, switches break up collision domains and routers break up broadcast domains. Okay, I feel better! Now we can move on.

In contrast to the networks of yesterday, which were based on collapsed backbones, today's network design is characterized by a flatter architecture—thanks to switches. So now what? How do we break up broadcast domains in a pure switched internetwork? By creating a virtual local area network (VLAN), that's how!

A VLAN is a logical grouping of network users and resources connected to administratively defined ports on a switch. When you create VLANs, you gain the ability to create smaller broadcast domains within a layer 2 switched internetwork by assigning the various ports on the switch to different subnetworks. A VLAN is treated like its own subnet or broadcast domain, meaning that frames broadcasted onto the network are only switched between the ports logically grouped within the same VLAN.

So, does this mean we no longer need routers? Maybe yes, maybe no—it really depends on what your specific goals and needs are. By default, hosts in a specific VLAN can't communicate with hosts that are members of another VLAN, so if you want inter-VLAN communication, the answer is yes, you still need a router.

VLAN Basics

Figure 11.13 shows how layer 2 switched networks are typically designed—as flat networks. With this configuration, every broadcast packet transmitted is seen by every device on the network regardless of whether the device needs to receive that data or not.

FIGURE 11.13   Flat network structure

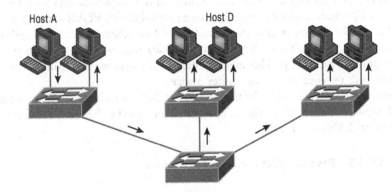

By default, routers allow broadcasts to occur only within the originating network, whereas switches forward broadcasts to all segments. Oh, and by the way, the reason it's called a *flat network* is because it's one *broadcast domain*, not because the actual design is physically flat. In Figure 11.13, you can see Host A sending out a broadcast and all ports on all switches forwarding it—all except each port that receives it.

Now check out Figure 11.14. It pictures a switched network and shows Host A sending a frame with Host D as its destination. What's important to get out of this figure is that the frame is forwarded only out of the port where Host D is located. This is a huge improvement over the old hub networks, unless having one collision domain by default is what you really want. (I'm guessing not!)

Okay, you already know that the coolest benefit you gain by having a layer 2 switched network is that it creates an individual collision domain segment for each device plugged into each port on the switch. But as is often the case, new advances bring new challenges with them. One of the biggest is that the greater the number of users and devices, the more broadcasts and packets each switch must handle.

FIGURE 11.14   The benefit of a switched network

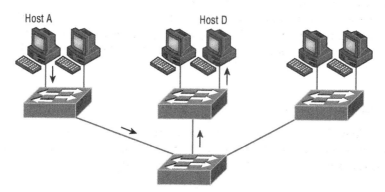

And of course, the all-important issue of security and its demands also must be considered—while simultaneously becoming more complicated! VLANs present a security challenge because by default, within the typical layer 2 switched internetwork, all users can see all devices. And you can't stop devices from broadcasting, plus you can't stop users from trying to respond to broadcasts. This means your security options are dismally limited to placing passwords on your servers and other devices.

To understand how a VLAN looks to a switch, it's helpful to begin by first looking at a traditional network. Figure 11.15 shows how a network used to be created using hubs to connect physical LANs to a router.

FIGURE 11.15   Physical LANs connected to a router

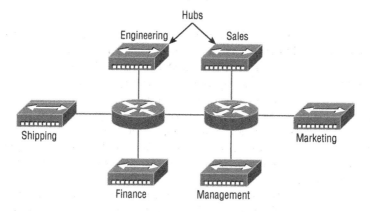

Here you can see that each network is attached with a hub port to the router (each segment also has its own logical network number, even though this isn't obvious looking at the figure). Each host attached to a particular physical network has to match that network's logical network number in order to be able to communicate on the internetwork. Notice that each department has its own LAN, so if we needed to add new users to, let's say, Sales, we would just plug them into the Sales LAN and they would automatically be part of the Sales collision and broadcast domain. This design actually did work well for many years.

But there was one major flaw: What happens if the hub for Sales is full and we need to add another user to the Sales LAN? Or, what do we do if there's no more physical space for a new employee where the Sales team is located? Hmmm, well, let's say there just happens to be plenty of room over in the Finance section of the building. That new Sales team member will just have to sit on the same side of the building as the Finance people, and we'll just plug the poor soul into the hub for Finance. Simple, right?

So wrong! Doing this obviously makes the new user part of the Finance LAN, which is very bad for many reasons. First and foremost, we now have a major security issue. Because the new Sales employee is a member of the Finance broadcast domain, the newbie can see all the same servers and access all network services that the Finance folks can. Second, for this user to access the Sales network services they need to get their job done, they would have to go through the router to log in to the Sales server—not exactly efficient.

Now, let's look at what a switch accomplishes for us. Figure 11.16 demonstrates how switches come to the rescue by removing the physical boundary to solve our problem. It also shows how six VLANs (numbered 2 through 7) are used to create a broadcast domain for each department. Each switch port is then administratively assigned a VLAN membership, depending on the host and which broadcast domain it's placed in.

FIGURE 11.16   Switches removing the physical boundary

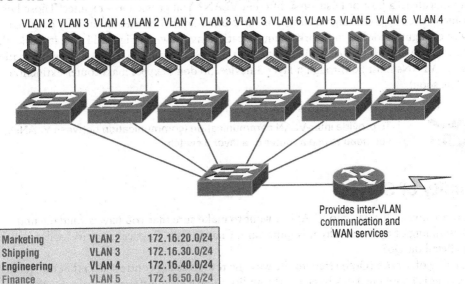

VLAN 2 VLAN 3 VLAN 4 VLAN 2 VLAN 7 VLAN 3 VLAN 3 VLAN 6 VLAN 5 VLAN 5 VLAN 6 VLAN 4

Provides inter-VLAN communication and WAN services

Marketing	VLAN 2	172.16.20.0/24
Shipping	VLAN 3	172.16.30.0/24
Engineering	VLAN 4	172.16.40.0/24
Finance	VLAN 5	172.16.50.0/24
Management	VLAN 6	172.16.60.0/24
Sales	VLAN 7	172.16.70.0/24

So now if we needed to add another user to the Sales VLAN (VLAN 7), we could just assign the port to VLAN 7 regardless of where the new Sales team member is physically located—nice! This illustrates one of the sweetest advantages to designing your network with VLANs over the old collapsed backbone design. Now, cleanly and simply, each host that needs to be in the Sales VLAN is merely assigned to VLAN 7.

Notice that I started assigning VLANs with VLAN number 2. The number is irrelevant, but you might be wondering what happened to VLAN 1. Well, that VLAN is an administrative VLAN, and even though it can be used for a workgroup, Cisco recommends that you use it for administrative purposes only. You can't delete or change the name of VLAN 1, and by default, all ports on a switch are members of VLAN 1 until you actually do change them.

Now, because each VLAN is considered a broadcast domain, it's got to also have its own subnet number (refer again to Figure 11.16). And if you're also using IPv6, then each VLAN must also be assigned its own IPv6 network number. So you don't get confused, just keep thinking of VLANs as separate subnets or networks.

Let's get back to that "because of switches, we don't need routers anymore" misconception. When looking at Figure 11.16, you can see that there are seven VLANs, or broadcast domains, counting VLAN 1 (not shown in the figure). The hosts within each VLAN can communicate with each other but not with anything in a different VLAN because the hosts in any given VLAN "think" that they're actually in a collapsed backbone, illustrated in Figure 11.15.

So what handy little device do you think we need to enable the hosts in Figure 11.16 to communicate to a host or hosts on a different VLAN? You guessed it—a router! Those hosts absolutely need to go through a router, or some other layer 3 device, just as they do when they're configured for internetwork communication (as shown in Figure 11.15). It works the same way it would if we were trying to connect different physical networks. Communication between VLANs must go through a layer 3 device. So don't expect mass router extinction anytime soon!

To provide inter-VLAN communication (communication between VLANs), you need to use a router or a layer 3 switch.

Quality of Service

Before we dive in further into VLANs, I want to make sure that you have a fundamental understanding of QoS and why it is important. Chapter 20, "Physical Security" will provide more detail on QoS.

Quality of service (QoS) refers to the way the resources are controlled so that the quality of services is maintained. It's basically the ability to provide a different priority for one or more types of traffic over other levels; priority is applied to different applications, data flows, or users so that they can be guaranteed a certain performance level.

QoS methods focus on one of five problems that can affect data as it traverses network cable:

- Delay
- Dropped packets
- Error
- Jitter
- Out-of-order delivery

QoS can ensure that applications with a required bit rate receive the necessary bandwidth to work properly. Clearly, on networks with excess bandwidth, this is not a factor, but the more limited your bandwidth is, the more important a concept like this becomes.

Quality of service (QoS) allows administrators to predict, monitor, and control bandwidth use to ensure it is available to programs and apps that need it.

VLAN Memberships

Most of the time, VLANs are created by a system administrator who proceeds to assign switch ports to each one. VLANs of this type are known as *static VLANs*. If you don't mind doing a little more work when you begin this process, assign all the host devices' hardware addresses into a database so your switches can be configured to assign VLANs dynamically anytime you plug a host into a switch. I hate saying things like "obviously," but obviously, this type of VLAN is known as a *dynamic VLAN*. I'll be covering both static and dynamic VLANs next.

Static VLANs

Creating static VLANs is the most common way to create a VLAN, and one of the reasons for that is because static VLANs are the most secure. This security stems from the fact that any switch port you've assigned a VLAN association to will always maintain it unless you change the port assignment manually.

Static VLAN configuration is pretty easy to set up and supervise, and it works really well in a networking environment where any user movement within the network needs to be controlled. It can be helpful to use network management software to configure the ports, but you don't have to use it if you don't want to.

In Figure 11.16, each switch port was configured manually with a VLAN membership based on which VLAN the host needed to be a member of—remember, the device's actual physical location doesn't matter one bit as long as the VLAN assignments are correctly configured. Which broadcast domain your hosts become members of is purely up to you. And again, remember that each host also has to have the correct IP address information. For instance, you must configure each host in VLAN 2 into the 172.16.20.0/24 network for it to become a member of that VLAN. It's also a good idea to keep in mind that if you plug a host into a switch, you have to verify the VLAN membership of that port. If the membership is different than what's needed for that host, the host won't be able to gain access to the network services that it needs, such as a workgroup server.

Static access ports are either manually assigned to a VLAN or assigned through a RADIUS server for use with IEEE 802.1X. It's easy to set an incorrect VLAN assignment on a port, so using a RADIUS server can help in your configurations.

Dynamic VLANs

On the other hand, a dynamic VLAN determines a host's VLAN assignment automatically. Using intelligent management software, you can base VLAN assignments on hardware (MAC) addresses, protocols, or even applications that work to create dynamic VLANs.

For example, let's say MAC addresses have been entered into a centralized VLAN management application and you hook up a new host. If you attach it to an unassigned switch port, the VLAN management database can look up the hardware address and both assign and configure the switch port into the correct VLAN. Needless to say, this makes management and configuration much easier because if a user moves, the switch will simply assign them to the correct VLAN automatically. But here again, there's a catch—initially, you've got to do a lot more work setting up the database. It can be very worthwhile, though!

And here's some more good news: You can use the VLAN Management Policy Server (VMPS) service to set up a database of MAC addresses to be used for the dynamic addressing of your VLANs. The VMPS database automatically maps MAC addresses to VLANs.

Identifying VLANs

Know that switch ports are layer 2–only interfaces that are associated with a physical port. A switch port can belong to only one VLAN if it is an access port or all VLANs if it is a trunk port, as I'll explain in a minute. You can manually configure a port as an access or trunk port, or you can let the Dynamic Trunking Protocol (DTP) operate on a per-port basis to set the switch port mode. DTP does this by negotiating with the port on the other end of the link.

Switches are definitely pretty busy devices. As frames are switched throughout the network, they've got to be able to keep track of all the different port types plus understand what to do with them depending on the hardware address. And remember—frames are handled differently according to the type of link they're traversing.

There are two different types of links in a switched environment: access ports and trunk ports.

Access Ports

An access port belongs to and carries the traffic of only one VLAN. Anything arriving on an access port is simply assumed to belong to the VLAN assigned to the port. Any device attached to an *access link* is unaware of a VLAN membership—the device just assumes it's part of the same broadcast domain, but it doesn't have the big picture, so it doesn't understand the physical network topology at all.

Another good thing to know is that switches remove any VLAN information from the frame before it's forwarded out to an access-link device. Remember that access-link devices can't communicate with devices outside their VLAN unless the packet is routed. And you can only create a switch port to be either an access port or a trunk port—not both. So you've got to choose one or the other, and know that if you make it an access port, that port can be assigned to one VLAN only.

Voice Access Ports

Not to confuse you, but all that I just said about the fact that an access port can be assigned to only one VLAN is really only sort of true. Nowadays, most switches will allow you to add a second VLAN to an access port on a switch port for your voice traffic; it's called the voice VLAN. The voice VLAN used to be called the auxiliary VLAN, which allowed it to be overlaid on top of the data VLAN, enabling both types of traffic through the same port. Even though this is technically considered to be a different type of link, it's still just an access port that can be configured for both data and voice VLANs. This allows you to connect both a phone and a PC device to one switch port but still have each device in a separate VLAN. If you are configuring voice VLANs, you'll want to configure quality of service (QoS) on the switch ports to provide a higher precedence to voice traffic over data traffic to improve sound quality.

Suppose you plug a host into a switch port and users are unable to access any server resources. The two typical reasons this happens is because the port is configured in the wrong VLAN membership or STP has shut down the port because STP thought there was possibly a loop.

Trunk Ports

Believe it or not, the term *trunk port* was inspired by the telephone system trunks that carry multiple telephone conversations at a time. So it follows that trunk ports can similarly carry multiple VLANs at a time.

A *trunk link* is a 100 Mbps or 1000 Mbps point-to-point link between two switches, between a switch and router, or even between a switch and server, and it carries the traffic of multiple VLANs—from 1 to 4,094 VLANs at a time.

Trunking can be a real advantage because with it, you get to make a single port part of a whole bunch of different VLANs at the same time. This is a great feature because you can actually set ports up to have a server in two separate broadcast domains simultaneously so your users won't have to cross a layer 3 device (router) to log in and access it. Another benefit of trunking comes into play when you're connecting switches. Information from multiple VLANs can be carried across trunk links, but by default, if the links between your switches aren't trunked, only information from the configured VLAN will be switched across that link.

Check out Figure 11.17. It shows how the different links are used in a switched network. All hosts connected to the switches can communicate to all ports in their VLAN because of the trunk link between them. Remember, if we used an access link between the switches, this would allow only one VLAN to communicate between switches. As you can see, these hosts are using access links to connect to the switch, so they're communicating in one VLAN only. That means that without a router, no host can communicate outside its own VLAN, but the hosts can send data over trunked links to hosts on another switch configured in their same VLAN.

FIGURE 11.17 Access and trunk links in a switched network

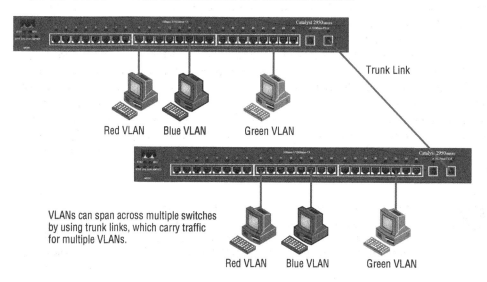

It's finally time to tell you about the VLAN identification methods.

VLAN Identification Methods

VLAN identification is what switches use to keep track of all those frames as they're traversing a switch fabric. All of our hosts connect together via a switch fabric in our switched network topology. It's how switches identify which frames belong to which VLANs, and there's more than one trunking method: ISL and 802.1Q.

Inter-Switch Link (ISL)

Inter-Switch Link (ISL) is a way of explicitly tagging VLAN information onto an Ethernet frame. This tagging information allows VLANs to be multiplexed over a trunk link through an external encapsulation method (ISL), which allows the switch to identify the VLAN membership of a frame over the trunked link.

By running ISL, you can interconnect multiple switches and still maintain VLAN information as traffic travels between switches on trunk links. ISL functions at layer 2 by encapsulating a data frame with a new header and cyclic redundancy check (CRC).

Of note is that this is proprietary to Cisco switches, and it's used for Fast Ethernet and Gigabit Ethernet links only. *ISL routing* is pretty versatile and can be used on a switch port, on router interfaces, and on server interface cards to trunk a server.

Port Tagging/IEEE 802.1Q

Created by the IEEE as a standard method of frame tagging, IEEE 802.1Q works by inserting a field into the frame to identify the VLAN. This is one of the aspects of 802.1Q that makes it your only option if you want to trunk between a Cisco switched link and another brand of switch. In a mixed environment, you've just got to use 802.1Q for the trunk to work!

Unlike ISL, which encapsulates the frame with control information, 802.1Q inserts an 802.1Q field along with tag control information, as shown in Figure 11.18.

FIGURE 11.18   IEEE 802.1Q encapsulation with and without the 802.1Q tag

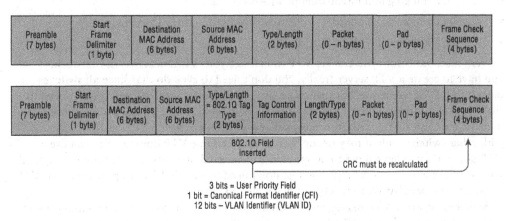

To meet the exam objectives, it's really the 12-bit VLAN ID that matters, so keep your focus on it. This field identifies the VLAN and can be 2^12 minus 2 for the 0 and 4,095 reserved VLANs, which means an 802.1Q tagged frame can carry information for 4,094 VLANs.

It works like this: You first designate each port that's going to be a trunk with 802.1Q encapsulation. The other ports must be assigned a specific VLAN ID in order for them to communicate. VLAN 1 is the default native VLAN, and when 802.1Q is used, all traffic for a native VLAN is *untagged*. The ports that populate the same trunk create a group with this native VLAN, and each port gets tagged with an identification number reflecting that membership. Again, the default is VLAN 1. The native VLAN allows the trunks to accept information that was received without any VLAN identification or frame tag.

> The basic purpose of ISL and 802.1Q frame-tagging methods is to provide inter-switch VLAN communication. Remember that any ISL or 802.1Q frame tagging is removed if a frame is forwarded out an access link—tagging is used internally and across trunk links only!

VLAN Trunking Protocol

The basic goals of *VLAN Trunking Protocol (VTP)* are to manage all configured VLANs across a switched internetwork and to maintain consistency throughout that network. VTP allows you to add, delete, and rename VLANs—and information about those actions is then propagated to all other switches in the VTP domain.

Here's a list of some of the cool features VTP has to offer:

- Consistent VLAN configuration across all switches in the network
- Accurate tracking and monitoring of VLANs
- Dynamic reporting of added VLANs to all switches in the VTP domain
- Adding VLANs using plug-and-play

Very nice, but before you can get VTP to manage your VLANs across the network, you have to create a VTP server (really, you don't need to even do that since all switches default to VTP server mode, but just make sure you have a server). All servers that need to share VLAN information must use the same domain name, and a switch can be in only one domain at a time. So basically, this means that a switch can share VTP domain information with other switches only if they're configured into the same VTP domain. You can use a VTP domain if you have more than one switch connected in a network, but if you've got all your switches in only one VLAN, you just don't need to use VTP. Do keep in mind that VTP information is sent between switches only via a trunk port.

Switches advertise VTP management domain information as well as a configuration revision number and all known VLANs with any specific parameters. But there's also something called *VTP transparent mode*. In it, you can configure switches to forward VTP information through trunk ports but not to accept information updates or update their VTP databases.

If you've got sneaky users adding switches to your VTP domain behind your back, you can include passwords, but don't forget—every switch must be set up with the same password. And as you can imagine, this little snag can be a real hassle administratively!

Switches detect any added VLANs within a VTP advertisement and then prepare to send information on their trunk ports with the newly defined VLAN in tow. Updates are sent out as revision numbers that consist of summary advertisements. Anytime a switch sees a higher revision number, it knows the information it's getting is more current, so it will overwrite the existing VLAN database with the latest information.

You should know these requirements for VTP to communicate VLAN information between switches:

- The VTP management domain name of both switches must be set the same.

- One of the switches has to be configured as a VTP server.

- Set a VTP password if used.

- No router is necessary and a router is not a requirement.

Now that you've got that down, we're going to delve deeper into the world of VTP with VTP modes.

VTP Modes of Operation

Figure 11.19 shows you all three different modes of operation within a VTP domain.

FIGURE 11.19   VTP modes

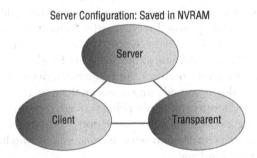

Server Configuration: Saved in NVRAM

Client Configuration: Not Saved in NVRAM   Transparent Configuration: Saved in NVRAM

Server   This is the default mode for all Catalyst switches. You need at least one server in your VTP domain to propagate VLAN information throughout that domain. Also important is that the switch must be in server mode for you to be able to create, add, and delete VLANs in a VTP domain. VLAN information has to be changed in server mode, and any change made to VLANs on a switch in server mode will be advertised to the entire VTP domain. In VTP server mode, VLAN configurations are saved in NVRAM on the switch.

Client   In client mode, switches receive information from VTP servers, but they also receive and forward updates, so in this way they behave like VTP servers. The difference is that they can't create, change, or delete VLANs. Plus, none of the ports on a client switch can be added to a new VLAN before the VTP server notifies the client switch of the new VLAN and the VLAN exists in the client's VLAN database. Also good to know is that VLAN information sent from a VTP server isn't stored in NVRAM, which is important because it means that if the switch is reset or reloaded, the VLAN information will be deleted. Here's a hint: If you want a switch to become a server, first make it a client so it receives all the correct VLAN information, then change it to a server—so much easier!

Transparent   Switches in transparent mode don't participate in the VTP domain or share its VLAN database, but they'll still forward VTP advertisements through any configured trunk links. An admin on a transparent switch can create, modify, and delete VLANs because they keep their own database—one they keep secret from the other switches. Despite being kept in NVRAM memory, the VLAN database in transparent mode is actually only locally significant. The whole purpose of transparent mode is to allow remote switches to receive the VLAN database from a VTP-server-configured switch through a switch that is not participating in the same VLAN assignments.

Do We Really Need to Put an IP Address on a Switch?

The answer is absolutely not! Switches have all ports enabled and ready to rock. Take the switch out of the box, plug it in, and the switch starts learning MAC addresses in the CAM. But since the switches are providing layer 2 services, why do we need an IP address? Because you still need an IP address for *in-band* management, which is used with your *virtual terminals*, that's why. Telnet, SSH, SNMP, and so on all require IP addresses to communicate with the switch, in-band, through the network. And remember, since all ports are enabled by default, you need to shut down unused ports or assign them to an unused VLAN. Configuring a switch *out-of-band* means you're not going through the network to configure the device; you're actually using a port, such as a console port, to configure the switch instead. Most of the time, you'll use the console port upon starting up the switch. After that, all the management will be completed in-band.

So now you know that the switch needs a management IP address for in-band management purposes, but exactly where do you want to place it? Conveniently, there's something predictably called the management VLAN interface, and that's clearly your target. It's a routed interface found on every switch, and it's referred to as interface VLAN 1. It's good to know that this management interface can be changed, and all manufacturers recommend changing it to a different management interface for security purposes.

Yes, you can buy switches that are *unmanaged*, but you would never ever want to do that for an enterprise network! The only environment in which doing that would make sense is in a home network, but that's about it. Anything you get for an office or larger network absolutely must be a *managed* switch!

With all that in mind, let's get down to configuring a switch now.

We'll begin our configuration by connecting into the switch via the console and setting the administrative functions. At this point, we'll also assign an IP address to each switch, but as I said, doing that isn't really necessary to make our network function. The only reason we're going to do that is so we can manage/administer it remotely—in-band—via a protocol like Telnet. Let's use a simple IP scheme like 192.168.10.16/28. And by the way, this mask should be familiar to you. Let's check out the following output:

```
Switch>enable
Switch#config t
Switch(config)#hostname S1
S1(config)#enable secret todd
S1(config)#int f0/15
S1(config-if)#description 1st connection to S3
S1(config-if)#int f0/16
S1(config-if)#description 2nd connection to S3
S1(config-if)#speed 1000
S1(config-if)#duplex full
S1(config-if)#line console 0
S1(config-line)#password console
S1(config-line)#login
S1(config-line)#line vty 0 15
S1(config-line)#password telnet
S1(config-line)#login
S1(config-line)#int vlan 1
S1(config-if)#ip address 192.168.10.17 255.255.255.240
S1(config-if)#no shut
S1(config-if)#exit
S1(config)#ip default-gateway 192.168.10.30
S1(config)#banner motd #this is my S1 switch#
S1(config)#exit
S1#copy run start
Destination filename [startup-config]? [enter]
Building configuration...
[OK]
S1#
```

In this output, the first thing to notice is that there aren't any IP addresses configured on the switch's physical interfaces. Since all ports on a switch are enabled by default, there's not really a whole lot to configure. But look again—I configured the speed and duplex of the switch to gigabit, full-on port 16. Most of the time you would just leave these as auto-detect, and I actually recommend doing that. This is not the same technology used between switches to determine the cable type which is auto Medium Dependent Interface Crossover (MDI-X).

My next step is to set the console password for out-of-band management and then the VTY (Telnet) password for in-band management. The next task is to set the default gateway of the switch and banner. So you don't get confused, I want to clarify that the *default gateway* is used to send management (in-band) traffic to a remote network so you can manage the switch remotely. Understand this is not the default gateway for the hosts—the default gateway would be the router interface address assigned to each VLAN.

The IP address is configured under a logical interface, called a management domain or VLAN. You can use default VLAN 1 to manage a switched network just as we're doing here, or you can be smart and opt to use a different VLAN for management.

The preceding configuration demonstrates how to configure the switch for local management, meaning that the passwords to log in to the switch are right there in the switch's configuration. You can also configure switches and routers to store their usernames and passwords remotely for ease of configuration using an AAA server. Doing this allows you to change the passwords at one device without having to telnet into each device separately to change passwords.

To get this done, use the following command:

```
S1(config)#aaa authentication login default
```

This tells the switch to use AAA when Telnet or SSH is used for in-band management. This next command tells the switch to use the AAA server if someone is trying to access the console of the switch:

```
S1(config)#aaa authentication login console
```

So remember, no IP addresses on physical switch interfaces, no routing protocols there either, and so on. We're performing layer 2 switching at this point, not routing!

Switch Port Protection

There are many features that are available to mitigate switch attacks. In the following sections, we'll examine some of these protections.

Port Security

Clearly, it's a bad idea to have your switches available for anyone to just plug into and play around with. Security is a big deal—even more of a concern regarding wireless security, so why wouldn't we demand switch security as much, if not more?

But just how do we actually prevent someone from simply plugging a host into one of our switch ports—or worse, adding a hub, switch, or access point into the Ethernet jack in their office? By default, MAC addresses dynamically appear in your MAC forward/filter database, but the good news is that you can stop bad guys in their tracks by using port security!

Figure 11.20 pictures two hosts connected to the single switch port Fa0/3 via either a hub or access point (AP).

FIGURE 11.20   Port security on a switch port restricts port access by MAC address.

Port Fa0/3 is configured to observe and allow only certain MAC addresses to associate with the specific port, so in this example, Host A is denied access, but Host B is allowed to associate with the port.

By using port security, you can limit the number of MAC addresses that can be assigned dynamically to a port, set static MAC addresses, and—here's my favorite part—set penalties for users who abuse your policy! Personally, I like to have the port shut down when the security policy is violated. Making abusers bring me a memo from their boss explaining why they violated the security policy brings with it a certain poetic justice, which is nice. And I'll also require something like that before I'll enable their port again. Things like this really seem to help people remember to behave!

DHCP Snooping

A rogue DHCP server (one not under your control that is giving out incompatible IP addresses) can be an annoyance that causes users to be unable to connect to network resources, or it may play a part in several types of attacks. In either case, DHCP snooping is a switch feature that can help to prevent your devices from communicating with illegitimate DHCP servers.

When enabled, DHCP snooping allows responses to client requests from only DHCP servers located on trusted switch ports (which you define). When only the ports where company DHCP servers are located are configured to be trusted, rogue DHCP servers will be unable to respond to client requests.

The protection doesn't stop there, however. The switch will also, over time, develop an IP address–to–MAC address table called the bindings table, derived from "snooping" on DHCP traffic to and from the legitimate DHCP server. The bindings table will alert the switch to any packets that have mappings that do not match the table. These frames will be dropped. The bindings table is also used with ARP inspection, which makes the configuration of DHCP snooping a prerequisite of ARP inspection.

ARP Inspection

Many on-path (previously known as man-in-the-middle) attacks are made possible by the attacker polluting the ARP cache of the two victims such that their cache maps each other's

IP addresses to the MAC address of the attacker, thus allowing the attacker to receive all traffic in the conversation.

Dynamic ARP inspection (DAI) is a feature that, when configured, uses the DHCP snooping database of IP address–to–MAC address mappings to verify the MAC address mappings of each frame going through the switch. In this way, any frames with incorrect or altered mappings are dropped by the switch, thus breaking any attacks depending on these bogus mappings. Because it uses the DHCP snooping database, the configuration of DHCP snooping is a prerequisite to enabling DAI.

Flood Guard

Switches can undergo an attack where some malicious individual floods the switch with unknown MAC addresses. Since switches record all MAC addresses of received frames, the switch will continue to update its MAC table with these MAC addresses until it pushes all legitimate MAC addresses out of the limited space provided for the MAC table in memory. Once this occurs, all traffic received by the switch will be unknown to the switch and it will flood this traffic out of all ports, basically turning the switch into a hub. Now the attacker can connect a sniffer to his port and receive all traffic rather than only the traffic destined for that port as would normally be the case. This attack is shown in Figure 11.21.

FIGURE 11.21   Flood guard process

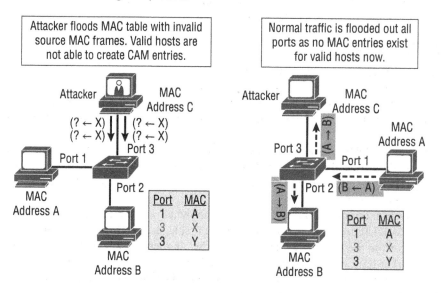

Flood guard is a feature that can be implemented to prevent this attack. It uses two mechanisms to accomplish this: unknown unicast flood blocking (UUFB) and unknown unicast flood rate-limiting (UUFRL).

The UUFB feature blocks unknown unicast and multicast traffic flooding at a specific port, only permitting egress traffic with MAC addresses that are known to exist on the port. The UUFRL feature applies a rate limit globally to unknown unicast traffic on all VLANs.

When these two features are combined, flooding attacks can be prevented in switches that support the features.

BPDU Guard

When a switch that is unknown to you and not under your control is connected to one of your switches, it can play havoc with your STP topology and may even allow the rogue switch to become the root bridge! As you know, when a switch starts receiving STP BPDUs from a new switch, the information in the BPDU (specifically the switch priority) is used to determine if the switch might be a new root bridge (causing a new election) or if the STP topology should be changed.

To prevent this from occurring, a feature called BPDU Guard can be implemented. This feature should be enabled on all switch ports that do not connect to known switches. Since most connections between switches and from the switch to a router are trunk ports, then it is typically enabled on all access ports or ports that connect to end devices.

The effect of enabling this feature is simple but effective. The ports on which it is enabled will be shut down when a BPDU is received. While reenabling the port can be done manually, you can also configure the port to wait a period and then reenable itself automatically as well.

Root Guard

Another feature that can be used to maintain the desired STP topology is called Root Guard. This feature is like BPDU Guard in that it also prevents a new switch from altering the topology. It is applied to all interfaces on the current root bridge and prevents these ports from becoming root ports. Despite the name, root ports are only present on non-root switches and represent the best path back to the root bridge.

The feature prevents this by disabling a port if a BPDU is received that, because of its superior priority number, would cause a new root bridge election. It differs from BPDU Guard in that BPDU Guard disables a port where it is configured when *any* BPDU is received. This would be undesirable behavior on the root bridge as it needs to receive those BPDUs to maintain the topology. So, in summary, it helps to maintain the current root bridge's role as the root bridge.

Port Bonding

Know that almost all Ethernet networks today will typically have multiple links between switches because this kind of design provides redundancy and resiliency. On a physical design that includes multiple links between switches, STP will do its job and put a port or ports into blocking mode. In addition to that, routing protocols like OSPF and EIGRP could see all these redundant links as individual ones, depending on the configuration, which can mean an increase in routing overhead.

We can gain the benefits from multiple links between switches by using port channeling. EtherChannel is a port channel technology that was originally developed by Cisco as a switch-to-switch technique for grouping several Fast Ethernet or Gigabit Ethernet ports into one logical channel.

Also important to note is that once your port channel is up and working, layer 2 STP and layer 3 routing protocols will treat those bundled links as a single one, which would stop STP from performing blocking. An additional nice result is that because the routing protocols now only see this as a single link, a single adjacency across the link can be formed—elegant!

Figure 11.22 shows how a network would look if we had four connections between switches, before and after configuring port channels.

FIGURE 11.22   Before and after port channels

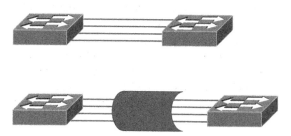

As usual, there's the Cisco version and the IEEE version of port channel negotiation protocols to choose from, and you can take your pick. Cisco's version is called Port Aggregation Protocol (PAgP), and the IEEE 802.3ad standard is called Link Aggregation Control Protocol (LACP). Both versions work equally well, but the way you configure each is slightly different. Keep in mind that both PAgP and LACP are negotiation protocols and that EtherChannel can actually be statically configured without PAgP or LACP. Still, it's better to use one of these protocols to help with compatibility issues as well as to manage link additions and failures between two switches.

Cisco EtherChannel allows us to bundle up to eight active ports between switches. The links must have the same speed, duplex setting, and VLAN configuration—in other words, you can't mix interface types and configurations into the same bundle.

Here are a few things to remember:

Port Channeling/Bonding   Refers to combining two to eight Fast Ethernet or Gigabit Ethernet ports together between two switches into one aggregated logical link to achieve more bandwidth and resiliency.

EtherChannel   Cisco's proprietary term for port channeling.

PAgP   This is a Cisco proprietary port channel negotiation protocol that aids in the automatic creation of EtherChannel links. All links in the bundle must match the same parameters (speed, duplex, VLAN info), and when PAgP identifies matched links, it groups the links into an EtherChannel. This is then added to STP as a single bridge port. At this point, PAgP's job is to send packets every 30 seconds to manage the link for consistency, any link additions and modifications, and failures.

LACP (802.3ad)   This has the exact same purpose as PAgP, but it's nonproprietary, so it can work between multivendor networks.

Device Hardening

A discussion of switch security would be incomplete without discussing device hardening. Actually, this Device Hardening section is applicable not only to the routers and switches in your network but to all devices, including endpoints such as laptops, mobile devices, and desktops.

One of the ongoing goals of operations security is to ensure that all systems have been hardened to the extent that is possible and still provide functionality. The hardening can be accomplished both on a physical and logical basis. From a logical perspective, do this:

- Remove unnecessary applications.
- Disable unnecessary services.
- Block unrequired ports.
- Tightly control the connecting of external storage devices and media if it's allowed at all.
- Keep firmware update.

Two Additional Advanced Features of Switches

Switches really expand our flexibility when we're designing our networks. The features that we need to cover for the CompTIA Network+ objectives are as follows:

- Power over Ethernet (PoE)/Power over Ethernet Plus (PoE+)
- Port mirroring/spanning (local vs. remote)

Power over Ethernet (802.3af, 802.3at)

Power over Ethernet (PoE and PoE+) technology describes a system for transmitting electrical power, along with data, to remote devices over standard twisted-pair cable in an Ethernet network. This technology is useful for powering IP telephones (Voice over IP, or VoIP), wireless LAN access points, network cameras, remote network switches, embedded computers, and other appliances—situations where it would be inconvenient, expensive, and possibly not even feasible to supply power separately. One reason for this is that the main wiring usually must be done by qualified and/or licensed electricians for legal and/or insurance mandates.

The IEEE has created a standard for PoE called 802.3af, and for PoE+ it's referred to as 802.3at. This standard describes precisely how a powered device is detected and also defines two methods of delivering Power over Ethernet to a given powered device. Keep in mind that the PoE+ standard, 802.3at, delivers more power than 802.3af, which is compatible with Gigabit Ethernet with four-wire pairs at 30 watts.

This process happens one of two ways: either by receiving the power from an Ethernet port on a switch (or other capable device) or via a power injector. And you can't use both approaches to get the job done. And this can lead to serious trouble, so be sure before connecting!

Real World Scenario

PoE

It would be rare for me not to design a network around PoE. Most of my consulting work is wireless networking, including large outdoor wireless networks. When I design the network, I order equipment based on the amount of power needed to run it, knowing I'll have only a few electrical outlets, or even no outlets if all my equipment is outside. This means that all my switches must run PoE to my access points and wireless bridges and must do this for long distances.

For me to accomplish this, I need to order the more expensive, large-scale enterprise switches. If you have devices that need PoE but do not have long-distance connections, you can use lower-end switches, but you must verify that they provide the right amount of power. There was a customer who called me because their network access points were going up and down. The bottom line is that they had purchased less expensive switches and there was not enough power to run the equipment. They ended up buying all new switches. So, before you buy a PoE switch, verify that the switch provides the right power for your environment.

Figure 11.23 shows an example of a switch that provides PoE to any PoE-capable device.

FIGURE 11.23   Switched Ethernet ports can provide power to devices.

As I just said, if you don't have a switch with PoE, then you can use a power injector. Figure 11.24 shows a picture of a typical power injector physically installed in a network.

FIGURE 11.24   An external power injector used for PoE

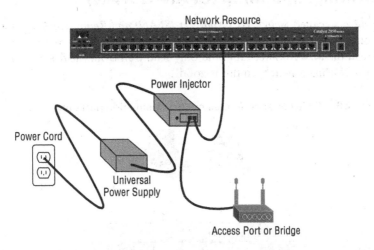

Use caution when using an external power injector! Take the time to make sure the power injector provides the voltage level for which your device was manufactured.

Because most higher-end switches provide PoE, we don't need to worry about injectors, but if you are adding a wireless bridge into an existing network that has switches without PoE, you need to add a power injector. Figure 11.25 shows a power injector used for a wireless bridge.

FIGURE 11.25   Wireless bridge power injector

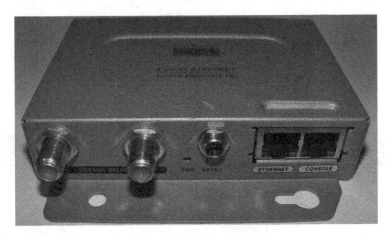

Now, let's discuss how we would troubleshoot a network that has a switch in the LAN instead of a hub.

Port Mirroring/Spanning (SPAN/RSPAN)

Port mirroring, also called *Switch Port Analyzer (SPAN) and Remote SPAN*, allows you to sniff traffic on a network when using a switch. In Figure 11.26, you can see how a typical switch will read the forward/filter table and only send traffic out the destination port (this is the whole idea of using a switch, so this is good!).

FIGURE 11.26   Switches send frames out the destination port only.

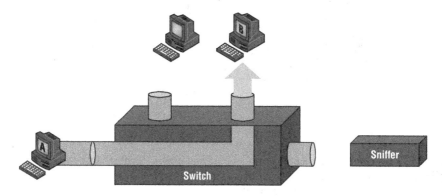

All good, but a problem with this arises when you need to sniff traffic on the network. Figure 11.26 illustrates this issue; the sniffer isn't seeing data coming from Host A to Host B. To solve this little snag, you can temporarily place a hub between Host A and Host B, as demonstrated in Figure 11.27.

FIGURE 11.27   Place a hub between two hosts to troubleshoot.

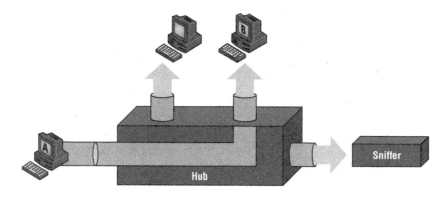

This method will allow you to see the frames sent from Host A to Host B. The bad news, however, is that by doing this, you'll bring down the network temporarily.

The port-mirroring option allows you to place a port in span mode so that every frame from Host A is captured by both Host B and the sniffer, as shown in Figure 11.28. This would also be a helpful option to take advantage of if you were connecting an IDS or IPS to the switch as well.

FIGURE 11.28 Port spanning/mirroring

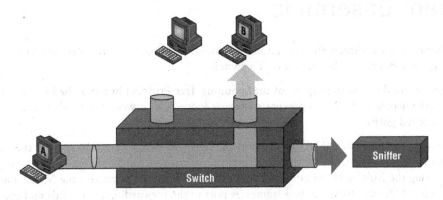

Be careful when using port mirroring because it can cause a lot of overhead on the switch and possibly crash your network. Because of this, it's a really good idea to use this feature at strategic times, and only for short periods if possible.

> The last thing I want you to bear in mind is that RSPAN extends SPAN by enabling remote monitoring of multiple switches across your network. The traffic for each RSPAN session is carried over a user-specified RSPAN VLAN, which is dedicated for a specific RSPAN session in all participating switches.

Summary

In this chapter, I talked about the differences between switches and bridges and how they both work at layer 2 and create a MAC address forward/filter table in order to make decisions about whether to forward or flood a frame.

I also discussed problems that can occur if you have multiple links between bridges (switches) and how to solve these problems by using the Spanning Tree Protocol (STP).

This chapter also introduced you to the world of virtual LANs and described how switches can use them. We talked about how VLANs break up broadcast domains in a switched internetwork—a very important, necessary thing because layer 2 switches only break up collision domains and, by default, all switches make up one large broadcast domain. I also described access links and went over how trunked VLANs work across a Fast Ethernet link.

Trunking is a crucial technology to understand well when you're dealing with a network populated by multiple switches that are running several VLANs.

Exam Essentials

Remember the three switch functions.   Address learning, forward/filter decisions, and loop avoidance are the functions of a switch.

Understand the main purpose of the Spanning Tree Protocol in a switched LAN.   The main purpose of STP is to prevent switching loops in a network with redundant switched paths.

Remember the states of STP.   The purpose of the blocking state is to prevent the use of looped paths. A port in the listening state prepares to forward data frames without populating the MAC address table. A port in the learning state populates the MAC address table but doesn't forward data frames. A port in the forwarding state sends and receives all data frames on the bridged port. Last, a port in the disabled state is virtually non-operational.

Remember to check a switch port's VLAN assignment when plugging in a new host.   If you plug a new host into a switch, then you must verify the VLAN membership of that port. If the membership is different than what is needed for that host, the host will not be able to reach the needed network services, such as a workgroup server.

Understand what PoE provides.   Power over Ethernet was created to provide power to devices that are connected to a switch port but that are not in a place that has a power outlet—for example, an access point in a ceiling.

List features that can be used to maintain the STP topology.   These include BPDU Guard, Root Guard, and flood guards.

Written Lab

You can find the answers to the written labs in Appendix A. Write the answers to the following questions:

1.   VLANs break up _____ domains in a layer 2 switched network.

2.   Switches, by default, only break up _____ domains.

3. What does trunking provide?

4. You need to power a device such as an access point or IP phone. What protocol can provide power to these devices over an Ethernet cable?

5. You plug a host into a switch port and the host receives an IP address, but the user can't get to the services it needs. What is possibly the problem?

6. If a destination MAC address is not in the forward/filter table, what will the switch do with the frame?

7. What are the three switch functions at layer 2?

8. If a frame is received on a switch port and the source MAC address is not in the forward/filter table, what will the switch do?

9. What is used at layer 2 to prevent switching loops?

10. You need to implement a separate network for contractors and guests working at your office. Which technology should you implement?

Review Questions

You can find the answers to the review questions in Appendix B.

1. You want to improve network performance by increasing the bandwidth available to hosts and limiting the size of the broadcast domains. Which of the following options will achieve this goal?

    A. Managed hubs

    B. Bridges

    C. Switches

    D. Switches configured with VLANs

2. The types of ports that can be found on a switch are _____ and _____. (Choose two.)

    A. VLAN Trunk Protocol

    B. Access

    C. 802.1Q

    D. Trunk

3. Which switching technology reduces the size of a broadcast domain?

    A. ISL

    B. 802.1Q

    C. VLANs

    D. STP

4. Which of the following are IEEE versions of STP? (Choose two.)

    A. 802.1X

    B. VLANs

    C. 802.1D

    D. 802.11

    E. 802.1w

5. You connect a host to a switch port, but the new host cannot log into the server that is plugged into the same switch. What could the problem be? (Choose two.)

    A. The router is not configured for the new host.

    B. The STP configuration on the switch is not updated for the new host.

    C. The host has an invalid MAC address.

    D. The switch port the host is connected to is not configured to the correct VLAN membership.

    E. STP shut down the port.

6. Which of the following are benefits of VLANs? (Choose three.)

   A. They increase the size of collision domains.

   B. They allow logical grouping of users by function.

   C. They can enhance network security.

   D. They increase the size of broadcast domains while decreasing the number of collision domains.

   E. They simplify switch administration.

   F. They increase the number of broadcast domains while decreasing the size of the broadcast domains.

7. Which of the following is a layer 2 protocol used to maintain a loop-free network?

   A. VTP

   B. STP

   C. RIP

   D. CDP

8. What is the result of segmenting a network with a bridge (switch)? (Choose two.)

   A. It increases the number of collision domains.

   B. It decreases the number of collision domains.

   C. It increases the number of broadcast domains.

   D. It decreases the number of broadcast domains.

   E. It makes smaller collision domains.

   F. It makes larger collision domains.

9. You connect your host to a switch that is running network analysis software. However, you are not seeing any packets from the server. What do you need to implement on the switch to see all the packet information?

   A. VLANs

   B. STP

   C. Port mirroring

   D. Authentication

10. Which of the following features of a switch will allow two switches to pass VLAN network information?

   A. PoE

   B. VLANs

   C. Trunking

   D. STP

11. What are the distinct functions of layer 2 switching that increase available bandwidth on the network? (Choose three.)

    A. Address learning

    B. Routing

    C. Forwarding and filtering

    D. Creating network loops

    E. Loop avoidance

    F. IP addressing

12. Which of the following statements is true?

    A. A switch creates a single collision domain and a single broadcast domain. A router creates a single collision domain.

    B. A switch creates separate collision domains but one broadcast domain. A router provides a separate broadcast domain.

    C. A switch creates a single collision domain and separate broadcast domains. A router provides a separate broadcast domain as well.

    D. A switch creates separate collision domains and separate broadcast domains. A router provides separate collision domains.

13. What does a switch do when a frame is received on an interface and the destination hardware address is unknown or not in the filter table?

    A. Forwards the switch to the first available link

    B. Drops the frame

    C. With the exception of the source port, floods the network with the frame looking for the device

    D. Sends back a message to the originating station asking for a name resolution

14. If a switch receives a frame and the source MAC address is not in the MAC address table but the destination address is, what will the switch do with the frame?

    A. Discard it and send an error message back to the originating host

    B. Flood the network with the frame

    C. Add the source address and port to the MAC address table and forward the frame out the destination port

    D. Add the destination to the MAC address table and then forward the frame

15. When would you configure VTP on a switch?

    A. When you have hubs connected in your network

    B. When you have redundant links between switches

    C. When you have multiple hosts in multiple VLANs and you want to share all the data between hosts without a router

    D. When you have multiple switches with multiple VLANs and you want to share the VLAN database from one switch to all the others

16. When is STP said to be converged on the root bridge? (Choose two.)

   A. When all ports are in the forwarding state

   B. When all ports are in the blocking state

   C. When all ports are in the listening state

   D. When all ports are in the learning state

17. In which two states is the MAC address table populated with addresses? (Choose two.)

   A. Blocking

   B. Listening

   C. Learning

   D. Forwarding

18. You have multiple departments all connected to switches, with crossover cables connecting the switches together. However, response time on the network is still very slow even though you have upgraded from hubs to switches. What technology should you implement to improve response time on the networks?

   A. STP

   B. VLANs

   C. Convergence

   D. OSPF

19. If you are configuring voice VLANs, which of the following should you configure on the switch ports to provide a higher precedence to voice traffic over data traffic to improve sound quality?

   A. Access VLANs

   B. VTP

   C. QoS

   D. STP

20. What is a disadvantage of using port spanning?

   A. It breaks up broadcast domains on all ports.

   B. It can create overhead on the switch.

   C. It makes the switch one large collision domain.

   D. It makes the switch fast between only two ports instead of all ports.

Chapter

12

Wireless Networking

THE FOLLOWING COMPTIA NETWORK+ EXAM OBJECTIVES ARE COVERED IN THIS CHAPTER:

✓ **2.1 Compare and contrast various devices, their features, and their appropriate placement on the network.**

- Networking devices
  - Access point
  - Wireless LAN controller

✓ **2.4 Given a scenario, install and configure the appropriate wireless standards and technologies.**

- 802.11 standards
  - a
  - b
  - g
  - n (WiFi 4)
  - ac (WiFi 5)
  - ax (WiFi 6)
- Frequencies and range
  - 2.4GHz
  - 5GHz
- Channels
  - Regulatory impacts
- Channel bonding
- Service set identifier (SSID)
  - Basic service set
  - Extended service set
  - Independent basic service set (Ad-hoc)
  - Roaming

- Antenna types
  - Omni
  - Directional
- Encryption standards
  - WiFi Protected Access (WPA)/WPA2 Personal [Advanced Encryption Standard (AES)/Temporal Key Integrity Protocol (TKIP)]
  - WPA/WPA2 Enterprise (AES/TKIP)
- Cellular technologies
  - Code-division multiple access (CDMA)
  - Global System for Mobile Communications (GSM)
  - Long-Term Evolution (LTE)
  - 3G, 4G, 5G
- Multiple input, multiple output (MIMO) and multi-user MIMO (MU-MIMO)

If you want to understand the basic wireless LANs (WLANs) most commonly used today, just think 10BaseT Ethernet with hubs. What this means is that our WLANs typically run half-duplex communication—everyone is sharing the same bandwidth, and only one user is communicating at a time.

This isn't necessarily bad; it's just not good enough. Because most people rely on wireless networks today, it's critical that they evolve faster than greased lightning to keep up with our rapidly escalating needs. The good news is that this is actually happening—and it even works securely! We'll discuss these newer, faster technologies in this chapter.

The goal in this chapter is to introduce you to wireless networks and the technologies in use today. I'll also cover the various components used, the IEEE 802.11 standards, wireless installation, and of course, wireless security.

To find Todd Lammle CompTIA videos and practice questions, please see www.lammle.com.

Introduction to Wireless Technology

Transmitting a signal using the basic 802.11 specifications works a lot like transmitting with a basic Ethernet hub: They're both two-way forms of communication, and they both use the same frequency to both transmit and receive, often referred to as *half-duplex*. Wireless LANs (WLANs) use radio frequencies (RFs) that are radiated into the air from an antenna that creates radio waves. These waves can be absorbed, refracted, or reflected by walls, water, and metal surfaces, resulting in low signal strength. So, because of this innate vulnerability to surrounding environmental factors, it's pretty apparent that wireless will never offer us the same robustness as a wired network can, but that still doesn't mean we're not going to run wireless. Believe me, we definitely will!

We can increase the transmitting power and we'd be able to gain a greater transmitting distance, but doing so can create some nasty distortion, so it has to be done carefully. By using higher frequencies, we can attain higher data rates, but this is, unfortunately, at the cost of decreased transmitting distances. And if we use lower frequencies, we get to transmit greater distances but at lower data rates. This should make it pretty clear to you that understanding all the various types of WLANs you can implement is imperative to creating the LAN solution that best meets the specific requirements of the unique situation you're dealing with.

Also important to note is the fact that the 802.11 specifications were developed so that there would be no licensing required in most countries—to ensure that the user has the freedom to install and operate without any licensing or operating fees. This means that any manufacturer can create wireless networking products and sell them at a local computer store or wherever. It also means that all our computers should be able to communicate wirelessly without configuring much, if anything at all.

Various agencies have been around for a very long time to help govern the use of wireless devices, frequencies, standards, and how the frequency spectrums are used. Table 12.1 shows the current agencies that help create, maintain, and even enforce wireless standards worldwide.

TABLE 12.1   Wireless agencies and standards

Agency	Purpose	Website
Institute of Electrical and Electronics Engineers (IEEE)	Creates and maintains operational standards	www.ieee.org
Federal Communications Commission (FCC)	Regulates the use of wireless devices in the US	www.fcc.gov
European Telecommunications Standards Institute (ETSi)	Chartered to produce common standards in Europe	www.etsi.org
Wi-Fi Alliance	Promotes and tests for WLAN interoperability	www.wi-fi.org
WLAN Association (WLANA)	Educates and raises consumer awareness regarding WLANs	www.wlana.org

Because WLANs transmit over radio frequencies, they're regulated by the same types of laws used to govern things like AM/FM radios. In the United States, it's the Federal Communications Commission (FCC) that regulates the use of wireless LAN devices, and the Institute of Electrical and Electronics Engineers (IEEE) takes it from there and creates standards based on what frequencies the FCC releases for public use.

The FCC has released three unlicensed bands for public use: 900 MHz, 2.4 GHz, and 5 GHz. The 900 MHz and 2.4 GHz bands are referred to as the Industrial, Scientific, and Medical (ISM) bands, and the 5 GHz band is known as the Unlicensed National Information Infrastructure (U-NII) band. Figure 12.1 shows where the unlicensed bands sit within the RF spectrum.

So it follows that, if you opt to deploy wireless in a range outside the three public bands shown in Figure 12.1, you need to get a specific license from the FCC to do so. Once the FCC opened the three frequency ranges for public use, many manufacturers were able to start offering myriad products that flooded the market, with 802.11AC/AX being the most widely used wireless network found today.

FIGURE 12.1   Unlicensed frequencies

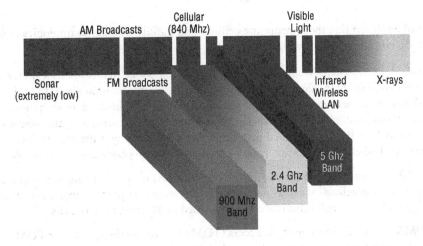

Figure 12.2 shows the WLAN history that is important to us. Although wireless transmissions date back many, many years, the type we really care about is wireless as related to WLANs starting in the 1990s. Use of the ISM band started in early 1990, and it's deployed today in multiple environments, including outdoor links, mesh networks, office buildings, healthcare facilities, warehouses, and homes.

FIGURE 12.2   Wireless LAN history

Speed	860 Kbps	1 and 2 Mbps		11 Mbps	54 Mbps
Network	Proprietary			Standards-Based	
Radio	900 MHz	2.4 GHz		5 GHz	

	IEEE 802.11 Drafting Begins	802.11 Ratified	802.11a,b Ratified	802.11g Ratified	802.11n Draft 2.0
	1992	1997	1999	2003	2007

802.11ac (now referred to as WiFi 5) was released in December 2013, 802.11ax (WiFi 6) was released in 2019, and although they are not shown in Figure 12.2, I'll discuss these in detail throughout this chapter.

The Wi-Fi Alliance grants certification for interoperability among 802.11 products offered by various vendors. This certification provides a sort of comfort zone for the users purchasing the many types of products, although in my personal experience, it's just a whole lot easier if you buy all your access points from the same manufacturer.

In the current US WLAN market, there are several accepted operational standards and drafts created and maintained by the IEEE. We'll now take a look at these standards and then talk about how the most commonly used standards work.

Cellular Technologies

As part of implementing the appropriate cellular and mobile wireless technologies and configurations, consider the following options:

GSM   Global System Mobile (GSM) is a type of cell phone that contains a subscriber identity module (SIM) chip. These chips contain all the information about the subscriber and must be present in the phone for it to function. One of the dangers with these phones is cell phone cloning, a process where copies of the SIM chip are made, allowing another user to make calls as the original user. Secret key cryptography is used (using a common secret key) when authentication is performed between the phone and the network.

FDMA   Frequency-division multiple access (FDMA) is one of the modulation techniques used in cellular wireless networks. It divides the frequency range into bands and assigns a band to each subscriber. This was used in 1G cellular networks.

TDMA   Time-division multiple access (TDMA) increases the speed over FDMA by dividing the channels into time slots and assigning slots to calls. This also helps to prevent eavesdropping in calls.

CDMA   Code division multiple access (CDMA) assigns a unique code to each call or transmission and spreads the data across the spectrum, allowing a call to make use of all frequencies.

3G   This third generation (3G) of cellular data networks was really a game changer at 1G and 2G and allowed the basics to get smartphones working and achieving usable data speeds (sort of), but 2 Mbps was a lot of bandwidth in the 1990s and really provided us with the start of smartphone applications, which lead to more research and technologies and of course the plethora of applications we now have.

The 2G networks handled phone calls, basic text messaging, and small amounts of data over a protocol called MMS. When 3G connectivity arrived, a number of larger data formats became much more accessible, such as HTML pages, videos, and music, and there was no going back!

4G   The term 4G stands for fourth generation of speed and connection standards for cellular data networks. The speeds really helped push smartphones to customers as it provided from 100 Mbps up to 1 Gbps, but you'd have to be in a 4G mobile hotspot to achieve the maximum speed.

LTE   Most of 4G networks were called Long-Term Evolution (LTE), which was also called 4G LTE. Although 5G has taken over and 6G is probably here to stay, LTE is still prevalent in many markets, and I still see it on my phones at times. The reality is that in the 2000s your phone would display "4G," but it couldn't really provide what the standard mandated.

When the cellular standards bodies set the minimum speeds for 4G, they could never reach those speeds, even though cell carriers spend millions trying to get them. Because of this, the regulating body decided that LTE (which really was just the pursuit of the

4G standard) could be labeled as 4G as long as it provided an improvement over the 3G technology speeds.

5G   This stands for "fifth generation" of cellular technology and is a standard for mobile telecommunications service that is significantly faster than today's 4G technology, up to 100xs faster.

Since this technology has been out for years, you know you can upload or download videos and use data-intensive apps or other applications much more quickly and smoothly than what we had in the past with 3G and 4G.

This is because 5G technology utilizes a higher-frequency band of the wireless spectrum called millimeter wave that allows data to be transferred much more rapidly than the lower-frequency band dedicated to 4G.

However, the millimeter wave signals don't travel as far so you need more antennas spaced closer together than the previous wireless 3G and 4G.

Table 12.2 shows us the comparisons between 3G, 4G, and 5G.

TABLE 12.2   Cellular comparisons

Technology	3G	4G	5G
Deployment	1990	2000	2014
Bandwidth	2 Mbps	200 to 1000 Mbps	1 to 10 Gbps
Standards	WCDMA, CDMA-2000	CDMA, LTE, WiMAX	OFDM, MIMO, nm Waves
Technology	CDMA/IP	Unified IP, LAN/WAN	Unified IP, LAN/WAN

The 802.11 Standards (Regulatory Impacts)

Building on what you learned in Chapter 1, "Introduction to Networks," wireless networking has its own 802 standards group—remember, Ethernet's committee is 802.3. Wireless starts with 802.11. And even cellular networks are becoming huge players in our wireless experience. But for now, we're going to concentrate on the 802.11 standards committee and subcommittees.

IEEE 802.11 was the first, original standardized WLAN at 1 Mbps and 2 Mbps. It runs in the 2.4 GHz radio frequency. It was ratified in 1997, although we didn't see many products pop up until around 1999 when 802.11b was introduced. All the committees listed in Table 12.3 made amendments to the original 802.11 standard except for 802.11F and 802.11T, which produced stand-alone documents.

TABLE 12.3   802.11 committees and subcommittees

Committee	Purpose
IEEE 802.11a	54 Mbps, 5 GHz standard
IEEE 802.11ac	1 Gbps, 5 GHz standard (WiFi 5)
IEEE 802.11ax	Published in Feb 2021, successor to WiFi 5, works in 1 to 6 GHz range to get over 10 Gbit/s
IEEE 802.11b	Enhancements to 802.11 to support 5.5 Mbps and 11 Mbps
IEEE 802.11c	Bridge operation procedures; included in the IEEE 802.1D standard
IEEE 802.11d	International roaming extensions
IEEE 802.11e	Quality of service
IEEE 802.11F	Inter-Access Point Protocol
IEEE 802.11g	54 Mbps, 2.4 GHz standard (backward compatible with 802.11b)
IEEE 802.11h	Dynamic Frequency Selection (DFS) and Transmit Power Control (TPC) at 5 GHz
IEEE 802.11i	Enhanced security
IEEE 802.11j	Extensions for Japan and US public safety
IEEE 802.11k	Radio resource measurement enhancements
IEEE 802.11m	Maintenance of the standard; odds and ends
IEEE 802.11n	Higher throughput improvements using multiple-input, multiple-output (MIMO) antennas (WiFi 4)
IEEE 802.11p	Wireless Access for the Vehicular Environment (WAVE)
IEEE 802.11r	Fast roaming
IEEE 802.11s	ESS Extended Service Set Mesh Networking
IEEE 802.11T	Wireless Performance Prediction (WPP)

IEEE 802.11u	Internetworking with non-802 networks (cellular, for example)
IEEE 802.11v	Wireless network management
IEEE 802.11w	Protected management frames
IEEE 802.11y	3650–3700 operation in the US

> One type of wireless networking that doesn't get a whole lot of attention is infrared wireless. Infrared wireless uses the same basic transmission method as many television remote controls—that's right, infrared technology. Infrared is used primarily for short-distance, point-to-point communications, like those between a peripheral and a PC, with the most widely used for peripherals being the IrDA standard.

Now let's discuss some important specifics of the most popular 802.11 WLANs.

2.4 GHz (802.11b)

First on the menu is the 802.11b standard. It was the most widely deployed wireless standard, and it operates in the 2.4 GHz unlicensed radio band that delivers a maximum data rate of 11 Mbps. The 802.11b standard has been widely adopted by both vendors and customers who found that its 11 Mbps data rate worked pretty well for most applications. But now that 802.11b has a big brother (802.11g), no one goes out and just buys an 802.11b card or access point anymore—why would you buy a 10 Mbps Ethernet card when you can score a 10/100 Ethernet card for the same price?

An interesting thing about all 802.11 WLAN products is that they have the ability to data-rate-shift while moving. This allows the person operating at 11 Mbps to shift to 5.5 Mbps, then 2 Mbps, and finally still communicate farthest from the access point at 1 Mbps. And furthermore, this rate shifting happens without losing the connection and with no interaction from the user. Rate shifting also occurs on a transmission-by-transmission basis. This is important because it means that the access point can support multiple clients at varying speeds depending on the location of each client.

The problem with all 802.11b communication lies in how the Data Link layer is dealt with. In order to solve problems in the RF spectrum, a type of Ethernet contention management was created called *carrier sense multiple access with collision avoidance (CSMA/CA)*.

CSMA/CA also has an optional implementation called a *Request to Send, Clear to Send (RTS/CTS)* because of the way that hosts must communicate with the access point (AP). For every packet sent, an RTS/CTS and acknowledgment must be received, and because of this rather cumbersome process, it's kind of hard to believe it all actually works when you use this!

To get a clear picture of this, check out Figure 12.3.

FIGURE 12.3 802.11b CSMA/CA

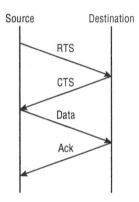

2.4 GHz (802.11g)

The 802.11g standard was ratified in June 2003 and is backward compatible to 802.11b. The 802.11g standard delivers the same 54 Mbps maximum data rate as you'll find in the 802.11a range but runs in the 2.4 GHz range—the same as 802.11b.

Because 802.11b/g operates in the same 2.4 GHz unlicensed band, migrating to 802.11g is an affordable choice for organizations with existing 802.11b wireless infrastructures. Just keep in mind that 802.11b products can't be "software upgraded" to 802.11g. This limitation is because 802.11g radios use a different chipset in order to deliver the higher data rate.

But still, much like Ethernet and Fast Ethernet, 802.11g products can be commingled with 802.11b products in the same network. Yet, for example, and completely unlike Ethernet, if you have four users running 802.11g cards and one user starts using an 802.11b card, everyone connected to the same access point is then forced to run the 802.11b signal modulation method—an ugly fact that really makes throughput suffer badly. So to optimize performance, it's recommended that you disable the 802.11b-only modes on all your access points.

To explain this further, 802.11b uses a *modulation technique* called *direct-sequence spread spectrum (DSSS)* that's just not as robust as the *orthogonal frequency-division multiplexing (OFDM)* modulation used by both 802.11g and 802.11a. 802.11g clients using OFDM enjoy much better performance at the same ranges as 802.11b clients do, but—and remember this—when 802.11g clients are operating at the 802.11b rates (11 Mbps, 5.5 Mbps, 2 Mbps, and 1 Mbps), they're actually using the same modulation 802.11b uses.

So, regarding the throughput of different WLAN standards, you know that 802.11b has a top throughput of 11 Mbps, and 802.11g has a top throughput of 54 Mbps. But with that said, do you really think we're actually getting that type of throughput? The answer is absolutely not! This is because in reality, about 70 percent or more of the RF bandwidth is used for the management of the wireless network itself! The actual bandwidth the user experiences using an application is called goodput, even though you won't hear this term used a lot. Just remember that *goodput* refers to the actual data throughput, not the theoretical number that the standards describe.

Figure 12.4 shows the 14 different channels (each 22 MHz wide) that the FCC released in the 2.4 GHz range.

FIGURE 12.4   ISM 2.4 GHz channels

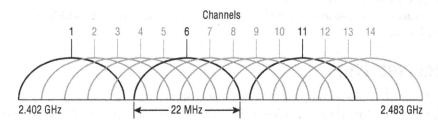

In the United States, only 11 channels are configurable, with channels 1, 6, and 11 being non-overlapping. This allows you to have three access points in the same area without experiencing interference. You must be aware of the channels when installing APs in a large environment so you do not overlap channels. If you configure one AP with channel 1, then the next AP would be configured in channel 11, the channel farthest from that configured on the first AP.

5 GHz (802.11a)

The IEEE ratified the 802.11a standard in 1999, but the first 802.11a products didn't begin appearing on the market until late 2001—and boy, were they pricey! The 802.11a standard delivers a maximum data rate of 54 Mbps with 12 non-overlapping frequency channels. Figure 12.5 shows the U-NII band.

FIGURE 12.5   U-NII 5 GHz band has 12 non-overlapping channels (US)

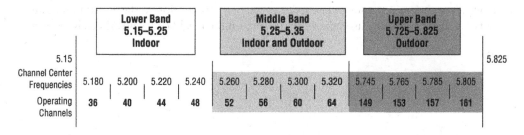

Operating in the 5 GHz radio band, 802.11a is also immune to interference from devices that operate in the 2.4 GHz band, like microwave ovens, cordless phones, and Bluetooth devices. 802.11a isn't backward compatible with 802.11b because they are different frequencies, so you don't get to just "upgrade" part of your network and expect everything to work together in perfect harmony. But no worries—there are plenty of dual-radio devices that will work in both types of networks. A definite plus for 802.11a is that it can work in the same physical environment without interference from 802.11b users.

Similar to the 802.11b radios, all 802.11a products also have the ability to data-rate-shift while moving. The 802.11a products allow the person operating at 54 Mbps to shift to 48 Mbps, 36 Mbps, 24 Mbps, 18 Mbps, 12 Mbps, and 9 Mbps, and finally, still communicate farthest from the AP at 6 Mbps.

There's also an extension to the 802.11a specification called 802.11h, which is described next.

5 GHz (802.11h)

The FCC added 11 new channels in February 2004, and in 2008, we were finally able to begin using these channels based on manufacturers' releases of more 802.11a 5 GHz products. This means that we gained access to up to 23 non-overlapping channels! And there are even two new features to the 5 GHz radio that are part of the 802.11h specification: *Dynamic Frequency Selection (DFS)* and *Transmit Power Control (TPC)*.

Dynamic Frequency Selection (DFS)   This cool feature continuously monitors a device's operating range for any radar signals that are allowed to operate in portions of the 5 GHz band as well as 802.11a before transmitting. If DFS discovers any radar signals, it'll either abandon the occupied channel or mark it as unavailable to prevent interference from occurring on the WLAN.

Transmit Power Control (TPC)   Even though it's been employed by the mobile phone industry for a long time, this technology has some handy new uses. You can set the client machine's adapter and the access point's transmit power to cover various size ranges—a feature that's useful for many reasons. For one, setting the access point's transmit power to 5 milliwatts (mW) reduces cell range, which works great if you've got a compact area with high-density usage.

Further advantages include the fact that TPC enables the client and the access point to communicate with less power. This means the client machine can fine-tune its transmit power dynamically so it uses just enough energy to preserve its connection to the access point and conserve its battery power plus reduce interference on the neighboring WLAN cells—sweet!

2.4 GHz/5 GHz (802.11n)

802.11n builds on previous 802.11 standards by adding *multiple-input, multiple-output (MIMO)*, which employs multiple transmitters and receiver antennas to increase data throughput. 802.11n can have up to eight antennas, but most of today's access points use four. These are sometimes referred to as *smart antennas*, and if you did have four of them, two would be used for transmitting simultaneously with the other two receiving simultaneously. This setup allowed for much higher data rates than 802.11a/b/g. In fact, the marketing people claim it provided about 250 Mbps, but personally, I've never really seen that level of throughput with 802.11n. Even if what they're saying is true, exactly how would that help if all you've got is a 100 Mbps DSL connection to the Internet?

 802.11n allows for communication at both the 2.4 GHz and 5 GHz frequencies by using channel bonding.

Unlike 802.11a and 802.11g, which are locked into using the 5.0 GHz and 2.4 GHz spectrums, respectively, with 802.11n you can allow one, the other, or both spectrums in your WLAN! Listed next are some additional components of 802.11n that give people reason to say 802.11n has greater reliability and predictability:

40 MHz Channels   802.11g and 802.11a use 20 MHz channels, and tones on the sides of each channel are not used to protect the main carrier, which means that 11 Mbps are unused or wasted. However, 802.11n aggregates two 40 MHz carriers to double the speed from 54 Mbps to 108 Mbps, and add the 11 Mbps that we gain from not wasting the side tones and we have 119 Mbps.

MAC Efficiency   802.11 protocols require acknowledgment of each and every frame. 802.11n can pass many packets before an acknowledgment is required, which saves you on overhead. This is called *block acknowledgment*.

Multiple-Input, Multiple-Output (MIMO)   Several frames are sent by several antennas over several paths and are then recombined by another set of antennas to optimize throughput and multipath resistance. This is called *spatial multiplexing*.

Multiuser Multiple-Input, Multiple-Output (MU-MIMO)   MU-MIMO is an enhancement over the original MIMO technology. It allows antennas to be spread over a multitude of independent access points. MU-MIMO does not directly affect data rates. What it does do, though, is help multiple devices like Wi-Fi routers coordinate when they communicate with one another better and faster than before. Overall, because MU-MIMO allows multiple devices to transmit at once, it makes more efficient use of channels.

So What Is Wi-Fi?

You may have seen products that are 802.11 compliant with a small sticker on them that says "Wi-Fi." You might be able to guess that this rather odd phrase stands for Wireless Fidelity, but you may not know what its implications are. Simply put, that sticker indicates that the product in question has passed certification testing for 802.11 interoperability by the Wi-Fi Alliance. This nonprofit group was formed to ensure that all 802.11a/b/g/n/ac/ax wireless devices would communicate seamlessly. So, Wi-Fi is a good thing.

---

5 GHz (802.11ac)

802.11ac is a Wi-Fi standard that works in the 5 GHz range and delivers up to 1 gigabit throughput that was approved by the 802.11 standards committee in January 2014. Still, just as it is with 802.11n, you won't find that the speeds described in the standard actually line up with the marketing material.

For example, for a single link, which is basically one host to AP, the best throughput you can hope to get would be 500 Mbps, which is fantastic if it actually happens! But unless you have a Gigabit Internet connection, 802.11ac won't really help so much. To be fair, in a small network, or if you're transferring files in your internal WLAN or to your internal network, this new specification could actually be useful.

At this point, you're probably wondering how these people can claim to achieve these theoretical rates, right? That's an excellent question! They get these values by increasing the RF band usage from 20 MHz wide channels with 802.11a/b/g to 40 MHz with 802.11n and up to 160 MHz wide channels with 802.11ac. But again, for typical commercial 802.11ac products, 80 MHz would be a lot more realistic. The problem with this scenario centers on the fact that if any interference is found in the 80 MHz wide channel, it drops down to 40 MHz wide channels. Worse, if interference is still found at that level, it will drop even further down to 20 MHz wide channels.

In addition to the wider channels, we can also get more MIMO spatial streams than we can with 802.11n—up to eight, where 802.11n only supported four. Furthermore, and optionally, a downlink of multiuser MIMO (MU-MIMO) supports up to four clients and, most important, a modulation of QAM-256 compared to QAM-64 with 802.11a/g.

The last thing I want to point out is the fact that 802.11n had added fields in the wireless frame to identify 802.11a and 802.11g as high throughput (HT), whereas 802.11ac adds four fields to identify the frames as very high throughput (VHT).

WiFi 6 (802.11ax)

So, what is WiFi 6 and is it faster than WiFi 5? Well, I would hope so since it is one number greater than 5, but that is only because this is the sixth generation of Wi-Fi with enough changes to possibly give us twice the speed, but only time will tell if that is true.

To say that 802.11ax and Wi-Fi 6 are the same thing would definitely be true, and it's great marketing right now for the Wi-Fi manufacturers.

Figure 12.6 shows the difference between 802.11ac (WiFi 5) and 802.11.ax (WiFi 6), and the first thing you should notice is that ax uses both 2.4 and 5 GHz, where ac uses only 5 GHz, and ax has more OFDM symbols and a higher modulation, which provides superior data rates.

FIGURE 12.6   Comparing WiFi 5 to WiFi 6

TABLE 1: COMPARING WIFI 5 AND WIFI 6 STANDARDS		
Parameter	WiFi 5 (802.11 ac)	WiFi 6 (802.11 ax)
Frequency	5 GHz	2.4 and 5.0 GHz
Bandwidths (channels)	20, 40, 80+80, 160 MHz	20, 40, 80+80, 160 MHz
Access	OFDM	OFDMA
Antennas	MU-MIMO (4 × 4)	MU-MIMO (8 × 8)
Modulation	256QAM	1024QAM
Maximum data rate	3.5 Gb/s	9.6 Gb/s
Maximum users/AP	4	8

This newer Wi-Fi 6 technology includes the following benefits:

- Denser modulation using 1024 Quadrature Amplitude Modulation (QAM), enabling a more than 35 percent speed burst.
- Orthogonal frequency-division multiple access (OFDMA) based scheduling to reduce overhead and latency.
- Robust high efficiency signaling for better operation at a significantly lower received signal strength Indicator (RSSI).
- Better scheduling and longer device battery life with Target Wake Time (TWT).

Comparing 802.11 Standards

Before I move on to wireless installations, take a look at Figure 12.7, which lists, for each of the IEEE standards in use today, the year of ratification as well as the frequency, number of non-overlapping channels, physical layer transmission technique, and data rates.

I mentioned earlier that 802.11b runs DSSS, whereas 802.11g and 802.11a both run the OFDM modulation technique (802.11ac runs up to OFDM 256-QAM).

FIGURE 12.7   Current standards for spectrums and speeds

	802.11	802.11b	802.11a	802.11g		802.11n	802.11ac
Ratified	1997	1999	1999	2003		2010	2013
Frequency Band	2.4 GHz	2.4 GHz	5 GHz	2.4 GHz		2.4 GHz–5 GHz	5 GHz
No. of Channels	3	3	Up to 23	3		Varies	Varies
Transmission	IR, FHSS, DSSS	DSSS	OFDM	DSSS	OFDM	DSSS, CCK, OFDM	OFDM
Data Rates (Mbps)	1, 2	1, 2, 5.5, 11	6, 9, 12, 18, 24, 36, 48, 54	1, 2, 5.5, 11	6, 9, 12, 18, 24, 36, 48, 54	100+	1000+

Range and Speed Comparisons

Now let's take a look at Table 12.4, which delimits the range comparisons of each 802.11 standard and shows these different ranges using an indoor open-office environment as a factor. (We'll be using default power settings.)

TABLE 12.4   Range and speed comparisons

Standard	802.11b	802.11a	802.11g	802.11n	802.11ac	802.11ax
Speed	11 Mbps	54 Mbps	54 Mbps	300 Mbps	1 Gbps	3.5+ Gbps
Frequency	2.4 GHz	5 GHz	2.4 GHz	2.4/5 GHz	5 GHz	2.4/5/6 GHz
Range ft.	100–150	25–75	100–150	>230	>230	Unknown

You can see that to get the full 54 Mbps benefit of both 802.11a and 802.11g, you need to be between 75 feet and 150 feet (maximum) away, which will likely be even less if there happen to be any obstructions between the client and the access point. 802.11n gives more distance than all three standards shown in figure 12.7 (up to twice the distance), and understand that 802.11ac won't give you more distance than 802.11n, but certainly more speed; however, 802.11ax is our future with more than three times the speed of 802.11ac.

Wireless Network Components

Though it might not seem this way to you right now, wireless networks are less complex than their wired cousins because they require fewer components. To make a wireless network work properly, all you really need are two main devices: a wireless access point and a wireless NIC, the latter of which is typically built into your laptop. This also makes it a lot easier to install a wireless network because, basically, you just need an understanding of these two components in order to do so.

Wireless Access Points

You'll find a central component—like a hub or switch—in the vast majority of wired networks that serves to connect hosts together and allow them to communicate with each other. It's the same idea with wireless networks. They also have a component that connects all wireless devices together, only that device is known as a *wireless access point (WAP)*, or just AP. Wireless access points have at least one antenna (typically two for better reception—a solution called *diversity*, and up to eight to support 802.11ac/ax) and an Ethernet port to connect them to a wired network. Figure 12.8 shows an example of a typical wireless access point.

FIGURE 12.8   A wireless access point

You can even think of an AP as a bridge between the wireless clients and the wired network. In fact, an AP can be used as a wireless bridge (depending on the settings) to bridge two wired network segments together.

In addition to the stand-alone AP, there is another type of AP that includes a built-in router, which you can use to connect both wired and wireless clients to the Internet (the most popular home brand being Linksys, a division of Cisco). In summary, an AP can operate as a repeater, bridge (switch), or router, depending on its hardware and its implementation.

These devices are usually known as (surprise) wireless routers. They're usually employed as network address translation (NAT) servers by using the one ISP-provided global IP address to multiplex numerous local IP addresses that are generally doled out to inside clients by the wireless router from a pool within the 192.168.*x.x* range.

Wireless Network Interface Card

Every host that wants to connect to a wireless network needs a wireless *network interface card (NIC)* to do so. Basically, a wireless NIC does the same job as a traditional NIC, but instead of having a socket to plug some cable into, the wireless NIC has a radio antenna. In addition to the different types of wireless networking (I'll talk about those in a minute), wireless NICs (like other NICs) can differ in the type of connection they use to connect to the host computer.

Figure 12.9 shows an example of a wireless NIC.

FIGURE 12.9   A wireless NIC

The wireless card shown in Figure 12.9 is used in a desktop PC. There are various options for laptops as well. All new laptops have wireless cards built into the motherboard.

These days, it's pretty rare to use an external wireless client card because all laptops come with them built in, and desktops can be ordered with them too. But it's good to know that you can still buy the client card shown in Figure 12.9. Typically, you would use cards like the one shown in the figure for areas of poor reception because they can have a better range—depending on the antenna you use, or because you want to upgrade the built-in card to 802.11n/ac/ax. It might be cheaper and easier to just buy a new PC these days.

Wireless Antennas

Wireless antennas act as both transmitters and receivers. There are two broad classes of antennas on the market today: *Omni directional* (or point-to-multipoint) and *directional,* or *Yagi* (point-to-point). Yagi antennas usually provide a greater range than Omni antennas of equivalent gain. Why? Because Yagis focus all their power in a single direction, whereas Omnis must disperse the same amount of power in all directions at the same time. A downside to using a directional antenna is that you've got to be much more precise when aligning communication points. This is why a Yagi is really only a good choice for point-to-point bridging of access points. It's also why most APs use Omnis, because often, clients and other APs could be located in any direction at any given moment.

To get a picture of this, think of the antenna on your car (if you still have an antenna on your car!). Yes, it's a non-networking example, but it's still a good one because it clarifies the fact that your car's particular orientation doesn't affect the signal reception of whatever radio station you happen to be listening to. Well, most of the time, anyway. If you're in the boonies, you're out of range—something that also applies to the networking version of Omnis.

The television aerials that *some* of us are old enough to remember rotating into a specific direction for a certain channel are examples of Yagi antennas. (How many of you labeled your set-top antenna dial for the actual TV stations you could receive?) Believe it or not, they still look the same to this day!

Both Omnis and Yagis are rated according to their signal gain with respect to an actual or theoretical laboratory reference antenna. These ratings are relative indicators of the corresponding production antenna's range. Range is also affected by the bit rate of the underlying technology, with higher bit rates extending shorter distances. Remember, a Yagi will always have a longer range than an equivalently rated Omni, but as I said, the straight-line Yagi will be very limited in its coverage area.

Both antennas are also rated in units of decibel isotropic (dBi) or decibel dipole (dBd), based on the type of reference antenna (isotropic or dipole) of equivalent frequency that was initially used to rate the production antenna. A positive value for either unit of measure represents a gain in signal strength with respect to the reference antenna. *Merriam-Webster* defines *isotropic* as "exhibiting properties (as velocity of light transmission) with the same values when measured along axes in all directions." Isotropic antennas are not able to be produced in reality, but their properties can be engineered from antenna theory for reference purposes.

It's pretty much a given that antennas operating with frequencies below 1 GHz are measured in dBd while those operating above 1 GHz are measured in dBi. But because this rule doesn't always work definitively, sometimes we have to compare the strength of one antenna measured in dBd with another measured in numerically equivalent dBi in order to determine which one is stronger. This is exactly why it's important to know that a particular numerical magnitude of dBd is more powerful than the same numerical magnitude of dBi.

I know this sounds pretty complicated, but because the relationship between these two values is linear, it really makes the conversion a lot easier than you might think. Here's how it works: At the same operating frequency, a dipole antenna has about 2.2 dB gain over a

0 dBi theoretical isotropic antenna, which means you can easily convert from dBd to dBi by adding 2.2 to the dBd rating. Conversely, subtract 2.2 from the dBi rating and you get the equivalent dBd rating.

Armed with what you've learned about the difference between Omni and Yagi antennas and the difference between dBd and dBi gain ratings, you should be able to compare the relative range of transmission of one antenna with respect to another based on a combination of these characteristics. For example, the following four antenna ratings are given in relative order from the greatest to the least range:

- 7 dBd Yagi (equivalent to a 9.2 dBi Yagi)
- 7 dBi Yagi (longer range than 7 dBi Omni)
- 4.8 dBd Omni (equivalent to a 7 dBi Omni)
- 4.8 dBi Omni (equivalent to a 2.6 dBd Omni)

If you're having an intermittent problem with hosts connecting to the wireless network and varying signal strengths at different locations, check the location of your antennas in the office or warehouse to make sure you're getting the best coverage possible.

So now that you understand the basic components involved in a wireless network, it's time to use what you learned about the standards we use in our everyday home and corporate wireless networks and the different ways that they're actually installed.

Installing a Wireless Network

Let's say you just bought a wireless AP for your laptop to use to connect to the Internet. What's next? Well, that all depends on the type of installation you want to create with your new toys. First, it's important you understand where to place the AP. For example, you don't want to place the AP on or near a metal filing cabinet or other obstructions. Once you decide on the AP's placement, you can configure your wireless network.

There are two main installation types, ad hoc and infrastructure mode, and each 802.11 wireless network device can be installed in one of these two modes, also called *service sets*.

Ad Hoc Mode: Independent Basic Service Set

This is the easiest way to install wireless 802.11 devices. In this mode, the wireless NICs (or other devices) can communicate directly without the need for an AP. A good example of this is two laptops with wireless NICs installed. If both cards were set up to operate in ad hoc mode, they could connect and transfer files as long as the other network settings, like protocols, were set up to enable this as well. We'll also call this an *independent basic service set (IBSS)*, which is created as soon as two wireless devices communicate.

To set up a basic ad hoc wireless network, all you need are two wireless NICs and two computers. First (assuming they aren't built in), install the cards into the computers according to the manufacturer's directions. During the software installation, you'll be asked if you want to set up the NIC in ad hoc mode or infrastructure mode. For an ad hoc network, you would obviously go with the ad hoc mode setting. Once that's done, all you've got to do is bring the computers within range (90–100 m) of each other, and voilà—they'll "see" each other and be able to connect to each other.

Figure 12.10 shows an example of an ad hoc wireless network. (Note the absence of an access point.)

FIGURE 12.10   A wireless network in ad hoc mode

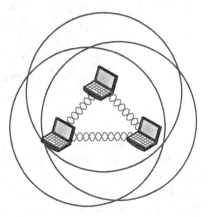

An ad hoc network would not scale well and really is not recommended due to collision and organization issues. With the low costs of APs, this type of network is just not needed today.

Infrastructure Mode: Basic Service Set

The most common use of wireless networking equipment is to give us the wireless equivalent of a wired network. To do this, all 802.11 wireless equipment has the ability to operate in what's known as infrastructure mode, also referred to as a *basic service set (BSS)*, which is provided by an AP. The term *basic service area (BSA)* is also used at times to define the area managed by the AP, but *BSS* is the most common term used to define the cell area.

In infrastructure mode, NICs communicate only with an access point instead of directly with each other as they do when they're in ad hoc mode. All communication between hosts, plus with any wired portion of the network, must go through the access point. A really important fact to remember is that in this mode, wireless clients actually appear to the rest of the network as though they were standard, wired hosts.

Figure 12.11 shows a typical infrastructure mode wireless network. Pay special attention to the access point and the fact that it's also connected to the wired network. This connection from the access point to the wired network is called the *distribution system (DS)* and is referred to as wireless bridging.

FIGURE 12.11 A wireless network in infrastructure mode

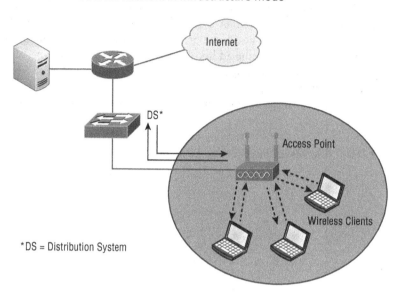

When you configure a client to operate in wireless infrastructure mode, you need to understand a couple of basic wireless concepts—namely, SSID and security. The *service set identifier (SSID)* refers to the unique 32-character identifier that represents a particular wireless network and defines the basic service set. Oh, and by the way, a lot of people use the terms *SSID* and *BSS* interchangeably, so don't let that confuse you! All devices involved in a particular wireless network must be configured with the same SSID.

It is good to know that if you set all your access points to the same SSID, mobile wireless clients can roam around freely within the same network. Doing this creates an *extended service set (ESS)* and provides more coverage than a single access point. Figure 12.12 shows two APs configured with the same SSID in an office, thereby creating the ESS network.

For users to be able to roam throughout the wireless network—from AP to AP without losing their connection to the network—all AP signal areas must overlap by 10 percent of their signal or more. To make this happen, be sure the channels on each AP are set differently. And remember, in an 802.11b/g network, there are only three non-overlapping channels (1, 6, 11), so careful design is super important here!

Wireless Controllers

You'd be hard pressed to find an enterprise WLAN that doesn't use wireless controllers. In fact, every wireless enterprise manufacturer has a controller to manage the APs in the network.

By looking at Figure 12.13, you can see the difference between what we call stand-alone APs and the controller solution. In a stand-alone solution, all the APs have a full operating system loaded and running, and each must be managed separately.

FIGURE 12.12   Extended service set (ESS)

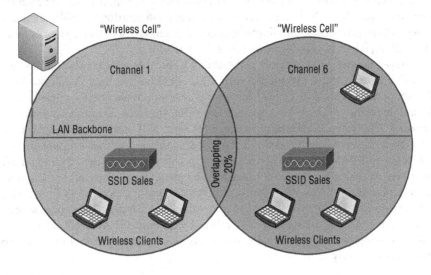

FIGURE 12.13   Stand-alone and controller-based wireless networks

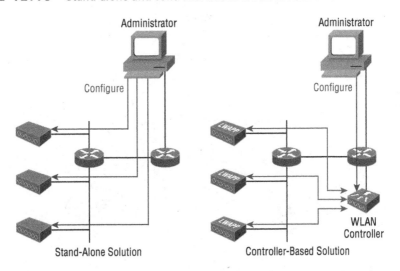

In the controller-based system, the APs are what we refer to as lightweight, meaning they do not have a full operating system running on them. The controller and AP split duties—a solution known as *split MAC*. APs running with a controller are referred to as lightweight, but you'll also hear the term *thin AP*, whereas you'll hear the term *thick* when referring to APs that run a full OS.

Take another look at Figure 12.13. You can also see that the administrator isn't managing each AP independently when using the WLAN controller solution. Instead, the administrator configures the controller, which in turn pushes out the configuration needed for each AP. Controllers allow us to design and implement larger enterprise wireless networks with less time and tedium, which is very important in today's world!

One feature that also gives controllers the ability to provide a great solution is when you're dealing with a location that's overloaded with clients because it utilizes VLAN pooling, or virtual LAN pooling. This is very cool because it allows you to partition a single large wireless broadcast domain into multiple VLANs and then either statically or randomly assign clients into a pool of VLANs. So, all clients get to keep the same SSID and stay connected to the wireless network, even when they roam. They're just in different broadcast domains.

In order for split MAC to work in a wireless controller network, the APs and controller run a protocol to enable them to communicate. The proprietary protocol that Cisco used was called Lightweight Access Point Protocol (LWAPP), and it's pictured in Figure 12.14.

Keep in mind that LWAPP isn't used too much these days, but a newer, more secure protocol called Control and Provisioning of Wireless Access Points (CAPWAP), which also happens to be nonproprietary, has replaced it to become the standard that most controller manufacturers use today.

FIGURE 12.14   LWAPP

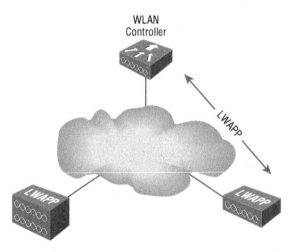

Mobile Hot Spots

Let's say you're in a location that doesn't have an AP installed, or they want to charge you for access, and you want to connect your laptop, tablet, or even play a game. What can you do?

You've got a couple of options, but they all include the cellular network as an infrastructure. Not to be an ad for AT&T, but Figure 12.15 shows a mobile hot spot device that connects your laptop, tablet, media devices, or even a gaming device to the Internet at decent speeds. Pretty much all cellular vendors sell a version of these hot spots now.

FIGURE 12.15   Mobile hot spot

But let's say you don't want to carry yet another device around with you, and you just want to use your phone instead. Figure 12.16 shows how I turned my iPhone into an AP for my laptop. First, I went to Settings and then chose Personal Hotspot. If that option doesn't show up for you, just give a quick shout to your carrier and have it enabled.

FIGURE 12.16   iPhone hot spot

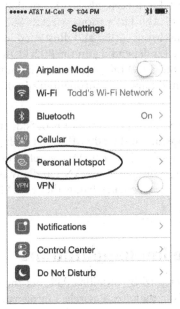

I pay very little to AT&T for my AP capability, but I still have to pay for my usage, so I use it only when I'm someplace like an airport and I want security without paying for access to their Internet wireless. Airport wireless hot spots are notoriously slow anyway, and you'd be dead in the water if you intend to use this type of wireless networking for something like gaming, which requires a ton of bandwidth!

Signal Degradation

Something that's really important to consider when installing a wireless network is signal degradation. Because the 802.11 wireless protocols use radio frequencies, the signal strength varies according to many factors. The weaker the signal, the less reliable the network connection will be and so the less usable as well. (Think dropped calls!) There are several key factors that affect signal strength:

Distance   This one is definitely on the obvious side—the farther away from the WAP you get, the weaker the signal you get. Most APs have a very limited maximum range that equals less than 100 meters for most systems. You can extend this range to some degree using amplifiers or repeaters, or even by using different antennas.

Walls and Other Barriers   Also easy to imagine is the fact that the more walls and other office barriers a wireless signal has to pass through, the more attenuated (reduced) the signal becomes. Also, the thicker the wall, the more it interrupts the signal. So in an indoor office area with lots of walls, the range of your wireless network could be as low as 25 feet! You really have to be careful where you place your APs!

Protocols Used   This one isn't so apparent, but it certainly is a factor that affects, and can even determine, the range of a wireless LAN. The various wireless 802.11 protocols have different maximum ranges. As discussed earlier and illustrated in Figure 12.7, the maximum effective range varies quite a bit depending on the 802.11 protocol used. For example, if you have a client running the 802.11ac protocol but it connects to an AP running only the 802.11n protocol, you'll only get a throughput of 600 Mbps to the client.

Interference   The final factor that affects wireless performance is outside interference. Because 802.11 wireless protocols operate in the 900 MHz, 2.4 GHz, and 5 GHz ranges, interference can come from many sources. These include wireless devices like Bluetooth, cordless telephones, cell phones, other wireless LANs, and any other device that transmits a radio frequency (RF) near the frequency bands that 802.11 protocols use.

Other Network Infrastructure Implementations

We've discussed the wireless LANs (WLANs) created by installing APs, but there are other technologies, like personal area networks (PANs), that create wireless infrastructures too.

By far, the best known is the ever-popular Bluetooth, but there are other wireless technologies we can use as well, and we'll take some time to explore these soon.

For now, it's back to Bluetooth, which happens to have a fantastic history behind it! The technology was actually named after a fabled 10th century Viking king, Harald I (Harald "Blatand" Gormsson), who was faced with the challenge of dealing with many disparate tribes; he needed to communicate with them all and they needed to get along with each other. Blatand, who it's said got his unique nickname due to sporting an unfortunately prominent blue tooth, was having a really tough time getting this to happen. However, the Viking king was a famously great diplomat possessing a wonderful way with words, and he effectively and nonviolently united ancient Norway and Denmark into a single territory via his powerful communication skills. Incidentally, *Blatand* just happens to translate into *Bluetooth* in English.

Fast-forward to modern times and a Scandinavian company called Ericsson and a highly gifted technological innovator, Jim Kardach. As one of the founders of Bluetooth, Kardach's challenge was a decent, modern-day analogy of the ancient Viking king's—he was faced with making disparate phones, computers, and other devices communicate and cooperate effectively. To answer the challenge, Kardach came up with an elegant, technological wireless solution to make all these disparate devices communicate and play well with each other. To come up with an equally cool name for the brilliant innovation, he did some research, discovered the legend of the ancient Viking king, and codenamed the new technology Bluetooth. It stuck! Now all that was left was to create a super slick logo for it. Today's Bluetooth icon is actually the legendary king's initials in ancient Viking runes merged together—how cool is that?

Bluetooth 1.0 was far slower than what we have now. Data speeds capped off at 1 Mbps and the range only reached as far as 10 meters.

When Bluetooth 2.0 came out, GFSK was taken out in favor of two newer schemes: p/4-DQPSK and 8DPSK, which used changes in the waveforms' phase to carry information, as opposed to frequency modulation. These two schemes resulted in unprecedented data speeds of 2 Mbps and 3 Mbps, respectively. Bluetooth 3.0 further improved data speeds with the addition of 802.11 for up to 24 Mbps of data transfer, although this was not a mandatory part of the 3.0 specification.

Because of the large amount of energy that was required from Bluetooth versions 1.0 to 3.0, also known as Bluetooth Classic, small devices would continue to suffer from short battery life, making early versions of Bluetooth impractical for IoT use.

In order to meet the increasing demand for wireless connectivity between small devices, Bluetooth 4.0 was introduced to the market with a new category of Bluetooth: Bluetooth Low Energy (BLE). Geared toward applications requiring low power consumption, BLE returns to a lower data throughput of 1 Mbps using the GFSK modulation scheme. Although BLE's max data throughput of 1 Mbps may not be suitable for products that require a continuous stream of data like wireless headphones, other IoT applications only need to send small bits of data periodically. An example are fitness wearables that relay small amounts of temperature data to your smartphone only when requested (from a mobile app, perhaps).

With the focus on keeping energy demands low, Bluetooth Low Energy makes many coin-cell battery-operated IoT applications (e.g., beacons) feasible. The most recent version of the Bluetooth protocol, Bluetooth 5.0, is an improvement of the previous BLE standards. It is still geared toward low-powered applications but also improves upon BLE's data rate and range. Unlike version 4.0, Bluetooth 5.0 offers four different data rates to accommodate a variety of transmission ranges: 2 Mbps, 1 Mbps, 500 kbps, and 125 kbps. Because an increase in transmission range requires a reduction in data rate, the lower data rate of 125 kbps was added to support applications that benefit more from improved range.

To delve a little deeper into wireless technologies, the idea of PANs is to allow personal items such as keyboards, mice, and phones to communicate to our PC/laptop/display/TV wirelessly instead of having to use any wires at all—over short distances of up to 30 feet, of course. This idea of the wireless office hasn't quite come to fruition completely yet, but you have to admit that Bluetooth really has helped us out tremendously in our offices and especially in our cars!

There are two other network infrastructure implementations in the PAN area: infrared (IR) and near-field communication (NFC).

Like Bluetooth, IR has some history behind it, but the technology's idea only goes back to about 1800 because that's when it was first said that the energy from the sun radiates to Earth in infrared. We can use IR to communicate short range with our devices, like Bluetooth-enabled ones, but it isn't really as popular as Bluetooth to use within network infrastructures. Unlike Wi-Fi and Bluetooth, the infrared wireless signals cannot penetrate walls and only work line-of-sight. The rates are super slow and most transfers are only 115 Kbps—up to 4 Mbps on a really good day!

The other implementation I want to cover is called near-field communication (NFC). For NFC to work, the actual antenna must be smaller than the wavelength on both the transmitter and receiver. For instance, if you look at a 2.4 GHz or 5 GHz antenna, they are the exact length of one wavelength for that specific frequency. With NFC, the antenna is about one-quarter the size of the wavelength, which means that the antenna can create either an electric field or a magnetic field but not an electromagnetic field.

NFC can be used for wireless communication between devices like smartphones and/or tablets, but you need to be near the device transmitting the RF to pick up the signal—really close. A solid example would be when you're swiping your phone over a QR code or contactless payment terminal.

Technologies That Facilitate the Internet of Things (IoT)

Internet of Things (IoT) is the newest buzzword in IT and it means the introduction of all sorts of devices to the network (and Internet) that were not formerly there. Refrigerators, alarm systems, building service systems, elevators, and power systems are now equipped with networked sensors allowing us to monitor and control these systems from the Internet.

These systems depend on several technologies to facilitate their operations:

Z-Wave   Z-Wave is a wireless protocol used for home automation. It uses a mesh network using low-energy radio waves to communicate from appliance to appliance.

Residential appliances and other devices, such as lighting control, security systems, thermostats, windows, locks, swimming pools, and garage door openers can use this system.

ANT+   ANT+ is another wireless protocol for monitoring sensor data such as a person's heart rate or a bicycle's tire pressure as well as for controlling systems like indoor lighting and television sets. ANT+ is designed and maintained by the ANT+ Alliance, which is owned by Garmin.

Bluetooth   Some systems use Bluetooth. Bluetooth was discussed earlier in this chapter.

NFC   Some systems use near-field communication. NFC was discussed earlier in this chapter.

IR   Some systems use infrared. Infrared was discussed earlier in this chapter.

RFID   While RFID is mostly known for asset tracking, it can also be used in the IoT. Objects are given an RFID tag so they are uniquely identifiable. Also, an RFID tag allows the object to wirelessly communicate certain types of information.

Truly smart objects will be embedded with both an RFID tag and a sensor to measure data. The sensor may capture fluctuations in the surrounding temperature, changes in quantity, or other types of information.

802.11   Finally, 802.11 can also be used for IoT communication. 802.11 was discussed earlier in this chapter.

Installing and Configuring WLAN Hardware

As I said earlier, installing 802.11 equipment is actually fairly simple—remember that there are really only two main types of components in 802.11 networks: APs and NICs. Wireless NIC installation is just like installing any other network card, but nowadays most, if not all, laptops have wireless cards preinstalled, and that's as easy as it gets! And just as with connecting an Ethernet card to a LAN switch, you need the wireless network card to connect to an access point.

The AP installation can be fairly simple as well. Take it out of the box, connect the antenna(s) if necessary, connect the power, and then place the AP where it can reach the highest number of clients. This last part is probably the trickiest, but it really just involves a little common sense and maybe a bit of trial and error. Knowing that walls obstruct the signal means that putting the AP out in the open—even indoors—works better. And you also know it should be placed away from sources of RF interference, so putting it next to the microwave or phone system is probably a really bad idea too. Near a metal filing cabinet is also not so good. So just experiment and move your AP around to find the spot that gives you the best signal strength for all the clients that need to use it.

Now that you have the hardware installed, it's time to configure it, right? Let's get started.

No worries—configuring your AP and NIC to work together isn't as tricky as it sounds. Most wireless equipment is designed to work almost without configuration, so by default, you can pretty much turn things on and start working. The only things you need to configure are customization settings (name, network address, and so on) and security settings, and even these aren't required. But because I do highly recommend configuring them, I'll take you through that now.

NIC Configuration

Windows hosts and servers include software to automatically configure a wireless connection, and they do so automatically if you install a wireless NIC—assuming that somehow you have a Windows machine without a wireless NIC installed on the motherboard. And if you have one without a NIC installed, your Windows machine is really old!

Configuring a Windows client is pretty simple, but what do you do if you can't get it to actually work afterward? If this happens to you, searching for the solution could eat up a serious amount of your time! Following these steps could save you from that frustrating quest:

1. To find a wireless network, just go to the lower-right corner of your screen and click the icon that looks like a wireless wave. You will see the box below.

2. Double-click the network you want to join, and click Connect Anyway, even if it's an unsecured network. You'll then see a screen showing that it's trying to connect.

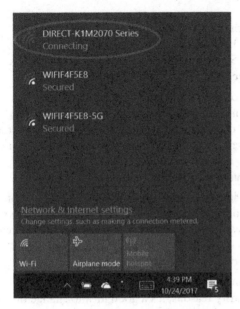

3. If you're using security, the AP will ask you for your credentials.

4. Check your TCP/IP settings to find out if you're not really connected to the Internet and troubleshoot from there.

AP Configuration

Once you've successfully configured your workstation(s), it's time to move on and configure the AP. There are literally hundreds of different APs out there, and of course, each uses a different method to configure its internal software. The good news is that for the most part, they all follow the same general patterns:

1. First of all, out of the box, the AP should come configured with an IP address that's usually something similar to 192.168.1.1. But check the documentation that comes with the AP to be sure. You can just take the AP out of its box, plug it into a power outlet, and connect it to your network, but in order to manage the AP, you've got to configure its IP address scheme to match your network's.

2. You should receive a DHCP address from the AP when you connect, but if you don't get one, start by configuring a workstation on the wired network with an IP address (192.168.1.2 or similar) and subnet mask on the same subnet as the AP's. You should then be able to connect to the AP to begin the configuration process. Usually, you do this via a web browser or with a manufacturer-supplied configuration program.

3. Once you have successfully connected to the AP, you then get to configure its parameters.

Following are the minimum parameters common to APs that you should configure for your AP to work properly. (Remember, typically an AP works right out of the box, but it is unsecure too!)

SSID As I mentioned earlier, this is the name of the wireless network that your AP will advertise. If this new AP is to be part of an existing wireless network, it needs to be configured with the same SSID as the existing network. In a network with only one AP, you can think of the SSID as the "name" of the AP.

AP IP Addresses Remember, even though most APs come preconfigured with an IP address, it may not be one that matches the wired network's IP addressing scheme. So it follows that you should configure the AP's IP addresses (including the address, subnet mask, and default gateway addresses) to match the wired network you want it connected to. An AP does not need an IP address to work in your network. The IP address of the AP is used only to manage the AP.

Operating Mode (Access Point or Bridging) Access points can operate in one of two main modes: *Access Point mode* or *Bridging mode*. Access Point mode allows the AP to operate as a traditional access point to allow a wireless client transparent access to a wired network. Alternatively, two APs set to Bridging mode provide a wireless bridge between two wired network segments.

Password Every access point has some kind of default password that's used to access the AP's configuration. For security reasons, it's a good idea to change this as soon as you can to connect to and configure the AP.

Wireless Channel 802.11 wireless networks can operate on different channels to avoid interference. Most wireless APs come set to work on a particular channel from the factory, and you can change it if other networks in the area are using that channel, but be aware that no particular channel is any more secure than another. Wireless stations do *not* use channel numbers as the criteria when seeking a connection. They only pay attention to SSIDs!

WEP/WPA Although it isn't a requirement per se, I definitely recommend enabling security right from the start as soon as you turn on the AP. Commercial APs typically come configured as an open network so that it's easy to log in, whereas enterprise APs come unconfigured and don't work until they are configured. WEP and Wi-Fi Protected Access (WPA) allow data to be encrypted before it's sent over the wireless connection, and all configuring entails is to enable it and pick a key to be used for the connections. Simple, easy-to-configure security is certainly worth your time!

So here's what you do: First, you'll be asked to enter one or more human-readable passphrases called *shared keys*—secret passwords that won't ever be sent over the wire. After entering each one, you'll generally click a button to initiate a one-way hash to produce a WEP key of a size related to the number of bits of WEP encryption you want. Entering the same passphrase on a wireless client causes the hash (not the passphrase) to be sent from the wireless client to the AP during a connection attempt. Most configuration utilities allow you to create multiple keys in case you want to grant someone temporary access to the network, but you still want to keep the primary passphrase a secret. You can just delete the key you enabled to permit temporary access after you don't need it anymore without affecting access by any primary LAN participants.

Here's an example of connecting to a Linksys access point (not a Linksys wireless router, which is a different device):

1. The first screen shows that I've connected using HTTP to configure the device. The IP address of the Linksys AP is 192.168.1.245. If it was a Linksys wireless router instead—the typical home DSL/cable modem wireless connection device around today—then the address would be 192.168.1.1.

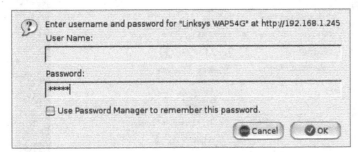

2. As you can see, there's no username required, and the password is just *admin*. Again, be sure not to leave this login configuration as the default! Once I click OK, I get taken to a screen where I can change my IP address.

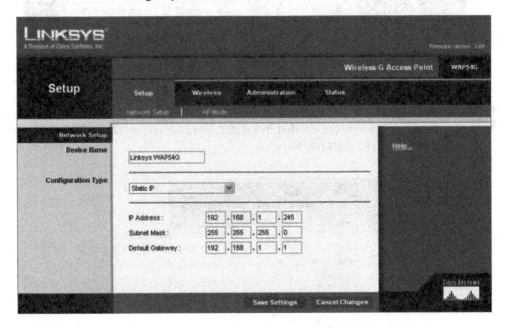

3. It isn't vital for an AP to have an IP address, but it comes in handy for management purposes. You can change the IP address as well as the device name from this screen if you want to. I clicked the Wireless tab on top and this screen appeared.

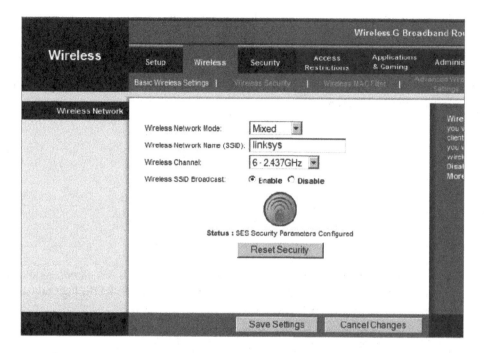

4. From here, you can set the device to run b/g, only g, or hopefully the newer technologies, but if all you have is g, that will work too. You can also change the SSID from Linksys to another name, and I *highly* recommend doing this. The AP channel can also be changed, and you can turn off the AP beacons as well, which is also recommended, but understand that if you do this, you'll have to set the new SSID name in each of your clients! Last thing—you can see that by default, there's no encryption. Click the Wireless Security tab, and you'll get this screen.

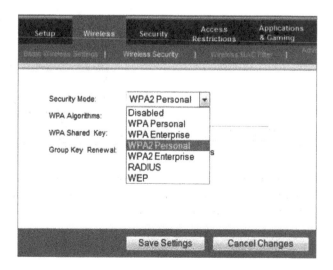

5. From the pull-down menu, you get to choose from various wireless security options if you want to.

I'll talk more about security after I hammer on about site surveys for a bit—they really are that important!

Site Survey

I want to be sure you're completely clear about where I stand regarding site surveys. They are absolutely and vitally imperative to bringing a premium-quality—even just a reasonably viable—WLAN into this world! You should carry out a predeployment survey and a postdeployment survey, but keep in mind that your predeployment survey isn't actually your first step to begin this key process.

So, because you positively must know how to formulate and implement a solid site survey, I'm going to walk you through executing the three major steps to doing that effectively. And just to be really thorough, I'm also going to cover some issues commonly encountered as we progress through these steps.

Information Gathering   This is actually your first step, and during this stage, you must determine three key factors:

- The scope of the network, including all applications that will be used, data types that will be present, and how sensitive these data types are to delay
- The areas that must be covered and the expected capacity at each location
- The types of wireless devices that will need to be supported, such as, for example, laptops, tablets, smartphones, IP phones, and barcode readers

During this phase, a key goal of mine would be to create a coverage model that maps to all areas that need coverage, along with those that don't, and have my client sign off in agreement to this document before I do anything else. You definitely want to do this too—just trust me!

Predeployment Site Survey   In this phase, I use live APs to verify the optimal distances between their prospective locations. I base this placement on the expected speed at the edge of the cell, the anticipated number of devices, and other information gathered in step 1. Usually, after I get one AP positioned, I'll place the next one based on the distance from the first, with special consideration given to any sources of interference I've found.

Postdeployment Site Survey   I utilize the postdeployment survey phase to confirm and verify that the original design and placements are happily humming along and problem free, when all stations are using the network. This pretty much never happens, so at this point, it's likely changes will need to be made—sometimes, significant ones—in order to optimize the performance of a WLAN operating under full capacity.

Providing Capacity

Now here's a big issue that frequently rears its ugly head: providing enough capacity in areas where many wireless stations will be competing for the airwaves. Remember that stations share access to the RF environment with all other stations in the BSS, as well as with the AP, so really, the only way to increase capacity is by increasing the number of APs in an area requiring serious density.

This can get complicated, but basically it comes down to placing APs on non-overlapping channels while still sharing the same SSID. Take a look at Figure 12.17 for an example of this scenario.

FIGURE 12.17 Basic coverage

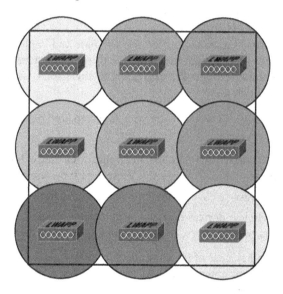

In Figure 12.17, nine APs have been configured in the same area using the three non-overlapping channels in the 2.4 GHz frequency (1, 6, and 11). Each shade represents a different channel. Even though the APs on the same channel have been positioned far enough away from one another so that they don't overlap much and/or cause interference, surprisingly, it's actually better if there is some overlap. But bear in mind that the channels should be used in a way that no APs on the same channel overlap in a detrimental way. Another thing I want to point out that's not so ideal about this arrangement is that all the APs would have to run at full power. This isn't a good way to go because it doesn't give you much fault tolerance at all!

So, we've got two problems with our design: lack of overlap and lack of fault tolerance. To address both issues, you need more APs using 802.11ac or later, which would get you more channels and provide better throughput, as shown in Figure 12.18.

FIGURE 12.18   Enterprise design

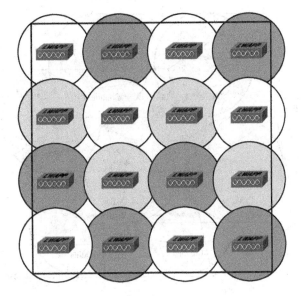

A key benefit to this design is it would also gain the critical ability to run the APs at less than full power. This allows the controller to strategically boost the power of specific APs in the event of an AP outage in a given area.

When you know exactly the type of applications and activity a WLAN will need to support, you can then determine the data rate that must be attained in a particular area. Since received signal strength indicator (RSSI), signal-to-noise ratio (SNR), and data rate are correlated, the required data rate will tell you what the required RSSI or SNR should be as seen at the AP from the stations. Keep in mind that stations located at the edge of the cell will automatically drop the data rate and that the data rate will increase as a station moves toward the AP.

Multiple Floors

Another special challenge is a multistory building where WLANs are located on all floors. In these conditions, you've got to think about channel usage in a three-dimensional way, and you'll have to play nicely with the other WLANs' administrators to make this work! Facing this scenario, your channel spacing should be deployed as shown in Figure 12.19.

To prevent bleed from one floor to another, use semi-directional or patch antennas to control radiation patterns.

FIGURE 12.19   A multifloor installation

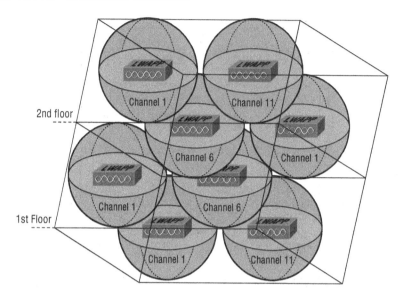

Location-Based WLAN

When using a location device such as the Cisco 2710, your restrictions get even tighter. The additional requirements for the location device to operate properly are as follows:

- APs should be placed at the edge even when they're not needed there for normal coverage purposes so that devices at the edge can be located.

- The density of APs must be higher. Each AP should be 50 to 70 feet apart—much closer than is normally required.

- Some APs will need to be set in monitor or scanner mode so that they won't transmit and interfere with other APs.

All of this means that the final placement will be denser and a bit more symmetrical than usual.

Site Survey Tools

There are some highly specialized, very cool site survey tools that can majorly help you achieve your goals. The AirMagnet Survey and Ekahau Site Survey tools make it possible to do a client walk-through with the unit running and you can click each location on the map.

These tools will gather RSSI and SNR from each AP in the range, and at the end of your tour, global heat map coverage will be magically displayed, as shown in Figure 12.20.

FIGURE 12.20   A heat map of a building

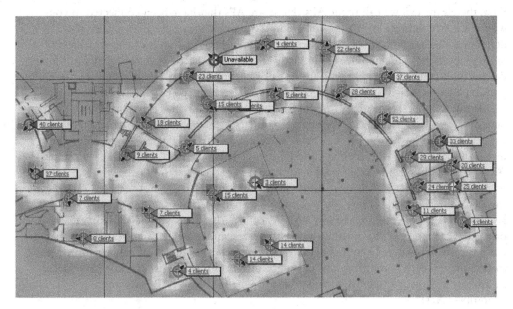

Wireless Security

So, wireless security is basically nonexistent on access points and clients. The original 802.11 committee just didn't imagine that wireless hosts would one day outnumber bounded media hosts, but that's actually where we're headed now. Also, unfortunately, just as with the IPv4 routed protocol, engineers and scientists didn't include security standards that are robust enough to work in a corporate environment. So we're left with proprietary solution add-ons to aid us in our quest to create a secure wireless network. And no—I'm not sitting here bashing the standards committees, because the security problems we're experiencing were also created by the US government because of export issues with its own security standards. Our world is a complicated place, so it follows that our security solutions would have to be as well.

Wireless Threats

Protection of data and the authentication processes are certainly key threats, but there are other wireless security perils lurking out there as well. We'll dive deeper into the processes and procedures designed to mitigate these dangers in Chapter 14, "Organizational Documents and Policies," but I want to briefly discuss them here.

Rogue APs

First, there's the evil we call rogue APs. These are APs that have been connected to your wired infrastructure without your knowledge. The rogue may have been placed there by a determined hacker who snuck into your facility and put it in an out-of-the-way location or, more innocently, by an employee who just wants wireless access and doesn't get just how dangerous doing this is. Either way, it's just like placing an open Ethernet port out in the parking lot with a sign that says "Corporate LAN access here—no password required!"

Clearly, the worst type of rogue AP is the one some hacker has cleverly slipped into your network. It's particularly nasty because the bad guy probably didn't do it to simply gain access to your network. Nope—the hacker likely did it to entice your wireless clients to disastrously associate with their rogue AP instead! This ugly trick is achieved by placing their AP on a different channel from your legitimate APs and then setting its SSID in accordance with your SSID. Wireless clients identify the network by the SSID, not the MAC address of the AP or the IP address of the AP, so jamming the channel that your AP is on will cause your stations to roam to the bad guy's AP instead. With the proper DHCP software installed on the AP, the hacker can issue the client an address, and once that's been done, the bad guy has basically "kidnapped" your client over to their network and can freely perform a peer-to-peer attack. Believe it or not, this can all be achieved from a laptop while Mr. Hacker simply sits in your parking lot, because there are many types of AP software that will run on a laptop—yikes!

Mitigation

But you're not helpless—one way to keep rogue APs out of the wireless network is to employ a wireless LAN controller (WLC) to manage your APs. This is a nice mitigation technique because APs and controllers communicate using Lightweight Access Point Protocol (LWAPP) or the newer CAPWAP, and it just so happens that one of the message types they share is called Radio Resource Management (RRM). Basically, your APs monitor all channels by momentarily switching from their configured channel and by collecting packets to check for rogue activity. If an AP is detected that isn't usually managed by the controller, it's classified as a rogue, and if a wireless control system is in use, that rogue can be plotted on a floor plan and located. Another great benefit to this mitigation approach is that it enables your APs to also prevent workstations from associating with the newly exposed rogue.

Ad Hoc Networks

As you already know, ad hoc networks are created peer to peer or directly between stations and not through an AP. This can be a dangerous configuration because there's no corporate security in place, and since these networks are often created by unsophisticated users, you end up with the scenario I just described that's primed for, and wide open to, a peer-to-peer attack. It's even uglier if the laptop happens to connect to the corporate LAN through an Ethernet connection at the same time the ad hoc network is created, because the two connections could be bridged by a hacker to gain access straight up into the wired LAN itself!

Mitigation

When you've got a Cisco Unified Wireless Network (CUWN) in operation, ad hoc networks can be identified over the air by the kind of frames they send, which are different from those belonging to an infrastructure network. When these frames are identified, the CUWN can prevent harmful intrusions by sending out something known as deauthentication frames to keep your stations from associating via ad hoc mode.

Denial of Service

Not all attacks are aimed at the goal of stealing information. Sometimes the hacker just wants to cause some major network grief, like jamming the frequency where your WLAN lives to cause a complete interruption of service until you manage to ferret out the jamming signal and disable it. This type of assault is known as a denial of service (DoS) attack.

Mitigation

And this is how we deal with them. First, if someone is jamming the frequency, there isn't much, if anything, you can do. However, many DoS, on-path (formerly known as man-in-the-middle), and penetration attacks operate by deauthenticating, or disassociating, stations from their networks. Some DoS attacks take the form of simply flooding the wireless network with probe requests or association frames, which effectively makes the overwhelmed network unavailable for normal transmissions. These types of management frames are sent unauthenticated and unencrypted. Since deauthentication and disassociation frames are classified as management frames, the Management Frame Protection (MFP) mechanism can be used to prevent the deluge. There are two types of MFP you can use, referred to as infrastructure and client. Let's take a look at each of them now.

Infrastructure Mode

This sweet strategy doesn't require configuration on the station—only the AP. Controllers generate a specific signature for each WLAN, which is added to each management frame it sends, and any attempt to alter this is detected by the message integrity check (MIC) in the frame. Therefore, when an AP receives a management frame from an unknown SSID, it reports the event to the controller and an alarm is generated.

When an AP receives an MFP protected frame from an unknown SSID, it queries the controller for the key. If the BSSID isn't recognized by the controller, it will return an "unknown BSSID" message, which causes the AP to drop the frame.

Client Mode

Often rogue APs attempt to impersonate the company AP. With client MFP, all management frames between the AP and the station are protected because clients can detect and drop spoofed or invalid management frames.

Passive Attacks

So far, the attacks I've talked about are in a category referred to as active attacks because in deploying them, the hacker is interacting with stations, the AP, and the network in real time. But beware—there are other ways into the fort!

Passive attacks are most often used to gather information to be used in an active attack a hacker is planning to execute later, and they usually involve wireless sniffing. During a passive attack, the hacker captures large amounts of raw frames to analyze online with sniffing software used to discover a key and decrypt it "on the fly." Or the data will be analyzed offline, which simply means the bad guy will take the data away and analyze it later.

Mitigation

In addition to the tools already described, you can use an intrusion detection system (IDS) or an intrusion protection system (IPS) to guard against passive attacks:

IDS   An intrusion detection system (IDS) is used to detect several types of malicious behaviors that can compromise the security and trust of your system. These malicious behaviors include network attacks against vulnerable services; data-driven attacks on applications; host-based attacks like privilege escalation; unauthorized logins; access to sensitive files; and malware like viruses, Trojan horses, and worms.

IPS   An intrusion prevention system (IPS) is a computer security device that monitors network and/or system activities for malicious or unwanted behavior and can react, in real time, to block or prevent those activities. For example, a network-based IPS will operate inline to monitor all network traffic for malicious code or attacks. When either is detected, it can drop the offending packets while still allowing all other traffic to pass.

Which approach you'll opt to go with depends on the size of your wireless network and how tight your security needs to be. The goal of a security mechanism is to provide three features:

- Confidentiality of the data
- Data integrity
- An assured identification process

And when faced with decisions about security, you need to consider these three things:

- The safety of the authentication process
- The strength of the encryption mechanism
- Its ability to protect the integrity of the data

 **Real World Scenario**

War Driving

It's a fact—wireless networks are pretty much everywhere these days. You can get your hands on a wireless access point for less than $100.00, and they're flying off the shelves. You can find APs in public places like shopping malls, coffee shops, airports, and hotels, and in some cities, you can just hang out in a downtown area and zero in on a veritable menu of APs operating in almost every nearby business.

Predictably, this proliferation of APs has led to a new hobby for those with enough skill: It's called *war driving*. Not for the technologically challenged, war driving involves driving around in a car with a laptop, a wireless NIC, and a high-gain antenna, trying to locate open APs. If one with high-speed Internet access is found, it's like hitting the jackpot. People do this aided by various software programs and Global Positioning Systems (GPSs) to make their game even easier. But it's not always innocent—war drivers can be a serious security threat because they can potentially access anything on your wireless LAN as well as anything it's attached to! Even though they're not a sinister threat most of the time, realize that in the very least, they're consuming precious resources from your network. So, if you happen to notice unusually slow-moving vehicles outside your home or business—especially those with computer equipment inside—know that you're the potential target of a war driver.

A good place to start discussing Wi-Fi security is by talking about the basic security that was incorporated into the original 802.11 standards and why those standards are still way too flimsy and incomplete to help us create a secure wireless network relevant to today's challenges.

Open Access

All Wi-Fi Certified small-office, home-office (SOHO) wireless LAN products are shipped in "open-access" mode, with their security features turned off. Although open access or no security may be appropriate and acceptable for public hot spots such as coffee shops, college campuses, and maybe airports, it's definitely not an option for an enterprise organization, and it's probably not even adequate for your private home network.

With what I've told you so far, I'm sure you agree that security needs to be enabled on wireless devices during their installation in enterprise environments. Yet surprisingly, many companies actually don't enable any WLAN security features. Obviously, the companies that don't enable security features are exposing their networks to tremendous risk.

The reason that the products are shipped with open access is so that any person who knows absolutely nothing about computers can just buy an access point, plug it into their cable or DSL modem, and voilà—they're up and running. It's marketing, plain and simple, and simplicity sells.

Service Set Identifiers, Wired Equivalent Privacy, and Media Access Control Address Authentication

What the original designers of 802.11 did to create basic security was to include the use of SSIDs, open or shared-key authentication, static WEP, and optional *Media Access Control (MAC) authentication/MAC filtering*. Sounds like a lot, but none of these really offer any type of serious security solution—all they may be close to adequate for is use on a common home network. But we'll go over them anyway.

An SSID is a common network name for the devices in a WLAN system that create the wireless LAN. An SSID prevents access by any client device that doesn't have the SSID. The thing is, by default, an access point broadcasts its SSID in its beacon many times a second. And even if SSID broadcasting is turned off, a bad guy can discover the SSID by monitoring the network and just waiting for a client response to the access point. Why? Because, believe it or not, that information, as regulated in the original 802.11 specifications, must be sent in the clear—how secure!

 If you cannot see an AP when trying to perform a site survey, verify that the AP has SSID beaconing enabled.

Two types of authentication were specified by the IEEE 802.11 committee: open authentication and shared-key authentication. Open authentication involves little more than supplying the correct SSID—but it's the most common method in use today. With shared-key authentication, the access point sends the client device a challenge-text packet that the client must then encrypt with the correct WEP key and return to the access point. Without the correct key, authentication will fail and the client won't be allowed to associate with the access point. But shared-key authentication is still not considered secure because all an intruder has to do to get around this is detect both the clear-text challenge and the same challenge encrypted with a WEP key and then decipher the WEP key. Surprise—shared key isn't used in today's WLANs because of clear-text challenge.

With open authentication, even if a client can complete authentication and associate with an access point, the use of WEP prevents the client from sending and receiving data from the access point unless the client has the correct WEP key. A WEP key is composed of either 40 or 128 bits, and in its basic form, it's usually statically defined by the network administrator on the access point and all clients that communicate with that access point. When static WEP keys are used, a network administrator must perform the time-consuming task of entering the same keys on every device in the WLAN. Obviously, we now have fixes for this because tackling this would be administratively impossible in today's huge corporate wireless networks!

Finally, client MAC addresses can be statically typed into each access point, allowing MAC filtering, and any frames that show up to the AP without a known MAC address in the filter table will be denied access. Sounds good, but of course all MAC layer information must be sent in the clear—anyone equipped with a free wireless sniffer can just read the client packets sent to the access point and spoof their MAC address. If you have a small number of wireless clients and you don't want to deploy an encryption-based access method, MAC address filters may be sufficient.

 If you cannot connect to an AP and you've verified that your DHCP configuration and WEP key are correct, check the MAC address filtering on the AP.

WEP can actually work if administered correctly. But basic static WEP keys are no longer a viable option in today's corporate networks without some of the proprietary fixes that run on top of WEP.

Geofencing

Geofencing is the process of defining the area in which an operation can be performed by using global positioning (GPS) or radio frequency identification (RFID) to define a geographic boundary. An example of usage involves a location-aware device of a location-based service (LBS) user entering or exiting a geofence. This activity could trigger an alert to the device's user as well as messaging to the geofence operator.

Remote Authentication Dial-In User Service (802.1X)

Remote Authentication Dial-In User Service (RADIUS) is a networking protocol that offers us several security benefits: authorization, centralized access, and accounting supervision regarding the users and/or computers that connect to and access our networks' services. Once RADIUS has authenticated the user, it allows us to specify the type of rights a user or workstation has, plus control what it, or they, can do within the network. It also creates a record of all access attempts and actions. The provision of authentication, authorization, and accounting is called AAA, which is pronounced just like the automobile insurance company, "triple A," and it's part of the IEEE 802.1X security standard.

RADIUS has risen to stardom because of its AAA features and is often employed by ISPs, web servers, wireless networks, and APs as well as network ports—basically, by anybody who wants or needs a AAA server. And these servers are only becoming more critically important in large corporate environments, and that's because they offer security for wireless networks. From the Linksys security screen shown earlier, you can see that RADIUS is an available option. If you choose it, you'll be asked for the IP address of the RADIUS server so the AP can send authentication packets.

Figure 12.21 shows how the AP becomes an authenticator when you choose the RADIUS authentication method.

FIGURE 12.21   RADIUS authentication server

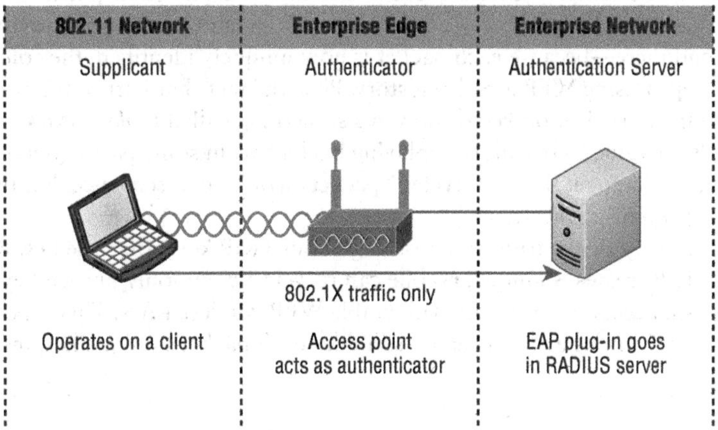

Now packets must pass through the AP until the user and/or host gets authenticated by the RADIUS server.

Temporal Key Integrity Protocol

Put up a fence, and it's only a matter of time until bad guys find a way over, around, and through it. And true to form, they indeed found ways to get through WEP's defenses, leaving our Wi-Fi networks vulnerable—stripped of their Data Link layer security! So someone had to come to the rescue. In this case, it happened to be the IEEE 802.11i task group and the Wi-Fi Alliance, joining forces for the cause. They came up with a solution called Temporal Key Integrity Protocol (TKIP). The Wi-Fi Alliance unveiled it back in late 2002 and introduced it as *Wi-Fi Protected Access (WPA)*. This little beauty even saved us lots of money because TKIP—say this like "tee kip"—didn't make us upgrade all our legacy hardware equipment in order to use it. Then, in the summer of 2004, the IEEE put its seal of approval on the final version and added even more defensive muscle with goodies like 802.1X and AES-CCMP (AES-Counter Mode CBC-MAC Protocol) upon publishing IEEE 802.11i-2004. The Wi-Fi Alliance responded positively by embracing the now-complete specification and dubbing it WPA2 for marketing purposes.

A big reason that TKIP doesn't require buying new hardware to run is that it just wraps around the preexisting WEP encryption key (which was way too short) and upgrades it a whole lot to much more impenetrable 128-bit encryption. Another reason for TKIP's innate compatibility is that both its encryption mechanism and the RC4 algorithm used to power and define WEP, respectively, remained the same.

But there are still significant differences that help make it the seriously tough shield it is, one of them being that it actually changes each packet's key. Let me explain: Packet keys are made up of three things: a base key, the transmitting device's MAC address, and the packet's serial number. It's an elegant design because, although it doesn't place a ton of stress on workstations and APs, it serves up some truly formidable cryptographic force. Here's how it works: Remember the packet serial number part of the transmission key? Well, it's not just your average serial number; it's special—very special.

TKIP-governed transmission ensures that each packet gets its very own 48-bit serial number, which is augmented with a sequence number whenever a new packet gets sent out, and not only serves as part of the key but also acts as the initialization vector. And the good news doesn't end there—because each packet is now uniquely identified, the collision attacks that used to happen using WEP are also history. Plus, the fact that part of the packet's serial number is also the initialization vector prevents something called *replay attacks*. It takes an ice age for a 48-bit value to repeat, so replaying packets from some past wireless connection is just not going to happen; those "recycled" packets won't be in sequence, but they will be identified, thus preventing the attack.

Now for what may be the truly coolest thing about TKIP keys: the base key. Because each base key that TKIP creates is unique, no one can recycle a commonly known key over and over again to gain access to a formerly vulnerable WEP wireless LAN. This is because TKIP throws the base key into the mix when it assembles each packet's unique key, meaning that even if a device has connected to a particular access point a bunch of times, it won't be permitted access again unless it has a completely new key granting it permission.

Even the base key itself is a fusion of something called *nonces*—an assortment of random numbers gleaned from the workstation, the access point, and each of these devices' MAC addresses, so this should also be referred to as a *session secret*. So basically, if you've got IEEE 802.1X authentication working for you, rest assured that a session secret absolutely will be transmitted securely to each machine every time it initiates a connection to the wireless LAN by the authentication server—unless you're using preshared keys, that is, because if you happen to be using them, that important session secret always remains the same. Using TKIP with preshared keys is kind of like closing an automatically locking security door but not enabling its security settings and alarm—anyone who knows where the secret latch is can get right in!

Wi-Fi Protected Access or WPA2 Pre-Shared Key

These are both essentially another form of basic security that's really just an add-on to the specifications. Even though you can totally lock the vault, as I mentioned in the previous section, WPA/WPA2 Pre-Shared Key (PSK) is a better form of wireless security than any other basic wireless security method I've talked about so far. And note that I did say basic! But if you are using only MAC address filters and/or WEP, and you find that interlopers are still using your network and dragging down the performance, adding this layer of security should help tremendously since it's a better form of access control than either of those measures.

Wi-Fi Protected Access (WPA) is a standard developed by the Wi-Fi Alliance, formerly known as the Wireless Ethernet Compatibility Alliance (WECA). WPA provides a standard for authentication and encryption of WLANs that's intended to solve known security problems. The standard takes into account the well-publicized AirSnort and on-path (man-in-the-middle) WLAN attacks. So of course we use WPA2 to help us with today's security issues.

The PSK verifies users via a password or identifying code (also called a *passphrase*) on both the client machine and the access point. A client gains access to the network only if its password matches the access point's password. The PSK also provides keying material that TKIP or Advanced Encryption Standard (AES) uses to generate an encryption key for each packet of transmitted data.

Although more secure than static WEP, PSK still has a lot in common with static WEP in that the PSK is stored on the client station and can be compromised if the client station is lost or stolen (even though finding this key isn't all that easy to do). It's a definite recommendation to use a strong PSK passphrase that includes a mixture of letters, numbers, and non-alphanumeric characters. With WPA, it's still actually possible to specify the use of dynamic encryption keys that change each time a client establishes a connection.

The benefit of WPA over a static WEP key is that WPA can change dynamically while the system is used.

WPA is a step toward the IEEE 802.11i standard and uses many of the same components, with the exception of encryption—802.11i (WPA2) uses AES-CCMP encryption. The IEEE 802.11i standard replaced WEP with a specific mode of AES known as the CCMP, as mentioned earlier. This allows AES-CCMP to provide both data confidentiality (encryption) and data integrity.

 The highest level of wireless encryption you can run is WPA3-SAE.

The following screen shows that if you choose WPA2 Personal on the Linksys AP, you can then enter your passphrase—it's really called WPA2 Pre-Shared Key, but whatever.

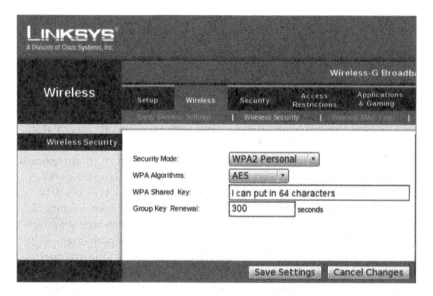

You have a choice of TKIP or AES as the encryption, and by the way, you can choose up to a 64-character key—pretty tight!

WPA's mechanisms are designed to be implementable by current hardware vendors, meaning that users should be able to implement WPA on their systems with only a firmware/software modification.

 The IEEE 802.11i standard has been sanctioned by WPA and is called WPA version 2.

Certificates and PKI

WPA2 can use the Extensible Authentication Protocol (EAP) method for authentication.

EAP isn't a single method but a framework that enhances the existing 802.1X framework. The EAP framework describes a basic set of actions that will take place, and each EAP type differs in the specifics of how it operates within the framework. These variables include things like whether they use passwords or certificates as well as the ultimate level of security provided. Some of the EAP methods require that certificates be used as the credential during authentication. This means that to implement those methods, you must have a Public Key Infrastructure (PKI) in your network. A PKI requires a certificate server that issues certificates to your users and/or devices. These certificates, which consist of a public/private key pair, must be securely installed on the devices and renewed at regular intervals.

In symmetric encryption, the two encryption keys are the same, just as they are with WEP keys, but in asymmetric encryption, the key used to encrypt is different from the key used to decrypt. In PKI, asymmetric keys are used, and the keys are called a public/private key pair. Certificates are binding regulations of a public/private key pair generated by a certificate server to a user or computer. As long as two parties trust the same certificate source, called the trusted certificate authority (CA), they can trust the certificate they're presented with for authentication. These keys can also be used for encryption and as digital signatures.

Despite the other uses of public/private keys, our focus here is the use of the certificates as a form of authentication and authorization. And as a means of identifying the device or the user, this is considered the highest form of authentication and authorization when compared to names and passwords. What all this means is that as long as the AP or controller and the station or user trust the CA that issued the certificates, the certificate is trusted as a means of identification as well.

EAP   Extensible Authentication Protocol (EAP) is not a single protocol but a framework for port-based access control that uses the same three components that are used in RADIUS. A wide variety of these include certificates, a PKI, or even simple passwords.

PEAP   Protected Extensible Authentication Protocol, also known as Protected EAP or simply PEAP, is a protocol that encapsulates the Extensible Authentication Protocol (EAP) within an encrypted and authenticated Transport Layer Security (TLS) tunnel. It requires only a server-side PKI certificate to create a secure TLS tunnel to protect user authentication.

EAP-FAST   EAP-FAST works in two stages. In the first stage, a TLS tunnel is established. Unlike PEAP, however, EAP-FAST's first stage is established by using a pre-shared key called a Protected Authentication Credential (PAC). In the second stage, a series of type/length/value (TLV)-encoded data is used to carry a user authentication.

EAP-TLS   EAP Transport Layer Security (EAP-TLS) is the most secure method, but it's also the most difficult to configure and maintain. To use EAP-TLS, you must install a certificate on both the authentication server and the client. An authentication server pair of keys and a client pair of keys need to be generated first, signed using a PKI, and installed on the devices. On the station side, the keys can be issued for the machine itself and/or for the user.

In the authentication stage, the station, along with the authentication server (RADIUS, etc.), exchange certificates and identify each other. Mutual authentication is a solid beneficial feature, which ensures that the station it's communicating with is the proper authentication server. After this process is completed, random session keys are created for encryption.

Preshared Key   Finally, a preshared key can be used to secure wireless transmissions. This is most labor intensive as it requires that all devices use the same key as the AP and that the keys be changed frequently to provide adequate security.

Tunneled Transport Layer Security (TTLS) provides authentication as strong as EAP-TLS, but it doesn't require each user to be issued a certificate. Instead, only the servers are issued certificates.

Summary

Like rock 'n' roll, wireless technologies are here to stay. And for those of us who have come to depend on wireless technologies, it's actually pretty hard to imagine a world without wireless networks—what did we do before cell phones?

So we began this chapter by exploring the essentials and fundamentals of how wireless networks function. Springing off that foundation, I then introduced you to the basics of wireless radio frequencies (RFs) and the IEEE standards. We discussed 802.11 from its inception through its evolution to current and near-future standards and talked about the subcommittees that create these standards.

All of this led into a discussion of wireless security—or rather, nonsecurity for the most part—which we went over in detail.

We finished the chapter by bringing you up to speed on TKIP and WPA/WPA2 security solutions—important tools used to protect the wireless LANs of today.

Exam Essentials

Understand the IEEE 802.11a specification.   802.11a runs in the 5 GHz spectrum, and if you use the 802.11h extensions, you have 23 non-overlapping channels. 802.11a can run up to 54 Mbps, but only if you are less than 50 feet from an access point.

Understand the IEEE 802.11b specification.   IEEE 802.11b runs in the 2.4 GHz range and has three non-overlapping channels. It can handle long distances but with a maximum data rate of up to 11 Mbps.

Understand the IEEE 802.11g specification.   IEEE 802.11g is 802.11b's big brother and runs in the same 2.4 GHz range, but it has a higher data rate of 54 Mbps if you are less than 100 feet from an access point.

Understand the IEEE 802.11n specification. IEEE 802.11n operates in the 2.4 GHz and 5 GHz range. Support for 5 GHz bands is optional. Its net data rate ranges from 54 Mbit/s to 600 Mbit/s. The standard also added support for multiple-input, multiple-output (MIMO) antennas.

Understand the IEEE 802.11ac specification. IEEE 802.11ac-2013 is an amendment that builds on 802.11n. Changes include wider channels (80 or 160 MHz versus 40 MHz) in the 5 GHz band, more spatial streams (up to eight versus four). Wave 2 products include additional features like MU-MIMO, 160 MHz channel width support, support for more 5 GHz channels, and four spatial streams with four antennas.

Understand the IEEE 802.11ax specification. IEEE 802.11ax is the successor to 802.11ac. It's marketed as Wi-Fi 6 (2.4 GHz and 5 GHz) and Wi-Fi 6E (6 GHz). It is also known as High Efficiency Wi-Fi, for the overall improvements to Wi-Fi 6. Data rates against the predecessor (802.11ac) is only 39 percent. For comparison, this improvement was nearly 500 percent for the other predecessors.

Understand the different WiFi standards, frequencies, and ranges. WiFi standards are 802.11a/b/g/n/ac/ax using 2.4 GHz and 5 GHz.

Remember the various service set identifiers (SSIDs). SSIDs can use a basic service set, an extended service set, an independent service set (ad hoc), and a roaming service set.

Remember the antenna types. WiFi antennas can be Omni directional or directional.

Remember the encryption standards. Encryption standards include Wi-Fi Protected Access (WPA), WPA2 Personal (Advanced Encryption Standard-AES), Temporal Key Integrity Protocol (TKIP), and WPA/WPA2 Enterprise (AES/TKIP).

Remember the cellular technologies. Technologies used in cellular communications include code division multiple access (CDMA), global System Mobile (GSM), Long-Term Evolution (LTE), and 3g, 4g, and 5g.

Understand MIMO/MU-MIMO. MIMO is multiple-input, multiple output, which is widely used in 802.11n and 802.11ac. MU-MIMO is multiuser multiple input, multiple output, which is used in the new 802.11ax protocol.

Remember the wireless LAN modulation techniques. Direct-sequence spread spectrum (DSSS) is the most widely used modulation technique, but it has speeds only to 11 Mbps. To get the higher speeds needed in today's WLANs, we use orthogonal frequency-division multiplexing (OFDM) in 802.11g/a/n and 802.11ac/ax networks.

Understand how WPA works in a WLAN. Wi-Fi Protected Access (WPA) is the security of choice in today's home and corporate networks. It provides both authentication and encryption (either TKIP or AES).

Written Lab

You can find the answers to the written labs in Appendix A. Write the answers to the following questions about wireless networking:

1. What is the maximum data rate of IEEE 802.11b?

2. What is the maximum data rate of IEEE 802.11g?

3. What is the maximum data rate of IEEE 802.11a?

4. What is the frequency range of IEEE 802.11b?

5. What is the frequency range of IEEE 802.11g?

6. What is the frequency range of IEEE 802.11a?

7. What is the possible bandwidth of 802.11ac?

8. Why would we use WPA instead of basic WEP?

9. Which IEEE committee has been sanctioned by WPA and is called WPA2?

10. The IEEE 802.11b/g basic standard has how many non-overlapping channels?

Review Questions

You can find the answers to the review questions in Appendix B.

1. You need to install wireless Internet access in an open warehouse environment. After installing the equipment, the technician notices varying signal strengths throughout the warehouse. How do you make sure there is full coverage?

   A. Turn on broadcast key rotation.

   B. Change the encryption method used on all the APs.

   C. Change the antenna placement.

   D. Use channel bonding.

   E. Use channel shaping.

2. Which of the following uses a certificate on both the server and client to provide the best wireless security with 802.1X (and is hardest to implement)?

   A. AES

   B. TTLS

   C. TLS

   D. TKIP

3. What is the frequency range of the IEEE 802.11g standard?

   A. 2.4 Gbps

   B. 5 Gbps

   C. 2.4 GHz

   D. 5 GHz

4. Which devices can interfere with the operation of a wireless network because they operate on similar frequencies? (Choose two.)

   A. Copier

   B. Microwave oven

   C. Toaster

   D. Cordless phone

   E. IP phone

   F. AM radio

5. Which wireless standard allows you to channel-bond to increase bandwidth and uses both the 2.4 GHz and 5 GHz frequencies?

   A. 802.11b

   B. 802.11g

   C. 802.11a

   D. 802.11n

   E. 802.11ac

6. Which of the following is considered a PAN?

    A. AES

    B. BSS

    C. SSID

    D. Bluetooth

7. How many non-overlapping channels are available with 802.11a?

    A. 3

    B. 12

    C. 23

    D. 40

8. What is the maximum data rate for the 802.11a standard?

    A. 6 Mbps

    B. 11 Mbps

    C. 22 Mbps

    D. 54 Mbps

9. You need to install wireless on multiple floors of a large building and maintenance area. What is your first concern before installing the APs?

    A. Authentication

    B. Encryption

    C. Channel overlap

    D. AP configuration

10. What is the maximum data rate for the 802.11b standard?

    A. 6 Mbps

    B. 11 Mbps

    C. 22 Mbps

    D. 54 Mbps

11. You connect a new host to your company's wireless network. The host is set to receive a DHCP address and the WPA2 key is entered correctly. However, the host cannot connect to the network. What can the problem be?

    A. DNS is not configured on the host.

    B. MAC filtering is enabled on the AP.

    C. The network has run out of wireless connections.

    D. The host is enabled to run 802.11b and 802.11g.

12. Which is the highest encryption that WPA2 can use?

    A. AES-CCMP

    B. PPK via IV

    C. PSK

    D. TKIP/MIC

13. Which additional configuration step is necessary in order to connect to an access point that has SSID broadcasting disabled?

   A. Set the SSID value in the client software to public.

   B. Configure open authentication on the AP and the client.

   C. Set the SSID value on the client to the SSID configured on the AP.

   D. Configure MAC address filtering to permit the client to connect to the AP.

14. Which spread-spectrum technology does the 802.11b standard define for operation?

   A. IR

   B. DSSS

   C. FHSS

   D. DSSS and FHSS

   E. IR, FHSS, and DSSS

15. Which wireless LAN design ensures that a mobile wireless client will not lose connectivity when moving from one access point to another (roaming)?

   A. Using adapters and access points manufactured by the same company

   B. Overlapping the wireless cell coverage by at least 10 percent

   C. Configuring all access points to use the same channel

   D. Utilizing MAC address filtering to allow the client MAC address to authenticate with the surrounding APs

16. You have installed a point-to-point connection using wireless bridges and Omni directional antennas between two buildings. The throughput is low. What can you do to improve the link?

   A. Replace the bridges with APs.

   B. Replace the Omni directional antennas with Yagis.

   C. Configure 802.11a on the links.

   D. Install amps to boost the signal.

17. What does extended service set (ESS) ID mean?

   A. That you have more than one access point, and they are in the same SSID connected by a distribution system

   B. That you have more than one access point, and they are in separate SSIDs connected by a distribution system

   C. That you have multiple access points, but they are placed physically in different buildings

   D. That you have multiple access points, but one is a repeater access point

18. What is one reason that WPA encryption is preferred over WEP?

   A. A WPA key is longer and requires more special characters than the WEP key.

   B. The access point and the client are manually configured with different WPA key values.

   C. WPA key values remain the same until the client configuration is changed.

   D. The values of WPA keys can change dynamically while the system is used.

19. How wide are the channels used in 802.11n in order to gain the large bandwidth that the specification provides?

   A. 22 MHz

   B. 20 MHz

   C. 40 MHz

   D. 100 MHz

20. 802.11n uses MIMO. How does this optimize throughput to gain the high-speed advantage that 802.11n provides?

   A. By specifying an acknowledgment of each and every frame, 802.11n provides better overhead.

   B. Several frames are sent by several antennas over several paths and are then recombined by another set of antennas.

   C. One frame at a time is sent, but faster than in 802.11g because multiple antennas are used (multiple-in, multiple-out).

   D. MIMO packs smaller packets into a single unit, which improves throughput.

Chapter

13

Using Statistics and Sensors to Ensure Network Availability

THE FOLLOWING COMPTIA NETWORK+ EXAM OBJECTIVES ARE COVERED IN THIS CHAPTER:

✓ **3.1 Given a scenario, use the appropriate statistics and sensors to ensure network availability.**

- Performance metrics/sensors
    - Device/chassis
        - Temperature
        - Central processing unit (CPU) usage
        - Memory
    - Network metrics
        - Bandwidth
        - Latency
        - Jitter
- SNMP
    - Traps
    - Object identifiers (OIDs)
    - Management information bases (MIBs)
- Network device logs
    - Log reviews
        - Traffic logs

- Audit logs
- Syslog
- Logging levels/severity levels
- Interface statistics/status
  - Link state (up/down)
  - Speed/duplex
  - Send/receive traffic
  - Cyclic redundancy checks (CRCs)
  - Protocol packet and byte counts
- Interface errors or alerts
  - CRC errors
  - Giants
  - Runts
  - Encapsulation errors
- Environmental factors and sensors
  - Temperature
  - Humidity
  - Electrical
  - Flooding
- Baselines
- NetFlow data
- Uptime/downtime

All organizations detest downtime. It costs money and it damages their reputation. So they spend millions trying to solve the issue. One of the keys to stopping downtime is to be listening to what the devices may be telling you about their current state of health. Doing so forms a sort of early warning system that alerts you before a system goes down so there is time to address it. In this chapter you'll learn what sort of data you should be monitoring and some of the ways to do so.

To find Todd Lammle CompTIA videos and practice questions, please see www.lammle.com.

Performance Metrics/Sensors

Let's imagine you were just brought from the 1800s to the present in a time machine, and on your first trip in a car, you examine the dashboard. Speed, temperature, tire inflation, tachometer, what does all that stuff mean? It would be meaningless to you and useless for monitoring the state of the car's health. Likewise, you cannot monitor the health of a device or a network unless you understand the metrics. In these opening sections, you will learn what these are and how to use them.

Device/Chassis

There are certain basic items to monitor when dealing with physical computing devices, regardless of whether it's a computer, router, or switch. While not the only things to monitor, these items would be on the dashboard (if they had dashboards).

Temperature

Heat and computers do not mix well. Many computer systems require both temperature and humidity control for reliable service. The larger servers, communications equipment, and drive arrays generate considerable amounts of heat; this is especially true of mainframes and older minicomputers. An environmental system for this type of equipment is a significant expense beyond the actual computer system costs. Fortunately, newer systems operate in a wider temperature range. Most new systems are designed to operate in an office environment.

Overheating is also a big cause of reboots. When CPUs get overheated, a cycle of reboots can ensue. Make sure the fan is working on the heat sink and the system fan is also working. If required, vacuum the dust from around the vents.

Under normal conditions, the PC cools itself by pulling in air. That air is used to dissipate the heat created by the processor (and absorbed by the heat sink). When airflow is restricted by clogged ports, a bad fan, and so forth, heat can build up inside the unit and cause problems. Chip creep—the loosening of components—is one of the more common by—products of overheating and cooling cycles inside the system.

Since the air is being pulled into the machine, excessive heat can originate from outside the PC as well because of a hot working environment. The heat can be pulled in and cause the same problems. Take care to keep the ambient air within normal ranges (approximately 60°F to 90°F) and at a constant temperature.

Replacing slot covers is vital. Computers are designed to circulate air with slot covers in place or cards plugged into the ports. Leaving slots on the back of the computer open alters the air circulation and causes more dust to be pulled into the system.

Finally, make sure the fan is working; if it stops, that is a major cause of overheating.

Central Processing Unit (CPU) Usage

When monitoring the CPU, the specific counters you use depend on the server role. Consult the vendor's documentation for information on those counters and what they mean to the performance of the service or application. The following counters are commonly monitored:

- Processor\% Processor Time—The percentage of time the CPU spends executing a non-idle thread. This should not be over 85 percent on a sustained basis.

- Processor\% User Time—The percentage of time the CPU spends in user mode, which means it is doing work for an application. If this value is higher than the baseline you captured during normal operation, the service or application is dominating the CPU.

- Processor\% Interrupt Time—The percentage of time the CPU receives and services hardware interrupts during specific sample intervals. If this is over 15 percent, there could be a hardware issue.

- System\Processor Queue Length—The number of threads (which are smaller pieces of an overall operation) in the processor queue. If this value is over two times the number of CPUs, the server is not keeping up with the workload.

Memory

Different system roles place different demands on the memory, so there may be specific counters of interest you can learn by consulting the documentation provided by the vendor of the specific service. Some of the most common counters monitored by server administrators are listed here:

- Memory\% Committed Bytes in Use—The amount of virtual memory in use. If this is over 80 percent, you need more memory.

- Memory\Available Mbytes—The amount of physical memory, in megabytes, currently available. If this is less than 5 percent you need more memory.

- Memory\Free System Page Table Entries—The number of entries in the page table not currently in use by the system. If the number is less than 5000, there may well be a memory leak.

- Memory\Pool Non-Paged Bytes—The size, in bytes, of the non-paged pool, which contains objects that cannot be paged to the disk. If the value is greater than 175 MB, you may have a memory leak (an application is not releasing its allocated memory when it is done).

- Memory\Pool Paged Bytes—The size, in bytes, of the paged pool, which contains objects that *can* be paged to disk. (If this value is greater than 250 MB, there may be a memory leak.)

- Memory\Pages per Second—The rate at which pages are written to and read from the disk during paging. If the value is greater than 1000, as a result of excessive paging, there may be a memory leak.

Network Metrics

The health of a network's operation can also be monitored so you can maintain its performance at peak efficiency. Just as you can avoid a problem issue with a workstation or server, so you can react to network conditions before they cause an issue by monitoring these items.

Bandwidth

In a perfect world, there would be unlimited bandwidth, but in reality, you're more likely to find Bigfoot. So, it's helpful to have some great strategies up your sleeve.

If you look at what computers are used for today, there's a huge difference between the files we transfer now versus those transferred even three to five years ago. Now we do things like watch movies online without them stalling, and we can send huge email attachments. Video teleconferencing is almost more common than Starbucks locations. The point is that the files we transfer today are really large compared to what we sent back and forth just a few years ago. And although bandwidth has increased to allow us to do what we do, there are still limitations that cause network performance to suffer miserably.

The following are metrics to follow for bandwidth on a system:

- Network Interface\Bytes Total/Sec—The percentage of bandwidth the NIC is capable of that is currently being used. If this value is more than 70 percent of the bandwidth of the interface, the interface is saturated or not keeping up.

- Network Interface\Output Queue Length—The number of packets in the output queue. If this value is over 2, the NIC is not keeping up with the workload.

Latency

Latency is the delay typically incurred in the processing of network data. A low-latency network connection is one that generally experiences short delay times, while a high-latency connection generally suffers from long delays. Many security solutions may negatively affect latency. For example, routers take a certain amount of time to process and forward any communication. Configuring additional rules on a router generally increases latency, thereby resulting in longer delays. An organization may decide not to deploy certain security solutions because of the negative effects they will have on network latency.

Auditing is a great example of a security solution that affects latency and performance.

When auditing is configured, it records certain actions as they occur. The recording of these actions may affect the latency and performance.

Measuring latency is typically done using a metric called round-trip time (RTT). This metric is calculated using a ping, a command-line tool that bounces a user request off a server and calculates how long it takes to return to the user device.

Jitter

Jitter occurs when the data flow in a connection is not consistent; that is, it increases and decreases in no discernable pattern. Jitter results from network congestion, timing drift, and route changes. Jitter is especially problematic in real-time communications like IP telephony and videoconferencing.

SNMP

Simple Network Management Protocol (SNMP), which uses ports 161 and 162, collects and manipulates valuable network information. It gathers data by polling the devices on the network from a management station at fixed or random intervals, requiring them to disclose certain information. When all is well, SNMP receives something called a baseline—a report delimiting the operational traits of a healthy network. This protocol can also stand as a watchdog over the network, quickly notifying managers of any sudden turn of events. The network watchdogs are called agents, and when aberrations occur, agents send an alert called a trap to the management station. In addition, SNMP can help simplify the process of setting up a network as well as the administration of your entire network.

SNMP has three versions, with version 1 being rarely, if ever, implemented today. Here's a summary of these three versions:

- SNMPv1—Supports plaintext authentication with community strings and uses only UDP.

- SNMPv2c—Supports plaintext authentication with MD5 or SHA with no encryption but provides GET BULK, which is a way to gather many types of information at once and minimize the number of GET requests. It offers a more detailed error message reporting method, but it's not more secure than v1. It uses UDP even though it can be configured to use TCP.

- SNMPv3—Supports strong authentication with MD5 or SHA, providing confidentiality (encryption) and data integrity of messages via DES or DES-256 encryption between agents and managers. GET BULK is a supported feature of SNMPv3, and this version also uses TCP. (Note: MD5 and DES are no longer considered secure.)

Traps

SNMP provides a message format for agents on a variety of devices to communicate with network management stations (NMSs)—for example, Cisco Prime or HP OpenView. These agents send messages to the NMS station, which then either reads or writes information in the database, stored on the NMS, that's called a management information base (MIB).

The NMS periodically queries or polls the SNMP agent on a device to gather and analyze statistics via GET messages. These messages can be sent to a console or alert you via email or SMS. The command `snmpwalk` uses the SNMP GET NEXT request to query a network for a tree of information.

End devices running SNMP agents will send an SNMP trap to the NMS if a problem occurs. This is demonstrated in Figure 13.1.

FIGURE 13.1   SNMP GET and TRAP messages

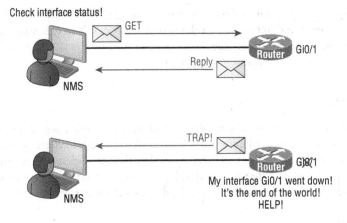

In addition to polling to obtain statistics, SNMP can be used for analyzing information and compiling the results in a report or even a graph. Thresholds can be used to trigger a notification process when exceeded. Graphing tools are used to monitor the CPU statistics of devices like a core router. The CPU should be monitored continuously, and the NMS can graph the statistics. Notification will be sent when any threshold you have set has been exceeded.

Object Identifiers (OIDs)

Object identifiers (OIDs) are an identifier mechanism standardized by the International Tele-communications Union (ITU) and ISO/IEC for naming any object, concept, or "thing" with a globally unambiguous persistent name.

Each physical component can possess a number of OIDs to describe the current state of a system. In Simple Network Management Protocol (SNMP), each node in a management information base (MIB) is identified by an OID.

Management Information Bases (MIBs)

OIDs are organized into a hierarchical structure called management information bases (MIBs). A managed object (sometimes called a MIB object or object) is one of any number of specific characteristics of a managed device. Managed objects are made up of one or more object instances, which are essentially variables. An OID uniquely identifies a managed object in the MIB hierarchy.

Network Device Logs

While SMTP should be in your toolbox when monitoring the network, there is also a wealth of information to be found in the logs on the network devices. You will now learn about the main log types and methods to manage the volume of data that exists in these logs. Baseline configurations are covered in detail in Chapter 14.

Log Reviews

High-quality documentation should include a baseline for network performance because you and your client need to know what "normal" looks like in order to detect problems before they develop into disasters. Don't forget to verify that the network conforms to all internal and external regulations and that you've developed and itemized solid management procedures and security policies for future network administrators to refer to and follow.

Traffic Logs

Some of your infrastructure devices will have logs that record the network traffic that has traversed the device. Examples include firewalls and intrusion detection and prevention devices. Those devices were covered in Chapter 5.

Many organizations choose to direct the traffic logs from these devices to a syslog server or to security information and event management (SIEM) systems (both covered later in this section).

Audit Logs

Audit logs record the activities of the users. Windows Server 2019 (and most other Windows operating systems) comes with a tool called Event Viewer that provides you with several logs containing vital information about events happening on your computer. Other server operating systems have similar logs, and many connectivity devices like routers and switches also have graphical logs that gather statistics on what's happening to them. These logs can go by various names, such as history logs, general logs, or server logs. Figure 13.2 shows an Event Viewer security log display from a Windows Server 2019 machine.

FIGURE 13.2   Event Viewer security log

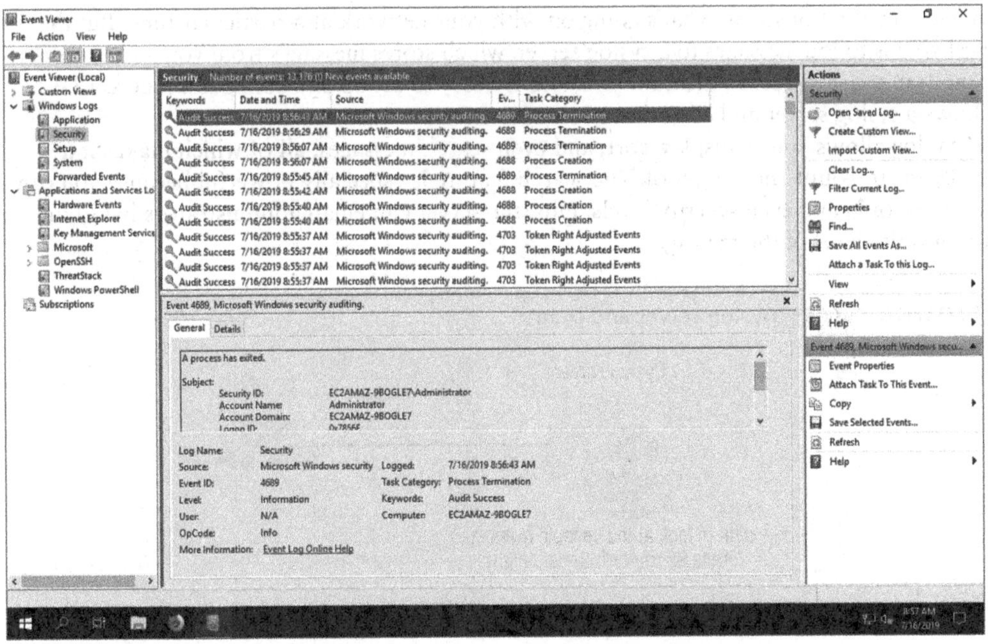

On Windows servers and client systems, a minimum of three separate logs hold different types of information:

- Application log: Contains events triggered by applications or programs determined by their programmers. Example applications include LiveUpdate, the Microsoft Office suite, and SQL and Exchange servers.

- Security log: Contains security events like valid or invalid logon attempts and potential security problems.

- System log: Contains events generated by Windows system components, including drivers and services that started or failed to start.

The basic "Big Three" can give us lots of juicy information about who's logging on, who's accessing the computer, and which services are running properly (or not). If you want to find out whether your Dynamic Host Configuration Protocol (DHCP) server started up its DHCP service properly, just check out its system log.

Syslog

Reading system messages from a switch's or router's internal buffer is the most popular and efficient method of seeing what's going on with your network at a particular time. But the best way is to log messages to a syslog server, which stores messages from you and can even time-stamp and sequence them for you, and it's easy to set up and configure! Figure 13.3 shows a syslog server and client in action.

Syslog allows you to display, sort, and even search messages, all of which makes it a really great troubleshooting tool. The search feature is especially powerful because you can use keywords and even severity levels. Plus, the server can email administrators based on the severity level of the message.

FIGURE 13.3   Syslog server and client

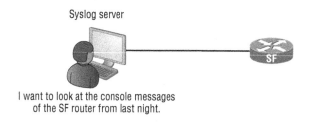

Syslog server

I want to look at the console messages
of the SF router from last night.

Network devices can be configured to generate a syslog message and forward it to various destinations. These four examples are popular ways to gather messages from Cisco devices:

- Logging buffer (on by default)
- Console line (on by default)
- Terminal lines (using the terminal monitor command)
- Syslog server

All system messages and debug output generated by the IOS go out only through the console port by default and are also logged in buffers in RAM. And you also know that routers aren't exactly shy about sending messages! To send message to the VTY lines, use the `terminal monitor` command.

So, by default, we'd see something like this on our console line:

```
*Oct 21 17:33:50.565:%LINK-5-CHANGED:Interface FastEthernet0/0, changed state
to administratively down

*Oct 21 17:33:51.565:%LINEPROTO-5-UPDOWN:Line protocol on Interface
FastEthernet0/0, changed state to down
```

And the router would send a general version of the message to the syslog server that would be formatted something like this:

```
Seq no:timestamp: %facility-severity- MNEMONIC:description
```

The system message format can be broken down in this way:

- **seq no:** This stamp logs messages with a sequence number, but not by default. If you want this output, you've got to configure it.
- **Timestamp:** Date and time of the message or event.
- **Facility:** The facility to which the message refers.
- **Severity:** A single-digit code from 0 to 7 that indicates the severity of the message.
- **MNEMONIC:** Text string that uniquely describes the message.
- **Description:** Text string containing detailed information about the event being reported.

SIEM

Security information and event management (SIEM) is a term for software products and services combining security information management (SIM) and security event management (SEM). SIEM technology provides real-time analysis of security alerts generated by network hardware and applications. You can get this as a software solution or a hardware appliance, and some businesses sell managed services using SIEM. Any one of these solutions provides log security data and can generate reports for compliance purposes.

The acronyms SEM, SIM, and SIEM are used interchangeably; however, SEM is typically used to describe the management that deals with real-time monitoring and correlation of events, notifications, and console views.

The term SIM is used to describe long-term storage, analysis, and reporting of log data.

Recently, vSIEM (voice security information and event management) was introduced to provide voice data visibility.

SIEM can collect useful data about the following items:

- Data aggregation
- Correlation
- Alerting
- Dashboards
- Compliance
- Retention
- Forensic analysis

Notifications

SIEM systems not only assess the aggregated logs in real time, they generate alerts or notifications when an issue is discovered. This allows for continuous monitoring of the environment in a way not possible with other log centralization approaches such as syslog.

Logging Levels/Severity Levels

In most cases you need to know what to filter so you get the information you really need and nothing else. For example, with syslog you can filter by the security level. Severity levels, from the most severe level to the least severe, are explained in Table 13.1. Informational is the default and will result in all messages being sent to the buffers and console.

TABLE 13.1   Severity levels

Severity Level	Explanation
Emergency (severity 0)	System is unusable.
Alert (severity 1)	Immediate action is needed.
Critical (severity 2)	Critical condition.
Error (severity 3)	Error condition.
Warning (severity 4)	Warning condition.
Notification (severity 5)	Normal but significant condition.
Information (severity 6)	Normal information message.
Debugging (severity 7)	Debugging message.

Understand that only emergency-level messages will be displayed if you've configured severity level 0. But if, for example, you opt for level 4 instead, levels 0 through 4 will be displayed, giving you emergency, alert, critical, error, and warning messages too. Level 7 is the highest-level security option and displays everything, but be warned that going with it could have a serious impact on the performance of your device. So always use debugging commands carefully with an eye on the messages you really need to meet your specific business requirements!

Servers also create useful logs that you may or may not be using. Even if you are using the logs (and you should!), you shouldn't allow them to slowly eat up all of the space. You can control the behavior of log files in Windows in several ways:

- You can limit the amount of space used for each log.
- You can determine the behavior when the log is full.
- You can choose to save a log for later viewing.

To set the maximum size for a log file, access the properties of the log in Event Viewer. In the Maximum Log Size option, use the spinner control to set the value you want and click OK as shown in Figure 13.4.

FIGURE 13.4   Event log properties

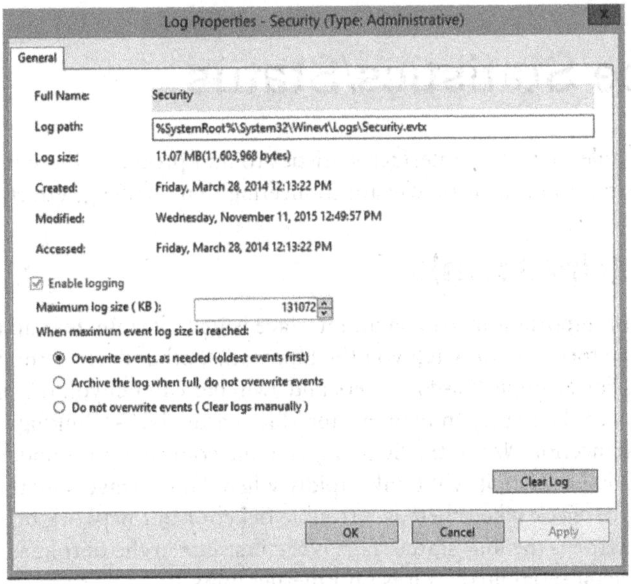

This can also be done at the command line using the following command, inserting the name of the log file and the maximum size in bytes:

```
wevtutil sl <LogName> /ms:<MaxSizeInBytes>
```

To determine what happens when the log is full, access the same dialog box shown in Figure 13.4 and select one of the three options:

- Overwrite events as needed (oldest events first)
- Archive the log when full, do not overwrite events
- Do not overwrite events (Clear logs manually)

This can also be done at the command line using the following command:

```
wevtutil sl <LogName> /r:{true | false} /ab:{true | false}
```

The r parameter specifies whether to retain the log, and the ab parameter specifies whether to automatically back up the log.

Therefore, use the following combinations to achieve the desired result:

- Overwrite events as needed: `r = false, ab = false`
- Archive the log when full, do not overwrite events: `r = true, ab = true`
- Do not overwrite events. (Clear logs manually): `r = true, ab = false`

Interface Statistics/Status

You've got to be able to analyze interface statistics to find problems there if they exist, so let's pick out the important factors relevant to meeting that challenge effectively now.

Link State (Up/Down)

Typically, the most important metric on an interface is its link state. Is it up (functional) or down? While some tools can only tell you the link status, other devices and tools can tell you what the issue is. For example, Cisco routers and switches can tell you the link state along with an indication of the issue. On network interface cards (NICs), link lights can also tell the state of the connection. When the light is green, the connection is good, and when it's amber, there is an issue. Also, it will blink rapidly when data is traversing the NIC.

The first thing to check when there is a trouble ticket or our network management tools alert us of a link error is the link status. This is the first line in the output as shown. This would be the same on serial links as it is on Ethernet links.

```
Router#sh int fa0/0
FastEthernet0/0 is up, line protocol is up
```

The first up listed is carrier detect. If this shows down, then you have a physical layer problem locally and you need to get to that port immediately and check the cable and port. The second statistic, which is `protocol is up` in this example, is keepalives from the remote end. If you see up/down, then you know your local end is good but you're not getting a digital signal from the remote end.

The utilities known as ipconfig (in Windows) and ifconfig (in Unix/Linux/macOS) will display the current configuration of TCP/IP on a given workstation—including the current IP address, DNS configuration, Windows Internet Naming Service (WINS) configuration, and default gateway. In Chapter 23 you will learn more about using these tools.

Speed/Duplex

As you will learn in Chapter 11, in full-duplex communication, both devices can send and receive communication at the same time.

This means that the effective throughput is doubled and communication is much more efficient. Full-duplex is typical in most of today's switched networks.

You also learned that two interfaces on the end of a common link should be set to both the same duplex and the same speed to function correctly. Later in this chapter you will learn how to interpret the output of an interface to determine when a speed mismatch is indicated and when duplex mismatch is the issue.

To determine the status on a router or switch, execute the following command:

```
R2#show run
Building configuration…
Current configuration : 1036 bytes
<output omitted>
version 12.4
interface FastEthernet0/0
ip address 10.1.1.2 255.255.255.0
duplex auto
speed auto
!
interface FastEthernet1/0
ip address 10.2.2.2 255.255.255.0
duplex auto
speed auto
```

In this case both interfaces are set for auto-detect.

To verify speed and duplex settings on a Windows device use Device Manager as shown on the Advanced tab of the interface properties (Figure 13.5).

FIGURE 13.5 Speed and duplex

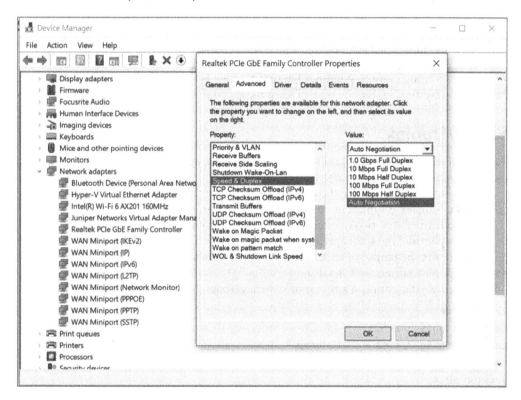

Send/Receive Traffic

Sometimes you need to check how well traffic is flowing into and out of a device, without regard to the type. The show run command will show this as well. In this case, the interface is down so there is no traffic flowing in either direction.

```
Router#sh int s0/0
Serial0/0 is up, line protocol is down
Hardware is PowerQUICC Serial
<output omitted>
Input queue: 0/75/0/0 (size/max/drops/flushes); Total output drops: 0
Queueing strategy: fifo
```

```
Output queue: 0/40 (size/max)
5 minute input rate 0 bits/sec, 0 packets/sec
5 minute output rate 0 bits/sec, 0 packets/sec
```

To check the latest input and output statistics on a Windows interface, use the netsh command as shown below.

```
netsh interface ipv4>show ipstats
MIB-II IP Statistics

--------------------------------------------------------

Forwarding is:              Disabled
Default TTL:                     128
In Receives:                 5696170
In Header Errors:                  0
In Address Errors:             81691
Datagrams Forwarded:               0
In Unknown Protocol:               0
In Discarded:                   2972
In Delivered:                2898662
Out Requests:                1907432
Routing Discards:                  0
Out Discards:                   1965
Out No Routes:                     6
Reassembly Timeout:               60
Reassembly Required:               0
Reassembled Ok:                    0
Reassembly Failures:               0
Fragments Ok:                      0
Fragments Failed:                  0
Fragments Created:                 0
netsh interface ipv4>
```

Cyclic Redundancy Checks (CRCs)

As you learned in Chapter 11, the function of Ethernet stations is to pass data frames between each other using a group of bits known as a MAC frame format. This provides error detection from a cyclic redundancy check (CRC). But remember—this is error detection, not error correction. Just know that when CRC errors occur, something has corrupted the received packet.

Protocol Packet and Byte Counts

It is also possible to determine the number of packets received from protocols and the number of bytes received. This is also contained in a section of the output of the show run command as shown here:

```
FastEthernet0/0 is up, line protocol is up
[output cut]
Full-duplex, 100Mb/s, 100BaseTX/FX
ARP type: ARPA, ARP Timeout 04:00:00
5 minute input rate 0 bits/sec, 0 packets/sec
5 minute output rate 0 bits/sec, 0 packets/sec
1325 packets input, 157823 bytes
Received 1157 broadcasts (0 IP multicasts)
0 runts, 0 giants, 0 throttles
0 input errors, 0 CRC, 0 frame, 0 overrun, 0 ignored
0 watchdog
0 input packets with dribble condition detected
2294 packets output, 244630 bytes, 0 underruns
0 output errors, 0 collisions, 3 interface resets
347 unknown protocol drops
0 babbles, 0 late collision, 0 deferred
4 lost carrier, 0 no carrier
0 output buffer failures, 0 output buffers swapped out
```

Interface Errors or Alerts

Let's take a look at an example to clarify how to use this information for interface monitoring to scrutinize errors, utilization, discards, packet drops, interface resets, and duplex issues:

```
Router#sh int fa0/0
FastEthernet0/0 is up, line protocol is up
[output cut]
Full-duplex, 100Mb/s, 100BaseTX/FX
ARP type: ARPA, ARP Timeout 04:00:00
WAN Troubleshooting 625
Last input 00:00:05, output 00:00:01, output hang never
Last clearing of "show interface" counters never
Input queue: 0/75/0/0 (size/max/drops/flushes); Total output drops: 0
```

```
Queueing strategy: fifo
Output queue: 0/40 (size/max)
5 minute input rate 0 bits/sec, 0 packets/sec
5 minute output rate 0 bits/sec, 0 packets/sec
1325 packets input, 157823 bytes
Received 1157 broadcasts (0 IP multicasts)
0 runts, 0 giants, 0 throttles
0 input errors, 0 CRC, 0 frame, 0 overrun, 0 ignored
0 watchdog
0 input packets with dribble condition detected
2294 packets output, 244630 bytes, 0 underruns
0 output errors, 0 collisions, 3 interface resets
347 unknown protocol drops
0 babbles, 0 late collision, 0 deferred
4 lost carrier, 0 no carrier
0 output buffer failures, 0 output buffers swapped out
```

If you have a duplex mismatch, a telling sign is that the late collision counter will increment.

- **Input Queue Drops:** If the input queue drops counter increments, this tells you that more traffic is being delivered to the router than it can process. If this value is consistently high, try to determine exactly when these counters are increasing and how the events relate to CPU usage. Know that you'll see the ignored and throttle counters increment as well.

- **Output Queue Drops:** This counter indicates that packets were dropped due to interface congestion, leading to lost data and queuing delays. When this occurs, applications like VoIP will experience performance issues. If you observe this constantly incrementing, consider QoS as the culprit.

- **Input Errors:** Input errors often indicate high-level errors such as CRCs. This can point to cabling problems, hardware issues, or duplex mismatches.

- **Output Errors:** This issue equals the total number of frames that the port tried to transmit when an issue such as a collision occurred.

CRC Errors

CRC errors mean that packets have been damaged. This can be caused by a faulty port on the device or a bad Ethernet cable. Changing the cable or swapping the port is a relatively easy fix. Occasionally, they are generated on layer 2 by a duplex mismatch. It can also be the result of collisions or a station transmitting bad data.

Giants and Runts

Giants are packets that are discarded because they exceed the maximum packet size of the medium. For example, any Ethernet packet that is greater than 1518 bytes is considered a giant. They also have an incorrect frame check sequence (FCS). What causes this? In many cases, this is the result of a bad NIC.

Because collisions are a normal aspect of half-duplex communications, runt (packets that are discarded because they do not meet minimum packet size requirements) and giant frames are common by-products of those operations. A malfunctioning NIC can also place frames on the network that are either too short or longer than the maximum allowed length. CRC errors can result from using the wrong type of cable or from electrical interference. Using a cable that is too long can result in late collisions rather than runts and giants.

Encapsulation Errors

As you have learned in Chapter 2, encapsulation is the process of adding headers and trailers to data. When a host transmits data to another device over a network, the data is encapsulated, with protocol information at each layer of the OSI reference model. Each layer uses protocol data units (PDUs) to communicate and exchange information from the source to the destination.

A failed encapsulation error message indicates that the router has a layer 3 packet to forward and is lacking some element of the layer 2 header that it needs to be able to forward the packet toward the next hop. You may see this in the logs of a router as shown here:

```
Dec 26 18:18:38.081 PST: IP: s=0.0.0.0 (FastEthernet0/0), d=255.255.255.255,
len 328, rcvd 2

Dec 26 18:18:38.081 PST: UDP src=68, dst=67

Dec 26 18:18:38.085 PST: IP: s=10.209.2.254 (local), d=10.69.96.30
(FastEthernet0/0), len 328, sending

Dec 26 18:18:38.085 PST: UDP src=67, dst=67

Dec 26 18:18:38.085 PST: IP: s=10.209.2.254 (local), d=10.69.96.30
(FastEthernet0/0), len 328, encapsulation failed

Dec 26 18:18:38.085 PST: UDP src=67, dst=67
```

Environmental Factors and Sensors

All of the equipment discussed in this chapter—switches, routers, hubs, and so on—require proper environmental conditions to operate correctly. These devices have the same needs as any computing device. The environmental concerns and methods to address these concerns are covered in the following sections.

Temperature

Like any device with a CPU, infrastructure devices such as routers, switches, and specialty appliances must have a cool area to operate. When temperatures rise, servers start rebooting and appliance CPUs start overworking as well. The room(s) where these devices are located should be provided with heavy-duty HVAC systems and ample ventilation.

It may even be advisable to dedicate a suite for this purpose and put the entire system on an uninterruptable power supply (UPS) with a backup generator in the case of a loss of power.

Humidity

The air around these systems can be neither too damp nor too dry; it must be "just right." If it is too dry, static electricity will build up in the air, making the situation ripe for damaging a system. It takes very little static electricity to fry some electrical components.

If it is too damp, connections start corroding and shorts begin to occur. A humidifying system should be used to maintain the level above 50 percent. The air conditioning should keep it within acceptable levels on the upper end.

Check On It

Recommendations change, so techs should keep up with new ASHRAE recommendations: https://www.ashrae.org/File%20Library/ Technical%20Resources/Standards%20and%20Guidelines/ Standards%20Addenda/62.1-2016/62_1_2016_ae_20190826.pdf.

Environmental Monitors

Environmental monitors are designed to monitor the temperature, humidity, power, and air flow in an area or in a device.

High humidity cannot be tolerated because it leads to corrosion of electrical parts followed by shorts and other failures. Low humidity sounds good on paper, but with it comes static electricity buildup in the air, which can fry computer parts if it reaches them. Both of these conditions should be monitored.

A temperature and humidity monitor can save you and your precious devices from a total meltdown. By their very nature, networks often include lots of machines placed close together in one or several location(s)—like server rooms. Clearly, these devices, all humming along at once, generate quite a bit of heat.

Just like us, electronics need to "breathe," and they're also pretty sensitive to becoming overheated, which is why you'll often need a jacket in a chilly server room. It's also why we need to set up and use temperature-monitoring devices. Twenty years ago or so, these devices didn't send alerts or give off any kind of alarms; they were just little plastic boxes that had pieces of round graph paper to graph temperature. The paper was good for a month, and for that duration, it would just spin around in a circle. As the temperature moved up or down, the pen attached to the temperature coil moved in or out, leaving a circle line around the paper. All of this allowed you to manually monitor the temperature modulation in the server room over time. Although intended to "alert" you when and if there were climate changes, it usually did so after the fact, and therefore, too late.

Today, these temperature/humidity systems can provide multiple sensors feeding data to a single control point—nice. Now we can much more accurately track the temperature in our server rooms dynamically in real time. The central control point is usually equipped with HTTPS software that can send alerts and provide alarms via a browser should your server room experience a warming event.

Temperature/humidity monitors also come in a variety of flavors. They vary in size and cost and come in hardware and/or software varieties. The kind you need varies and is based on the size of the room and the number of devices in it. You can even get one that will just monitor your PC's internal heat.

What else will indicate you have a temperature problem in your server room? When you install new servers in a rack and you have network instability and other issues across all the servers in the rack but the power resources and bandwidth have been tested, this would be a good time to check your temperature monitor and verify that the servers are staying cool enough. Another red flag when it comes to environmental issues is a problem that occurs every day at the same time. This could be the time of day when the room temperature reaches the problematic stage.

Electrical

Power is the lifeline of the data center. One of your goals is to ensure that all systems have a constant clean source of power. In the following sections, we'll look at the proper use of uninterruptable power supplies (UPSs). We'll also talk about how to plan to ensure you have sufficient capacity to serve your devices. Finally, we'll explore the use of redundant power supplies and the use of multiple circuits to enhance availability.

UPS

All systems of any importance to the continued functioning of the enterprise should be connected to a UPS. You probably already know that UPSs have a battery attached that can provide power to your devices in the event of a power outage. You may also be aware that these systems are designed to only provide short-term power to the devices, that is, a length of time sufficient to allow someone to gracefully shut down the devices. We'll now dig a bit deeper and identify some of the features of these devices. We'll also go over some best practices with regard to ensuring your UPS solution provides the protection you intended.

Runtime vs. Capacity

Two important metrics that are related but are *not* the same when assessing a UPS are its runtime and its capacity. The runtime is the amount of time the UPS can provide power at a given power level. This means you can't really evaluate this metric without knowing the amount of load you will be placing on the UPS. Documentation that comes with the UPS should reveal to you the number of minutes expected at various power levels. So if you doubled the number of similar devices attached to the UPS, you should expect the time to be cut in half (actually, it will cut more than half in reality because the batteries discharge quicker at higher loads).

Capacity, on the other hand, is the maximum amount of power the UPS can supply at any moment in time. So, if the UPS has a capacity of 650 volt amperes (VA) and you attempt to pull 800 VA from the UPS, it will probably shut itself down. So both of the values must be considered. You need to know the total amount of power the devices may require (capacity) and, based on that figure, select a UPS that can provide that for the amount of time you will need to shut all the devices down.

One good thing to know is that some UPS vendors can supply expansion packs for existing units that increase their capacity and runtime. That would be a favorable feature to insist on to allow your system to grow.

Automated Graceful Shutdown of Attached Devices

Many of today's enterprise-level UPS systems offer the ability to shut down a server to which it is attached when the power is lost. A proper shutdown is called a graceful shutdown. If all devices were thus equipped, it could reduce the amount of runtime required and eliminate the race to shut servers down.

There are several approaches that vendors have taken to this. In some cases, if you purchase a special network card for the UPS, a single UPS can provide the automatic shutdown to multiple servers. The agent on each server communicates with the network card in the UPS.

Another option is to use a dedicated UPS for each server and attach the server to the UPS using a serial or USB cable. The disadvantage of this approach is that it requires a UPS for each device and you will be faced with the cable length limitations of serial and USB cables.

In either case, using the software that comes with the UPS, you can also have scripts run prior to the shutdown, and you can configure the amount of time to wait for the shutdown so the script has time to execute, as shown in Figure 13.6. You can also set a notification of this event.

FIGURE 13.6   Automatic shutdown

Periodic Testing of Batteries

Just as you would never wait until there is a loss of data to find out if the backup system is working, you should never wait until the power goes out to see the UPS does its job. Periodically, you should test the batteries to ensure they stand ready to provide the expected runtime.

While the simplest test would be to remove power and see what happens, if you have production servers connected when you do this, it could be a resume generating event (RGE). In most cases the software that came with the UPS will have the ability to report the current expected runtime based on the current state of the battery, as shown in Figure 13.7.

FIGURE 13.7   Checking battery level

Even with this information, it is probably advisable to test the units from time to time with devices that you don't care about connected just to make sure the process of switching over to the battery succeeds and the correct runtime is provided.

Maximum Load

While the capacity of a UPS is rated in volts ampere (VA), that is not the same as maximum load. The capacity value assumes that all of the attached devices are pulling the maximum amount of power, which they rarely do. As a rule of thumb, if you multiply the VA times .6, you will get a rough estimate of the maximum load your UPS may undergo at any particular time. So a UPS that is rated for 650 VA cannot provide more than 390 watts. If either of these values are exceeded during operation, the UPS will fail to provide the power you need.

Bypass Procedures

Putting a UPS in bypass mode removes the UPS from between the device and the wall output conceptually, without disconnecting it. A static bypass is one in which the UPS, either by the administrator invoking the bypass manually or by an inverter failure in the UPS, switches the power path back to the main line and removes itself from the line.

A maintenance bypass is possible when the UPS is augmented with an external appliance called the bypass cabinet. This allows for enabling the bypass and then working with the UPS without concerns about the power being on (although it can be enabled while leaving the power to the UPS on). This concept is shown in Figure 13.8. Notice the two switches on the bypass cabinet that can be opened and shut to accomplish this power segregation.

FIGURE 13.8   Maintenance bypass

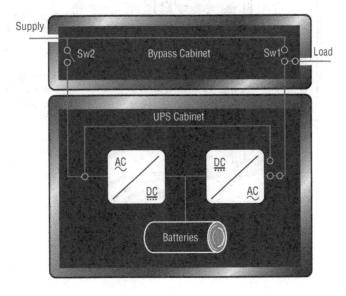

Multiple Circuits

If you have a single power circuit and it fails, you will only be up as long as your batteries last or as long as the generator can run. Many data centers commission multiple power circuits to prevent this. A comparison of a center with a single circuit to one with two circuits is shown in Figure 13.9. In this particular case, the engineers have gone beyond circuit redundancy and also implemented main power panel, auto transfer switch, power panel, MBP, and UPS redundancy.

FIGURE 13.9   Multiple circuits

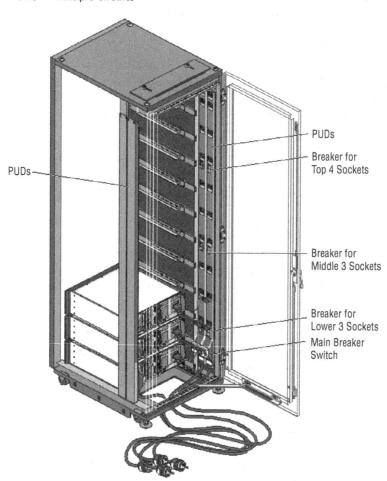

Flooding

In some parts of the country, floods are a constant source of concern. For this reason, server rooms and data centers should be located on upper floors if possible. If not, raised floors should be deployed to help prevent the water from reaching the equipment, as shown in Figure 13.10.

FIGURE 13.10   Flooding

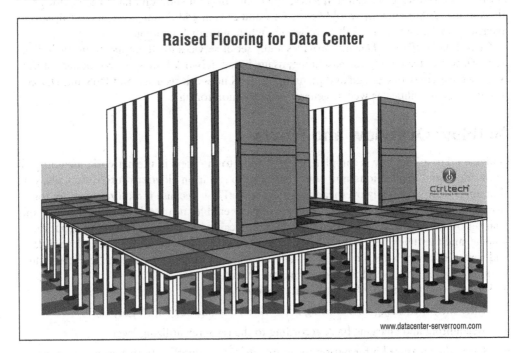

Baselines

As you learned earlier in this chapter, a baseline can refer to the standard level of performance of a certain device or to the normal operating capacity for your whole network. Please review the coverage of baselines in the section "Network Device Logs" earlier in this chapter.

NetFlow Data

SNMP can be a powerful tool to help you manage and troubleshoot your network, but Cisco knew it would be very helpful for engineers to be able to track TCP/IP flows within the network as well.

That's why we have NetFlow as an application for collecting IP traffic information. Cisco compares NetFlow informational reports to receiving a phone bill with detailed call information to track calls, call frequency, and even calls that shouldn't have been made at all. A more current analogy would be the CIA and certain additional government "alphabet agencies" watching who has talked to whom, when, and for how long.

Cisco IOS NetFlow efficiently provides a key set of services for IP applications, including network traffic accounting for baselining, usage-based network billing for consumers of network services, network design and planning, general network security, and DoS and DDoS monitoring capabilities as well as general network monitoring.

NetFlow Overview and Flows

Understand that NetFlow is completely transparent to the users in the network, including all end stations and applications, and you don't need to run it on all your routers. Actually, you shouldn't; there's definitely overhead when using NetFlow because it requires memory for storing information in cache on the device. NetFlow enables near real-time visualization and analysis of recorded and aggregated flow data. You can specify the router, the aggregation scheme, and the time interval for when you want to view and then retrieve the relevant data and sort it into bar charts, pie charts, and so on. The components used with NetFlow include a router enabled with NetFlow and a NetFlow collector.

Service providers use NetFlow to do the following:

- Efficiently measuring who is using network service and for which purpose
- Accounting and charging back according to the resource utilizing level
- Using the measured information for more effective network planning so that resource allocation and deployment are well aligned with customer requirements
- Using the information to better structure and customize the set of available applications and services to meet user needs and customer service requirements

Moreover, there are different types of analyzers available to gather NetFlow statistics and analyze the traffic on your network by showing the following:

- Major users of the network, meaning top talkers, top listeners, top protocols, and so on
- Websites that are routinely visited, plus what's been downloaded
- Who's generating the most traffic and using excessive bandwidth
- Descriptions of bandwidth needs for an application as well as your available bandwidth

NetFlow is built around TCP/IP communication for statistical record-keeping using the concept of a flow. A flow is a unidirectional stream of packets between a source and destination host or system. With an understanding of TCP/IP, you can figure out that NetFlow is using socket information, meaning source and destination IP addresses and source and destination port numbers. But there are a few more fields that NetFlow uses. Here is a list of commonly used NetFlow flows:

- Source IP address
- Destination IP address
- Source port number
- Destination port number
- Layer 3 protocol field
- Type of Service (ToS) marking
- Input logical interface

The operation of NetFlow is shown in Figure 13.11.

FIGURE 13.11   NetFlow

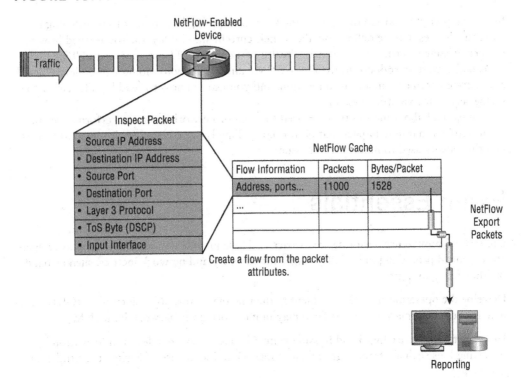

As mentioned, the first four listings are the sockets used between the source and destination host, which identify the application. The protocol field identifies the data the packet is carrying, and ToS in the IPv4 header describes how QoS rules are applied to the packets in the flow. If a packet has a key field that's different from another packet, it's considered to belong to another flow.

Uptime/Downtime

Uptime is the amount of time the system is up and accessible to your end users, so the more uptime you have the better. And depending on how critical the nature of your business is, you may need to provide four-nine or five-nine uptime on your network—that's a lot. Why is this a lot? Because you write out four nines as 99.99 percent, or better, you write out five nines as 99.999 percent. Now that is some serious uptime!

Summary

In this chapter you learned that one of the keys to stopping downtime is to be listening to what the devices may be telling you about their current state of health. You learned how to use performance metrics to monitor the health of a device's CPU, memory, and NIC.

You also were introduced to the use of SNMP and NetFlow to monitor both device health and network traffic from a central location, and you learned how to send log files either to a syslog server or to a SIEM system.

You learned about metrics that are used to monitor network interface performance and about settings that may impact that performance. Finally, we covered environmental factors and the sensors used to monitor these issues.

Exam Essentials

Understand how to use performance metrics.   These include device metrics such as temperature, central processing unit (CPU) usage, and memory and network metrics, such as bandwidth, latency, and jitter.

Describe the operation of SNMP.   Identify the role that traps, object identifiers (OIDs), and management information bases (MIBs) play in monitoring the network with SNMP.

Utilize network device logs in addressing system issues.   Locate relevant information by reviewing logs such as traffic logs and audit logs. Describe the use of Syslog in centralizing these logs.

Interpret interface statistics and settings.   Identify issues based on interface statistics and error messages. These include values for link state (up/down), speed/duplex, send/receive traffic, cyclic redundancy checks (CRCs), protocol packet and byte counts, CRC errors, giants, runts, and encapsulation errors. Finally, understand the importance of matching speed and duplex settings.

Identify critical environmental factors and sensors that monitor them.   These factors include temperature, humidity, electrical issues, and flooding mitigation.

Written Lab

Complete the table by filling in the appropriate term for the description provided. You can find the answers in Appendix A.

Description	Term
The percentage of time the CPU spends executing a non-idle thread.	
The amount of physical memory in megabytes currently available.	
The percentage of bandwidth the NIC is capable of that is currently being used.	
The delay typically incurred in the processing of network data.	
Occurs when the data flow in a connection is not consistent; that is, it increases and decreases in no discernable pattern.	
Supports plaintext authentication with MD5 or SHA with no encryption but provides GET BULK.	
Sent by SNMP agents to the NMS if a problem occurs.	
Identifier mechanism standardized by the International Telecommunications Union (ITU) and ISO/IEC for naming any object, concept, or "thing" with a globally unambiguous persistent name.	
Hierarchical structure into which SNMP OIDs are organized.	

Refers to the standard level of performance of a certain device or to the normal operating capacity for your whole network.	
Centralizes and stores log messages and can even time-stamp and sequence them.	
Provides real-time analysis of security alerts generated by network hardware and applications.	
Errors that mean packets have been damaged.	

Review Questions

You can find the answers to the review questions in Appendix B.

1. Which of the following represents the percentage of uptime provided when four nines of fault tolerance are present?

   A. 9.999 percent

   B. 99.99 percent

   C. 99.999 percent

   D. 90.9 percent

2. Which of the following is *not* a commonly used NetFlow identifier?

   A. Source IP

   B. Destination port number

   C. Layer 2 protocol field

   D. Input logical interface

3. Which service can identify major users of the network, meaning top talkers?

   A. Syslog

   B. SIEM

   C. NetFlow

   D. SNMP

4. Which of the following refers to the standard level of performance of a certain device or to the normal operating capacity for your whole network?

   A. Baseline

   B. Target

   C. Normal

   D. Utilization

5. Raised floors are used to address which of the following?

   A. Electrical issues

   B. Flooding

   C. Terrorism

   D. Theft

6. Which of the following removes the UPS from between the device and the wall output conceptually, without disconnecting it?

   A. Inline mode

   B. Offline mode

    C. Bypass mode

    D. Maintenance mode

    E. Pie a la mode (just seeing if you're paying attention)

7. Which UPS value assumes that all of the attached devices are pulling the maximum amount of power?

    A. Maximum load

    B. Volts ampere

    C. UPC

    D. Capacity

8. Which value is the amount of time a UPS can operate based on the current battery charge?

    A. Runtime

    B. Remaining life

    C. Lifetime

    D. Live time

9. The proper shutdown of a system is called which of the following?

    A. Stateful

    B. Graceful

    C. Stateless

    D. Quick

10. Which of the following is the maximum amount of power the UPS can supply at any moment in time?

    A. Maximum load

    B. Volts ampere

    C. UPC

    D. Capacity

11. What devices have a battery attached that can provide power to the devices in the event of a power outage?

    A. NFC

    B. VA

    C. UPS

    D. Syslog server

12. Which condition leads to shorts?

    A. High temperature

    B. High humidity

    C. Low temperature

    D. Low humidity

13. Damage from static electricity can occur when which of the following is present?

   A. High temperature

   B. High humidity

   C. Low temperature

   D. Low humidity

14. Which of the following causes system reboots?

   A. High temperature

   B. High humidity

   C. Low temperature

   D. Low humidity

15. A humidifying system should be used to maintain the level above what percent?

   A. 30 percent

   B. 40 percent

   C. 50 percent

   D. 60 percent

16. Which error message indicates that the router has a layer 3 packet to forward and is lacking some element of the layer 2 header that it needs to be able to forward the packet toward the next hop?

   A. CRC error

   B. Encapsulación error

   C. Duplex mismatch

   D. Speed mismatch

17. Any Ethernet packet that is greater than 1518 bytes is which of the following?

   A. Giant

   B. Runt

   C. Outlier

   D. Exception

18. Using a cable that is too long can result in which if the following?

   A. Runt

   B. Giant

   C. Collisions

   D. CRC errors

19. Which of the following means that packets have been damaged?

   A. Runt

   B. Giant

    C. Collisions

    D. CRC errors

20. If you have a duplex mismatch, which counter will increment?

    A. Late collisions

    B. Babbles

    C. Watchdog

    D. Unknown protocol drops

Chapter

14

Organizational Documents and Policies

THE FOLLOWING COMPTIA NETWORK+ EXAM OBJECTIVES ARE COVERED IN THIS CHAPTER:

✓ **3.2 Explain the purpose of organizational documents and policies.**

- Plans and procedures
  - Change management
  - Incident response plan
  - Disaster recovery plan
  - Business continuity plan
  - System life cycle
  - Standard operating procedures
- Hardening and security policies
  - Acceptable use policy
  - Password policy
  - Bring your own device (BYOD) policy
  - Remote access policy
  - Onboarding and offboarding policy
  - Security policy
  - Data loss prevention
- Common documentation
  - Physical network diagram
    - Floor plan
    - Rack diagram

- Intermediate distribution frame (IDF)/main distribution frame (MDF) documentation
- Logical network diagram
- Wiring diagram
- Site survey report
- Audit and assessment report
- Baseline configurations
- Common agreements
  - Non-disclosure agreement (NDA)
  - Service-level agreement (SLA)
  - Memorandum of understanding (MOU)

It's up to us, individually and corporately, to nail down exactly what solid guidelines there should be for policies and procedures for network installation and operation. Some organizations are bound by regulations that also affect how they conduct their business, and that kind of thing clearly needs to be involved in their choices.

One of the most important aspects of any policy or procedure is that it's given high-level management support. This is because neither will be very effective if there aren't any consequences for not following the rules!

To find Todd Lammle CompTIA videos and practice questions, please see www.lammle.com.

Plans and Procedures

Let's take some time to examine the difference between policies and procedures.

Policies govern how the network is configured and operated as well as how people are expected to behave on it. They're in place to direct things like how users access resources and which employees and groups get various types of network access and/or privileges. Basically, policies give people guidelines as to what they are expected to do. Procedures are precise descriptions of the appropriate steps to follow in a given situation, such as what to do when an employee is terminated or what to do in the event of a natural disaster. They often dictate precisely how to execute policies as well.

Procedures are the actions to be taken in specific situations:

- Disciplinary action to be taken if a policy is broken
- What to do during an audit
- How issues are reported to management
- What to do when someone has locked themselves out of their account
- How to properly install or remove software on servers
- What to do if files on the servers suddenly appear to be "missing" or altered
- How to respond when a network computer has a virus

- What actions to take if it appears that a hacker has broken into the network
- What actions to take if there is a physical emergency like a fire or flood

So you get the idea, right? For every policy on your network, there should be a credible related procedure that clearly dictates the steps to take in order to fulfill it. And you know that policies and procedures are as unique as the wide array of companies and organizations that create and employ them. But all this doesn't mean you can't borrow good ideas and plans from others and tweak them a bit to meet your requirements.

 An example of a network access policy is a time-of-day restriction on logging into the network.

Change Management

Change should be introduced in a managed fashion. For this to occur, an organization must have a formal change management process in place. The purpose of this process is to ensure that all changes are approved by the proper personnel and are implemented in a safe and logical manner. Let's look at some of the key items that should be included in these procedures.

Document Reason for a Change

Clearly, every change should be made for a reason, and before the change is even discussed, that reason should be documented. During all stages of the approval process (discussed later), this information should be clearly communicated and attached to the change under consideration.

Change Request

A change should start its life as a change request. This request will move through various stages of the approval process and should include certain pieces of information that will guide those tasked with approving or denying it.

Configuration Procedures

The exact steps required to implement the change and the exact devices involved should be clearly detailed. Complete documentation should be produced and submitted with a formal report to the change management board.

Rollback Process

Changes always carry a risk. Before any changes are implemented, plans for reversing changes and recovering from any adverse effects from them should be identified. Those making the changes should be completely briefed in these rollback procedures, and they should exhibit a clear understanding of them prior to implementing the changes.

Potential Impact

While unexpected adverse effects of a change can't always be anticipated, a good-faith effort should be made to identity all possible systems that could be impacted by the change. One of the benefits of performing this exercise is that it can identify systems that may need to be more closely monitored for their reaction to the change as the change is being implemented.

Notification

When all systems and departments that may be impacted by the change are identified, system owners and department heads should be notified of all changes that could potentially affect them. One of the associated benefits of this is that it creates additional monitors for problems during the change process.

Approval Process

Requests for changes should be fully vetted by a cross section of users, IT personnel, management, and security experts. In many cases, it's wise to form a change control board to complete the following tasks:

- Assure that changes made are approved, tested, documented, and implemented correctly.
- Meet periodically to discuss change status accounting reports.
- Maintain responsibility for assuring that changes made do not jeopardize the soundness of the verification system.

Maintenance Window

A maintenance window is an amount of time a system will be down or unavailable during the implementation of changes. Before this window of time is specified, all affected systems should be examined to identify how essential they are in supporting mission-critical operations. It may be that the time required to make the change may exceed the allowable downtime a system can suffer during normal business hours, and the change may need to be implemented during a weekend or in the evening.

Authorized Downtime

Once the time required to make the change has been compared to the maximum allowable downtime a system can suffer and the optimum time for the change is identified, the authorized downtime can be specified. This amounts to a final decision on when the change will be made.

Notification of Change

When the change has been successfully completed and a sufficient amount of time has elapsed for issues to manifest themselves, all stakeholders should be notified that the change is complete. At that time, the stakeholders (those possibly affected by the change) can continue to monitor the situation for any residual problems.

Documentation

The job isn't complete until the paperwork is complete. In this case, the following should be updated to reflect the changed state of the network:

- Network configurations
- Additions to network
- Physical location changes

Incident Response Plan

Often, when an attack or security breach occurs in the network, valuable time and information are lost in the critical first minutes and hours after the incident occurs. In some cases, evidence is inadvertently destroyed, making prosecution of the offending party impossible. In other cases, attacks that could have been interrupted and prevented before damage occurs are allowed to continue.

An incident response plan or policy is designed to prevent this by establishing in advance the procedures that should be followed when an attack occurs. It may categorize incidents in such a way that certain event types (such as an active port scan) may require a response (such as disabling certain services) within 10 minutes while other events (such as an attempt to access a file without proper credentials) may only require a notation and follow-up in the next few days. The point is to establish these rules ahead of time to ensure that events are handled in a way that minimizes damage and preserves evidence.

Disaster Recovery Plan

A disaster is an emergency that goes beyond the normal response of resources. The causes of disasters are categorized into three main areas according to origin:

- Technological disasters (device failures)
- Manmade disasters (arson, terrorism, sabotage)
- Natural disasters (hurricanes, floods, earthquakes)

The severity of financial and reputational damage to an organization is largely determined by the amount of time it takes the organization to recover from the disaster. A properly designed disaster recovery plan (DRP) minimizes the effect of a disaster. The DRP is implemented when the emergency occurs and includes the steps to restore systems so the organization can resume normal operations. The goal of a DRP is to minimize or prevent property damage and prevent loss of life.

Business Continuity Plan

One of the parts of a DRP is a plan to keep the business operational while the organization recovers from the disaster; this is known as a business continuity plan (BCP). Continuity planning deals with identifying the impact of any disaster and ensuring that a viable recovery plan for each function and system is implemented. By prioritizing each process and its supporting technologies, the company can ensure that mission-critical systems are recovered first and systems that are considered luxuries can be recovered as time allows.

One document that should be created to drive this prioritization is the business impact analysis (BIA). In this document, the impact each system has on the ability of the organization to stay operational is determined. The results list the critical and necessary business functions, their resource dependencies, and their level of criticality to the overall organization.

System Life Cycle

The steps in the system life cycle are defined, including acquisition, implementation, maintenance, and decommissioning. The life cycle specifies certain due diligence activities to be performed in each phase.

Asset disposal is usually a subset of the system life cycle and prescribes methods of ensuring that sensitive data is removed from devices before disposal.

Standard Operating Procedures

Once your business is launched, each department leader will need to develop practical methods to implement their assigned tasks using the specific part of the business model's blueprint that relates to their branch. These practical methods, or protocols, must be compiled into a standard operating procedures manual and followed closely. The procedures in your manual will have been included for different reasons and have varying degrees of importance and implementation. If you form a partnership or acquire another company, it will be crucial for its business protocols to either match or be compatible with yours.

Hardening and Security Policies

One of the ongoing goals of operations security is to ensure that all systems have been hardened to the extent that is possible and still provide functionality. The hardening can be accomplished on both a physical and logical basis. From a logical perspective:

- Remove unnecessary applications.
- Disable unnecessary services.
- Block unrequired ports.
- Tightly control the connecting of external storage devices and media if it's allowed at all.

But hardening is only a part of the picture. There needs to be a set of security policies that are enforced through the use of security profiles, sometimes also called baselines. Let's look at some of the more important policies that should be implemented.

Acceptable Use Policy

Acceptable use policies should be as comprehensive as possible and should outline every action that is allowed in addition to those that are not allowed. They should also specify the devices and websites that are allowed and the proper use of company equipment.

 Real World Scenario

Implement the appropriate policies or procedures.

You operate a mid-sized network for Acme Inc. Recently a rogue access point was discovered in the network, which constituted a security breach. While the original fear was that it was installed as an evil twin, further investigation revealed it was placed there by an employee so his department could have wireless access. It has now been removed.

Question: What two actions do you need to take and what security policy document do you need to access?

Answer: Remind/inform the employee of the security policy prohibiting this activity and discipline the employee. This will require access to an acceptable use policy, specifically the one that the employee signed when hired.

To prevent this in the future, you should schedule a training session for employees that reinforces the rules contained in the acceptable use policy and explains the motivation behind each of these rules.

Password Policy

The password policy defines the requirements for all passwords, including length, complexity, and age. Password management considerations include, but may not be limited to, the following:

- **Password life:** How long a password will be valid. For most organizations, passwords are valid for 60 to 90 days.

- **Password history:** How long before a password can be reused. Password policies usually remember a certain number of previously used passwords.

- **Authentication period:** How long a user can remain logged in. If a user remains logged in for the specified period without activity, the user will be automatically logged out.

- **Password complexity:** How the password will be structured. Most organizations require upper- and lowercase letters, numbers, and special characters.

The following are some recommendations:

- Passwords shouldn't contain the username or parts of the user's full name, such as their first name.
- Passwords should use at least three of the four available character types: lowercase letters, uppercase letters, numbers, and symbols.
- **Password length:** How long the password must be. Most organizations require 8 to 12 characters.

Bring Your Own Device (BYOD) Policy

Increasingly, users are doing work on their mobile devices that they once performed on laptops and desktop computers. Moreover, they are demanding that they be able to use their personal devices to work on the company network. This presents a huge security issue for the IT department because they have to secure these devices while simultaneously exercising much less control over them.

The security team must have a way to prevent these personal devices from introducing malware and other security issues to the network. Bring your own device (BYOD) initiatives can be successful if implemented correctly. The key is to implement control over personal devices that leave the safety of your network and return later after potentially being exposed to environments that are out of your control.

Educating users on the risks related to mobile devices and ensuring that they implement appropriate security measures can help protect against threats involved with these devices. Some of the guidelines that should be provided to mobile device users include implementing a device locking PIN, using device encryption, implementing GPS location services, and implementing remote wipe. Also, users should be cautioned on downloading apps without ensuring that they are coming from a reputable source. In recent years, mobile device management (MDM) and mobile application management (MAM) systems have become popular in enterprises. They are implemented to ensure that an organization can control mobile device settings, applications, and other parameters when those devices are attached to the enterprise.

Remote Access Policy

Remote access policies define the requirements for all remote access connections to the enterprise. This may cover VPN, dial-up, and wireless access methods. One method of securing remote access connections is through the use of Network Access Control (NAC), which you will learn about in Chapter 19.

Onboarding and Offboarding Policy

Every new user that is hired undergoes what is called an onboarding process that should be guided by a consistent onboarding policy. This policy prescribes the way in which users are assigned accounts and access to resources as well as the issuance of equipment to them. The following items should be defined and standardized by the onboarding policy:

- Required training
- Account creation
- Resource access

Also, several documents should be executed and signed prior to starting work:

- Acceptable use agreement
- Nondisclosure agreement

There also should be an offboarding policy that defines what actions take place when a user leaves the organization. Special items of concern are as follows:

- Proper recovery of all equipment
- Secure removal of all resource access
- Deletion or disablement of account

Security Policy

So what, exactly, is a security policy? Ideally, it should precisely define how security is to be implemented within an organization and include physical security, document security, and network security. Plus, you have to make sure these forms of security are implemented completely and solidly because if they aren't, your security policy will be a lot like a block of Swiss cheese—some areas are covered, but others are full of holes.

Before a network can be truly secure, the network support staff should post the part of the security policy that applies to employee conduct on bulletin boards. It should, for example, forbid posting any company and/or employee information that's not absolutely necessary—like, believe it or not, sticking Post-its with usernames and passwords on computer screens. Really clean desks, audits, and recordings of email communications and, in some cases, phone calls should also be requirements. And don't forget to also post the consequences of not complying with the security policy.

Security Audit

Let's examine each of these aspects of security policy a little more closely, beginning with security audits. A *security audit* is a thorough examination of your network that includes testing all its components to make sure everything is secure. You can do this internally, but you can also contract an audit with a third party if you want the level of security to be certified. A valid and verified consultant's audit is a good follow-up to an internal audit. One reason for having your network's security certified like this is that government agencies usually require it before they'll grant you contract work, especially if that work is considered confidential, secret, or top secret.

Clean-Desk Policy

That clean-desk policy doesn't just end with "get rid of the crumbs from your last snack." It means requiring that all potentially important documents like books, schematics, confidential letters, notes to self, and so on aren't left out in the open when someone's away from their desk. Instead, they're locked away, securely out of sight. And make sure it's clear that this rule applies to users' PC desktops too. Policies like this apply to offices, laboratories, and workbenches as well as desks, and it's really important for employees who share workspaces and/or workstations.

It's super easy to nick something off someone's desk or screen. Because most security problems involve people on the inside, implementing and enforcing a clean-desk policy is a simple way to guard against security breaches.

It might sound really nitpicky, but for a clean-desk policy to be effective, users have to clean up their desks every time they walk away from them—without exception. The day someone doesn't will be the very day when some prospective tenant is being shown the building's layout and a sensitive document suddenly disappears. You should make sure workstations are locked to desks and do random spot checks once in a while to help enforce the policy. For obvious reasons, before company picnics and parties and before "bring your child to work day" are good times to do this.

 The ICSA is a vendor-neutral organization that certifies the functionality of security products as well as makes recommendations on security in general.

Recording Equipment

Recording equipment—such as tape recorders, cell phones, and small memory devices like USB flash memory keychains—can contain sensitive, confidential information, so a good security policy should prohibit their unauthorized presence and use.

Just walk into almost any large technology company and you'll be immediately confronted with signs. A really common one is a camera with a circle surrounding it and a slash through the center of the circle. Read the text below the sign and you'll be informed that you can't bring any recording devices onto the premises.

Here's a good example. The National Security Agency (NSA) has updated its policy to include prohibiting Furby dolls on government premises because they have reasonably sophisticated computers inside them, complete with a digital recording device. The doll repeats what it hears at a certain interval of time, which is either cute or creepy but pretty much harmless—maybe even protective—in a children's daycare center. Not so much at the NSA, though—no recording conversations there. Maybe, at least in some locations, it's not such a good idea for your company either.

Other Common Security Policies

So you get the idea—security policies can cover literally hundreds of items. Here are some common ones:

Notification   Security policies aren't much good if no one knows about them, right? So make sure you give users a copy of the security policy when you give them their usernames and passwords. It's also a good idea to have computers display a summarized version of the policy when any user attempts to connect. Here's an example: "Unauthorized access is prohibited and will be prosecuted to the fullest extent of the law." Remember—your goal is to close loopholes. One hacker actually argued that because a computer didn't tell him otherwise, anyone was free to connect to it and use the system!

Equipment Access   Disable all unused network ports so that any nonemployees who happen to be in the building can't connect a laptop to an unused port and gain access to the network. And don't forget to place all network equipment under lock and key.

Wiring   Your network's wires should never run along the floor where they can be easily accessed (or tripped over, getting you sued). Routers, switches, and concentrators should live in locked closets or rooms, with access to those rooms controlled by anything ranging from a good lock to a biometric access system, depending on the level of security your specific network and data require.

Door Locks/Swipe Mechanisms   Be sure that only authorized people know the combination to the cipher lock on your data-center doors or that only the appropriate people have badges that allow access to the data center. Change lock combinations often, and never ever leave server room doors open or unlocked.

Badges   Require everyone to wear an ID badge, including contractors and visitors, and assign appropriate access levels to everyone.

Tracking   Require badge access to all entrances to buildings and internal computer rooms. Track and record all entry to and exits from these rooms.

Passwords   Reset passwords at least every month. Train everyone on how to create strong passwords. Set BIOS/UEFI passwords on every client and server computer to prevent BIOS/UEFI changes.

Monitor Viewing   Place computer monitors strategically so that visitors or people looking through windows can't see them, and make sure unauthorized users/persons can't see security-guard stations and server monitors. Use monitor privacy screens if necessary.

Accounts   Each user should have their own, unique user account, and employees should never share user accounts. Even temporary employees should have their own account. Otherwise, you won't be able to isolate a security breach.

Testing   Review and audit your network security at least once a year.

Background Checks   Do background checks on all network support staff. This may include calling their previous employers, verifying their college degrees, requiring a drug test, and checking for a criminal background.

Firewalls   Use a firewall to protect all Internet connections, and use the appropriate proxies and dynamic-packet-filtering equipment to control access to the network. Your firewall should provide as much security as your company requires and your budget allows.

Intrusion Detection   Use intrusion detection and logging software to discover security breaches, and be sure you're logging the events you want to monitor.

Cameras   Cameras should cover all entrances to the building and the entire parking lot. Be sure that cameras are in weatherproof and tamper-proof housings, and review the output at a security-monitoring office. Record everything on extended-length tape recorders.

Mail Servers   Provide each person with their own email mailbox, and attach an individual network account to each mailbox. If several people need to access a mailbox, don't give all of them the password to a single network account. Instead, assign individual privileges to each person's network account so you can track activity down to a single person, even with a generic address like `info@mycompany.com`.

DMZ   Use a demilitarized zone (DMZ) for all publicly viewable servers, including web servers, FTP servers, and email relay servers. Figure 14.1 shows a common DMZ setup.

FIGURE 14.1   A common DMZ configuration

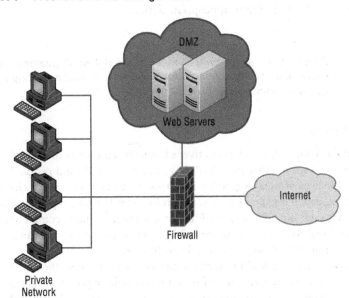

It is not advisable to put a DMZ outside the firewall because any servers outside your firewall defeat the whole purpose of having one. However, it is possible that you may see a DMZ outside the firewall in some networks. You will learn more about DMZs in Chapter 16.

Mail Relay   Mail servers relay to other email servers by design. When the email server relays from any server that requests it, it is called *open relay*. Hackers use this feature to forward spam. Modern email systems allow you to control which servers your email server will relay from which helps to prevent this.

Patches   Make sure the latest security updates are installed after being properly tested on a nonproduction computer.

Backups   Store backup tape cartridges securely, not on a shelf or table within reach of someone working at the server. Lock tapes in a waterproof, fireproof safe, and keep at least some of your backups off site.

Modems   Do not ever allow desktop modems because they can be used to get to the Internet without your knowledge. Restrict modem access to approved server-based modem pools.

Guards   If you need security guards, they shouldn't patrol the same station all the time. As people become familiar with an environment and situation, they tend to become less observant about that environment, so rotating guards to keep their focus at the highest possible level makes a lot of sense. Clearly, guards are people who need breaks to ensure alertness, but make sure that all patrol areas are covered during shift changes, rotations, and breaks. Guards should also receive periodic training and testing to make sure they can recognize a threat and take appropriate action.

WARNING   Believe it or not, covering all these bases still won't guarantee that your network or facility is secure. All of this is really just a starting point that's meant to point you in the right direction.

Breaking Policy

You know that for your policy to be effective it has to be enforced consistently and completely. Nobody is so special that they don't have to adhere to it. And people have to understand the consequences of breaking policy too. Your network users need to have a clearly written document, called a *security policy*, that fully identifies and explains what's expected of them and what they can and can't do. Plus, people must be made completely aware of the consequences of breaking the rules, and penalties have to match the severity of the offense and be carried out quickly, if not immediately, to be effective.

Let's take a minute and talk about those penalties. As far back as the mid-1980s, employees were immediately terminated for major technology policy infractions. For example, one guy from a large computer company immediately got his pink slip when pornography was found on his computer's hard drive. The situation was handled decisively—his manager informed him that he was being immediately terminated and that he had one hour to vacate the premises. A security guard stood watch while he cleaned out his desk to make sure the employee only touched personal items—no computer equipment, including storage media—and when he had finished gathering his personal things, the guard then escorted him from the building.

Downloading and installing software from the Internet to your PC at work is not as major (depending on where you work), but from the things we've been over so far, you know that doing that can compromise security. Beta products, new software, and patches need to be tested by the IT department before anyone can use them, period! Here's an example: After an employee installed the untested beta release of a web browser and rebooted their PC, the production Windows server at a national telephone company crashed. The resulting action was to revoke that employee's Internet FTP privileges for three months.

Data Loss Prevention

The data loss prevention policy defines all procedures for preventing the egress of sensitive data from the network and may include references to the use of data loss prevention (DLP) software.

Data leakage occurs when sensitive data is disclosed to unauthorized personnel either intentionally or inadvertently. Data loss prevention (DLP) software attempts to prevent data leakage. It does this by maintaining awareness of actions that can and cannot be taken with respect to a document. For example, it might allow printing of a document but only at the company office. It might also disallow sending the document through email. DLP software uses ingress and egress filters to identify sensitive data that is leaving the organization and can prevent such leakage.

Another scenario might be the release of product plans that should be available only to the Sales group. A security professional could set a policy like the following for that document:

- It cannot be emailed to anyone other than Sales group members.
- It cannot be printed.
- It cannot be copied.

There are two locations where a DLP can be implemented:

- Network DLP: Installed at network egress points near the perimeter, network DLP analyzes network traffic.
- Endpoint DLP: Endpoint DLP runs on end-user workstations or servers in the organization.

Common Documentation

Building a great network requires some really solid planning before you buy even one device for it. And planning includes thoroughly analyzing your design for potential flaws and optimizing configurations everywhere you can to maximize the network's future throughput and performance. If you fail in this phase, trust me—you'll pay dearly later in bottom-line costs and countless hours consumed troubleshooting and putting out the fires of faulty design.

Start planning by creating an outline that precisely delimits all goals and business requirements for the network, and refer back to it often to ensure that you don't deliver a network that falls short of your client's present needs or fails to offer the scalability to grow with those needs. Drawing out your design and jotting down all the relevant information really helps in spotting weaknesses and faults. If you have a team, make sure everyone on it gets to examine the design and evaluate it, and keep that network plan up throughout the installation phase. Hang on to it after implementation has been completed because having it is like having the keys to the kingdom—it will enable you to efficiently troubleshoot any issues that could arise after everything is in place and up and running.

Physical Network Diagram

A physical network diagram contains all the physical devices and connectivity paths on your network and should accurately picture how your network physically fits together in glorious detail. Again, I know it seems like overkill, but ideally, your network diagram should list and map everything you would need to completely rebuild your network from scratch if you had to. This is actually what this type of diagram is designed for. But there's still another physical network diagram variety that includes the firmware revision on all the switches and access points in your network. Remember, besides having your physical network accurately detailed, you must also clearly understand the connections, types of hardware, and their firmware revisions. I'm going to say it again—you will be so happy you have this documentation when troubleshooting! It will prevent much suffering and enable you to fix whatever the problem is so much faster!

 Real World Scenario

Avoiding Confusion

Naming your network devices is no big deal, but for some reason, coming up with systems for naming devices and numbering connections can really stress people out.

Let me ease the pain. Let's say your network has two racks of switches, creatively named Block A and Block B. (Sounds like a prison, I know, but it's just to keep things simple for this example. In the real world, you can come up with whatever naming system works for you.)

Anyway, I'm going to use the letters *FETH* for Fast Ethernet; and because each rack has six switches, I'm going to number them (surprise!) 1 through 6. Because we read from left to right, it's intuitive to number the ports on each switch that way too.

Having a solid naming system makes thing so much more efficient—even if it's a bit of a hassle to create. For instance, if you were the system administrator in this example and suddenly all computers connected to FETHB-3 couldn't access any network resources, you would have a pretty good idea of where to look first, right?

If you can't diagram everything, at least make sure all network devices are listed. As I said, physical network diagrams can run from simple, hand-drawn models to insanely complex monsters created by software packages like SmartDraw, Visio, and AutoCAD. Figure 14.2 shows a simple diagram that most of us could draw by hand.

FIGURE 14.2   Simple network physical diagram

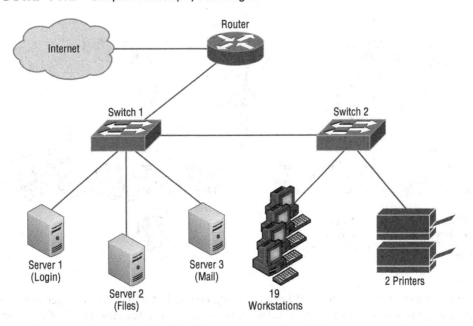

For the artistically impaired, or if you just want a flashier version, Figure 14.3 exhibits a more complex physical diagram. This is an actual sample of what SmartDraw can do for you, and you can get it at www.smartdraw.com. In addition, Microsoft Visio provides many or possibly more of these same functions.

FIGURE 14.3 Network diagram with firewalls from SmartDraw

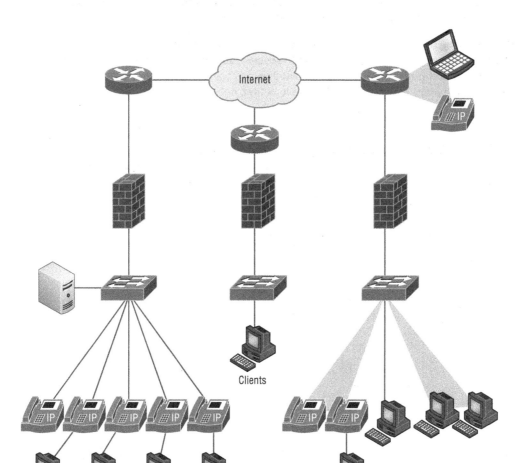

Don't throw anything at me, but I need to bring up one last thing: Never forget to mirror any changes you make to your actual network in the network's diagram. Think of it like an updated snapshot. If you give the authorities your college buddy's baby picture after he goes missing, will that really help people recognize him? Not without the help of some high-tech, age-progression software, that's for sure—and they don't make that for networks, so it's better to just keep things up-to-date.

Floor Plan

It's always helpful to have a floor diagram. One of the uses of this is when performing a WLAN site survey. When it's input to the survey software, you can indicate the types of materials found in all walls, doors, and so on, and the survey software can determine the best location for APs.

It can serve as a plotting bed if you have a wireless IPS that has at least three sensors. In that case, when the system sees a rogue AP or evil twin, the software can triangulate the location of the rogue AP and plot it on the floor plan, making it simple to physically locate it and remove it.

Rack Diagram

My next example, also courtesy of SmartDraw, includes diagrams of hardware racks, as revealed in Figure 14.4.

FIGURE 14.4   Hardware-rack diagram from SmartDraw

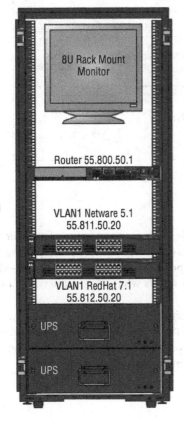
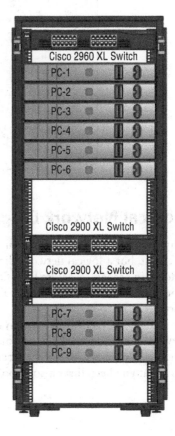

Intermediate Distribution Frame (IDF)/Main Distribution Frame (MDF) Documentation

The main distribution frame (MDF) connects equipment (inside plant) to cables and sub-scriber carrier equipment (outside plant). It also terminates cables that run to intermediate distribution frames distributed throughout the facility.

An intermediate distribution frame (IDF) serves as a distribution point for cables from the MDF to individual cables connected to equipment in areas remote from these frames. The relationship between the IDFs and the MDF is shown in Figure 14.5. This should also be clearly documented and continually updated.

FIGURE 14.5   MDF and IDFs

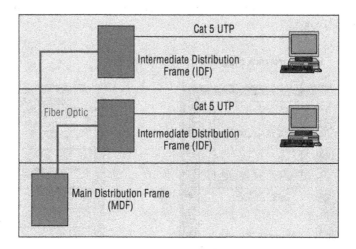

Logical Network Diagram

Physical diagrams depict how data physically flows from one area of your network to the next, but a logical network diagram includes things like protocols, configurations, addressing schemes, access lists, firewalls, types of applications, and so on—all things that apply logically to your network. Figure 14.6 shows what a logical network diagram could look like.

And just as you mirror any physical changes you make to the network (like adding devices or even just a cable) on your physical diagram, you map logical changes (like creating a new subnet, VLAN, or security zone) on your logical network diagram. It is important that you keep this oh-so-important document up-to-date.

FIGURE 14.6 Logical network diagram

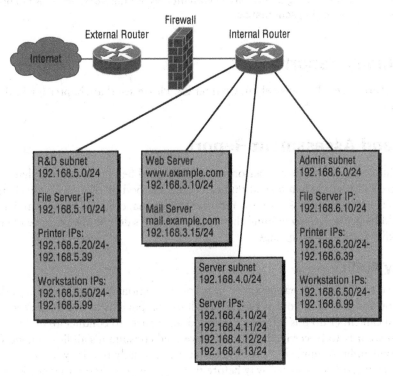

Wiring Diagram

Wireless is definitely the wave of the future, but for now even the most extensive wireless networks have a wired backbone they rely on to connect them to the rest of humanity.

That skeleton is made up of cabled physical media like coax, fiber, and twisted pair. Surprisingly, it is the latter—specifically, unshielded twisted-pair (UTP)—that screams to be pictured in a diagram.

When you're troubleshooting a network, having a diagram is golden. Let's say you discover a connectivity problem between two hosts. Because you've got the map, you know the cable running between them is brand new and custom made. This should tell you to go directly to that new cable because it's likely it was poorly made and is therefore causing the snag.

Another reason it's so important to diagram all things wiring is that all wires have to plug into something somewhere, and it's really good to know what and where that is. Whether it's into a hub, a switch, a router, a workstation, or the wall, you positively need to know the who, what, where, when, and how of the way the wiring is attached.

After adding a new cable segment on your network, you need to update the wiring schematics.

Site Survey Report

Site surveys are covered extensively in Chapter 24. Please see that chapter for in-depth information.

Audit and Assessment Report

When audits and assessments are performed, there should be reports created that organize the collected information in a format that can be understood by those who are charged with making security decisions based on the reports. The language should be clear and all terms used should be defined. Keep in mind that decision makers do not always have the same security skills as those they manage.

Security Audit

As discussed earlier in this chapter's "Security Policy" section, a security audit is a thorough examination and testing of your network and all its components to make sure everything is secure. You can either do this internally or hire a third party to conduct an audit if you want the level of security to be certified. A valid and verified consultant's audit is a good follow-up to an internal audit. A number of government agencies usually require you to have your network's security certified in such a way before they'll grant you contract work, particularly if that work is considered confidential, secret, or top secret.

Results of security audits or assessments should be kept and used to perform gap analysis. The results of the latest audit are compared with those of the previous audit to determine if issues have been corrected or if there are still "gaps" to close.

 Real World Scenario

Walk Your Beat

A great way to begin a basic security audit to get a feel for any potential threats to your network is to simply take a walk through the company's halls and offices. I've done this a lot, and it always pays off because invariably I happen upon some new and different way that people are trying to "beat the system" regarding security. This doesn't necessarily indicate that a given user is trying to cause damage on purpose; it's just that following the rules can be a little inconvenient—especially when it comes to adhering to strict password policies. Your average user just doesn't get how important their role is in maintaining the security of the network (maybe even their job security as well) by sticking to the network's security policy, so you have to make sure they do.

Think about it. If you can easily discover user passwords just by taking a little tour of the premises, so can a bad guy, and once someone has a username and a password, it's pretty easy to hack into resources. I wasn't kidding about people slapping sticky notes with their usernames and/or passwords right on their monitors—this happens a lot more than you would think. Some users, thinking they're actually being really careful, glue them to the back of their keyboards instead, but you don't have to be James Bond to think about looking there either, right? People wouldn't think of leaving their cars unlocked with the windows down and the keys in the ignition, but that's exactly what they're doing by leaving sensitive info anywhere on or near their workstations.

Even though it might not make you Mr. or Ms. Popularity when you search workspaces or even inside desks for notes with interesting or odd words written on them, do it anyway. People will try to hide these goodies anywhere. Or sometimes, not so much. I kid you not—I had a user who actually wrote his password on the border of his monitor with a Sharpie, and when his password expired, he just crossed it off and wrote the new one underneath it. Sheer genius! But my personal favorite was when I glanced at this one guy's keyboard and noticed that some of the letter keys had numbers written on them. All you had to do was follow the numbers that (surprise!) led straight to his password. Oh sure—he'd followed policy to the, ahem, letter by choosing random letters and numbers, but a lot of good that did—he had to draw himself a little map in plain sight on his keyboard to remember the password.

So, like it or not, you have to walk your beat to find out if users are managing their accounts properly. If you find someone doing things the right way, praise them for it openly. If not, it's time for more training—or maybe worse, termination.

Baseline Configurations

In networking, baseline can refer to the standard level of performance of a certain device or to the normal operating capacity for your whole network. For instance, a specific server's baseline describes norms for factors like how busy its processors are, how much of the memory it uses, and how much data usually goes through the NIC at a given time. A network baseline delimits when a bandwidth is available and the amount of that bandwidth. For networks and networked devices, baselines include information about four key components:

- Processor
- Memory
- Hard-disk (or other storage) subsystem
- Wired/wireless utilization

After everything is up and running, it's a good idea to establish performance baselines on all vital devices and your network in general. To do this, measure things like network usage at three different strategic times to get an accurate assessment. For instance, peak usage usually happens around 8:00 a.m. Monday through Friday, or whenever most people log in to the network in the morning. After hours or on weekends is often when usage is the lowest. Knowing these values can help you troubleshoot bottlenecks or determine why certain system resources are more limited than they should be. Knowing what your baseline is can even tell you if someone's complaints about the network running like a slug are really valid—nice!

It's good to know that you can use network-monitoring software to establish baselines. Even some server operating systems come with software to help with network monitoring, which can help find baselines, perform log management, and even do network graphing as well so you can compare the logs and graphs at a later period of time on your network.

In my experience, it's wise to re-baseline network performance at least once a year. And always pinpoint new performance baselines after any major upgrade to your network's infrastructure.

Common Agreements

In the course of supporting mergers and acquisitions, and in providing support to departments within the organization, it's always important to keep the details of agreements in writing to reduce the risk of misunderstandings. In the following sections, I'll discuss standard documents that are used in these situations. You should be familiar with the purpose of these documents.

Nondisclosure Agreement (NDA)

A nondisclosure agreement (NDA) is an agreement between two parties that defines what information is considered confidential and cannot be shared outside the two parties. An organization may implement NDAs with personnel regarding the intellectual property of the organization. NDAs can also be used when two organizations work together to develop a new product. Because certain information must be shared to make the partnership successful, NDAs are signed to ensure that each partner's data is protected.

While an NDA cannot ensure that confidential data is not shared, it usually provides details on the repercussions for the offending party, including but not limited to fines, jail time, and forfeiture of rights. For example, an organization should decide to implement an NDA when it wants to legally ensure that no sensitive information is compromised through a project with a third party or in a cloud-computing environment.

Service-Level Agreement (SLA)

This is an agreement that defines the allowable time in which a party must respond to issues on behalf of the other party. Most service contracts are accompanied by an SLA, which often include security priorities, responsibilities, guarantees, and warranties.

Memorandum of Understanding (MOU)

This is an agreement between two or more organizations that details a common line of action. It is often used in cases where parties do not have a legal commitment or in situations where the parties cannot create a legally enforceable agreement. In some cases, it is referred to as a letter of intent.

Summary

In this chapter you learned that plans and procedures should be developed to manage operational issues such as change management, incident response, disaster recovery, business continuity, and the system life cycle. You also learned that standard operating procedures should be developed to guide each of these processes.

We also discussed the hardening of systems and the use of security policies that help mitigate security issues such as acceptable use, password, bring your own device (BYOD), remote access. and onboarding and offboarding policies.

Finally, you learned about the importance of critical network documentation such as physical network diagrams, floor plans, rack diagrams, intermediate distribution frame (IDF)/main distribution frame (MDF) documentation, logical network diagrams, and wiring diagrams. We also covered common agreements such as nondisclosure agreements (NDA), service-level agreements (SLA), and memorandums of understanding (MOUs).

Exam Essentials

Understand the importance of plans and procedures.   These include change management, incident response, disaster recovery, business continuity, and the system life cycle.

Describe hardening and security policies.   Among these are acceptable use, password, bring your own device (BYOD), remote access, and onboarding and offboarding policies.

Utilize common documentation.   These include physical network diagrams, floor plans, rack diagrams, intermediate distribution frame (IDF)/main distribution frame (MDF) documentation, logical network diagrams, wiring diagrams, and site survey reports.

Identify common business agreements.   These agreements include nondisclosure agreements (NDA), service-level agreements (SLA), and memorandums of understanding (MOUs).

Written Lab

Complete the table by filling in the appropriate plan of which the given step is a part. Choose from the following list:

- Change management plan
- Incident response plan
- Disaster recovery plan
- Business continuity plan
- System life cycle plan

You can find the answers in Appendix A.

Step	Plan
Utilization of three network interfaces on the DNS server	
Phased introductions of security patches	
Degaussing of all discarded hard drives	
Security issue escalation list	
System recovery priority chart	

Review Questions

You can find the answers to the review questions in Appendix B.

1. The way to properly install or remove software on the servers is an example of which of the following?

   A. Plan

   B. Policy

   C. Procedure

   D. Code

2. Which of the following is a plan for reversing changes and recovering from any adverse effects from the changes?

   A. Backup

   B. Secondary

   C. Rollback

   D. Failover

3. Which of the following is the amount of time a system will be down or unavailable during the implementation of changes?

   A. Downtime

   B. Maintenance window

   C. MTBF

   D. Work factor

4. Which of the following is *not* a device hardening technique?

   A. Remove unnecessary applications.

   B. Deploy an access control vestibule.

   C. Block unrequired ports.

   D. Disable unnecessary services.

5. Which policy automatically logs a user out after a specified period without activity?

   A. Password complexity

   B. Password history

   C. Password length

   D. Authentication period

6. BYOD policies apply to what type of device?

   A. Mobile

   B. Desktop

   C. Server

   D. Firewall

7. Which tool can prevent the emailing of a document to anyone other than Sales group members?

    A. SSS

    B. STP

    C. DLP

    D. VBA

8. Which of the following connects equipment (inside plant) to cables and subscriber carrier equipment (outside plant)?

    A. IDF

    B. MDF

    C. Plant rack

    D. Access control vestibule

9. Which of the following is not part of the Information Gathering step of a site survey?

    A. Determine the scope of the network with respect to applications in use.

    B. Verify optimal distances between prospective AP locations.

    C. Identify areas that must be covered.

    D. Assess types of wireless devices that will need to be supported.

10. Device baselines include information about all but which of the following components?

    A. CPU

    B. Memory

    C. Hard disk

    D. Display

Chapter

15

High Availability and Disaster Recovery

THE FOLLOWING COMPTIA NETWORK+ EXAM OBJECTIVES ARE COVERED IN THIS CHAPTER:

✓ **3.3 Explain high availability and disaster recovery concepts and summarize which is the best solution.**

- Load balancing
- Multipathing
- Network interface card (NIC) teaming
- Redundant hardware/clusters
  - Switches
  - Routers
  - Firewalls
- Facilities and infrastructure support
  - Uninterruptible power supply (UPS)
  - Power distribution units (PDUs)
  - Generator
  - HVAC
  - Fire suppression
- Redundancy and high availability (HA) concepts
  - Cold site
  - Warm site
  - Hot site
  - Cloud site
  - Active-active vs. active-passive

- Multiple Internet service providers (ISPs)/ diverse paths
- Virtual Router Redundancy Protocol (VRRP)/ First Hop Redundancy Protocol (FHRP)
- Mean time to repair (MTTR)
- Mean time between failure (MTBF)
- Recovery time objective (RTO)
- Recovery point objective (RPO)
- Network device backup/restore
  - State
  - Configuration

High availability is a system-design protocol that guarantees a certain amount of operational uptime during a given period. The design attempts to minimize unplanned downtime—the time users are unable to access resources. In almost all cases, high availability is provided through the implementation of duplicate equipment (multiple servers, multiple NICs, etc.). Organizations that serve critical functions obviously need this; after all, you really don't want to rush to a hospital ER only to find that they can't treat you because their network is down!

Fault tolerance means that even if one component fails, you won't lose access to the resource it provides. To implement fault tolerance, you need to employ multiple devices or connections that all provide a way to access the same resource(s).

A familiar form of fault tolerance is configuring an additional hard drive to be a mirror image of the original so that if either one fails, there's still a copy of the data available to you. In networking, fault tolerance means that you have multiple paths from one point to another. What's really cool is that fault-tolerant connections can be configured to be available either on a standby basis only or all the time if you intend to use them as part of a load-balancing system.

In this chapter you will learn about redundancy concepts, fault tolerance, and the process of disaster recovery.

Planned Downtime

There's a difference between planned downtime and unplanned downtime. Planned downtime is good—it's occasionally scheduled for system maintenance and routine upgrades. Unplanned downtime is bad—it's a lack of access due to system failure, which is exactly the issue high availability resolves.

To find Todd Lammle CompTIA videos and practice questions, please see www.lammle.com.

Load Balancing

Load balancing refers to a technique used to spread work out to multiple computers, network links, or other devices.

Using load balancing, you can provide an active/passive server cluster in which only one server is active and handling requests. For example, your favorite Internet site might actually consist of 20 servers that all appear to be the same exact site because that site's owner wants to ensure that its users always experience quick access. You can accomplish this on a network by installing multiple, redundant links to ensure that network traffic is spread across several paths and to maximize the bandwidth on each link.

Think of this as similar to having two or more different freeways that will both get you to your destination equally well—if one is really busy, just take the other one.

Multipathing

Multipathing is the process of configuring multiple network connections between a system and its storage device. The idea behind multipathing is to provide a backup path in case the preferred connection goes down. For example, a SCSI hard disk drive may connect to two SCSI controllers on the same computer, or a disk may connect to two Fibre Channel ports.

The ease with which multipathing can be set up in a virtual environment is one of the advantages a virtual environment provides. A multipath configuration is shown in Figure 15.1.

FIGURE 15.1   Multipathing

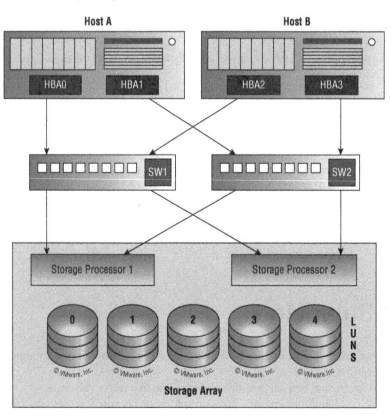

Both Host A and Host B have multiple host bus adapters (NICs) and multiple connections through multiple switches and are mapped to multiple storage processors as well. This is a highly fault-tolerant arrangement that can survive an HBA failure, a path failure, a switch failure, and a storage processor failure.

Network Interface Card (NIC) Teaming

NIC teaming allows multiple network interfaces to be placed into a team for the purposes of bandwidth aggregation and/or traffic failover to prevent connectivity loss in the event of a network component failure. The cards can be set to active/active state, where both cards are load balancing, or active/passive, where one card is on standby in case the primary card fails. Most of the time, the NIC team will use a multicast address to send and receive data, but it can also use a broadcast address so all cards receive the data at the same time.

This can be done with a single switch or multiple switches. Figure 15.2 shows what is called static teaming, where a single switch is in use. This would provide failover only for the connection but would not protect against a switch failure.

FIGURE 15.2   Static teaming

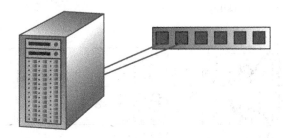

A more redundant arrangement is shown in Figure 15.3, where a switch-independent setup is in use. This provides fault tolerance for both switches and connections.

FIGURE 15.3   Switch independent setup

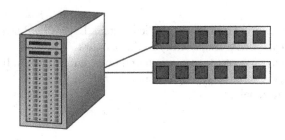

Redundant Hardware/Clusters

By now it must be clear that redundancy is a good thing. While this concept can be applied to network connections, it can also be applied to hardware components and even complete servers. In the following sections, you'll learn how this concept is applied to severs and infrastructure devices.

Switches

As you saw in the last section, multiple switches can be deployed to provide for failover if a switch fails. When this is done, it sometimes creates what is called a switching loop. Luckily, as you learned in Chapter 11, there is a protocol called Spanning Tree Protocol that can prevent these loops from forming. There are two forms of switch redundancy, switch stacking and switch clusters.

Switch Stacking

Switch stacking is the process of connecting multiple switches together (usually in a stack) and managing them as a single switch. Figure 15.4 shows a typical configuration.

FIGURE 15.4 Switch stacking

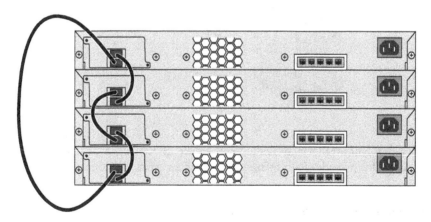

The stack members work together as a unified system. Layer 2 and layer 3 protocols present the entire switch stack as a single entity to the network.

A switch stack always has one active switch and one standby switch. If the active switch becomes unavailable, the standby switch assumes the role of the active switch and continues to keep the stack operational.

The active switch controls the operation of the switch stack and is the single point of stack-wide management.

Hard to believe that Cisco is using switch stacking to start its "Evolution of Intelligent Networks" objectives since switch stacking has been around since the word *cloud* meant 4/20 in my home town of Boulder, but I digress.

A typical access closet contains one or more access switches placed next to each other in the same rack and uses high-speed redundant links with copper, or more typically fiber, to the distribution layer switches.

Here are three big drawbacks to a typical switch topology:

- Overhead of management.

- STP will block half of the uplinks.

- No direct communication between switches.

Cisco StackWise technology connects switches that are mounted in the same rack together so they basically become one larger switch. By doing this, you clearly get more access ports for each closet while avoiding the cost of upgrading to a bigger switch. So you're adding ports as you grow your company instead of front loading the investment into a pricier, larger switch all at once. And since these stacks are managed as a single unit, it reduces the management in your network.

All switches in a stack share configuration and routing information so you can easily add or remove switches at any time without disrupting your network or affecting its performance. Figure 15.4 shows a typical switch stack.

To create a StackWise unit, you combine switches into a single, logical unit using special stack interconnect cables as shown in Figure 15.4. This creates a bidirectional closed-loop path in the stack.

Here are some other features of StackWise:

- Any changes to the network topology or routing information are updated continuously through the stack interconnect.

- A master switch manages the stack as a single unit. The master switch is elected from one of the stack member switches.

- You can join up to nine separate switches in a stack.

- Each stack of switches has only a single IP address and the stack is managed as a single object. You'll use this single IP address for all the management of the stack, including fault detection, VLAN database updates, security, and QoS controls. Each stack has only one configuration file, which is distributed to each switch in the StackWise.

- Using Cisco StackWise will produce some management overhead, but at the same time, multiple switches in a stack can create an EtherChannel connection, eliminating the need for STP.

Here's a list of the benefits to using StackWise technology:

- StackWise provides a method to join multiple physical switches into a single logical switching unit.

- Switches are united by special interconnect cables.
- The master switch is elected.
- The stack is managed as a single object and has a single management IP address.
- It reduces management overhead.
- STP is no longer needed if you use EtherChannel.
- Up to 9 switches can be in a StackWise unit.

One more very cool thing—when you add a new switch to the stack, the master switch automatically configures the unit with the currently running IOS image as well as the configuration of the stack. So you don't have to do anything to bring up the switch before its ready to operate. Nice!

Switch Clustering

A switch cluster is another option. This is a set of connected and cluster-capable switches that are managed as a single entity without interconnecting stack cables. This is possible by using Cluster Management Protocol (CMP). The switches in the cluster use the switch clustering technology so that you can configure and troubleshoot a group of different switch platforms through a single IP address. In those switches, one switch plays the role of cluster command switch, and the other switches are cluster member switches that are managed by the command switch. Figure 15.5 shows a switch cluster. Notice that the cluster is managed by using the CMP address of the cluster commander.

FIGURE 15.5   Switch cluster

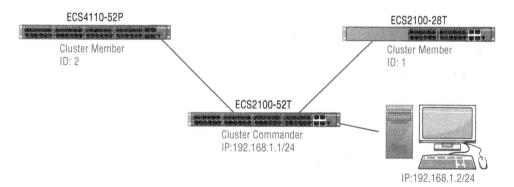

Routers

Routers can also be set up in a redundant fashion. When we provide router redundancy, we call it providing first-hop redundancy since the router will be the first hop from any system to get to a destination. To accomplish first-hop redundancy requires an FHRP protocol.

First-hop redundancy protocols (FHRPs) work by giving you a way to configure more than one physical router to appear as if they were only a single logical one. This makes client configuration and communication easier because you can simply configure a single default gateway and the host machine can use its standard protocols to communicate. First hop is a reference to the default router being the first router, or first router hop, through which a packet must pass.

So how does a redundancy protocol accomplish this? The protocols I'm going to describe to you do this basically by presenting a virtual router to all of the clients. The virtual router has its own IP and MAC addresses. The virtual IP address is the address that's configured on each of the host machines as the default gateway. The virtual MAC address is the address that will be returned when an ARP request is sent by a host. The hosts don't know or care which physical router is actually forwarding the traffic, as you can see in Figure 15.6.

FIGURE 15.6   FHRPs use a virtual router with a virtual IP address and virtual MAC address.

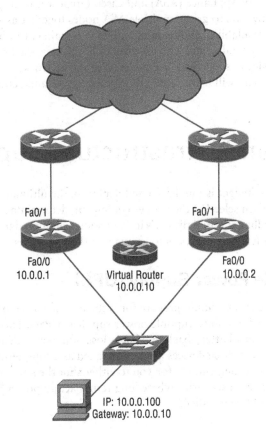

It's the responsibility of the redundancy protocol to decide which physical router will actively forward traffic and which one will be placed in standby in case the active router fails. Even if the active router fails, the transition to the standby router will be transparent to the hosts because the virtual router, identified by the virtual IP and MAC addresses, is now used by the standby router. The hosts never change default gateway information, so traffic keeps flowing.

Fault-tolerant solutions provide continued operation in the event of a device failure, and load-balancing solutions distribute the workload over multiple devices. Later in this chapter you will learn about the two most common FHRPs.

Firewalls

Firewalls can also be clustered, and some can also use FHRPs. A firewall cluster is a group of firewall nodes that work as a single logical entity to share the load of traffic processing and provide redundancy. Clustering guarantees the availability of network services to the users.

Cisco Adaptive Security Appliance (ASA) and Cisco Firepower next-generation firewall (NGFW) clustering allow you to group multiple ASA nodes together as a single logical device to provide high availability and scalability. The two main clustering options discussed in this chapter are active/standby and active/active. In both cases, the firewall cluster looks like a single logical device (a single MAC/IP address) to the network.

Later in this chapter you will learn more about active/active and active/standby operations.

Facilities and Infrastructure Support

When infrastructure equipment is purchased and deployed, the ultimate success of the deployment can depend on selecting the proper equipment, determining its proper location in the facility, and installing it correctly. Let's look at some common data center and server room equipment and a few best practices for managing these facilities.

Uninterruptible Power Supply (UPS)

One risk that all organizations should prepare for is the loss of power. All infrastructure systems should be connected to uninterruptible power supplies (UPSs). These devices can immediately supply power from a battery backup when a loss of power is detected. You should keep in mind, however, that these devices are not designed as a long-term solution. They are designed to provide power long enough for you to either shut the system down gracefully or turn on a power generator. In scenarios where long-term backup power is called for, a gas-powered generator should be installed.

Power Distribution Units (PDUs)

Power distribution units (PDUs) simply provide a means of distributing power from the input to a plurality of outlets. Intelligent PDUs normally have an intelligence module that allows for remote management of power metering information, power outlet on/off control, and/or alarms. Some advanced PDUs allow users to manage external sensors such as temperature, humidity, and airflow.

While these can be as simple as a power strip, in data centers, larger PDUs are needed to power multiple server cabinets. Each server cabinet or row of cabinets may require multiple high current circuits, possibly from different phases of incoming power or different UPSs. Stand-alone cabinet PDUs are self-contained units that include main circuit breakers, individual circuit breakers, and power monitoring panels. Figure 15.7 shows a standard rack-mounted PDU.

FIGURE 15.7   Rack-mounted PDU

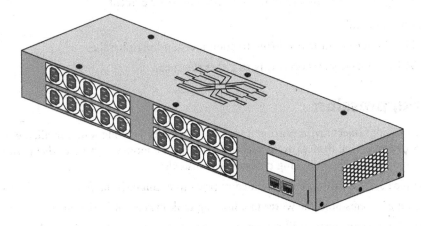

Generator

As you learned earlier in this chapter, a UPS is not designed for long-term power supply. The battery will run out. This should be supplemented with a backup generator if more than an hour or so of backup is required. The amount of backup time supplied by a generator is limited only by the amount of fuel you keep on hand.

HVAC

The heating and air-conditioning systems must support the massive amounts of computing equipment deployed by most enterprises. Computing equipment and infrastructure devices like routers and switches do not like the following conditions:

- Heat. Excessive heat causes reboots and crashes.

- High humidity. It causes corrosion problems with connections.

- Low humidity. Dry conditions encourage static electricity, which can damage equipment.

The American Society of Heating, Refrigerating and Air-Conditioning Engineers (ASHRAE) publishes standards for indoor air quality and humidity. Their latest recommendations are as follows:

- A class A1 data center

- Can range in temperature from 59°F to 89.6°F

- Can range in relative humidity from 20 percent to 80 percent

Also keep in mind:

- At 175°F, damage starts occurring to computers and peripherals.

- At 350°F, damage starts occurring to paper products.

Fire Suppression

While fire extinguishers are important and should be placed throughout a facility, when large numbers of computing devices are present, it is worth the money to protect them with a fire-suppression system. The following types of systems exist:

- Wet pipe systems use water contained in pipes to extinguish the fire.

- Dry pipe systems hold the water in a holding tank instead of in the pipes.

- Preaction systems operate like a dry pipe system except that the sprinkler head holds a thermal-fusible link that must melt before the water is released.

- Deluge systems allow large amounts of water to be released into the room, which obviously makes this not a good choice where computing equipment will be located.

At one time, fire suppression systems used halon gas, which works well by suppressing combustion through a chemical reaction. However, the US Environmental Protection Agency banned halon manufacturing in 1994 as it has been found to damage the ozone layer.

The EPA has approved the following replacements for halon:

- Water

- Argon

- NAF-S-III

Another fire suppression system that can be used in computer rooms that will not damage computers and is safe for humans is FM-200.

Redundancy and High Availability (HA) Concepts

All organizations should identify and analyze the risks they face. This is called risk management. In the following sections, you'll find a survey of topics that all relate in some way to addressing risks that can be mitigated with redundancy and high availability techniques.

Recovery Sites

Although a secondary site that is identical in every way to the main site with data kept synchronized up to the minute would be ideal, the cost cannot be justified for most organizations. Cost-benefit analysis must be applied to every business issue, even disaster recovery. Thankfully, not all secondary sites are created equally. They can vary in functionality and cost. We're going to explore four types of sites: cold sites, warm sites, hot sites, and cloud sites.

Cold Site

A cold site is a leased facility that contains only electrical and communications wiring, air conditioning, plumbing, and raised flooring. No communications equipment, networking hardware, or computers are installed at a cold site until it is necessary to bring the site to full operation. For this reason, a cold site takes much longer to restore than a hot or warm site.

A cold site provides the slowest recovery, but it is the least expensive to maintain. It is also the most difficult to test.

Warm Site

The restoration time and cost of a warm site is somewhere between that of a hot site and a cold site. It is the most widely implemented alternate leased location. Although it is easier to test a warm site than a cold site, a warm site requires much more effort for testing than a hot site.

A warm site is a leased facility that contains electrical and communications wiring, full utilities, and networking equipment. In most cases, the only thing that needs to be restored is the software and the data. A warm site takes longer to restore than a hot site but less than a cold site.

Hot Site

A hot site is a leased facility that contains all the resources needed for full operation. This environment includes computers, raised flooring, full utilities, electrical and communications wiring, networking equipment, and uninterruptible power supplies (UPSs). The only resource that must be restored at a hot site is the organization's data, usually only partially. It should only take a few minutes to bring a hot site to full operation.

Although a hot site provides the quickest recovery, it is the most expensive to maintain. In addition, it can be administratively hard to manage if the organization requires proprietary hardware or software. A hot site requires the same security controls as the primary facility and full redundancy, including hardware, software, and communication wiring.

Cloud Site

A cloud recovery site is an extension of the cloud backup services that have developed over the years. These are sites that, while mimicking your on-premises network, are totally virtual, as shown in Figure 15.8.

FIGURE 15.8   Cloud recovery site

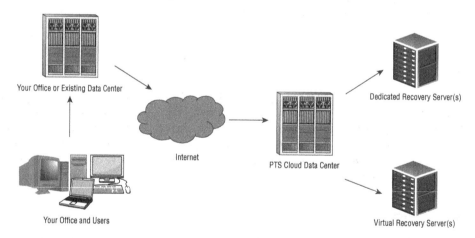

Organizations that lack either the expertise of the resources to develop even a cold site may benefit from engaging with a cloud vendor of these services.

Active/Active vs. Active/Passive

When systems are arranged for fault tolerance or high availability, they can be set up in either an active/active arrangement or an active/passive configuration. Earlier in this chapter you learned that when set to active/active state, both or all devices (servers, routers, switches, etc.) are performing work, and set to active/passive, at least one device is on standby in case a working device fails. Active/active increases availability by providing more systems for work, while active/passive provides fault tolerance by holding at least one system in reserve in case of a system failure.

Multiple Internet Service Providers (ISPs)/Diverse Paths

Redundancy may also be beneficial when it comes to your Internet connection. There are two types of redundancy that can be implemented.

Path redundancy is accomplished by configuring paths to the ISP. This is shown in Figure 15.9. There is a single ISP with two paths extending to the ISP from two different routers.

FIGURE 15.9 Path redundancy

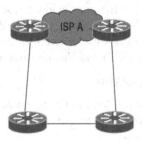

That's great, but what if the ISP suffers a failure (it does happen)? To protect against that you could engage two different ISPs with a path to each from a single router, as shown in Figure 15.10.

FIGURE 15.10 ISP redundancy

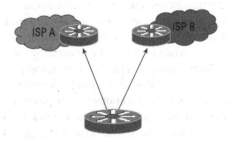

For complete protection you could combine the two by using a separate router connection to each ISP, thus protecting against an issue with a single router or path in your network, as shown in Figure 15.11.

FIGURE 15.11   Path and ISP redundancy

Virtual Router Redundancy Protocol (VRRP)/First-Hop Redundancy Protocol (FHRP)

Earlier in this chapter I mentioned FHRPs and said we would come back to them. Now's the time. There are three first-hop redundancy protocols: HSRP, VRRP, and GLBP. HSRP and GLBP are Cisco proprietary protocols, while VRRP is a standards-based protocol. Let's look at Hot Standby Router Protocol (HSRP) and Virtual Router Redundancy Protocol (VRRP).

Hot Standby Router Protocol (HSRP)

HSRP is a Cisco proprietary protocol that can be run on most, but not all, of Cisco's router and multilayer switch models. It defines a standby group, and each standby group that you define includes the following routers:

- Active router
- Standby router
- Virtual router
- Any other routers that may be attached to the subnet

The problem with HSRP is that only one router is active and two or more routers just sit there in standby mode and won't be used unless a failure occurs—not very cost effective or efficient! Figure 15.12 shows how only one router is used at a time in an HSRP group.

The standby group will always have at least two routers participating in it. The primary players in the group are the one active router and one standby router that communicate to each other using multicast Hello messages. The Hello messages provide all of the required communication for the routers. The Hellos contain the information required to accomplish the election that determines the active and standby router positions. They also hold the key to the failover process. If the standby router stops receiving Hello packets from the active router, it then takes over the active router role, as shown in Figure 15.13.

FIGURE 15.12   HSRP active and standby routers

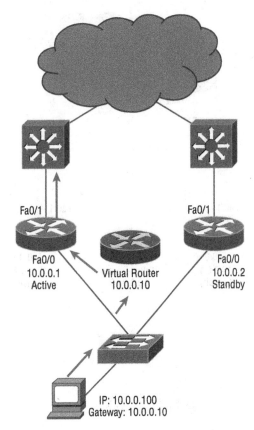

As soon as the active router stops responding to Hellos, the standby router automatically becomes the active router and starts responding to host requests.

VIRTUAL MAC ADDRESS

A virtual router in an HSRP group has a virtual IP address and a virtual MAC address. So where does that virtual MAC address come from? The virtual IP address isn't that hard to figure out; it just has to be a unique IP address on the same subnet as the hosts defined in the configuration. But MAC addresses are a little different, right? Or are they? The answer is yes—sort of. With HSRP, you create a totally new, made-up MAC address in addition to the IP address.

FIGURE 15.13 HSRP active and standby routers

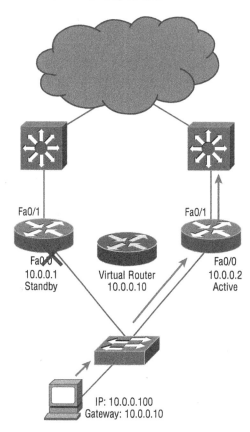

The HSRP MAC address has only one variable piece in it. The first 24 bits still identify the vendor who manufactured the device (the organizationally unique identifier, or OUI). The next 16 bits in the address tell us that the MAC address is a well-known HSRP MAC address. Finally, the last 8 bits of the address are the hexadecimal representation of the HSRP group number.

Let me clarify all this with an example of what an HSRP MAC address would look like:

0000.0c07.ac0a

- The first 24 bits (0000.0c) are the vendor ID of the address; in the case of HSRP being a Cisco protocol, the ID is assigned to Cisco.

- The next 16 bits (07.ac) are the well-known HSRP ID. This part of the address was assigned by Cisco in the protocol, so it's always easy to recognize that this address is for use with HSRP.

- The last 8 bits (0a) are the only variable bits and represent the HSRP group number that you assign. In this case, the group number is 10 and is converted to hexadecimal when placed in the MAC address where it becomes the 0a that you see.

You can see this MAC address added to the ARP cache of every router in the HSRP group. There will be the translation from the IP address to the MAC address as well as the interface on which it's located.

HSRP TIMERS

Before we get deeper into the roles that each of the routers can have in an HSRP group, I want to define the HSRP timers. The timers are very important to the HSRP function because they ensure communication between the routers, and if something goes wrong, they allow the standby router to take over. The HSRP timers include hello, hold, active, and standby.

Hello Timer   The hello timer is the defined interval during which each of the routers send out Hello messages. Their default interval is 3 seconds, and they identify the state that each router is in. This is important because the particular state determines the specific role of each router and, as a result, the actions each will take within the group. Figure 15.14 shows the Hello messages being sent, and the router uses the hello timer to keep network traffic flowing in case of a failure.

FIGURE 15.14   HSRP active and standby routers

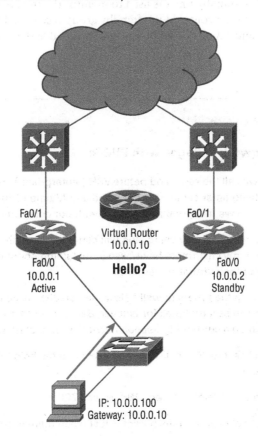

This timer can be changed, and people used to avoid doing so because it was *thought* that lowering the hello value would place an unnecessary load on the routers. That isn't true with most of the routers today; in fact, you can configure the timers in milliseconds, meaning the failover time can be in milliseconds! Still, keep in mind that increasing the value will cause the standby router to wait longer before taking over for the active router when it fails or can't communicate.

Hold Timer   The hold timer specifies the interval the standby router uses to determine whether the active router is offline or out of communication. By default, the hold timer is 10 seconds, roughly three times the default for the hello timer. If one timer is changed for some reason, I recommend using this multiplier to adjust the other timers too. By setting the hold timer at three times the hello timer, you ensure that the standby router doesn't take over the active role every time there's a short break in communication.

Active Timer   The active timer monitors the state of the active router. The timer resets each time a router in the standby group receives a Hello packet from the active router. This timer expires based on the hold time value that's set in the corresponding field of the HSRP Hello message.

Standby Timer   The standby timer is used to monitor the state of the standby router. The timer resets anytime a router in the standby group receives a Hello packet from the standby router and expires based on the hold time value that's set in the respective Hello packet.

 Real World Scenario

Large Enterprise Network Outages with FHRPs

Years ago, when HSRP was all the rage, and before VRRP, enterprises used hundreds of HSRP groups. With the hello timer set to 3 seconds and a hold time of 10 seconds, these timers worked just fine and we had great redundancy with our core routers.

However, as we've seen in the last few years, and will certainly see in the future, 10 seconds is now a lifetime! Some of my customers have been complaining about the failover time and loss of connectivity to their virtual server farms.

So lately I've been changing the timers to well below the defaults. Cisco had changed the timers so you could use sub-second times for failover. Because these are multicast packets, the overhead that is seen on a current high-speed network is almost nothing.

The hello timer is typically set to 200 milliseconds (msec) and the hold time is 700 msec. The command is as follows:

```
(config-if)#Standby 1 timers msec 200 msec 700
```

This almost ensures that not even a single packet is lost when there is an outage.

VIRTUAL ROUTER REDUNDANCY PROTOCOL

Like HSRP, Virtual Router Redundancy Protocol (VRRP) allows a group of routers to form a single virtual router. In an HSRP or VRRP group, one router is elected to handle all requests sent to the virtual IP address. With HSRP, this is the active router. An HSRP group has only one active router, at least one standby router, and many listening routers. A VRRP group has one master router and one or more backup routers and is the open standard implementation of HSRP.

COMPARING VRRP AND HSRP

The LAN workstations are configured with the address of the virtual router as their default gateway, just as they are with HSRP, but VRRP differs from HSRP in these important ways:

- VRRP is an IEEE standard (RFC 2338) for router redundancy; HSRP is a Cisco proprietary protocol.

- The virtual router that represents a group of routers is known as a VRRP group.

- The active router is referred to as the master virtual router.

- The master virtual router may have the same IP address as the virtual router group.

- Multiple routers can function as backup routers.

- VRRP is supported on Ethernet, Fast Ethernet, and Gigabit Ethernet interfaces as well as on Multiprotocol Label Switching (MPLS), virtual private networks (VPNs), and VLANs.

VRRP REDUNDANCY CHARACTERISTICS

VRRP has some unique features:

- VRRP provides redundancy for the real IP address of a router or for a virtual IP address shared among the VRRP group members.

- If a real IP address is used, the router with that address becomes the master.

- If a virtual IP address is used, the master is the router with the highest priority.

- A VRRP group has one master router and one or more backup routers.

- The master router uses VRRP messages to inform group members.

Mean Time to Repair (MTTR)

One of the metrics that's used in planning both SLAs and IT operations in general is mean time to repair (MTTR). This value describes the average length of time it takes a vendor to repair a device or component. By building these into SLAs, IT can assure that the time taken to repair a component or device will not be a factor that causes them to violate the SLAs' requirements. Sometimes MTTR is considered to be from the point at which the failure is first discovered until the point at which the equipment returns to operation. In other cases, it is a measure of the elapsed time between the point where repairs actually begin until the point at which the equipment returns to operation. It is important that there is a clear understanding by all parties with regard to when the clock starts and ends when calculating MTTR.

Mean Time Between Failure (MTBF)

Another valuable metric typically provided is the mean time between failures (MTBF), which describes the amount of time that elapses between one failure and the next. Mathematically, this is the sum of mean time to failure (MTTF) and MTTR, which is the total time required to get the device fixed and back online.

Recovery Time Objective (RTO)

This is the shortest time period after a disaster or disruptive event within which a resource or function must be restored in order to avoid unacceptable consequences. RTO assumes that an acceptable period of downtime exists.

Recovery Point Objective (RPO)

An RPO is a measurement of time from the failure, disaster, or comparable loss-causing event. RPOs measure back in time to when your data was preserved in a usable format, usually to the most recent backup.

Network Device Backup/Restore

When devices are backed up it is important to know that backing up the data and the underlying system are two separate actions. Let's look at protecting the system itself.

State/Configuration

We create device configurations over time that can be quite complicated, and in some cases where multiple technicians have played a role, no single person has a complete understanding of the configuration. For this reason, configurations should be backed up.

Configurations may sometimes exist as text files, such as in a router or switch. Other times, such as with a Microsoft server, you will back up what is called the system state. This backs up only the configuration of the server and not the data. In this case, a system state backup and a data backup should be performed. It is also possible to back up the entire computer, which would include both datasets.

Considering the time it takes to set up a new device, install the operating system, and reconfigure it to replace a defective device, it makes great sense to keep backups of configurations so that if a device fails, you can quickly reimage a new machine and simply apply the system state to it or apply the configuration file (in the case of routers and switches).

Summary

In this chapter you learned the importance of providing both fault tolerance and high availability. You also learned about disaster recovery concepts.

We discussed ensuring continued access to resources with load balancing, multipathing, and NIC teaming. Expanding on that concept, we looked at setting up clusters of routers, switches, and firewalls. Finally, we explored facilities redundancy with techniques such as UPS systems, PDUs, and generators and environmental issues such as HVAC systems and fire suppression systems.

In disaster recovery you learned about hot, cold, warm, and cloud sites and how they fit into a disaster recovery plan. You also learned terms critical to planning for disaster recovery, such as MTTR, MTBF, RTO, and RPO.

Finally, we covered backup operations for both configurations and system state.

Exam Essentials

Understand the importance of fault tolerance and high availability techniques. These include load balancing, multipathing, NIC teaming, and router, switch, and firewall clusters.

Describe facilities and infrastructure redundancy techniques. Among these are uninterruptible power supplies (UPSs), power distribution units (PDUs), generators, HVAC systems, fire suppression, and multiple Internet service providers (ISPs)/diverse paths.

Utilize disaster recovery techniques. These include physical cold sites, warm sites, hot sites, and cloud sites. It also requires an understanding of RPO, MTTR, MTBF, and RTO.

Identify applications of active/active and active/passive configurations. These include switch clusters, VRRP and HSRP, and firewall clusters.

Written Lab

Complete the table by filling in the appropriate term for each definition.
You can find the answers in Appendix A.

Definition	Term
Technique used to spread work out to multiple computers, network links, or other devices	
Allows multiple network interfaces to be placed into a team for the purposes of bandwidth aggregation	
Devices that can immediately supply power from a battery backup when a loss of power is detected	
A leased facility that contains all the resources needed for full operation	
A Cisco proprietary FHRP	

Review Questions

You can find the answers to the review questions in Appendix B.

1. Which of the following backup types does *not* include the data?
    A. Full
    B. System state
    C. Clone
    D. Differential

2. Which of the following is a measure back in time to when your data was preserved in a usable format, usually to the most recent backup?
    A. RTO
    B. MTBF
    C. RPO
    D. MTD

3. Which of the following is an IEEE standard (RFC 2338) for router redundancy?
    A. HSRP
    B. VRRP
    C. HDLC
    D. MLPS

4. Which of the following is the defined interval during which each of the routers send out Hello messages in HSRP?
    A. Hold timer
    B. Hello timer
    C. Active timer
    D. Standby timer

5. What is the HSRP group number of the group with the following HSRP MAC address?

    0000.0c07.ac0a
    A. 10
    B. 15
    C. 20
    D. 25

6. Which of the following only provides fault tolerance?
    A. Two servers in an active/active configuration
    B. Three servers in an active/passive configuration with one on standby

C. Three servers in an active/passive configuration with two on standby

D. Three servers in an active/active configuration

7. Which site type mimics your on-premises network yet is totally virtual?

A. Cold site

B. Cloud site

C. Warm site

D. Hot site

8. Which of the following fire suppression systems is not a good choice where computing equipment will be located?

A. Deluge

B. Wet pipe

C. Dry pipe

D. Preaction

9. Which of the following protocols gives you a way to configure more than one physical router to appear as if they were only a single logical one?

A. FHRP

B. NAT

C. NAC

D. CMS

10. Which of the following provides a method to join multiple physical switches into a single logical switching unit?

A. Stacking

B. Daisy chaining

C. Segmenting

D. Federating

Chapter

16

Common Security Concepts

THE FOLLOWING COMPTIA NETWORK+ EXAM OBJECTIVES ARE COVERED IN THIS CHAPTER:

✓ **4.1 Explain common security concepts.**

- Confidentiality, integrity, availability (CIA)
- Threats
  - Internal
  - External
- Vulnerabilities
  - Common vulnerabilities and exposures (CVE)
  - Zero-day
- Exploits
- Least privilege
- Role-based access
- Zero Trust
- Defense in depth
  - Network segmentation enforcement
  - Screened subnet [previously known as demilitarized zone (DMZ)]
  - Separation of duties
  - Network access control
  - Honeypot
- Authentication methods
  - Multifactor
  - Terminal Access Controller Access Control System Plus (TACACS+)

- Single sign-on (SSO)
- Remote Authentication Dial in User Service (RADIUS)
- LDAP
- Kerberos
- Local authentication
- 802.1X
- Extensible Authentication Protocol (EAP)
- Risk Management
  - Security risk assessments
    - Threat assessment
    - Vulnerability assessment
    - Penetration testing
    - Posture assessment
  - Business risk assessment
    - Process assessment
    - Vendor assessment
- Security information and event management (SIEM)

To operate securely in a network environment, one must understand how to speak the language of security. As in any field, there is terminology that must be understood to discuss more involved topics.

In this chapter you will learn the basic concepts, terms, and principles that all network professionals should understand to secure an enterprise network.

To find Todd Lammle CompTIA videos and practice questions, please see www.lammle.com.

Confidentiality, Integrity, and Availability (CIA)

The three fundamentals of security are confidentiality, integrity, and availability (CIA), often referred to as the CIA triad. Most security issues result in a violation of at least one facet of the CIA triad. Understanding these three security principles will help ensure that the security controls and mechanisms implemented protect at least one of these principles.

Confidentiality

To ensure confidentiality, you must prevent the disclosure of data or information to unauthorized entities. As part of confidentiality, the sensitivity level of data must be determined before putting any access controls in place. Data with a higher sensitivity level will have more access controls in place than data at a lower sensitivity level. Identification, authentication, authorization, and encryption can be used to maintain data confidentiality.

Integrity

Integrity, the second part of the CIA triad, ensures that data is protected from unauthorized modification or data corruption. The goal of integrity is to preserve the consistency of data, including data stored in files, databases, systems, and networks.

Availability

Availability means ensuring that data is accessible when and where it is needed. Only individuals who need access to data should be allowed access to that data. The two main areas where availability is affected are (1) when attacks are carried out that disable or cripple a system and (2) when service loss occurs during and after disasters. Technologies that provide fault tolerance, such as RAID or redundant sites, are examples of controls that help to improve availability.

Threats

The first line of defense in providing CIA is to know about the types of threats out there because you can't do anything to protect yourself from something you don't know about. But once you understand the threats, you can begin to design defenses to combat bad guys lurking in the depths of cyberspace just waiting for an opportunity to strike. Threats come in two forms, internal and external.

Internal

Internal threats are those that are sourced within your own network. These attacks come from inside the firewall. Sadly, we have more to fear from our own users than we do from external hackers (maybe we should treat them better). They have already discovered and penetrated the network, which is two-thirds of the hacking process.

External

External threats come from outside the firewall. These are typically hackers of all abilities. They include script kiddies (amateurs) and advanced persistent threats (APT, usually a state-sponsored team) and all types in between. Later you will learn that these two types require a different approach when performing penetration testing for vulnerabilities.

Vulnerabilities

A vulnerability is the absence of a countermeasure or a weakness in a countermeasure that is in place. Vulnerabilities can occur in software, hardware, or personnel. An example of a vulnerability is unrestricted access to a folder on a computer. Most organizations implement a vulnerability assessment to identify vulnerabilities. In the following sections, you'll learn about a method of classifying vulnerabilities and about one special type of vulnerability.

Common Vulnerabilities and Exposures (CVE)

The *Common Vulnerability Scoring System (CVSS)* is a system of ranking vulnerabilities that are discovered based on predefined metrics. This system ensures that the most critical vulnerabilities can be easily identified and addressed after a vulnerability test is met.

The output of using this classification system is a database of known vulnerabilities called *Common Vulnerabilities and Exposures (CVE)*. It is maintained by the MITRE Corporation and each entry describes a vulnerability in detail, using a number and letter system to describe what it endangers, the environment it requires to be successful, and, in many cases, the proper mitigation. This system is used by security professionals to share and inform one another as new CVEs are discovered.

Zero-Day

Antivirus software uses definition files that identify known malware. These files must be updated frequently, but the update process can usually be automated so that it requires no help from the user. If a new virus is created that has not yet been identified in the list, you will not be protected until the virus definition is added and the new definition file is downloaded.

This condition is known as a *zero-day* attack because it is the first day the virus has been released and therefore no known fix exists. This term may also be applied to an operating system bug that has not been corrected.

Exploits

An exploit occurs when a threat agent takes advantage of a vulnerability and uses it to advance an attack. When a network attack takes advantage of a vulnerability, it is somewhat of an indictment of the network team as most vulnerabilities can be identified and mitigated. A good example of a vulnerability that was exploited was the unpatched Apache server that was compromised and led to the Equifax breach.

Least Privilege

The first step to mitigating damage that may be caused by disgruntled or malicious employees is to adhere to the principle of *least privilege*. This concept prescribes that users should be given access only to resources required to do their job. So if Ralph's job only requires read permission to the Sales folder, that's all he should get even if you know he's completely trustworthy. By doing this, you also limit the damage that could be done if Ralph's account is compromised.

Role-Based Access

Role-based access control prescribes creating roles or sets of permissions required for various job roles and assigning those permissions to security groups. When a new employee is assigned a role, they are simply placed in the group and thus inherit all required permissions.

When you create a role-based group, you should define what actions this role will be capable of. The choice of permissions or rights you assign to the group that represents this role (for example, customer service rep) should be driven by the tasks required and the resources required to do that job. This is an area where you should exercise least privilege. This principle states that no user should be given access to any resource that is not required to do their job.

Zero Trust

The *Zero Trust* concept supports least privilege. It prescribes that when a resource is created, the default permission should be No Access. It also means that when configuring ACLs on routers, all traffic should be blocked by default and only specific traffic allowed.

Defense in Depth

A *defense-in-depth* strategy refers to the practice of using multiple layers of security between data and the resources on which it resides and possible attackers. The first layer of a good defense-in-depth strategy is appropriate access control strategies. Access controls exist in all areas of an Information Systems (IS) infrastructure (more commonly referred to as an IT infrastructure), but a defense-in-depth strategy goes beyond access control. It also considers software development security, cryptography, and physical security. In the following sections, we'll look at some of the options you should consider in developing defense in depth.

Network Segmentation Enforcement

Maintaining security in the network can be made easier by segmenting the network and controlling access from one segment to another. Segmentation can be done at several layers of the OSI model.

One of the biggest reasons for implementing segmentation is for security purposes. At layer 1, this means complete physical separation. However, if you don't want to go with complete segmentation, you can also segment at layer 2 on switches by implementing VLANs and port security. This can prevent connections between systems that are connected to the same switch. They can also be used to organize users into common networks regardless of their physical location.

If segmentation at layer 3 is required, it's achieved using access control lists on routers to control access from one subnet to another or from one VLAN to another. Firewalls can implement these types of access lists as well.

Screened Subnet (aka Demilitarized Zone)

Use a screened subnet—previously known as a demilitarized zone (DMZ)—for all publicly viewable servers, including web servers, FTP servers, and email relay servers. A *screened subnet* is a version of the DMZ that is created with two firewalls (each of the routers are operating as a firewall) and the DMZ (also called the perimeter between them), as shown in Figure 16.1.

FIGURE 16.1   Screened subnet

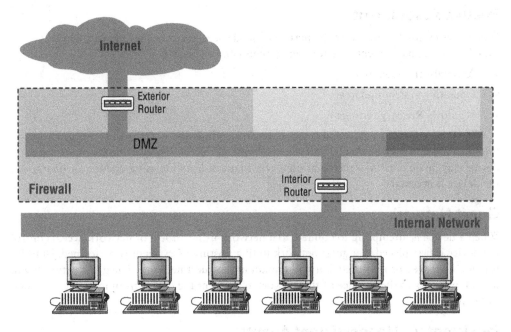

In this case, two firewalling routers are used, and traffic must be inspected at both firewalls to enter the internal network. It is called a screened subnet because there is a subnet between the two firewalls that can act as a DMZ for resources from the outside world.

Separation of Duties

Separation of duties is a concept that specifies that any operation that is susceptible to fraud or abuse by employees should be broken into two tasks and then these two tasks should be assigned to different individuals. While there is no guarantee that these two individuals don't collude, the chance of that occurring are much less than the chance of a single individual committing fraud.

Network Access Control

Network Access Control (NAC) is a method of securing network hosts before they're allowed to access the network. Network Access Control systems that control access to devices based on their security settings include Cisco's Network Admission Control (NAC) and Microsoft's Network Policy and Access Services (NPAS). These systems examine the state of a computer's operating system updates and antimalware updates before allowing access, and in some cases, they can even remediate the devices prior to permitting access. In the following sections, key components of Network Access Control systems are covered.

Posture Assessment

When devices attempt to access the network, the devices are examined closely, which is called a posture assessment. The following items can be checked:

- Antimalware updates
- Operating system updates
- Windows Registry settings

When the assessment is complete and is positive, admission is granted. If problems are found, admission may be denied and the user notified that action must be taken, or the device may be directed to a remediation server that can install missing updates or quarantine the device if necessary.

Guest Network

When a device is attempting to connect to a network using a form of network access control, the device is first placed in a guest network until a posture assessment is performed. Until it is either approved or remediated, it will remain in the guest network. The guest network will not allow access to the balance of the network to prevent the device from introducing issues to the network.

Persistent vs. Nonpersistent Agents

Network Access Control systems can be deployed using either persistent or nonpersistent agents on the devices. A persistent agent is one that is installed on an NAC client and starts when the operating system loads. This agent provides functionality that may not be present in the nonpersistent agent, such as system-wide notifications and alerts and auto and manual remediation.

A nonpersistent agent is one that is used to assess the device only during the onetime check-in at login, usually through a captive web portal. The nonpersistent or dissolvable agent is removed from the device when the authentication web page is closed. It can be used to support the assessment of endpoints not owned by the organization and as such can help to make a bring your own device (BYOD) policy possible.

Honeypot

Another segmentation tactic is to create honeypots and honeynets. *Honeypots* are systems strategically configured to be attractive to hackers and to lure them into spending enough time attacking them while information is gathered about the attack. In some cases, entire networks called *honeynets* are attractively configured for this purpose. You need to make sure that either of these types of systems do not provide direct connections to any important systems. Their ultimate purpose is to divert attention from valuable resources and to gather as much information about an attack as possible. A tarpit is a type of honeypot designed to provide a very slow connection to the hacker so that the attack takes enough time to be properly analyzed.

Authentication Methods

A whole bunch of authentication schemes are used today, and although it's important to know about the different schemes and how they work, all that knowledge doesn't make a difference if your network's users aren't schooled on how to manage their account names and passwords correctly. In the following sections, you'll learn about authentication systems and techniques.

Multifactor

Multifactor authentication is designed to add an additional level of security to the authentication process by verifying more than one characteristic of a user before allowing access to a resource. Users can be identified in one of five ways:

- By something they know (password)
- By something they are (retinas, fingerprint, facial recognition)
- By something they possess (smart card)
- By somewhere they are (location)
- By something they do (behavior)

Two-factor authentication is when two of the above factors are being tested, while multifactor is when more than two of the above factors are being tested. An example of two-factor authentication would be requiring both a smart card and a PIN to log onto the network. The possession of either by itself would not be sufficient to authenticate.

This protects against the loss and theft of the card as well as the loss of the password. An example of multifactor authentication would be when three items are required, such as a smart card, a PIN, and a username and password.

This process can get as involved as the security requires. In an extremely high-security situation, you might require a smart card, a password, a retina scan, and a fingerprint scan. The trade-off to all the increased security is an inconvenient authentication process for the user and the high cost of biometric authentication devices.

Authentication, Authorization, and Accounting (AAA)

In computer security speak, AAA (triple A, like the auto club) refers to authentication, authorization, and accounting. AAAA is a more robust version that adds auditing into the mix. AAA and AAAA aren't really protocols; instead, they're systematized, conceptual models for managing network security through one central location. Two common implementations of AAA are RADIUS and TACACS+.

Remote Authentication Dial-In User Service (RADIUS)

Although its name implies it, the *Remote Authentication Dial-In User Service (RADIUS)* is not a dial-up server. Like pretty much everything else, it originated that way, but it's evolved into more of a verification service. Today, RADIUS is an authentication and accounting service that's used for verifying users over various types of links, including dial-up. Many ISPs use a RADIUS server to store the usernames and passwords of their clients in a central spot through which connections are configured to pass authentication requests. RADIUS servers are client-server based authentication and encryption services maintaining user profiles in a central database.

RADIUS is also used in firewalls. When they're purposed this way, a user must provide a username and a password when they want to access a particular TCP/IP port. The firewall then contacts the RADIUS server to verify the credentials given. If the verification is successful, the user is granted access to that port.

RADIUS is an authentication server that allows for domain-level authentication on both wired and wireless networks.

Terminal Access Controller Access Control System Plus (TACACS+)

The *Terminal Access Controller Access-Control System Plus (TACACS+)* protocol is also a AAA method and an alternative to RADIUS. Like RADIUS, it is capable of performing authentication on behalf of multiple wireless APs, RAS servers, or even LAN switches that are 802.1X capable. Based on its name, you would think it's an extension of the TACACS protocol (and in some ways it is), but the two definitely are not compatible.

Here are two major differences between TACACS+ and RADIUS:

- RADIUS combines user authentication and authorization into one profile, but TACACS+ separates the two.

- TACACS+ utilizes the connection-based TCP, but RADIUS uses UDP instead.

Even though both are commonly used today, because of these two reasons TACACS+ is considered more stable and secure than RADIUS.

Figure 16.2 shows how TACACS+ works.

FIGURE 16.2 TACACS+ login and logout sequence

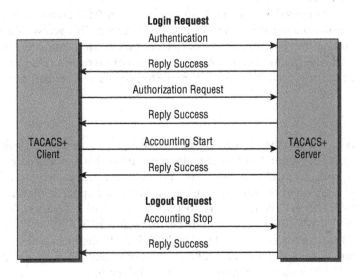

Just to clarify things, in the IT world, accounting has nothing to do with money. Here's what I mean: When a TACACS+ session is closed, the information in the following list is logged, or accounted for. This isn't a complete list; it's just meant to give you an idea of the type of accounting information TACACS+ gathers:

- Connection start time and stop time

- The number of bytes sent and received by the user

- The number of packets sent and received by the user

- The reason for the disconnection

The only time the accounting feature has anything to do with money is if your service provider is charging you based on the amount of time you've spent logged in or for the amount of data sent and received.

Single Sign-On (SSO)

In today's modern enterprises, users can be overwhelmed by the number of points in the network where they may be challenged to identify themselves. Most users have to log onto the domain to have network access at all, and then there may be company websites that require an authentication process to access databases, SharePoint sites, secured drives, personal folders, and on and on!

When users must remember multiple passwords, as the number increases, they begin to resort to unsafe security practices such as writing passwords on sticky notes, hiding passwords in their drawers, and even sharing them with coworkers. All of these practices undermine the security of the network.

Single sign-on addresses this problem. With *single sign-on (SSO)*, when the user logs into the domain, the domain controller issues them an access token. This access token contains a list of all the resources (which can include folders, drives, websites, databases, and so on) to which they should have access. As a result, anytime the user accesses a resource, the token is verified behind the scenes, and the user never needs to provide another password!

LDAP

A directory service is a database designed to centralize data management regarding network subjects and objects. A typical directory contains a hierarchy that includes users, groups, systems, servers, client workstations, and so on. Because the directory service contains data about users and other network entities, it can be used by many applications that require access to that information. A common directory service standard is *Lightweight Directory Access Protocol (LDAP)*, which is based on the earlier standard X.500.

X.500 uses Directory Access Protocol (DAP). In X.500, the distinguished name (DN) provides the full path in the X.500 database where the entry is found. The relative distinguished name (RDN) in X.500 is an entry's name without the full path.

LDAP is simpler than X.500. LDAP supports DN and RDN, but it includes more attributes, such as the common name (CN), domain component (DC), and organizational unit (OU) attributes. Using a client-server architecture, LDAP uses TCP port 389 to communicate. If advanced security is needed, LDAP over SSL communicates via TCP port 636.

Kerberos

Kerberos, created at MIT, isn't just a protocol, it's an entire security system that establishes a user's identity when they first log on to a system that's running it. It employs strong encryption for all transactions and communication, and it's readily available. The source code for Kerberos can be freely downloaded from lots of places on the Internet.

Kerberos works by issuing tickets to users who log in, kind of like going to an amusement park—as long as you have your ticket to ride, you're good to go. Even though the tickets expire quickly, they're automatically refreshed as long as you remain logged in. Because of this refresh feature, all systems participating in a Kerberos domain must have synchronized clocks.

This synchronicity is a bit complicated to set up, although in Microsoft servers and domains the process is automatic, requiring only access to a recognized time server (which Microsoft also operates). The real negative hits happen if you have only one Kerberos authentication server—if it goes down, no one can log into the network. So when running Kerberos, having redundant servers is clearly vital. You should also know that because all users' secret keys are stored in one centralized database, if that's compromised, you have a security tsunami on your hands. Luckily these keys are stored in an encrypted state. Figure 16.3 shows Kerberos in action.

FIGURE 16.3 Kerberos authentication

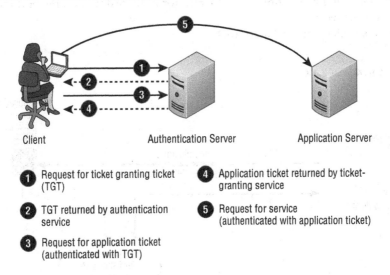

1 Request for ticket granting ticket (TGT)	**4** Application ticket returned by ticket-granting service
2 TGT returned by authentication service	**5** Request for service (authenticated with application ticket)
3 Request for application ticket (authenticated with TGT)	

Local Authentication

When users authenticate to their computer, the authentication can be either to a domain or to the local machine. When local authentication is performed, the user's local account and password are verified with the local user database. This local user database is called Security Accounts Manager (SAM) and is located in C:\windows\system32\config\. In Linux, the database is a text file, /etc/passwd (called the password file), which lists all valid user-names and their associated information.

802.1X

Another form of network access control is 802.1X. This is a standard that defines a frame-work for centralized port-based authentication. It can be applied to both wireless and wired networks and uses three components:

- Supplicant: The user or device requesting access to the network
- Authenticator: The device through which the supplicant is attempting to access the network
- Authentication server: The centralized device that performs authentication

The role of the authenticator can be performed by a wide variety of network access devices, including remote access servers (both dial-up and VPN), switches, and wireless access points. The role of the authentication server can be performed by a Remote Authentication Dial-In User Service (RADIUS) or Terminal Access Controller Access-Control System Plus (TACACS+) server. The authenticator requests credentials from the supplicant and, upon receipt of those credentials, relays them to the authentication server, where they are validated. Upon successful verification, the authenticator is notified to open the port for the supplicant to allow network access.

This process is illustrated in Figure 16.4.

FIGURE 16.4 802.1X

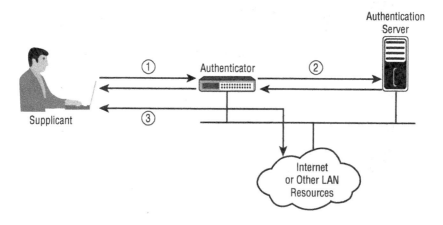

Extensible Authentication Protocol (EAP)

Extensible Authentication Protocol (EAP) isn't a single method but a framework that enhances the existing 802.1X framework. The EAP framework describes a basic set of actions that will take place, and each EAP type differs in the specifics of how it operates within the framework. These variables include things like whether they use passwords or certificates as well as the ultimate level of security provided. Some of the EAP methods require that certificates be used as the credential during authentication. This means that to implement those methods, you must have a Public Key Infrastructure (PKI) in your network.

PEAP

Protected Extensible Authentication Protocol, also known as Protected EAP or simply PEAP, is a protocol that encapsulates the Extensible Authentication Protocol (EAP) within an encrypted and authenticated Transport Layer Security (TLS) tunnel. It requires only a server-side PKI certificate to create a secure TLS tunnel to protect user authentication.

EAP-FAST

EAP-FAST works in two stages. In the first stage, a TLS tunnel is established. Unlike PEAP, EAP-FAST's first stage is established by using a pre-shared key called a Protected Authentication Credential (PAC). In the second stage, a series of type/length/value (TLV)–encoded data is used to carry a user authentication.

EAP-TLS

EAP Transport Layer Security (EAP-TLS) is the most secure method, but it's also the most difficult to configure and maintain. To use EAP-TLS, you must install a certificate on both the authentication server and the client. An authentication server pair of keys and a client pair of keys need to be generated first, signed using a PKI, and installed on the devices. On the station side, the keys can be issued for the machine itself and/or for the user.

In the authentication stage, the station, along with the authentication server (RADIUS, etc.), exchange certificates and identify each other. Mutual authentication is a solid beneficial feature, which ensures that the station it's communicating with is the proper authentication server. After this process is completed, random session keys are created for encryption.

Preshared Key

Finally, a preshared key can be used to secure wireless transmissions. This is most labor intensive as it requires that all devices use the same key as the AP and that the keys be changed frequently to provide adequate security.

Security Risk Assessments

Security assessments are used to identify security weakness with the goal of eliminating them. This section of the chapter covers various assessment types that can be utilized to define where you are and help you define where you need to go.

Threat Assessment

Prior to performing a vulnerability or a penetration test, it is useful to identity the types of risk with which you are concerned. This effort can be enhanced by subscribing to threat feeds. Threat intelligence feeds are constantly updating streams of indicators or artifacts derived from a source outside the organization. These feeds are used to inform the organization as quickly as possible about new threats that have occurred. They contain the following information:

- Suspicious domains
- Lists of known malware hashes
- IP addresses associated with malicious activity

Later in this chapter, you will learn how security information and event management (SIEM) systems aggregate the log from various security devices into a single log for analysis. The reason for this is that by analyzing this single aggregated log, inferences can be made about potential issues or attacks that would not be possible if the logs were analyzed separately.

Using SIEM (or other aggregation tools) to aggregate threat feeds can also be beneficial, and there are tools and services for this. Among them are the following:

- Combine: Gathers threat intelligence feeds from publicly available sources.
- Palo Alto Networks AutoFocus: Provides intelligence, correlation, added context, and automated prevention workflows.
- Anomali ThreatStream: Helps deduplicate data, remove false positives, and feed intelligence to security tools.
- ThreatQuotient: Helps accelerate security operations with an integrated threat library and shared contextual intelligence.
- ThreatConnect: Combines external threat data from trusted sources with in-house data.

Vulnerability Assessment

Part of the security policy of an organization should address the type and frequency of vulnerability scans. These scans are designed to identify any security vulnerabilities that exist.

A vulnerability scanner can probe for a variety of security weaknesses, including misconfigurations, out-of-date software, missing patches, and open ports. One of the most widely used is Nessus, a proprietary vulnerability scanner developed by Tenable Network Security. A partial screen shot is shown in Figure 16.5. In the output, the issues found on a host are rated, and issues with the highest severity are at the top by default.

FIGURE 16.5 Nessus

Plugin ID	Count	Severity	Name	Family
32315	1	High	Firebird Default Credentials	Databases
51192	2	Medium	SSL Certificate Cannot Be Trusted	General
18405	1	Medium	Microsoft Windows Remote Desktop Protocol Server Man-in-the-Middle Weakness	Windows
24244	1	Medium	Microsoft .NET Custom Errors Not Set	Web Servers
57608	1	Medium	SMB Signing Disabled	Misc.
57690	1	Medium	Terminal Services Encryption Level is Medium or Low	Misc.
30218	1	Low	Terminal Services Encryption Level is not FIPS-140 Compliant	Misc.
14272	15	Info	netstat portscanner (SSH)	Port scanners
10736	7	Info	DCE Services Enumeration	Windows

Penetration Testing

A penetration test is designed to simulate an attack on a system, network, or application. Its value lies in its potential to discover security holes that may have gone unnoticed. It differs from vulnerability testing in that it attempts to exploit vulnerabilities rather than simply identify them.

Strategies for penetration testing are based on the testing objectives as defined by the organization:

- **Blind Test:** The testing team is provided with limited knowledge of the network systems and devices, using publicly available information. The organization's security team knows that an attack is coming. This test requires more effort by the testing team.

- **Double-Blind Test:** This test is like a blind test except the organization's security team does not know that an attack is coming. This test usually requires equal effort for both the testing team and the organization's security team.

- **Target Test:** Both the testing team and the organization's security team are given maximum information about the network and the type of test that will occur. This is the easiest test to complete, but it will not provide a full picture of the organization's security.

Business Risk Assessments

Although penetration testing can identify vulnerabilities, it is not the recommended way to do so. An organization should have a well-defined risk management process in place that includes the evaluation of risk that is present. When this process is carried out properly, threat modeling allows organizations to identify threats and potential attacks and implement the appropriate mitigations against these threats and attacks. These facets ensure that any security controls implemented are in balance with the operations of the organization.

Once all assets have been identified and their value to the organization has been established, specific threats to each asset are identified. An attempt must be made to establish both the likelihood of the threat's realization and the impact to the organization if it occurs. Only then can cost-effective mitigation be identified.

Process Assessment

Process assessment is the examination of all processes, policies and procedures that govern the way we do things. As technologies change and more options become available, new methods and approaches may be called for. The goal is continuous improvement.

Vendor Assessment

A business risk assessment should also include a careful review of all vendor relationships, asking the following questions:

- Are SLAs as robust as they should be and do they focus on security requirements?

- Are we too reliant on a single vendor for critical supplies and services? Is there a single point of failure in the supply chain?

- Does the access required indicate the need for additional agreements such as an interconnection agreement?

Security Information and Event Management (SIEM)

Security information and event management (SIEM) is a term for software products and services combining security information management (SIM) and security event management (SEM). SIEM technology provides real-time analysis of security alerts generated by network hardware and applications. You can get this as a software solution or a hardware appliance, and some businesses sell managed services using SIEM. Any one of these solutions provides log security data and can generate reports for compliance purposes.

The acronyms SEM, SIM, and SIEM are used interchangeably; however, SEM is typically used to describe the management that deals with real-time monitoring and correlation of events, notifications, and console views.

The term SIM is used to describe long-term storage, analysis, and reporting of log data. Recently, vSIEM (voice security information and event management) was introduced to provide voice data visibility.

SIEM can collect useful data about the following items:

- Data aggregation
- Correlation
- Alerting
- Dashboards
- Compliance
- Retention
- Forensic analysis

Notifications

SIEM systems not only assess the aggregated logs in real time, they generate alerts or notifications when an issue is discovered. This allows for continuous monitoring of the environment in a way not possible with other log centralization approaches such as syslog.

Summary

In this chapter you learned the basic concepts, terms, and principles that all network professionals should understand to secure an enterprise network. We covered concepts such as the CIA triad, internal and external threats, and how vulnerabilities can be classified using the CVE database.

You also learned that the defense-in-depth approach to security is the best and that utilizing design techniques such as a screened subnet along with other forms of segmentation makes addressing risks easier.

Finally, you learned about the various types of assessments that can be performed to test security, such as vulnerability assessments, penetration testing, risk assessments, and posture assessments.

Exam Essentials

Explain common security concepts.   These include the CIA triad, least privilege, zero-trust model, defense in depth, and separation of duties.

Describe key security terms.   Among these are *vulnerabilities*, *exploits*, and *threats*.

Know how to utilize segmentation.   You should know how to properly deploy screened subnets, VLANs, and broadcast domains as layer 1, 2, and 3 segmentations.

Identify common authentication methods.   These include multifactor, Terminal Access Controller Access-Control System Plus (TACACS+), single sign-on (SSO), Remote Authentication Dial-In User Service (RADIUS), LDAP, Kerberos, local authentication, 802.1X, and Extensible Authentication Protocol (EAP).

Differentiate assessment types.   These include vulnerability assessments, penetration testing, risk assessments, and posture assessments.

Written Lab

Complete the table by filling in the appropriate term for each authentication method. You can find the answers in Appendix A.

Authentication Method	Term
Utilizes the connection-based TCP protocol.	
When a user logs into the domain, the domain controller issues them an access token.	
The user's local account and password are verified with the local user database.	
Defines a framework for centralized port-based authentication.	
Combines user authentication and authorization into one profile.	

Review Questions

You can find the answers to the review questions in Appendix B.

1. In which of the following access methods are new employees simply placed in the group and thus inherit all required permissions?
   A. Discretionary
   B. Role-based
   C. Mandatory
   D. Rule-based

2. Which principle prescribes that users should be given access only to resources required to do their job?
   A. Least privilege
   B. Need to know
   C. Separation of duties
   D. Zero trust

3. Which of the following occurs when a threat agent takes advantage of a weakness and uses it to advance an attack?
   A. Threat
   B. Breach
   C. Vulnerability
   D. Exploit

4. Which of the following is an attack where no known fix exists?
   A. Advanced persistent
   B. Zero-day
   C. Pretexting
   D. Prime exploit

5. Which of the following is maintained by the MITRE Corporation and includes entries that describe a vulnerability in detail, using a number and letter system?
   A. ISACA
   B. WHOIS
   C. CVE
   D. NIST

6. Which of the following is *not* an external threat?
   A. Accidental file deletion by an employee
   B. DoS attack

C. Fake contractor on site

D. Malware infection by email

7. Which concern do you have when you encrypt data before sending it?

A. Accounting

B. Availability

C. Integrity

D. Confidentiality

8. You have decided that the default permission for all files will be NO access. What principle are you following?

A. Defense in depth

B. Need to know

C. Separation of duties

D. Zero Trust

9. What are you following if you encrypt a file, apply access permissions to it, and lock the door to the room where the server on which the file resides is located?

A. Defense in depth

B. Need to know

C. Separation of duties

D. Zero Trust

10. Which of the following is a method of checking the security health of network hosts before they're allowed to access the network?

A. NAC

B. DAC

C. CVE

D. CVSS

Chapter

17

Common Types
of Attacks

It's true . . . you're not paranoid if they really are out to get you. Although "they" probably aren't after you personally, your network—no matter the size—is seriously vulnerable, so it's wise to be very concerned about keeping it secure. Unfortunately, it's also true that no matter how secure you think your network is, it's a good bet that there are still some very real threats out there that could breach its security and totally cripple your infrastructure!

I'm not trying to scare you; it's just that networks, by their very nature, are not secure environments. Think about it—the whole point of having a network is to make resources available to people who aren't at the same physical location as the network's resources.

Because of this, it follows that you've got to open access to those resources to users you may not be able to identify. One network administrator I know referred to a server running a much-maligned network operating system as "a perfectly secure server until you install the NIC." You can see the dilemma here, right?

Okay, with all this doom and gloom, what's a network administrator to do? Well, the first line of defense is to know about the types of threats out there because you can't do anything to protect yourself from something you don't know about. But once you understand the threats, you can begin to design defenses to combat bad guys lurking in the depths of cyberspace just waiting for an opportunity to strike.

I'm going to introduce you to some of the more common security threats and teach you about the ways to mitigate them. I'll be honest—the information I'll be giving you in this chapter is definitely not exhaustive. Securing computers and networks is a huge task and there are literally hundreds of books on this subject alone. To operate securely in a network environment, one must understand how to speak the language of security. As in any field there is specific terminology.

In this chapter you will learn the common types of attacks that all network professionals should understand to secure an enterprise network.

To find Todd Lammle CompTIA videos and practice questions, please see www.lammle.com.

Technology-Based Attacks

Technology-based attacks are those that take advantage of weaknesses in software and the protocols that systems use to communicate with one another. This is in contrast to attacks that target environmental or human weaknesses (covered later in this chapter). In the following sections, you'll learn about attacks that target technologies.

Denial of Service (DoS)/Distributed Denial of Service (DDoS)

A denial of service (DoS) attack does exactly what it sounds like it would do—it prevents users from accessing the network and/or its resources. Today, DoS attacks are commonly launched against a major company's intranet and especially its websites. "Joe the Hacker" (formerly a plumber) thinks that if he can make a mess of, say, Microsoft's or Amazon's website, he's done that company some serious damage. And you know what?

He's right!

Even though DoS attacks are nasty, strangely, hackers don't respect other hackers who execute them because they're really easy to deploy. It's true—even a pesky little 10-year-old can execute one and bring you to your knees. (That's just wrong!) This means that "real" bad guys have no respect for someone who uses DoS attacks, and they usually employ much more sophisticated methods of wreaking havoc on you instead. I guess it comes down to that "honor among thieves" thing. Still, know that even though a DoS-type attack won't gain the guilty party any esteemed status among "real" hackers, it's still not exactly a day at the beach to deal with.

Worse, DoS attacks come in a variety of flavors. Let's talk about some of them now.

The Ping of Death

Ping is primarily used to see whether a computer is responding to IP requests. Usually, when you ping a remote host, what you're really doing is sending four normal-sized Internet Control Message Protocol (ICMP) packets to the remote host to see if it's available. But during a Ping of Death attack, a humongous ICMP packet is sent to the remote host victim, totally flooding the victim's buffer and causing the system to reboot or helplessly hang there, drowning. It's good to know that patches are available for most operating systems to prevent a Ping of Death attack from working.

Distributed DoS (DDoS)

Denial of service attacks can be made more effective if they can be amplified by recruiting helpers in the attack process. In the following sections, some terms and concepts that apply to a distributed denial of service attack are explained.

Botnet/Command and Control

A botnet is a group of programs connected on the Internet for the purpose of performing a task in a coordinated manner. Some botnets, such as those created to maintain control of Internet Relay Chat (IRC) channels, are legal, while others are illegally created to foist a DDoS. An attacker can recruit and build a botnet to help amplify a DoS attack, as illustrated in Figure 17.1.

FIGURE 17.1 Botnet

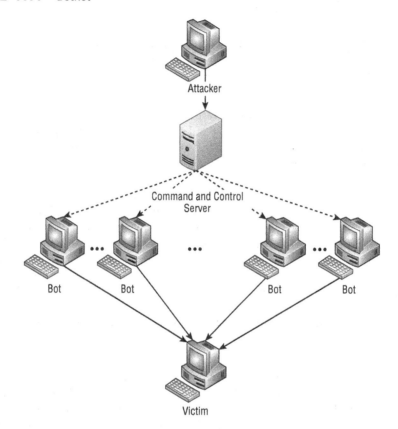

The steps in the process of building a botnet are as follows:

1. A botnet operator sends out viruses or worms whose payloads are malicious applications, the bots, infecting ordinary users' computers.

2. The bots on the infected PCs log into a server called a command and control (C&C) server under the control of the attacker.

3. At the appropriate time, the attacker, through the C&C server, sends a command to all bots to attack the victim at the same time, thereby significantly amplifying the effect of the attack.

Traffic Spike

One of the hallmarks of a DDoS attack is a major spike in traffic in the network as bots that have been recruited mount the attack. For this reason, any major spike in traffic should be regarded with suspicion. A network intrusion detection system (IDS) can recognize these traffic spikes and may be able to prevent them from growing larger or in some cases prevent the traffic in the first place.

Some smaller organizations that cannot afford some of the pricier intrusion prevention systems (IPSs) or IDSs make use of features present on their load balancers. Many of these products include DDoS mitigation features such as the TCP SYN cookie option. This allows the load balancer to react when the number of SYN requests reaches a certain point. At that point, the device will start dropping requests when the SYN queue is full.

Coordinated Attack

Another unmistakable feature of a DDoS attack is the presence of a coordinated attack. As shown in Figure 17.1 and as just described in the section "Botnet/Command and Control," to properly amplify the attack, the bots must attack the victim at the same time. The coordination of the bots is orchestrated by the command and control server depicted in Figure 17.1. If all the bots can be instructed to attack at precisely the same second, the attack becomes much more dangerous to the victim.

Friendly/Unintentional DoS

An unintentional DoS attack (also referred to as attack from "friendly fire") is not one that is not caused by malicious individuals; instead, it's a spike in activity to a website or resource that overpowers its ability to respond. In many cases, it is the result of a relatively unknown URL suddenly being shared in a larger medium such as a popular TV or news show. For example, when Michael Jackson died, the amount of Twitter and Google traffic spiked so much that at first it was thought that an automated attack was under way.

Physical Attack

Physical attacks are those that cause hardware damage to a device. These attacks can be mitigated, but not eliminated, by preventing physical access to the device. Routers, switches, firewalls, servers, and other infrastructure devices should be locked away and protected by strong access controls. Otherwise, you may be confronted with a permanent DoS, which is discussed next.

Permanent DoS

A permanent DoS attack is one in which the device is damaged and must be replaced. It requires physical access to the device, or does it? Actually, it doesn't! An attack called a phlashing denial of service (PDoS) attacks the firmware located in many systems. Using tools that fuzz (introduce errors) the firmware, attackers cause the device to be unusable.

Another approach is to introduce a firmware image containing a Trojan or other types of malware.

Smurf

Smurfs are happy little blue creatures that like to sing and dance, but a Smurf attack is far more nefarious. It's a version of a DoS attack that floods its victim with spoofed broadcast ping messages. I'll talk about spoofing in more detail later; for now, understand that it basically involves stealing someone else's IP address.

Here's how it works: The bad guy spoofs the intended victim's IP address and then sends a large number of pings (IP echo requests) to IP broadcast addresses. The receiving router responds by delivering the broadcast to all hosts in the subnet, and all the hosts respond with an IP echo reply—all of them at the same time. On a network with hundreds of hosts, this results in major network gridlock because all the machines are kept busy responding to each echo request. The situation is even worse if the routers have not been configured to keep these types of broadcasts confined to the local subnet (which thankfully they are by default!). Figure 17.2 shows a Smurf attack in progress.

FIGURE 17.2   Smurf attack

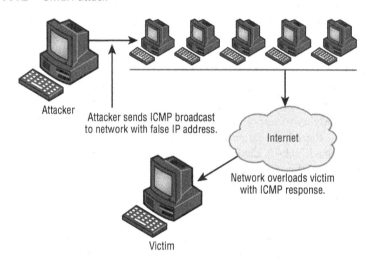

Fortunately, Smurf attacks aren't very common anymore because most routers are configured in a way that prevents them from forwarding broadcast packets to other networks. Plus, it's really easy to configure routers and hosts so they won't respond to ping requests directed toward broadcast addresses.

SYN Flood

A SYN flood is also a DoS attack that inundates the receiving machine with lots of packets that cause the victim to waste resources by holding connections open. In normal communications, a workstation that wants to open a Transmission Control Protocol/Internet Protocol (TCP/IP) communication with a server sends a TCP/IP packet with the SYN flag set to 1. The server automatically responds to the request, indicating that it's ready to start communicating with a SYN-ACK. In the SYN flood, the attacker sends a SYN, the victim sends back a SYN-ACK, and the attacker leaves the victim waiting for the final ACK. While the server is waiting for the response, a small part of memory is reserved for it. As the SYNs continue to arrive, memory is gradually consumed.

Figure 17.3 shows an example of a simple DoS/SYN flood attack.

FIGURE 17.3   SYN flood

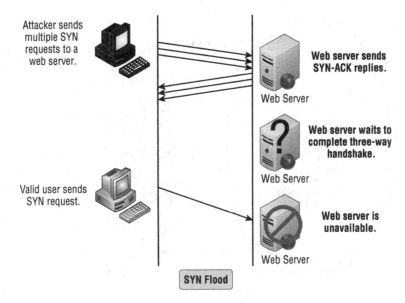

You can see that the preyed-upon machine can't respond to any other requests because its buffers are already overloaded, and it therefore rejects all packets requesting connections, even valid ones, which is the idea behind the attack. The good news is that patches to help guard against this type of attack are available for the various network operating systems today.

Reflected/Amplified Attacks

Reflected or amplified attacks increase the effectiveness of a DoS attack. Two of the more effective of these types of attacks involve leveraging two functions that almost all networks use, DNS and NTP. In the next two sections these attacks are described.

DNS

A DNS amplification attack is a form of reflection attack in that the attacker delivers traffic to the victim by reflecting it off a third party. Reflection conceals the source of the attack. It relies on the exploitation of publicly accessible open DNS servers to deluge victims with DNS response traffic.

The attacker sends a small DNS message using the victim's IP address as the source to an open resolver. The type of request used returns all known information about the DNS zone, which allows for the maximum level of response amplification directed to the victim's server. The attack is magnified by recruiting a botnet to send the small messages to a large list of open resolvers (DNS servers). The response from the DNS server overwhelms the victim, as shown in Figure 17.4.

FIGURE 17.4 DNS amplification attack

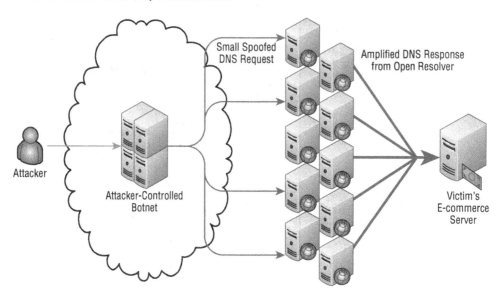

NTP

While NTP refection attacks use the same process of recruiting bots to aid the attack, the attacks are not reflected off DNS servers; they are instead reflected off Network Time Protocol (NTP) servers. These servers are used to maintain time synchronization between devices in a network.

The attacker (and his bots) sends a small spoofed 8-byte UDP packet to vulnerable NTP servers that requests a large amount of data (megabytes worth of traffic) to be sent to the DDoS's target IP address. The attackers use the `monlist` command, a remote command in older versions of NTP, that sends the requester a list of the last 600 hosts who have connected to that server. This attack can be prevented by using at least the NTP version 4.2.7 (which was released in 2010).

On-Path Attack (Previously Known as Man-in-the-Middle Attack)

Interception! But it's not a football, it's a bunch of your network's packets—your precious data. An on-path attack (previously known as a man-in-the-middle attack) happens when someone intercepts packets intended for one computer and reads the data. A common guilty party could be someone working for your very own ISP using a packet sniffer and augmenting it with routing and transport protocols. Rogue ATM machines and even credit-card swipers are tools that are also increasingly used for this type of attack. Figure 17.5 shows an on-path/man-in-the-middle attack.

FIGURE 17.5   On-path attack

Client   Man in the Middle   Server

DNS Poisoning

DNS clients send requests for name to IP address resolution (called queries) to a DNS server. The search for the IP address that goes with a computer or domain name usually starts with a local DNS server that is not authoritative for the DNS domain in which the requested computer or website resides. When this occurs, the local DNS server makes a request of the DNS server that does hold the record in question. After the local DNS server receives the answer, it returns it to the local DNS client. After this, the local DNS server maintains that record in its DNS cache for a period called the time to live (TTL), which is usually an hour but can vary.

In a DNS cache poisoning attack, the attacker attempts to refresh or update that record when it expires with a different address than the correct address. If the attacker can convince the DNS server to accept this refresh, the local DNS server will then be responding to client requests for that computer with the address inserted by the attacker. Typically, the address they now receive is for a fake website that appears to look in every way like the site the client is requesting. The hacker can then harvest all the name and password combinations entered on his fake site.

To prevent this type of attack, the DNS servers should be limited in the updates they accept. In most DNS software, you can restrict the DNS servers from which a server will accept updates. This can help prevent the server from accepting these false updates.

VLAN Hopping

VLANs, or virtual LANs, are layer 2 subdivisions of the ports in a single switch. A VLAN may also span multiple switches. When devices are segregated into VLANs, access control lists (ACLs) can be used in a router to control access between VLANs in the same way it is done between real LANs. When VLANs span switches, the connection between the switches is called a trunk link, and it carries the traffic of multiple VLANs. Trunk links are also used for the connection from the switch to the router.

A VLAN hopping attack results in traffic from one VLAN being sent to the wrong VLAN. Normally, this is prevented by the trunking protocol placing a VLAN tag in the packet to identify the VLAN to which the traffic belongs. The attacker can circumvent this by a process called double tagging, which is placing a fake VLAN tag into the packet along with the real tag. When the frame goes through multiple switches, the real tag is taken off by the first switch, leaving the fake tag. When the frame reaches the second switch, the fake tag is read and the frame is sent to the VLAN to which the hacker intended the frame to go.

This process is shown in Figure 17.6.

FIGURE 17.6 VLAN hopping

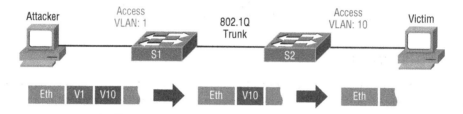

ARP Spoofing

ARP spoofing is the process of adopting another system's MAC address for the purpose of receiving data meant for that system. It usually also entails ARP cache poisoning. ARP cache poisoning is usually a part of an on-path/man-in-the middle attack. The ARP cache contains IP address–to–MAC address mappings that a device has learned through the ARP process. One of the ways this cache can be poisoned is by pinging a device with a spoofed IP address. In this way, an attacker can force the victim to insert an incorrect IP address–to–MAC address mapping into its ARP cache. If the attacker can accomplish this with two computers having a conversation, they can effectively be placed in the middle of the transmission. After the ARP cache is poisoned on both machines, they will be sending data packets to the attacker, all the while thinking they are sending them to the other member of the conversation.

Rogue DHCP

Dynamic Host Configuration Protocol (DHCP) is used to automate the process of assigning IP configurations to hosts. When configured properly, it reduces administrative overload, reduces the human error inherent in manual assignment, and enhances device mobility. But it introduces a vulnerability that when leveraged by a malicious individual can result in an inability of hosts to communicate (constituting a DoS attack) and peer-to-peer attacks.

When an illegitimate DHCP server (called a rogue DHCP server) is introduced to the network, unsuspecting hosts may accept DHCP Offer packets from the illegitimate DHCP server rather than the legitimate DHCP server. When this occurs, the rogue DHCP server will not only issue the host an incorrect IP address, subnet mask, and default gateway address (which makes a peer-to-peer attack possible), it can also issue an incorrect DNS server address, which will lead to the host relying on the attacker's DNS server for the IP addresses of websites (such as those resembling major banks' websites) that lead to phishing attacks. An example of how this can occur is shown in Figure 17.7.

FIGURE 17.7   Rogue DHCP

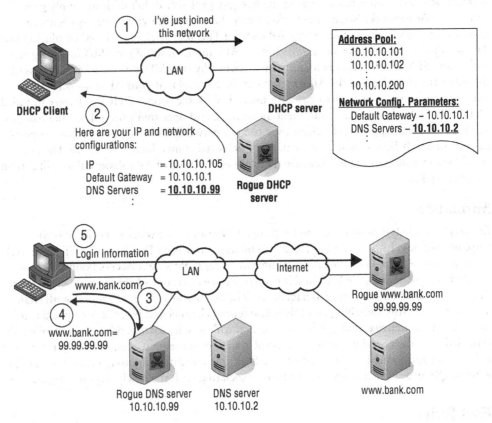

In Figure 17.7, after receiving an incorrect IP address, subnet mask, default gateway, and DNS server address from the rogue DHCP server, the DHCP client uses the attacker's DNS server to obtain the IP address of his bank. This leads the client to unwittingly connect to the attacker's copy of the bank's website. When the client enters his credentials to log in, the attacker now has the client's bank credentials and can proceed to empty out his account.

Rogue Access Point (AP)

These are APs that have been connected to your wired infrastructure without your knowledge. The rogue AP may have been placed there by a determined hacker who snuck into your facility and put it in an out-of-the-way location or, more innocently, by an employee who just wants wireless access and doesn't get just how dangerous doing this is. Either way, it's just like placing an open Ethernet port out in the parking lot with a sign that says "Corporate LAN access here—no password required!"

Clearly, the worst type of rogue AP is the one some hacker has cleverly slipped into your network. It's particularly nasty because the bad guy probably didn't do it to simply gain access to your network. Nope—the hacker likely did it to entice your wireless clients to disastrously associate with their rogue AP instead! This ugly trick is achieved by placing their AP on a different channel from your legitimate APs and then setting its SSID in accordance with your SSID. Wireless clients identify the network by the SSID, not the MAC address of the AP or the IP address of the AP, so jamming the channel that your AP is on will cause your stations to roam to the bad guy's AP instead. With the proper DHCP software installed on the AP, the hacker can issue the client an address, and once that's been done, the bad guy has basically "kidnapped" your client over to their network and can freely perform a peer-to-peer attack. Believe it or not, this can all be achieved from a laptop while Mr. Hacker simply sits in your parking lot, because there are many types of AP software that will run on a laptop—yikes!

Mitigation

But you're not helpless—one way to keep rogue APs out of the wireless network is to employ a wireless LAN controller (WLC) to manage your APs. This is a nice mitigation technique because APs and controllers communicate using Lightweight Access Point Protocol (LWAPP) or the newer CAPWAP, and it just so happens that one of the message types they share is called Radio Resource Management (RRM). Basically, your APs monitor all channels by momentarily switching from their configured channel and by collecting packets to check for rogue activity. If an AP is detected that isn't usually managed by the controller, it's classified as a rogue, and if a wireless control system is in use, that rogue can be plotted on a floor plan and located. Another great benefit of this mitigation approach is that it enables your APs to also prevent workstations from associating with the newly exposed rogue.

Evil Twin

An evil twin is an AP that is not under your control but is used to perform a hijacking attack. A hijacking attack is one in which the hacker connects one or more of your users' computers to their network for the purpose of a peer-to-peer attack.

The attack begins with the introduction of an access point that is under the hacker's control. This access point will be set to use the same network name or SSID your network uses, and it will be set to require no authentication (creating what is called an open network).

Moreover, this access point will be set to use a different channel than the access point under your control.

To understand how the attack works, you must understand how wireless stations (laptops, tablets, and so on) choose an access point with which to connect. It is done by SSID and not by channel. The hacker will "jam" the channel on which your access point is transmitting. When a station gets disconnected from an access point, it scans the area for another access point with the same SSID. The stations will find the hacker's access point and will connect to it.

Once the station is connected to the hacker's access point, it will receive an IP address from a DHCP server running on the access point and the user will now be located on the same network as the hacker. At this point, the hacker is free to commence a peer-to-peer attack.

Ransomware

Ransomware is a class of malware that prevents or limits users from accessing their information or systems. In many cases the data is encrypted and the decryption key is only made available to the user when the ransom has been paid.

Password Attacks

Password attacks are one of the most common attacks there are. Cracked or disclosed passwords can lead to severe data breaches. The end game of a phishing attack is often to learn a password. In the following sections, you'll learn about the two major approaches to cracking a password.

Brute-Force

A brute-force attack is a form of password cracking. The attacker attempts every possible combination of numbers and letters that could be in a password. Theoretically, given enough time and processing power, any password can be cracked. When long, complex passwords are used, however, it can take years.

Setting an account lockout policy is the simplest mitigation technique to defeat brute-force attacks. With such a policy applied, the account becomes locked after a set number of failed attempts.

Dictionary

Similar to a brute-force attack, a dictionary attack uses all the words in a dictionary until a key is discovered that successfully decrypts the ciphertext. This attack requires considerable time and processing power and is very difficult to complete. It also requires a comprehensive dictionary of words.

An automated program uses the hash of the dictionary word and compares this hash value to entries in the system password file. Although the program comes with a dictionary, attackers also use extra dictionaries that are found on the Internet.

To protect against these attacks, you should implement a security rule that says that a password must *not* be a word found in the dictionary. You can also implement an account lockout policy so that an account is locked out after a certain number of invalid login attempts.

MAC Spoofing

MAC spoofing is the assumption of another system's MAC address for the following purposes:

- To pass through a MAC address filter
- To receive data intended for another system
- To impersonate a gateway (router interface) for the purpose of receiving all data leaving a subnet.

MAC spoofing is the reason we don't rely solely on security at layer 2 (MAC address filters), while best practices call for basing access on user accounts rather than device properties such as IP addresses or MAC addresses.

IP Spoofing

IP spoofing is the process of changing a source IP address so that one computer appears to be a different computer. It's usually done to get traffic through a firewall that would normally not be allowed. It may also be used to access a server to which the hacker would normally be disallowed access by their IP address.

Deauthentication

A wireless deauthentication attack is a form of a DoS attack in which the attacker sends a large number of management packets called deauthentication frames on the WLAN, causing stations to be disconnected from the access point.

Malware

Malicious software (or *malware*) is a term that describes any software that harms a computer, deletes data, or takes actions the user did not authorize. There is a wide array of malware types, including ones you have probably heard of, like viruses. Some types of malware require the assistance of a user to spread, while others do not.

A worm is a type of malware that can spread without the assistance of the user. A worm is a small program that, like a virus, is used to deliver a payload. One way to help mitigate the effects of worms is to place limits on sharing, writing, and executing programs.

However, the real solution is to deploy antivirus and antimalware software to all devices in the network. This software is designed to identify viruses, Trojans, and worms and delete them, or at least quarantine them until they can be removed.

Viruses

Viruses with catchy names like Chernobyl, Michelangelo, Melissa, I Love You, and Love Bug are probably the best-known threats to your computer's security because they get a lot of media coverage as they proliferate and cause tons of damage to legions of people. In their simplest form, viruses are basically little programs that cause a variety of very bad things to happen on your computer, ranging from merely annoying to totally devastating. They can display a message, delete files, or even send huge amounts of meaningless data over a network to block legitimate messages. A key trait of viruses is that they can't replicate themselves to other computers or systems without a user doing something like opening an executable attachment in an email to propagate them. Figure 17.8 shows how fast a virus can spread through an email system.

FIGURE 17.8   An email virus spreading rapidly

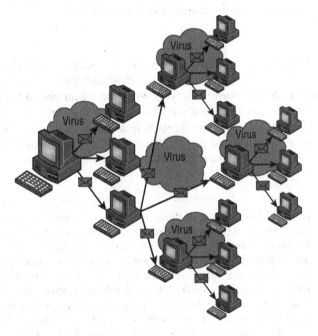

There are several different kinds of viruses, but the most popular ones are file viruses, macro (data file) viruses, and boot-sector viruses. Each type differs slightly in the way it works and how it infects your system. Predictably, many viruses attack popular applications like Microsoft Word, Excel, and PowerPoint because those programs are easy to use so it's easy to create a virus for them. Unlike with DoS attacks, writing a unique virus is considered a programming challenge, so the scoundrel who's able to come up with it not only gains respect from the hacking community but also gets to bask in the glow of the media frenzy that results from their creation and relish their 15 minutes of fame. This is also a big reason why viruses are becoming more and more complex and harder to eliminate.

Logic Bomb

A logic bomb is a type of malware that executes when a particular event takes place. For example, that event could be a time of day or a specific date or it could be the first time you open notepad.exe. Some logic bombs execute when forensics are being undertaken, and in that case the bomb might delete all digital evidence.

Ransomware

Ransomware is a class of malware that prevents or limits users from accessing their information or systems. In many cases the data is encrypted and the decryption key is only made available to the user when the ransom has been paid.

File Viruses

A file virus attacks executable application and system program files like those with filenames ending in .com, .exe, and .dll. These viruses do their damage by replacing some or all of the target program's code with their own. Only when the compromised file is executed can the virus do its dirty work. First, it loads itself into memory and waits to infect other executables, propagating its destructive effects throughout a system or network. A couple of well-known file viruses are Jerusalem and Nimda, the latter of which is actually an Internet worm that infects common Windows files and other files with filename extensions like .html, .htm, and .asp.

> Don't fall into the trap of thinking that just because you have a Mac, you don't need to worry about viruses. It's a common misconception that Mac operating systems are immune to viruses, but they're not. Today's Macs are really BSD Unix machines with a couple of proprietary programs running on top that provide users with a slick interface. And although it's true that more sophisticated programming skills are required to write viruses for Mac, BSD Unix, and Linux operating systems than for DOS-based operating systems like Windows, all operating systems are vulnerable to attacks. True, it's a lot easier for a bad guy to write malicious code for Windows machines, but the real reason few programmers spend their time creating viruses for Sun workstations and Macs is that there aren't nearly as many people using them. On the other hand, Windows machines are everywhere, so viruses written for them will clearly infect multitudes, giving bad guys who want to infect as many computers as possible a lot more bang for their evil programming buck!

Macro Viruses

A macro is basically a script of commonly enacted commands used to automatically carry out tasks without requiring a user to initiate them. Some popular programs even give you the option of creating your own, personal scripts to perform tasks you do repeatedly in a single step instead of having to enter the individual commands one by one.

Similar to this, a macro virus uses something known as the Visual Basic macro-scripting language to perform nasty things in data files created with programs like those in the Microsoft Office Suite. Because macros are so easy to write, they're really common and usually fairly harmless, but they can be super annoying! People frequently find them infecting the files they're working on in Microsoft Word and PowerPoint. Suddenly you can't save the file even though the Save function is working, or you can't open a new document, only a template. As I said, these viruses won't crash your system, but they can ruin your day. Cap and Cap A are examples of macro viruses.

Boot-Sector Viruses

Boot-sector viruses work their way into the master boot record that's essentially the ground-zero sector on your hard disk where applications aren't supposed to live. When a computer boots up, it checks this area to find a pointer for its operating system. Boot-sector viruses overwrite your boot sector, making it appear as if there's no pointer to your operating system. You know you've got this type of virus when you power up the computer and get a Missing Operating System or Hard Disk Not Found error message. Monkey B, Michelangelo, Stoned, and Stealth Boot are a few examples of boot-sector viruses.

Multipartite Viruses

A multipartite virus is one that affects both the boot sector and files on your computer, making such a virus particularly dangerous and exasperatingly difficult to remove. Figure 17.9 gives you an idea of how a multipartite virus works. You can see that it is attacking the boot sector, memory, and the disk at once.

FIGURE 17.9   Botnet

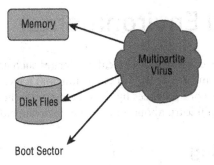

Anthrax and Tequila are both multipartite viruses. These viruses are so nasty that you might end up reformatting your computer if you get one. The Anthrax virus, however, was more of a hoax then a real virus; what is really interesting about the Tequila virus is that it does nothing until the next reboot—it was no hoax!

Although many software companies can handle these, the best way to save your computer from a complete overhaul is to make sure you do not get a virus in the first place by using a good virus scan program as well as Windows Defender.

 Some viruses infect your system through something known as a Trojan horse. Troy was successfully invaded by troops hidden inside a giant horse; a Trojan virus hides within other programs and is launched when the program it's lurking in starts up.

Often viruses come as attachments to emails with double filename extensions to hide the true extension. A virus called `love-letter-for-you .txt.vbs` is an example. Displaying filename extensions for known file types can help spot naming tricks like these, but they make up only a short list of the viruses out there. For a more complete inventory, see your antivirus software manufacturer's website.

Zero-Day Attacks

Antivirus software uses definition files that identify known malware. These files must be updated frequently, but the update process can usually be automated so that it requires no help from the user. If a new virus is created that has not yet been identified in the list, you will not be protected until the virus definition is added and the new definition file is downloaded.

This condition is known as a zero-day attack because it is the first day the virus has been released and therefore no known fix exists. This term may also be applied to an operating system bug that has not been corrected.

Human and Environmental

While some vulnerabilities come from technical challenges such as attacks on cryptography and network protocols, many are a result of environmental issues within the facility or of human error and poor network practices by the users (we call these self-inflicted wounds). In the following sections, you'll learn about human and environmental vulnerabilities.

Social Engineering

Hackers are more sophisticated today than they were 10 years ago, but then again, so are network administrators. Because most of today's sys admins have secured their networks well enough to make it pretty tough for an outsider to gain access, hackers decided to try an easier route to gain information: they just asked the network's users for it.

Social engineering attacks occur when attackers use believable language and user gullibility to obtain user credentials or some other confidential information. The best countermeasure against social engineering threats is to provide user security awareness training. This training should be required and must occur on a regular basis because social engineering techniques evolve constantly.

Phishing

Phishing is a social engineering attack in which attackers try to learn personal information, including credit card information and financial data. This type of attack is usually carried out by implementing a fake website that is nearly identical to a legitimate website. Users are led there by fake emails that appear to come from a trusted source. Users enter data, including credentials, on the fake website, allowing the attackers to capture any information entered. Spear phishing is a phishing attack carried out against a specific target by learning about the target's habits and likes. The best defense is security awareness training for the users.

Environmental

Some attacks become possible because of the security environment we have allowed to develop. The following are issues that are created by user behavior.

Tailgating

Tailgating is the term used for someone being so close to you when you enter a building that they are able to come in right behind you without needing to use a key, a card, or any other security device. Many social-engineering intruders who need physical access to a site will use this method of gaining entry. Educate users to beware of this and other social-engineering ploys and prevent them from happening.

 Access control vestibules (mantraps) are a great way to stop tailgating. An access control vestibule (mantrap) is a series of two doors with a small room between them that helps prevent unauthorized people from entering a building.

Piggybacking

Piggybacking and tailgating are similar but not the same. Piggybacking is done with the authorization of the person with access. Tailgating is done when the attacker sneaks inside without the person with access knowing. This is why access control vestibules (mantraps) and turnstiles deter tailgating and live guards and security training deter piggybacking.

Shoulder Surfing

Shoulder surfing involves nothing more than watching someone when they enter their sensitive data. They can see you entering a password, typing in a credit card number, or entering any other pertinent information. The best defense against this type of attack is simply to survey your environment before entering personal data. Privacy filters can be used that make the screen difficult to read unless you are directly in front of it.

Summary

In this chapter you learned about common attack types that one might expect on an enterprise network. These attack types can be categorized into technology-based attacks and those that are the result of human failure or of the network environment that exists.

Technology-based attacks include denial of service (DoS)/distributed denial of service (DDoS) attacks, on-path attacks, DNS poisoning, VLAN hopping, ARP spoofing, rogue DHCP and rogue access point (AP) attacks, evil twin attacks, ransomware, and password attacks.

Human and environmental attacks include social engineering, phishing, tailgating, piggybacking, and shoulder surfing.

Exam Essentials

Explain common technology-based attacks. These include denial of service (DoS)/distributed denial of service (DDoS) attacks, on-path attacks, DNS poisoning, VLAN hopping, ARP spoofing, rogue DHCP and rogue access point (AP) attacks, evil twin attacks, ransomware, and password attacks.

Describe (DoS)/distributed denial-of-service (DDoS) attacks. This includes the architecture and behavior of a botnet and of the role of the command and control server.

Identify human and environmental attacks. These include social engineering, phishing, tailgating, piggybacking, and shoulder surfing.

Written Lab

Complete the table by filling in the appropriate countermeasure for each attack method. You can find the answers in Appendix A.

Attack	Countermeasure
Shoulder surfing	
Piggybacking	
Tailgating	
Phishing	
Brute-force attack	

Review Questions

You can find the answers to the review questions in Appendix B.

1. Which of the following is *not* a technology-based attack?
   A. DoS
   B. Ping of death
   C. Shoulder surfing
   D. Malware

2. A command and control server is a part of which of the following attacks?
   A. DDoS
   B. Ping of death
   C. Shoulder surfing
   D. Malware

3. Which of the following is a DoS attack that floods its victim with spoofed broadcast ping messages?
   A. SYN flood
   B. Smurf
   C. Land attack
   D. Ping of death

4. Which of the following is an attack that inundates the receiving machine with lots of packets that cause the victim to waste resources by holding connections open?
   A. Ping of death
   B. Zero day
   C. Smurf
   D. SYN flood

5. In which of the following does the attacker (and his bots) send a small spoofed 8-byte UDP packet to vulnerable NTP servers that requests a large amount of data (megabytes worth of traffic) be sent to the DDoS's target IP address?
   A. SYN flood
   B. NTP amplification
   C. Smurf
   D. DNS amplification

6. Which of the following was previously known as a man-in-the-middle attack?
   A. VLAN hopping
   B. On-path attack
   C. LAND attack
   D. Smurf

7. Double tagging is a part of which of the following attacks?
   A. VLAN hopping
   B. Smurf
   C. DDoS
   D. Malware

8. Which of the following is the process of adopting another system's MAC address for the purpose of receiving data meant for that system?
   A. Certificate spoofing
   B. ARP spoofing
   C. IP spoofing
   D. URL spoofing

9. Which of the following is connected to your wired infrastructure without your knowledge?
   A. Rogue AP
   B. Command and control server
   C. Zombies
   D. Botnet

10. Which of the following uses the same SSID as your AP?
    A. Rogue AP
    B. Rogue DHCP
    C. Evil twin
    D. Zombie

Chapter

18

Network Hardening Techniques

THE FOLLOWING COMPTIA NETWORK+ EXAM OBJECTIVES ARE COVERED IN THIS CHAPTER:

✓ **4.3 Given a scenario, apply network hardening techniques.**

- Best practices
    - Secure SNMP
    - Router Advertisement (RA) Guard
    - Port security
    - Dynamic ARP inspection
    - Control plane policing
    - Private VLANs
    - Disable unneeded switchports
    - Disable unneeded network services
    - Change default passwords
    - Password complexity/length
    - Enable DHCP snooping
    - Change default VLAN
    - Patch and firmware management
    - Access control list
    - Role-based access
- Firewall rules
    - Explicit deny
    - Implicit deny
- Wireless security
    - MAC filtering
    - Antenna placement

- Power levels
- Wireless client isolation
- Guest network isolation
- Preshared keys (PSKs)
- EAP
- Geofencing
- Captive portal
- IoT access considerations

It's true . . . you're not paranoid if you think they really are out to get you. Although "they" probably aren't after you personally. Your network—no matter the size—is seriously vulnerable, so it's wise to be very concerned about keeping it secure. Unfortunately, it's also true that no matter how secure you think your network is, it's a good bet that there are still some very real threats out there that could breach its security and totally cripple your infrastructure!

One of the ongoing goals of operations security is to ensure that all systems have been hardened to the extent that is possible and still provide functionality. The hardening can be accomplished both on a physical and logical basis. From a logical perspective, this is accomplished if you do this:

- Remove unnecessary applications.
- Disable unnecessary services.
- Block or disable unrequired ports.
- Tightly control the connecting of external storage devices and media if it's allowed at all.

In this chapter, you'll learn best practices for hardening devices and for hardening the network environment in which these devices reside. At the end of the chapter, you'll learn about the newest challenge to secure, the Internet of Things (IoT).

To find Todd Lammle CompTIA videos and practice questions, please see www.lammle.com.

Best Practices

While hardening devices may present a challenge, you are not alone in your efforts to meet that challenge. Over time, best practices have been developed by those that came before you in this battle. These are lessons that have been learned the hard way and are certainly concepts and principles that you can utilize to ensure you don't make the same mistakes that led to these hard-earned lessons. In the following sections, you'll learn some of the more common best practices for hardening devices and the network environment.

Secure SNMP

In Chapter 13, "Using Statistics and Sensors to Ensure Network Availability," you learned that SNMP has three versions. SNMPv3 supports strong authentication with confidentiality (encryption) and data integrity of messages via encryption between agents and managers. For this reason, you should always ensure that the version you are using is version 3.

Version 3 offers two methods of securing SNMP. The Transport Security Model (TSM) component of SNMPv3 enables security to be applied at the Transport layer. Protocols used by the Transport Security Model, such as TLS, are based on asymmetric cryptography.

RFC 3414 describes a user-based security model (USM) that provides message-based security and uses symmetric encryption along with usernames and passwords.

Router Advertisement (RA) Guard

In Chapter 10, "Routing Protocols," you learned about how routers running IPv6 use a Router Advertisement in neighbor discovery and solicitation. Capturing these packet types could reveal information about the routers and their neighbors. These packet types can also be spoofed as well. IPv6 Router Advertisement (RA) Guard is not yet a standard but a proposal on a method of allowing the network administrator to block or reject unwanted or rogue RA Guard messages that arrive at the network device platform.

RA Guard compares configuration information on the switch with the information found in the received RA frame. Once the switch has validated the content of the RA frame, it forwards the RA to its unicast or multicast destination. If the RA frame content is not validated, the RA is dropped. As you see in Figure 18.1, the switch only validates RA packets from the two configured IPv6 addresses.

FIGURE 18.1   RA Guard

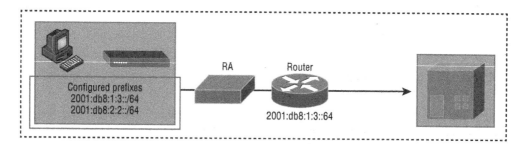

Port Security

In Chapter 11, "Switching and Virtual LANs," you learned about the use of port security on a switch. This can be used as a device hardening technique in instances where you would like to provide layer 2 separation between devices connected to the same switch or residing in the same VLAN (in the case of VLANs spanning multiple switches).

This is also a network hardening technique in that it can help prevent a hacker from disconnecting a device from the wall and using that port for access. While your unused ports should always be disabled, legitimate ports are always at danger of misuse this way. By limiting network access on a port to a single MAC address (or in the case of an IP phone, two), access by any other MAC address can be prevented.

Finally, it can be used to prevent the connections of a hub to a switch port by limiting the number of MAC addresses that can transmit on a port to one or two addresses.

Dynamic ARP Inspection

Many on-path/man-in-the-middle attacks are made possible by the attacker polluting the ARP cache of the two victims such that their cache maps each other's IP addresses to the MAC address of the attacker, thus allowing the attacker to receive all traffic in the conversation.

Dynamic ARP inspection (DAI) is a feature that, when configured, uses the DHCP snooping database of IP address–to–MAC address mappings to verify the MAC address mappings of each frame going through the switch. In this way, any frames with incorrect or altered mappings are dropped by the switch, thus breaking any attacks depending on these bogus mappings. Because it uses the DHCP snooping database, the configuration of DHCP snooping is a prerequisite to enabling DAI.

Control Plane Policing

In a network, three planes typically form the networking architecture:

- **Control plane:** This plane carries signaling traffic originating from or destined for a router. This is the information that allows routers to share information and build routing tables.
- **Data plane:** Also known as the forwarding plane, this plane carries user traffic.
- **Management plane:** This plane administers the router.

Control plane policing is a feature that can be implemented to protect and secure packets on the control plane. It is a quality of service (QoS) policy that is applied by the router's control plane. By rate limiting the control packets that can arrive to the router processor, it can prevent denial of service (DoS) attacks.

Private VLANs

In Chapter 11 you learned about VLANs. You saw that devices that reside in different VLANs reside in different layer 3 networks as well. Private VLANs are a type you can implement on a switch to segregate devices that reside in the same layer 3 network.

When this is done, the private VLAN (called secondary) is simply a subsection of the main VLAN (called primary). The secondary VLAN can be of two types, community (which can contain multiple devices that can talk to one another) or an isolated VLAN (in which a single device can only talk to the switch). The second VLAN type is excellent for isolating a device from other devices.

Disable Unneeded Switchports

All unused ports on the switch should be disabled to prevent the connection of a rogue device into an unused wall outlet. Each switchport to which unused wall outlets are connected should be identified and disabled.

Disable Unneeded Network Services

Destination services and applications are specified in a packet in terms of a port number. When a device is open to receiving a connection to a service or application, it is said to be listening on the corresponding port. Therefore, closing or disabling a port eliminates the possibility of a malicious user connecting to that port and leveraging any weakness that may be known to be present with that service.

It is a standard device hardening practice to close any ports not required for the proper functioning of a device based on its role in the network. For example, a DNS server should have no other ports open but port 53, which is used to service DNS.

Change Default Passwords

Many network devices are configured with default administrator accounts and their default passwords. These accounts should be disabled and renamed if possible. At the very least, the passwords for these accounts should be changed from the default because they are well-known, available in documentation that comes with the product, and also widely available on the Internet.

Password Complexity/Length

Strong passwords should be at least 8 characters (the more, the merrier), but they shouldn't be any longer than 15 characters to make them easier to remember. You absolutely must specify a minimum length for passwords because a short password is easily cracked— after all, there are only so many combinations of three characters, right? The upper limit depends on the capabilities of your operating system and the ability of your users to remember complex passwords. Here's what I call "The Weak List" for passwords—never use them!

- The word *password* (Not kidding—people actually do this!)
- Proper names
- Your pet's name
- Your spouse's name
- Your children's names
- Any word in the dictionary

- A license plate number
- Birth dates
- Anniversary dates
- Your username
- The word *server*
- Any text or label on the PC or monitor
- Your company's name
- Your occupation
- Your favorite color
- Any of the above with a leading number
- Any of the above with a trailing number
- Any of the above spelled backward

There are more, but you get the idea, and these really are the most commonly used brainless passwords. These settings on a Windows machine are shown in Figure 18.2.

FIGURE 18.2   Password Policy settings

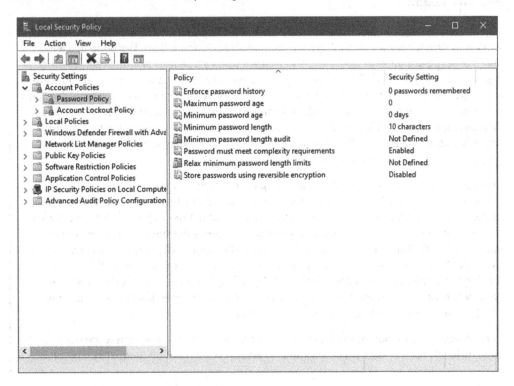

Using Characters to Make a Strong Password

The good news is that solid passwords don't have to be in ancient Mayan to be hard to crack. They just need to include a combination of numbers, letters, and special characters—that's it. Special characters aren't letters or numbers but symbols like $ % ^ # @). Here's an example of a strong password: tqbf4#jotld. Looks like gibberish, but remember that famous sentence, "The quick brown fox jumped over the lazy dog"? Well, this particular password uses the first letter of each word in that sentence with a 4# thrown in the middle of it.

Sweet—solid and easy to remember. You can do this with favorite quotes, song lyrics, and so on, with a couple of numbers and symbols stuck in the middle. Just make sure you don't sing the song or quote Shakespeare every time you log in!

If you want to test the strength of passwords to make sure they're nice and tight, you can use auditing tools like crack programs that try to guess passwords. Clearly, if that program has a really tough time or even fails to crack the password, you have a good one. By the way, don't just use a regular word preceded by or ending with a special character because good crack programs strip off the leading and trailing characters during decryption attempts.

 Real World Scenario

Security Audits

A great way to begin a basic security audit to get a feel for any potential threats to your network is to simply take a walk through the company's halls and offices. I've done this a lot, and it always pays off because invariably I happen upon some new and different way that people are trying to "beat the system" regarding security. This doesn't necessarily indicate that a given user is trying to cause damage on purpose; it's just that following the rules can be a little inconvenient—especially when it comes to adhering to strict password policies. Your average user just doesn't get how important their role is in maintaining the security of the network (maybe even their job security as well) by sticking to the network's security policy, so you have to make sure they do.

Think about it. If you can easily discover user passwords just by taking a little tour of the premises, so can a bad guy, and once someone has a username and a password, it's pretty easy to hack into resources. I wasn't kidding about people slapping sticky notes with their usernames and/or passwords right on their monitors—this happens a lot more than you would think. Some users, thinking they're actually being really careful, glue them to the back of their keyboards instead, but you don't have to be James Bond to think about looking there either, right? People wouldn't think of leaving their cars unlocked with the windows down and the keys in the ignition, but that's exactly what they're doing by leaving sensitive info anywhere on or near their workstations.

Even though it might not make you Mr. or Ms. Popularity when you search workspaces or even inside desks for notes with interesting or odd words written on them, do it anyway.

People will try to hide these goodies anywhere. Or sometimes, not so much. I kid you not —I had a user who actually wrote his password on the border of his monitor with a Sharpie, and when his password expired, he just crossed it off and wrote the new one underneath it. Sheer genius! But my personal favorite was when I glanced at this one guy's keyboard and noticed that some of the letter keys had numbers written on them. All you had to do was follow the numbers that (surprise!) led straight to his password. Oh sure—he'd followed policy to the, ahem, letter by choosing random letters and numbers, but a lot of good that did—he had to draw himself a little map in plain sight on his keyboard to remember the password.

So, like it or not, you have to walk your beat to find out if users are managing their accounts properly. If you find someone doing things the right way, praise them for it openly. If not, it's time for more training—or maybe worse, termination.

Enable DHCP Snooping

A rogue DHCP server (one not under your control that is giving out incompatible IP addresses) can be an annoyance that causes users to be unable to connect to network resources, or it may play a part in several types of attacks. In either case, DHCP snooping is a switch feature that can help to prevent your devices from communicating with illegitimate DHCP servers.

When enabled, DHCP snooping allows responses to client requests from only DHCP servers located on trusted switch ports (which you define). When only ports where company DHCP servers are located are configured to be trusted, rogue DHCP servers will be unable to respond to client requests.

The protection doesn't stop there, however. The switch will also, over time, develop an IP address–to–MAC address table called the bindings table, derived from "snooping" on DHCP traffic to and from the legitimate DHCP server. The bindings table will alert the switch to any packets that have mappings that do not match the table. These frames will be dropped. The bindings table is also used with ARP inspection, which makes the configuration and enabling of DHCP snooping a prerequisite of ARP inspection.

Change Default VLAN

All switches have a VLAN by default called VLAN1. You can't change or even delete the default VLAN; it is mandatory. The default VLAN is simply the VLAN to which all access ports are assigned to until they are explicitly placed in another VLAN. While you can't change the default VLAN, you can create a new VLAN and move all switch ports to that VLAN. Since VLAN1 is typically set as the default for most vendors, it becomes a well-known configuration for attackers to abuse.

Patch and Firmware Management

In some cases, applying patches, especially device driver updates, can be problematic. Issues can include the device no longer working, loss of some key functionality, or generation of odd error messages. When this occurs, you may want to make use of the procedure covered in the next section.

Rollback

While *rollback* is a general term that applies to reversing any operation related to device drivers, it means to remove the newer driver and go back to using the previous driver. This is typically an available option if the last driver you used is the driver to which you want to roll back.

If you don't have automatic updates set up, you can download patches and hotfixes manually. A hotfix is just like a patch that updates software, but this term is reserved for a solution to potentially serious issues that could compromise your network and hosts. When a company like Microsoft used to create a whole bunch of patches, hotfixes, and upgrades, it would put them together in a larger bundle called a service pack. For instance, you could download Windows 7 Service Pack 1 (SP1) or Windows Server 2008 Service Pack 2 (SP2), which will update lots of components and address security, performance, and stability issues all at the same time. Windows 10 is different as there are no service packs. Instead, Microsoft issue updates when they are ready rather than batching them together in one huge update.

Firmware Updates

While keeping operating system and application patches up-to-date gets most of the attention, there are devices on your network that may require firmware updates from time to time. Firmware is a form of program code and related data that is stored in persistent memory of some sort, such as non-volatile RAM (NVRAM).

In many cases, firmware updates are designed to increase the functionality of a device.

In other cases, they may correct a bug or flaw in the system. Firmware updates are much more infrequent than other types of updates, so it's easy to forget about them. You should always agree to be contacted by manufacturers regarding these updates because they are not as widely publicized as other types of updates.

Updating firmware is a process sometimes called flashing, in which the old firmware instructions are overwritten by the new ones. You should carefully follow the process described in the manufacturer's documentation because failure to do so can lead to the device being made useless (sometimes called bricking the device).

Driver Updates

Drivers are files that allow a peripheral or component to talk to the hardware layer of the hosting device. In most cases, the drivers you need for a device will already be present in the drive cache that is installed with the operating system, but sometimes, especially with new devices, this will not be the case. In those instances, you will have to allow the system to locate the driver file from the media that came with the device, or in extreme instances, you may have to search for it on the Internet. You should always start your search on the website of the manufacturer. Drivers found elsewhere may be problematic and, in some cases, may introduce malware.

Drivers also need to be updated from time to time. If you have computers set to receive updates automatically, updated drivers can be among the items you select to receive. Not all devices can benefit from automatic updating, and you may be required to check manually from time to time for driver updates for other devices, such as printers, scanners, and cameras.

Access Control List

It's rare to find a network around these days that isn't connected to the Internet. The Internet is clearly a public internetwork that anyone can connect to, but your company's or personal network is, and should definitely be, a private one. The catch here is that every time you connect to the Internet (where everyone is welcome) from a private network, you're instantly vulnerable to security break-ins. This is where something we call a firewall comes into play. Firewalls are basically tools that you can implement to prevent any unauthorized users roaming around on public networks from gaining access to your private network.

Firewalls can be either stand-alone devices or combined with another hardware device like a server or a router. And although firewalls can use a lot of various technologies to restrict information flow, their primary weapon is known as an access control list (ACL).

Access control lists (ACLs) typically reside on routers to determine which packets are allowed to route through them based on the requesting device's source or destination Internet Protocol (IP) address. Oh, and just so you know, ACLs have been around for decades and have other uses apart from firewalls.

Figure 18.3 demonstrates how ACLs prevent users on Network B from accessing Network A.

FIGURE 18.3 Two networks with an ACL-enabled router

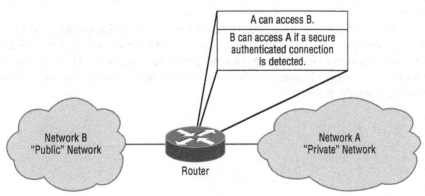

Okay, what we see here is that users in Network A can pass through the router into Network B. This means that an IP spoofing attack, when someone pretends to have a network address on the inside of a firewall to gain network access, can still happen if a user in Network B pretends to be located in Network A.

You can create a wide array of ACLs, from the very simple to the highly complex, depending on exactly what you want to have them do for you. One example is placing separate inbound and outbound ACLs on a router to ensure that the data that's leaving your network comes from a different source than the data that's coming into it.

When configuring ACLs between the Internet and your private network to mitigate security problems, it's a good idea to include these four conditions:

- Deny any addresses from your internal networks.
- Deny any local host addresses (127.0.0.0/8).
- Deny any reserved private addresses.
- Deny any addresses in the IP multicast address range (224.0.0.0/4).

None of these addresses should ever be allowed to enter your internetwork. Interestingly enough, because of the way in which in-public IP addresses are issued, with some research you can create a filter that blocks a country, state, or even locale based on IP addresses!

Role-Based Access

Role-based access control (RBAC) is commonly used in networks to simplify the process of assigning new users the permission required to perform a job role. In this arrangement, users are organized by job role into security groups, which are then granted the rights and permissions required to perform that job. This process is pictured in Figure 18.4. The role is implemented as a security group possessing the required rights and permissions, which are inherited by all security group or role members.

This is not a perfect solution, however, and it carries several security issues. First, RBAC is only as successful as the organization policies designed to support it. Poor policies can result in the proliferation of unnecessary roles, creating an administrative nightmare for the person managing user access. This can lead to mistakes that reduce rather than enhance access security.

A related issue is that those managing user access may have an incomplete understanding of the process, and this can lead to a serious reduction in security. There can be additional costs to the organization to ensure proper training of these individuals. The key to making RBAC successful is proper alignment with policies and proper training of those implementing and maintaining the system.

FIGURE 18.4   RBAC

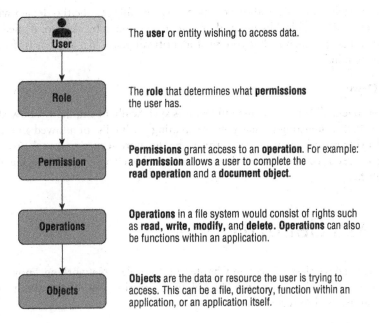

User — The **user** or entity wishing to access data.

Role — The **role** that determines what **permissions** the user has.

Permission — **Permissions** grant access to an **operation**. For example: a **permission** allows a user to complete the **read operation** and a **document object**.

Operations — **Operations** in a file system would consist of rights such as **read, write, modify,** and **delete. Operations** can also be functions within an application.

Objects — **Objects** are the data or resource the user is trying to access. This can be a file, directory, function within an application, or an application itself.

Firewall Rules

In Chapter 5, "Networking Devices," you learned about firewalls. If the access control lists are misconfigured on a firewall, the damage will fall into one of three categories:

- Traffic is allowed that shouldn't be allowed.
- Traffic that should be allowed is blocked.
- No traffic is allowed at all.

The first two problems are a matter of specifying the wrong traffic type in a permit or deny rule. Because in many cases the traffic type is specified in terms of a port number, it is critical to know the port numbers of the traffic you are dealing with.

The last problem can be either a simple omission or a complete misunderstanding of how ACLs work. At the end of every ACL is an implied rule that blocks all traffic that has not been allowed by earlier rules in the rule set. This means that all ACLs should have a rule at the end that allows all traffic that should be allowed. An ACL with no permit statements will block all traffic.

When developing rules for firewalls there are two basic approaches.

Explicit Deny

Using this approach, all traffic is allowed unless it is specially (explicitly) denied with a rule. This is also referred to as blacklisting in that you are creating a blacklist of denied traffic. The issue with this approach is that you must identify all possible malicious traffic, which can be overwhelming.

Implicit Deny

With this approach, all traffic is denied unless it is specifically or implicitly allowed by a rule. This is also called whitelisting in that you are creating a whitelist of allowed traffic with the denial of all other traffic. Many consider this to be the more secure approach. You need only identify what is required traffic, a much more manageable effort than identifying all possible malicious traffic.

Wireless Security

While we discussed wireless security in Chapter 12, "Wireless Networking," now let's focus on some of the issues to be found with WLAN. In this section you'll learn about some techniques that can be used to secure them.

MAC Filtering

Client MAC addresses can be statically typed into each access point, allowing MAC filtering, and any frames that show up to the AP without a known MAC address in the filter table will be denied access. Sounds good, but of course all MAC layer information must be sent in the clear—anyone equipped with a free wireless sniffer can just read the client packets sent to the access point and spoof their MAC address. If you have a small number of wireless clients and you don't want to deploy an encryption-based access method, MAC address filters may be sufficient.

Antenna Placement

In Chapter 12 you learned about the importance of a site survey in identifying proper antenna placement. The security aspect of antenna placement is also critical. Since you cannot prevent the capture of wireless frames being broadcast by the AP, limiting the exposed areas of the broadcast signal helps to limit eavesdropping.

In the next section you will learn about using power levels to expand and contract the size of the cell around the AP. While this is an available option, keep in mind that as you raise and lower the power, you are expanding and contracting the signal in *all* directions. In some cases, there is a need to reshape the cell rather than expand or contract it.

When you need to reshape the cell, you use antennas to accomplish this. For example, you may want to send the signal down a long hallway while not transmitting outside the hallway into the parking lot. That could be done with a directional antenna. For more on antennas, see Chapter 12.

Power Levels

Location, location, location. You've got only two worries with this one: Your clients are either too far or not far enough from the AP. If your AP doesn't seem to have enough power to provide a connectivity point for your clients, you can move it closer to them, increase the distance that the AP can transmit by changing the type of antenna it uses, or use multiple APs connected to the same switch or set of switches to solve the problem. If the power level or signal is too strong, and it reaches out into the parking area or farther out to other buildings and businesses, place the AP as close as possible to the center of the area it's providing service for. And don't forget to verify that you've got the latest security features in place to keep bad guys from authenticating to and using your network.

Wireless Client Isolation

Wireless client isolation prevents wireless stations within an SSID from communicating directly with one another or with any devices on the wired network to which the wireless network might be connected. They can only access the Internet. The setting is shown in Figure 18.5.

FIGURE 18.5   Isolation

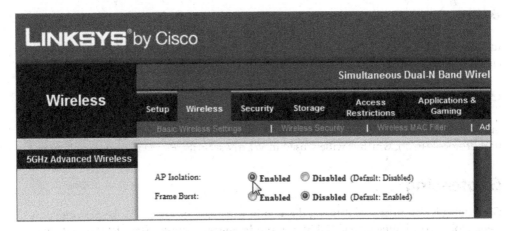

Guest Network Isolation

A similar setting to client isolation is the guest network isolation feature. When enabled it creates two networks in one. One, the guest network, has client isolation in effect and has access only to the Internet. The second serves as the regular WLAN. Guests who join the guest Wi-Fi network are confined to an entirely separate network and given Internet access, but they can't communicate with the main wired network or the primary wireless network.

The setting is shown in Figure 18.6.

FIGURE 18.6   Guest network

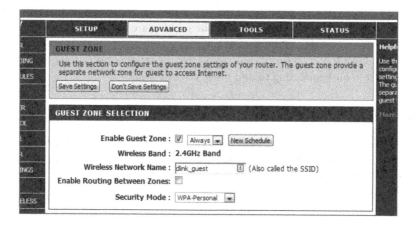

Preshared Keys (PSKs)

In Chapter 12 you learned about preshared keys (PSK) used in some authentication and encryption systems. Please review that chapter.

EAP

In Chapter 16, "Common Security Concepts," you learned about the Extensible Authentication Protocol (EAP), which is widely used in WLAN security. Please review that chapter.

Geofencing

Geofencing is the process of defining the area in which an operation can be performed by using global positioning system (GPS) or radio frequency identification (RFID) to define a geographic boundary. An example of usage involves a location-aware device of a location-based service (LBS) user entering or exiting a geofence. This activity could trigger an alert to the device's user as well as messaging the geofence operator.

Captive Portal

When a wireless network is in use, one method of securing access to a WLAN is using a captive portal. This is a web page to which users are directed when they attempt to connect to a WLAN. This web page may ask for network credentials, or in the case of a guest network such as at a coffee shop, hotel, or airport, it may only ask for agreement to the usage policy of the guest network.

IoT Access Considerations

In Chapter 5 you learned about the Internet of Things (IoT) devices. Many of these devices use a wireless connection to communicate with the systems gathering data from the sensors. These systems were not designed with security in mind.

IoT devices are easy recruits to a botnet, which is a group of systems that an attacker controls and directs to foist a DoS attack. Consider using VLANs and other forms of segmentation to prevent this. The role an IoT device will play is that of a zombie.

Summary

In this chapter you learned network hardening techniques, including securing SNMP, using Router Advertisement (RA) Guard, implementing port security and utilizing Dynamic ARP inspection. We also talked about wireless security hardening methods, including MAC filtering, proper antenna placement and proper power levels. Finally, we identified IoT access considerations.

Exam Essentials

Explain network hardening techniques. These include securing SNMP, Router Advertisement (RA) Guard, port security, Dynamic ARP inspection, control plane policing, private VLANs, disabling unneeded switchports, disabling unneeded network services, changing default passwords, and enabling DHCP snooping.

Describe wireless security hardening. The techniques used for wireless security hardening include MAC filtering, proper antenna placement, proper power levels, wireless client isolation, guest network isolation, preshared keys (PSKs), EAP, geofencing, and captive portal.

Mitigate IoT threats. These include segmenting the IoT devices to help prevent their recruitment to a botnet.

Written Lab

Complete the table by filling in the appropriate term for each authentication method. You can find the answers in Appendix A.

Authentication Method	Term
Method of blocking rogue router advertisements	
Can prevent many on-path/man-in-the-middle attacks	
Can limit network access on a port to a single (or in the case of an IP phone, two) MAC address	
Carries signaling traffic originating from or destined for a router	
Carries user traffic	

Review Questions

You can find the answers to the review questions in Appendix B.

1. Which of the following is a web page to which users are directed when they attempt to connect to the WLAN?
    A. Captive portal
    B. Evil twin
    C. PSK
    D. LBS

2. Which of the following defines the area in which an operation can be performed?
    A. Captive portal
    B. Geofencing
    C. VLAN
    D. API

3. Which of the following is a role that an IoT device can play in a botnet?
    A. Command and control
    B. Handler
    C. Zombie
    D. Broker

4. Which of the following creates two WLANs in one?
    A. VLAN
    B. Client isolation
    C. Evil twin
    D. Guest network isolation

5. Which of the following provides the best way to shape a broadcast cell?
    A. Antennas
    B. Power setting
    C. Repeaters
    D. Multiple APs

6. Which of the following can be defeated with a wireless sniffer?
    A. VLAN hopping
    B. MAC address filters
    C. ARP poisoning
    D. RBAC

7. Which of the following is also called whitelisting?

   A. Implicit allow

   B. Least privilege

   C. Implicit deny

   D. Need to know

8. In which of the following systems are users organized by job into security groups, which are then granted the rights and permissions required to perform that job?

   A. RBAC

   B. MAC

   C. DAC

   D. BBAC

9. When configuring ACLs between the Internet and your private network to mitigate security problems, it's a good idea to include all but which of the following?

   A. Deny any public addresses.

   B. Deny any addresses from your internal networks.

   C. Deny any local host addresses (127.0.0.0/8).

   D. Deny any reserved private addresses.

10. Where should you always start your search for driver updates?

   A. `Drivers.com`

   B. Website of the manufacturer

   C. Windows Update

   D. Doesn't matter

Chapter

19

Remote Access Security

Think of remote access as a telecommuting tool because it's used by companies to allow remote employees to connect to the internal network and access resources that are in the office. Remote access is great for users who work from home or travel frequently, but clearly, to a stalking hacker, using an unsecured remote access connection is like stealing candy from a baby.

Using remote access requires a server configured to accept incoming calls and also requires remote access software to be installed on the client. Microsoft Windows operating systems, since Windows 95, have had remote access client software built in, and there are many third-party remote access clients available as well. Several different methods exist to create remote access connections. In this chapter we'll look at remote access and the VPN types that make it secure.

To find Todd Lammle CompTIA videos and practice questions, please see www.lammle.com.

Site-to-Site VPN

Site-to-site VPNs, or intranet VPNs, allow a company to connect its remote sites to the corporate backbone securely over a public medium like the Internet instead of requiring more expensive wide area network (WAN) connections like Frame Relay. This is probably the best solution for connecting a remote office to a main company office because all traffic that goes between the offices will be encrypted with no effort on the part of the users.

In this scenario, all traffic that goes between the offices will go through the VPN tunnel. A site-to-site VPN is shown in Figure 19.1, along with a remote access called a *client-to-site VPN* covered in the next section. This solution requires a remote access client on the user device.

Client-to-Site VPN

Remote access VPNs or client-to-site VPN allow remote users like telecommuters to securely access the corporate network wherever and whenever they need to. It is typical that users can connect to the Internet but not to the office via their VPN client because they don't have the correct VPN address and password. This is the most common problem and one you should always check first.

In this scenario *only* the traffic between the user and the office will go through the VPN tunnel. A remote access VPN is shown in Figure 19.1. This solution requires a remote access client on the user device.

FIGURE 19.1   Site-to-site and client-to-site VPN

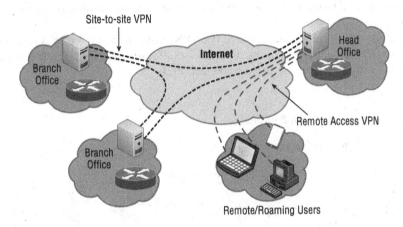

Clientless VPN

A *clientless* VPN enables end users to securely access resources on the corporate network from anywhere using an SSL/TLS-enabled web browser. They need no remote access client to do this, only a browser that can perform SSL or the more secure TLS. A clientless VPN is shown in Figure 19.2.

FIGURE 19.2   Clientless VPN

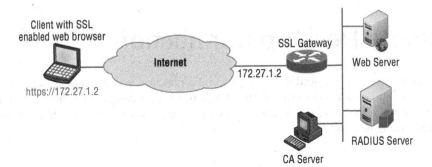

Split Tunnel vs. Full Tunnel

When a client-to-site VPN is created it is possible to do so in two ways, split tunnel and full tunnel. The difference is whether the user use the VPN for connecting to the Internet as well as for connecting to the office.

Split tunneling works by using two connections at the same time: the secure VPN connection and an open connection to the Internet. So in split tunneling, *only* traffic to the office goes through the VPN. Internet traffic does not. The security issue with this is that while the user is connected to the VPN, they are also connected to the most untrusted network, the Internet.

With full tunnel, all traffic goes through the VPN, which means the user is accessing the Internet through the connection of the office and so all traffic will be examined by the office security. Split and full tunnel are shown in Figure 19.3.

FIGURE 19.3   Split and full tunnel

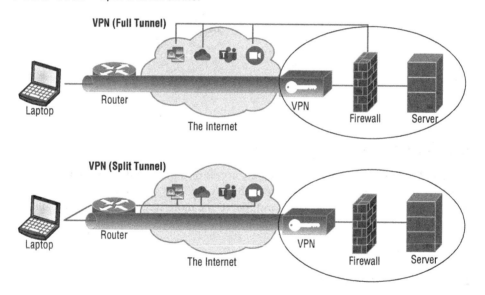

Remote Desktop Connection

There are times when you need to make a remote connection to a machine to perform troubleshooting but you are miles away. Connectivity software is designed to allow you to make a connection to a machine, see the desktop, and perform any action you could perform if you were sitting in front of it.

Microsoft has made what it calls Remote Desktop software available for free with Windows products since Windows NT. When this software is installed (installed by default in later versions) on both source and destination computers, a remote desktop connection can be made.

Commercial tools are also available that (of course) claim to have more functionality, and they probably do have a few extra bells and whistles. These include LogMeIn.com, GoTo-MyPC, and others.

The advantages of these connectivity tools are obvious. With these tools, you can do anything you need to on the machine as long as you can connect. They also allow you to see what a user is actually doing when they encounter a problem rather than having to rely on what they tell you they are doing. You can even show a user what they are doing wrong. Most of these tools allow for chat sessions and for either end of the connection to take control of the machine. You can also transfer files to them if required (maybe a DLL got deleted, for example).

Remote Desktop Gateway

Remote Desktop Protocol (RDP) is a proprietary protocol developed by Microsoft. It allows you to connect to another computer and run programs. RDP operates somewhat like Telnet, except instead of getting a command-line prompt as you do with Telnet, you get the actual graphical user interface (GUI) of the remote computer. Clients exist for most versions of Windows, and Macs now come with a preinstalled RDP client.

Microsoft currently calls its official RDP server software Remote Desktop Services; it was called Terminal Services for a while. Microsoft's official client software is currently referred to as Remote Desktop Connection, which was called Terminal Services Client in the past.

RDP is an excellent tool for remote clients, allowing them to connect to their work computer from home, for example, and get their email or perform work on other applications without running or installing any of the software on their home computer.

RDP allows users to connect to a computer running Microsoft's Remote Desktop Services, but a remote computer must have the right kind of client software installed for this to happen. Most Windows-based operating systems include an RDP client, and so do most other major operating systems, like Linux, Solaris, and macOS. Microsoft began calling all terminal services products Remote Desktop with Windows Server 2008 R2. RDP uses TCP port 3389.

After establishing a connection, the user sees a terminal window that's basically a preconfigured window that looks like a Windows desktop or another operating system's desktop. From there, the user on the client computer can access applications and files available to them by using the remote desktop.

The most current version of RDC is RDC 1.2.1953. When logged in using RDP, clients are able to access local files and printers from the remote desktop just as if they were logged into the network.

RDP Gateway

RDP Gateway is a more secure version of RDP created by RouterHosting. It is more secure than the public or MS version in the following ways:

- You don't need to use a VPN. Using the SSL channel, RDP Gateway can tunnel directly to the remote server to increase the security of RDS.
- No pass through a third-party website or service.
- Native Windows Server service.
- Can be combined with Network Access Protection.
- Can be used along with Microsoft Internet Security and Acceleration (ISA), the Microsoft implementation of RADIUS.

SSH

Secure Shell is a network protocol that is designed as an alternative to command-based utilities such as Telnet that transmit requests and responses in clear text. It creates a secure channel between the devices and provides confidentiality and integrity of the data transmission.

It uses public-key cryptography to authenticate the remote computer and allow the remote computer to authenticate the user, if necessary. This public key is placed on any computer that must allow access to the owner of a matching private key (the owner keeps the private key in secret). The private key is never transferred through the network during authentication.

Don't use Telnet! Telnet is totally insecure because it sends all data in crystal-clear text—including your name and password. And I'm pretty sure you know that's a really bad thing these days. If Microsoft doesn't even enable it on its latest OSs, then you know it really must be insecure.

Some configuration is usually necessary if you want things to work as they really should, and yes, sometimes it's a little painful to get everything running smoothly, but it's all worth it in the long run. Personally, I disable Telnet on all my routers and use SSH exclusively. No lie—I never use Telnet anymore if I can help it. Even so, you should still understand Telnet and get in some practice with it in case you do ever need it.

Virtual Network Computing (VNC)

Virtual Network Computing (VNC) is a remote desktop sharing system that uses the Remote Frame Buffer (RFB) protocol. It is platform independent and provides an experience much like Remote Desktop Protocol (RDP).

VNC includes the following components:

- VNC server: Software that runs on the machine sharing its screen
- VNC client (or viewer): Software on the machine that is remotely receiving the shared screen
- VNC protocol (RDP)

One big difference in VNC and RDP is that VNC sends raw pixel data (which does make it work on any desktop type) while RDP uses graphic primitives or higher-level commands for the screen transfer process.

Virtual Desktop

Using operating system images for desktop computers is not a new concept. Nor is delivering these desktop images to users from a virtual environment when they start their computer. This allows for the user desktop to require less computing power, especially if the applications are also delivered virtually and those applications are running in a VM in the cloud rather than in the local desktop eating up local resources. Another benefit of using virtual desktops is the ability to maintain a consistent user environment (same desktop, applications, etc.), which can enhance user support.

Authentication and Authorization Considerations

The most effective way to control both authentication of remote users and the application of their permissions is to provision an AAA server. AAA services is covered in Chapter 5, "Networking Devices," and Chapter 16, "Common Security Concepts."

In-Band vs. Out-of-Band Management

Out-of-band management refers to any method of managing the server that does use the network. An example of this technology is Integrated Lights-Out, or iLO, a technology embedded into HP servers that allows for out-of-band management of the server. The physical connection is an Ethernet port that will be on the server and will be labeled ILO. In Figure 19.4, one of these ILO ports is shown (labeled number 2) in an HP Moonshot chassis (these hold blade servers). HP iLO functions out-of-the-box without additional software installation regardless of the server's state of operation, giving you complete access to the server from any location via a web browser or the iLO Mobile app.

FIGURE 19.4   ILO port

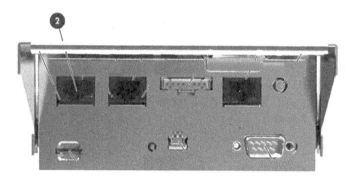

Summary

In this chapter you learned the importance of providing both fault tolerance and high availability. You also learned about VPN architectures. These include site-to-site VPNs, client-to-site VPN, clientless VPN, split tunnel vs. full, and SSH VPN.

We also looked at SSL and TLS, including common applications with respect to VPNs. Finally, we identified other remote access solutions., such as VNC, RDP, remote desktop gateway, remote desktop connections, and virtual connections.

Exam Essentials

Explain VPN architectures.   These include site-to-site VPNs, client-to-site VPN, clientless VPN, split tunnel vs. full, and SSH VPN.

Describe SSL and TLS.   This includes the differences between the two and the advantages of TLS. It also includes common applications with respect to VPNs.

Identify other remote access solutions.   These include VNC, RDP, remote desktop gateway, remote desktop connections, and virtual connections.

Written Lab

Complete the table by filling in the appropriate definition for each term.
    You can find the answers in Appendix A.

Term	Definition
Clientless VPN	
Full tunnel	
Site-to-site VPN	
Split tunnel	
Client-to-site VPN	

Review Questions

You can find the answers to the review questions in Appendix B.

1. Integrated Lights-Out is an example of which of the following technologies?

   A. Captive portal

   B. Out-of-band management

   C. Clientless VPN

   D. AAA

2. The most effective way to control both authentication of remote users and the application of their permissions is to provision which of the following?

   A. Captive portal

   B. AAA

   C. LDAP

   D. RDP

3. Which of the following is an operating system image delivered over the network at each startup?

   A. VNC

   B. Virtual desktop

   C. Remote desktop

   D. RDP

4. Which of the following is *not* a component of Virtual Network Computing (VNC)?

   A. VNC server

   B. VNC client

   C. VNC desktop

   D. VNC protocol

5. Which of the following is a network protocol that is designed as an alternative to command-based utilities such as Telnet?

   A. SSL

   B. SSH

   C. STP

   D. STFP

6. Which of the following allows you to tunnel directly to the remote server with no VPN?

   A. Split tunnel

   B. RDP Gateway

   C. Full tunnel

   D. VNC

7. Which of the following was formerly called Terminal Services Client?

   A. Virtual desktop

   B. Remote Desktop Connection

   C. VNC

   D. RDP Gateway

8. Which of the following operates somewhat like Telnet, except instead of getting a command-line prompt as you do with Telnet, you get the actual graphical user interface (GUI) of the remote computer?

   A. RBAC

   B. SSH

   C. RDP

   D. SSL

9. Which of the following is *not* an example of a remote desktop connection?

   A. RDP

   B. LogMeIn

   C. GoToMyPC

   D. SSH

10. Split tunnel and full tunnel are examples of which type of VPN?

   A. Client-to-site

   B. Site-to-site

   C. RDP VPN

   D. Clientless VPN

Chapter

20

Physical Security

THE FOLLOWING COMPTIA NETWORK+ EXAM OBJECTIVES ARE COVERED IN THIS CHAPTER:

✓ **Explain the importance of physical security.**

- Detection methods
    - Camera
    - Motion detection
    - Asset tags
    - Tamper detection
- Prevention methods
    - Employee training
    - Access control hardware
        - Badge readers
        - Biometrics
    - Locking racks
    - Locking cabinets
- Access control vestibule (previously known as a mantrap)
- Smart lockers
- Asset disposal
    - Factory reset/wipe configuration
    - Sanitize devices for disposal

Over the years, I've visited lots of different companies, large and small, public and private, and analyzed, advised, troubleshot, designed, and implemented their networks. Without fail, the system administrators I've met along the way have been really eager to tell me all about the security systems they have in place. "Look at this awesome firewall setup!", "Check out the cool Group Policy structure we have!" "Watch how quickly our fault tolerance springs into action!" They're very proud, and rightly so, of what they've worked so hard to set up, because doing that isn't easy.

But interestingly, one of the things few people brag about is physical security—like it's some kind of afterthought. Maybe the server room has a locked door, maybe it doesn't. Maybe the badges that open that door are owned by the right people, or maybe they aren't. I guess that on a subconscious level, we tend to inherently trust the people working within the walls and focus our fears, suspicions, and ammo on mysterious outside forces that we're sure are incessantly trying to break in, steal data, or totally murder our networks. Some of the sharpest, most talented, and savvy system administrators I've ever met still have a tendency to neglect inside security and fail to reasonably monitor things going on within the building.

And there are some seriously vital things to nail down on the inside. For instance, does it really matter if your network has a secured subnet for the servers, with its own dedicated internal firewall? Definitely—I've actually found servers in racks like sitting ducks in a hallway right across from the lunch room. When I pointed out the fact that this was not so good, I was assured that it was only temporary until the server room construction was complete. I don't know about you, but for some reason, that didn't cut it and didn't make me feel anywhere near okay with the situation. At another company, I found the door to the server room propped open because otherwise "it got too hot in there." Because that toasty server room didn't exactly have a guard posted, anyone could just walk in and do whatever; the backup tapes were clearly marked and sitting there on a shelf—yikes! And don't even get me started about the heat. The bottom line is that if your system is not physically secured, you're basically sending out an open invitation to a Pandora's box of problems without even realizing it.

 Real World Scenario

Beware the Big Gulp

Several years ago when I was teaching a networking class, one of my best students challenged me. He was proud of the security configuration on his server computer in the classroom and went so far as to tell me there was no way I could get to or damage any files on his system. He was really sure about that. Well, it just so happens I like a good challenge.

The students went off to lunch, and I stayed behind to work on a few things. While they were gone, I got out my handy Partition Magic diskette (I said this was a while ago) and popped it into his system. One reset button push later, I was in business. I wiped out the partitions on his hard drive and shut down the system.

When he came back from lunch, he looked a bit confused. He clearly remembered leaving his computer on, and upon booting up and playing around for a minute, he realized that his hard drive was gone. At first, he was more than a little angry at me for doing that, but then I asked him to give me a chance to prove a point—an important one. That is, when someone has access to your computer, they can do whatever they want. Yes, they might not be able to read your files (although I could have done that too), but they can still do a lot of damage. My tool of destruction was a partitioning program, but going back to that "servers out in the open across from the lunch room" situation, all it would take is a spilled soft drink to cause mass destruction. In any case, the data clearly was not safe, so physical security needs to be a top priority.

To find Todd Lammle CompTIA videos and practice questions, please see www.lammle.com.

Detection Methods

You can't react to and address a security issue if you don't even know its occurring. As one fellow security expert once said, "if you're going to get hacked, at least realize you've been hacked." Detection technologies and procedures are designed to alert you when bad things might be occurring. In the following sections, we'll look at some of the most common detection mechanisms.

Cameras

In many high-security scenarios it may be advisable to visually monitor the area 24 hours a day. When this is the case, it will make sense to deploy video monitoring. We'll look at two options, IP cameras and CCTV systems.

IP Cameras

IP video systems are a good example of the benefits of networking applications. These systems can be used both for surveillance of the facility and for facilitating collaboration.

CCTVs

While an IP camera is a type of digital video camera commonly employed for surveillance, analog closed-circuit television (CCTV) cameras are unable to send their images across IP networks. CCTV cameras record directly to a medium such as video tape or hard drive. It is possible to convert the signal to digital in cases where you need to send it across an IP network.

Cameras should cover all entrances to the building and the entire parking lot. Be sure that cameras are in weather-proof and tamper-proof housings and review the output at a security-monitoring office. Record everything on extended-length tape recorders.

Motion Detection

In areas that require constant attention to security, it may be advisable to install motion detectors of some sort. Server rooms, wiring closets, and other critical areas may need these. Let's look at a few types.

Infrared Sensors

Passive infrared (PIR) systems operate by identifying changes in heat waves in an area. Because the presence of an intruder would raise the temperature of the surrounding air particles, the system alerts or sounds an alarm when this occurs.

Electromechanical Systems

Electromechanical systems operate by detecting a break in an electrical circuit. For example, the circuit might cross a window or door, and when the window or door is opened, the circuit is broken, setting off an alarm of some sort. Another example might be a pressure pad placed under the carpet to detect the presence of individuals.

Photoelectric Systems

Photometric or photoelectric systems operate by detecting changes in the light and thus are used in windowless areas. They send a beam of light across the area and if the beam is interrupted (by a person, for example), the alarm is triggered.

Acoustical Detection Systems

Acoustical systems use strategically placed microphones to detect any sound made during a forced entry. These systems only work well in areas where there is not a lot of surrounding noise. They are typically very sensitive, which would cause many false alarms in a loud area, such as a door next to a busy street.

Wave Motion Detector

These devices generate a wave pattern in the area and detect any motion that disturbs the wave pattern. When the pattern is disturbed, an alarm sounds.

Capacitance Detector

These devices emit a magnetic field and monitor that field. If the field is disrupted, which will occur when a person enters the area, the alarm will sound.

Asset Tags

Proper asset management is not rocket science. It boils down to knowing exactly what you have, when you got it, where it is, and where the license to use it is. The devil as they say is in the details. Most server administrators don't set out to intentionally exercise poor asset management; they simply don't give it the importance it requires to be done correctly.

Labeling or tagging servers, workstations, printers, ports on infrastructure devices (routers and switches), and other items is another form of asset documentation that often doesn't receive enough attention. Not only does this make your day-to-day duties easier, it makes the process of maintaining accurate records simpler and supports a proper asset management plan. When periodic inventories are taken (you are doing that, right?), having these items labeled makes the process so much quicker. This goes for cables in the server room as well.

Tamper Detection

Tamper detection refers to any method that alerts you when a device or the enclosure in which it resides has been opened or an attempt has been made to open it. A good example is computer chassis intrusion detection.

You should use settings in the BIOS/UEFI to alert you when the case has been opened. These settings are shown in Figure 20.1. In this case, the open case warning has not been enabled yet.

FIGURE 20.1   Open case warning in the BIOS

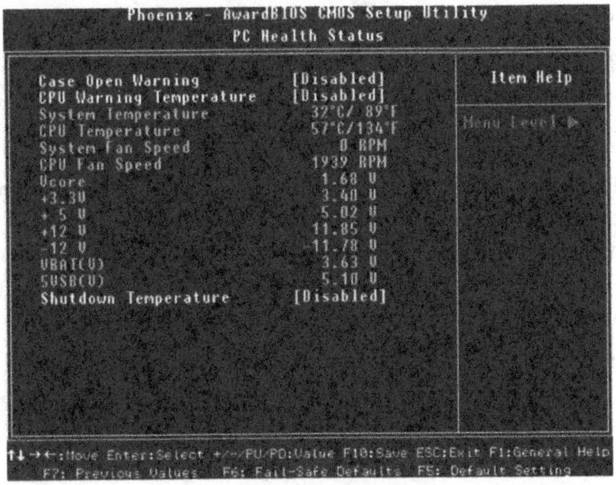

Prevention Methods

While detection mechanism are great, wouldn't it be even better if we could just avoid the issue altogether? There are some measures we can take to prevent some of the issues that detection mechanisms are designed to identify. In the following sections, you'll learn about some of the more common methods.

Employee Training

This brings us to the human element of network security. It's true that most of your users want to do the right thing to protect the company from the prying eyes of hackers (and in the process protect their jobs), but the problem is that people don't always know the right thing to do. That's why training is so vital. It can include classroom sessions and/or web-based training, but experience has shown me that actual classroom-based instruction works the best. It's also a good idea to have separate training classes for IT personnel and end users.

End-User Training

End-user training is pretty easy—it can take just an hour or so to bring employees up to speed. The "keep it short and simple" rule applies here or you'll just end up with nap time. This is a great time to include detailed security protocol training. But if you see eyes beginning to glaze over or hear anyone snoring, you might want to make security protocol training a separate session because, as I said, it's really important to the effectiveness of your security policy for everyone to know about and understand it. You can even use a year-end bonus or something else cool as a motivational reward for the employees who complete their training and test well on it.

And you have to back up your training by providing your end users with hard-copy, printed reference manuals in case they forget something (which they will). Include things like the following items:

- Recommended policies for creating safe passwords
- The number to call if they've locked themselves out of their accounts
- What to do if they think someone is phishing for information
- What to do if they think their computer has a virus

Clearly, new employees to the company or division should be required to go through training, but requiring that everybody attend refresher courses is also a good idea. And don't hesitate to call a meeting if new threats arise or any sudden changes occur to keep everyone up to date.

Administrator Training

Obviously, training sessions for your IT personnel have to be a lot more in depth because they'll be the ones who set up and configure policies, and they'll also be the first responders to any security emergency.

It's important to cover every aspect of your security policy with these people. And be sure they understand the correct ways to escalate issues in case of an emergency. Reacting to a security emergency is pretty stressful, and you don't want your administrators to panic or feel isolated if one occurs. Making sure they know where their lifelines are and how to reach them quickly if they need backup will relieve a lot of pressure when something nasty happens.

Access Control Hardware

Access control hardware comprises a category of devices that are used to identify and authenticate users. They combine a technical physical control (the device) and administrative controls (password policies and procedures) to create an access control system.

While access control vestibules/mantraps may justify their cost in some high-security scenarios, not all situations require them. Door controls should be used to prevent physical access to important infrastructure devices such as routers, switches, firewalls, and servers.

Proximity or badge readers are door controls that read a card from a short distance and are used to control access to sensitive rooms. These devices can also provide a log of all entries and exits. Usually, a card contains the user information required to authenticate and authorize the user to enter the room.

Biometrics

Biometric systems are designed to operate using characteristic and behavioral factors. While knowledge factors (password, PIN, or something you know) are the most common authentication factors used, characteristic factors represent something you are (fingerprint, iris scan), while behavioral factors represent something you do (signature analysis).

Multifactor authentication is achieved by combining authentication factors. When two factors are combined, such as a retina scan (characteristic factor) and a password (knowledge factor), dual-factor authentication is required. When three factors are combined, such as a retina scan (characteristic factor), a password (knowledge factor), and signature analysis (behavioral factor), then multifactor authentication is in effect.

One of the issues with biometrics is the occurrence of false positives and false negatives. A false positive is when a user that should not be allowed access is indeed allowed access. A false negative, on the other hand, is when an authorized individual is denied passage by mistake.

Locking Racks

Rack devices should be secured from theft. There are several locking systems that can be used to facilitate this. These locks are typically implemented in the doors on the front of a rack cabinet:

- Swing handle/wing knob locks with common key
- Swing handle/wing knob locks with unique key

- Swing handle with number and key lock
- Electronic locks
- Radio-frequency identification (RFID) card locks

Locking Cabinets

There are many items that should not be left just lying around a facility. These items include laptops, smartphones, and sensitive documents. A good example of a locking cabinet is shown in Figure 20.2. Each drawer is secured by a lock.

FIGURE 20.2 Locking cabinet

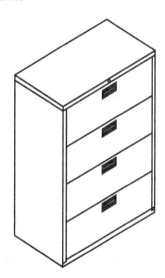

Access Control Vestibule (Previously Known as a Mantrap)

A mantrap or vestibule is used to control access to the vestibule of a building. It is a series of two doors with a small room between them. The user is authenticated at the first door and then allowed into the room. At that point, additional verification will occur (such as a guard visually identifying the person) and then they are allowed through the second door. These doors are typically used only in very high-security situations. They can help prevent tail-gating. A mantrap design is shown in Figure 20.3.

FIGURE 20.3   Access Control Vestibule/Mantrap

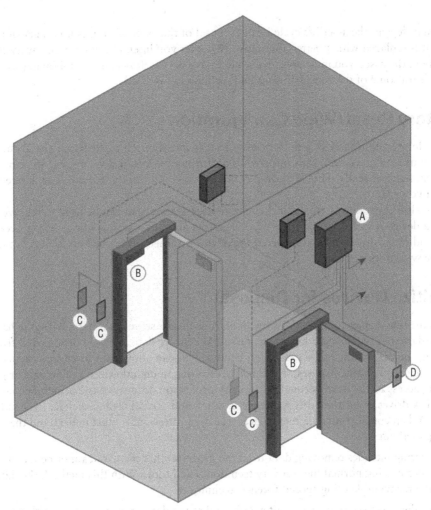

Smart Lockers

Smart lockers comprise a new storage locker option born in the last decade. A smart lock is an electromechanical lock that is designed to perform locking and unlocking operations on a door when it receives such instructions from an authorized device using a wireless protocol and a cryptographic key to execute the authorization process. With smart locks, lockers can be assigned on-the-fly, reset, audited, and reassigned using simple desktop or mobile software. They can utilize many lock choices (RFID or NFC, others with digital touch pads).

Asset Disposal

The final steps in the asset life cycle is the disposal of the asset when it is no longer of use or when it is replaced with a better alternative. Whether you intend to donate, throw away, or repurpose the asset, you must consider what data is on the device. In the following sections, you'll learn some of the considerations and techniques involved.

Factory Reset/Wipe Configuration

Many device vendors offer a factory reset that is mostly used to clear out the accumulated gunk and start over, thus improving performance. Yes, it does appear to remove all data, but not really. This is not a technique on which to rely if there is sensitive data involved.

You also hear quite often about the remote wipe feature that can be used to remove data when a device is stolen. While these wipe processes are different, it is not generally accepted to get rid of sensitive data. Moreover, if the device is turned off or the battery has run down, remote wipe does not work.

Sanitize Devices for Disposal

When the time comes to decommission an asset such as a server or a hard drive, the handling of any data that remains is a big security issue. Whenever data is erased or removed from a storage media, residual data can be left behind. This can allow data to be reconstructed when the organization disposes of the media, resulting in unauthorized individuals or groups gaining access to the data. Media that security professionals must consider include magnetic hard disk drives, solid-state drives, magnetic tapes, and optical media, such as CDs and DVDs. When considering data remanence, security professionals must understand the following methods:

- Clearing includes removing data from the media so that the data cannot be reconstructed using normal file recovery techniques and tools. With this method, the data is only recoverable using special forensic techniques.

- Purging, also referred to as sanitization, makes the data unreadable even with advanced forensic techniques. With this technique, data should be unrecoverable.

- Overwriting is a technique that writes data patterns over the entire media, thereby eliminating any trace data.

- Degaussing exposes the media to a powerful, alternating magnetic field, removing any previously written data and leaving the media in a magnetically randomized (blank) state.

- Encryption scrambles the data on the media, thereby rendering it unreadable without the encryption key.

- Physical destruction involves physically breaking the media apart or chemically altering it. For magnetic media, physical destruction can also involve exposure to high temperatures.

Most of the countermeasures given work for magnetic media. However, solid-state drives present unique challenges because they cannot be overwritten. Most solid-state drive vendors provide sanitization commands that can be used to erase the data on the drive. Security professionals should research these commands to ensure that they are effective. Another option for these drives is to erase the cryptographic key. Often a combination of these methods must be used to fully ensure that the data is removed.

Data remanence is also a consideration when using any cloud-based solution for an organization. Security professionals should work with their organization when negotiating any contract with a cloud-based provider to ensure that the contract covers data remanence issues, although it is difficult to determine that the data is properly removed. Using data encryption is a great way to ensure that data remanence is not a concern when dealing with the cloud.

Summary

In this chapter you learned the basic concepts, terms, and principles that all network professionals should understand to physically secure a network.

You learned about detection methods such as cameras and motion detection systems. We also discussed prevention methods such as training, locking cabinets, and rack locks. Finally you learned about the proper way to dispose of assets in a secure manner.

Exam Essentials

Explain detection methods. These include cameras, motion-detection systems, asset tags, and tamper-detection software.

Describe common prevention methods. This includes the employee training, access control hardware, badge readers, biometrics, locking racks, locking cabinets, access control vestibules/mantraps, and smart lockers.

Identify asset disposal issues. These consist of proper identification and application of the proper destruction method, including factory reset, remote wipe, purging, degaussing, and overwriting.

Written Lab

Complete the table by filling in the appropriate definition for each term.
You can find the answers in Appendix A.

Term	Definition
Purging	
Clearing	
Destruction	
Overwriting	

Review Questions

You can find the answers to the review questions in Appendix B.

1. Which of the following would *not* be considered a detection method?
    A. Camera
    B. Motion sensor
    C. Tamper alert software
    D. Employee training

2. Which motion detection system operates by identifying changes in heat waves in an area?
    A. Infrared
    B. Electromechanical
    C. Photelectric
    D. Acoustical

3. Which motion-detection system operates by emitting a magnetic field and monitoring that field?
    A. Infrared
    B. Capacitance
    C. Wave motion
    D. Acoustical

4. An open case warning is an example of which of the following?
    A. Motion detection
    B. Asset tagging
    C. Tamper detection
    D. Dynamic alert

5. Which of the following is the *most* effective way to stop social engineering attacks?
    A. Policies
    B. Penalties
    C. Training
    D. Auditing

6. Which of the following uses a characteristic factor for authentication?
    A. Biometrics
    B. Secondary authentication
    C. Identity proofing
    D. Hybrid authentication

7. Which of the following is *not* an example of multifactor authentication?

   A. Password and PIN

   B. Password and iris scan

   C. Retina scan and USB fob

   D. USB fob and smart card

8. Which of the following occurs when a legitimate user is denied authentication in a biometric system?

   A. False negative

   B. True negative

   C. True positive

   D. False positive

9. Which of the following is also known as an access control vestibule?

   A. Trapdoor

   B. Mantrap

   C. Smart door

   D. Turnstile

10. Which of the following is managed using simple desktop or mobile software?

   A. Proximity door

   B. Smart locker

   C. Faraday cage

   D. Black box

Chapter

21

Data Center Architecture and Cloud Concepts

THE FOLLOWING COMPTIA NETWORK+ EXAM OBJECTIVES ARE COVERED IN THIS CHAPTER:

✓ **1.7 Explain basic corporate and datacenter network architecture.**

- Three-tiered
    - Core
    - Distribution/aggregation layer
    - Access/edge
- Software-defined networking
    - Application layer
    - Control layer
    - Infrastructure layer
    - Management plane
    - Spine and leaf
    - Software-defined network
    - Top-of-rack switching
    - Backbone
- Traffic flows
    - North-South
    - East-West
- Branch office vs. on-premises datacenter vs. colocation

- Storage area networks
    - Connection types
        - Fibre Channel over Ethernet (FCoE)
        - Fibre Channel
        - Internet Small Computer Systems Interface (iSCSI)

✓ **1.8 Summarize cloud concepts and connectivity options.**

- Deployment models
    - Public
    - Private
    - Hybrid
    - Community
- Service models
    - Software as a service (SaaS)
    - Infrastructure as a service (IaaS)
    - Platform as a service (PaaS)
    - Desktop as a service (DaaS)
- Infrastructure as code
    - Automation/orchestration
- Connectivity options
    - Virtual private network (VPN)
    - Private-direct connection to cloud provider
- Multitenancy
- Elasticity
- Scalability
- Security implications

If you didn't just skip toward the end of this book, you've trekked through enough material to know that, without a doubt, the task of designing, implementing, and maintaining a state-of-the-art network doesn't happen magically. Ending up with a great network requires some really solid planning before you buy even one device for it. And planning includes thoroughly analyzing your design for potential flaws and optimizing configurations everywhere you can to maximize the network's future throughput and performance. If you blow it in this phase, trust me—you'll pay dearly later in bottom-line costs and countless hours consumed troubleshooting and putting out the fires of faulty design.

Start planning by creating an outline that precisely delimits all goals and business requirements for the network, and refer back to it often to ensure that you don't deliver a network that falls short of your client's present needs or fails to offer the scalability to grow with those needs. Drawing out your design and jotting down all the relevant information really helps in spotting weaknesses and faults. If you have a team, make sure everyone on it gets to examine the design and evaluate it, and keep that network plan active throughout the installation phase. Hang on to this plan even after implementation has been completed because having it is like having the keys to the kingdom; it will enable you to efficiently troubleshoot any issues that could arise after everything is in place and up and running.

High-quality documentation should include a baseline for network performance because you and your client need to know what "normal" looks like in order to detect problems before they develop into disasters. Don't forget to verify that the network conforms to all internal and external regulations and that you've developed and itemized solid management procedures and security policies for future network administrators to refer to and follow.

I'll begin this chapter by going over fundamentals like plans, diagrams, baselines, rules, and regulations and then move on to cover critical hardware and software utilities you should have in your problem resolution arsenal, like packet sniffers, throughput testers, connectivity packages, and even different types of event logs on your servers. And because even the best designs usually need a little boost after they've been up and running for a while, I'll wrap things up by telling you about some cool ways you can tweak things to really jack up a network's performance, optimize its data throughput, and, well, keep it all humming along as efficiently and smoothly as possible.

To find Todd Lammle CompTIA videos and practice questions, please see www.lammle.com.

Data Center Network Architectures

Modern data center networking divides the task up into three sections called tiers or layers, as shown in Figure 21.1. Each layer has a specific function in the data center for various connectivity types. In addition to the traditional data center architectures, I will show you some of the newer designs that are often called the fabric or spine-leaf.

FIGURE 21.1 Data center three-tier architecture

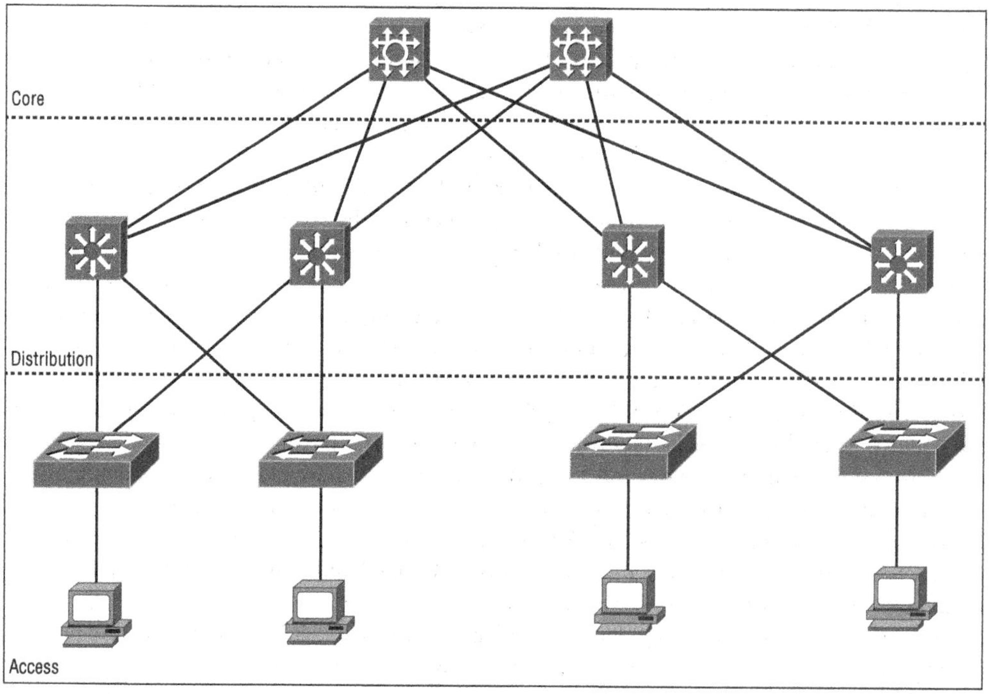

Access/Edge Layer

Starting at the outside of the network and working toward the middle is the access layer, which is also referred to as the edge. This is where all of the devices in the data center attach to the network. This could include servers and Ethernet-based storage devices. The access layer consists of a large number of switches that are often installed at the top or end of each rack to keep cable runs to the servers at a minimum to reduce cable clutter.

Access Ethernet switches are usually fixed port configurations ranging from 12 to 48 ports and are layer two/VLAN based in the most common architecture. The Spanning Tree Protocol (STP) is implemented to prevent network loops from occurring. Access switches will feature high-speed uplink ports from 1G all the way up to 100G to connect to the rest of the network at the distribution layer.

In today's data centers, much of the data flows are between servers, sometimes called East-West traffic. Since the data often stays inside the data center and is server to server, the access switches provide high-speed, low-latency local interconnections between the servers.

Distribution Layer

The middle tier of the three-tier network is called the distribution or aggregation layer. The task of the distribution layer is to provide redundant interconnections for all of the access switches, connect to the core switches, and implement security and access control and layer 3 routing. Distribution switches are chassis-based with modules for different connection types, redundant power, fans, and control logic. Also, the distribution layer provides network redundancy; if one switch should fail, the other can assume the traffic load without incurring any downtime. So, as you would guess, there will always be at least two distribution switches and sometimes more depending on the size of the network. All of the access switches have high-speed uplinks to each of the distribution switches and the distribution switches are all interconnected.

Core Layer

The core layer provides the interconnectivity between all of the network pods in the data center. These are highly redundant and very high-speed interconnection devices. The core switches are usually high-end chassis-based switches with full hardware redundancy as is used in the distribution layer. All of the distribution switches will be connected to redundant core switches to exchange traffic. The core devices can be either routers or switches, depending on the architecture of the data center backbone network, but they do not implement advanced features such as security since the job of the core is to exchange traffic with minimal delays.

Software-Defined Networking

As modern networks grew in complexity and size, it has become increasingly difficult to configure, manage, and control them. There has traditionally been no centralized control plane, which means to make even the simplest of changes often many switches had to be individually accessed and configured.

With the introduction of software-defined networking, a centralized controller is implemented and all of the networking devices are managed as a complete set and not individually. This greatly reduces the amount of configuration tasks required to make changes to the network and allows the network to be monitored as a single entity instead of many different independent switches and routers.

Application Layer

The application layer contains the standard network applications or functions like intrusion detection/prevention appliances, load balancers, proxy servers, and firewalls that either explicitly and programmatically communicate their desired network behavior or provide their network requirements to the SDN controller.

Control Layer

The control layer, or management plane, translates the instructions or requirements received from the application layer devices, proceeds the requests, and configures the SDN-controlled network devices in the infrastructure layer.

The control layer also pushes to the application layer devices information received from the networking devices.

The SDN Controller sits in the control layer and processes configuration, monitoring, and any other application-specific information between the application layer and infrastructure layer.

The northbound interface is the connection between the controller and applications, while the southbound interface is the connection between the controller and the infrastructure layer.

Infrastructure Layer

The infrastructure layer, or forwarding plane, consists of the actual networking hardware devices that control the forwarding and processing for the network. This is where the -/ leaf switches sit and are connected to the SDN controller for configuration and operation commands.

The spine and leaf switches handle packet forwarding based on the rules provided by the SDN controller.

The infrastructure layer is also responsible for collecting network health and statistics such as traffic, topology, usage, logging, errors, and analytics and sending this information to the control layer.

Management Plane

SDN network architectures are often broken into three main functions: the management plane, the control plane, and the forwarding plane.

The management plane is the configuration interface to the SDN controllers and is used to configure and manage the network. The protocols commonly used are HTTP/HTTPS for web browser access, Secure Shell (SSH) for command-line programs, and application programming interfaces (APIs) for machine-to-machine communications.

The management plane is responsible for monitoring, configuring, and maintaining the data center switch fabric. It is used to configure the forwarding plane. It is considered to be a subset of the control plane.

The control plane includes the routing and switching functions and protocols used to select the patch used to send the packets or frames as well as a basic configuration of the network.

The data plane refers to all the functions and processes that forward packets/frames from one interface to another; it moves the bits across the fabric.

Spine-Leaf–Based Two-Tier Networks

Data center networks are evolving into two-tier fabric-based networks that are also referred to as spine-leaf architecture as is shown in Figure 21.2.

FIGURE 21.2   Spine-leaf fabric architecture

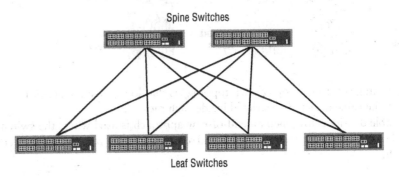

Spine Switches

Leaf Switches

Spine switches have extremely high-throughput, low-latency, and port-dense switches that have direct high-speed (10, 25, 40 to 100 Gbps) connections to each leaf switch.

Leaf switches are very similar to traditional top-of-rack access switches in that they are often 24- or 48-port 1, 10, 25, or 40 Gbps access layer connections but have the increased capability of either 40, 100, or higher uplinks to each spine switch.

The two-tier architecture offers the following advantages over the traditional three-tier designs:

Resiliency: Each leaf switch connects to every spine switch, the spanning tree is not needed, and due to layer 3 routing protocols being used, now every uplink can be used concurrently.

Latency: There is a maximum of two hops for any East-West packet flow over very high-speed links, so ultra-low latency is standard.

Performance: True active-active uplinks enable traffic to flow over the least congested high-speed links available.

Scalability: You can increase leaf switch quantity to desired port capacity and add spine switches as needed for uplinks.

Adaptability: Multiple spine-leaf networks across a multitenant or private cloud design are often managed from software-defined networking controllers.

Top-of-Rack Switching

Top-of-rack switching refers to the access switches in the data center network. The objective is to place the switch at the top of each rack and cable the devices in the rack to the local switch as shown in Figure 21.3. The top-of-rack (TOR) switch connects to the distribution or spine switches with high-speed links such as 10G, 25G, 40G, or 100G Ethernet interfaces.

FIGURE 21.3   Top-of-rack switching

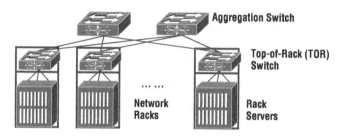

The advantage of using a top-of-rack topology is that lower-cost copper or coax cabling is used and the cable density is restricted inside each rack.

If the cable density is low, then an end-of-row approach is used where the switch is placed at the end of a row of data center cabinets and all devises in the row cable to the end-of-row switch.

Backbone

The data center backbone switches or routers are either a spine switch or core switches depending on your topology. Backbone switches have very high-speed interfaces and are used to interconnect the access or leaf switches. The backbone does not have any direct server connections, only connections to other network devices. It is common for backbone switches to have 10G and higher interface speeds and to be highly redundant.

Traffic Flows

In a data center there are server-to-server communications and also communications to the outside word. These are called North-South and East-West.

Today, there is a substantial amount of traffic between devices in the data center that is often much greater than the flows into and out of the network. It is important to understand your network and make sure it is designed properly so there are no congestion points that could cause slowdowns.

North-South

North-South traffic typically indicates data flow that either enters or leaves the data center from/to a system physically residing outside the data center, such as user to server.

North-South traffic (or data flow) is the traffic into and out of a data center. as shown in Figure 21.4.

FIGURE 21.4   North-South data flow

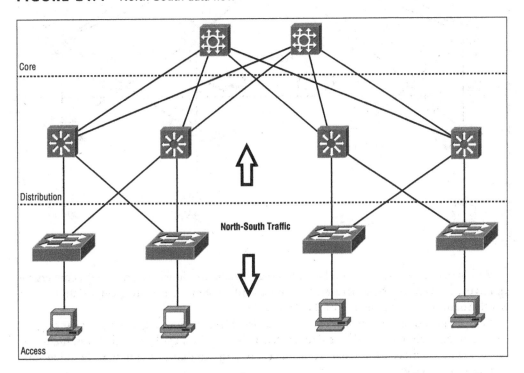

Southbound traffic is data entering the data center from the outside, such as from the Internet or a private network. Usually the border network consists of a router and firewall to define the border of the data center network with the outside world.

Data leaving the data center is referred to as northbound traffic.

East-West

East-West traffic describes the traffic flow inside a data center and refers to the data sent and received between devices, as shown in Figure 21.5.

FIGURE 21.5   East-West data flow in a data center

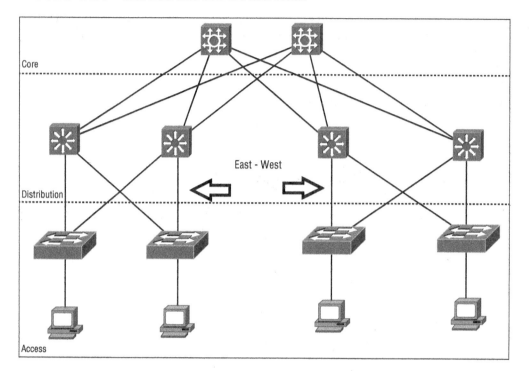

With modern decentralized application designs, virtualizations, private clouds, converged and hyper-converged infrastructures, East-West traffic volume is usually greater than the North-South traffic into and out of the data center.

Many applications, containers, servers, and virtualized networking devices exchange data between each other inside the data center. This East-West traffic benefits from high-speed interconnections for low-latency transfers of large amounts of data that the spine-leaf architecture provides.

Branch Office vs. On-premises Data Center vs. Colocation

When deciding where to place a data center, there are many variables that must be taken into account. These factors can often be in conflict with each other when deciding how to deploy your compute and storage resources. Do you place them nearest to the end users? Do you build and manage your own data center? Maybe leasing space would be a better solution?

A branch office can be a large office campus or a remote retail or distribution center. The common factor is that you put the data center nearest the people who access and rely on the services they provide. This can increase uptime because there are no remote links that can go down. It can also add to the fragility unless redundant and backup systems are put in place, which can drive up costs due to the increased number of data centers rather than a larger, centralized data center. Branch office data centers often do not have local technical expertise, and it is generally more difficult to monitor and maintain a large number of small data centers over a more centralized approach. With hyper-converged architectures, it is feasible to place some of your compute and storage resources at the remote locations for backup and local processing while still maintaining a central data center.

The traditional approach has been to maintain one or more private on-premises data centers. This puts everything under your control. A company can place staff and security in the data center and handle all of the operations themselves. It is recommended that a backup data center be deployed that is some distance away in case of an outage at the primary data center due to man-made or natural disasters. With a distance of several hundred miles separating the primary and backup data centers, a hurricane, for example, would not affect the backup if the primary data center fails.

Many companies choose to use the services of co-located (colo) data centers. Specialized co-location data center providers build, manage, and maintain high-end data center facilities and lease space. This allows you to access high-end services such as redundant power, cooling, and telco circuits for less cost than if you were to implement these in an in-house data center.

Cloud Computing and Its Effect on the Enterprise Network

Cloud computing is by far one of the hottest topics in today's IT world. Basically, cloud computing can provide virtualized processing, storage, and computing resources to users remotely, making the resources transparently available regardless of the user connection. To put it simply, some people just refer to the cloud as "someone else's hard drive." This is true, of course, but the cloud is much more than just storage.

The history of the consolidation and virtualization of our servers tells us that this has become the de facto way of implementing servers because of basic resource efficiency. Two physical servers will use twice the amount of electricity as one server, but through virtualization, one physical server can host two virtual machines, hence the main thrust toward virtualization. With it, network components can simply be shared more efficiently.

Users connecting to a cloud provider's network, whether it be for storage or applications, really don't care about the underlying infrastructure because, as computing becomes a service rather than a product, it's then considered an on-demand resource, as shown in Figure 21.6.

FIGURE 21.6 Cloud computing is on demand.

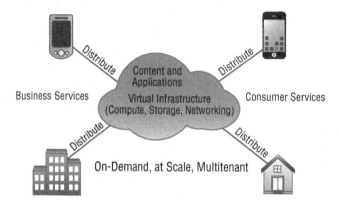

Centralization/consolidation of resources, automation of services, virtualization, and standardization are just a few of the big benefits cloud services offer. Let's take a look at Figure 21.7.

FIGURE 21.7 Advantages of cloud computing

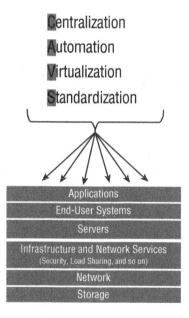

Cloud computing has several advantages over the traditional use of computer resources. The following are the advantages to the provider and to the cloud user.

The advantages to a cloud service builder or provider are:

- Cost reduction, standardization, and automation
- High utilization through virtualized, shared resources
- Easier administration
- Fall-in-place operations model

The advantages to cloud users are:

- On-demand, self-service resource provisioning
- Fast deployment cycles
- Cost effectiveness
- Centralized appearance of resources
- Highly available, horizontally scaled application architectures
- No local backups

Having centralized resources is critical for today's workforce. For example, if you have your documents stored locally on your laptop and your laptop gets stolen, you've pretty much lost everything unless you're doing constant local backups. That is so 2005!

After I lost my laptop and all the files for the book I was writing at the time, I swore (yes, I did that too) to never have my files stored locally again. I started using only Google Drive, OneDrive, and Dropbox for all my files, and they became my best backup friends. If I lose my laptop now, I just need to log in from any computer from anywhere to my service provider's logical drives and presto, I have all my files again. This is clearly a simple example of using cloud computing, specifically SaaS (which is discussed next), and it's wonderful!

So cloud computing provides for the sharing of resources, lower cost operations passed to the cloud consumer, computing scaling, and the ability to dynamically add new servers without going through the procurement and deployment process.

Service Models

Cloud providers can offer you different available resources based on your needs and budget. You can choose just a vitalized network platform or go all in with the network, OS, and application resources.

Figure 21.8 shows the three service models available, depending on the type of service you choose to get from a cloud.

You can see that Infrastructure as a Service (IaaS) allows the customer to manage most of the network, whereas Software as a Service (SaaS) doesn't allow any management by the customer, and Platform as a Service (PaaS) is somewhere in the middle of the two. Clearly, choices can be cost-driven, so the most important thing is that the customer pays only for the services or infrastructure they use.

FIGURE 21.8   Cloud computing services

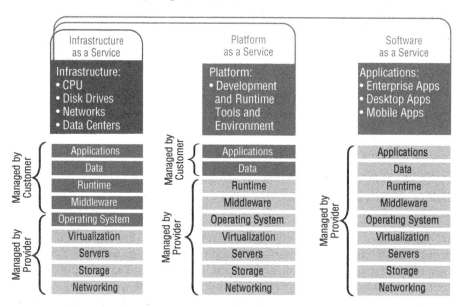

Let's take a look at each service:

IaaS: Provides only the network.   Delivers computer infrastructure—a platform virtualization environment—where the customer has the most control and management capability.

PaaS: Provides the operating system and the network.   Delivers a computing platform and solution stack, allowing customers to develop, run, and manage applications without the complexity of building and maintaining the infrastructure typically associated with developing and launching an application. An example is Windows Azure.

SaaS: Provides the required software, operating system, and network.   SaaS consists of common application software such as databases, web servers, and email software that's hosted by the SaaS vendor. The customer accesses this software over the Internet. Instead of having users install software on their computers or servers, the SaaS vendor owns the software and runs it on computers in its data center. Microsoft Office 365 and many Amazon Web Services (AWS) offerings are perfect examples of SaaS.

DaaS: Provides the desktop and other resources.   DaaS hosts the desktop operating system, such as Windows or Linux, plus the storage, infrastructure, and network resources inside the data center. A data stream of the desktop is accessed from the user's remote device, usually via a web browser or a small application residing on the user's computer, tablet, or phone. This allows all applications, data, and security standards to be hosted inside the data center for centralized management.

So depending on your business requirements and budget, cloud service providers market a very broad offering of cloud computing products, from highly specialized offerings to a large selection of services.

What's nice here is that you're offered a fixed price for each service that you use, which allows you to easily budget wisely for the future. It's true—at first, you'll have to spend a little cash on staff training, but with automation you can do more with less staff because administration will be easier and less complex. All of this works to free up the company resources to work on new business requirements and allows the company to be more agile and innovative in the long run.

Overview of Network Programmability in Enterprise Network

Right now in our current, traditional networks, our router and switch ports are the only devices that are not virtualized. So this is what we're really trying to do here—virtualize our physical ports.

First, understand that our current routers and switches run an operating system, such as Cisco IOS, that provides network functionality. This has worked well for us for 25 years or so, but it is way too cumbersome now to configure, implement, and troubleshoot these autonomous devices in today's large, complicated networks. Before you even get started, you have to understand the business requirements and then push that out to all the devices. This can take weeks or even months since each device is configured, maintained, and monitored separately.

Before we can talk about the new way to network our ports, you need to understand how our current networks forward data, which happens via these two planes:

Data Plane   This plane, also referred to as the forwarding plane, is physically responsible for forwarding frames of packets from its ingress to egress interfaces using protocols managed in the control plane. Here, data is received, the destination interface is looked up, and the forwarding of frames and packets happens, so the data plane relies completely on the control plane to provide solid information.

Control Plane   This plane is responsible for managing and controlling any forwarding table that the data plane uses. For example, routing protocols such as OSPF, EIGRP, RIP, and BGP as well as IPv4 ARP, IPv6 NDP, switch MAC address learning, and STP are all managed by the control plane.

Now that you understand that there are two planes used to forward traffic in our current or legacy network, let's look at the future of networking.

Software-Defined Networking

Traditional networks comprised many discreet devices that were managed and configured individually. Today, SDN controllers are deployed that contain the management plane operations for the complete network.

Now, all of the hardware infrastructure devices are not individually configured by network administrators. All commands and operations are now performed on the SDN controller, which is a computer, or cluster of computers, running specialized applications to monitor and configure the complete network. SDN controllers communicate southbound to the underlying hardware at the infrastructure layer for all control and management operations. There are software portals, or application programming interfaces (APIs), that communicate northbound to other applications that need to monitor and access the data center network fabric. The northbound applications could be any number of devices or applications, such as load balancers, ticketing systems, analytics applications, firewalls, authentication servers, or any application that needs to access the network traffic.

The software-defined network allows for very large-scale deployments to be automated and managed much more efficiently than in the past where each device was a stand-alone system.

SDN controllers also allow the fabric to be partitioned into virtual private clouds that different entities or companies can utilize and still be separated from the other networks running on the same platform.

Application Programming Interfaces (APIs)

If you have worked on any enterprise Wi-Fi installations in the past decade, you would have designed your physical network and then configured a type of network controller that managed all the wireless APs in the network. It's hard to imagine that anyone would install a wireless network today without some type of controller in an enterprise network, where the access points (APs) receive their directions from the controller on how to manage the wireless frames and the APs have no operating system or brains to make many decisions on their own.

The same is now true for our physical router and switch ports, and it's precisely this centralized management of network frames and packets that software-defined networking (SDN) provides to us.

SDN removes the control plane intelligence from the network devices by having a central controller manage the network instead of having a full operating system (Cisco IOS, for example) on the devices. In turn, the controller manages the network by separating the control and data (forwarding) planes, which automates configuration and the remediation of all devices.

So instead of the network devices each having individual control planes, we now have a centralized control plane, which consolidates all network operations in the SDN controller. APIs allow for applications to control and configure the network without human intervention. The APIs are another type of configuration interface just like the CLI, SNMP, or GUI interfaces, which facilitate machine-to-machine operations.

The SDN architecture slightly differs from the architecture of traditional networks by adding a third layer, the application plane, as described here and shown in Figure 21.9:

FIGURE 21.9   The SDN architecture

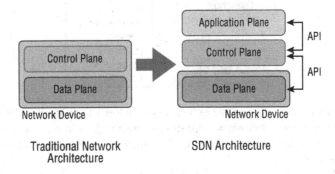

Data (or Forwarding) Plane   Contains network elements, meaning any physical or virtual device that deals with data traffic.

Control Plane   Usually a software solution, the SDN controllers reside here to provide centralized control of the router and switches that populate the data plane, removing the control plane from individual devices.

Application Plane   This new layer contains the applications that communicate their network requirements toward the controller using APIs.

SDN is pretty cool because your applications tell the network what to do based on business needs instead of you having to do it. Then the controller uses the APIs to pass instructions on to your routers, switches, or other network gear. So instead of taking weeks or months to push out a business requirement, the solution now only takes minutes.

There are two sets of APIs that SDN uses and they are very different. As you already know, the SDN controller uses APIs to communicate with both the application and data plane. Communication with the data plane is defined with southbound interfaces, while services are offered to the application plane using the northbound interface. Let's take a deeper look at this oh-so-vital CCNA objective.

Southbound APIs

Logical southbound interface (SBI) APIs (or device-to-control-plane interfaces) are used for communication between the controllers and network devices. They allow the two devices to communicate so that the controller can program the data plane forwarding tables of your routers and switches. SBIs are shown in Figure 21.10.

FIGURE 21.10 Southbound interfaces

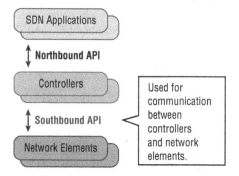

Since all the network drawings had the network gear below the controller, the APIs that talked to the devices became known as southbound, meaning, "out the southbound interface of the controller." And don't forget that with SDN, the term *interface* is no longer referring to a physical interface!

Unlike northbound APIs, southbound APIs have many standards, and you absolutely must know them well for the objectives. Let's talk about them now:

OpenFlow Describes an industry-standard API, which the ONF (opennetworking. org) defines. It configures white label switches, meaning that they are nonproprietary, and as a result defines the flow path through the network. All the configuration is done through NETCONF.

NETCONF Although not all devices support NETCONF yet, what this provides is a network management protocol standardized by the IETF. Using RPC, you can use XML to install, manipulate, and delete the configurations of network devices.

NETCONF is a protocol that allows you to modify the configuration of a networking device, but if you want to modify the device's forwarding table, then the OpenFlow protocol is the way to go.

onePK A Cisco proprietary SBI that allows you to inspect or modify the network element configuration without hardware upgrades. This makes life easier for developers by providing software development kits for Java, C, and Python.

OpFlex The name of the southbound API in the Cisco ACI world is OpFlex, an open-standard, distributed control system. Understand that OpenFlow first sends detailed and complex instructions to the control plane of the network elements in order to implement a new application policy—something called an imperative SDN model. On the other hand, OpFlex uses a declarative SDN model because the controller, which Cisco calls the APIC, sends a more abstract, "summary policy" to the network elements. The summary policy makes the controller believe that the network elements will implement the required changes using their own control planes, since the devices will use a partially centralized control plane.

Northbound APIs

To communicate from the SDN controller and the applications running over the network, you'll use northbound interfaces (NBIs), shown in Figure 21.11.

FIGURE 21.11   Northbound interfaces

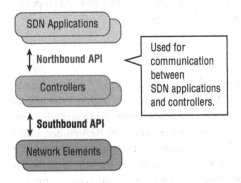

By setting up a framework that allows the application to demand the network setup with the configuration that it needs, the NBIs allow your applications to manage and control the network. This is priceless for saving time because you no longer need to adjust and tweak your network to get a service or application running correctly.

The NBI applications include a wide variety of automated network services, from network virtualization and dynamic virtual network provisioning to more granular firewall monitoring, user identity management, and access policy control. This allows for cloud orchestration applications that tie together, for server provisioning, storage, and networking that enables a complete rollout of new cloud services in minutes instead of weeks!

Sadly, at the time of this writing, there is no single northbound interface that you can use for communication between the controller and all applications. So instead, you use various and sundry northbound APIs, with each one working only with a specific set of applications.

Most of the time, applications used by NBIs will be on the same system as the APIC controller, so the APIs don't need to send messages over the network since both programs run on the same system. However, if they don't reside on the same system, REST (Representational State Transfer) comes into play; it uses HTTP messages to transfer data over the API for applications that sit on different hosts.

Managing Network Documentation

I'll admit it—creating network documentation is one of my least favorite tasks in network administration. It just isn't as exciting to me as learning about the coolest new technology or tackling and solving a challenging problem. Part of it may be that I think I know my networks well enough—after all, I installed and configured them, so if something comes up, it should be easy to figure it out and fix it, right? And most of the time I can do that, but as networks get bigger and more complex, it gets harder and harder to remember it all. Plus, it's an integral part of the service I provide for my clients to have seriously solid documentation at hand to refer to after I've left the scene and turned their network over to them. So while I'll admit that creating documentation isn't something I get excited about, I know from experience that having it around is critical when problems come up—for myself and for my clients' technicians and administrators, who may not have been part of the installation process and simply aren't familiar with the system.

Using SNMP

In Chapter 6, "Introduction to the Internet Protocol," I introduced you to Simple Network Management Protocol (SNMP), which is used to gather information from and send settings to devices that are SNMP compatible. Make sure to thoroughly review the differences between versions 1, 2, and 3 that we discussed there! Remember, I told you SNMP gathers data by polling the devices on the network from a management station at fixed or random intervals, requiring them to disclose certain information. This is a big factor that really helps to simplify the process of gathering information about your entire internetwork.

SNMP uses UDP to transfer messages back and forth between the management system and the agents running on the managed devices. Inside the UDP packets (called *datagrams*) are commands from the management system to the agent. These commands can be used either to get information from the device about its state (SNMP `GetRequest`) or to make a change in the device's configuration (`SetRequest`). If a `GetRequest` command has been sent, the device will respond with an SNMP response. If there's a piece of information that's particularly interesting to an administrator about the device, the administrator can set something called a *trap* on the device.

So, no whining! Like it or not, we're going to create some solid documentation. But because I'm guessing that you really don't want to redo it, it's a very good idea to keep it safe in at least three forms:

- An electronic copy that you can easily modify after configuration changes

- A hard copy in a binder of some sort, stored in an easily accessible location

- A copy on an external drive to keep in a really safe place (even off site) in case something happens to the other two or the building or part of it burns to the ground

So why the hard copy? Well, what if the computer storing the electronic copy totally crashes and burns at exactly the same time a major crisis develops? Good thing you have that paper documentation on hand for reference! Plus, sometimes you'll be troubleshooting on the run—maybe literally, as in running down the hall to the disaster's origin. Having that binder containing key configuration information on board could save you a lot of time and trouble, and it's also handy for making notes to yourself as you troubleshoot. Also, depending on the size of the intranet and the amount of people staffing the IT department, it might be smart to have several hard copies. Just always make sure they're only checked out by staff who are cleared to have them and that they're all returned to a secure location at the end of each shift. You definitely don't want that information in the wrong hands!

Now that I've hopefully convinced you that you absolutely must have tight documentation, let's take a look at the different types you need on hand so you can learn how to assemble them.

Schematics and Diagrams

Now reading network documentation doesn't exactly compete with racing your friends on jet skis, but it's really not that bad. It's better than eating canned spinach, and sometimes it's actually interesting to check out schematics and diagrams—especially when they describe innovative, elegant designs or when you're hunting down clues needed to solve an intricate problem with an elusive solution. I can't tell you how many times, if something isn't working between point A and point B, a solid diagram of the network that precisely describes what exists between point A and point B has totally saved the day. Another time when these tools come in handy is when you need to extend your network and want a clear picture of how the expanded version will look and work. Will the new addition cause one part of the network to become bogged down while another remains underutilized? You get the idea.

Diagrams can be simple sketches created while brainstorming or troubleshooting on the fly. They can also be highly detailed, refined illustrations created with some of the snappy software packages around today, like Microsoft Visio, SmartDraw, and a host of computer-aided design (CAD) programs. Some of the more complex varieties, especially CAD programs, are super pricey. But whatever tool you use to draw pictures about your networks, they basically fall into these groups:

- Wiring diagrams/schematics
- Physical network diagrams
- Logical network diagrams
- Asset management
- IP address utilization
- Vendor documentation

Wiring Schematics

Wireless is definitely the wave of the future, but for now, even the most extensive wireless networks have a wired backbone they rely on to connect them to the rest of humanity.

That skeleton is made up of cabled physical media like coax, fiber, and twisted-pair. Surprisingly, it is the latter—specifically, unshielded twisted-pair (UTP)—that screams to be represented in a diagram. You'll see why in a minute. To help you follow me, let's review what we learned in Chapter 3, "Networking Connectors and Wiring Standards." We'll start by checking out Figure 21.12 (a diagram!) that describes the fact that UTP cables use an RJ-45 connector (*RJ* stands for *registered jack*).

FIGURE 21.12 RJ-45 connector

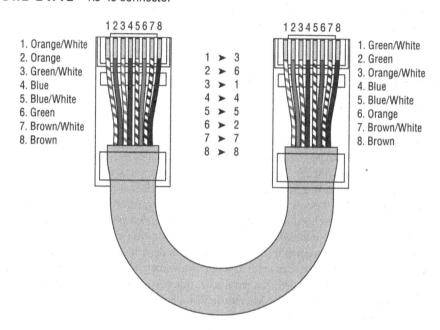

What we see here is that pin 1 is on the left and pin 8 is on the right, so clearly, within your UTP cable, you need to make sure the right wires get to the right pins. No worries if you got your cables premade from the store, but making them yourself not only saves you a bunch of money, it allows you to customize cable lengths, which is really important!

Table 21.1 matches the colors for the wire associated with each pin, based on the Electronic Industries Association and the Telecommunications Industry Alliance (TIA/EIA) 568B wiring standard.

NOTE | In the print edition the figure is in black and white and you cannot see the color, however, in the e-books the figures are all in color.

TABLE 21.1   Standard TIA/EIA 568B wiring

Pin	Color
1	Orange/White
2	Orange
3	Green/White
4	Blue
5	Blue/White
6	Green
7	Brown/White
8	Brown

Standard drop cables, or *patch cables*, have the pins in the same order on both connectors. If you're connecting a computer to another computer directly, you should already know that you need a *crossover cable* that has one connector with flipped wires. Specifically, pins 1 and 3 and pins 2 and 6 get switched to ensure that the send port from one computer's network interface card (NIC) gets attached to the receive port on the other computer's NIC. Crossover cables were also used to connect older routers, switches, and hubs through their uplink ports. Figure 21.13 shows you what this looks like.

FIGURE 21.13   Two ends of a crossover cable

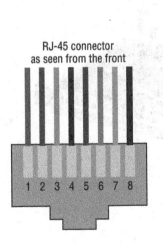
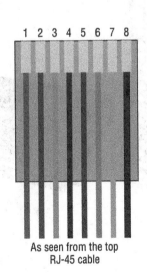

RJ-45 connector as seen from the front

As seen from the top RJ-45 cable

The crossover cable shown in Figure 21.13 is for connections up to 100BaseTX. If you are using 1000BaseT4, all four pairs of wires get crossed at the opposite end, meaning pins 4 and 7 and pins 5 and 8 get crossed as well. The Automatic MDI/MDI+ Configuration standard—an optional feature of the 1000BaseT standard—makes the need for cross-over cables between Gigabit-capable interfaces a thing of the past.

This is where having a diagram is golden. Let's say you're troubleshooting a network and discover connectivity problems between two hosts. Because you've got the map, you know the cable running between them is brand-new and custom made. This should tell you to go directly to that new cable because it's likely it was poorly made and is therefore causing the snag.

Another reason it's so important to diagram all things wiring is that all wires have to plug into something somewhere, and it's really good to know what and where that is. Whether it's into a hub, a switch, a router, a workstation, or the wall, you positively need to know the who, what, where, when, and how of the way the wiring is attached.

After adding a new cable segment on your network, you need to update the wiring schematics.

For medium to large networks, devices like switches and routers are rack-mounted and would look something like the switch in Figure 21.14.

FIGURE 21.14 Rack-mounted switches

Knowing someone's or something's name is important because it helps us differentiate between people and things—especially when communicating with each other. If you want to be specific, you can't just say, "You know that router in the rack?" This is why coming up with a good naming system for all the devices living in your racks will be invaluable for ensuring that your wires don't get crossed.

Okay, I know it probably seems like we're edging over into OCD territory, but stay with me here; in addition to labeling, well, everything so far, you should actually label both ends of your cables too. If something happens (earthquake, tsunami, temper tantrum, even repairs) and more than one cable gets unplugged at the same time, it can get really messy scrambling to reconnect them from memory—fast!

Physical Network Diagrams

Physical diagrams were covered in Chapter 14, "Organizational Documents and Policies"; please refer to it for a detailed explanation.

Logical Network Diagrams

Logical diagrams were also covered in Chapter 14; please refer to that chapter for a detailed explanation.

Asset Management

Asset management involves tracking all network assets like computers, routers, switches, and hubs through their entire life cycles. Most organizations find it beneficial to utilize asset identification numbers to facilitate this process. The ISO has established standards regarding asset management. The ISO 19770 family consists of four major parts:

- 19770-1 is a process-related standard that outlines best practices for IT asset management in an organization.

- 19770-2 is a standard for machine encapsulation (in the form of an XML file known as a SWID tag) of inventory data—allowing users to easily identify what software is deployed on a given device.

- 19770-3 is a standard that provides a schema for machine encapsulation of entitlements and rights associated with software licenses. The records (known as ENTs) will describe all entitlements and rights attendant to a piece of software and the method for measurement of license/entitlement consumption.

- 19770-4 allows for standardized reporting of utilization of resources. This is crucial when considering complex data center license types and for the management of cloud-based software and hardware (Software as a Service, or SaaS, and Infrastructure as a Service, or IaaS).

IP Address Utilization

Documenting the current IP addressing scheme can also be highly beneficial, especially when changes are required. Not only is this really helpful to new technicians, it's very useful when identifying IP addressing issues that can lead to future problems. In many cases IP addresses are configured over a long period of time with no real thought or planning on the macro level.

Current and correct documentation can help administrators identify discontiguous networks (where subnets of a major network are separated by another major network) that can cause routing protocol issues. Proper IP address design can also facilitate summarization, which makes routing tables smaller, speeding the routing process. None of these wise design choices can be made without proper IP address documentation.

Vendor Documentation

Vendor agreements often have beneficial clauses that were negotiated during the purchase process. Many also contain critical details concerning SLAs and deadlines for warranties. These documents need to be organized and stored safely for future reference. Creating a spreadsheet or some other form of tracking documentation that alerts you of upcoming dates of interest can be a huge advantage!

Network Monitoring

Identifying performance issues within the network is only one of the reasons to perform structured monitoring. Security issues also require constant monitoring. In the following sections, we'll look into both types of monitoring and cover some of the best practices and guidelines for success.

Baselines

Baselines were covered in Chapter 14; please refer to that chapter for a detailed explanation.

Processes

When monitoring baselines, there are methods that can be used to enhance the process. In this section we'll look at three particularly helpful processes:

Log Reviewing   While regular log review is always recommended anyway, it can have benefits when monitoring baselines. In some cases you may be able to identify a non-compliant device by the entries in its log or in the logs of infrastructure devices.

Patch Management Issues   In some cases, applying patches, especially device driver updates, can be problematic. Issues can include the device no longer working, loss of some key functionality, or generation of odd error messages.

Rollback   While *rollback* is a general term that applies to reversing any operation about device drivers, it means to remove the newer driver and go back to using the previous driver. This is typically an available option if the last driver you used is the driver to which you want to roll back.

Onboarding and Offboarding of Mobile Devices

Increasingly, users are doing work on their mobile devices that they once performed on laptops and desktop computers. Moreover, they are demanding that they be able to use their personal devices to work on the company network. This presents a huge security issue for the IT department because they have to secure these devices while simultaneously exercising much less control over them.

The security team must have a way to prevent these personal devices from introducing malware and other security issues to the network. Bring your own device (BYOD) initiatives can be successful if implemented correctly. The key is to implement control over these personal devices that leave the safety of your network and return later after potentially being exposed to environments that are out of your control. One of the methods that has been employed successfully to accomplish this goal is network access control (NAC), covered in the next section.

NAC

Today's network access control (NAC) goes beyond simply authenticating users and devices before they are allowed into the network. Today's mobile workforce presents challenges that require additional services. These services are called Network Access Control in the Cisco world, and Network Access Protection in the Microsoft world, but the goals of these features are the same: to examine all devices requesting network access for malware, missing security updates, and any other security issues any device could potentially introduce to the network.

In some cases NAC goes beyond simply denying access to systems that fail inspection. NAC can even redirect the failed system to a remediation server, which will then apply patches and updates before allowing the device access to the network. These systems can be especially helpful in supporting a BYOD initiative while still maintaining the security of the network.

Policies, Procedures, and Regulations

It's up to us, individually and corporately, to nail down solid guidelines for the necessary *policies* and *procedures* for network installation and operation. Some organizations are bound by regulations that also affect how they conduct their business, and that kind of thing clearly needs to be involved in their choices. But let me take a minute to make sure you understand the difference between policies and procedures.

Policies govern how the network is configured and operated as well as how people are expected to behave on it. They're in place to direct things like how users access resources and which employees and groups get various types of network access and/or privileges. Basically, policies give people guidelines as to what they are expected to do. Procedures are precise descriptions of the appropriate steps to follow in a given situation, such as what to do when an employee is terminated or what to do in the event of a natural disaster. They often dictate precisely how to execute policies as well.

One of the most important aspects of any policy or procedure is that it's given high-level management support. This is because neither will be very effective if there aren't any consequences for not following the rules!

Policies

I talked extensively about security policies in Chapter 16, "Common Security Concepts," so if you're drawing a blank, you can go back there for details. Here's a summary list of factors that most policies cover:

Security Policies   These are policies applied to users to help maintain security in the network:

- Clean-desk policies: These policies are designed to prevent users from leaving sensitive documents on unattended desks.

- Network access (who, what, and how): These policies control which users can access which portions of the network. They should be designed around job responsibilities.

- Acceptable-use policies (AUPs): These policies should be as comprehensive as possible and should outline *every* action that is allowed in addition to those that are *not* allowed. They should also specify which devices are allowed, which websites are allowed, and the proper use of company equipment.

- Consent to monitoring: These policies are designed to constantly remind users that their activities are subject to monitoring as they are using company equipment and as such they should have no expectation of privacy.

- Privileged user agreement: Whenever a user is given some right normally possessed by the administrator, they obtain a privileged user account. In this agreement, they agree to use these rights responsibly.

- Password policy: This policy defines the requirements for all passwords, including length, complexity, and age.

- Licensing restrictions: These restrictions define the procedures used to ensure that all software license agreements are not violated.

- International export controls: in accordance with all agreements between countries in which the organization does business, all allowable export destinations and import sources are defined.

- Data loss prevention: This policy defines all procedures for preventing the egress of sensitive data from the network and may include references to the use of data loss prevention (DLP) software.

- Remote access policies: These policies define the requirements for all remote access connections to the enterprise. This may cover VPN, dial-up, and wireless access methods.

- Incident response policies: These policies define a scripted and repeatable process for responding to incidents and responsibilities of various roles in the network in this process.

- Nondisclosure agreement (NDA): All scenarios in which contractors and other third parties must execute a nondisclosure agreement are defined.

- System life cycle: The steps in the asset life cycle are defined, including acquisition, implementation, maintenance, and decommissioning. It specifies certain due diligence activities to be performed in each phase.

- Asset disposal: This is usually a subset of the system life cycle and prescribes methods of ensuring that sensitive data is removed from devices before disposal.

Change Management   These policies ensure a consistent approach to managing changes to network configurations:

- Disposal of network equipment

- Use of recording equipment

- How passwords are managed (length and complexity required, and how often they need to be changed)

- Types of security hardware in place

- How often to do backups and take other fault-tolerance measures

- What to do with user accounts after an employee leaves the company

Procedures

These are the actions to be taken in specific situations:

- Disciplinary action to be taken if a policy is broken

- What to do during an audit

- How issues are reported to management

- What to do when someone has locked themselves out of their account

- How to properly install or remove software on servers

- What to do if files on the servers suddenly appear to be "missing" or altered

- How to respond when a network computer has a virus

- Actions to take if it appears that a hacker has broken into the network

- Actions to take if there is a physical emergency like a fire or flood

So you get the idea, right? For every policy on your network, there should be a credible related procedure that clearly dictates the steps to take in order to fulfill it. And you know that policies and procedures are as unique as the wide array of companies and organizations that create and employ them. But all this doesn't mean you can't borrow good ideas and plans from others and tweak them a bit to meet your requirements.

An example of a network access policy is a time-of-day restriction on logging into the network.

Standard Business Documents

In the course of supporting mergers and acquisitions, and in providing support to departments within an organization, it's always important to keep the details of agreements in writing to reduce the risk of misunderstanding. In this section, I'll discuss standard documents that are used in these situations. You should be familiar with the purpose of the following documents:

Statement of Work (SOW)   This document spells out all details concerning what work is to be performed, deliverables, and the required timeline for a vendor to perform the specified work.

Memorandum of Understanding (MOU)   This is an agreement between two or more organizations that details a common line of action. It is often used when parties do not have a legal commitment or they cannot create a legally enforceable agreement. In some cases, it is referred to as a letter of intent.

Master License Agreement (MLA)   This is an agreement whereby one party is agreeing to pay another party for the use of a piece of software for a period of time. These agreements, as you would expect, are pretty common in the IT world.

Service-Level Agreement (SLA)   This is an agreement that defines the allowable time in which a party must respond to issues on behalf of the other party. Most service contracts are accompanied by an SLA, which often includes security priorities, responsibilities, guarantees, and warranties.

Regulations

Regulations are rules imposed on your organization by an outside agency, like a certifying board or a government entity, and they're usually totally rigid and immutable. The list of possible regulations that your company could be subjected to is so exhaustively long, there's no way I can include them all in this book. Different regulations exist for different types of organizations, depending on whether they're corporate, nonprofit, scientific, educational, legal, governmental, and so on, and they also vary by where the organization is located.

For instance, US governmental regulations vary by county and state, federal regulations are piled on top of those, and many other countries have multiple regulatory bodies as well. The Sarbanes-Oxley Act of 2002 (SOX) is an example of a regulation system imposed on all publicly traded companies in the United States. Its main goal was to ensure corporate responsibility and sound accounting practices, and although that may not sound like it would have much of an effect on your IT department, it does because a lot of the provisions in this act target the retention and protection of data. Believe me, something as innocent sounding as deleting old emails could get you in trouble—if any of them could've remotely had a material impact on the company's financial disclosures, deleting them could actually be breaking the law. All good to know, so be aware, and be careful!

I'm not going to give you a laundry list of regulations to memorize here, but I will tell you that IT regulations center around something known as the CIA triad:

- Confidentiality: Only authorized users have access to the data.
- Integrity: The data is accurate and complete.
- Availability: Authorized users have access to the data when access is needed.

One of the most commonly applied regulations is the ISO/IEC 27002 standard for information security, previously known as ISO 17799, renamed in 2007 and updated in 2013. It was developed by the International Organization for Standardization (ISO) and the International Electrotechnical Commission (IEC), and it is based on British Standard (BS) 7799-1:1999.

The official title of ISO/IEC 27002 is *Information technology - Security techniques - Code of practice for information security controls*. Although it's beyond our scope to get into the details of this standard, know that the following items are among the topics it covers:

- Risk assessment
- Security policy
- Organization of information security
- Asset management
- Human-resources security
- Physical and environmental security
- Communications and operations management
- Access control
- Information systems acquisition, development, and maintenance
- Information security incident management
- Business-continuity management
- Compliance

So, what do you take with you from this? Your mission is clear. Know the regulations your company is expected to comply with, and make sure your IT policies and procedures are totally in line with any regulations so it's easy for you to comply with them. No sense getting hauled off to jail because you didn't archive an email, right?

Safety Practices

In the course of doing business, it's the responsibility of the company to protect the safety of its workers, customers, vendors, and business partners. In the following sections, some of the issues that affect safety are considered, along with best practices and guidelines for preventing injuries and damage to equipment.

Electrical Safety

IT personnel spend a great deal of time dealing with electrical devices. Therefore, electrical safety should be stressed in all procedures. In this section, we'll look at key issues involved with electrical safety, including those that are relevant to preventing injuries to people and damage to computer equipment.

Grounding   *Grounding* is the electrical term for providing a path for an electrical charge to follow to return to earth. To prevent injuring yourself when you are working with equipment, you should ensure that you are grounded. To avoid damaging the equipment with which you are working, it should also be grounded.

You can provide grounding to yourself or the equipment with either a grounding strap or a grounding mat. Either of these should be plugged into the ground of an electrical outlet.

ESD   *Electrostatic discharge (ESD)* is the technical term for what happens whenever two objects of dissimilar charge come in contact. ESD can be generated easily by walking across a carpeted floor. While the amount of ESD generated doing that may shock you if you touch a doorknob, it's really not enough to harm you. However, even that small amount is enough to seriously damage sensitive parts of computers.

This is exactly why we ground both ourselves and the equipment—to prevent ESD damage. Always use mats and straps to prevent damage when working with computing equipment.

Static   When ESD is created, it's a form of static energy. Extremely dry conditions in the area where computers are utilized make the problem of static electricity worse. This is why the humidity of the area must be controlled; the area must not be too humid, which causes corrosion of electrical connections, and it should not be too dry, which causes static buildup and potential for damage.

Installation Safety

While protecting yourself from electrical injury is very important, it's not the only safety issue you've got to take into consideration. Other types of injuries can also occur, ranging from a simple pulled muscle to a more serious incident requiring a trip to the hospital. The following issues related to installing equipment should also be taken into consideration.

Lifting Equipment   Oftentimes when a piece of equipment is being installed, the time pressures involved and the rush to "get 'er done" can lead to improper lifting. Always keep in mind these safe lifting techniques:

- Be careful to not twist when lifting. Keep the weight at the center of your body.
- Keep objects as close to your body as possible and at waist level.
- Lift with your legs, not your back. When you have to pick up something, bend at the knees, not at the waist. You want to maintain the natural curve of the back and spine when lifting.
- Whenever possible, push instead of pull.

Rack Installation   Even for a small business, it's bad business to operate computing equipment in a poor environment such as on a shelf. There is a reason so many devices come "rack ready." Racks not only make for a neat and clean server room or closet, but when combined with proper cable management and environmental control, they provide an environment that allows the devices to breathe and stay cool.

When installing racks, always follow the manufacturer's directions and always use the correct tools! Countless screws have been ruined using the wrong tool.

Server racks are measured in terms of rack units, usually written as RU or simply U. One rack unit equals 1.75 inches (44.45 mm) in height, with compliant equipment measured in multiples of U. Network switches are generally 1U to 2U, servers can range from 1U to 4U, and blade servers can be anywhere from 5U to 10U or more.

I'll cover the types of racks you're likely to encounter in more detail later in this chapter.

Placement   The most important issue when placing devices is to ensure proper cooling and protection from moisture. It's a good idea to align the racks and install your equipment in hot and cold aisles. The goal of a hot aisle/cold aisle configuration is to conserve energy and lower cooling costs by managing air flow.

Hot aisle/cold aisle design involves lining up racks in alternating rows with cold air intakes facing one way and hot air exhausts facing the other. The rows composed of rack fronts are called cold aisles. Typically, cold aisles face air conditioner output ducts. The rows the heated exhausts pour into are called hot aisles and face air conditioner return ducts. Moreover, all of the racks and the equipment they hold should never be on the floor. There should be a raised floor to provide protection against water.

Figure 21.15 shows a solid arrangement.

FIGURE 21.15   Hot and cold aisles

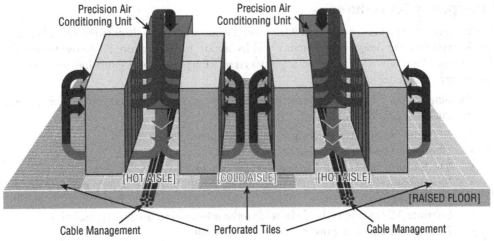

Tool Safety   It's worth mentioning again that the first step on safely using tools is to make sure you're properly grounded. Besides practicing tool safety for your own welfare, you should do so to protect the equipment. Here are some specific guidelines to follow:

- Avoid using pencils inside a computer. They can become a conductor and cause damage.

- Be sure that the tools you are using have not been magnetized. Magnetic fields can be harmful to data stored on magnetic media.

- When using compressed air to clean inside the computer, blow the air around the components with a minimum distance of 4 inches (10 centimeters) from the nozzle.

- Clean the contacts on components with isopropyl alcohol. Do not use rubbing alcohol.

- Never use a standard vacuum cleaner inside a computer case. The plastic parts of the vacuum cleaner can build up static electricity and discharge to the components. Use only vacuums that are approved for electronic components.

MSDS   In the course of installing, servicing, and repairing equipment, you'll come in contact with many different types of materials. Some are safer than others. You can get all the information you need regarding the safe handling of materials by reviewing the *Material Safety Data Sheet (MSDS)*.

Any type of chemical, equipment, or supply that has the potential to harm the environment or people has to have an MSDS associated with it. These are traditionally created by the manufacturer and describe the boiling point, melting point, flash point, and potential health risks. You can obtain them from the manufacturer or from the Environmental Protection Agency (EPA).

Emergency Procedures

Every organization should be prepared for emergencies of all types. If possible, this planning should start with the design of the facility and its layout. In this section, I'll go over some of the components of a well-planned emergency system along with some guidelines for maintaining safety on a day-to-day basis.

Building Layout   Planning for emergencies can start with the layout of the facility. Here are some key considerations:

- All walls should have a two-hour minimum fire rating.
- Doors must resist forcible entry.
- The location and type of fire suppression systems should be known.
- Flooring in server rooms and wiring closets should be raised to help mitigate flooding damage.
- Separate AC units must be dedicated to the information processing facilities.
- Backup and alternate power sources should exist.

Fire Escape Plan   You should develop a plan that identifies the escape route in the event of a fire. You should create a facility map showing the escape route for each section of the building, keeping in mind that it's better to use multiple exits to move people out quickly. These diagrams should be placed in all areas.

Safety/Emergency Exits   All escape routes on the map should have the following characteristics:

- Clearly marked and well lit
- Wide enough to accommodate the expected number of people
- Clear of obstructions

Fail Open/Fail Close   Door systems that have electronic locks may lose power during a fire. When they do, they may lock automatically (fail close) or unlock automatically (fail open). While a fail close setting may enhance security during an electrical outage, you should consider the effect it will have during an evacuation and take steps to ensure that everyone can get out of the building when the time comes.

Emergency Alert System   All facilities should be equipped with a system to alert all employees when a fire or any other type of emergency occurs. It might be advisable to connect the facility to the Emergency Alert System (EAS), which is a national warning system in the United States. One of the functions of this system is to alert the public of local weather emergencies such as tornadoes and flash floods. EAS messages are transmitted via AM and FM radio, broadcast television, cable television, and the Land Mobile Radio Service as well as VHF, UHF, and FiOS (wireline video providers).

Fire-Suppression Systems   While fire extinguishers are important and should be placed throughout a facility, when large numbers of computing devices are present, it is worth the money to protect them with a fire-suppression system. The following types of systems exist:

- Wet pipe systems use water contained in pipes to extinguish the fire.
- Dry pipe systems hold the water in a holding tank instead of in the pipes.
- Preaction systems operate like a dry pipe system except that the sprinkler head holds a thermal-fusible link that must melt before the water is released.
- Deluge systems allow large amounts of water to be released into the room, which obviously makes this not a good choice where computing equipment will be located.
- Today, most companies use a fire suppressant like halon, which is known as a "Clean Agent, an electrically non-conducting, volatile, or gaseous fire extinguisher that does not leave a residue upon evaporation." Leaving no residue means not rendering inoperative expensive networking equipment as water can do if released in a data center. It's remarkably safe for human exposure, meaning that it won't poison living things, and it will allow you to leave the area safely, returning only after the fire department gives the all-clear.

HVAC

The heating and air-conditioning systems must support the massive amounts of computing equipment deployed by most enterprises. Computing equipment and infrastructure devices like routers and switches do not like the following conditions:

- Heat. Excessive heat causes reboots and crashes.

- High humidity. It causes corrosion problems with connections.

- Low humidity. Dry conditions encourage static electricity, which can damage equipment.

  Here are some important facts to know about temperature:

- At 100 degrees, damage starts occurring to magnetic media.

- At 175 degrees, damage starts occurring to computers and peripherals.

- At 350 degrees, damage starts occurring to paper products.

Implementing Network Segmentation

Maintaining security in the network can be made easier by segmenting the network and controlling access from one segment to another. Segmentation can be done at several layers of the OSI model. The most extreme segmentation would be at layer 1 if the networks are actually physically separated from one another. In other cases, it may be sufficient to segment a network at layer 2 or layer 3. Coming up next, we'll look at some systems that require segmentation from other networks at one layer or another.

SCADA Systems/Industrial Control Systems

Industrial control system (ICS) is a general term that encompasses several types of control systems used in industrial production. The most widespread is supervisory control and data acquisition (SCADA). SCADA is a system operating with coded signals over communication channels to provide control of remote equipment. It includes the following components:

- Sensors, which typically have digital or analog I/O, and these signals are not in a form that can be easily communicated over long distances

- Remote terminal units (RTUs), which connect to the sensors and convert sensor data to digital data (includes telemetry hardware)

- Programmable logic controllers (PLCs), which connect to the sensors and convert sensor data to digital data (does not include telemetry hardware)

- Telemetry systems, which connect RTUs and PLCs to control centers and the enterprise

- Human interface, which presents data to the operator

- ICS server, also called a data acquisition server, which uses coded signals over communication channels to acquire information about the status of the remote equipment for display or for recording functions

The distributed control system (DCS) network should be a closed network, meaning it should be securely segregated from other networks. The Stuxnet virus hit the SCADA used for the control and monitoring of industrial processes.

Medianets

Medianets are networks primarily devoted to VoIP and video data that often require segmentation from the rest of the network at some layer. We implement segmentation for two reasons: first, to ensure the security of the data, and second, to ensure that the network delivers the high performance and low latency required by these applications. One such high-demand application is video teleconferencing (VTC), which I'll cover next.

Video Teleconferencing (VTC)

IP video has ushered in a new age of remote collaboration. This has saved a great deal of money on travel expenses and enabled more efficient use of time. When you're implementing IP video systems, consider and plan for the following issues:

- Expect a large increase in the need for bandwidth.
- QoS will need to be configured to ensure performance.
- Storage will need to be provisioned for the camera recordings.
- Initial cost may be high.

There are two types of VTC systems. Let's look at both:

ISDN The first VTC systems were ISDN based. These systems were based on a standard called H.320. While the bandwidth in each ISDN line is quite low by today's standard (128 Kbps per line), multiple lines could be combined or bonded.

IP/SIP VTC systems based on IP use a standard called H.323. Since these work on a packet-switched network, you don't need a direct ISDN link between the sites. Session Initiation Protocol (SIP) can also be used, and it operates over IP but lacks many of the structured call control functions that H.323 provides.

Legacy Systems

Legacy systems are systems that are older and incompatible with more modern systems and equipment. They may also be less secure and no longer supported by the vendor. In some cases, these legacy systems, especially with respect to industrial control systems, use propriety protocols that prevent them from communicating on the IP-based network. It's a good idea to segment these systems to protect them from security issues they aren't equipped to handle or even just to allow them to function correctly.

Separate Private/Public Networks

Public IP addressing isn't typically used in a modern network. Instead, private IP addresses are used and network address translation (NAT) services are employed to convert traffic to a public IP address when the traffic enters the Internet. While this is one of the strategies used to conserve the public IP address space, it also serves to segment the private network from the public network (Internet). Hiding the actual IP address (private) of the hosts inside the network makes it very difficult to make an unsolicited connection to a system on the inside of the network from the outside.

Honeypot/Honeynet

Another segmentation tactic is to create honeypots and honeynets. Honeypots are systems strategically configured to be attractive to hackers and to lure them into spending enough time attacking them to allow information to be gathered about the attack. In some cases, entire networks called honeynets are attractively configured for this purpose.

You need to make sure that either of these types of systems do not provide direct connections to any important systems. Their ultimate purpose is to divert attention from valuable resources and to gather as much information about an attack as possible. A tarpit is a type of honeypot designed to provide a very slow connection to the hacker so that the attack takes enough time to be properly analyzed.

Testing Lab

Testing labs are used for many purposes. Sometimes they're created as an environment for developers to test applications. They may also be used to test operating system patches and antivirus updates. These environments may even be virtual environments. Virtualization works well for testing labs because it makes it easier to ensure that the virtual networks have no physical connection to the rest of the network, providing necessary segmentation.

Security

One of the biggest reasons for implementing segmentation is for security purposes. At layer 1, this means complete physical separation. However, if you don't want to go with complete segmentation, you can also segment at layer 2 on switches by implementing VLANs and port security. This can prevent connections between systems that are connected to the same switch. They can also be used to organize users into common networks regardless of their physical location.

If segmentation at layer 3 is required, this is achieved using access control lists on routers to control access from one subnet to another or from one VLAN to another. Firewalls can implement these types of access lists as well.

Compliance

Finally, network segmentation may be required to comply with an industry regulation. For example, while it's not strictly required, the Payment Card Industry Data Security Standard (PCI DSS) strongly recommends that a credit card network should be segmented from the regular network. If you choose not to do this, your entire network must be compliant with all sections of the standard.

Network Optimization

Regardless of how well a network is functioning, you should never stop trying to optimize its performance. This is especially true when latency-sensitive applications such as VoIP, streaming video, and web conferencing are implemented. In the next several sections, I'll discuss some techniques you can use to ensure that these applications and services deliver on their promise of increased functionality.

Reasons to Optimize Your Network's Performance

So why do we have networks, anyway? I don't mean this in a historical sense; I mean pragmatically. The reason they've become such precious resources is that as our world becomes increasingly smaller and more connected we need to be able to keep in touch now more than ever. Networks make accessing resources easy for people who can't be in the same location as the resources they need—including other people.

In essence, networks of all types are really complex tools we use to facilitate communication from afar and to allow lots of us to access the resources we need to keep up with the demands imposed on us in today's lightning-paced world. And use them we do—a lot! And when we have many, many people trying to access one resource like a valuable file server or a shared database, our systems can get as bogged down and clogged as a freeway at rush hour. Just as road rage can result from driving on one of those not-so-expressways, frustrated people can direct some serious hostility at you if the same thing happens when they're trying to get somewhere using a network that's crawling along at snail speed.

This is why optimizing performance is in everyone's best interest—it keeps you and your network's users happily humming along. Optimization includes things like splitting up network segments, stopping unnecessary services on servers, offloading one server's work onto another, and upgrading outmoded hardware devices to newer, faster models. I'll get to exactly how to make all this happen coming up soon, but first, I'm going to talk about the theories behind performance optimization and even more about the reasons for making sure performance is at its best.

In a perfect world, there would be unlimited bandwidth, but in reality, you're more likely to find Bigfoot. So, it's helpful to have some great strategies up your sleeve.

If you look at what computers are used for today, there's a huge difference between the files we transfer now versus those transferred even three to five years ago. Now we do things like watch movies online without them stalling, and we can send huge email attachments. Video teleconferencing is almost more common than Starbucks locations. The point is that the files we transfer today are really large compared to what we sent back and forth just a few years ago. And although bandwidth has increased to allow us to do what we do, there are still limitations that cause network performance to suffer miserably. Let's start with a few reasons why you need to carefully manage whatever amount of precious bandwidth you've got.

Latency Sensitivity

Most of us have clicked to open an application or clicked a web link only to have the computer just sit there staring back at us, helplessly hanging. That sort of lag comes when the resources needed to open the program or take us to the next page are not fully available. That kind of lag on a network is called *latency*—the time between when data is requested and the moment it actually gets delivered. The more latency, the longer the delay and the longer you have to stare blankly back at your computer screen, hoping something happens soon.

Latency affects some programs more than others. If you are sending an email, it may be annoying to have to wait a few seconds for the email server to respond, but that type of delay isn't likely to cause physical harm to you or a loved one. Applications that are adversely affected by latency are said to have high *latency sensitivity*. A common example of this is online gaming. Although it may not mean actual life or death, playing certain online games with significant delays can mean the untimely demise of your character—and you won't even know it. Worse, it can affect the entire experience for those playing with you, which can get you booted from some game servers. On a much more serious level, applications like remote surgery also have high latency sensitivity.

High-Bandwidth Applications

Many of the applications we now use over the network would have been totally unserviceable in the past because of the high amount of bandwidth they consume. And even though technology is constantly improving to give us more bandwidth, developers are in hot pursuit, developing new applications that gobble up that bandwidth as soon as it becomes—even in advance of it becoming—available. A couple of good examples of high-bandwidth applications are VoIP and video streaming:

VoIP   *Voice over Internet Protocol (VoIP)* describes several technologies that work to deliver voice communications over the Internet or other data networks. In many cases, VoIP includes not only voice but video transmissions as well. VoIP allows us to send voice, video, and data all over the same connection to another location. Its most common application is video teleconferencing.

Many companies are investing in VoIP systems to reduce travel costs. Ponying up for pricey plane tickets, lodging, and rental cars adds up fast, so investing in a good VoIP system that allows the company to have virtual conferences with people in another state or country pays for itself in no time.

But sadly, VoIP installations can be stressed heavily by things like really low bandwidth, latency issues, packet loss, jitter, security flaws, and reliability concerns. And in some cases, routing VoIP through firewalls and routers using address translation can prove pretty problematic as well.

Video Applications   Watching real-time video on the Internet today is great if you have a decent high-speed connection. You can watch the news, sports, movies, and pretty much anything else that you watch on television. Although viewing digital media online is so common that anyone born after the year 2000 won't be able to remember a time when we had to watch videos on anything other than a computer, again, this requires lots of bandwidth. And excessive use can cause traffic problems even on the most robust networks!

Other Real-Time Services

While VoIP and video traffic certainly require the most attention with respect to performance and latency, other real-time services are probably in use in your network. We're going to briefly look at presence, another example of real-time services you may not give a lot of thought to, and then I'll compare the use of unicast and multicast in real-time services.

Presence   Presence is a function provided by many collaboration solutions that indicates the availability of a user. It signals to other users whether a user is online, busy, in a meeting, and so forth. If enabled across multiple communication tools, such as IM, phone, email, and videoconferencing, it also can help determine the communication channel on which the user is currently active and therefore which channel provides the best possibility of an immediate response.

Multicast vs. Unicast   Unicast transmissions represent a one-to-one conversation, that is, data sent from a single device to another single device. On the other hand, multicast is a technology that sends information for a single source to multiple recipients and is far superior to using unicast transmission when it comes to video streaming and conferencing.

While unicast transmission creates a data connection and stream for each recipient, multicast uses the same stream for all recipients. This single stream is replicated as needed by multicast routers and switches in the network. The stream is limited to branches of the network topology that actually have subscribers to the stream. This greatly reduces the use of bandwidth in the network.

Uptime

Uptime is the amount of time the system is up and accessible to your end users, so the more uptime you have the better. And depending on how critical the nature of your business is, you may need to provide four-nines or five-nines uptime on your network—that's a lot. Why is this a lot? Because you write out four nines as 99.99 percent, or better, you write out five nines as 99.999 percent! Now that is some serious uptime!

How to Optimize Performance

You now know that bandwidth is to networking as water is to life, and you're one of the lucky few if your network actually has an excess of it. Cursed is the downtrodden administrator who can't seem to find enough, and more fall into this category than the former. At times, your very sanity may hinge upon ensuring that your users have enough available bandwidth to get their jobs done on your network, and even if you've got a 10 Gbps connection, it doesn't mean all your users have that much bandwidth at their fingertips. What it really means is that they get a piece of it, and they share the rest with other users and network processes. Because it's your job to make sure as much of that 1 Gbps as possible is there to use when needed, I'm going to discuss some really cool ways to make that happen for you.

Quality of Service

Quality of service (QoS) refers to the way the resources are controlled so that the quality of service is maintained. It's basically the ability to provide a different priority to one or more types of traffic over other levels for different applications, data flows, or users so that they can be guaranteed a certain performance level.

QoS methods focus on one of five problems that can affect data as it traverses network cable:

Delay   Data can run into congested lines or take a less-than-ideal route to the destination, and delays like these can make some applications, such as VoIP, fail. This is the best reason to implement QoS when real-time applications are in use in the network—to prioritize delay-sensitive traffic.

Dropped Packets   Some routers will drop packets if they receive them while their buffers are full. If the receiving application is waiting for the packets but doesn't get them, it will usually request that the packets be retransmitted—another common cause of service delays.

Error   Packets can be corrupted in transit and arrive at the destination in an unacceptable format, again requiring retransmission and resulting in delays.

Jitter   Not every packet takes the same route to the destination, so some will be more delayed than others if they travel through a slower or busier network connection. The variation in packet delay is called *jitter*, and this can have a nastily negative impact on programs that communicate in real time.

Out-of-Order Delivery   Out-of-order delivery is also a result of packets taking different paths through the network to their destinations. The application at the receiving end needs to put them back together in the right order for the message to be completed, so if there are significant delays or the packets are reassembled out of order, users will probably notice degradation of an application's quality.

QoS can ensure that applications with a required bit rate receive the necessary bandwidth to work properly. Clearly, on networks with excess bandwidth, this is not a factor, but the more limited your bandwidth is, the more important a concept like this becomes.

DSCP

One of the methods that can be used for classifying and managing network traffic and providing quality of service (QoS) on modern IP networks is Differentiated Services Code Point (DSCP), or DiffServ. DiffServ uses a 6-bit code point (DSCP) in the 8-bit Differentiated Services field (DS field) in the IP header for packet classification. This allows for the creation of traffic classes that can be used to assign priorities to various traffic classes.

In theory, a network could have up to 64 different traffic classes using different DSCPs, but most networks use the following traffic classifications:

- Default, which is typically best-effort traffic
- Expedited Forwarding (EF), which is dedicated to low-loss, low-latency traffic
- Assured Forwarding (AF), which gives assurance of delivery under prescribed conditions
- Class Selector, which maintains backward compatibility with the IP Precedence field (a field formerly used by the Type of Service (ToS) function)

Class of Service (COS)

The second method of providing traffic classification and thus the ability to treat the classes differently is a 3-bit field called the Priority Code Point (PCP) within an Ethernet frame header when VLAN tagged frames as defined by IEEE 802.1Q are used.

This method is defined in the IEEE 802.1p standard. It describes eight different classes of service as expressed through the 3-bit PCP field in an IEEE 802.1Q header added to the frame. These classes are shown in Table 21.2.

TABLE 21.2   Eight levels of QoS

Level	Description
0	Best effort
1	Background
2	Standard (spare)
3	Excellent load (business-critical applications)
4	Controlled load (streaming media)
5	Voice and video (interactive voice and video, less than 100 ms latency and jitter)
6	Layer 3 Network Control Reserved Traffic (less than 10 ms latency and jitter)
7	Layer 2 Network Control Reserved Traffic (lowest latency and jitter)

QoS levels are established per call, per session, or in advance of the session by an agreement known as a service-level agreement (SLA).

Unified Communications

Increasingly, workers and the organizations for which they work are relying on new methods of communicating and working together. Unified communications (UC) is the integration of real-time communication services such as instant messaging with non-real-time communication services such as unified messaging (integrated voicemail, email, SMS, and fax). UC allows an individual to send a message on one medium and receive the same communication on another medium.

UC systems are made of several components that make sending a message on one medium and receiving the same communication on another medium possible. The following may be part of a UC system:

UC Servers   The UC server is the heart of the system. It provides call control mobility services and administrative functions. It may be a stand-alone device or in some cases a module that is added to a router.

UC Devices   UC devices are the endpoints that may participate in unified communications. This includes computers, laptops, tablets, and smartphones.

UC Gateways   UC gateways are used to tie together geographically dispersed locations that may want to make use of UC facilities. They are used to connect the IP-based network with the public switched telephone network (PSTN).

Traffic Shaping

Traffic shaping, or packet shaping, is another form of bandwidth optimization. It works by delaying packets that meet a certain criteria to guarantee usable bandwidth for other applications. Traffic shaping is basically traffic triage—you're really just delaying attention to some traffic so other traffic gets A-listed through. Traffic shaping uses *bandwidth throttling* to ensure that certain data streams don't send too much data in a specified period of time as well as *rate limiting* to control the rate at which traffic is sent.

Most often, traffic shaping is applied to devices at the edge of the network to control the traffic entering the network, but it can also be deployed on devices within an internal network. The devices that control it have what's called a *traffic contract* that determines which packets are allowed on the network and when. You can think of this as the stoplights on busy freeway on-ramps, where only so much traffic is allowed onto the road at one time, based on predefined rules. Even so, some traffic (like carpools and emergency vehicles) is allowed on the road immediately. Delayed packets are stored in the managing device's first-in, first-out (FIFO) buffer until they're allowed to proceed per the conditions in the contract. If you're the first car at the light, this could happen immediately. If not, you get to go after waiting briefly until the traffic in front of you is released.

Load Balancing

Load balancing refers to a technique used to spread work out to multiple computers, network links, or other devices.

Using load balancing, you can provide an active/passive server cluster in which only one server is active and handling requests. For example, your favorite Internet site might actually consist of 20 servers that all appear to be the same exact site because that site's owner wants to ensure that its users always experience quick access. You can accomplish this on a network by installing multiple, redundant links to ensure that network traffic is spread across several paths and to maximize the bandwidth on each link.

Think of this as having two or more different freeways that will both get you to your destination equally well—if one is really busy, just take the other one.

High Availability

High availability is a system-design protocol that guarantees a certain amount of operational uptime during a given period. The design attempts to minimize unplanned downtime—the time users are unable to access resources. In almost all cases, high availability is provided through the implementation of duplicate equipment (multiple servers, multiple NICs, etc.). Organizations that serve critical functions obviously need this; after all, you really don't want to blaze your way to a hospital ER only to find that they can't treat you because their network is down!

There's a difference between planned downtime and unplanned downtime. Planned downtime is good—it's occasionally scheduled for system maintenance and routine upgrades. Unplanned downtime is bad: It's a lack of access due to system failure, which is exactly the issue high availability resolves.

One of the highest standards in uptime is the ability to provide the five-nines availability I mentioned earlier. This actually means the network is accessible 99.999 percent of the time—way impressive! Think about this. In one non-leap year, there are 31,536,000 seconds. If you are available 99.999 percent of the time, it means you can be down only 0.001 percent of the time, or a total of 315.36 seconds, or 5 minutes and 15.36 seconds per year—wow!

There's a difference between uptime and availability. For example, your servers may be up but not accessible if a cable gets cut, and that outage would definitely count against your availability time.

Caching Engines

A *cache* is a collection of data that duplicates key pieces of original data. Computers use caches all the time to temporarily store information for faster access, and processors have both internal and external caches available to them, which speeds up their response times.

A *caching engine* is basically a database on a server that stores information people need to access fast. The most popular implementation of this is with web servers and proxy servers, but caching engines are also used on internal networks to speed up access to things like database services.

Fault Tolerance

Fault tolerance means that even if one component fails, you won't lose access to the resource it provides. To implement fault tolerance, you need to employ multiple devices or connections that all provide a way to access the same resource(s).

A familiar form of fault tolerance is configuring an additional hard drive to be a mirror image of another so that if either one fails, there's still a copy of the data available to you. In networking, fault tolerance means that you have multiple paths from one point to another. What's really cool is that fault-tolerant connections can be configured to be available either on a standby basis only or all the time if you intend to use them as part of a load-balancing system.

Archives/Backups

While providing redundancy to hardware components is important, the data that resides on the components must also be archived in case a device where the data is stored has to be replaced. It could be a matter of replacing a hard drive on which the data cannot be saved and restoring the data from tape backup. Or suppose RAID has been enabled in a system; in that case, the loss of a single hard drive will not present an immediate loss of access to the data (although a replacement of the bad drive will be required to recover from another drive failure).

With regard to the data backups, they must be created on a schedule and tested regularly to ensure that a data restoration is successful. The three main data backup types are full backups, differential backups, and incremental backups. But to understand them, you must grasp the concept of archive bits. When a file is created or updated, the archive bit for the file is enabled. If the archive bit is cleared, the file will not be archived during the next backup. If the archive bit is enabled, the file will be archived during the next backup.

The end result is that each type of backup differs in the amount of time taken, the amount of data backed up, whether unchanged data is backed up repeatedly, and the number of tapes required to restore the data. Keep these key facts in mind:

- If you use a full backup once a week and differential backups the other days of the week, to restore you will only need the last full backup tape and the last differential tape. This is the fastest restore.

- If you use a full backup once a week and incremental backups the other days of the week, to restore you will need the last full backup tape and all of the incremental tapes. This is the slowest restore.

A comparison of the three main backup types is shown in Figure 21.16.

FIGURE 21.16 Backup types

Backup Type	Data Backed Up	Backup Time	Restore Time	Storage Space
Full backup	All data	Slowest	Fast	High
Incremental backup	Only new/modified files/folders	Fast	Moderate	Lowest
Differential backup	All data since last full	Moderate	Fast	Moderate

Common Address Redundancy Protocol

Common Address Redundancy Protocol (CARP) provides IP-based redundancy, allowing a group of hosts on the same network segment (referred to as a *redundancy group*) to share an IP address. One host is designated the *master* and the rest are *backups*. The master host responds to any traffic or ARP requests directed toward it. Each host may belong to more than one redundancy group at a time.

One of its most common uses is to provide redundancy for devices such as firewalls or routers. The virtual IP address (this is another name for the shared group IP address) will be shared by a group of routers or firewalls.

The client machines use the virtual IP address as their default gateway. In the event that the master router suffers a failure or is taken offline, the IP will move to one of the backup routers and service will continue. Other protocols that use similar principles are Virtual Router Redundancy Protocol (VRRP) and the Hot Standby Router Protocol (HSRP).

Virtual Networking

Over the last few years, one of the most significant developments helping to increase the efficient use of computing resources—leading to an increase in network performance without an increase in spending on hardware—has been the widespread adoption of virtualization technology. You can't read an industry publication without coming across the term *cloud computing* within 45 seconds!

The concept of virtualization is quite simple. Instead of dedicating a physical piece of hardware to every server, run multiple instances of the server operating system, each in its own "virtual environment" on the same physical piece of equipment. This saves power, maximizes the use of memory and CPU resources, and can even help to "hide" the physical location of each virtual server.

Virtual computing solutions come from a number of vendors. The following are some of the more popular currently:

- VMware vSphere
- Microsoft Hyper-V
- Citrix XenServer

All of these solutions work on the same basic concept but each has its own unique features, and of course all claim to be the best solution. In the following sections, I will discuss the building blocks of virtualization rather than the specific implementation from any single vendor.

On-site vs. Off-site

Often you hear the terms *public cloud* and *private cloud. Clouds* can be thought of as virtual computing environments where virtual servers and desktops live and can be accessed by users. A private cloud is one in which this environment is provided to the enterprise by a third party for a fee. This is a good solution for a company that has neither the expertise nor the resources to manage its own cloud yet would like to take advantage of the benefits that cloud computing offers:

- Increased performance
- Increased fault tolerance
- Constant availability
- Access from anywhere

These types of clouds might be considered off-site or public. On the other hand, for the organization that has the expertise and resources, a private or on-site solution might be better and might be more secure. This approach will enjoy the same benefits as a public cloud and may offer more precise control and more options to the organization.

Virtual Networking Components

The foundation of virtualization is the host device, which may be a workstation or a server. This device is the physical machine that contains the software that makes virtualization possible and the containers or virtual machines for the guest operating systems. The host provides the underlying hardware and computing resources, such as processing power, memory, and disk and network I/O, to the VMs. Each guest is a separate and independent instance of an operating system and application software. From a high level, the relationship is shown in Figure 21.17.

Virtualization can be deployed in several different ways to deliver cost-effective solutions to different problems. Each of the following components can have its place in the solution:

Hypervisor   The host is responsible for allocating compute resources to each of the VMs as specified by the configuration. The software that manages all of this is called the *hypervisor*. Based on parameters set by the administrator, the hypervisor may take various actions to maintain the performance of each guest as specified by the administrator. This may include the following actions:

- Turning off a VM not in use
- Taking CPU resources away from one VM and allocating them to another
- Turning on additional VMs when required to provide fault tolerance

FIGURE 21.17 Guests and hosts

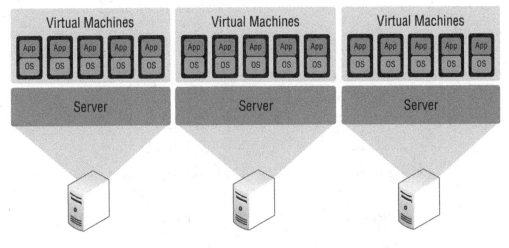

Physical Servers

The exact nature of the relationship between the hypervisor, the host operating system, and the guest operating systems depends on the type of hypervisor in use. There are two types of hypervisors in use today. Let's review both of these.

Type 1 A Type 1 hypervisor (or native, bare metal) runs directly on the host's hardware to control the hardware and to manage guest operating systems. A guest operating system runs on another level above the hypervisor. Examples of these are VMware vSphere and Microsoft Hyper-V.

Type 2 A Type 2 hypervisor runs within a conventional operating system environment. With the hypervisor layer as a distinct second software level, guest operating systems run at the third level above the hardware. VMware Workstation and VirtualBox exemplify Type 2 hypervisors. A comparison of the two approaches is shown in Figure 21.18.

Virtual Servers Virtual servers can perform all the same functions as physical servers but can enjoy some significant advantages. By clustering a virtual server with other virtual servers located on different hosts, you can achieve fault tolerance in the case of a host failure. Increased performance can also be derived from this approach.

The virtualization software can allow you to allocate CPU and memory resources to the virtual machines (VMs) dynamically as needed to ensure that the maximum amount of computing power is available to any single VM at any moment while not wasting any of that power on an idle VM. In fact, in situations where VMs have been clustered, they may even be suspended or powered down in times of low demand in the cluster.

FIGURE 21.18   Hypervisors

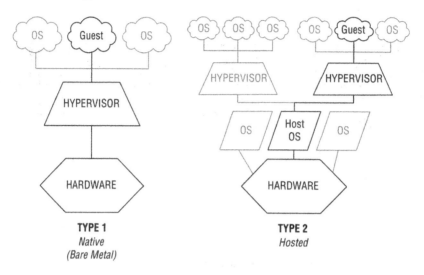

Virtual Switches   Virtual switches are software versions of a layer 2 switch that can be used to create virtual networks. They can be used for the same purposes as physical switches. VLANs can be created, virtual servers can be connected to the switches, and the virtual network can be managed, all while residing on the same physical box. These switches can also span multiple hosts (the physical machines that house multiple virtual servers, desktops, and switches are called hosts).

Distributed virtual switches are those switches that span multiple hosts, and they are what links together the VMs that are located on different hosts yet are members of the same cluster.

Virtual vs. Physical NICs   Figure 21.19 shows the relationship between a physical server and the virtual servers and virtual switches that it hosts. The virtual servers, called virtual machines (VMs), have virtual network cards (vNICs) that connect to the virtual switch. Keep in mind that all three of these components are software running on the same physical server. Then the virtual switch makes a software connection to the physical NIC on the physical host, which makes a physical connection to the physical switch in the network.

It is interesting to note and important to be aware of the fact that the IP address of the physical NIC in Figure 21.19 will actually be transmitting packets from multiple MAC addresses since each of the virtual servers will have a unique virtual MAC address.

Virtual Routers   In virtualized environments, virtual routers are typically implemented as specialized software. They consist of individual routing and forwarding tables, each of which could be considered a virtual router.

Virtual Firewall   Virtual firewalls are also implemented as software in the virtualized environment. Like their physical counterparts, they can be used to restrict traffic between virtual subnets created by virtual routers.

FIGURE 21.19   Virtualization

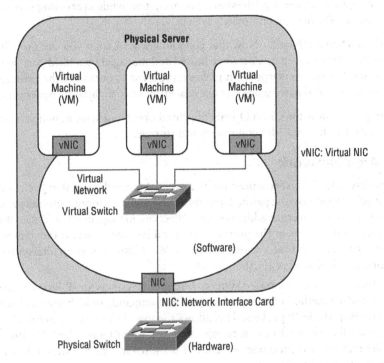

Software-Defined Networking   Software-defined networking (SDN) is an approach to computer networking that allows network administrators to manage network services through abstraction of lower-level functionality. SDN architectures decouple network control and forwarding functions, enabling network control to become directly programmable and the underlying infrastructure to be abstracted from applications and network services.

Virtual Desktops   Using operating system images for desktop computers is not a new concept, but delivering these desktop images to users from a virtual environment when they start their computer is. This allows for the user desktop to require less computing power, especially if the applications are also delivered virtually and those applications are running in a VM in the cloud rather than in the local desktop eating up local resources. Another benefit of using virtual desktops is the ability to maintain a consistent user environment (same desktop, applications, etc.), which can enhance user support.

Thin computing takes this a step further. In this case, all of the computing is taking place on the server. A *thin client* is simply displaying the output from the operating system running in the cloud, and the keyboard is used to interact with that operating system in the cloud. Does this sound like dumb terminals with a GUI to anyone yet? Back to the future indeed! The thin client needs very little processing power for this job.

Virtual PBX   Virtual PBX is an example of what is called *Software as a Service* (SaaS). A hosting company manages the entire phone system for the company, freeing the organization from the need to purchase and manage the physical equipment that would be required otherwise to provide the same level of service. To the outside world, the company appears to have a professional phone system while everything is actually being routed through the hosting company's system.

Network as a Service (NaaS)   Now that you know what SaaS is you can probably guess what NaaS is. You guessed it: a network hosted and managed by a third party on behalf of the company. For many enterprises, it makes more sense to outsource the management of the network to a third party when it is not cost effective to maintain a networking staff.

An example of this is the Cisco OpenStack cloud operating system, which is an open-source platform that provides computers and storage.

Storage Area Network

Storage area networks (SANs) comprise high-capacity storage devices that are connected by a high-speed private network (separate from the LAN) using a storage-specific switch. This storage information architecture addresses the collection, management, and use of data. In this section, we'll take a look at the protocols that can be used to access the data and the client systems that can use those various protocols. We'll also look at an alternative to a SAN: network-attached storage (NAS).

iSCSI   *Internet Small Computer Systems Interface (iSCSI)* is an IP-based networking storage standard method of encapsulating SCSI commands (which are used with storage area networks) within IP packets. This allows the use of the same network for storage as is used for the balance of the network. A comparison of a regular SAN that uses the Fibre Channel protocol, and one using iSCSI is shown in Figure 21.20. I'll talk more about Fibre Channel later in this list.

FIGURE 21.20   Classic SAN vs. iSCSI

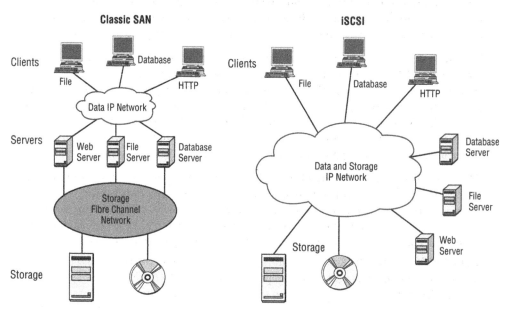

InfiniBand   InfiniBand is a communications standard that provides high performance and low latency. It is utilized as a direct, or switched, interconnect between servers and storage systems as well as an interconnect between storage systems. It uses a switched fabric topology. The adaptors can exchange information on QoS.

Fibre Channel   Fibre Channel, or FC, is a high-speed network technology (commonly running at 2, 4, 8, and 16 gigabits per second rates) primarily used to connect computer data storage. It operates on an optical network that is not compatible with the regular IP-based data network. As you can see in Figure 21.20, this protocol runs on a private network that connects the servers to the storage network.

Fibre-Channel over Ethernet (FCoE), on the other hand, encapsulates Fibre Channel traffic within Ethernet frames much like iSCSI encapsulates SCSI commands in IP packets. However, unlike iSCSI, FCoE does not use IP at all, but does allow this traffic on the IP network.

Jumbo Frames   Jumbo frames are Ethernet frames with more than 1500 bytes of payload. Jumbo frames with more than 9000-byte payloads have the potential to reduce overhead and CPU cycles. In high-speed networks such as those typically used in a SAN, it may be advisable to enable jumbo frames to improve performance.

Network Attached Storage   Network attached storage (NAS) serves the same function as SAN, but clients access the storage in a different way. In a NAS configuration, almost any machine that can connect to the LAN (or is interconnected to the LAN through a WAN) can use protocols such as NFS, SMB2/3, and HTTPS to connect to the NAS and share files. In a SAN configuration, only devices that can use the Fibre Channel SCSI network can access the data, so it's typically done through a server with this capability. A comparison of the two systems is shown in Figure 21.21.

FIGURE 21.21   NAS and SAN

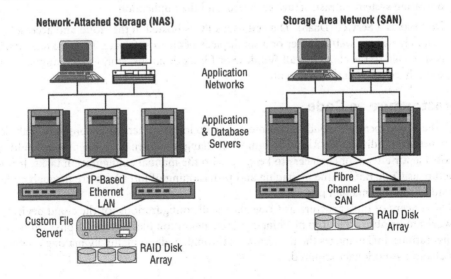

Cloud Concepts

Cloud storage locates the data on a central server, but unlike with an internal data center in the LAN, the data is accessible from anywhere and in many cases from a variety of device types. Moreover, cloud solutions typically provide fault tolerance and dynamic computer resource (CPU, memory, network) provisioning.

Cloud deployments can differ in two ways:

- The entity that manages the solution
- The percentage of the total solution provided by the vendor

First, let's look at the options relative to the entity that manages the solution:

- **Private cloud:** This is a solution owned and managed by one company solely for that company's use.
- **Public cloud:** This is a solution provided by a third party. It offloads the details to the third party but gives up some control and can introduce security issues.
- **Hybrid cloud:** This is some combination of private and public. For example, perhaps you only use the facilities of the provider but still manage the data yourself.
- **Community cloud:** This is a solution owned and managed by a group of organizations that create the cloud for a common purpose.

There are several levels of service that can be made available through a cloud deployment:

- **Infrastructure as a Service (IaaS).** The vendor provides the hardware platform or data center, and the company installs and manages its own operating systems and application systems.
- **Platform as a Service (PaaS).** The vendor provides the hardware platform or data center and the software running on the platform.
- **Software as a Service (SaaS).** The vendor provides the entire solution. This includes the operating system, infrastructure software, and the application.
- **Desktop as a Service (DaaS).** The end user's PC is hosted in the cloud and accessed remotely using a web browser or a small piece of client software. The desktop interface is streamed to the client but all Window or Linux desktops, storage, and applications are securely running in the data center.

Infrastructure as Code

With the new hyperscale cloud data centers, it is no longer practical to configure each device in the network individually. Also, configuration changes happen so frequently it would be impossible for a team of engineers to keep up with the manual configuration tasks. Infrastructure as Code (IaC) is the managing and provisioning of infrastructure through code instead of through manual processes.

The concept of Infrastructure as Code allows all configurations for the cloud devices and networks to be abstracted into machine-readable definition files instead of physical hardware configurations. IaC manages the provisioning through code so manually making configuration changes is no longer required.

These configuration files contain the infrastructure requirements and specifications. They can be stored for repeatable use, distributed to other groups, and versioned as you make changes. Faster deployment speeds, fewer errors, and consistency are advantages of Infrastructure as Code over the older, manual process.

Deploying your infrastructure as code allows you to divide your infrastructure into modular components that can be combined in different ways using automation. Code formats include JSON and YAML, and they are used by tools such as Ansible, Salt, Chef, Puppet, Terraform, and AWS CloudFormation.

Automation/Orchestration

Automation and orchestration define configuration, management, and the coordination of cloud operations. Automation involves individual tasks that do not require human intervention and are used to create workflows that are referred to as orchestration. This allows you to easily manage very complex and large tasks using code instead of a manual process.

Automation is a single task that orchestration uses to create the workflow. By using orchestration in the cloud, you can create a complete virtual data center that includes all compute, storage, database, networking, security, management, and any other required services. Very complex tasks can be defined in code and used to create your environment.

Common automation tools used today include Puppet, Docker, Jenkins, Terraform, Ansible, Kubernetes, CloudBees, CloudFormation, Chef, and Vagrant.

Connectivity Options

By default, traffic into and out of your public cloud traverses the Internet. This is a good solution in many cases, but if you require additional security when accessing your cloud resources and exchanging your data, there are two common solutions that we will discuss. The first is a virtual private network (VPN) that sends data securely over the Internet or dedicated connections. The second solution is to install a private non-Internet connection and then a direct connection can be configured.

Virtual Private Network (VPN)

Cloud providers offer site-to-site VPN options that allow you to establish a secure and protected network connection across the public Internet. The VPN connection verifies that both ends of the connection are legitimate and then establishes encrypted tunnels to route traffic from your data center to your cloud resources. If a bad actor intercepts the data, they will not be able to read it due to the encryption of the traffic.

VPNs can be configured with redundant links to back up each other or to load-balance the traffic for higher-speed interconnections.

Another type of VPN allows desktops, laptops, tablets, and other devices to establish individual secure connections into your cloud deployment.

Private Direct Connection

A dedicated circuit can be ordered and installed between your data center and an interconnection provider or directly to the cloud company. This provides a secure, low latency connection with predictable performance.

Direct connection speeds usually range from 1 Gbps to 10 Gbps and can be aggregated together. For example, four 10 Gbps circuits can be installed from your data center to the cloud company for a total aggregate bandwidth of 40 Gbps.

It is also a common practice to establish a VPN connection over the private link for encryption of data in transit.

There are often many options when connecting to the cloud provider that allow you to specify which geographic regions to connect to as well as which areas inside of each region, such as storage systems or your private virtual cloud.

Internet exchange providers maintain dedicated high speed connections to multiple cloud providers and will connect a dedicated circuit from your facility to the cloud providers as you specify.

There are several ways to connect to a virtual server that is in a cloud environment:

- Remote Desktop: While the VPN connection connects you to the virtual network, an RDP connection can be directly connected to a server. If the server is a Windows server, then you will use the Remote Desktop Connection (RDC) client. If it is a Linux server, then the connection will most likely be an SSH connection to the command line.

- File Transfer Protocol (FTP) and Secure File Transfer Protocol (SFTP): The FTP/FTPS server will need to be enabled on the Windows/Linux server and then you can use the FTP/FTPS client or work at the command line. This is best when performing bulk data downloads.

- VMware Remote Console: This allows you to mount a local DVD, hard drive, or USB drive to the virtual server. This is handy for uploading ISO or installation media to the cloud server.

Multitenancy

Public clouds host hundreds of thousands of different customer accounts in the same cloud. This is often referred to as multitenancy, and it presents a number of technical considerations. Tenants and even networks inside of a customer's account need complete isolation from each other and the ability to selectively and securely interconnect to each other. Multitenancy can also be an issue in a private cloud where the development, test, and production networks should be securely isolated.

In a private cloud, the tenants may be different groups or departments within a single company, while in a public cloud, entirely different organizations share services such as compute and storage systems that are isolated from each other.

Multitenant clouds offer isolated space in the data centers to run services such as compute, storage, databases, development applications, artificial intelligence, network applications (such as firewalls and load balancers), and many other services. Think of this as your own private data center in the cloud.

Each tenant controls access, security roles, permissions inside your space, and traffic in and out of your virtual private cloud. All resources are not accessible unless you explicitly allow them to be.

Software multitenancy refers to an architecture where a single instance of an application runs on a server and is shared by multiple tenants.

With software multitenancy, the application software is designed to provide every tenant a dedicated instance of the application, including the data, security, and configuration management. Many instances of the same application support different tenants.

Elasticity

One of the benefits of deploying your workloads in the cloud is to take advantage of the dynamic allocation of cloud resources. Elasticity allows you to meet the fluctuating workload requirements by adding or removing resources in near real time.

Elasticity is the process that cloud providers offer to allocate the desired amount of service resources needed to run your workloads at any given moment.

Elasticity provides on-demand resources such as computing instances or stage space that can meet your existing workloads and automatically adds or subtracts capacity to meet peak and off-peak workloads.

For example, you could be hosting an e-commerce site in the public cloud and expect a large increase in traffic for a big sale you are advertising. Your deployment can be configured to monitor activity and, if needed, add more capacity to meet the demand. When the demand lowers, by using network automation, you can automatically remove that capacity, allowing you to only pay for the cloud resources you actually need and use.

Elasticity allows you to add services such as storage and compute on-demand, often in seconds or minutes.

Scalability

Scalability is a cloud feature that allows you to use cloud resources that meet your current workload needs and later migrate to a larger system to handle growth. Scalability allows you to better manage static resources. With the pay-as-you-go pricing model of the cloud, you do not have to buy expensive hardware that you may outgrow. You can use the cloud to stop the lower-performing services and migrate to larger instances. There are two types of scalabilities, scaling up to a larger server instance or scaling out by adding additional cloud servers in parallel to handle the larger workloads.

Scalability enables you to reliably grow your cloud deployments based on demand, whereas elasticity enables you to scale resources up or down based on real-time workload requirements. This allows you to efficiently manage resources and costs.

Security Implications/Considerations

While an entire book could be written on the security implications of the cloud, there are some concerns that stand above the others. Among them are these:

- While clouds increasingly contain valuable data, they are just as susceptible to attacks as on-premises environments. Cases such as the `Salesforce.com` incident in which a technician fell for a phishing attack that compromised customer passwords remind us of this.

- Customers are failing to ensure that the provider keeps their data safe in multitenant environments. They are failing to ensure that passwords are assigned, protected, and changed with the same attention to detail they might desire.

- No specific standard has been developed to guide providers with respect to data privacy.

- Data security varies greatly from country to country, and customers have no idea where their data is located at any point in time.

Relationship Between Local and Cloud Resources

When comparing the advantages of local and cloud environments and the resources that reside in each, several things stand out:

- A cloud environment requires very little infrastructure investment on the part of the customer, while a local environment requires an investment in both the equipment and the personnel to set it up and manage it.

- A cloud environment can be extremely scalable and at a moment's notice, while scaling a local environment either up or out requires an investment in both equipment and personnel.

- Investments in cloud environments involve monthly fees rather than capital expenditures as would be required in a local environment.

- While a local environment provides total control for the organization, a cloud takes some of that control away.

- While you always know where your data is in a local environment, that may not be the case in a cloud, and the location may change rapidly.

Locating and Installing Equipment

When infrastructure equipment is purchased and deployed, the ultimate success of the deployment can depend on selecting the proper equipment, determining its proper location in the facility, and installing it correctly. Let's look at some common data center or server room equipment and a few best practices for managing these facilities.

Main Distribution Frame

The main distribution frame connects equipment (inside plant) to cables and subscriber carrier equipment (outside plant). It also terminates cables that run to intermediate distribution frames distributed throughout the facility.

Intermediate Distribution Frame

An intermediate distribution frame (IDF) serves as a distribution point for cables from the main distribution frame (MDF) to individual cables connected to equipment in areas remote from these frames. The relationship between the IDFs and the MDF is shown in Figure 21.22.

FIGURE 21.22   MDF and IDFs

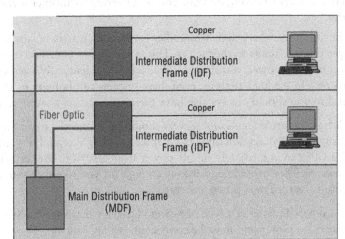

Cable Management

While some parts of our network may be wireless, the lion's share of the network will be connected with cables. The cables come together in large numbers at distribution points where managing them becomes important both to protect the integrity of the cables and to prevent overheating of the infrastructure devices caused by masses of unruly cabling. The points of congestion typically occur at the patch panels.

Patch panels terminate cables from wall or data outlets. These masses of wires that emerge from the wall in a room will probably feed to the patch panel in a cable tray, which I'll talk more about soon. The critical maintenance issues at the patch panel are to ensure that cabling from the patch panel to the switch is neat, that the patch cables are as short as possible without causing stress on the cables, and that the positioning of the cabling does not impede air flow to the devices, which can cause overheating.

Power Management

Computing equipment of all types needs clean and constant power. Power fluctuations of any sort, especially complete outages and powerful surges, are a serious matter. In this section, we'll look at power issues and devices that can be implemented to avoid or mitigate them.

Power Converters   Power conversion is the process of converting electric energy from one form to another. This conversion could take several forms:

- AC to DC
- From one voltage level to another
- From one frequency to another

Power converters are devices that make these conversions, and they typically are placed inline, where the energy flowing into one end is converted to another form when it exits the converter.

Circuits   In situations where high availability is required, it may be advisable to provision multiple power circuits to the facility. This is sometimes called A+B or A/B power. To provision for A+B power, you should utilize a pair of identically sized circuits (e.g., 2 × 20 amperes). In the final analysis, even these systems can fail you in some natural disasters and so you should always also have power generators as well as a final backup.

UPS   All infrastructure systems and servers should be connected to an uninterruptible power supply (UPS). As described in Chapter 15, "High Availability and Disaster Recovery," a UPS can immediately supply power from a battery backup when a loss of power is detected. They provide power long enough for you to either shut the system down gracefully or turn on a power generator.

Inverters   A power inverter is a type of power converter that specifically converts DC to AC. It produces no power and must be connected to a DC source.

Power Redundancy   While the facility itself needs redundant power circuits and backup generators, a system can still fail if the power supply in the device fails. Mission-critical devices should be equipped with redundant power supplies, which can mitigate this issue.

Device Placement

When locating equipment in a data center, server room, or wiring closet, you should take several issues into consideration when placing the equipment.

Air Flow   Air flow around the equipment is crucially important to keep devices running. When hot air is not removed from the area and replaced with cooler air, the devices overheat and start doing things like rebooting unexpectedly. Even if the situation doesn't reach that point, the high heat will shorten the life of costly equipment.

One of the approaches that has been really successful is called hot/cold aisles. As explained earlier in this chapter, hot aisle/cold aisle design involves lining up racks in alternating rows with cold air intakes facing one way and hot air exhausts facing the other. The rows composed of rack fronts are called cold aisles. Typically, cold aisles face air conditioner output ducts. The rows the heated exhausts pour into are called hot aisles. They face air conditioner return ducts. Moreover, all of the racks and the equipment they hold should never be on the floor. There should be a raised floor to provide some protection against water.

Cable Trays   Masses of unruly cables can block air flow and act as a heat blanket on the equipment if the situation is bad enough. Cable trays are metal trays used to organize the cabling neatly and keep it away from the areas where it can cause heat buildup. In Figure 21.23, some examples of cable tray components are shown. These are used to organize the cables and route them as needed.

FIGURE 21.23   Cable trays

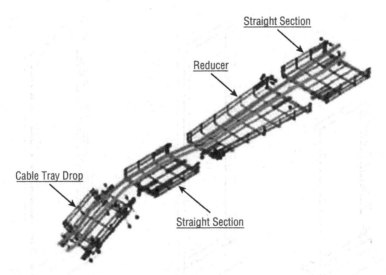

Rack Systems   Rack systems are used to hold and arrange the servers, routers, switches, firewalls, and other rack-ready equipment. Rack devices are advertised in terms of Us. U is the standard unit of measure for designating the vertical usable space, or the height of racks. 1U is equal to 1.75 inches. For example, a rack designated as 20U has 20 rack spaces for equipment and 35 (20 × 1.75) inches of vertical usable space. You should be familiar with the following types of rack systems and components:

Server Rail Racks   Server rail racks are used to hold servers in one of the types of racks described next. They are designed to hold the server while allowing the server to be slid out from the rack for maintenance.

Two-Post Racks   A two-post rack is one in which only two posts run from the floor. These posts may reach to the ceiling or they may not (freestanding). Several sizes of two-post racks are shown in Figure 21.24.

Four-Post Racks   As you would expect, these racks have four rails and can be either floor to ceiling or freestanding. One is shown in Figure 21.25.

Freestanding racks   A freestanding rack is one that does not reach the ceiling and stands on its own. A four-post freestanding rack is shown in Figure 21.26.

FIGURE 21.24 Two-post racks

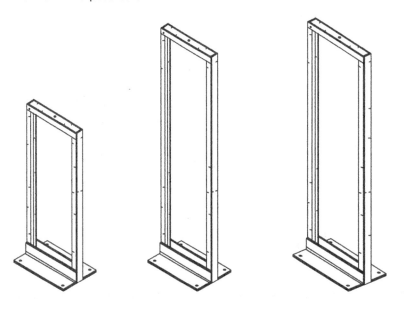

FIGURE 21.25 Four-post rack

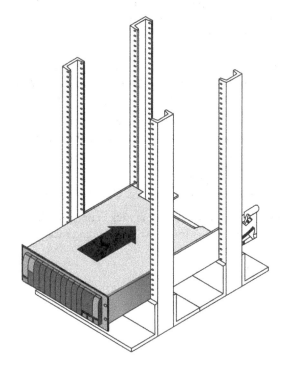

FIGURE 21.26   Freestanding rack

 Real World Scenario

Applying Your Knowledge

You have been assigned the job of positioning the following pieces of equipment in the network for maximum performance and security:

Firewall

Patch server

Main distribution frame (MDF)

Intermediate distribution frame (IDF)

Public web server

Using the following table, match the five pieces of equipment in the left column with the correct position in the right column. The answer follows.

(continues)

(continued)

Device	Position
Firewall	In the screened subnet/DMZ
Patch server	Just after the Internet router
MDF	In the server room or closet on each floor
IDF	Inside the LAN
Public web server	In the server room or closet that is connected to the service provider

Firewall	Just after the Internet router
Patch server	Inside the LAN
MDF	In the server room or closet that is connected to the service provider
IDF	In the server room or closet on each floor
Public web server	In the screened subnet/DMZ

Labeling

In a data center, server room, or wiring closet, correct and updated labeling of ports, systems, circuits, and patch panels can prevent a lot of confusion and mistakes when configuration changes are made. Working with incorrect or incomplete (in some cases nonexistent) labeling is somewhat like trying to locate a place with an incorrect or incomplete map. In this section, we'll touch on some of the items that should be correctly labeled.

Port Labeling   Ports on switches, patch panels, and other systems should be properly labeled, and the wall outlets to which they lead should match! You should arrive at an agreement as to the naming convention to use so that all technicians are operating from the same point of reference. They also should be updated any time changes are made that require an update.

System Labeling   Other systems that are installed in racks, such as servers, firewall appliances, and redundant power supplies, should also be labeled with IP addresses and DNS names that the devices possess.

Circuit Labeling   Circuits entering the facility should also be labeled. Label electrical receptacles, circuit breaker panels, and power distribution units. Include circuit information, voltage and amperage, the type of electrical receptacle, and where in the data center the conduit terminates.

Naming Conventions   A naming system or convention guides and organizes labeling and ensures consistency. No matter what name or numbering system you use, be consistent.

Patch Panel Labeling   The key issue when labeling patch panels is to ensure that they're correct. Also, you need to make sure that the wall outlet they're connected to is the same. The American National Standards Institute/Telecommunications Industry Association (ANSI/TIA) 606-B.1 Administration Standard for Telecommunications Infrastructure for identification and labeling approved in April 2012 provides clear specifications for labeling and administration best practices across all electrical and network systems premise classes, including large data centers.

Rack Monitoring

Racks should contain monitoring devices that can be operated remotely. These devices can be used to monitor the following issues:

- Temperature
- Humidity
- Physical security (open doors)
- Smoke
- Water leaks
- Vibration

Rack Security

Rack devices should be secured from theft. There are several locking systems that can be used to facilitate this. These locks are typically implemented in the doors on the front of a rack cabinet:

- Swing handle/wing knob locks with common key
- Swing handle/wing knob locks with unique key
- Swing handle with number and key lock
- Electronic locks
- Radio-frequency identification (RFID) card locks

Change Management Procedures

Throughout this chapter I've stressed that network operations need to occur in a controlled and managed fashion. For this to occur, an organization must have a formal change management process in place. The purpose of this process is to ensure that all changes are approved by the proper personnel and are implemented in a safe and logical manner. Let's look at some of the key items that should be included in these procedures.

Document Reason for a Change

Clearly, every change should be made for a reason, and before the change is even discussed, that reason should be documented. During all stages of the approval process (discussed later), this information should be clearly communicated and attached to the change under consideration.

Change Request

A change should start its life as a change request. This request will move through various stages of the approval process and should include certain pieces of information that will guide those tasked with approving or denying it.

Configuration Procedures

The exact steps required to implement the change and the exact devices involved should be clearly detailed. Complete documentation should be produced and submitted with a formal report to the change management board.

Rollback Process

Changes always carry a risk. Before any changes are implemented, plans for reversing the changes and recovering from any adverse effects should be identified. Those making the changes should be completely briefed in these rollback procedures, and they should exhibit a clear understanding of them prior to implementing the changes.

Potential Impact

While unexpected adverse effects of a change can't always be anticipated, a good-faith effort should be made to identity all possible systems that could be impacted by the change. One of the benefits of performing this exercise is that it can identify systems that may need to be more closely monitored for their reaction to the change as the change is being implemented.

Notification

When all systems and departments that may be impacted by the change are identified, system owners and department heads should be notified of all changes that could potentially affect them. One of the associated benefits of this is that it creates additional monitors for problems during the change process.

Approval Process

Requests for changes should be fully vetted by a cross section of users, IT personnel, management, and security experts. In many cases, it's wise to form a change control board to complete the following tasks:

- Assure that changes made are approved, tested, documented, and implemented correctly.
- Meet periodically to discuss change status accounting reports.
- Maintain responsibility for assuring that changes made do not jeopardize the soundness of the verification system.

Maintenance Window

A maintenance window is an amount of time a system will be down or unavailable during the implementation of changes. Before this window of time is specified, all affected systems should be examined with respect to their criticality in supporting mission-critical operations. It may be that the time required to make the change may exceed the allowable downtime a system can suffer during normal business hours, and the change may need to be implemented during a weekend or in the evening.

Authorized Downtime

Once the time required to make the change has been compared to the maximum allowable downtime a system can suffer and the optimum time for the change is identified, the authorized downtime can be specified. This amounts to a final decision on when the change will be made.

Notification of Change

When the change has been successfully completed and a sufficient amount of time has elapsed for issues to manifest themselves, all stakeholders should be notified that the change is complete. At that time, these stakeholders (those possibly affected by the change) can continue to monitor the situation for any residual problems.

Documentation

The job isn't complete until the paperwork is complete. In this case, the following should be updated to reflect the changed state of the network:

- Network configurations
- Additions to network
- Physical location changes

Summary

In this chapter, I talked a lot about the layout and basic architectures in modern data centers. I started off discussing the tiering of the data center networks, including the access/distribution/core designs, and then you learned about the newer spine-leaf architectures. Next you learned about the placement of network hardware in the data center with top of rack and backbone switching being introduced and discussed. The flow of data inside the data center was introduced with North-South traffic going into and out of a data center and East-West traffic being inside the data center between servers and storage or server-to-server flows.

We went into great detail on cloud computing because it continues to evolve and take on more and more IT workloads. You learned about the most common services models, including Infrastructure as a Service, Platform as a Service, and Software as a Service.

You learned about software-defined networking and how SDN is used to centrally configure large networks. We discussed the components of a software-defined network, including the management and forwarding planes, the use of application programming interfaces, and the north- and southbound configuration flows.

Next we looked at managing network documentation and the tools needed for that, such as SNMP and schematics. You learned about both physical and logical diagrams, managing IP addresses, and vendor documentation.

Network monitoring helps address performance issues in the network and includes creating baselines, defining processes such as log viewing, and patch management. You learned about the documentation processes including change management, security policies, statements of work, service-level agreements, and master license agreements. Next, we touched on the regulations you may need to adhere to depending on your business.

Safety is important in the data center, including proper electrical grounding and preventing static discharge. Installation safety includes handling of heavy equipment, rack installations, and tool safety. Fire suppression, emergency alerting, and HVAC systems are all a part of safely operating a data center.

We discussed network optimization and the network requirements for real-time applications such as voice and video, including low latency and jitter. Quality of service can be implemented in the network to prioritize applications.

You were introduced to the modern cloud designs and architectures that are highly virtualized. The two types of hypervisors were discussed along with the virtual machines and NICs that are part of virtualization. I compared private, public, and hybrid clouds and you learned about cloud operations using infrastructure as code, automation, orchestration, scalability, and elasticity.

Finally we ended with device placement in the data center and how to design for air flow and cabling.

I talked a lot about the documentation aspects of network administration. I started off discussing physical diagrams and schematics and moved on to the logical form as well as configuration-management documentation. You learned about the importance of these diagrams as well as the simple to complex forms they can take and the tools used to create them—from pencil and paper to high-tech AutoCAD schematics. You also found out a great deal about creating performance baselines. After that, I delved deep into a discussion of network policies and procedures and how regulations can affect how you manage your network.

Next, you learned about network monitoring and optimization and how monitoring your network can help you find issues before they develop into major problems. You learned that server operating systems and intelligent network devices have built-in graphical monitoring tools to help you troubleshoot your network.

We got into performance optimization and the many theories and strategies you can apply to optimize performance on your network. All of them deal with controlling the traffic in some way and include methods like QoS, traffic shaping, load balancing, high availability, and the use of caching servers. We discussed how Common Address Redundancy Protocol (CARP) can be used to increase availability of gateways and firewalls. You also learned how important it is to ensure that you have plenty of bandwidth available for any applications that vitally need it, like critical service operations, VoIP, and real-time multimedia streaming.

Exam Essentials

Compare and contrast cloud technologies.   Understand the differences between IaaS, SaaS, PaaS, and DaaS. Also know the difference between a NAS and a SAN.

Understand common data center network architectures.   Data center architectures include the standard three-tier core, distribution/aggregation, and access/edge model. Newer architectures use a spine and leaf design for a higher throughput switching fabric. Traffic flows in the data center or cloud are often referred to as North-South, which refers to traffic into and out of the data center. East-West traffic refers to the flows inside the data center between devices such as storage and servers.

Know the basic concepts of software-defined networking.   SDN controllers are centralized management plane systems that use application programming interfaces (APIs) to configure the data network as a whole, which eliminates the need to log in and make changes individually to a large number of individual networking devices. Infrastructure as Code allows you to divide your infrastructure into modular components that can be combined in different ways using automation.

Know the basic cloud architectures.   Having many different customers or groups all sharing the same cloud provider's data centers is called multitenancy. Understand that elasticity is the ability to scale your resources up and down on demand and scalability is the ability to reliably grow your cloud deployment based on demand. The public cloud relies on the Internet for access, however, private direct connections can be deployed for secure, reliable, low-latency connections from your data center to your cloud operations.

Understand the difference between a physical network diagram and a logical network diagram.   A physical diagram shows all of the physical connections and devices, and in many cases, the cables or connections between the devices. It's a very detail-oriented view of the hardware on your network. A logical network diagram takes a higher-level view, such as your subnets and the protocols those subnets use to communicate with each other.

Identify the elements of unified communications technology.   This includes the proper treatment of traffic types such as VoIP and video. You should also understand what UC servers, devices, and gateways are. Finally, describe the methods used to provide QoS to latency-sensitive traffic.

Understand the difference between policies, procedures, and regulations.   A policy is created to give users guidance as to what is acceptable behavior on the network. Policies also help resolve problems before they begin by specifying who has access to what resources and how configurations should be managed. Procedures are steps to be taken when an event occurs on the network, such as what to do when a user is fired or how to respond to a natural disaster. Regulations are imposed on your organization; you are required to follow them, and if you don't, you may be subject to punitive actions.

Know how your servers and network devices can help you monitor your network.   Most servers and network devices have monitoring tools built in that are capable of tracking data and events on your network. These include graphical tools as well as log files.

Understand several theories of performance optimization.   There are several ways to manage traffic on your network to speed up access and in some cases guarantee available bandwidth to applications. These include QoS, traffic shaping, load balancing, high availability, and using caching servers.

Know some examples of bandwidth-intensive applications.   Two examples of high-bandwidth applications are Voice over IP (VoIP) and real-time video streaming.

Describe the major building blocks of virtualization.   Understand how virtual servers, virtual switches, and virtual desktops are used to supply the infrastructure to deliver cloud services. Differentiate on-site or private clouds from off-site or public cloud services. Identify services that can be provided, such as Network as a Service (NaaS) and Software as a Service (SaaS).

Summarize safety and environmental issues in the data center.   Understand electrical safety as it relates to both devices and humans. Understand the use of fire suppression systems. Describe proper emergency procedures.

Written Lab

You can find the answers to the written labs in Appendix A. In this section, write the answers to the following management questions:

1.   _____ and _____ are the two main components of modern data center fabric-based networks.

2.   Traffic flow inside the data center is referred to as _____.

3.   _____ and orchestration define configuration, management, and the coordination of cloud operations.

4.   _____ is a single task that orchestration uses to create the workflow.

5.   _____ allows you to add cloud services such as storage and compute on demand, often in seconds or minutes.

6.   A standard of normal network performance is called _____.

7.   If you need to connect two PCs directly together using their network adapters, what type of cable do you need?

8.   What is another name for using virtualization to provide services?

9.   List at least three major components of virtualization.

10.   _____ is the managing and provisioning of resources through software instead of through manual processes.

Review Questions

You can find the answers to the review questions in Appendix B.

1. On a three-tiered network, servers connect at which level?
   A. Core
   B. Distribution
   C. Aggregation
   D. Access

2. Which type of cable will have the pins in the same order on both connectors?
   A. Crossover cable
   B. Straight-through cable
   C. Console cable
   D. Telephone cable

3. Which pins are switched in a crossover cable?
   A. 1 and 2, 3 and 4
   B. 1 and 3, 2 and 6
   C. 2 and 4, 5 and 7
   D. 1 and 4, 5 and 8

4. UTP cable has specific colors for the wire associated with each pin. Based on the TIA/EIA 568B wiring standard, what is the correct color order, starting with pin 1?
   A. White/Orange, Orange, Blue, White/Green, White/Blue, Green, White/Brown, Brown
   B. Orange, White/Orange, White/Green, Blue, White/Blue, White/Brown, Brown, Green
   C. White/Orange, Orange, White/Green, Blue, White/Blue, Green, White/Brown, Brown
   D. White/Green, Green, White/Orange, Blue, White/Blue, Orange, White/Brown, Brown

5. What is used to describe network traffic flows that remain inside the data center?
   A. Ingress
   B. Aggregation
   C. East-West
   D. North-South

6. Which of the following govern how the network is configured and operated as well as how people are expected to behave on the network?
   A. Baselines
   B. Laws
   C. Policies
   D. Procedures

7. You have upgraded the firmware on your switches and access points. What documentation do you need to update?

   A. Baselines and configuration documentation

   B. Physical network diagram

   C. Logical network diagram

   D. Wiring schematics

8. Where does the SDN controller interface with the switching fabric?

   A. Spine

   B. Control plane

   C. Forwarding plane

   D. P Core

9. Load testing, connectivity testing, and throughput testing are all examples of what?

   A. Load balancing

   B. Network monitoring

   C. Packet sniffing

   D. Traffic shaping

10. Abstracting the Cloud hardware into software objects for automated configuration is referred to as _____.

   A. Application programming interface

   B. Elasticity

   C. Infrastructure as Code

   D. Software-defined networking

11. Which of the following identifies steps to recover from adverse effects caused by a change?

   A. Rollback process

   B. Approvable process

   C. Notification process

   D. Impact assessment

12. After a network configuration change has been made, which three of the following is *not* a document that needs to be updated?

   A. Network configurations

   B. Additions to the network

   C. Physical location changes

   D. Application document

13. When the vendor provides the hardware platform or data center, and the company installs and manages its own operating systems and application systems, which service type is being used?

    A. Software as a Service

    B. Infrastructure as a Service

    C. Platform as a Service

    D. Desktop as a Service

14. You have added a new cable segment to your network. You need to make sure you document this for troubleshooting purposes. What should you update?

    A. The disaster recovery plan

    B. The wiring schematics

    C. The router connections document

    D. The baseline document

15. Machine to machine configuration interfaces are called _____ .

    A. Northbound interfaces

    B. Southbound interfaces

    C. APIs

    D. SDN

16. Public clouds are divided into logical groupings that allow many different customers to access a section as if it were their own private data center. This is known as _____ .

    A. Multi-fabric

    B. Elasticity

    C. Multitenancy

    D. Platform as a Service

17. Which of the following are methods used to connect a private cloud to a public cloud? (Choose all that apply.)

    A. Internet

    B. SDN

    C. VPN

    D. Direct Connect

    E. Virtual switches

18. Which of the following are reasons to optimize network performance? (Choose all that apply.)

    A. Maximizing uptime

    B. Minimizing latency

    C. Using VoIP

    D. Using video applications

    E. None of the above

19. What term describes technologies that can deliver voice communications over the Internet?

   A. Jitter

   B. Uptime

   C. Voice over Internet Protocol

   D. None of the above

20. Which virtualization approach is run as an application?

   A. Type 1 hypervisor

   B. Type 2 hypervisor

   C. SDN

   D. Virtual switch

   E. None of the above

Chapter
22

Ensuring Network Availability

THE FOLLOWING COMPTIA NETWORK+ EXAM OBJECTIVES ARE COVERED IN THIS CHAPTER:

✓ **3.1 Given a scenario, use the appropriate statistics and sensors to ensure network availability.**

- Performance metrics/sensors
- Device/Chassis
    - Temperature
    - Central processing unit (CPU) usage
    - Memory
- Network metrics
    - Bandwidth
    - Latency
    - Jitter
- SNMP
    - Traps
    - Object identifiers (OIDs)
    - Management Information bases (MIBs)
- Network device Logs
    - Log reviews
        - Traffic logs
        - Audit logs
        - Syslog
    - Logging levels/severity levels

- Interface statistics/status
    - Link state (up/down)
    - Speed/duplex
    - Send/receive traffic
    - Cyclic redundancy checks (CRCs)
    - Protocol packet and byte counts
- Interface errors or alerts
    - CRC errors
    - Giants
    - Runts
    - Encapsulation errors
- Environmental factors and sensors
    - Temperature
    - Humidity
    - Electrical
    - Flooding
- Baselines
- NetFlow Data
- Uptime/downtime

In this chapter you will learn about network availability and some of the ways to achieve a stable network. The environmental parameters include heat and humidity and must remain in satisfactory ranges. CPU load and memory utilization cannot exceed a maximum value without the network suffering low-performance problems.

We'll discuss common networking interface issues such as bandwidth; latency, which is the delay incurred as data crosses the network; and jitter, which is the variation in delay.

SNMP is a common and widely used network management protocol and application. SNMP systems use OIDs to identify individual parameters on devices and MIBs to define the data structure on the SNMP management system.

We'll also cover logging. Logging is used to collect, store, and analyze events occurring on the network as reported by the networking devices. Various types of logs can be collected to analyze traffic and audit reporting and general events using a syslog server.

Let's go ahead and get started on ensuring network availability.

To find Todd Lammle CompTIA videos and practice questions, please see www.lammle.com

Performance Metrics/Sensors

Most of today's modern networking equipment is wired up with sensors that collect very useful data on the health of your network. By effectively collecting, storing, and analyzing this data, you can determine what metrics are in the normal range and, more importantly, take action when they stray outside of the safe zone.

Temperature   When a piece of networking equipment overheats, bad things usually happen (trust me on this). Modern technology platforms have become increasingly dense silicon chips that give off heat that needs to be dissipated. There are elaborate mechanisms in the devices and data centers to remove this heat so they operate in their safe ranges. All devices will come with parameters for both maximum and minimum storage and operating ranges. Sensors in the room, cabinets, and enclosures can report operating temperatures to management systems that can take action if out of range. This can include automatically powering them off, increasing the airflow, or sending out an alert to the staff to take action.

Central Processing Unit (CPU) Usage   It is a good practice to use as much of the CPU cycles as you can. After all, you paid for them, and if they are not used, they are wasted. But wait, there is a line you don't want to cross and that's high CPU utilization. This is part hard science, part vendor recommendations, and part intuition on your part based on your experience. However, if a CPU stays pegged at 90 percent or higher all day long, you are pushing your luck. If a CPU pegs at 100 percent, the operating system or application software may become unstable, leading to failures. It is a good practice to monitor the CPU load and turn off unneeded services or upgrade to a higher-performing platform if required.

Memory   High memory utilization can be as severe as a saturated CPU. The operating system and applications require access to high-speed memory to function. If you run out of memory, the system may crash or have severe performance degradation. You can use your network monitoring tools to monitor memory and alarm if the utilization gets too high.

Network Metrics

Collecting and comparing metrics over time is a valuable exercise. Once a baseline has been established for these metrics, you can determine when an issue has gotten better or worse over time. It also allows you to determine if measures you have taken to improve a scenario have done so.

Bandwidth   In a perfect world, there would be unlimited *bandwidth*, but in reality, you're more likely to find Bigfoot. So, it's helpful to have some great strategies up your sleeve.

If you look at what computers are used for today, there's a huge difference between the files we transfer now versus those transferred even three to five years ago. Now we do things like watch movies online without them stalling, and we can send huge email attachments. Video teleconferencing is almost more common than Starbucks locations. The point is that the files we transfer today are really large compared to what we sent back and forth just a few years ago. And although bandwidth has increased to allow us to do what we do, there are still limitations that cause network performance to suffer miserably. Let's start with a few reasons why you need to carefully manage whatever amount of precious bandwidth you've got.

You now know that bandwidth is to networking as water is to life, and you're one of the lucky few if your network actually has an excess of it. Cursed is the downtrodden administrator who can't seem to find enough, and more fall into this category than the former. At times, your very sanity may hinge upon ensuring that your users have enough available bandwidth to get their jobs done on your network, and even if you've got a 1 Gbps connection, it doesn't mean all your users have that much bandwidth at their fingertips. What it really means is that they get a piece of it, and they share the rest with other users and network processes. Because it's your job to make sure as much of that 1 Gbps as possible is there to use when needed.

Latency   Most of us have clicked to open an application or clicked a web link only to have the computer just sit there staring back at us, helplessly hanging. That sort of lag comes when the resources needed to open the program or take us to the next page are not fully available. That kind of lag on a network is called *latency*—the time between when data is requested and the moment it actually gets delivered. The more latency, the longer the delay and the longer you have to stare blankly back at your computer screen, hoping something happens soon.

Latency affects some programs more than others. If you are sending an email, it may be annoying to have to wait a few seconds for the email server to respond, but that type of delay isn't likely to cause physical harm to you or a loved one. Applications that are adversely affected by latency are said to have high *latency sensitivity*. A common example of this is online gaming. Although it may not mean actual life or death, playing certain online games with significant delays can mean the untimely demise of your character—and you won't even know it. Worse, it can affect the entire experience for those playing with you, which can get you booted from some game servers. On a much more serious level, applications like remote surgery also have high latency sensitivity.

Jitter   Not every packet takes the same route to the destination, so some will be more delayed than others if they travel through a slower or busier network connection. The variation in packet delay is called *jitter*, and this can have a nastily negative impact on programs that communicate in real time.

Jitter occurs when the data flow in a connection is not consistent; that is, it increases and decreases in no discernable pattern. Jitter results from network congestion, timing drift, and route changes. Jitter is especially problematic in real-time communications like IP telephony and videoconferencing.

SNMP

Although *Simple Network Management Protocol (SNMP)* certainly isn't the oldest protocol ever, it's still pretty old, considering it was created way back in 1988 (RFC 1065)! SNMP is an Application layer protocol that provides a message format for agents on a variety of devices to communicate with network management stations (NMSs)—for example, Cisco Prime or SolarWinds Orion. These agents send messages to the NMS station, which then either reads or writes information in the database that's stored on the NMS and called a *management information base (MIB)*.

The NMS periodically queries or polls the SNMP agent on a device to gather and analyze statistics via GET messages. These messages can be sent to a console or alert you via email or SMS.

The command `snmpwalk` uses the SNMP GET NEXT request to query a network for a tree of information. Each piece of data on the device is identified by a string of numbers called an organizational identifier, or OID for short. For example, end devices running SNMP agents would send an SNMP trap to the NMS if a problem occurs. This is demonstrated in Figure 22.1.

FIGURE 22.1   SNMP GET and TRAP messages

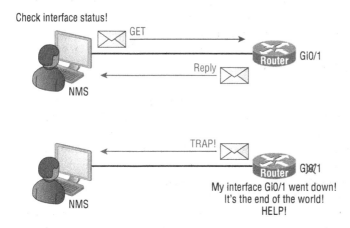

Admins can also use SNMP to provide some configuration to agents as well, called
SET messages. In addition to polling to obtain statistics, SNMP can be used for analyzing
information and compiling the results in a report or even a graph. Thresholds can be used to
trigger a notification process when exceeded. Graphing tools are used to monitor the CPU
statistics of devices like a core router. The CPU should be monitored continuously, and the
NMS can graph the statistics. Notification will be sent when any threshold you've set has
been exceeded.

SNMP has three versions, with version 1 being rarely, if ever, implemented today. Here's a
summary of these three versions:

SNMPv1   Supports plaintext authentication with community strings and
uses only UDP.

SNMPv2c   Supports plaintext authentication with MD5 or SHA with no encryption
but provides GET BULK, which is a way to gather many types of information at once
and minimize the number of GET requests. It offers a more detailed error message
reporting method, but it's not more secure than v1. It uses UDP even though it can be
configured to use TCP.

SNMPv3   Supports strong authentication with MD5 or SHA, providing confidentiality
(encryption) and data integrity of messages via DES or DES-256 encryption between
agents and managers. SNMPv3 Security with 256-bit AES encryption is available in
many products today. AES-256 enhances encryption capabilities of SNMPv3 beyond
the SNMPv3 standard. Some network devices, including most Cisco devices, support
SNMP with 256-bit AES. Some other devices do not. The net-snmp agent does not
support AES-256 with SNMPv3/USM. While most operating system platforms like Windows, Linux, and FreeBSD do not support it off-the-shelf, there are third-party SNMPv3
agents available for these platforms that support SNMPv3 with AES-256. GET BULK is
a supported feature of SNMPv3, and this version also uses TCP.

Network Device Logs

All network devices will record events taking place that offer invaluable information to us network engineers. In this section, we will look at logging with reviews, specific logs of traffic flows, and logs that are used for auditing your network, and we'll end with the most widely used method of logging called the syslog.

Log Reviews   Generating a mountain of logging data does no good if you never review it and look for critical information on the health of your network. There are many amazing tools offered by commercial companies, tools such as Splunk and Cisco Tetration that analyze log data for very useful information. These tools can establish benchmarks and detect anomalies. Tools such as Kibana can mine your data and supply visualizations in many different formats that are good for monitoring dashboards and making pretty reports.

Traffic Logs   By collecting traffic logs at various points in your network, you can collect the needed data to establish baselines and monitor for events that exceed the baselines. Also, storing traffic logs allows you to search for events based on the time of day or user session. Network management systems can be configured to send out warnings if traffic utilization is outside of standard boundaries.

Audit Logs   By saving log data and using business intelligence tools in the data lake, you can provide audit reports configured to meet your needs. Many devices can export specific data and reports to meet general audit log requirements.

Syslog   Reading system messages from a switch's or router's internal buffer is the most popular and efficient method of seeing what's going on with your network at a particular time. But the best way is to log messages to a *syslog* server, which stores messages from you and can even time-stamp and sequence them for you, and it's easy to set up and configure! Figure 22.2 shows a syslog server and client in action.

Syslog allows you to display, sort, and even search messages, all of which makes it a really great troubleshooting tool. The search feature is especially powerful because you can use keywords and even severity levels. Plus, the server can email admins based on the severity level of the message.

FIGURE 22.2   Syslog server and client

Syslog server

I want to look at the console messages
of the SF router from last night.

Network devices can be configured to generate a syslog message and forward it to various destinations. These four examples are popular ways to gather messages from Cisco devices:

- Logging buffer (on by default)
- Console line (on by default)
- Terminal lines (using the terminal monitor command)
- Syslog server

As you already know, all system messages and debug output generated by the IOS go out only the console port by default and are also logged in buffers in RAM. And you also know that routers aren't exactly shy about sending messages! To send message to the VTY lines, use the terminal monitor command.

So, by default, we'd see something like this on our console line:

```
*Oct 21 17:33:50.565:%LINK-5-CHANGED:Interface FastEthernet0/0,
changed state to administratively down
*Oct 21 17:33:51.565:%LINEPROTO-5-UPDOWN:Line protocol on
Interface FastEthernet0/0, changed state to down
```

And the router would send a general version of the message to the syslog server that would be formatted something like this:

```
Seq no:timestamp: %facility-severity-MNEMONIC:description
```

The system message format can be broken down in this way:

seq no   This stamp logs messages with a sequence number, but not by default. If you want this output, you've got to configure it.

timestamp   Date and time of the message or event.

facility   The facility to which the message refers.

severity   A single-digit code from 0 to 7 that indicates the severity of the message. (See Table 22.1 for more information on the severity levels.)

MNEMONIC   Text string that uniquely describes the message.

description   Text string containing detailed information about the event being reported.

The severity levels, from the most severe to the least severe, are explained in Table 22.1. Informational is the default and will result in all messages being sent to the buffers and console.

If you are studying for your CompTIA Network+ exam, you need to memorize Table 22.1.

Understand that only emergency-level messages will be displayed if you've configured severity level 0. But if, for example, you opt for level 4 instead, level 0 through 4 will be

TABLE 22.1 Severity levels

Severity Level	Explanation
Emergency (severity 0)	System is unusable.
Alert (severity 1)	Immediate action is needed.
Critical (severity 2)	Critical condition.
Error (severity 3)	Error condition.
Warning (severity 4)	Warning condition.
Notification (severity 5)	Normal but significant condition.
Information (severity 6)	Normal information message.
Debugging (severity 7)	Debugging message.

displayed, giving you emergency, alert, critical, error, and warning messages too. Level 7 is the highest-level security option and displays everything, but be warned that going with it could have a serious impact on the performance of your device. So always use debugging commands carefully with an eye on the messages you really need to meet your specific business requirements!

Interface Statistics/Status

When troubleshooting, I usually take a look at the interface statistics when first investigating an issue. If the link is down, nothing else will work, so it is a good place to start. Most device manufacturers will show interface statistics either in a generalized format showing all of the links or on a highly detailed link statistics page for each individual interface. You can also enter specific commands to drill down to exactly what you are wanting to look at.

Link State Up/Down   Look to see if the physical link is down and also check to see if there is a protocol error causing the link to be down. Also, the link can be forced down by the administrator in the configuration.

Speed and Duplex   There are generally three duplex settings on each port of a network switch: full, half, and auto. In order for two devices to connect effectively, the duplex setting has to match on both sides of the connection. If one side of a connection is set to full and the other is set to half, they're mismatched. More elusively, if both sides are set to auto but the devices are different, you can also end up with a mismatch because the device on one side defaults to full and the other one defaults to half.

Duplex mismatches can cause lots of network and interface errors, and even the lack of a network connection. This is partially because setting the interfaces to full-duplex disables the CSMA/CD protocol. This is definitely not a problem in a network that has no hubs (and therefore no shared segments in which there could be collisions), but it can make things really ugly in a network where hubs are still being used. This means the settings you choose are based on the type of devices you have populating your network. If you have all switches and no hubs, feel free to set all interfaces to full-duplex, but if you've got hubs in the mix, you have shared networks, so you're forced to keep the settings at half-duplex. With all new switches produced today, leaving the speed and duplex setting to auto (the default on both switches and hosts) is the recommended way to go.

For Windows 10, right-click on Ethernet and then select Properties. Click Configure. Click the Advanced tab and set the Ethernet card's Speed & Duplex settings to 100 Mbps Full Duplex.

The option in the Property field may be named Link Speed & Duplex or just Speed & Duplex.

Send/Receive Traffic   When looking at the interface statistics, it is a good practice to look at the counters of the send and receive traffic. If it is incrementing or not will tell you the current activity and usually the activity in the recent past as well as the total values. By clearing the counters on the interface, you can see current information on the total traffic coming into and out of an interface.

Cyclic Redundancy Checks (CRCs)   By looking at an interface's CRC counters, you can determine if there are any errors on the link. If you see the CRC counter incrementing, you should check the physical interfaces on each end and the cabling interconnecting the interfaces.

Protocol Packet and Byte Counts   Some network devices have the added intelligence to provide detailed information on the traffic flowing through them by reporting protocol-level information. For example, firewalls can provide detailed information on HTTP and HTPS traffic. This can be helpful in troubleshooting protocol-specific problems.

Interface Errors

Your network's main purpose is to send and receive traffic as quickly and error free as possible. By monitoring your interface statistics and knowing the parameters to look for, you can identify and take action to correct the problem before an outage or degradation occurs.

CRC Errors The cyclic redundancy check (CRC) is used to detect data corruption of a received frame. The network hardware runs a mathematical formula on the received data and the result is a value known as the CRC. This value is then compared to the value received that was calculated by the sender and included in the received frame. If they do not match, you'll receive a CRC error, which means the received data is not good. It would be a good time to check your network cabling and the sending and receiving physical interfaces as the source of the problem.

Giants We have all been taught that bigger is always better. And while this can be true, it can also create some problems for us. Let us descend into the murky world of giant, baby giant, jumbo, and super jumbo frames. The Ethernet specification clearly calls out that the maximum transmission unit (MTU) of an Ethernet frame is 1500 bytes long. So, what is the problem? Well with all the enhancements and the natural evolution of Ethernet, frames have slowly begun to grow all the way up to 9000 bytes!

The problem arises when a giant frame larger than 1500 bytes tries to cross an interface that is set at the standard MTU of 1500. This clearly does not work! There are two things we can do here: either configure the sending device to that standard MTU size or change the configuration on your network interface to accept a larger MTU. If you have giant or jumbo frames on your network, you will need to make sure that all devices in the data path are configured to accept the larger size.

Runts It would only make sense that if we can have giants running through our network, we may have a few runts too. The smallest an Ethernet frame can be is 64 bytes. Any frames of data that are smaller than this are not supposed to be there and are called runts. Where do they come from? Well, there should never be runts on your network, and if you see them, they are usually caused by collisions, bad network interface hardware, a buffer underrun, a duplex mismatch, or a software driver bug.

Encapsulation Errors Data encapsulation means that additional information is added to the frame by the various layers in the OSI stack. Data can be added either before or after the existing data and at the other end of the process it is de-encapsulated by removing that information. This is often called headers and trailers.

An Ethernet frame can be encapsulated into other protocols for transmission, such as VXLAN, OTV, and virtualized networks such as hypervisors and the public cloud. When the software performs the encapsulation, if there is a failure in the process, it is logged as an encapsulation error. This is usually either a configuration problem or an issue with the software performing the process.

Environmental Factors and Sensors

Environmental monitors are designed to monitor the temperature, humidity, power, and air flow in an area or in a device. Temperature and humidity are both critical factors in the health of computing equipment. High temperatures lead to CPU overheating, and shortly thereafter, systems start rebooting.

High humidity cannot be tolerated because it leads to corrosion of electrical parts followed by shorts and other failures. Low humidity sounds good on paper, but with it comes static electricity buildup in the air, which can fry computer parts if it reaches them. Both of these conditions should be monitored.

A *temperature and humidity monitor* can save you and your precious devices from a total meltdown. By their very nature, networks often include lots of machines placed close together in one or several locations—like server rooms. Clearly, these devices, all humming along at once, generate quite a bit of heat.

Just like us, electronics need to "breathe," and they're also pretty sensitive to becoming overheated, which is why you'll often need a jacket in a chilly server room. It's also why we need to set up and use temperature-monitoring devices. Twenty years ago or so, these devices didn't send alerts or give off any kind of alarms; they were just little plastic boxes that had pieces of round graph paper to graph temperature. The paper was good for a month, and for that duration, it would just spin around in a circle. As the temperature moved up or down, the pen attached to the temperature coil moved in or out, leaving a circle line around the paper. All of this allowed you to manually monitor the temperature modulation in the server room over time. Although intended to "alert" you when and if there were climate changes, it usually did so after the fact, and therefore, too late.

Today, these temperature/humidity systems can provide multiple sensors feeding data to a single control point—nice. Now we can much more accurately track the temperature in our server rooms dynamically in real time. The central control point is usually equipped with HTTP/HTTPS software that can send alerts and provide alarms via a browser should your server room experience a warming event.

Temperature/humidity monitors also come in a variety of flavors. They vary in size and cost and come in hardware and/or software varieties. The kind you need varies and is based on the size of the room and the number of devices in it. You can even get one that will just monitor your PC's internal heat.

What else will indicate you have a temperature problem in your server room? When you install new servers in a rack and you have network instability and other issues across all the servers in the rack but the power resources and bandwidth have been tested, this would be a good time to check your temperature monitor and verify that the servers are staying cool enough. Another red flag when it comes to environmental issues is a problem that occurs every day at the same time. This could be the time of day when the room temperature reaches the problematic stage.

Baseline

High-quality documentation should include a baseline for network performance because you and your client need to know what "normal" looks like in order to detect problems before they develop into disasters. Don't forget to verify that the network conforms to all internal and external regulations and that you've developed and itemized solid management procedures and security policies for future network administrators to refer to and follow.

In networking, *baseline* can refer to the standard level of performance of a certain device or to the normal operating capacity for your whole network. For instance, a specific server's baseline describes norms for factors like how busy its processors are, how much of the memory it uses, and how much data usually goes through the NIC at a given time.

A network baseline delimits the amount of bandwidth available and when it is available. For networks and networked devices, baselines include information about four key components:

- Processor
- Memory
- Hard-disk (or other storage) subsystem
- Wired/wireless utilization

After everything is up and running, it's a good idea to establish performance baselines on all vital devices and your network in general. To do this, measure things like network usage at three different strategic times to get an accurate assessment. For instance, peak usage usually happens around 8:00 a.m., Monday through Friday, or whenever most people log in to the network in the morning. After hours or on weekends is often when usage is the lowest. Knowing these values can help you troubleshoot *bottlenecks* or determine why certain system resources are more limited than they should be. Knowing what your baseline is can even tell you if someone's complaints about the network running like a slug are really valid—nice!

It's good to know that you can use network-monitoring software to establish baselines. Even some server operating systems come with software to help with network monitoring, which can help find baselines, perform log management, and even do network graphing as well so you can compare the logs and graphs at a later period of time on your network.

In my experience, it's wise to re-baseline network performance at least once a year. And always pinpoint new performance baselines after any major upgrade to your network's infrastructure.

NetFlow

What if we could take an X-ray of the traffic flows in your network to see what is connecting where? Well, with NetFlow, now you can! NetFlow can collect more granular information on traffic flows than SNMP is able to. After setting up your network routers, firewalls, and other devices such as VPN concentrators to collect information on the data that flows through them, you send this information over to a NetFlow collector for analysis.

The NetFlow collectors are software management applications running on servers that analyze the received information from your network. They show which devices are talking to each other and what the traffic flows look like; add timestamps, traffic peaks, and valleys; and produce nice charts and graphs of the data flowing through your network. This information is valuable for establishing baselines and troubleshooting. It is also used by the security team to help identify potentially suspicious activity.

The network devices send information such as source and destination IP address and applications such as if the traffic is web or e-mail traffic or from any other application.

Uptime

Uptime is the amount of time the system is up and accessible to your end users, so the more uptime you have the better. And depending on how critical the nature of your business is, you may need to provide four nines or five nines uptime on your network—that's a lot. Why is this a lot? Because you write out four nines as 99.99 percent, or better, you write out five nines as 99.999 percent! Now that is some serious uptime!

 There's a difference between uptime and availability. Your servers may be up but not accessible if a cable gets cut or something, and that outage would definitely count against your availability time.

Downtime

What can I say... your late-night call comes in right after a network failure. Downtime can be a serious issue, or the impacts can be reduced with a good network design. As we all say, it depends.

All networks will eventually fail, and that is a strike in the downtime column.

High availability is a system-design protocol that guarantees a certain amount of operational uptime during a given period. The design attempts to minimize unplanned downtime—the time users are unable to access resources. In almost all cases, high availability is provided through the implementation of duplicate equipment (multiple servers, multiple NICs, etc.). Organizations that serve critical functions obviously need this; after all, you really don't want to blaze your way to a hospital ER only to find that they can't treat you because their network is down!

 There's a difference between planned downtime and unplanned downtime. Planned downtime is good—it's occasionally scheduled for system maintenance and routine upgrades. Unplanned downtime is bad—it's a lack of access due to system failure, which is exactly the issue high availability resolves.

One of the highest standards in uptime is the ability to provide the five nines availability I mentioned earlier. This actually means the network is accessible 99.999 percent of the time—way impressive! Think about this. In one non-leap year, there are 31,536,000 seconds. If you are available 99.999 percent of the time, it means you can be down only 0.001 percent of the time, or a total of 315.36 seconds, or 5 minutes and 15.36 seconds per year—wow!

Summary

In this chapter you learned about network availability and some of the ways to achieve a stable network. The environmental parameters include heat and humidity and must remain in satisfactory ranges. CPU load and memory utilization cannot exceed a maximum value without the network suffering low-performance problems.

We discussed common networking interface issues such as bandwidth; latency, which is the delay incurred as data crosses the network; and jitter, which is the variation in delay.

SNMP is a common and widely used network management protocol and application. SNMP systems use OIDs to identify individual parameters on devices and MIBs to define the data structure on the SNMP management system.

Logging is used to collect, store, and analyze events occurring on the network as reported by the networking devices. Various types of logs can be collected to analyze traffic and audit reporting and general events using a syslog server.

Interface statistics report on the health of individual device interfaces and can include that state of the link, speed/duplex, the volume of traffic sent and received, the error rates using CRC checks, and sometimes protocol-specific data.

Interface errors are important to understand, and you should know what jumbo and runt frames are and what an encapsulation error is.

Baselines help you determine what normal operations are and when your network events are outside of what is considered to be normal operation.

NetFlow is an advanced protocol with which network devices send detailed traffic information for NetFlow application data from your devices to a centralized application. That centralized application then reports application and endpoint traffic flow information.

Exam Essentials

Describe the critical need to monitor environment readings such as the temperature of the networking equipment.   Excessive temperature readings can permanently destroy networking hardware and steps must be taken to monitor and react to high temperature conditions.

Explain why high CPU and memory usage can affect network hardware performance.   Both CPU and memory starvation can cause the networking platform to fail, reload, or have unpredictable results when there is not enough available CPU and memory on the platform.

Describe SNMP.   The Simple Network Management Protocol collects, monitors, and reports on the data retrieved from networking devices.

Know what device logging is and the different uses for collecting log files.   The syslog protocol is the standard for collecting events and logs sent from networking equipment. Various logs types include traffic, error, and audit logs. The syslog server stores these logs; each network device can also store logging information locally.

Describe the various statistics generated by network interfaces. Network interfaces can report that status of a link, whether it is up or down, the speed and duplex, traffic/packet counters, and errors using the CRC checksums.

Describe the different types of interface errors. Network interface errors include CRC checksum comparison errors indicating the frame has been corrupted. Giant frames are above the standard maximum Ethernet frame size of 1500 bytes and runts are under the minimum frame size of 64 bytes. Encapsulation errors indicate the process of adding or removing header data has failed.

Know what a baseline is and why it is needed. To determine what is normal on your network, you must collect data in a baseline and then you can track ongoing operations to see if you exceed these values, which may indicate a problem in your network.

Describe NetFlow. NetFlow is a standardized protocol that sends detailed traffic flow information to a collector station that shows which devices are talking to each other, at what time, and using what applications.

Written Lab

You can find the answers to the written labs in Appendix A. Write the answers to the following questions about statistics, sensors, and network availability.

1. Which two device parameters should never reach full utilization?

2. What are the average metrics collected over time?

3. You want to collect logging data on ongoing operations on a centralized server. What application allows you to do this?

4. Which interface operation determines if the data flow is one way or two way?

5. In what per-second value are interface speeds recorded?

6. You want to log in to a server and transfer files. What application will you use?

7. Which interface parameter uses a mathematical calculation to derive errors?

8. What is an Ethernet frame that is larger than the standard size called?

9. What protocol collects detailed application-level traffic information?

10. Which network management protocol is used to poll and collect information from networking devices?

Review Questions

You can find the answers to the review questions in Appendix B.

1. What protocol provides detailed information on traffic flows between endpoints?
   A. Syslog
   B. SNMP
   C. NetFlow
   D. SPAN

2. What networking protocol uses OIDs and MIBs for data collection?
   A. SPAN
   B. NetFlow
   C. Syslog
   D. SNMP

3. What is a below-standard frame size called?
   A. Undercount
   B. Runt
   C. Nibble
   D. Short Frame

4. What is one-way traffic flow called?
   A. Duplex
   B. Asymmetric
   C. Half-duplex
   D. Receive only auto-negotiation

5. What is the average of collected metrics called?
   A. NetFlow
   B. SNMPv2c
   C. Management information base
   D. Baseline
   E. Syslog

6. Which device components should never be allowed to reach full capacity? (Choose two.)
   A. Memory
   B. Voltage
   C. CPU
   D. Delay

7. Which of the following mathematically determines network errors?

   A. SNMP

   B. NetFlow

   C. CRC

   D. Syslog

8. What protocol is used to poll and collect information from networking devices?

   A. SPAN

   B. NetFlow

   C. Syslog

   D. SNMP

9. What is the term for when a segment of data fails the addition or deletion of header information?

   A. Encapsulation error

   B. CRC

   C. NetFlow

   D. Frame reject

10. What are two environmental variables that are commonly monitored? (Choose two.)

   A. Temperature

   B. Airflow

   C. Humidity

   D. Utilization

11. Baselines commonly include which of the following?

   A. Processor

   B. Memory

   C. Storage subsystems

   D. Wired/wireless utilization

   E. All of the above

12. What are two metrics that are tracked to account for utilization in operations?

   A. Syslog

   B. Uptime

   C. Downtime

   D. SNMP

13. What is a system-design protocol that guarantees a certain amount of operational uptime during a given period?

    A. High availability

    B. Redundancy

    C. Hot standby

    D. Backup systems

14. What is bi-directional traffic flow across an Ethernet interface?

    A. Full-duplex

    B. Two-way

    C. Duplex

    D. Symmetric

15. What syslog severity level denotes that the system is unusable?

    A. Emergency

    B. Alert

    C. Critical

    D. Error

16. What protocol is commonly used to collect audit information?

    A. SNMP

    B. NetFlow

    C. Syslog

    D. Kibana

17. Which SNMP version added support for GET BULK operations?

    A. SNMPv1

    B. SNMPv2a

    C. SNMPv2c

    D. SNMPv3

18. What is the variation in delay?

    A. Jitter

    B. Bandwidth variance

    C. Latency

    D. Egress latency

19. What is end-to-end delay?

    A. Jitter

    B. Bandwidth variance

    C. Latency

    D. Egress latency

20. Resource starvation of which of the following can cause a networking device to fail? (Choose two.)

   A. Memory

   B. bandwidth

   C. CRC utilization

   D. CPU utilization

Chapter 23

Cable Connectivity Issues and Tools

THE FOLLOWING COMPTIA NETWORK+ EXAM OBJECTIVES ARE COVERED IN THIS CHAPTER:

✓ **5.2 Given a scenario, troubleshoot common cable connectivity issues and select the appropriate tools.**

- Specifications and limitations

    - Throughput

    - Speed

    - Distance

- Cable considerations

    - Shielded and unshielded

    - Plenum and riser-rated

- Cable application

    - Rollover cable/console cable

    - Crossover cable

    - Power over Ethernet

- Common issues

    - Attenuation

    - Interference

    - Decibel (dB) loss

    - Incorrect pinout

    - Bad ports

    - Open/short

    - Light emitting diode (LED) status indicators

    - Incorrect transceivers

- Duplexing issues
- Transmit and received (TX/RX) reversed
- Dirty optical cables
- Common tools
  - Cable Crimper
  - Punch-down tool
  - Tone generator
  - Loopback adapter
  - Optical time-domain reflectometer (OTDR)
  - Multimeter
  - Cable tester
  - Wire map
  - Tap
  - Fusion splicers
  - Spectrum analyzers
  - Snips/cutters
  - Fiber light meter

Specialized tasks require specialized tools, and installing network components is no exception. We use some of these tools, on an everyday basis, but most of the hardware tools I'll be covering in this chapter are used mainly in the telecommunications industry.

Still, in order to meet the CompTIA Network+ objectives, and also because you're likely to come across them in today's networking environments, it's very important that you're familiar with them.

To find Todd Lammle CompTIA videos and practice questions, please see www.lammle.com.

Specifications and Limitations

When working on the Physical layer, you must understand the specifications of the equipment you are working with to ensure that you are not exceeding cable and interface capabilities.

Throughput Network throughput capabilities are always increasing with speeds of 100 gigabits per second becoming very common and 400 G interfaces starting to appear more and more in the larger data centers, carrier networks, and large cloud computing locations. With the higher speeds come more stringent cable requirements. It is critical that we check the interface specifications that detail the supported cable types.

Speed Distance Generally, the higher the speed of an interface the more sensitive it is to distance. New optical technologies overcome this imitation. However, high-end optics are very expensive and not required if the distances needed are, for example, just inside a data center. If the distances are short, say 5 meters, copper/coax cables can be used in place of optical for significant cost savings.

Cable Considerations

Understanding cable types and use cases is important to meet local regulatory requirements that are usually related to fire safety and to keep costs down by selecting the correct cable type for your needs.

Shielded and Unshielded   Copper Ethernet cabling comes in both unshielded twisted-pair (UTP) and shielded twisted-pair (STP) types.

With UTP, the wires are twisted together in pairs to reduce noise and crosstalk, and multiple pairs are enclosed in a standard nonmetal outer covering. These are the basic Ethernet cables found in most installations.

With STP, we still twist wires into pairs, but for added protection from electromagnetic interference, the cable is wrapped with a foil or mesh shielded outer wrapper.

Plenum and Riser-Rated   Cabling inside a building will use either plenum or riser-rated cabling depending on the needs.

Plenum cables are highly fire resistant and have a low emittance of fumes. Plenum cables can be installed in air ducts.

Riser cables are less costly and are used for building runs between floors that do not traverse air ducts.

Cable Applications

There are so many types of cables that choosing what cable is needed for your requirements can be confusing. In the networking world, we primarily see copper and optical for Ethernet and always need to carry a few console cables in our tool pack to connect directly to servers and network gear when busy troubleshooting problems.

Rollover Cable/Console Cable   Since the beginning of time (well almost), the serial RS232 interface has been with us. Today it is still used for local connections into network equipment and servers for configuration and troubleshooting. These serial port to laptop cables use a standard four-pair cable that is crossed over end to end. For example, wire 1 goes to 8 on the other end, wire 2 goes to 7, and so on. This is commonly referred to as a rollover cable and is the most common console cable configuration in the industry.

Crossover Cable   Copper Ethernet cables come in two different types of pinout configurations. When an end device such as a computer or printer is plugged into a port on a piece of networking gear, straight-through cables are used. This is pin 1 to pin 1, pin 2 to pin 2, and so on.

However, a networking engineer's life is never that simple. If you are connecting a PC directly to another PC or connecting two Ethernet switches together, you end up with a situation where you have the transmitters on each end connected to each other and the same for the receivers. This won't work! So, we need to cross the cables over so we have the transmitter on one end connected to the receiver at the other end. Some network gear can auto-detect and automatically adjust so we do not have to run around looking for a crossover cable to install.

You may have noticed on many Ethernet switches several interfaces off to the side have a "X" label next to them. These are crossover interfaces used to connect switch to switch, which saves you the need to use a crossover cable.

Power over Ethernet   As the networking world evolved and it became common to attach devices such as IP phones and remote Wi-Fi access points to the network, the requirement to supply power to these devices arose. Many IP phones could be powered from a central access Ethernet switch to save having to find a power outlet at every desk. With Wi-Fi access ports, many are located in office ceilings or remote locations where local power may not be available or may be costly to install.

The network switch manufacturers responded with a Power over Ethernet (PoE) option for these use cases. This is standardized under the 802.3af and 802.3at specifications that offer per-port power of 15.4 to 30 watts, respectively.

Common Issues

A surprising number of network troubleshooting takes place at the Physical layer of the OSI model. Remember that the OSI model is additive in that if the layer below has a problem, all of the other layers above it probably won't work! Therefore, it is important to understand all of the issues with cabling and how to identify and resolve them to get the network back up and running.

Attenuation   As a signal moves through any medium, the medium itself will degrade the signal—a phenomenon known as *attenuation* that's common in all kinds of networks. True, signals traversing fiber-optic cable don't attenuate as fast as those on copper cable, but they still do eventually. You know that all copper twisted-pair cables have a maximum segment distance of 100 meters before they'll need to be amplified, or *repeated*, by a hub or a switch, but single-mode fiber-optic cables can sometimes carry signals for miles before they begin to attenuate (degrade). If you need to go far, use fiber, not copper. Although there is attenuation/dB loss in fiber, it can go much farther distances than copper cabling can before being affected by attenuation.

Interference   EMI and *radio frequency interference (RFI)* occur when signals interfere with the normal operation of electronic circuits. Computers happen to be really sensitive to sources of this, such as TV and radio transmitters, which create a specific radio frequency as part of their transmission process. Two other common culprits are two-way radios and cellular phones.

Your only way around this is to use shielded network cables like shielded twisted-pair (STP) and coaxial cable (rare today) or to run EMI/RFI-immune but pricey fiber-optic cable throughout your entire network.

Decibel (dB) Loss   Cables will have signal loss regardless of whether they are copper or optical. The measurement for loss is in power decibels (dB). The dB measurement is the ratio of watts out/watts in on a base 10 logarithmic scale. The longer the cable or higher the frequency, the greater the loss.

If you have too much loss end to end on a cable, the signal strength may not be strong enough for the receiver to bring up the link. Some higher-end network gear can determine the loss and report it via the interface statistics. Generally, however, a cable tester would be required to collect end-to-end loss and see if it is in or out of the specification for the cable type you are using.

Incorrect Pinouts   If you have the wrong type of cable pinout, chances are good that you are not going to get the light up. The standard Ethernet cable uses two out of the four available pairs; one pair is for transmit and the other for receive. These are on pins 1, 2, 3, and 6 of a R-J45 plug. For a straight-through cable, the correct pinouts are 1-1, 2-2, 3-3, and 6-6. For a crossover cable we use 1-3, 2-6, 3-1, and 6-2. Thankfully, the R-J45 jacks are clear plastic and can be held up to a light to confirm the pinouts of the cable.

Bad Ports   Sometimes it's not the cable but the actual port on the networking equipment. When troubleshooting cable issues, it is important to keep your mind open to all possibilities. The device console can help in identifying a bad port, or you can move the cable over to an unused port and see if the problem remains on the original port.

Open/Short   Basically, a *short circuit*, or *short*, happens when the current flows through a different path within a circuit than it's supposed to; in networks, they're usually caused by some type of physical fault in the cable. You can find shorts with circuit-testing equipment, but because sooner is better when it comes to getting a network back up and running, replacing the ailing cable until it can be fixed (if it can be) is your best option.

Light-Emitting Diode (LED) Status Indicators   LED indicators on network devices can be your best friend when trying to resolve a connection issue. They provide a quick visual reference. Remember, green is good, amber may be a problem, and if there is no light, there is no connection. They are also handy when you have someone on the phone in a distant location and you have no access to the network. The visual indications can be invaluable. The general setting is green and means there is a link to the device at the other end, and when it flashes, traffic is being either sent or received.

Incorrect Transceivers   Transceivers convert the electrical signals inside the device to the correct Ethernet specification to communicate with the remote end. For example, you would need a 1G copper transceiver on both ends of the cable for the link to communicate if you are connecting two 1G copper interfaces together that have copper interfaces. Many networking devices now have modular interfaces where you can slide in a transceiver that meets your requirements. For example, you may want to run single-mode fiber-optic to support a 10G link. In this case, you would need 10G-MMF transceivers on both ends. Since transceivers can all look alike, this can be an easy mistake to make and certainly something to look at if the link does not come up.

Duplexing Issues   Ethernet interconnections were originally half-duplex, where one end would transmit while the other received but only in one direction at a time. This is old school and rarely seen in today's networks. Now everything is full-duplex, where both transmit and receive are active on both ends of the link.

However, to maintain backward compatibility, Ethernet interfaces can support both full- and half-duplex. The problem arises when one end thinks it's half-duplex while the other is convinced it's on a full-duplex connection. They will talk, just not very well!

This is usually caused by one end configured to autonegotiation while the other end is not. The one not configured to negotiate ends up with the lowest common denominator, which, you guessed it right, is half-duplex. The other end thinks it's full-duplex and you get a lot of collisions. The way around this is to either set both ends to negotiate their speed and duplex or hard-code in the interface configuration on both ends the speed and duplex setting you require.

Transmit and Received (TX/RX) Reversed   When connecting from a PC-type device into a switch, for the PC use pins 1 and 2 to transmit and 3 and 6 to receive a digital signal. This means that the pins must be reversed on the switch, using pins 1 and 2 for receiving and 3 and 6 for transmitting the digital signal. If your connection isn't working, check the cable end pinouts.

Dirty Optical Cables   This is just what it means: when the ends of a fiber-optic cable are dirty or have oily substances on them, there can be a substantial loss of signal or attenuation. Fiber testers can uncover this or you can simply clean off the ends of both fiber cables to see if you can bring the link up.

Split Pairs   A split pair is a wiring error where two connections that are supposed to be connected using the two wires of a twisted pair are instead connected using two wires from different pairs. Such wiring causes errors in high-rate data lines. If you buy your cables precut, you won't have this problem.

Bent Pins   Many of the connectors you will encounter have small pins on the end that must go into specific holes in the interface to which they plug. If these pins get bent, either they won't go into the correct hole or they won't go into a hole, period. When this occurs, the cable either will not work at all or will not work correctly. Taking care not to bend these fragile pins when working with these cable types will prevent this issue from occurring.

Identifying Hardware Tools

A great example of when the hardware tools and testers I'm about to cover would come in really handy is if you're dealing with failed fiber links between structures. As a system administrator running a network with a server, routers, and switches, it's entirely possible you'll never find yourself in a situation that calls for these tools. But if you're in network design or a field that requires you to install cabling, then these hardware tools are going to be really valuable to you. None of these goodies are free, but they do come in a variety of flavors that run the gamut from real bargains to "You're joking—how much?" Some of them can indeed free you of thousands of dollars!

Cable testers are the most widely used hardware tool in today's LANs, so let's start with them.

Cable Testers

The best way to deal with a faulty cable installation is to avoid the problem in the first place by purchasing high-quality components and installing them carefully. Still, this isn't a perfect world—no matter how careful you are, problems are bound to arise anyway. The tools that I'm going to cover can be used to test cables at the time of their installation and afterward, if and when you need to troubleshoot cabling problems. Cable-testing tools can range from simple, inexpensive mechanical devices to elaborate electronic testers that automatically supply you with a litany of test results in an easy-to-read pass/fail format. Figure 23.1 shows an example of an inexpensive cable tester for twisted-pair wiring testing.

FIGURE 23.1   An inexpensive cable tester

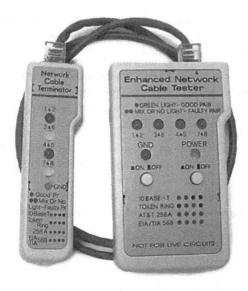

This little box can verify the connection through the cable and tell you if the cable is straight-through or crossover. It can also identify problems such as grounding issues. Sometimes the problem is not a complete lack of connectivity. Sometimes performance is slow, which can also be a cabling issue that a cable tester can identify. This tool is as cheap as they come.

Let's focus on the types of tools available for both copper and fiber-optic cable testing. This is not to say that you need all of the tools listed here. In fact, I'll try to steer you away from certain types of tools. Sometimes you'll get lucky and have the luxury of choosing between high-tech and low-tech devices that perform roughly the same function. You can choose which ones you prefer according to the requirements of your network, your operational budget, even your temperament and time constraints. Some of the tools are extremely complicated and require extensive training to use effectively, whereas others can be used by pretty much anybody equipped with a functioning brain.

Other important considerations to keep in mind when selecting the types of tools that you need are based on the descriptions of cable tests given earlier in this chapter, the test results required by the standards you're using to certify your network, and the capabilities of the people who will be doing the actual work. And don't forget the potentially painful cost of some of them.

Loopback Adapter (Plug)

A *loopback adapter* can be used to loop an Ethernet interface's transmit back to its receiver. This does not loop the data back on an Ethernet interface. Loopback adapters are only useful to verify that the port's transmit and receive electronics are working. Also, you can insert the loopback adapter at one end of a cable and use a cable tester at the other to verify your cable drop.

A loopback test is a diagnostic procedure in which a signal is transmitted and returned to the sending device after passing through all or a portion of a network or circuit. The returned signal is compared with the transmitted signal to evaluate the integrity of the equipment or transmission path. A computer needs a loopback plug that is inserted into a port in order to perform a loopback test.

Loopback adapters are more useful in the telecom world of T1s and DS0 interfaces where the send traffic will be returned to the receiver for testing.

Loopback plugs are made for both Ethernet and fiber applications. Figure 23.2 shows an Ethernet loopback plug.

FIGURE 23.2   Ethernet loopback plug

Figure 23.3 shows a plug for fiber applications.

FIGURE 23.3   Fiber loopback plug

Wire-Map Testers

A *wire-map tester* is a device that transmits signals through each wire in a copper twisted-pair cable to determine if it's connected to the correct pin at the other end. Wire mapping is the most basic test for twisted-pair cables because the eight separate wire connections involved in each cable run are a common source of installation errors. Wire-map testers detect transposed wires, opens (broken or unconnected wires), and shorts (wires or pins improperly connected to each other). All of these problems can render a cable run completely inoperable.

Wire-map testing is nearly always included in multifunction cable testers, but sometimes it's just not worth spending serious cash on a comprehensive device. Dedicated wire-map testers that run about $200–$300 are relatively inexpensive options that enable you to test your installation for the most common faults that occur during installation and afterward. If, say, you're installing voice-grade cable, a simple wire-mapping test is probably all that's needed.

A wire-map tester essentially consists of a remote unit that you attach to the far end of a connection and a battery-operated, handheld main unit that displays the results. Typically, the tester displays various codes that indicate the specific type of fault that it finds. You can also purchase a tester with multiple remote units that are numbered so that one person can test several connections without constantly traveling back and forth from one end of the connections to the other to move the remote unit.

> The one wiring fault that is not detectable by a dedicated wire-map tester is something known as *split pairs*. This fault flies under the radar because even though the pinouts are incorrect, the cable is still wired straight through. To detect split pairs, you must use a device that tests the cable for the near-end crosstalk that split pairs cause.

Continuity Testers

A *continuity tester*, or *line tester*, is an even simpler and less-expensive device than a wire-map tester. It's designed to check a copper cable connection for basic installation problems like opens, shorts, and crossed pairs. It will set you back only a few dollars, but such a device usually can't detect the more complicated twisted-pair wiring faults. It's still a nice option for basic cable testing, especially for coaxial cables that have only two conductors and so don't easily confuse whoever is installing them.

Like a wire-map tester, a continuity tester consists of two separate units that you connect to each end of the cable you want to test. Most of the time, the two units can snap together for storage and easy testing of patch cables. But remember, a continuity tester simply tests continuity, equivalent to data at one bit per minute (or slower), and cannot tell you whether or not a cable will reliably pass Ethernet data at network speeds. For that, you need a real cable tester that can test cables up to Gigabit speeds or higher.

Protocol Analyzer

A *protocol analyzer* is often confused with a packet sniffer because some products really are both. Remember—a packet sniffer looks at all traffic on a network segment. On the other hand, a protocol analyzer (surprise!) analyzes protocols. These tools come in both software and hardware versions, but compared to sniffer and similar products, a network protocol analyzer is likely to give you more information and help. This is because a bona fide protocol analyzer can actually help you troubleshoot problems, whereas most sniffers just provide information for you to enjoy deciphering.

A network protocol analyzer can perform the following functions:

- Help troubleshoot hard-to-solve problems

- Help you detect and identify malicious software (malware)

- Help gather information such as baseline traffic patterns and network-utilization metrics

- Help you identify unused protocols so that you can remove them from the network

- Provide a traffic generator for penetration testing

- Possibly even work with an IDS

And last, and perhaps most important for you, they can really help you learn about networking in general. This means if you just want to find out why a network device is functioning in a certain way, you can use a protocol analyzer to sniff (there's that word again) the traffic and expose the data and protocols that pass along the wire.

Free Network Analyzers

I've found a whole bunch of network analyzers you can use for free at the following location:

`https://www.snapfiles.com/freeware/network/fwpacketsniffer.html`

But understand that there's no way I can verify the validity of this link after this book is published. Again, the terms *sniffer* and *analyzer* are used to define the same products found at this link. For example, both Microsoft's Network Monitor (NetMon) and Wireshark are called sniffers and analyzers, and they both are—at least to some degree.

Certifiers

Certification testers—or *certifiers*—are used to determine whether your network meets specific International Organization for Standardization (ISO) or Telecommunications Industry Association (TIA) standards (Cat 5e, Cat 6, Cat 7, or Cat 8). A certification tester is the only option for you in this case. Also, if your network is wired with both copper and fiber, you really must use a certification tester.

Basically, a certifier is a combination cable tester and network analyzer, only better because it comes with more options. This is wonderful because it makes your job easier and makes you seem smarter to everyone around you—you're only as good as your tools, right? A good certifier will test the performance and response times of network resources like web, file, email, and even DNS and Dynamic Host Configuration Protocol (DHCP) servers. And, at the same time, it will certify your full Category 6 cable installation. After it finishes all this, you can provide your boss with a detailed network test report complete with dazzling, colorful graphics to make it simple to explain and understand—voilà! You're instantly the genius of the day.

To get these smarts, all you need is a lot of money. These products are not for the small office, home office (SOHO) market because they cost literally thousands of dollars, starting at about $5,000.

Time-Domain Reflectometer

A *time-domain reflectometer (TDR)* is a tool that finds and describes faults in metallic cables like twisted wire pairs and coaxial cables. The equivalent device for optical fiber is an optical time-domain reflectometer (OTDR), which I'll talk about in a minute.

A TDR works in the same basic way that radar does. It transmits a short rise time pulse along the conductor, and if it turns out to be of a uniform impedance and properly terminated, the entire transmitted pulse is absorbed in the far-end termination; no signal is reflected back to the TDR. Any impedance interruptions will cause some of the incident signal to be sent back toward the source, letting you know all is not well.

So basically, any increases in the impedance create a reflection that reinforces the original pulse and decreases the impedance, thereby creating a reflection that opposes the original pulse. The resulting reflected pulse that's measured at the output/input to the TDR is displayed or plotted in measures of time. And because the speed of signal propagation is pretty consistent for a given type of transmission medium, the reading can also tell you about the cable length.

Because of this sensitivity to any variation in impedance, you can use a TDR to verify these things:

- Speed and condition of the cable
- How long it takes to send a signal down a cable and how long it takes to come back
- Cable impedance characteristics
- Splice and connector locations and their associated loss amounts
- Estimated cable lengths

Now, let's take a look at a device that tests fiber-optic cables.

Optical Time-Domain Reflectometer

An *optical time-domain reflectometer (OTDR)* is an optoelectronic instrument used to give you the skinny on optical fibers, typically referred to as light meters. It works by putting out a series of optical pulses into the specific fiber you want to test. From the same end that sent these impulses, it collects and measures the light that is scattered and reflected along the length of the fiber. It then records the change in the amount of refraction at various points. This is a lot like the way an electronic TDR measures reflections caused by impedance changes in a cable that you're testing. The strength of the return pulses is incorporated into a measure of time, which also conveniently gives you the fiber's length.

We use OTDRs to give us the following information:

- The fiber's estimated length
- Its overall attenuation, including splice and mated-connector losses
- The location faults, such as breaks

Figure 23.4 shows the output from an OTDR testing a fiber connection.

FIGURE 23.4   Sample OTDR output

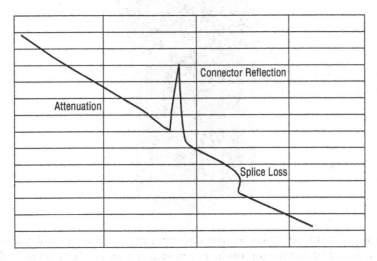

The spike shows where a splice in the fiber is located, which has resulted in the signal being degraded. This is a very typical output. As the signal attenuates, you see a gradual but quick drop in decibels (dB). Any connector will actually show a reflection, which, as mentioned, shows up as a spike in the OTDR output. The connector then creates more attenuation and loss of more db. The more splices, the less distance you can run with fiber.

Multimeter

A *multimeter*, or a multitester (also called a volt/ohm meter [VOM]), is a multitasking electronic measuring instrument. Your average multimeter typically includes features like the ability to measure voltage, current, and resistance. Multimeters come in analog and digital versions, and they range from basic handheld devices useful for simple fault-finding and field-service work to more complex bench instruments that will give you measurements with a very high degree of accuracy.

They can be used to troubleshoot electrical problems in a wide array of electrical devices like batteries, motor controls, appliances, power supplies, and wiring systems. Figure 23.5 shows output of the multimeter that I use to help troubleshoot my networks.

FIGURE 23.5   A multimeter

Multimeters come in lots of flavors with different ranges of features and prices. Cheap ones cost less than $10, but the top-of-the-line models can set you back up to $5,000.

Spectrum Analyzer

A spectrum analyzer is a tool that focuses on the physical layer, which will vary based on the type of analyzer. Although vendors make these analyzers for both audio and optical signals, in most cases spectrum analyzers are used to analyze wireless or radio frequency signals. Spectrum analyzers are primarily used to identify and measure the strength of radio signals that are present in the area. They can visually display these signals by frequency on the device. These devices are used to locate sources of interference that may impact the operation of a wireless network. Figure 23.6 is a screenshot of a spectrum analyzer showing the relative use of each channel in the area.

FIGURE 23.6   Spectrum analyzer output

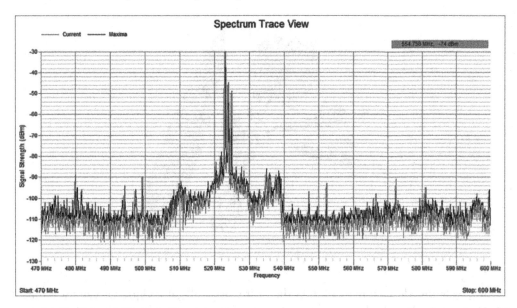

Toner Generator (Probe)

A *toner probe*, also called a tone generator, is a simple copper cable tester that is simple to use and can be used to trace a wire in a wall. It is a two-piece unit that's basically a tone generator and probe, sometimes called a "fox and hound" wire tracer. This type of device consists of one part that you connect to a cable with a standard jack—or to an individual wire with alligator clips that transmit a signal over the cable or wire—and another part that's a penlike probe that emits an audible tone when it touches the other end of the cable, the wire, or even its insulating sheath.

Most often, you will use a toner probe to locate a specific connection in a punch-down block because (annoyingly) some installers run all the cables for a network to the central punch-down block without labeling them. They (or you, if you're unlucky enough) then have to use a tone generator to identify which block is connected to which wall plate and label the punch-down block accordingly. This tool can identify a particular cable at any point between the two ends, and because the probe can detect the cable containing the tone signal through its sheath, it can help you to locate one specific cable out of a massive cable-spaghetti bundle in a ceiling conduit or other type of raceway.

Just connect the tone generator to one end, and touch the probe to each cable in the bundle until you hear the tone. Figure 23.7 shows a picture of my toner and the probe I use to find the tone on the other end of the cable.

FIGURE 23.7   A toner probe

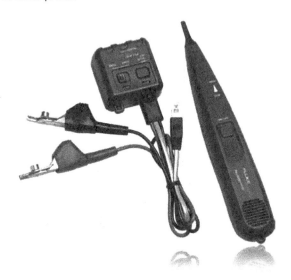

Also, by testing the continuity of individual wires using alligator clips, you can use a tone generator and probe to find opens, shorts, and miswires. An open wire won't produce a tone at the other end, a short will produce a tone on two or more wires at the other end, and an improperly connected wire will produce a tone on the wrong pin at the other end.

Sound like fun to you? Well, not so much—it takes a really long time, and it's super tedious. Worse, the whole process is almost as prone to errors as the cable installation itself. You have to either continually travel from one end of the cable to the other to move the tone generator unit or use a partner to test each connection, keeping in close contact by using radios or some other means of communication to avoid confusion. So, considering the time and effort involved, investing in a wire-map tester is just a much more practical solution unless you're numbingly bored or really easily amused.

Tap

A tap is a network hardware device that lets you passively insert test equipment in the traffic flow between two devices. This allows you to connect a network traffic analyzer to a third port of a tap that also has two ports that are connected between the two communicating devices. Taps can be used to monitor for intrusions and for packet captures during trouble-shooting. Taps are only used for monitoring the data flow in a cable; they are receive only and cannot be used to insert frames into the stream.

Metrics

When using any of the tools discussed in the preceding sections, especially the network testing tools, collecting and comparing metrics over time is a valuable exercise. Once a baseline has been established for these metrics, you can determine when an issue has gotten better or worse over time. It also allows you to determine if measures you have taken to improve a scenario have done so.

Error Rate

One of the key metrics for which a baseline should be established is network error rate. Since network errors typically lead to retransmissions, they also result in reduced throughput because each retransmission represents a lost opportunity to use that time slot to send new data.

Butt Set

A *butt set* is essentially a portable telephone that allows you to test analog wet or dry lines and is used to monitor those lines. The most common type, shown in Figure 23.8, can both monitor and transmit.

FIGURE 23.8   A butt set

You may see this with telco guys up on the telephone poles. They use their butt sets to connect to telephone lines, test them, and even make phone calls.

Another handy tool that will take the place of a butt set is a *hound*. This noncanine device is nothing more than an inductively coupled amplifier with a small speaker in a handheld tool. It's used to monitor the audio on a given line to verify that you have the right pair before connecting it and typically used with a toner probe. It will also monitor for noise.

Punch-Down Tool

Most networks today are built using twisted-pair cable of some sort. This cable is usually terminated in wiring closets using a tool known as a *punch-down tool*. It's called that because that's exactly what the tool does—punches down the wire into some kind of insulation displacement connector (IDC).

There are different types of punch-down tools. The most common is a punch-down with replaceable blades for the different types of connectors (either 66 or 110). Figure 23.9 shows an example of this type of punch-down tool.

FIGURE 23.9   An example of a punch-down tool

IDCs make contact by cutting through, or displacing, the insulation around a single conductor inside a twisted-pair cable.

As shown in Figure 23.10, the punch-down tool pushes a conductor between the sides of a V inside an IDC, in this example a keystone connector, allowing the small metal blade inside the connector to make contact with the inner conductor deep inside the wire.

FIGURE 23.10   Using a punch-down tool on a small keystone connector

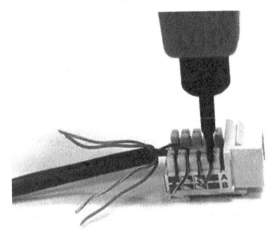

Now let's take a look at how to put a cable end together.

Cable Snips/Cutters

A *wire crimper*, often simply called a crimper, is a handy tool found in most network technicians' tool bags. Crimpers are primarily used for attaching ends onto different types of network cables via a process known as—that's right—*crimping*. Crimping involves using your hands to apply a certain amount of force to press some kind of metal teeth into the inner conductors of a cable. Before you can crimp a connector onto the end, you've got to strip the cable with a type of *cable stripper* (or snip) and then properly put the wires into the connector.

Figure 23.11 shows what a cable stripper and snip looks like (this particular tool also includes a crimper).

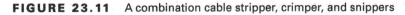

FIGURE 23.11   A combination cable stripper, crimper, and snippers

Often, network technicians will make patch cables with a crimper. They'll take a small piece of Category 5e, 6, 7, or 8 unshielded twisted-pair (UTP), strip the cable, and crimp two RJ-45 ends onto it to create the cable. Snips will create the type of cable needed to connect a host to a wall jack connection, for example. There are strippers and crimpers for the other types of cable as well—even specialized crimpers for fiber-optic ends.

Voltage Event Recorder (Power)

Alternating current (AC) is basically the food that PCs and other network devices require in specific amounts to function properly. In the United States, it's normally 110 volts and changes polarity 60 cycles a second (60 hertz). These values are referred to as *line voltage*. Any deviation from these values can create some major problems for your PC or other electronics—like death. While we're on the subject, you should also know that when a telephone rings, the phone company central office puts 140 VAC on the line to ring that bell;

telephone lines are not always the "low-voltage" devices we think they are. Do all phone systems do this, even PBX systems within buildings? Are you willing to bet your life that they don't? Didn't think so.

This is why we have *surge protectors*. These little saviors use a special electronic circuit that monitors the incoming voltage level and trips a circuit breaker when the voltage level reaches critical mass, which is known as the *overvoltage threshold*. Even though having a surge protector is definitely better than nothing, they too can fall victim to overvoltage events—I'm reminded of a friend whose home was struck by lightning during a thunderstorm and he found his surge protectors literally melted into the carpet! But they're still cool because even though they're really only somewhat protective, they are multiple-outlet strips that give us a lot more places to plug in our stuff.

By contrast, a quality *voltage event recorder* can troubleshoot and even provide preventative maintenance on your entire electrical system, whether it's for a home or a huge factory. Although they do big things, they're typically small devices that just plug into a wall and record, over time, the power quality of a given circuit. You would typically use a voltage event recorder for the following applications:

Recording Voltage   The voltage event recorder monitors and records the supply voltage and checks whether the socket outlet is providing voltage within specifications.

Measuring Distortion   The device measures frequency and harmonics, and it checks whether your uninterruptible power supply (UPS) system is functioning correctly.

Measuring Flicker   It checks the switching loads on lighting systems.

Capturing Voltage Transients   It can help you find intermittent, momentary events that may be affecting your equipment; the full waveform is captured with date, time stamp, and duration.

But you still have to do more to ensure the vitality of your electronic devices because they're very sensitive to temperature as well. This means you also need a way to monitor the temperature of the place(s) where your equipment is stored.

Fiber Light Meter

Some fiber-optic transmitters use LEDs as the source while more advanced and long-distance fiber types use lasers. Lasers can damage your eyesight, and it is best to never look directly at a fiber cable to see if there is light. A fiber light meter can tell you the receive levels and wavelengths to test and verify your fiber cable runs.

Fiber Fusion Splicer

When two fiber cables need to be spliced, a fusion splicer fuses the two cables together and minimizes the light scattering or being reflected back in the cable. They also ensure that the splice is strong and resistant to separation.

Summary

You need network tools, and you need to know how to use them. And as I said, you can get your hands on many of them for free, so download them and use them as soon as possible to get the experience you'll need to pass the CompTIA Network+ exam.

This chapter covered network scanners. I also covered hardware tools, which are rarely free. The good news is that you don't need many of them yourself, but the company that owns all the equipment definitely does. Even though I've used all of the tools I talked about in this chapter, I don't own most of them personally—only the ones that are free or relatively inexpensive.

In the hardware tools section, I covered cable testers, analyzers, certifiers, TDR/OTDRs, and other critical tools that help you test the cables and devices in your network, monitor them, and keep them up and running smoothly.

Exam Essentials

Understand what network scanners are and how to use each one. Packet sniffers, IDS/IPS software, and port scanners are all network scanners. These devices can help you both troubleshoot and fix your network as well as find and stop hackers in their tracks.

Remember the basic purpose of a packet sniffer. The basic purpose of packet sniffers or network analyzers is to collect and analyze each individual packet that is captured on a specific network segment to determine if problems are happening.

Understand what an OTDR is used for. An optical time-domain reflectometer (OTDR) is an optoelectronic instrument used to test fiber-optic cabling. You can learn the cable's estimated length and attenuation (loss in dB) and the location of faults.

Understand the difference between cable testers and certifiers. Cable testers simply tell you if the cable will function. Cable certifiers run much more sophisticated tests that determine if the cable performs according to specifications called for in the standard.

Understand the value of temperature and humidity monitors. These devices can monitor environmental conditions and alert you if either the temperature or the humidity in a server room or area falls below or rises above the prescribed range of safe values.

Written Lab

You can find the answers to the written labs in Appendix A. Answer the following questions about software and hardware tools.

1. True/False: A tap can be used to insert data into a link between two devices.

2. True/False: A crossover cable is needed between two directly connected PCs.

3. True/False: Plenum cables can be installed in air-conditioning ducts.

4. True/False: An OTDR is used to test fiber connections.

5. True/False: A network analyzer will see every packet on every segment of your network at the same time.

6. What type of device determines if a cable meets standards specifications?

7. True/False: It is okay to scan the DoD network servers with a port scanner.

8. You need to monitor the temperature of your server room. What device should you use?

9. You want to monitor your UPS systems and make sure they are functioning correctly. What device should you use?

10. What type of device is used to put an RJ-45 end on a Cat 5e, 6, 7, or 8 cable?

Review Questions

You can find the answers to the review questions in Appendix B.

1. Which is a tool in the network scanner category? (Choose all that apply.)
    A. Packet sniffers
    B. IDS/IPS software
    C. Port scanners
    D. None of the above

2. What is the purpose of packet sniffers?
    A. Discarding frames
    B. Sending transmissions from one port to another port
    C. Looking inside every packet on a network segment
    D. Stopping malicious behavior on the network

3. You need to trace cables in multiple-pair wiring. What tool will you use?
    A. Toner probe
    B. Cable stripper/snips
    C. Cable tester
    D. Butt set

4. What tool would you use to both find a break in a fiber-optic connection and test the fiber connectivity on the network?
    A. Multimeter
    B. OTDR
    C. Butt set
    D. Toner probe

5. You need to create a cable that will connect your host to a wall jack connection. Which of the following will you use?
    A. IDS/IPS
    B. Snips
    C. Coax cable strippers
    D. Multimeter

6. End-to-end loss across an Ethernet cable is called _____.
    A. Degradation
    B. Attenuation
    C. Runts
    D. Spectrum loss

7. What is the purpose of a port scanner?

   A. Scan UDP for closed ports

   B. Sweep TCP for closed ports

   C. Search the network host for open ports

   D. Validate operations

8. What is the purpose of wire-map testers?

   A. Check copper cable for crossed pairs only

   B. Analyze protocols in software

   C. Help find unused protocols and remove them from the network

   D. Detect transposed wires, opens, and shorts in twisted-pair cables

9. Which of the following can check the speed and condition of the signal on a cable, measure the time it takes to send a signal down the wire and back, and find the exact location of a break?

   A. Multimeter

   B. TDR

   C. Tone generator

   D. Event recorder

10. Which device should be used if you need to determine whether your network meets ISO or TIA standards?

   A. Angry IP

   B. Certifiers

   C. Nmap

   D. Routing table

11. Which software tool is used to view network traffic at the frame level?

   A. TDR

   B. Multimeter

   C. Port scanner

   D. Packet sniffer

12. Which of the following options is not a function of a TDR?

   A. Estimate cable lengths

   B. Find splice and connector locations and their associated loss amounts

   C. Display unused services

   D. Determine cable-impedance characteristics

   E. Send a signal down a cable and measure how long it takes to come back

13. Which device would be used to measure voltage?

    A. Multimeter

    B. OTDR

    C. Butt set

    D. Toner probe

14. Which device would most likely be used to locate a specific connection in an unlabeled punch-down block?

    A. VOM

    B. Certifier

    C. TDR

    D. Toner probe

15. Which tool would be used to connect wire between two punch-down block blades?

    A. Punch-down tool

    B. Crimper

    C. Snips

    D. Strippers

16. Which tool is used to attach an RJ-45 connector to a Cat 5e, 6, 7, or 8 cable?

    A. Punch-down tool

    B. Crimper

    C. Snips

    D. Strippers

17. On which of the following would a technician use a punch-down tool?

    A. RJ-45 connector

    B. CSU/DSU

    C. 110 block

    D. Fiber ST connector

18. Which device monitors incoming voltage levels and overvoltage thresholds?

    A. Repeater

    B. Toner probe

    C. VOM

    D. Surge protector

19. Which of the following tools can test a port on a device?

    A. Cable certifier

    B. Loopback plug

    C. Butt set

    D. Toner probe

20. You install new switches in your server room and are now experiencing network instability and other issues across all servers in the rack. Which device would be used to alert you of a system overheating?

    A. Voltage event recorder

    B. Temperature monitor

    C. Surge protector

    D. Probe

Chapter

24

Network Troubleshooting Methodology

THE FOLLOWING COMPTIA NETWORK+ EXAM OBJECTIVES ARE COVERED IN THIS CHAPTER:

✓ **5.1 Explain the network troubleshooting methodology.**

- Identify the problem
    - Gather information
    - Question users
    - Identify symptoms
    - Determine if anything has changed
    - Duplicate the problem, if possible
    - Approach multiple problems individually
- Establish a theory of probable cause
    - Question the obvious
    - Consider multiple approaches
        - Top-to-bottom/bottom-to-top OSI model
        - Divide and conquer
- Test the theory to determine the cause
    - If the theory is confirmed, determine the next steps to resolve the problem
    - If the theory is not confirmed, reestablish a new theory or escalate
- Establish a plan of action to resolve the problem and identify potential effects
- Implement the solution or escalate as necessary

- Verify full system functionality and, if applicable, implement preventive measures

- Document findings, actions, and outcomes and lessons learned

✓ **5.4 Given a scenario, troubleshoot common wireless connectivity issues.**

- Specifications and Limitations

    - Throughput

    - Speed

    - Distance

    - Received Signal Strength indication (RSSI) signal strength

    - Effective isotropic radiated power (EIRP)/ power settings

- Considerations

    - Antennas

    - Placement

    - Type

    - Polarization

- Channel utilization

- AP association time

- Site survey

- Common issues

    - Interference

    - Channel overlap

    - Antenna cable attenuation/signal loss

    - RF attenuation/signal loss

    - Wrong SSID

    - Incorrect passphrase

    - Encryption protocol mismatch

- Insufficient wireless coverage
- Captive portal issues
- Client disassociation issues

✓ **5.5 Given a scenario, troubleshoot general networking issues.**

- Considerations
    - Device configuration review
    - Routing tables
    - Interface status
    - VLAN assignment
    - Network performance baselines
- Common issues
    - Collisions
    - Broadcast storm
    - Duplicate MAC address
    - Duplicate IP address
    - Multicast flooding
    - Asymmetrical routing
    - Switching loops
    - Routing loops
    - Rogue DHCP server
    - DHCP scope exhaustion
    - IP subnetting issues
    - Incorrect gateway
    - Incorrect subnet mask
    - Incorrect IP address
    - Incorrect DNS
    - Missing route
    - Low optical link budget

- Certificate issues
- Hardware failure
- Host-based/network-based firewall settings
- Blocked services, ports, or addresses
- Incorrect VLAN
- DNS issues
- NTP issues
- BYOD challenge
- Licensed feature issues
- Network performance issues

There is no way around it. Troubleshooting computers and networks is a combination of art and science, and the only way to get really good at it is by doing it—a lot! So it's practice, practice, and practice with the basic yet vitally important skills you'll attain in this chapter. Of course, I'm going to cover all the troubleshooting topics you'll need to sail through the Network+ exam, but I'm also going to add some juicy bits of knowledge that will really help you tackle the task of troubleshooting successfully in the real world.

First, you'll learn to check quickly for problems in the "super simple stuff" category, and then we'll move into a hearty discussion about a common troubleshooting model that you can use like a checklist to go through and solve a surprising number of network problems. We'll finish the chapter with a good briefing about some common troubleshooting resources, tools, tips, and tricks to keep up your sleeve and equip you even further.

I won't be covering any new networking information in this chapter because you've gotten all the foundational background material you need for troubleshooting in the previous chapters. But no worries. I'll go through each of the issues described in this chapter's objectives, one at a time, in detail, so that even if you've still got a bit of that previous material to nail down yet, you'll be good to go and fix some networks anyway.

To find Todd Lammle CompTIA videos and practice questions, please see www.lammle.com.

Narrowing Down the Problem

When initially faced with a network problem in its entirety, it's easy to get totally overwhelmed. That's why it's a great strategy to start by narrowing things down to the source of the problem. To help you achieve that goal, it's always wise to ask the right questions. You can begin doing just that with this list of questions to ask yourself:

- Did you check the super simple stuff (SSS)?
- Is hardware or software causing the problem?
- Is it a workstation or server problem?
- Which segments of the network are affected?
- Are there any cabling issues?

Did You Check the Super Simple Stuff?

Yes—it sounds like a snake's hiss (appropriate for a problem, right?), but exactly what's on the SSS list that you should be checking first, and why? Well, as the saying goes, "All things being equal, the simplest explanation is probably the correct one," so you probably won't be stunned and amazed when I tell you that I've had people call me in and act like the sky is falling when all they needed to do was check to make sure their workstation was plugged in or powered on. (I didn't say "super simple stuff" for nothing!) Your SSS list really does include things that are this obvious—sometimes so obvious no one thinks to check for them. Even though anyone experienced in networking has their own favorite "DUH" events to tell about, almost everyone can agree on a few things that should definitely be on the SSS list:

- Check to verify login procedures and rights.
- Look for link lights and collision lights.
- Check all power switches, cords, and adapters.
- Look for user errors.

The Correct Login Procedure and Rights

You know by now that if you've set up everything correctly, your network's users absolutely have to follow the proper login procedure to the letter (or number, or symbol) in order to successfully gain access to the network resources they're after. If they don't do that, they will be denied access, and considering that there are truly tons of opportunities to blow it, it's a miracle, or at least very special, that anyone manages to log in to the network correctly at all.

Think about it. First, a user must enter their username and password flawlessly. Sounds easy, but as they say, "in a perfect world . . ." In this one, people mess up, don't realize it, and freak out at you about the "broken network" or the imaginary IT demon that changed their password on them while they went to lunch and now they can't log in. (The latter could be true—you may have done exactly that. If you did, just gently remind them about that memo you sent about the upcoming password-change date and time that they must have forgotten about due to the tremendous demands placed on them.)

Anyway, it's true. By far, the most common problem is bad typing—people accidentally enter the wrong username or password, and they do that a lot. With some operating systems, a slight brush of the Caps Lock key is all it takes: The user's username and password are case sensitive, and suddenly, they're trying to log in with what's now all in uppercase instead—oops.

Plus, if you happen to be running one of the shiny new operating systems around today, you can also restrict the times and conditions under which users can log in, right? So, if your user spent an unusual amount of time in the bathroom upon returning from lunch, or if they got distracted and tried to log in from their BFF's workstation instead of their own, the network's operating system would've rejected their login request even though they still can type impressively well after two martinis.

And remember—you can also restrict how many times a user can log in to the network simultaneously. If you've set that up, and your user tries to establish more connections than you've allowed, access will again be denied. Just know that most of the time, if a user is denied access to the network and/or its resources, they're probably going to interpret that as a network problem even though the network operating system is doing what it should.

Real World Scenario

Can the Problem Be Reproduced?

The first question to ask anyone who reports a network or computer problem is, "Can you show me what 'not working' looks like?" This is because if you can reproduce the problem, you can identify when it happens, which may give you all the information you need to determine the source of the problem and maybe even solve it in a snap. The hardest problems to solve are those of the random variety that occur intermittently and can't be easily reproduced.

Let's pause for a minute to outline the steps to take during any user-oriented network problem-solving process:

1. Make sure the username and password are being entered correctly.

2. Check that Caps Lock key.

3. Try to log in yourself from another workstation, assuming that doing this doesn't violate the security policy. If it works, go back to the user-oriented login problems, and go through them again.

4. If none of this solves the problem, check the network documentation to find out whether any of the aforementioned kinds of restrictions are in place; if so, find out whether the user has violated any of them.

Remember, if intruder detection is enabled on your network, a user will get locked out of their account after a specific number of unsuccessful login attempts. If this happens, either they'll have to wait until a predetermined time period has elapsed before their account will unlock and give them another chance or you'll have to go in and manually unlock it for them.

Network Connection LED Status Indicators

The link light is that little light-emitting diode (LED) found on both the network interface card (NIC) and the switch. It's typically green and labeled Link or some abbreviation of that. If you're running 100/1000BaseT, a link light indicates that the NIC and switch are making a logical (Data Link layer) connection. If the link lights are lit up on both the workstation's NIC and the switch port to which the workstation is connected, it's usually safe to assume that the workstation and switch are communicating just fine.

> The link lights on some NICs don't activate until the driver is loaded. So, if the link light isn't on when the system is first turned on, you'll just have to wait until the operating system loads the NIC driver. But don't wait forever!

The *collision light* is also a small LED, but it's typically amber in color, and it can usually be found on both Ethernet NICs and hubs. When lit, it indicates that an Ethernet collision has occurred. If you've got a busy Ethernet network on which collisions are somewhat common, understand that this light is likely to blink occasionally; if it stays on continuously, though, it could mean that there are way too many collisions happening for legitimate network traffic to get through. Don't assume this is really what's happening without first checking that the NIC, or other network device, is working properly because one or both could simply be malfunctioning.

> Don't confuse the collision light with the network-activity or network-traffic light (which is usually green) because the latter just indicates that a device is transmitting. This particular light *should* be blinking on and off continually as the device transmits and receives data on the network.

The Power Switch

Clearly, to function properly, all computer and network components must be turned on and powered up first. Obvious, yes, but if I had a buck for each time I've heard, "My computer is on, but my monitor is all dark," I'd be rolling in money by now.

When this kind of thing happens, just keep your cool and politely ask, "Is the monitor turned on?" After a little pause, the person calling for help will usually say, "Ohhh . . . ummmm . . . thanks," and then hang up ASAP. The reason I said to be nice is that, embarrassing as it is, this, or something like it, will probably happen to you, too, eventually.

Most systems include a power indicator (a Power or PWR light). The power switch typically has an On indicator, but the system or device could still be powerless if all the relevant power cables aren't actually plugged in—including the power strip.

> Remember that every cable has two ends, and both must be plugged into something. If you're thinking something like, "Sheesh—a four-year-old knows that," you're probably right. But again, I can't count the times this has turned out to be the root cause of a "major system failure."

The best way to go about troubleshooting power problems is to start with the most obvious device and work your way back to the power-service panel. There could be a number of power issues between the device and the service panel, including a bad power cable, bad outlet, bad electrical wire, tripped circuit breaker, or blown fuse, and any of these things could be the actual cause of the problem that appears to be device-death instead.

Operator Error

Or, the problem may be that you've got a user who simply doesn't know how to be one. Maybe you're dealing with someone who doesn't have the tiniest clue about the equipment they're using or about how to perform a certain task correctly—in other words, the problem may be due to something known as *operator error (OE)*. Here's a short list of the most common types of OEs and their associated acronyms:

- Equipment exceeds operator capability (EEOC)
- Problem exists between chair and keyboard (PEBCAK)
- ID Ten T error (an ID10T)

A word of caution here, though—assuming that all your problems are user related can quickly make an ID10T error out of you.

Although it can be really tempting to take the easy way out and blow things off, remember that the network's well-being and security are ultimately your responsibility. So, before you jump to the operator-error conclusion, ask the user in question to reproduce the problem in your presence, and pay close attention to what they do. Understand that doing this can require a great deal of patience, but it's worth your time and effort if you can prevent someone who doesn't know what they're doing from causing serious harm to pricey devices or leaving a gaping hole in your security. You might even save the help desk crew's sanity from the relentless calls of a user with the bad habit of flipping off the power switch without following proper shutdown procedures. You just wouldn't know they always do that if you didn't see it for yourself, right?

And what about finding out that that pesky user was, in fact, trained really badly by someone and that they aren't the only one? This is exactly the kind of thing that can turn the best security policy to dust and leave your network and its resources as vulnerable to attack as that goat in *Jurassic Park*.

The moral here is, always check out the problem thoroughly. If the problem and its solution aren't immediately clear to you, try the procedure yourself, or ask someone else at another workstation to do so. Don't just leave the issue unsettled or make the assumption that it is user error or a chance abnormality because that's exactly what the bad guys out there are hoping you'll do.

This is only a partial list of super simple stuff. No worries. Rest assured you'll come up with your own expanded version over time.

Is Hardware or Software Causing the Problem?

A hardware problem often rears its ugly head when some device in your computer skips a beat and/or dies. This one's pretty easy to discern because when you try to do something requiring that particular piece of hardware, you can't do it and instead get an error telling you that you can't do it. Even if your hard disk fails, you'll probably get warning signs before it actually kicks, like a Disk I/O error or something similar.

Other problems drop out of the sky and hit you like something from the wrong end of a seagull. No warning at all—just splat! Components that were humming along fine a second ago can and do suddenly fail, usually at the worst possible time, leaving you with a mess of lost data, files, everything—you get the idea.

Solutions to hardware problems usually involve one of three things:

- Changing hardware settings
- Updating device drivers
- Replacing dead hardware

If your hardware has truly failed, it's time to get out your tools and start replacing components. If this isn't one of your skills, you can either send the device out for repair or replace it. Your mantra here is "back up, back up, back up," because in either case, a system could be down for a while—anywhere from an hour to several days—so it's always good to keep backup hardware around. And I know everyone and your momma has told you this, but here it is one more time: Back up all data, files, hard drive, everything, and do so on a regular basis.

Software problems are muddier waters. Sometimes you'll get General Protection Fault messages, which indicate a Windows or Windows program (or other platform) error of some type, and other times the program you're working in will suddenly stop responding and hang. At their worst, they'll cause your machine to randomly lock up on you. When this type of thing happens, I'd recommend visiting the manufacturer's support website to get software updates and patches or searching for the answer in a knowledge base.

Sometimes you get lucky and the ailing software will tell the truth by giving you a precise message about the source of the problem. Messages saying the software is missing a file or a file has become corrupt are great because you can usually get your problem fixed fast by providing that missing file or by reinstalling the software. Neither solution takes very long, but the downside is that whatever you were doing before the program froze will probably be at least partially lost; so again, back up your stuff, and save your data often.

Make sure you have carefully read Chapter 22, "Ensuring Network Availability," and Chapter 23, "Cable Connectivity Issues and Tools," and use the software and hardware tools discussed in those two chapters to help you troubleshoot network problems.

It's time for you to learn how to troubleshoot your workstations and servers.

Is It a Workstation or a Server Problem?

The first thing you've got to determine when troubleshooting this kind of problem is whether it's only one person or a whole group that's been affected. If the answer is only one person (think, a single workstation), solving the issue will be pretty straightforward. More than that and your problem probably involves a chunk of the network, like a segment. A clue that the source of your grief is the latter case is if there's a whole bunch of users complaining that they can't discover neighboring devices/nodes.

So either way, what do you do about it? Well, if it's the single-user situation, your first line of defense is to try to log in from another workstation within the same group of users. If you can do that, the problem is definitely the user's workstation, so look for things like cabling faults, a bad NIC, power issues, and OSs.

But if a whole department can't access a specific server, take a good, hard look at that particular server, and start by checking all user connections to it. If everyone is logged in correctly, the problem may have something to do with individual rights or permissions. If no one can log in to that server, including you, the server probably has a communication problem with the rest of the network. And if the server has totally crashed, either you'll see messages telling you all about it on the server's monitor or you'll find its screen completely blank—screaming indicators that the server is no longer running. And keep in mind that these symptoms do vary among network operating systems.

Which Segments of the Network Are Affected?

Figuring this one out can be a little tough. If multiple segments are affected, you may be dealing with a network-address conflict. If you're running Transmission Control Protocol/Internet Protocol (TCP/IP), remember that IP addresses must be unique across an entire network. So, if two of your segments have the same static IP subnet addresses assigned, you'll end up with duplicate IP errors—an ugly situation that can be a real bear to troubleshoot and can make it tough to find the source of the problem.

If all of your network's users are experiencing the problem, it could be a server everyone accesses. Thank the powers that be if you nail it down to that because if not, other network devices like your main router or hub may be down, making network transmissions impossible and usually meaning a lot more work on your part to fix.

Adding wide area network (WAN) connections to the mix can complicate matters exponentially, and you don't want to go there if you can avoid it, so start by finding out if stations on both sides of a WAN link can communicate. If so, get the champagne—your problem isn't related to the WAN—woo hoo! But if those stations can't communicate, it's not a happy thing: You've got to check everything between the sending station and the receiving one, including the WAN hardware, to find the culprit. The good news is that most of the time, WAN devices have built-in diagnostics that tell you whether a WAN link is working okay, which really helps you determine if the failure has something to do with the WAN link itself or with the hardware involved instead.

Is It Bad Cabling?

Back to hooking up correctly . . . Once you've figured out whether your plight is related to one workstation, a network segment, or the whole tamale (network), you must then examine the relevant cabling. Are the cables properly connected to the correct port? More than once, I've seen a Digital Subscriber Line (DSL) modem connection to the wall cabled all wrong—it's an easy mistake to make and an easy one to fix.

And you know that nothing lasts forever, so check those patch cables running between a workstation and a wall jack. Just because they don't come with expiration dates written on them doesn't mean they don't expire. They do go bad—especially if they get moved, trampled on, or tripped over a lot. (I did tell you that it's a bad idea to run cabling across the office floor, didn't I?) Connection problems are the tell here—if you check the NIC and there is no link light blinking, you may have a bad patch cable to blame.

It gets murkier if your cable in the walls or ceiling is toast or hasn't been installed correctly. Maybe you've got a user or two telling you the place is haunted because they only have problems with their workstations after dark when the lights go on. Haunted? No . . . some genius probably ran a network cable over a fluorescent light, which is something that just happens to produce lots of electromagnetic interference (EMI), which can really mess up communications in that cable.

Next on your list is to check the medium dependent interface/medium dependent interface-crossover (MDI/MDI-X) port setting on small, workgroup hubs and switches. This is a potential source of trouble that's often overlooked, but it's important because this port is the one that's used to uplink to a switch on the network's backbone.

First, understand that the port setting has to be set to either MDI or MDI-X depending on the type of cable used for your hub-to-hub or switch-to-switch connection. For instance, the crossover cables I talked about way back in Chapter 3, "Networking Connectors and Wiring Standards," require that the port be set to MDI, and a standard network patch cable requires that the port be set to MDI-X. You can usually adjust the setting via a regular switch or a dual inline package (DIP) switch, but to be sure, if you're still using hubs, check out the hub's documentation. (You did keep that, right?)

Other Important Cable Issues You Need to Know About

They may be basic, but they're still vital—an understanding of the physical issues that can happen on a network when a user is connected via cable (usually Ethernet) is critical information to have in your troubleshooting repertoire.

Because many of today's networks still consist of large amounts of copper cable, they suffer from the same physical issues that have plagued networking since the very beginning. Newer technologies and protocols have helped to a degree, but they haven't made these issues a thing of the past yet. Some physical issues that still affect networks are listed and defined next:

Incorrect Pinout/TX/RX Reverse/Damaged Cable   The first things to check when working on cabling are the cable connectors to make sure they haven't gone bad. After that, make sure the wiring is correct on both ends by physically checking the cable pinouts. Important to remember is that if you have two switches, you need a crossover cable where you cross pins 1 and 2 with 3 and 6. On the other hand, if you have a PC going into a switch, you need a straight-through cable where pins 1 and 2 correspondingly connect to pins 1 and 2 on each side—the same with 3 and 6. Finally, make sure the termination pins on both ends are the correct type for the kind of cable you're using.

Bad Port   In some cases, the issue is not the cable but the port into which the cable is connected. On many devices, ports have LEDs that can alert you to a bad port. For example, a Cisco router or switch will have an LED for each port and the color of the LED will indicate its current state. In most cases, a lack of any light whatsoever indicates an issue with the port. Loopback plugs can be used to test the functionality of a port. These devices send a signal out and then back in the port to test it.

Transceiver Mismatch   Interfaces that send and receive are called transceivers. When a NIC is connected to a port, the two transceivers must have certain settings the same or issues will occur. These settings are the duplex and the speed settings. If the speed settings do not match, there will be no communication. If the duplex settings are incorrect, there may be functionality but the performance will be poor.

Crosstalk   Again, looking back to Chapter 3, remember that crosstalk is what happens when there's signal bleed between two adjacent wires that are carrying a current. Network designers minimize crosstalk inside network cables by twisting the wire pairs together, putting them at a 90-degree angle to each other. The tighter the wires are twisted, the less crosstalk you have, and newer cables like Cat 6 cable really make a difference. But like I said, not completely—crosstalk still exists and affects communications, especially in high-speed networks. This is often caused by using the wrong category of cable or by mismatching the member of one pair with a member of another when terminating a cable.

Near-End/Far-End Crosstalk   Near-end crosstalk is a specific type of crosstalk measurement that has to do with the EMI bled from a wire to adjoining wires where the current originates. This particular point has the strongest potential to create crosstalk issues because the crosstalk signal itself degrades as it moves down the wire. If you have a problem with it, it's probably going to show up in the first part of the wire where it's connected to a switch or a NIC. Far-end crosstalk is the interference between two pairs of a cable measured at the far end of the cable with respect to the interfering transmitter.

This condition is often caused by improperly terminating a cable. For example, it's important to maintain the twist right up to the punch-down or crimp connector. In the case of crimp connectors, it's critical to select the correct grade of connector even though one grade may look identical to another.

Attenuation/dB Loss/Distance Limitation   As a signal moves through any medium, the medium itself will degrade the signal—a phenomenon known as *attenuation* that's common in all kinds of networks. True, signals traversing fiber-optic cable don't attenuate as fast as those on copper cable, but they still do eventually. You know that all copper twisted-pair cables have a maximum segment distance of 100 meters before they'll need to be amplified, or *repeated*, by a hub or a switch, but single-mode fiber-optic cables can sometimes carry signals for miles before they begin to attenuate (degrade). If you need to go far, use fiber, not copper. Although there is attenuation/dB loss in fiber, it can go much farther distances than copper cabling can before being affected by attenuation.

Latency   Latency is the delay typically incurred in the processing of network data. A low-latency network connection is one that generally experiences short delay times, while a high-latency connection generally suffers from long delays. Many security solutions may negatively affect latency. For example, routers take a certain amount of time to process and forward any communication. Configuring additional rules on a router generally increases latency, thereby resulting in longer delays. An organization may decide not to deploy certain security solutions because of the negative effects they will have on network latency.

Auditing is a great example of a security solution that affects latency and performance. When auditing is configured, it records certain actions as they occur. The recording of these actions may affect the latency and performance.

Jitter   Jitter occurs when the data flow in a connection is not consistent; that is, it increases and decreases in no discernable pattern. Jitter results from network congestion, timing drift, and route changes. Jitter is especially problematic in real-time communications like IP telephony and videoconferencing.

Collisions   A network *collision* happens when two devices try to communicate on the same physical segment at the same time. Collisions like this were a big problem in the early Ethernet networks, and a tool known as *carrier sense multiple access with collision detection* (CSMA/CD) was used to detect and respond to them in Ethernet_II. Nowadays, we use switches in place of hubs because they can separate the network into multiple collision domains, learn the Media Access Control (MAC) addresses of the devices attached to them, create a type of permanent virtual circuit between all network devices, and prevent collisions.

Shorts   Basically, a *short circuit*, or *short*, happens when the current flows through a different path within a circuit than it's supposed to; in networks, they're usually caused by some type of physical fault in the cable. You can find shorts with circuit-testing equipment, but because sooner is better when it comes to getting a network back up and running, replacing the ailing cable until it can be fixed (if it can be) is your best option.

Open Impedance Mismatch (echo)   Open impedance on cable-testing equipment tells you that the cable or wires connect into another cable and there is an impedance mismatch. When that happens, some of the signal will bounce back in the direction it came from, degrading the strength of the signal, which ultimately causes the link to fail.

Interference/Cable Placement   EMI and *radio frequency interference (RFI)* occur when signals interfere with the normal operation of electronic circuits. Computers happen to be really sensitive to sources of this, such as TV and radio transmitters, which create a specific radio frequency as part of their transmission process. Two other common culprits are two-way radios and cellular phones.

Your only way around this is to use shielded network cables like shielded twisted-pair (STP) and coaxial cable (rare today) or to run EMI/RFI-immune but pricey fiber-optic cable throughout your entire network.

Split Pairs   A split pair is a wiring error where two connections that are supposed to be connected using the two wires of a twisted pair are instead connected using two wires from different pairs. Such wiring causes errors in high-rate data lines. If you buy your cables precut, you won't have this problem.

TX/RX Reverse   Just like the first item discussed in this section, incorrect pinout, when connecting from a PC-type device into a switch, for the PC use pins 1 and 2 to transmit and 3 and 6 to receive a digital signal. This means that the pins must be reversed on the switch, using pins 1 and 2 for receiving and 3 and 6 for transmitting the digital signal. If your connection isn't working, check the cable end pinouts.

Bent Pins   Many of the connectors you will encounter have small pins on the end that must go into specific holes in the interface to which they plug. If these pins get bent, either they won't go into the correct hole or they won't go into a hole at all. When this occurs, the cable will either not work at all or not work correctly. Taking care not to bend these fragile pins when working with these cable types will prevent this issue from occurring.

Bottlenecks   Bottlenecks are areas of the network where the physical infrastructure is not capable of handling the traffic. In some cases, this is a temporary issue caused by an unusual burst of traffic. In other scenarios, it is a wake-up call to upgrade the infrastructure or reorganize the network to alleviate the bottleneck. The obvious result of a bottleneck is poor performance.

Fiber Cable Issues

Fiber is definitely the best kind of wiring to use for long-distance runs because it has the least attenuation at long distances compared to copper. The bad news is that it's also the hardest to troubleshoot. Here are some common fiber issues to be aware of:

SFP/GBIC (Cable Mismatch)   The small form-factor pluggable (SFP) is a compact, hot-pluggable transceiver used for networking and other types of equipment. It interfaces a network device motherboard for a switch, router, media converter, or similar device to a fiber-optic or copper networking cable. Due to its smaller size, the SFP obsolesces the formerly ubiquitous gigabit interface converter (GBIC), so the SFP is sometimes referred to as a mini-GBIC. Always make sure you have the right cable for each type of connector and that they are not mismatched.

Bad SFP/GBIC (Cable or Transceiver)   If your link is down, verify that your cable or transceiver hasn't gone bad. Also, if the termination end is GBIC or SFP based, many network systems have console commands that output statistics on the status of the device. You can also swap out the SFP/GBIC to verify if it is faulty or not.

Wavelength Mismatch One of the more confusing terms used regarding fiber networks is *wavelength*. Though it sounds very complicated and scientific, it's actually just the term used to define what we think of as the color of light. Wavelength mismatch occurs when two different fiber transmitters at each end of the cable are using either a longer or shorter wavelength. This means you've got to make sure your transmitters match on both ends of the cable.

Fiber Type Mismatch Fiber type mismatches, at each of the transceivers, can cause wavelength issues, massive attenuation, and dB loss.

Dirty Connectors It's important to verify your connectors to make sure no dirt or dust has corrupted the cable end. You need to polish your cable ends with a soft cloth, but do not look into the cable if the other end is transmitting—it could damage your eyes!

Connector Mismatch Just because it fits doesn't mean it works. Make sure you have precisely the right connectors for each type of cable end or transceiver.

Bend Radius Limitations Fiber, whether it is made of glass or plastic, can break. You need to make sure you understand the bend radius limitations of each type of fiber you purchase and that you don't exceed the specifications when installing fiber in your rack.

Distance Limitations The pros of fiber are that it's completely immune to EMI and RFI, and that it can transmit up to 40 kilometers—about 25 miles! Add some repeater stations and you can go between continents. But all fiber types aren't created equally. For example, single mode can perform at much greater distances than multimode can. And again, make sure you have the right cable for the distance you'll require to run your fiber!

Unbounded Media Issues (Wireless)

Now let's say your problem-ridden user is telling you they only use a wireless connection. Well, you can definitely take crosstalk and shorts off the list of suspects, but don't get excited, because with wireless, you've got a whole new bunch of possible Physical layer problems to sort through.

Wireless networks are really convenient for the user but not so much for administrators. They can require a lot more configuration, and understand that with wireless networks, you don't just get to substitute one set of challenges for another—you pretty much add all those fresh new issues on top of the wired challenges you already have on your plate.

The following list includes some of those new wireless challenges:

Interference Because wireless networks rely on radio waves to transmit signals, they're more subject to interference, even from other wireless devices like Bluetooth keyboards, mice, or cell phones that are all close in frequency ranges. Any of these—even microwave ovens!—can cause signal bleed that can slow down or prevent wireless communications. Factors like the distance between a client and a wireless access point (WAP) and the stuff between the two can also affect signal strength and even intensify the interference from other signals. So, careful placement of that WAP is a must.

Device Saturation/Bandwidth Saturation   Clearly it's important to design and implement your wireless network correctly. Be sure to understand the number of hosts that will be connecting to each AP that you'll be installing. If you have too much device saturation on an AP, it will result in low available bandwidth. Just think about when you're in a hotel and how slow the wireless is. This is directly due to device/bandwidth saturation for each AP. And more APs don't always solve the problem—you need to design correctly!

Simultaneous Wired/Wireless Connections   It's not unusual to find that a laptop today will have both a wired and wireless connection at the same time. Typically, this doesn't create a problem, but don't think you get more bandwidth or better results because of it. It's possible that the configurations can cause a problem, although that's rare today. For instance, if each provides a DNS server with a different address, it can cause name resolution issues, or even default gateway issues. Most of the time, it just causes confusion in your laptop, which will make it work harder to determine the correct DNS or default gateway address to use. And it's possible for the laptop to give up and stop communicating completely! Because of this, you need to remind the user to turn off their wireless when they take it into their office and connect it to their dock.

Configurations   Mistakes in the configuration of the wireless access point or wireless router or inconsistencies between the settings on the AP and the stations can also be the source of problems. The following list describes some of the main sources of configuration problems:

Incorrect Encryption/Security Type Mismatch   You know that wireless networks can use encryption to secure their communications and that different encryption flavors are used for wireless networks, like Wired Equivalent Privacy (WEP) and Wi-Fi Protected Access 3 (WPA3) with Advanced Encryption Standard (AES). WPA3 is the latest standard and it is common now. To ensure the tightest security, configure your wireless networks with the highest encryption protocol that both the WAP and the clients can support. Oh, and make sure the AP and its clients are configured with the same type of encryption. This is why it's a good idea to disable security before troubleshooting client problems, because if the client can connect once you've done that, you know you're dealing with a security configuration error.

Incorrect, Overlapping, or Mismatched Channels   Wireless networks use many different frequencies within the 2.4 GHz or 5 GHz band, and I'll bet you didn't know that these frequencies are sometimes combined to provide greater bandwidth for the user. You actually do know about this—has anyone heard of something called a *channel*? Well, that's exactly what a channel is, and it's also the reason some radio stations come in better than others—they have more bandwidth because their channel has more combined frequencies. You also know what happens when the AP and the client aren't quite matching up. Have you ever hit the scan button on your car's radio and only kind of gotten a station's static-ridden broadcast? That's because the AP (radio station) and the client (your car's radio) aren't quite on the same channel. Most of the time, wireless networks use channel 1, 6, or 11, and because clients auto-configure themselves to any channel the AP is broadcasting on, it's not usually a configuration issue unless someone has forced a client onto an incorrect channel. Also, be sure not to use the same channel on APs within the same area. Overlapping channels cause your signal-to-noise ratio to drop because you'll get a ton of interference and signal loss!

Incorrect Frequency/Incompatibilities   So, setting the channel also sets the frequency or frequencies that wireless devices will use. But some devices, such as an AP running 802.11a/c and a/x, allow you to tweak those settings and choose a specific frequency such as 2.4 GHz or 5 GHz. As with any relationship, it works best if things are mutual. So if you do this on one device, you've got to configure the same setting on all the devices with which you want to communicate, or they won't—they'll argue, and you don't want that. Incorrect-channel and frequency-setting problems on a client are rare, but if you have multiple APs and they're in close proximity, you need to make sure they're on different channels/frequencies to avoid potential interference problems.

Wrong Passphrase   When a passphrase is used as an authentication method, the correct passphrase must be entered when authenticating to the AP or to the controller. When an incorrect passphrase is provided, access will be denied. This is another issue that will impair functionality.

SSID Mismatch   When a wireless device comes up, it scans for service set identifiers (SSIDs) in its immediate area. These can be basic service set identifiers (BSSIDs) that identify an individual access point or extended service set identifiers (ESSIDs) that identify a set of APs. In your own wireless LAN, you clearly want the devices to find the ESSID that you're broadcasting, which isn't usually a problem: Your broadcast is closer than the neighbor's, so it should be stronger—unless you're in an office building or apartment complex that has lots of different APs assigned to lots of different ESSIDs because they belong to lots of different tenants in the building. This can definitely give you some grief because it's possible that your neighbor's ESSID broadcast is stronger than yours, depending on where the clients are in the building. So if a user reports that they're connected to an AP but still can't access the resources they need or authenticate to the network, you should verify that they are, in fact, connected to your ESSID and not your neighbor's. This is very typical in an open security wireless network. You can generally just look at the information tool tip on the wireless software icon to find this out. However, you can easily solve this problem today by making the office SSID the preferred network in the client software.

Wireless Standard Mismatch   As you found out in Chapter 12, "Wireless Networking," wireless networks have many standards that have evolved over time, like 802.11a, 802.11b, 802.11g, 802.11n, 802.11ac, and 802.11ax. Standards continue to develop that make wireless networks even faster and more powerful. The catch is that some of these standards are backward compatible and others aren't. For instance, most devices you buy today can be set to all standards, which means they can be used to communicate with other devices of all four standards. So, make sure the standards on the AP match the standards on the client, or that they're at least backward compatible. It's either that or tell all your users to buy new cards for their machines. Be sure to understand the throughput, frequency, distance capabilities, and available channels for each standard you use.

Untested Updates   It's really important to push updates to the APs in your wireless network, but not before you test them. Just like waiting for an update from Microsoft or Apple to become available for weeks or months before you update, you need to wait for the OS or patch updates for your AP. Then, you need to test the updates thoroughly on your bench before pushing them to your live network.

Distance/Signal Strength/Power Levels   Location, location, location. You've got only two worries with this one: Your clients are either not far enough away or too far from the AP. If your AP doesn't seem to have enough power to provide a connectivity point for your clients, you can move it closer to them, increase the distance that the AP can transmit by changing the type of antenna it uses, or use multiple APs connected to the same switch or set of switches to solve the problem. If the power level or signal is too strong, and it reaches out into the parking area or farther out to other buildings and businesses, place the AP as close as possible to the center of the area it's providing service for. And don't forget to verify that you've got the latest security features in place to keep bad guys from authenticating to and using your network.

Latency and Overcapacity   When wireless users complain that the network is slow (latency) or that they are losing their connection to applications during a session, it is usually a capacity or distance issue. Remember, 802.11 is a shared medium, and as more users connect, all user throughput goes down. If this becomes a constant problem as opposed to the occasional issue where 20 guys with laptops gather for a meeting every six months in the conference room, it may be time to consider placing a second AP in the area. When you do this, place the second AP on a different non-overlapping channel from the first and make sure the second AP uses the same SSID as the first. In the 2.4 GHz frequency, the three non-overlapping channels are 1, 6, and 11. Now the traffic can be divided between them and users will get better performance. It is also worth noting that when clients move away from the AP, the data rate drops until at some point it is insufficient to maintain the connection.

Bounce   For a wireless network spanning large geographical distances, you can install repeaters and reflectors to bounce a signal and boost it to cover about a mile. This can be a good thing, but if you don't tightly control signal bounce, you could end up with a much bigger network than you wanted. To determine exactly how far and wide the signal will bounce, make sure you conduct a thorough wireless site survey. However, bounce can also refer to multipath issues, where the signal reflects off objects and arrives at the client degraded because it is arriving out of phase. The solution is pretty simple. APs use two antennas, both of which sample the signal and use the strongest signal and ignore the out-of-phase signal. However, 802.11ac and ax takes advantage of multipath and can combine the out-of-phase signals to increase the distance hosts can be from the AP.

Incorrect Antenna Type or Switch Placement   Most of the time, the best place to put an AP and/or its antenna is as close to the center of your wireless network as possible. But you can position some antennas a distance from the AP and connect to it with a cable—a method used for a lot of the outdoor installations around today. If you want to use multiple APs, you've also got to be a little more sophisticated about deciding where to put them all; you can use third-party tools like the packet sniffers Wireshark and Air-Magnet on a laptop to survey the site and establish how far your APs are actually transmitting. You can also hire a consultant to do this for you—there are many companies that specialize in assisting organizations with their wireless networks and the placement of antennas and APs. This is important because poor placement can lead to interference and poor performance, or even no performance at all.

Environmental Factors   It's vital to understand your environmental factors when designing and deploying your wireless network. Do you have concrete walls, window film, or metal studs in the walls? All of these will cause a degradation of dB or power level and result in connectivity issues. Again—plan your wireless network carefully!

Reflection   When a wave hits a smooth object that is larger than the wave itself, depending on the media the wave may bounce in another direction. This behavior is categorized as reflection.

Reflection can be the cause of serious performance problems in a WLAN. As a wave radiates from an antenna, it broadens and disperses. If portions of this wave are reflected, new wave fronts will appear from the reflection points. If these multiple waves all reach the receiver, the multiple reflected signals cause an effect called multipath.

Multipath can degrade the strength and quality of the received signal or even cause data corruption or canceled signals. APs mitigate this behavior by using multiple antennas and constantly sampling the signal to avoid a degraded signal.

Refraction   Refraction is the bending of an RF signal as it passes through a medium with a different density, thus causing the direction of the wave to change. RF refraction most commonly occurs as a result of atmospheric conditions.

In long-distance outdoor wireless bridge links, refraction can be an issue. An RF signal may also refract through certain types of glass and other materials that are found in an indoor environment.

Absorption Some materials will absorb a signal and reduce its strength. While there is not much that can be done about this, this behavior should be noted during a site survey, and measures such as additional APs or additional antenna types may be called for.

Signal-to-Noise Ratio Signal-to-noise ratio (SNR) is the difference in decibels between the received signal and the background noise level (noise floor).

If the amplitude of the noise floor is too close to the amplitude of the received signal, data corruption will occur and result in layer 2 retransmissions, negatively affecting both throughput and latency. An SNR of 25 dB or greater is considered good signal quality, and an SNR of 10 dB or lower is considered very poor signal quality.

Now that you know all about the possible physical network horrors that can befall you on a typical network, it's a good time for you to memorize the troubleshooting steps that you've got to know to ace the CompTIA Network+ exam.

Troubleshooting Steps

In the Network+ troubleshooting model, there are seven steps you need to follow:
1. Identify the problem.
2. Establish a theory of probable cause.
3. Test the theory to determine cause.
4. Establish a plan of action to resolve the problem and identify potential effects.
5. Implement the solution or escalate as necessary.
6. Verify full system functionality, and if applicable, implement preventative measures.
7. Document findings, actions, outcomes, and lessons learned.

To get things off to a running start, let's assume that the user has called you yet again, but now they're almost in tears because they can't connect to the server on the intranet and they also can't get to the Internet. (By the way, this happens a lot, so pay attention—it's only a matter of time before it happens to you!)

 Absolutely, positively make sure you memorize this seven-step troubleshooting process in the right order when studying for the Network+ exam!

Step 1: Identify the Problem

Before you can solve the problem, you've got to figure out what it is, right? Again, asking the right questions can get you far along this path and really help clarify the situation. Identifying the problem involves steps that together constitute *information gathering*.

Gather Information by Questioning Users

A good way to start is by asking the user the following questions:

- Exactly which part of the Internet can't you access? A particular website? A certain address? A type of website? None of it at all?

- Can you use your web browser?

- Is it possible to duplicate the problem?

- If the hitch has to do with an internal server to the company, ask the user if they can ping the server and talk them through doing that.

- Ask the user to try to SSH/telnet or SFTP/FTP to an internal server to verify local network connectivity; if they don't know how, talk them through it.

- If there are multiple complaints of problems occurring, look for the big stuff first, then isolate and approach each problem individually.

Here's another really common trouble ticket that just happens to build on the last scenario: Now let's say you've got a user who's called you at the help desk. By asking the previous questions, you found out that this user can't access the corporate intranet or get out to any sites on the Internet. You also established that the user can use their web browser to access the corporate FTP site, but only by IP address, not by the FTP server name. This information tells you two important things: that you can rule out the host and the web browser (application) as the source of the problem and that the physical network is working.

Duplicate the Problem, If Possible

When a user reports an issue, you should attempt to duplicate the issue. When this is possible, it will aid in discovering the problem. When you cannot duplicate the issue, your challenge becomes harder because you are dealing with an intermittent problem. These issues are difficult to solve because they don't happen consistently.

Determine If Anything Has Changed

Moving right along, if you can reproduce the problem, your next step is to verify what has changed and how. Drawing on your knowledge of networking, you ask yourself and your user questions like these:

Were you ever able to do this?   If not, then maybe it just isn't something the hardware or software is designed to do. You should then tell the user exactly that, as well as advise them that they may need additional hardware or software to pull off what they're trying to do.

If so, when did you become unable to do it?   If, once upon a time, the computer was able to do the job and then suddenly could not, whatever conditions surrounded and were involved in this turn of events become extremely important. You have a really good shot at unearthing the root of the problem if you know what happened right before things changed. Just know that there's a high level of probability that the cause of the problem is directly related to the conditions surrounding the change when it occurred.

Has anything changed since the last time you could do this?   This question can lead you right to the problem's cause. Seriously—the thing that changed right before the problem began happening is almost always what caused it. It's so important that if you ask it and your user tells you, "Nothing changed. . .it just happened," you should rephrase the question and say something like, "Did anyone add anything to your computer?" or "Are you doing anything differently from the way you usually do it?"

Were any error messages displayed?   These are basically arrows that point directly at the problem's origin; error messages are designed by programmers for the purpose of pointing them to exactly what it is that isn't working properly in computer systems. Sometimes error messages are crystal clear, like Disk Full, or they can be cryptically annoying little puzzles in and of themselves. If you pulled the short straw and got the latter variety, it's probably best to hit the software or hardware vendor's support site, where you can usually score a translation from the "programmerese" in which the error message is written into plain English so you can get back to solving your riddle.

Are other people experiencing this problem?   You've got to ask this one because the answer will definitely help you target the cause of the problem. First, try to duplicate the problem from your own workstation because if you can't, it's likely that the issue is related to only one user or group of users—possibly their workstations. (A solid hint that this is the case is if you're being inundated with calls from a bunch of people from the same workgroup.)

Is the problem always the same?   It's good to know that when problems crop up, they're almost always the same each time they occur. But their symptoms can change slightly as the conditions surrounding them change. A related question would be, "If you do x, does the problem get better or worse?" For example, ask a user, "If you use a different file, does the problem get better or worse?" If the symptoms lighten up, it's an indication that the problem is related to the original file that's being used. It's important to try to duplicate the problem to find the source of the issue as soon as possible!

 Understand that these are just a few of the questions you can use to get to the source of a problem.

Okay, so let's get back to our sample scenario. So far, you've determined that the problem is unique to one user, which tells you that the problem is specific to this one host. Confirming that is the fact that you haven't received any other calls from other users on the network.

And when watching the user attempt to reproduce the problem, you note that they're typing the address correctly. Plus, you've got an error message that leads you to believe that the problem has something to with Domain Name Service (DNS) lookups on the user's host. Time to go deeper . . .

Identify Symptoms

I probably don't need to tell you that computers and networks can be really fickle—they can hum along fine for months, suddenly crash, and then continue to work fine again without ever seizing up that way again. That's why it's so important to be able to reproduce the problem and identify the affected area to narrow things down so you can cut to the chase and fix the issue fast. This really helps—when something isn't working, try it again, and write down exactly what is and is not happening.

Most users' knee-jerk reaction is to straight up call the help desk the minute they have a problem. This is not only annoying but also inefficient, because you're going to ask them exactly what they were doing when the problem occurred and most users have no idea what they were doing with the computer at the time because they were focused on doing their jobs instead. This is why if you train users to reproduce the problem and jot down some notes about it *before* calling you, they'll be much better prepared to give you the information you need to start troubleshooting it and help them.

So with that in mind, here we go. The problem you've identified results in coughing out an error message to your user when they try to access the corporate intranet. It looks like Figure 24.1.

FIGURE 24.1   Cannot connect

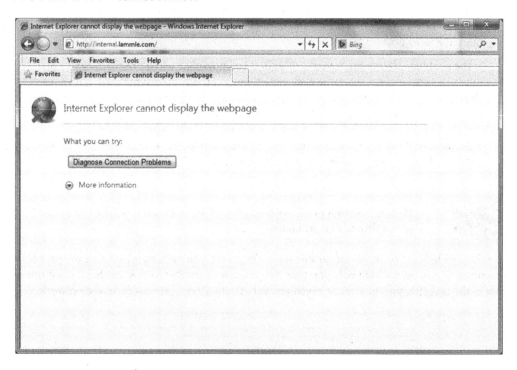

And when this user tries to ping the server using the server's hierarchical web name, it fails, too (see Figure 24.2).

FIGURE 24.2 Host could not be found.

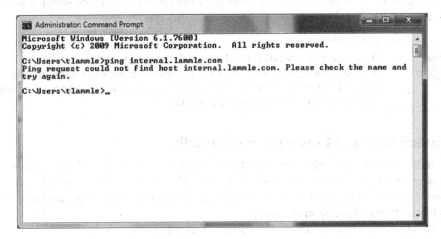

You're going to respond by checking to see whether the server is up by pinging the server by its IP address (see Figure 24.3).

FIGURE 24.3 Successful ping

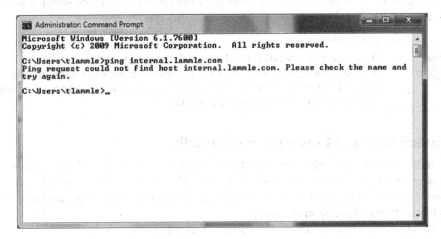

Nice—that worked, so the server is up, but you could still have a server problem. Just because you can ping a host, it doesn't mean that host is 100 percent up and running, but in this case, it's a good start.

And you're in luck because you've been able to re-create this problem from this user's host machine. By doing that, you now know that the URL name is not being resolved from Internet Explorer, and you can't ping it by the name either. But you can ping the server IP address from your limping host, and when you try this same connection to the internal .lammle.com server from another host nearby, it works fine, meaning the server is working fine. So, you've succeeded in isolating the problem to this specific host—yes!

It is a huge advantage if you can watch the user try to reproduce the problem themselves because then you know for sure whether the user is performing the operation correctly. It's a really bad idea to assume the user is typing in what they say they are.

Approach Multiple Problems Individually

You should never mix possible solutions when troubleshooting. When multiple changes are made, interactions can occur that muddy the results. Always attack one issue at a time and make only a single change at a time. When a change does not have a beneficial effect, reverse the change before making another change.

Great—now you've nailed down the problem. This leads us to step 2

Step 2: Establish a Theory of Probable Cause

After you observe the problem and identify the symptoms, next on the list is to establish its most probable cause. (If you're stressing about it now, don't, because even though you may feel overwhelmed by all this, it truly does get a lot easier with time and experience.)

You must come up with at least one possible cause, even though it may not be completely on the money. And you don't always have to come up with it yourself. Someone else in the group may have the answer. Also, don't forget to check online sources and vendor documentation.

Again, let's get back to our scenario, in which you've determined the cause is probably an improperly configured DNS lookup on the workstation. The next thing to do is to verify the configuration (and probably reconfigure DNS on the workstation; we'll get to this solution later, in step 4).

Understand that there are legions of problems that can occur on a network—and I'm sorry to tell you this, but they're typically not as simple as the example we've been using. They can be, but I just don't want you to expect them to be. Always consider the physical aspects of a network, but look beyond them into the realm of logical factors like the DNS lookup issue we've been using.

Question the Obvious

The probable causes that you've got to thoroughly understand to meet the Network+ objectives are as follows:

- Port speed
- Port duplex mismatch

- Mismatched MTU
- Incorrect virtual local area network (VLAN)
- Incorrect IP address/duplicate IP address
- Wrong gateway
- Wrong DNS
- Wrong subnet mask
- Incorrect interface/interface misconfiguration
- Duplicate MAC addresses
- Expired IP address
- Rogue DHCP server
- Untrusted SSL certificate
- Incorrect time
- Exhausted DHCP scope
- Blocked TCP/UDP ports
- Incorrect host-based firewall settings
- Incorrect ACL settings
- Unresponsive service
- Multicast flooding
- Metrics outside of baseline measurements
- Asymmetrical routing
- Low optical link budget
- Network Time Protocol issues
- Bring your own device challenges
- Licensed features

Let's talk about these logical issues, which can cause an abundance of network problems. Most of these happen because a device has been improperly configured.

Port Speed   Because networks have been evolving for many years, there are various levels of speed and sophistication mixed into them—often within the same network. Most of the newest NICs can be used at 10 Mbps, 100 Mbps, and 1000 Mbps. Most switches can support at least 10 Mbps and 100 Mbps, and an increasing number of switches can also support 1G or 25/40/100 Gbps. Plus, many switches can also autosense the speed of the NIC that's connected and use different speeds on various ports. As long as the switches are allowed to autosense the port speed, it's rare to have a problem develop that results in a complete lack of communication. But if you decide to set the port speed manually, make positively sure to set the same speed on both sides of a link.

Port Duplex Mismatch   There are generally three duplex settings on each port of a network switch: full, half, and auto. In order for two devices to connect effectively, the duplex setting has to match on both sides of the connection. If one side of a connection is set to full and the other is set to half, they're mismatched. More elusively, if both sides are set to auto but the devices are different, you can also end up with a mismatch because the device on one side defaults to full and the other one defaults to half.

Duplex mismatches can cause lots of network and interface errors, and even the lack of a network connection. This is partially because setting the interfaces to full duplex disables the CSMA/CD protocol. This is definitely not a problem in a network that has no hubs (and therefore no shared segments in which there could be collisions), but it can make things really ugly in a network where hubs are still being used. This means the settings you choose are based on the type of devices you have populating your network. If you have all switches and no hubs, feel free to set all interfaces to full duplex, but if you've got hubs in the mix, you have shared networks, so you're forced to keep the settings at half duplex. With all new switches produced today, leaving the speed and duplex setting to auto (the default on both switches and hosts) is the recommended way to go.

Mismatched MTU   Ethernet LANs enforce what is called a maximum transmission unit (MTU). This is the largest size packet that is allowed across a segment. In most cases, this is 1500 bytes. Left alone this is usually not a problem, but it is possible to set the MTU on a router interface, which means it is possible for a mismatch to be present between two router interfaces. This can cause problems with communications between the routers, resulting in the link failing to pass traffic. To check the MTU on an interface, execute the command show interface.

Incorrect VLAN   Switches can have multiple VLANs each, and they can be connected to other switches using trunk links. As you now know, VLANs are often used to represent departments or the occupations of a group of users. This makes the configurations of security policies and network access lists much easier to manage and control. On the other hand, if a port is accidentally assigned to the wrong VLAN in a switch, it's as if that client was magically transported to another place in the network. If that happens, the security policies that should apply to the client won't anymore, and other policies will be applied to the client that never should have been. The correct VLAN port assignment of a client is as important as air; when I'm troubleshooting a single-host problem, this is the first place I look.

It's pretty easy to tell if you have a port configured with a wrong VLAN assignment. If this is the case, it won't be long before you'll get a call from some user screaming something at you that makes the building shake, like, "I can get to the Internet but I can't get to the Sales server, and I'm about to lose a huge sale. DO SOMETHING!" When you check the switch, you will invariably see that this user's port has a membership in another VLAN, like Marketing, which has no access to the Sales server.

Incorrect IP Address/Duplicate IP Address   The most common addressing protocol in use today is IPv4, which provides a unique IP address for each host on a network. Client computers usually get their addresses from Dynamic Host Configuration Protocol (DHCP) servers. But sometimes, especially in smaller networks, IP addresses for servers and router interfaces are statically assigned by the network's administrator. An incorrect or duplicate IP address on a client will keep that client from being able to communicate and may even cause a conflict with another client on the network, and a bad address on a server or router interface can be disastrous and affect a multitude of users. This is exactly why you need to be super careful to set up DHCP servers correctly and also when configuring the static IP addresses assigned to servers and router interfaces.

Wrong Gateway   A *gateway*, sometimes called a *default gateway* or an *IP default gateway*, is a router interface's address that's configured to forward traffic with a destination IP address that's not in the same subnet as the device itself. Let me clarify that one for you: If a device compares where a packet wants to go with the network it's currently on and finds that the packet needs to go to a remote network, the device will send that packet to the gateway to be forwarded to the remote network. Because every device needs a valid gateway to obtain communication outside its own network, it's going to require some careful planning when considering the gateway configuration of devices in your network.

If you're configuring a static IP address and default gateway, you need to verify the router's address. Not doing so is a really common "wrong gateway" problem that I see all the time.

Wrong DNS   DNS servers are used by networks and their clients to resolve a computer's hostname to its IP addresses and to enable clients to find the server they need to provide the resources they require, like a domain controller during the login and authentication process. Most of the time, DNS addresses are automatically configured by a DHCP server, but sometimes these addresses are statically configured instead. Because lots of applications rely on hostname resolution, a botched DNS configuration usually causes a computer's network applications to fail just like the user's applications in our example scenario.

If you can ping a host using its IP address but not its name, you probably have some type of name-resolution issue. It's probably lurking somewhere within a DNS configuration.

Wrong Subnet Mask   When network devices look at an IP address configuration, they see a combination of the IP address and the subnet mask. The device uses the subnet mask to establish which part of the address represents the network address and which part represents the host address. So clearly, a subnet mask that is configured wrong has the same nasty effect as a wrong IP address configuration has on communications.

Again, a subnet mask is generally configured by the DHCP server; if you're going to enter it manually, make sure the subnet mask is tight or you'll end up tangling with the fallout caused by the entire address's misconfiguration.

Incorrect Interface/Interface Misconfiguration   If a host is plugged into a misconfigured switch port, or if it's plugged into the wrong switch port that's configured for the wrong VLAN, the host won't function correctly. Make sure the speed, duplex, and correct Ethernet cable is used. Get any of that wrong and either you'll get interface errors on the host and switch port or, worse, things just won't work at all!

Duplicate MAC Addresses   There should never be duplicate MAC addresses in your environment. Each interface vendor is issued an organizationally unique identifier (OUI), which will match on all interfaces produced by that vendor, and then the vendor is responsible for ensuring unique MAC addresses. That means duplicate MAC addresses usually indicate a MAC spoofing attack, in which some malicious individual changes their MAC address, which can be done quite easily in the properties of the NIC.

Expired IP Address   In almost all cases, when DHCP is used to allocate IP configurations to devices, the configuration is supplied to the DHCP client on a temporary basis. The lease period is configurable, and when the lease period and a grace period transpire, the lease is expired. The effect of an expired lease is the next time that client computer starts, it must enter the initialization state and obtain new TCP/IP configuration information from a DHCP server. There is nothing, however, to prevent the client from obtaining a new lease for the same IP address.

Rogue DHCP Server   Dynamic Host Configuration Protocol (DHCP) is used to automate the process of assigning IP configurations to hosts. When configured properly, it reduces administrative overload, reduces the human error inherent in manual assignment, and enhances device mobility. But it introduces a vulnerability that when leveraged by a malicious individual can result in an inability of hosts to communicate (constituting a DoS attack) and peer-to-peer attacks.

When an illegitimate DHCP server (called a rogue DHCP server) is introduced to the network, unsuspecting hosts may accept DHCP Offer packets from the illegitimate DHCP server rather than the legitimate DHCP server. When this occurs, the rogue DHCP server will not only issue the host an incorrect IP address, subnet mask, and default gateway address (which makes a peer-to-peer attack possible), it can also issue an incorrect DNS server address, which will lead to the host relying on the attacker's DNS server for the IP addresses of websites (such as major banks) that lead to phishing attacks. An example of how this can occur is shown in Figure 24.4.

In Figure 24.4, after receiving an incorrect IP address, subnet mask, default gateway, and DNS server address from the rogue DHCP server, the DHCP client uses the attacker's DNS server to obtain the IP address of his bank. This leads the client to unwittingly connect to the attacker's copy of the bank's website. When the client enters his credentials to log in, the attacker now has the client's bank credentials and can proceed to empty out his account.

FIGURE 24.4 Rogue DHCP

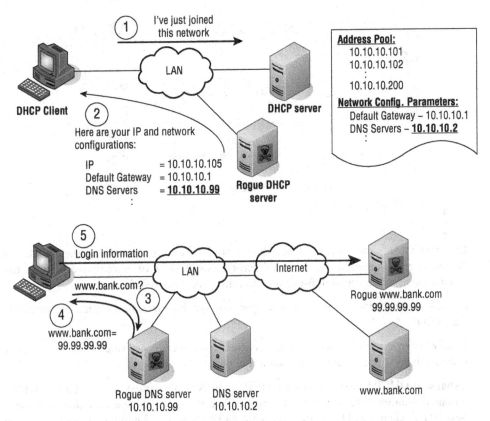

Untrusted SSL Certificate Reception of an untrusted SSL certificate error message can be for several reasons. In Figure 24.5, the possible reasons for the warning message are shown. The first reason, "The Security certificate presented by this website was not issued by a trusted certificate authority," means the CA that issued the certificate is not trusted by the local machine. This will occur if the certificate of the CA that issued the certificate is not found in the Trusted Root Certification Authorities Folder on the local machine.

The second reason this might occur is that the certificate is not valid. It may be that the certificate was presented before the validity period begins, or it may have expired, meaning the validity period is over.

The third reason is that the name on the certificate does not match the name listed on the certificate.

FIGURE 24.5   Certificate error

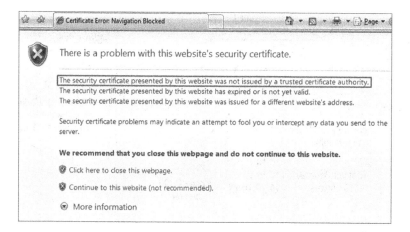

Incorrect Time   Incorrect time on a device can be the cause of several issues. First, in a Windows environment using Active Directory, a clock skew of more than 5 minutes between a client and server will prevent communication between the two.

Second, when certificates are in use, proper time synchronization is critical for successful operation.

Finally, when system logs are sent to a central server such as a syslog server, proper time synchronization is critical to understand the order of events.

Exhausted DHCP Scope   When a DHCP server is implemented, it is configured with a limited number of IP addresses. When the IP addresses in a scope are exhausted, any new DHCP clients will be unable to obtain an IP address and will be unable to function on the network.

DHCP servers can be set up to provide backup to another DHCP server for a scope. When this is done, it is important to ensure that while the two DHCP servers service the same scope, they do not have any duplicate IP addresses.

Blocked TCP/UDP Ports   When the ports used by common services and applications are blocked, either on the network firewall or on the personal firewall of a device, it will be impossible to make use of the service or application. One easy way to verify the open ports on a device is to execute the netstat command. An example of the output is shown in Figure 24.6.

FIGURE 24.6   Netstat -a output

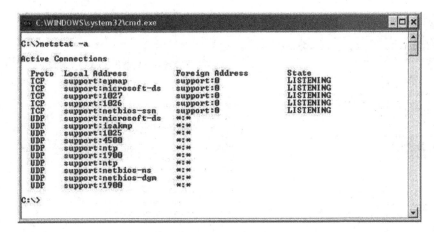

Incorrect Host-Based Firewall Settings   As you saw in the explanation of blocked TCP/ UDP ports, incorrect host-based firewall settings can either prevent transmissions or allow unwanted communications. Neither of these outcomes is desirable. One of the best ways to ensure that firewall settings are consistent and correct all the time is to control these settings with a group policy. When you do this, the settings will be checked and reset at every policy refresh interval.

Incorrect ACL Settings   Access control lists are used to control which traffic types can enter and exit ports on the router. When mistakes are made either in the construction of the ACLs or in their application, many devices may be affected. The creation and application of these tools should only be done by those who have been trained in their syntax and in the logic ACLs use in their operation.

Unresponsive Service   Services can fail for several reasons. Many services depend on other services for their operation. Therefore, the failure of one service sometimes causes a domino effect, taking down other services that depend on it. You can use the Services applet in Control Panel to identify these dependencies as well as start and stop services. To identify the services upon which a particular service depends, use the Dependencies tab on the Services applet, as shown in Figure 24.7.

In Figure 24.7, the spooler service is selected and the Dependencies tab is displayed. Here we see that the spooler service depends on the HTTP and RPC services. Therefore, if the spooler service will not start, we may need to restart one of these two services first.

FIGURE 24.7 Service dependencies

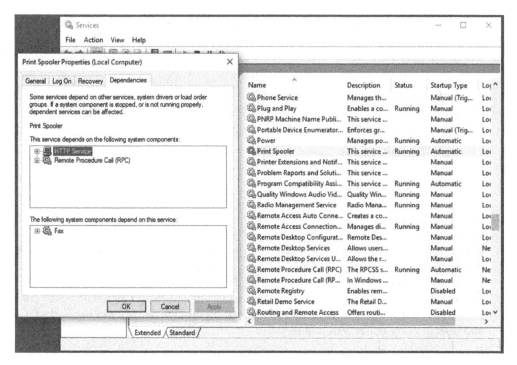

Multicast Flooding Multicasting is used for network devices to communicate with each other and to save network capacity by having only one sender but many listeners. This is handy for video because the content server does not have to generate an individual stream for every subscribed listener. However, multicast can flood a network with packets as they are sent to every networking device and potentially out every port, even if there are no listeners on the switch port. To resolve these issues, you must enable the multicast features on modern switches and routers that are designed to lessen the impact of multicast flooding.

Asymmetrical Routing Asymmetrical routing is when a session takes different paths through a network. Generally a routed network will have only one path for both send and receive traffic from a client to a server and vice versa. However, conditions can exist where a router sends traffic out and it comes back using another path. Check that you are not running multiple routing protocols inside your network or that your ISP is not returning traffic via another path than what you are sending out.

Low Optical Link Budget When you're troubleshooting fiber-optic links, a test set should be used to make sure the received light level is not too low as to be detected. If there is too much loss over a fiber link due to too many interconnects where additional loss is added, if the distance is greater than the standard dictates, or if there are dirty connections, a link may not be able to be established.

Network Time Protocol Issues   Networks and computers have the ability to sync their time clock to a central server called a Network Time Protocol (NTP) server. If communications are lost or NTP was never configured to begin with, time stamps for logging, application synchronizations, and licenses based on dates can all cause major headaches. It is always a good practice to use a central time sources and make sure all of your devices get their data and time data from the NTP servers.

Bring Your Own Devices (BYOD) Challenges   It has become more and more common for workers to want to bring their own smartphones, tablets, and laptops to work and connect them to the corporate network. This can raise a whole host of security issues for a company. There are several approaches to this dilemma. First, a device can be scanned for patches, virus software, and configuration parameters that meet corporate policy. This can be very complex to set up and administer.

A more common approach is to set up a separate Wi-Fi or LAN network for the BYOD devices that has little or no internal network connectivity but allows a connection out to the Internet. When troubleshooting network problems where a user can connect to some services but not others, it is a good idea to see what device they are using and if they are limited by design.

Licensed Features   If you are troubleshooting a device or application that is missing areas in its configuration, the issue could very well be that the feature has never been enabled. It is common for software to come with a basic feature set and then licenses must be purchased to enable enhanced features. Always take the time in your troubleshooting to investigate if the feature requires a license and if the license is active.

Network Performance Issues   If there is a problem with the network itself, trouble calls will arrive from many affected users. It is important to isolate the problem to see if it is local to a computer or more widespread. This can be a single switch or a whole building. Take the steps outlined in this chapter to really understand the problem and how widespread it is. By isolating it to network segments, you can focus your troubleshooting to determine the cause of the problem.

Consider Multiple Approaches

There are two standard approaches that you can use to establish a theory of probable cause. Let's take a look at them next.

Top-to-Bottom/Bottom-to-Top OSI Model   As its name implies, when you apply a *top-down* approach to troubleshooting a networking problem, you start with the user application and work your way down the layers of the OSI model. If a layer is *not* in good working condition, you inspect the layer below it. When you know that the current layer is not in working condition and you discover that a lower layer works, you can conclude that the problem is within the layer above the lower working layer. Once you've determined which layer is the lowest layer with problems, you can begin identifying their cause from within that layer.

The *bottom-up* approach to troubleshooting a networking problem starts with the physical components of the network and works its way up the layers of the OSI model. If you conclude that all the elements associated with a particular layer are in good working order, move on to inspect the elements associated with the next layer up until the causes of the problem are identified. The downside to the bottom-up approach is that it requires you to check every device, interface, and so on. In other words, regardless of the nature of the problem, the bottom-up approach starts with an exhaustive check of all the elements of each layer, starting with the physical layer and working its way up from there.

Divide and Conquer   Unlike the top-down and bottom-up troubleshooting strategies, the *divide-and-conquer* approach to network troubleshooting doesn't always begin the investigation at a particular OSI layer. When using the divide-and-conquer approach, you select a layer, test its health, and based on the results, you can move up or down through the model from the layer you began scrutinizing.

With all that in mind, let's move on with our troubleshooting steps.

Step 3: Test the Theory to Determine Cause

Once you've gathered information and established a plausible theory, you've got to determine the next steps to resolve your problem. If you can't confirm your theory during this step, you must formulate a new theory or escalate the problem.

Let's return to our troubleshooting example by first checking the IP configuration of the host that just happens to include DNS information. You use the `ipconfig /all` command to show the IP configuration. The `/all` switch will give you the DNS information you need, as shown in Figure 24.8.

FIGURE 24.8   Output from `ipconfig /all`

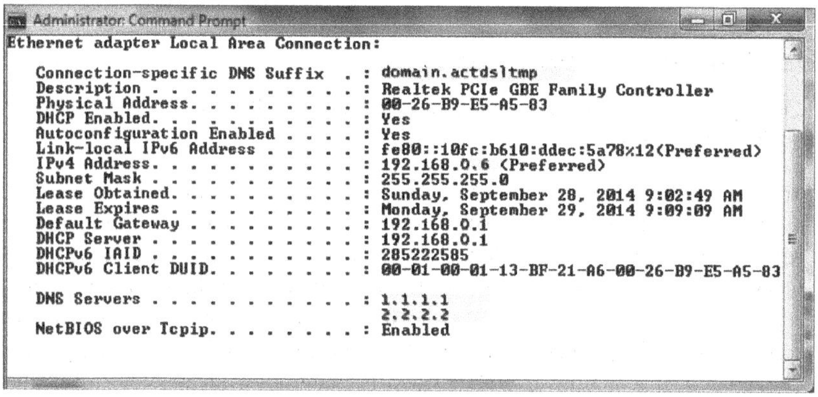

```
Administrator: Command Prompt
Ethernet adapter Local Area Connection:

   Connection-specific DNS Suffix  . : domain.actdsltmp
   Description . . . . . . . . . . . : Realtek PCIe GBE Family Controller
   Physical Address. . . . . . . . . : 00-26-B9-E5-A5-83
   DHCP Enabled. . . . . . . . . . . : Yes
   Autoconfiguration Enabled . . . . : Yes
   Link-local IPv6 Address . . . . . : fe80::10fc:b610:ddec:5a78%12(Preferred)
   IPv4 Address. . . . . . . . . . . : 192.168.0.6 (Preferred)
   Subnet Mask . . . . . . . . . . . : 255.255.255.0
   Lease Obtained. . . . . . . . . . : Sunday, September 28, 2014 9:02:49 AM
   Lease Expires . . . . . . . . . . : Monday, September 29, 2014 9:09:09 AM
   Default Gateway . . . . . . . . . : 192.168.0.1
   DHCP Server . . . . . . . . . . . : 192.168.0.1
   DHCPv6 IAID . . . . . . . . . . . : 285222585
   DHCPv6 Client DUID. . . . . . . . : 00-01-00-01-13-BF-21-A6-00-26-B9-E5-A5-83

   DNS Servers . . . . . . . . . . . : 1.1.1.1
                                       2.2.2.2
   NetBIOS over Tcpip. . . . . . . . : Enabled
```

Check out the DNS entries: 1.1.1.1 and 2.2.2.2. Is this right? What are they supposed to be? You can find this out by checking the addresses on a working host, but let's check the settings on your troubled host's adapter first. Click Start, then Control Panel, then Network And Sharing Center, and then Manage Network Connections on the left side of the screen, which will take you to the screen shown in Figure 24.9.

FIGURE 24.9   Manage Network Connections

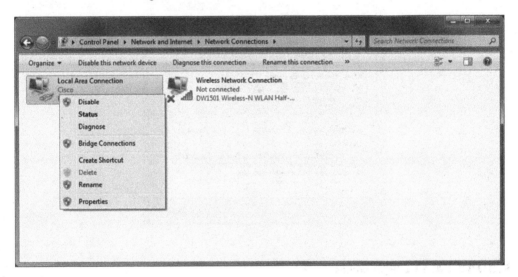

Now, click the interface in question, and click Properties. You receive the screen shown in Figure 24.10.

From here, you highlight Internet Protocol Version 4, and click Properties (or just double-click). From Figure 24.11, do you see what may be causing the problem?

As I said, you're using DHCP, right? But DNS is statically configured on this host. Interesting enough, when you set a static DNS entry on an interface, it will override the DHCP-provided DNS entry.

Once the theory is confirmed, determine the next steps to resolve the problem.   When the testing of the theory is complete, you will have determined if the suggested cause is correct. If you find you are correct, the next step (described in the next section) is to establish a plan of action to resolve the problem and identify potential effects.

If the theory is not confirmed, reestablish a new theory or escalate.   If you find that the suggested theory is not the cause of the issue, then you should move on to test any other theories you may have developed. In the event you have exhausted all theories you may have developed, it is advisable to escalate the issue to a more senior technician or, when it involves a system with which you are unfamiliar, the system owner or manager.

FIGURE 24.10   Interface properties

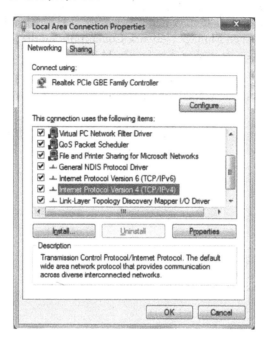

FIGURE 24.11   IP properties

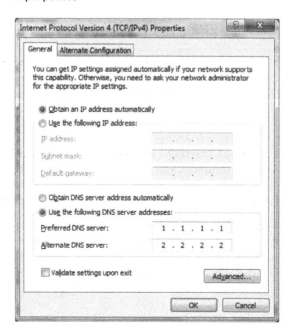

Step 4: Establish a Plan of Action to Resolve the Problem and Identify Potential Effects

Now that you've identified some possible changes, you've got to follow through and test your solution to see if you really solved the problem. In this case, you ask the user to try to access the intranet server (because that's what they called about). Basically, you just ask the user to try doing whatever it was they couldn't do when they called you in the first place. If it works—sweet—problem solved. If not, try the operation yourself.

Now you can test the proposed solution on the computer of the user who is still waiting for a solution. To do that, you need to check the DNS configuration on your host. But first, let me point out something about the neglected user's network. All hosts are using DHCP, so it's really weird that a single user is having a DNS resolution issue.

So, to fix the problem and get your user back in the game, just click Obtain DNS Server Address Automatically, and then click OK (see Figure 24.12). Voilà!

FIGURE 24.12   Obtain DNS Server Address Automatically

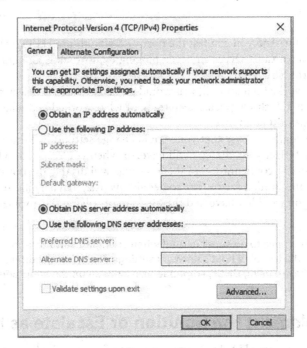

Let's take a look at the output of `ipconfig /all` in Figure 24.13 and see if you received new DNS server addresses.

FIGURE 24.13 `ipconfig /all` output

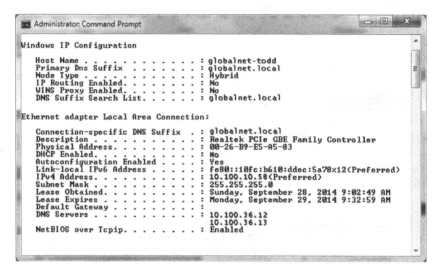

All good; you did it. And you can test the host by trying to use HTTP/HTTPS to connect to a web page on the intranet server and even pinging by hostname. Congratulations on solving your first trouble ticket!

If things hadn't worked out so well, you would go back to step 2, select a new possible cause, and redo step 3. If this happens, keep track of what worked and what didn't so you don't make the same mistakes twice.

It's pretty much common sense that you should change settings like this only when you fully understand the effect your changes will have, or when you're asked to by someone who does. The incorrect configuration of these settings will disable the normal operation of your workstation, and, well, it seems that someone (the user, maybe?) did something they shouldn't have or you wouldn't have had the pleasure of solving this problem.

 You have to be super careful when changing settings and always check out a troubled host's network settings. Don't just assume that because they're using DHCP, someone has screwed up the static configuration.

Step 5: Implement the Solution or Escalate as Necessary

Although it's true that CompTIA doesn't expect you to fix every single network problem that could possibly happen in the universe, they actually do expect you to get pretty close to determining exactly what the problem is. And if you can't fix it, you'll be expected to know how to escalate it and to whom. You are only as good as your resources—be they your own skill set, a book like this one, other more reference-oriented technical books, the Internet, or even a guru at a call center.

I know it seems like I talked to death the physical and logical issues that cause problems in a network, but trust me, with what I've taught you, you're just getting started. There's a galaxy of networking evils that we have not even touched on because they're far beyond the objectives for Network+ certification and, therefore, the scope of this book. But out there in the real world, you'll get calls about them anyway, and because you're not yet equipped to handle them yourself, you need to escalate these nasties to a senior network engineer who has the additional experience and knowledge required to resolve the problems.

Some of the calamities that you should escalate are as follows:

- Switching loops
- Missing routes
- Routing loops
- Routing problems
- MTU black hole
- Bad modules
- Proxy Address Resolution Protocol (ARP)
- Broadcast storms
- NIC Teaming misconfiguration
- Power failures/power anomalies

 If you can't implement a solution and instead have to escalate the problem, there is no need for you to go on with steps 6 and 7 of the seven-step troubleshooting model. You now need to meet with the emergency response team to determine the next step.

And just as with other problems, you have to be able to identify these events because if you can't do that, how else will you know that you need to escalate them?

Switching Loops   Today's networks often connect switches with redundant links to provide for fault tolerance and load balancing. Protocols such as Spanning Tree Protocol (STP) prevent switching loops and simultaneously maintain fault tolerance. If STP fails, it takes some expertise to reconfigure and repair the network, so you just need to be concerned with being able to identify the problem so you can escalate it. Remember, when you hear users complaining that the network works fine for a while, then unexpectedly goes down for about a minute, and then goes back to being fine, it's definitely an STP convergence issue that's pretty tough to find and fix. Escalate this problem ASAP!

Missing Routes   Routers must have routes either configured or learned to function. There are a number of issues that can prevent a router from learning the routes that it needs. To determine if a router has the route to the network in question, execute the show ip route command and view the routing table. This can save a lot of additional troubleshooting if you can narrow the problem to a missing route.

Routing Loops   Routing protocols are often used on networks to control traffic efficiently while preventing routing loops that happen when a routing protocol hasn't been configured properly or network changes didn't get the attention they deserved. Routing loops can also happen if you or the network admin blew the static configuration and created conflicting routes through the network. This evil event affects the traffic flow for all users, and although it's pretty complicated to fix, it's very important to address. You can expect routing loops to occur if your network is running old routing protocols like Routing Information Protocol (RIP) and RIPv2. Just upgrading your routing protocol to Enhanced Interior Gateway Routing Protocol (EIGRP), Open Shortest Path First (OSPF), or Intermediate System-to-Intermediate System (IS-IS) will usually take care of the problem once and for all. Anyway, escalate this problem to the router group—which hopefully is soon to be you.

Routing Problems   Routing packets through the many subnets of a large enterprise while still maintaining security can be a tremendous challenge. A router's configuration can include all kinds of stuff like access lists, network address translation (NAT), port address translation (PAT), and even authentication protocols like Remote Authentication Dial-In User Service (RADIUS) and Terminal Access Controller Access-Control System Plus (TACACS+). Particularly diabolical, errant configuration changes can trigger a domino effect that can derail traffic down the wrong path or even cause it to come to a grinding halt and stop traversing the network completely. To identify routing problems, check to see if someone has simply set a wrong default route on a router. This can easily create routing loops. I see it all the time. These configurations can be highly complex and specific to a particular device, so they need to be escalated to the top dogs—get the problem to the best sys admin in the router group.

MTU Black Hole   On a WAN connection, communication routes may fail if an intermediate network segment has an MTU that is smaller than the maximum packet size of the communicating hosts—and if the router does not send an appropriate Internet Control Message Protocol (ICMP) response to this condition. If ICMP traffic is allowed, the routers will take care of this problem using ICMP messages. However, as ICMP traffic is increasingly being blocked, this can create what is called a black hole. This will probably be an issue you will escalate.

Bad Modules   Some multilayer switches and routers have slots available to add new features. The hardware that fits in these slots is called a module. These modules can host fiber connections, wireless connections, and other types as well. A common example is the Cisco Small Form-Factor Pluggable (SFP) Gigabit Interface Ethernet Converter (GBIC). This is an input-output device that plugs into an existing Gigabit Ethernet port or slot, providing a variety of additional capabilities to the device hosting the slot or port. Conversions can happen in all types of cables, from Ethernet to fiber, for example. Like any piece of hardware made by humans, the modules can fail. It is always worth checking if there are no other reasons a link is not functioning.

Proxy ARP   Address Resolution Protocol (ARP) is a service that resolves IP addresses to MAC addresses. Proxy ARP is just wrong to use in today's networks, but hosts and routers still have it on by default. The idea of Proxy ARP was to solve the problem of a host being able to have only one configured default gateway. To allow redundancy, Proxy ARP running on a router will respond to an ARP broadcast from a host that's sending a packet to a remote network—but the host doesn't have a default gateway set. So the router responds by being the proxy for the remote host, which in turn makes the local host think the remote host is really local; as a result, the local host sends the packets to the router, which then forwards the packets to the remote host. Most of the time, in today's networks, this does not work well, if at all. Disable Proxy ARP on your routers, and make sure you have default gateways set on all your hosts. If you need router redundancy, there are much better solutions available than Proxy ARP! This is another job for the routing group.

Broadcast Storms   When a switch receives a broadcast, it will normally flood the broadcast out all the ports except for the one the broadcast came in on. If STP fails between switches or is disabled by an administrator, it's possible that the traffic could continue to be flooded repeatedly throughout the switch topology. When this happens, the network can get so busy that normal traffic can't traverse it—an event referred to as a *broadcast storm*. As you can imagine, this is a particularly gruesome thing to have to troubleshoot and fix because you need to find the one bad link that is causing the mess while the network is probably still up and running—but at a heavily congested crawl. Escalate ASAP to experts!

NIC Teaming Misconfiguration   NIC Teaming, also known as load balancing/failover (LBFO), allows multiple network interfaces to be placed into a team for the purposes of bandwidth aggregation and/or traffic failover to prevent connectivity loss in the event of a network component failure. The cards can be set to active-active state, where both cards are load-balancing, or active-passive, where one card is on standby in case the primary card fails. Most of the time, the NIC team will use a multicast address to send and receive data, but it can also use a broadcast address so all cards receive the data at the same time. If these are not configured correctly, either they will operate at a severely diminished capacity or, worse, neither card will work at all!

Power Failures/Power Anomalies   When you have power issues, whether it's a full-blown power outage or intermittent power surges, it can cause some serious issues with your network devices. Your servers and core network devices require a fully functional UPS system.

Step 6: Verify Full System Functionality, and If Applicable, Implement Preventative Measures

A trap that any network technician can fall into is solving one problem and thinking it's all fixed without stopping to consider the possible consequences of their solution. The cure can be worse than the disease, and it's possible that your solution falls into this category. So before you fully implement the solution to a problem, make sure you totally understand the ramifications of doing so—clearly, if it causes more problems than it fixes, you should toss it and find a different solution that does no harm.

 Many people update a router's operating system or firmware just because a new version of code is released from the manufacturer. Do not do this on your production routers—just say no! Always test any new code before upgrading your production routers: Like a bad solution, sometimes the new code provides new features but creates more problems, and the cons outweigh the pros.

Step 7: Document Findings, Actions, Outcomes, and Lessons Learned

I can't stress enough how vital network documentation is. Always document problems and solutions so that you have the information at hand when a similar problem arises in the future. With documented solutions to documented problems, you can assemble your own database of information that you can use to troubleshoot other problems. Be sure to include information like the following:

- A description of the conditions surrounding the problem
- The OS version, the software version, the type of computer, and the type of NIC
- Whether you were able to reproduce the problem
- The solutions you tried
- The ultimate solution
- The lessons you learned to achieve great success in the future

 Real World Scenario

Network Documentation

I don't know how many times I've gone into a place and asked where their documentation was only to be met with a blank stare. I was recently at a small business that was experiencing network problems. The first question I asked was, "Do you have any kind of network documentation?" I got the blank stare. So, we proceeded to search through lots of receipts and other paperwork—anything we could find to help us understand the network layout and figure out exactly what was on the network. It turned out they had recently bought a WAP, and it was having trouble connecting—something that would've taken me five minutes to fix instead of searching through a mess for a couple hours!

Documentation doesn't have to look like a sleek owner's manual or anything—it can consist of a simple three-ring binder with an up-to-date network map; receipts for network equipment; a pocket for owner's manuals; and a stack of loose-leaf paper to record services, changes, network-addressing assignments, access lists, and so on. Just this little bit of documentation can save lots of time and money and prevent grief, especially in the critical first few months of a new network install.

Troubleshooting Tips

Now that you've got the basics of network troubleshooting down pat, I'm going to go over a few really handy troubleshooting tips for you to arm yourself with even further in the quest to conquer the world's networking evils.

Don't Overlook the Small Stuff

The super simple stuff (SSS) I referred to at the beginning of this chapter should never be overlooked—ever! Here's a quick review: Just remember that problems are often caused by little things like a bad power switch; a power switch in the wrong position; a card or port that's not working, indicated by a link light that's not lit; or simply an operator error (OE). Even the most experienced system administrator has forgotten to turn on the power, left a cable unplugged, or mistyped a username and password—not me, of course, but others . . .

And make sure that users get solid training for the systems they use. An ounce of prevention is worth a pound of cure, and you'll experience dramatically fewer ID10T errors this way.

Prioritize Your Problems

Being a network administrator or technician of even a fairly small network can keep you hopping, and it's pretty rare that you'll get calls for help one at a time and never be interrupted by more coming in. Closer to reality is receiving yet another call when you already have three people waiting for service. So, you've got to prioritize.

You start this process by again asking some basic questions to determine the severity of the problem being reported. Clearly, if the new call is about something little and you already have a huge issue to deal with, you should put the new call on hold or get their info and get back to them later. If you establish a good set of priorities, you'll make much better use of your time. Here's an example of the rank you probably want to give to networking problems, from highest priority to lowest:

- Total network failure (affects everyone)
- Partial network failure (affects small groups of users)

- Small network failure (affects a small, single group of users)
- Total workstation failure (single user can't work at all)
- Partial workstation failure (single user can't do most tasks)
- Minor issue (single user has problems that crop up now and then)

Mitigating circumstances can, of course, change the order of this list. For example, if the president of the company can't retrieve email, you'd take the express elevator to their office as soon as you got the call, right? And even a minor issue can move up the ladder if it's persistent enough.

Don't fall prey to thinking that simple problems are easier to deal with because even though you may be able to bring up a crashed server in minutes, a user who doesn't know how to make columns line up in Microsoft Word could take a chunk out of your day. You'd want to put the latter problem toward the bottom of the list because of the time involved—it's a lot more efficient to solve problems for a big group of people than to fix this one user's problem immediately.

Some network administrators list all network-service requests on a chalkboard or a whiteboard. They then prioritize them based on the previously discussed criteria. Some larger companies have written support-call tracking software whose only function is to track and prioritize all network and computer problems. Use whatever method makes you comfortable, but prioritize your calls.

Check the Software Configuration

Often, network problems can be traced to software configuration, like our DNS configuration scenario; so when you're checking for software problems, don't forget to check types of configurations:

- DNS configuration/misconfiguration
- DHCP configuration/misconfiguration
- WINS configuration
- Hosts file
- The Registry

Software-configuration settings love to hide in places like these and can be notoriously hard to find (especially in the Registry).

Also, look for lines that have been commented out either intentionally or accidentally in text-configuration files—another place for clues. A command such as REM or REMARK, or asterisk or semicolon characters, indicates comment lines in a file.

 In the hosts file, a pound sign (#) is used to indicate a comment line.

Don't Overlook Physical Conditions

You want to make sure that from a network-design standpoint, the physical environment for a server is optimized for placement, temperature, and humidity. When troubleshooting an obscure network problem, don't forget to check the physical conditions under which the network device is operating. Check for problems like these:

- Excessive heat
- Excessive humidity (condensation)
- Low humidity (leads to electrostatic discharge [ESD] problems)
- EMI/RFI problems
- ESD problems
- Power problems
- Unplugged cables

Don't Overlook Cable Problems

Cables, generally speaking, work fine once they are installed properly. If the patch cable isn't the problem, use a cable tester (not a tone generator and locator) to find the source of the problem.

One of the easiest mistakes to make, especially if cables are not labeled, is to use a crossover cable where a straight-through cable should be used or vice versa. In either case, when you do this it causes TX/RX reversal. What's that? That's when the transmit wire is connected to Transmit and the receive wire to Receive. That sounds good, but it needs to be Transmit to Receive. See more about straight-through and crossover cables in Chapter 3.

Wires that are moved can be prone to breaking or shorting, and a short can happen when the wire conductor comes in contact with another conductive surface, changing the path of the electrical signal. The signal will go someplace else instead of to the intended recipient. You can use cable testers to test for many types of problems:

- Broken cables
- Incorrect connections
- Interference levels
- Total cable length (for length restrictions)
- Cable shorts
- Connector problems
- Testing the cable at all possible data rates

As a matter of fact, cable testers are so sophisticated that they can even indicate the exact location of a cable break, accurate to within 6 inches or better.

Check for Viruses

People overlook scanning for viruses because they assume that the network's virus-checking software has already picked them off. But to be effective, the software must be kept up-to-date, and updates are made available pretty much daily. You've got to run the virus-definition update utility to keep the virus-definition file current.

If you are having strange, unusual, irreproducible problems with a workstation, try scanning it with an up-to-date virus-scan or antimalware utility. You'd be surprised how many times people have spent hours and hours troubleshooting a strange problem only to run a virus-scan utility, find and clean out one or more viruses, and have the problem disappear like magic.

Summary

In this chapter, you learned about all things troubleshooting, and you now know how to sleuth out and solve a lot of network problems. You learned to first check all the SSS and about how to approach problem resolution by eliminating what the problem is *not*. You learned how to narrow the problem down to its basics and define it.

Next, you learned a systematic approach using a seven-step troubleshooting model to troubleshoot most of the problems you'll run into in networking. And you also learned about some resources you can use to help you during the troubleshooting process. In addition, you learned how important documentation is to the health of your network.

Finally, I gave you a bunch of cool tips to further equip you, tips about prioritizing issues, checking for configuration issues, considering environmental factors—even hunting down viruses. As you venture out into the real world, keep these tips in mind; along with your own personal experience, they'll really help make you an expert troubleshooter.

Exam Essentials

Know the seven troubleshooting steps, in order.

The steps, in order, are as follows:

1. Identify the problem.
2. Establish a theory of probable cause.
3. Test the theory to determine cause.

4. Establish a plan of action to resolve the problem and identify potential effects.
5. Implement the solution or escalate as necessary.
6. Verify full system functionality, and if applicable, implement preventative measures.
7. Document findings, actions, outcomes, and lessons learned.

Be able to identify a link light.   A link light is the small, usually green LED on the back of a network card. This LED is typically found next to the media connector on a NIC and is usually labeled Link.

Understand how proper network use procedures can affect the operation of a network.   If a user is not following a network use procedure properly (for example, not logging in correctly), that user may report a problem where none exists. A good network troubleshooter should know how to differentiate between a network hardware/software problem and a "lack of user training" problem.

Know how to narrow down a problem to one specific area or cause.   Most problems can be traced to one specific area or cause. You must be able to determine if a problem is specific to one user or a bunch of users, specific to one computer or a bunch of computers, and related to hardware or software. The answers to these questions will give you a very specific problem focus.

Know how to detect cabling-related problems.   Generally speaking, most cabling-related problems can be traced by plugging the suspect workstation into a known, working network port. If the problem disappears (or at the very least changes significantly), it is related to the cabling for that workstation.

Written Lab

In this section, write the answers to the following questions. You can find the answers in Appendix A.

1. What is step 3 of the seven-step troubleshooting model?

2. What is step 7 of the seven-step troubleshooting model?

3. How is crosstalk minimized in twisted-pair cabling?

4. If you plug a host into a switch port and the user cannot get to the server or other services they need to access despite a working link light, what could the problem be?

5. What is it called when a cable has two wires of a twisted pair connected to two wires from a different pair?

6. When a signal moves through any medium, the medium itself will degrade the signal. What is this called?

7. What is step 4 of the seven-step troubleshooting model?

8. What is step 5 of the seven-step troubleshooting model?

9. What are some of the problems that, if determined, should be escalated?

10. What cable issues should you know and understand for network troubleshooting?

Review Questions

You can find the answers to the review questions in Appendix B.

1. Which of the following are not steps in the Network+ troubleshooting model? (Choose all that apply.)

   A. Reboot the servers.

   B. Identify the problem.

   C. Test the theory to determine the cause.

   D. Implement the solution or escalate as necessary.

   E. Document findings, actions, outcomes, and lessons learned.

   F. Reboot all the routers.

2. You have a user who cannot connect to the network. What is the first thing you could check to determine the source of the problem?

   A. Workstation configuration

   B. Connectivity

   C. Patch cable

   D. Server configuration

3. When wireless users complain that they are losing their connection to applications during a session, what is the source of the problem?

   A. Incorrect SSID

   B. Latency

   C. Incorrect encryption

   D. MAC address filter

4. Several users can't log in to the server. Which action would help you to narrow the problem down to the workstations, network, or server?

   A. Run `tracert` from a workstation.

   B. Check the server console for user connections.

   C. Run `netstat` on all workstations.

   D. Check the network diagnostics.

5. A user can't log in to the network. She can't even connect to the Internet over the LAN. Other users in the same area aren't experiencing any problems. You attempt to log in as this user from your workstation with her username and password and don't experience any problems. However, you cannot log in with either her username or yours from her workstation. What is a likely cause of the problem?

   A. Insufficient rights to access the server

   B. A bad patch cable

    C. Server down

    D. Wrong username and password

6. A user is experiencing problems logging in to a Linux server. He can connect to the Internet over the LAN. Other users in the same area aren't experiencing any problems. You attempt logging in as this user from your workstation with his username and password and don't experience any problems. However, you cannot log in with either his username or yours from his workstation. What is a likely cause of the problem?

    A. The Caps Lock key is pressed.

    B. The network hub is malfunctioning.

    C. You have a downed server.

    D. You have a jabbering NIC.

7. You receive a call from a user who is having issues connecting to a new VPN. Which is the first step you should take?

    A. Find out what has changed.

    B. Reboot the workstation.

    C. Document the solution.

    D. Identify the symptoms and potential causes.

8. A workstation presents an error message to a user. The message states that a duplicate IP address has been detected on the network. After establishing what has changed in the network, what should be the next step using the standard troubleshooting model?

    A. Test the result.

    B. Select the most probable cause.

    C. Create an action plan.

    D. Identify the results and effects of the solution.

9. You have gathered information on a network issue and determined the affected areas of the network. What is your next step in resolving this issue?

    A. You should implement the best solution for the issue.

    B. You should test the best solution for the issue.

    C. You should check to see if there have been any recent changes to this affected part of the network.

    D. You should consider any negative impact to the network that might be caused by a solution.

10. A user calls you, reporting a problem logging in to the corporate intranet. You can access the website without problems using the user's username and password. At your request, the user has tried logging in from other workstations but has been unsuccessful. What is the most likely cause of the problem?

    A. The user is logging in incorrectly.

    B. The network is down.

C. The intranet server is locked up.

D. The server is not routing packets correctly to that user's workstation.

11. You have just implemented a solution and you want to celebrate your success. But what should you do next before you start your celebration?

A. Gather more information about the issue.

B. Document the issue and the solution that was implemented.

C. Test the solution and identify other effects it may have.

D. Escalate the issue.

12. You can ping the local router and web server that a local user is trying to reach, but you cannot reach the web page that resides on that server. From step 2 of the troubleshooting model, what is a possible problem that would lead to this situation?

A. Your network cable is unplugged.

B. There is a problem with your browser.

C. Your NIC has failed.

D. The web server is unplugged.

13. When troubleshooting an obscure network problem, what physical conditions should be reviewed to make sure the network device is operating correctly? (Choose all that apply.)

A. Excessive heat

B. Low/excessive humidity

C. ESD problems

D. None of the above

14. Which of the following is not a basic physical issue that can occur on a network when a user is connected via cable?

A. Crosstalk

B. Shorts

C. Open impedance mismatch

D. DNS configurations

15. You are troubleshooting a LAN switch and have identified the symptoms. What is the next step you should take?

A. Escalate the issue.

B. Create an action plan.

C. Implement the solution.

D. Determine the scope of the problem.

16. A user calls you, complaining that he can't access the corporate intranet web server. You try the same address, and you receive a Host Not Found error. Several minutes later, another user reports the same problem. You can still send email and transfer files to another server. What is the most likely cause of the problem?

    A. The hub is unplugged.

    B. The server is not routing protocols to your workstation.

    C. The user's workstation is not connected to the network.

    D. The web server is down.

17. You have implemented and tested a solution and identified any other effects the solution may have. What is your next step?

    A. Create an action plan.

    B. Close the case and head home for the day.

    C. Reboot the Windows server.

    D. Document the solution.

18. Users are reporting that they can access the Internet but not the internal company website. Which of the following is the most likely problem?

    A. The DNS entry for the server is non-authoritative.

    B. The intranet server is down.

    C. The DNS address handed out by DHCP is incorrect.

    D. The default gateway is incorrect.

19. Several users have complained about the server's poor performance as of late. You know that the memory installed in the server is sufficient. What could you use to determine the source of the problem?

    A. Server's NIC link light

    B. Protocol analyzer

    C. Performance-monitoring tools

    D. Server's system log file

20. You lose power to your computer room and the switches in your network do not come back up when everything is brought online. After you have identified the affected areas, established the cause, and escalated this problem, what do you do next?

    A. Start to implement a solution to get those users back online ASAP.

    B. Create an action plan and solution.

    C. Meet with the emergency response team to determine the next step.

    D. Copy all the working routers' configurations to the nonworking switches.

Chapter 25

Network Software Tools and Commands

THE FOLLOWING COMPTIA NETWORK+ EXAM OBJECTIVES ARE COVERED IN THIS CHAPTER:

✓ **5.3 Given a scenario, use the appropriate network software tools and commands.**

- Software tools
    - WiFi analyzer
    - Protocol analyzer/packet capture
    - Bandwidth speed tester
    - Port scanner
    - iperf
    - NetFlow analyzer
    - Trivial File Transfer Protocol (TFTP) server
    - Terminal emulator
    - IP scanner
- Command line tool
    - ping
    - ipconfig/ifconfig/ip
    - nslookup/dig
    - traceroute/tracert
    - arp
    - netstat
    - hostname
    - route
    - telnet

- tcpdump
- nmap
- Basic network platform commands
  - Show interface
  - Show config
  - Show route

Specialized tasks require specialized tools, and installing network components is no exception. We use some of these tools, such as network scanners, on an everyday basis, but most of the software tools I'll be covering in this chapter are used mainly in the telecommunications industry.

Still, in order to meet the CompTIA Network+ objectives and also because you're likely to run across them in today's networking environments, it's very important that you're familiar with them.

To find Todd Lammle CompTIA videos and practice questions, please see www.lammle.com.

Software Tools

To effectively test and troubleshoot networks, it is important to be aware of and know how to operate the many different types of tools available for you to use. We will start the chapter by going over many of the software applications designed for network testing and troubleshooting. Knowledge of how to use these tools allows you to locate, troubleshoot, and resolve any networking issues you may come across.

Wi-Fi Analyzers

When deploying and troubleshooting wireless networks, you must have some way to determine signal levers, noise readings, SSIDs, and interference to resolve most Wi-Fi related issues. Wi-Fi analyzers can look into the air and gather valuable information so you can see what is healthy and what is not. Using Wi-Fi analyzers, you can see the Wi-Fi coverage in an area and use that information for optimal access-point placement to get complete coverage and avoid dead spots.

Many vendors now have Wi-Fi analyzers built into access points and client software running on your laptop. Wireless controllers that manage multiple access points can also act as an analyzer and gather data from many access points in your network to give you a consolidated view of coverage, interference, and signal reception levels.

Protocol Analyzer/Packet Capture

Protocol analyzers, also called sniffers or network monitors, are used to capture packets in their raw format as they cross the network. Windows desktop operating systems before Windows Vista came with a built-in protocol analyzer called Network Monitor, but that is no longer the case, although you can download one for free that will work with the newer operating systems.

The Network Monitor tool that comes with these operating systems will capture only packets that are sourced from or destined to the computer on which the tool is running. Commercial sniffers like Wireshark and Omnipeek can capture any packets because they set the NIC to operate in promiscuous mode, which means the NIC processes all packets that it sees.

Protocol analyzers can be used to determine the type of traffic that you have in your network, and depending on the product and the bells and whistles contained therein, you may be able to sort the results based on port numbers, protocols, and so on. Another use of a sniffer is to examine the traffic that should be occurring on the network when something is not working to aid in troubleshooting. These devices can capture and display all packets involved in the connection setup, including, for example, request and response headers to a web server.

Let's review the series of four packet types that must occur for a DHCP client to receive an IP configuration from the server. As a review, those packets are as follows:

- DHCP Discover
- DHCP Offer
- DHCP Request
- DHCP ACK

If you turned on the analyzer and then executed the `ipconfig/release` and `ipconfig/renew` commands on the client (more on those commands later in this chapter), you should see these four packets in the analyzer's capture file. The packets would be interspersed with the hundreds and perhaps thousands of other packet types that would be captured, but by using the display filtering options in the software, you can easily segregate out the DHCP traffic. An example of the DHCP process, as seen in a capture, is shown in Figure 25.1.

FIGURE 25.1   DHCP capture

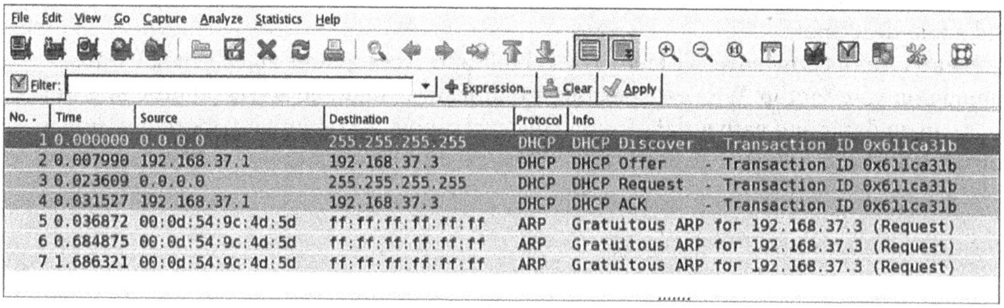

If all you saw in the capture were the DHCP Discover packets with no DHCP Offer packets, you could reasonably assert that the DHCP server is not receiving the DHCP Offer packets (perhaps the DHCP server is located in another broadcast domain or perhaps it is not on). Additionally, you could examine fields in the DHCP Offer packets that may tell you that the DHCP server is out of addresses. The point is that the tool can be used to troubleshoot the issue.

Bandwidth Speed Testers

Users of a network often complain about the speed of the network. Network "speed" is in some ways a personal perception because some people have more patience than others. To determine when a network slowdown is real as opposed to perceived, you need to actually measure the throughput. That's what throughput testers are used for.

These devices, typically software based, work much like a protocol analyzer in that they measure the traffic seen on the network and can also classify the types of traffic that are eating up your bandwidth (which is probably what you really need to know). Figure 25.2 shows one version of this software by TamoSoft.

FIGURE 25.2   Throughput

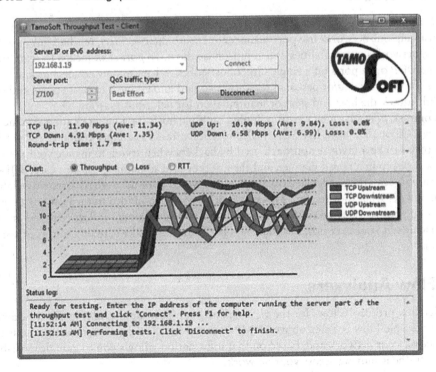

This software is installed on a server and also on a client. In the figure, the software is measuring traffic between the client and a server. It shows the throughput for traffic in real time and in this shot is breaking that traffic up by unicast (TCP) and broadcast (UDP) types and by direction.

Earlier in this book, I discussed the importance of baselines, and this is another area where they are important. Network throughput figures mean little without a baseline with which comparisons can be made. How do you know what is abnormal when you don't know what normal is? Baselines should be taken when the network is operating well, but they should also be taken when the traffic load is normal.

IPerf is an open-source software tool that measures network throughput and is very handy for testing and creating baselines of your network. The software runs as a server on one end and a client on the other.

IPerf can run on both Linux and Windows operating systems. It is highly customizable, allowing you to specify if you want to use TCP or UDP and also the port numbers and packet size to use.

After the test is run, reports are generated that give you throughput, the parameters used, and a timestamp.

Port Scanners

A *port scanner* is a software tool designed to search a host for open ports. Those of us administering our networks use port scanners to ensure their security, but bad guys use them to find a network's vulnerabilities and compromise them. To *port scan* means to scan for TCP and UDP open ports on a single target host either to legitimately connect to and use its services for business and/or personal reasons or to find and connect to those ports and subsequently attack the host and steal or manipulate it for nefarious reasons.

In contrast, *port sweeping* means scanning multiple hosts on a network for a specific listening TCP or UDP port, like SQL. (SQL injection attacks are super common today.) This just happens to be a favorite approach used by hackers when trying to invade your network. They port sweep in a broad manner, and then, if they find something—in this case, SQL— they can port scan the particular host they've discovered with the desired service available to exploit and get what they're after. This is why it's a really good idea to turn off any unused services on your servers and routers and to run only the minimum services required on every host machine in your network. Do yourself a big favor and make sure this is in your security policy.

NetFlow Analyzers

The NetFlow protocol allows for the viewing and analysis of application-level traffic across an interface. NetFlow is a step above SNMP in that it looks at the actual conversations taking place on your network and, based on that information, allows you to gain deep visibility of what traffic is moving across your network.

NetFlow collects information on each unique traffic flow into and out of a network device interfaces. NetFlow collects source and destination addresses, application information, and quality of service (QoS) data and is very helpful in troubleshooting causes of networking problems.

A flow exporter is a network device such as a router that monitors traffic flowing in and out of an interface and exports not the complete packet but a summary of its contents to a flow collector. A flow collector is a server on the network that receives the flows from multiple exporters and consolidates the NetFlow data in a centralized storage location.

A NetFlow application then analyzes the data and creates reports, charts, graphs, and sometimes analytics on the received information.

Trivial File Transfer Protocol (TFTP) Server

When the time comes to upgrade the software on a piece of networking equipment such as a switch or router, the code is downloaded from the vendor site to your laptop or a management server. Then steps are taken to transfer the code to the actual device. One of the most common methods is to use the Trivial File Transfer Protocol (TFTP) as it is supported by all vendors.

A TFTP server is a small application that is available from a wide variety of developers as freeware for Windows and Linux computers. All that is needed is to run the TFTP server on your local machine and point its source directory to the location of the file to upload. Then from the network device, specify the IP address of the TFTP server and the name of the file you want to upload. TFTP is designed to be a simple, effective, and fast method to upload code to a network device.

Connectivity Software

There are times when you need to make a remote connection to a machine to perform troubleshooting but you are miles away. Connectivity software is designed to allow you to make a connection to the machine, see the desktop, and perform any action you could perform if you were sitting in front of it.

Microsoft has made what it calls Remote Desktop software available for free with Windows products since Windows NT. When this software is installed (by default in later versions) on both source and destination computers, a remote desktop connection can be made.

Commercial tools are also available that (of course) claim to have more functionality, and they probably do have a few extra bells and whistles. These include LogMeIn.com, GoToMyPC, and others. Figure 25.3 shows the window for a LogMeIn.com session.

The advantages of these connectivity tools are obvious. With these tools, you can do anything you need to on the machine as long as you can connect. They also allow you to see what a user is actually doing when they encounter a problem rather than having to rely on what they tell you they are doing. You can even show a user what they are doing wrong. Most of these tools allow for chat sessions and for either end of the connection to take control of the machine. You can also transfer files to them if required (maybe a DLL got deleted, for example).

FIGURE 25.3   LogMeIn session window

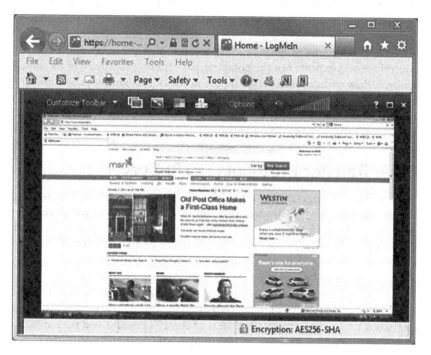

For networking, it is common to access the device's command-line interface remotely. This will require you to use terminal emulation software. Today the Telnet protocol is rarely used because it has no security and all data is sent unencrypted. Secure Shell (SSH) is the preferred method of accessing a remote device command line from across a network. There are many free and commercial terminal emulation packages for you to use. The most common open-source emulator is PuTTY, and it supports Telnet, SSH, and serial interfaces. PuTTY is widely used and found in almost every networking shop. As for commercial packages, Secu-reCRT is popular and has an extensive feature set.

IP Scanner

It is often very helpful to know what is running on a server or networking device. Scanners can tell you what IP addresses are active and what they are "listening for." All IP applications have an associated port number that is open for incoming connections, such as port 80 for HTTP and 443 for HTTPS. An IP scanner can be run on your local computer and will scan for open ports on each IP host. However, be very careful doing this on live production networks because security appliances such as Intrusion and firewall systems may generate an alarm when they detect scans as it may be an indication of fingerprinting your network by hackers.

Scanners can be used for network mapping by listing all of the active IP addresses in each subnet and what applications are running on them. There are many commercial and open-source scanners available on the market. Many have advanced features such as listing bugs and vulnerabilities of a scanned device and providing information on remediation.

Using *traceroute*

Most of us are running Transmission Control Protocol/Internet Protocol (TCP/IP) version 4 on our networks these days, so we absolutely need a way to test IP connectivity. But we also need to be able to test and verify IPv6 networks. The reason for this is that even though Microsoft makes the majority of client platforms, a lot of the commands used to test IP connectivity are really platform independent, and most of the platforms can now use both IPv4 and IPv6. Even so, keep in mind that the Network+ exam focuses on the basic concepts of the function and use of the TCP/IP utilities that come with Windows.

You can use several utilities, both command line and GUI, to verify TCP/IP function on Windows workstations, and most of them are listed in the chapter objectives. Here's a list of all the utilities I'm going to discuss:

- Traceroute (tracert in Microsoft)
- ipconfig (ifconfig in Linux/Unix)
- ping
- arp
- nslookup (dig in Linux/Unix)
- Resolving Names
- Mtr (pathping)
- Nmap
- route
- nbtstat
- netstat
- tcpdump
- ftp
- telnet

And by the way, it's very important that you don't just blow through the output that I've supplied for each command. Instead, pay serious attention to it because to meet the Network+ objectives, you'll be required to correctly identify each command's output.

So, let's cut right to the chase and take a look at some of these commands and their output. Oh, and do try and have fun with it!

For starters, let's pose these questions: Where do all those packets really go when we send them over the Internet? And, how do all the packets actually get to their destinations? Well, we can use the TCP/IP traceroute (tracert with Windows) command-line utility to help us answer both questions because its output will show us every router interface a TCP/IP packet passes through on the way to its destination.

Traceroute (trace for short) displays the path a packet takes to get to a remote device in all its glory by using something we call IP packet time to live (TTL) time-outs and Internet Control Message Protocol (ICMP) error messages. And it's also a handy tool for troubleshooting an internetwork because we can use it to figure out which router along a path through that internetwork happens to be causing a network failure when a certain destination machine or network is, or suddenly becomes, unreachable.

To use tracert, at a Windows command prompt, type **tracert**, a space, and the Domain Name Service (DNS) name or IP address of the host machine to which you want to find the route. The tracert utility will respond with a list of all the DNS names and IP addresses of the routers that the packet is passing through on its way. Plus, tracert uses TTL to indicate the time it takes for each attempt.

Following is the tracert output from my workstation in Boulder, Colorado, to my Lammle.com server in Dallas, Texas:

```
C:\Users\tlammle>tracert www.lammle.com


Tracing route to lammle.com [206.123.114.186]
over a maximum of 30 hops:


  1     1 ms     <1 ms     <1 ms   dslmodem.domain.actdsltmp [192.168.0.1]
  2    53 ms     52 ms     52 ms   hlrn-dsl-gw36-228.hlrn.qwest.net
[207.225.112.228]
  3    52 ms     53 ms     52 ms   hlrn-agw1.inet.qwest.net [71.217.189.25]
  4    75 ms     75 ms     74 ms   dal-core-01.inet.qwest.net [67.14.2.53]
  5    76 ms     76 ms     76 ms   dap-brdr-01.inet.qwest.net [205.171.225.49]
  6    76 ms     76 ms     76 ms   205.171.1.110
  7    75 ms     76 ms    106 ms   xe-0-0-0.er2.dfw2.us.above.net [64.125.26.206]
  8    76 ms     76 ms     76 ms   209.249.122.74.available.above.net
[209.249.122.74]
  9    76 ms     76 ms     76 ms   65.99.248.250
 10    76 ms     76 ms     76 ms   pageuppro.pageuppro.com [206.123.114.186]
Trace complete.
```

Were you able to see that the packet bounces through several routers before arriving at its destination? Good! This utility is useful if you are having problems reaching a web server on the Internet and you want to know if a wide area network (WAN) link is down or if the server just isn't responding. What this means to you is that, basically, wherever the trace stops is a great place to start troubleshooting. No worries here, though—the previous output shows that every router is up and responding. Last, notice the ms in the output. This is the latency of each hop, meaning the delay. Tracert (or traceroute) is a great trouble-shooting tool you can use to find out where your network bottlenecks are.

If you use traceroute or tracert and receive an asterisk, this indicates that the attempt to reach that router took longer than the default time-out value. This is very good to know because it can mean that either the router is extremely busy or a particular link is slow. Another reason for getting an asterisk could be that the administrator has disabled ICMP on the router that the packet is trying to hop through.

Why would someone want to do that? For security reasons, that's why. It happens to be a typical strategic move done on the routers that interface with the ISP to conceal their actual location so bad guys can't hack into them and therefore into your internetwork. It's a good idea, and I highly recommend doing it.

If you are running traceroute and see repeating addresses and TTL time-outs, you probably have a routing loop.

In addition to traceroute and tracert, you can use pathping, which is a lot like traceroute:

```
C:\Users\Todd Lammle>pathping lammle.com
Tracing route to lammle.com [184.172.53.52]
over a maximum of 30 hops:
  0  WIN-Q14VTD8DH0G.localdomain [192.168.133.147]
  1  192.168.133.2
  2    *         *         *
Computing statistics for 25 seconds...
            Source to Here    This Node/Link
Hop  RTT     Lost/Sent = Pct  Lost/Sent = Pct  Address
  0                            WIN-Q14VTD8DH0G.localdomain [192.168.133.147]
                                 0/ 100 =  0%   |
  1   0ms     0/ 100 =  0%      0/ 100 =  0%  192.168.133.2

Trace complete.


C:\Users\Todd Lammle>
```

This provides a nice feedback at the end of the output.

In addition to traceroute and tracert, which show the path of an IPv4 packet, you can use tracert -6 for a Windows trace, traceroute6 for MAC and Linux/Unix, and traceroute -6 for Cisco routers to trace an IPv6 packet through an internetwork.

Using ipconfig, ifconfig, and ip

The utilities known as ipconfig (in Windows) and ifconfig/ip (in Unix/Linux/Mac) will display the current configuration of TCP/IP on a given workstation—including the current IP address, DNS configuration, configuration, and default gateway. In the following sections, I will show you how to use both.

Using the *ipconfig* Utility

With the new Mac, Windows 10, and Windows Server 2019 operating systems, you can now see the IPv6 configuration because IPv6 is enabled by default. The output of the ipconfig command provides the basic routed protocol information on your machine. From a DOS prompt, type **ipconfig**, and you'll see something like this:

```
C:\Users\tlammle>ipconfig
Windows IP Configuration
Ethernet adapter Local Area Connection:
    Connection-specific DNS Suffix  . : domain.actdsltmp
    Link-local IPv6 Address . . . . . : fe80::2836:c43e:274b:f08c%11
    IPv4 Address. . . . . . . . . . . : 192.168.0.6
    Subnet Mask . . . . . . . . . . . : 255.255.255.0
    Default Gateway . . . . . . . . . : 192.168.0.1

Wireless LAN adapter Wireless Network Connection:
    Connection-specific DNS Suffix  . : qwest.net
    Link-local IPv6 Address . . . . . : fe80::20e7:7fb8:8a00:832b%10
    IPv4 Address. . . . . . . . . . . : 10.0.1.198
    Subnet Mask . . . . . . . . . . . : 255.255.255.0
    Default Gateway . . . . . . . . . : fe80::21b:63ff:fef3:3694%10
                                        10.0.1.1

Tunnel adapter Local Area Connection* 6:
    Media State . . . . . . . . . . . : Media disconnected
    Connection-specific DNS Suffix  . :

Tunnel adapter Local Area Connection* 7:
    Media State . . . . . . . . . . . : Media disconnected
    Connection-specific DNS Suffix  . :
[output cut for brevity]
```

Wow, there sure are a lot of options in this output compared to the output for earlier versions of Windows! First, what's up with all these interfaces showing? I only have two—one

Ethernet and one wireless. You can see that my Ethernet adapter shows up first, and it has an IP address, a mask, and a default gateway plus an IPv6 address and a DNS suffix. The next configured interface is the wireless local area network (LAN) adapter, which has an IP address, a mask, a default gateway, an IPv6 address, and the IPv6 default gateway as well. This IPv6 default gateway address is simply my router advertising that it runs IPv6 and saying, "I am the way out of the local LAN!"

The next adapters are disconnected because they are logical interfaces and I'm not using them—my machine actually shows eight, but I cut the output because it provides no new information. They're automatically inserted because IPv6 is installed and running on my machine, and these adapters allow me to run IPv6 over an IPv4-only network.

But just in case the ipconfig command doesn't provide enough information for you, try the ipconfig /all command—talk about details. Here's the beginning of that output:

```
C:\Users\tlammle>ipconfig /all
Windows IP Configuration
    Host Name . . . . . . . . . . . . : globalnet-todd
    Primary Dns Suffix  . . . . . . . : globalnet.local
    Node Type . . . . . . . . . . . . : Hybrid
    IP Routing Enabled. . . . . . . . : No
    WINS Proxy Enabled. . . . . . . . : No
    DNS Suffix Search List. . . . . . : globalnet.local
                                        domain.actdsltmp
                                        qwest.net


Ethernet adapter Local Area Connection:
    Connection-specific DNS Suffix  . : domain.actdsltmp
    Description . . . . . . . . . . . : Intel(R) 82566MM Gigabit
Network Connection
    Physical Address. . . . . . . . . : 00-1E-37-D0-E9-35
    DHCP Enabled. . . . . . . . . . . : Yes
    Autoconfiguration Enabled . . . . : Yes
    Link-local IPv6 Address . . . . . : fe80::2836:c43e:274b:f08c%11(Preferred)
    IPv4 Address. . . . . . . . . . . : 192.168.0.6(Preferred)
    Subnet Mask . . . . . . . . . . . : 255.255.255.0
    Lease Obtained. . . . . . . . . . : Monday, October 20, 2008 9:08:36 AM
    Lease Expires . . . . . . . . . . : Tuesday, October 21, 2008 9:08:39 AM
    Default Gateway . . . . . . . . . : 192.168.0.1
    DHCP Server . . . . . . . . . . . : 192.168.0.1
    DNS Servers . . . . . . . . . . . : 192.168.0.1
                                        205.171.3.65
    NetBIOS over Tcpip. . . . . . . . : Enabled
```

```
Wireless LAN adapter Wireless Network Connection:
   Connection-specific DNS Suffix  . : qwest.net
   Description . . . . . . . . . . . : Intel(R) Wireless WiFi Link 4965AGN
   Physical Address. . . . . . . . . : 00-1F-3B-3F-4A-D9
   DHCP Enabled. . . . . . . . . . . : Yes
   Autoconfiguration Enabled . . . . : Yes
   Link-local IPv6 Address . . . . . : fe80::20e7:7fb8:8a00:832b%10(Preferred)
   IPv4 Address. . . . . . . . . . . : 10.0.1.198(Preferred)
   Subnet Mask . . . . . . . . . . . : 255.255.255.0
   Lease Obtained. . . . . . . . . . : Monday, October 20, 2008 10:43:53 AM
   Lease Expires . . . . . . . . . . : Monday, October 20, 2008 2:43:53 PM
   Default Gateway . . . . . . . . . : fe80::21b:63ff:fef3:3694%10
                                       10.0.1.1
   DHCP Server . . . . . . . . . . . : 10.0.1.1
   DNS Servers . . . . . . . . . . . : 10.0.1.1
   NetBIOS over Tcpip. . . . . . . . : Enabled

Tunnel adapter Local Area Connection* 6:
   Media State . . . . . . . . . . . : Media disconnected
   Connection-specific DNS Suffix  . :
   Description . . . . . . . . . . . : isatap.globalnet.local
   Physical Address. . . . . . . . . : 00-00-00-00-00-00-00-E0
   DHCP Enabled. . . . . . . . . . . : No
   Autoconfiguration Enabled . . . . : Yes

Tunnel adapter Local Area Connection* 7:
   Media State . . . . . . . . . . . : Media disconnected
   Connection-specific DNS Suffix  . :
   Description . . . . . . . . . . . : isatap.{9572A79F-3A58-4E9B-
9BD0-8F6FF2F058FC}
   Physical Address. . . . . . . . . : 00-00-00-00-00-00-00-E0
   DHCP Enabled. . . . . . . . . . . : No
   Autoconfiguration Enabled . . . . : Yes
[output cut]
```

As you can see, it's more of the same—a whole lot more. The most important thing I want you to notice is that I've received the hardware information about each interface, including the Media Access Control (MAC) address. Also significant is that I can see the Dynamic Host Configuration Protocol (DHCP) lease times and DNS addresses now.

But why stop here? There are two more valuable options you need to use with the ipconfig command. They are /release and /renew.

When you change networks, you need to get the IP address of that subnet and/or virtual LAN (VLAN). Windows 10 works most of the time without doing anything, but sometimes

I do have to renew the IP configuration when changing networks. But that's easy—just type **ipconfig /renew** from a command prompt, and if you're connected to a DHCP server that's available, you'll then magically receive an IP address.

Now, if it still doesn't work, you'll need to release and renew your TCP/IP settings. To release your current DHCP TCP/IP information, you must elevate your command prompt or you'll get this warning:

```
C:\Users\tlammle>ipconfig /release
The requested operation requires elevation.
C:\Users\tlammle>
```

Should this happen to you, left-click in the search box in the lower-left menu bar, then type in **command prompt**, right-click on the command prompt icon, and choose Run As Administrator. (Of course, you'll have to enter your name and password to do this if you are using Windows 10. But we love Windows 10, right? Okay, maybe not always.) Figure 25.4 shows how I did this.

Once your command prompt has been duly elevated, you can use the ipconfig /release command and then the ipconfig /renew command to get new TCP/IP information for your host.

FIGURE 25.4   Elevating your command prompt

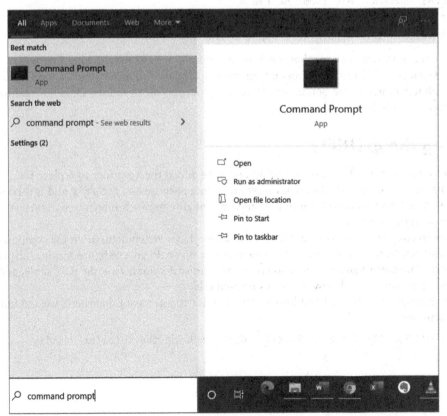

Using the *ifconfig* Utility

There is a utility in Linux/Unix/Mac that will give you information similar to what ipconfig shows. It's called ifconfig (short for *interface configuration*). Although ipconfig and ifconfig show similar information, there are major differences between these two utilities. The ipconfig utility is mainly used to view the TCP/IP configuration for a computer. You can use ifconfig to do the same thing, but ifconfig can also be used to configure a protocol or a particular network interface.

The general syntax of the ifconfig command is as follows:

```
ifconfig interface [address [parameters]]
```

The interface parameter equals the Unix name of the interface, such as eth0. If the optional address parameter is specified, the ifconfig command sets the IP address for the interface to the address you've specified. When the ifconfig command is used by itself with no parameters, all configured interfaces will be reported on. But if only the interface name is specified, you'll get output that looks like this:

```
# ifconfig eth0
eth0  Link encap 10Mbps Ethernet  HWaddr 00:00:C0:90:B3:42
inetaddr 172.16.0.2 Bcast 172.16.0.255 Mask 255.255.255.0 UP
BROADCAST RUNNING  MTU 1500  Metric 0
   RX packets 3136 errors 217 dropped 7 overrun 26
   TX packets 1752 errors 25 dropped 0 overrun 0
```

Looking at this, we can see that the eth0 interface is a 10 Mbps Ethernet interface. The interface's MAC and IP address information is displayed in this output as well. And, although not shown in the output, the ifconfig tool can show you the DNS information configured on the host.

Using the *ip* Utility

Newer versions of the Linux operating system have added the ip utility to replace the ifconfig command. This command serves the same purpose as ifconfig and is used to assign an address to a network interface and/or configure network interface parameters on Linux operating systems.

The ip command allows us to find out what interfaces are configured on the computer, view and configure their IP values, take an interface up or down, configure routing, display network status information, view and configure multicast values, view the ARP table, add or remove static routes, and view the host's routing table.

For example, to add the IP address of 192.168.1.1 to interface Ethenrnet0, use the following command:

```
#ip a add 192.168.1.1/255.255.255.0 dev eth0Using the iptables utility
```

Using the *iptables* Utility

While `iptables` is not part of the exam objectives, it is added here as it is an important Linux networking utility and good to be aware of. The `iptables` firewall utility is built for the Linux operating system. It is a command-line utility that uses what are called chains to allow or disallow traffic. When traffic arrives, `iptables` looks for a rule that addresses that traffic type, and if none exists, it will enforce the default rule. There are three different chain types:

- Input: Controls behavior for incoming connections
- Forward: Used for incoming connections that aren't being delivered locally (like a router would receive)
- Output: Used for outgoing connections

You can set the default action to accept, drop, or reject, with the difference between reject and drop being that reject sends an error message back to the source.

Examples of *iptables*

To block a connection from the device at 192.168.10.1, use this command:

```
iptables -A INPUT -s 192.168.10.1 -j DROP
```

To block all connections from all devices in the 172.16.0.0/16 network, use this command:

```
iptables -A INPUT -s 172.16.0.0/16 -j DROP
```

Here is the command to block SSH connections from 10.110.61.5:

```
iptables -A INPUT -p tcp --dport ssh -s 10.110.61.5 -j DROP
```

Use this command to block SSH connections from any IP address:

```
iptables -A INPUT -p tcp --dport ssh -j DROP
```

The following command is used to save the changes in Ubuntu:

```
sudo /sbin/iptables-save
```

In Red Hat/CentOS, use either of the following commands:

```
/sbin/service iptables save
/etc/init.d/iptables save
```

Using the *ping* Utility

The `ping` utility is the most basic TCP/IP utility, and it's included with most TCP/IP stacks for most platforms. Windows, again, is no exception. In most cases, `ping` is a command-line utility, although there are many GUI implementations available. You use the ping utility for two primary purposes:

- To find out if a host is responding
- To find out if you can reach a host

Here's the syntax (you can use either command):

```
ping hostname
ping IP address
```

If you ping any station that has an IP address, the ICMP that's part of that particular host's TCP/IP stack will respond to the request. The ICMP test and response looks something like this:

```
ping 204.153.163.2

Pinging 204.153.163.2 with 32 bytes of data:

Reply from 204.153.163.2: bytes=32 time<10ms TTL=128
Reply from 204.153.163.2: bytes=32 time=1ms TTL=128
Reply from 204.153.163.2: bytes=32 time<10ms TTL=128
Reply from 204.153.163.2: bytes=32 time<10ms TTL=128
```

Because I've received a reply from the destination station (204.153.163.2, in this case), I know that I can reach the host and that it's responding to basic IP requests. Don't forget that you can use name resolution and ping to a name, such as ping www.sybex.com, and as long as that name can be resolved, you're golden.

Most versions of ping work the same way, but there are some switches you can use to specify certain information, like the number of packets to send, how big a packet to send, and so on. And if you're running the Windows command-line version of ping, just use the /? or -? switch to display a list of the available options like this:

```
C:\Users\tlammle>ping /?

Usage: ping [-t] [-a] [-n count] [-l size] [-f] [-i TTL] [-v TOS]
            [-r count] [-s count] [[-j host-list] | [-k host-list]]
            [-w timeout] [-R] [-S srcaddr] [-4] [-6] target_name
```

The command will also output a table showing what each of the options does, presented here in Table 25.1.

NOTE   You can ping your local TCP/IP interface by typing **ping 127.0.0.1** or **ping localhost**. Understand that both addresses represent the local interface. Really, you can use any address in the 127.0.0.0 network range to provide a loopback test.

TABLE 25.1   Options for ping switches

Option	Description
-t	Pings the specified host until stopped. To see statistics and continue, press Ctrl+Break; to stop, press Ctrl+C.
-a	Resolves addresses to hostnames.
-n *count*	Specifies the number of echo requests to send.
-l *size*	Sends the buffer size.
-f	Sets the Don't Fragment flag in the packet (IPv4 only).
-i *TTL*	Specifies the time to live of the packet.
-v *TOS*	Specifies the type of service (IPv4 only).
-r *count*	Records the route for count hops (IPv4 only).
-s *count*	Specifies the time stamp for count hops (IPv4 only).
-j *host-list*	Uses a loose source route along the host list (IPv4 only).
-k *host-list*	Uses a strict source route along the host list (IPv4 only).
-w *timeout*	Specifies the time-out to wait for each reply in milliseconds.
-R	Uses the routing header to test the reverse route also (IPv6 only).
-S *srcaddr*	Specifies the source address to use.
-4	Forces using IPv4.
-6	Forces using IPv6.

As you can see, there's a plethora of options you can use with the ping command from a Windows DOS prompt. But I really want you to focus on a few from the previous output. (I'm going to go over only a few of them, but you can get on your host machine and play with all the options.)

The –a switch is very cool because if you have name resolution (such as a DNS server), you can see the name of the destination host even if you only know its IP address. The –n switch sets the number of echo requests to send, where four is the default, and the –w switch allows you to adjust the time-out in milliseconds. The default ping time-out is 1 second (1,000 ms).

The −6 is also nice if you want to ping an IPv6 host. By the way, unless you really love typing 128-bit addresses, this is a wonderful example of how important name resolution is. And then there's −t, which keeps the ping running. Here's an example of a ping to an IPv6 address:

```
C:\Users\tlammle>ping -6 fe80::1063:16af:3f57:fff9

Pinging fe80::1063:16af:3f57:fff9 from fe80::1063:16af:3f57:fff9%25
with 32 bytes of data:
Reply from fe80::1063:16af:3f57:fff9: time<1ms
Reply from fe80::1063:16af:3f57:fff9: time<1ms
Reply from fe80::1063:16af:3f57:fff9: time<1ms
Reply from fe80::1063:16af:3f57:fff9: time<1ms

Ping statistics for fe80::1063:16af:3f57:fff9:
Packets: Sent = 4, Received = 4, Lost = 0 (0% loss),
Approximate round trip times in milli-seconds:
Minimum = 0ms, Maximum = 0ms, Average = 0ms
C:\Users\tlammle>
```

From a MAC, you can use the ping6 command. Here are the options:

```
$ ping6
usage: ping6 [-DdfHmnNoqrRtvwW] [-a addrtype] [-b bufsiz] [-B boundif]
[-c count][-g gateway] [-h hoplimit] [-I interface] [-i wait] [-l preload]
[-p pattern] [-S sourceaddr] [-s packetsize] [-z tclass]
[hops ...] host
```

And if I want to have a continuous ping, I just use that −t option like this:

```
C:\Users\tlammle>ping -t 192.168.0.1

Pinging 192.168.0.1 with 32 bytes of data:
Reply from 192.168.0.1: bytes=32 time=7ms TTL=255
Reply from 192.168.0.1: bytes=32 time=1ms TTL=255
Reply from 192.168.0.1: bytes=32 time=1ms TTL=255
Reply from 192.168.0.1: bytes=32 time=1ms TTL=255
Reply from 192.168.0.1: bytes=32 time=1ms TTL=255
Reply from 192.168.0.1: bytes=32 time=1ms TTL=255

Ping statistics for 192.168.0.1:
Packets: Sent = 6, Received = 6, Lost = 0 (0% loss),
Approximate round trip times in milli-seconds:
Minimum = 1ms, Maximum = 7ms, Average = 2ms
```

```
Control-C
^C
C:\Users\tlammle>
```

This ping will just keep going and going like the Energizer Bunny until you press Ctrl+C. And by the way, it's an awesome tool for troubleshooting links.

Using the Address Resolution Protocol

The *Address Resolution Protocol (ARP)* is part of the TCP/IP protocol stack. It's used to translate TCP/IP addresses to MAC addresses using broadcasts. When a machine running TCP/IP wants to know which machine on an Ethernet network is using a certain IP address, it will send an ARP broadcast that says, in effect, "Hey . . . exactly who is IP address xxx. xxx.xxx.xxx?" The machine that owns the specific address will respond with its own MAC address, supplying the answer. The machine that made the inquiry will respond by adding the newly gained information to its own ARP table.

In addition to the normal usage, the ARP designation refers to a utility in Windows that you can use to manipulate and view the local workstation's ARP table.

The Windows ARP Table

The *ARP table* in Windows includes a list of TCP/IP addresses and their associated physical (MAC) addresses. This table is cached in memory so that Windows doesn't have to perform ARP lookups for frequently accessed TCP/IP addresses like those of servers and default gateways. Each entry contains an IP address and a MAC address plus a value for TTL that determines how long each entry will remain in the ARP table.

Remember that the ARP table contains two kinds of entries:

- Dynamic
- Static

Dynamic ARP table entries are created whenever the Windows TCP/IP stack performs an ARP lookup but the MAC address isn't found in the ARP table. When the MAC address of the requested IP address is finally found, or *resolved*, that information is then added into the ARP table as a dynamic entry. Whenever a request to send a packet to the host is sent to the Data Link layer, the ARP cache is checked first before an ARP broadcast is sent out. Remember, the ARP request is broadcast on the local segment—it does not go through a router.

   The ARP table is cleared of dynamic entries whose TTL has expired to ensure that the entries are current.

Static ARP table entries serve the same function as dynamic entries but are made manually using the arp utility.

Using the *arp* Utility

You now know that ARP is a protocol included in the TCP/IP suite. You also understand that ARP is used by IP to determine the MAC address of a device that exists on the same subnet as the requesting device. When a TCP/IP device needs to forward a packet to a device on the local subnet, it first looks in its own table, called an *ARP cache* or *MAC address lookup table*, for an association between the known IP address of the destination device on the local subnet and that same device's MAC address. The cache is called that because the contents are periodically weeded out.

If no association that includes the destination IP address can be found, the device will then send out an ARP broadcast that includes its own MAC and IP information as well as the IP address of the target device and a blank MAC address field. Filling in that blank is the object of the whole operation—it's the unknown value that the source device is requesting to be returned to it in the form of an ARP reply. Windows includes a utility called arp that allows us to check out the operating system's ARP cache. To view this, from a Windows DOS prompt, use the arp command like this:

```
C:\Users\tlammle>arp

Displays and modifies the IP-to-Physical address translation tables used
by address resolution protocol (ARP).

ARP -s inet_addr eth_addr [if_addr]
ARP -d inet_addr [if_addr]
ARP -a [inet_addr] [-N if_addr] [-v]
```

Table 25.2 describes the various options that you can use with the arp command.

Sheesh. Looking at that output really makes me wish we were all just running IPv6 because, as you already should know, IPv6 doesn't need ARP as well as many other annoying features and protocols required when running IPv4.

Of note, the Windows arp utility is primarily useful for resolving duplicate IP addresses. For example, let's say your workstation receives its IP address from a DHCP server but it accidentally receives the same address that some other workstation gets. And so, when you try to ping it, you get no response. Your workstation is basically confused—it's trying to determine the MAC address, and it can't because two machines are reporting that they have the same IP address. To solve this little snag, you can use the arp utility to view your local ARP table and see which TCP/IP address is resolved to which MAC address.

TABLE 25.2 arp options

Option	Description
-a	Displays current ARP entries by interrogating the current protocol data. If `inet_addr` is specified, the IP and physical addresses for only the specified computer are displayed. If more than one network interface uses ARP, entries for each ARP table are displayed.
-g	Same as -a.
-v	Displays current ARP entries in verbose mode. All invalid entries and entries on the loopback interface will be shown.
inet_addr	Specifies an Internet address.
-N	Displays the ARP entries for the network interface specified by `if_addr`.
-d	Deletes the host specified by `inet_addr`. `inet_addr` may be wildcarded with * to delete all hosts.
-s	Adds the host and associates the Internet address `inet_addr` with the physical address `eth_addr`. The physical address is given as six hexadecimal bytes separated by hyphens. The entry is permanent.
eth_addr	Specifies a physical address.
if_addr	If present, specifies the Internet address of the interface whose address translation table should be modified. If not present, the first applicable interface will be used.

To display the entire current ARP table, use the `arp` command with the –a switch like so to show you the MAC address lookup table:

```
C:\Users\tlammle>arp -a

Interface: 192.168.0.6 --- 0xb
Internet Address        Physical Address      Type
192.168.0.1             00-15-05-06-31-b0     dynamic
192.168.0.255           ff-ff-ff-ff-ff-ff     static
224.0.0.22              01-00-5e-00-00-16     static
224.0.0.252             01-00-5e-00-00-fc     static
239.255.255.250         01-00-5e-7f-ff-fa     static
255.255.255.255         ff-ff-ff-ff-ff-ff     static
```

```
Interface: 10.100.10.54 --- 0x10
Internet Address      Physical Address      Type
10.100.10.1           00-15-05-06-31-b0     dynamic
10.100.10.255         ff-ff-ff-ff-ff-ff     static
224.0.0.22            01-00-5e-00-00-16     static
224.0.0.252           01-00-5e-00-00-fc     static
239.255.255.250       01-00-5e-7f-ff-fa     static
```

 By the way, the –g switch will produce the same result.

Now, from this output, you can tell which MAC address is assigned to which IP address. Then, for static assignments, you can tell which workstation has a specific IP address and if it's indeed supposed to have that address by examining your network documentation—you do have that record, right?

For DHCP-assigned addresses, you can begin to uncover problems stemming from multiple DHCP scopes or servers doling out identical addresses and other common configuration issues. And remember that under normal circumstances, you shouldn't see IP addresses in the ARP table that aren't members of the same IP subnet as the interface.

 If the machine has more than one network card (as may happen in Windows servers and on laptops with both Ethernet and wireless cards), each interface will be listed separately.

It's good to know that in addition to displaying the ARP table, you can use the arp utility to manipulate the table itself. To add static entries to the ARP table, you use the arp command with the –s switch. These static entries will stay in the ARP table until the machine is rebooted. A static entry essentially hardwires a specific IP address to a specific MAC address so that when a packet needs to be sent to that IP address, it will automatically be sent to that MAC address. Here's the syntax:

```
arp -s [IP Address] [MAC Address]
```

Simply replace the [IP Address] and [MAC Address] sections with the appropriate entries, like so:

```
arp -s 204.153.163.5 00-a0-c0-ab-c3-11
```

Now, take a look at your new ARP table by using the arp -a command. You should see something like this:

```
Internet Address      Physical Address      Type
204.153.163.5         00-a0-c0-ab-c3-11     static
```

Finally, if you want to delete entries from the ARP table, you can either wait until the dynamic entries time out or use the –d switch with the IP address of the static entry you'd like to delete, like this:

```
arp -d 204.153.163.5
```

Doing so effectively deletes the entry from the ARP table in memory.

> The arp utility doesn't confirm successful additions or deletions (use arp -a or arp -g for that), but it will give you an error message if you use incorrect syntax.

Using the *nslookup* Utility

Whenever you're configuring a server or a workstation to connect to the Internet, you've got to start by configuring DNS if you want name resolution to happen (that is, if you want to be able to type **www.sybex.com** instead of an IP address). When configuring DNS, it's a very good thing to be able to test what IP address DNS is returning to ensure that it's working properly. The nslookup utility allows you to query a name server and quickly find out which name resolves to which IP address.

> The Linux/Unix dig (short for *domain information groper*) utility does the exact same thing as nslookup. It's primarily a command-line utility that allows you to perform a single DNS lookup for a specific entity, but it can also be employed in batch mode for a series of lookups. Detailed information on this command is beyond the scope of this study guide, but you can find more information on the Web by searching for "unix dig."

The nslookup utility comes with Windows 10 as well as with most versions of Unix and Linux. You can run it from a Windows command prompt. At the command prompt, you can start the nslookup utility by typing **nslookup** and pressing Enter. When you're inside this utility, the command prompt will change from something similar to a C:\> sign to a shorter > sign. It will also display the name and IP address of the default DNS server you will be querying (you can change it, if necessary). Then you can start using nslookup. The following output gives you a sample of the display after the nslookup command has been entered at the C:\> prompt.

```
C:\Users\tlammle>nslookup
Default Server:  gnt-corpdc1.globalnet.local
Address:  10.100.36.12

>
```

The primary job of nslookup is to tell you the many different features of a particular domain name, the names of the servers that serve it, and how they're configured. To get that, just type in a domain name at the > prompt, and the nslookup utility will then return this information:

```
> lammle.com
Server:   dslmodem.domain.actdsltmp
Address:  192.168.0.1
```

The non-authoritative answer is as follows:

```
Name:     lammle.com
Address:  206.123.114.186
```

What this tells you is that the server that returned the information is not responsible (authoritative) for the zone information of the domain for which you requested an address and that the name server for the domain lammle.com is located at the IP address 206.123.114.186.

You can also ask nslookup for other information by setting a different option within nslookup. Just type **set option** at the > prompt and replace option with the actual option you want to use—for example, use >set type=mx to determine the IP address of your email server. If you can't decide which one you want, use the question mark (?) at the greater than sign (>) to see all available options.

If you type in **nslookup** and receive this reply,

```
NS request timed out.
    timeout was 2 seconds.
***Can't find server name for address 206.123.114.186: Timed out
Default Server:  UnKnown
Address:  fec0:0:0:ffff::1
```

then you know your DNS servers are not answering. You need to get over to the DNS server, stat!

Resolving Names with the Hosts File

The hosts file is really a lot like DNS, except its entries are static for each and every host and server. Within the Hosts table, you'll find a collection of hostnames that devices reference for name-resolution purposes. And even though it works in both IPv4 and IPv6 environments, it's unlikely you will use it these days because the hosts file is a way-ancient relic left over from old Unix machines.

But just because it belongs in a museum, that doesn't mean you won't run into it now and then, which is the main reason I'm showing it to you. You can find the Hosts table in C:\ Windows\System32\drivers\etc. Just double-click the file, and then choose to open the file in Notepad or another text editor. Here's the default information—it's really nothing more than an explanation of how to use it and the local hosts for both IP and IPv6:

```
# Copyright (c) 1993-2006 Microsoft Corp.
#
```

```
# This is a sample HOSTS file used by Microsoft TCP/IP for Windows.
#
# This file contains the mappings of IP addresses to host names. Each
# entry should be kept on an individual line. The IP address should
# be placed in the first column followed by the corresponding host name.
# The IP address and the host name should be separated by at least one
# space.
#
# Additionally, comments (such as these) may be inserted on individual
# lines or following the machine name denoted by a '#' symbol.
#
# For example:
#
#      102.54.94.97      rhino.acme.com          # source server
#       38.25.63.10      x.acme.com              # x client host

127.0.0.1       localhost
::1             localhost
```

 Any information entered to the right of a pound sign (#) in a hosts file is ignored, so you can use this space for comments.

Because it's a plain ASCII text file, you add the IP address under the local hosts and then the name to which you want to resolve the IP address. It's a pretty simple configuration, and again, one I don't recommend using because you have to type in the names of every host on every machine in your network. DNS is definitely the name resolution of choice for networks today.

 Do not get the hosts file confused with the hostname command. The hostname command doesn't do much but display the name of your host, as shown here:

```
C:\Users\tlammle>hostname /?

Prints the name of the current host.

hostname

C:\Users\tlammle>hostname
globalnet-todd
```

Using the *Mtr* Command *(pathping)*

Mtr, or My traceroute, is a computer program that combines the functions of the traceroute and ping utilities in a single network diagnostic tool. It also adds round-trip time and packet loss to the output—very cool.

Mtr probes routers on the route path by limiting the number of hops individual packets are allowed to traverse and listening to news of their termination. It will regularly repeat this process (usually once per second) and keep track of the response times of the hops along the path.

Mtr is great if you have Linux or Unix, but by default, it's not installed on Windows devices. Third-party applications of Mtr are available to install on Windows, but Microsoft did respond with its own version of Mtr—it's called pathping and it provides the same functions as Mtr. Here's a look at the output and the options:

C:\Users\tlammle>**pathping**

```
Usage: pathping [-g host-list] [-h maximum_hops] [-i address] [-n]
                [-p period] [-q num_queries] [-w timeout]
                [-4] [-6] target_name
```

Table 25.3 lists the options of the Windows pathping command.

TABLE 25.3   pathping options

Option	Description
-g host-list	Uses a loose source route along the host list.
-h maximum_hops	Specifies the maximum number of hops to search for the target.
-i address	Uses the specified source address.
-n	Does not resolve addresses to hostnames.
-p period	Waits period milliseconds between pings.
-q num_queries	Specifies the number of queries per hop.
-w timeout	Waits timeout milliseconds for each reply.
-4	Forces using IPv4.
-6	Forces using IPv6.

The Mtr utility is basically the same as traceroute and ping, but it does give you some additional output that can help you troubleshoot your network.

Using the Nmap Utility

Nmap is one of the most popular port scanning tools used today. After performing scans with certain flags set in the scan packets, security analysts (and hackers) can make certain assumptions based on the responses received. These flags are used to control the TCP connection process and so are present only in TCP packets. Figure 25.5 shows a TCP header with the important flags circled. Normally flags are "turned on" because of the normal TCP process, but hackers can craft packets to check the flags they want to check.

FIGURE 25.5   TCP flags

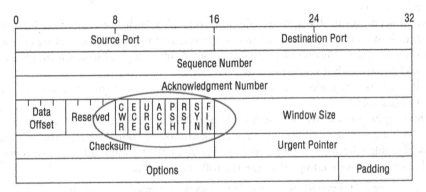

Figure 25.5 shows these flags, among others:

- URG: Urgent pointer field significant
- ACK: Acknowledgment field significant
- PSH: Push function
- RST: Reset the connection
- SYN: Synchronize sequence numbers
- FIN: No more data from sender

While application of a scan and interpretation of the responses are beyond the scope of this book, security analysts and hackers alike can perform scans with these flags set in the scan packets to get responses that allow them to determine the following information:

- If a port is open on a device
- If the port is blocked by a firewall before it gets to the device

Nmap can also be used as follows:

- To determine the live hosts on a network
- To create a logical "map" of the network

Using the *route* Command

I went over static routing in Chapter 9, "Introduction to IP Routing," so you know that Windows devices like routers perform routing. Most of the time, it's a good idea to leave Windows alone, but it's still good to know how to add and delete routes on your Windows machines.

Probably the biggest reason for manipulating the routing table on a Windows server is to create a firewall. For instance, let's say we're running an Application layer firewall on a Windows server located between a screen subnet, formerly known as a demilitarized zone (DMZ), and the internal network. This scenario would mean the routing that's happening on the server or hosts located in the DMZ wouldn't be able to reach the internal network's hosts and vice versa.

To circumvent this problem, we would need to employ both static and default routing because while Windows 10 and Windows Server versions support some routing protocols, running routing protocols on hosts and servers wouldn't be a good solution for today's networks, and Microsoft knows that.

To view the routing table on a Windows device, use the `route print` command, as shown in Figure 25.6.

In this output, you can see that each of the routes were added automatically when the system booted up. (This is all based on the configuration of your IP stack.) To see all the options available with the `route` command, type the `route` command and then press Enter. To add a route to your routing table, use the following syntax:

route [**-f**] [**-p**] [Command [*Destination*] [**mask** *Netmask*] [Gateway]
[**metric** *Metric*]] [**if** *Interface*]]

Using the *route* Command Options

Let's start with the switches you can use:

-f   Using this switch with any of the options like add, change, or delete will clear the routing table of all entries that aren't host routes (routes with the subnet mask 255.255.255.255), the loopback network route or routes (routes with a destination of 127.0.0.0 and the subnet mask 255.0.0.0), and any multicast routes (those with a destination of 224.0.0.0 and the subnet mask 240.0.0.0).

FIGURE 25.6   route print output

-p   If you use this with the add command, the individual route will be added to the Registry and then used to initialize the IP routing table whenever TCP/IP is started. Important to remember that by default, the routes you've statically added won't remain in the routing table the next time TCP/IP boots. And if you use -p with the print command, you'll get shown a list of the persistent routes that are stored in the Registry location of HKEY_LOCAL_MACHINE\SYSTEM\CurrentControlSet\Services\ Tcpip\Parameters\PersistentRoutes.

Now, let's take a look at how and when you would use the route command. Table 25.4 shows the command options available and what they do when you are using the route command with them.

TABLE 25.4   route command options

Command	Purpose
add	Adds a route
change	Modifies an existing route
delete	Deletes a route (or routes)
print	Prints a route (or routes)

Here's a description of some other tasks you can accomplish via the rest of the command's options:

Destination   This will give you the network destination of a given route. If the host bits of the network address are set to 0, it will be depicted with the destination's IP network address, an IP address for a specific host route, or the default route of 0.0.0.0.

mask *netmask*   This will provide you with the *netmask*—often referred to as the *subnet mask*—that's associated with the destination network. The default destination subnet mask is 0.0.0.0, and typically you'll see 255.255.255.255 representing a host route. It's really important to remember that the destination address can't be more specific than its corresponding subnet mask. What I'm saying is that there absolutely can't be a bit set to 1 in the destination address if the equivalent bit in the subnet mask is a 0.

Gateway   The gateway also depends on the network address and subnet mask, but it's even more specific and delimits what's called the *next-hop IP address*. For routes located on a local subnet, the gateway address maps directly to a particular interface. If the destination is on a remote network, the gateway IP address will direct packets to the neighboring router.

metric *metric*   Metric refers to the cost of a given route from the sending to the receiving device, and it's a value between 1 and 9999. Devices use this value to choose the best, or most efficient, routes among those in its routing table—the route with the lowest value wins. This decision can also include factors like the number of hops and the speed, reliability, and available bandwidth of the path being considered plus the various administrative aspects associated with it.

if *interface*   This tool depends on information from the gateway address and determines the interface index for the specific interface that needs to receive the data. You can get a list of interfaces along with their relevant interface indexes by typing the route print command.

/?   Using this will allow you to view help at the command prompt.

Some Examples of the *route* Command

Even though the finer points of the `route` command demand that you use caution when deploying some of the options, I'll still list the basics of the `route` command because it can be really useful. I highly recommend that you spend some time practicing them on a non-production server, though—especially at first.

- To display the entire IP routing table, type **route print**.
- To add a default route with the default gateway address 192.168.10.1, type **route add 0.0.0.0 mask 0.0.0.0 192.168.10.1**.
- To add a route to the destination 10.1.1.0 with the subnet mask 255.255.255.0 and the next-hop address 10.2.2.2, type **route add 10.1.1.0 mask 255.255.255.0 10.2.2.2**.
- If you want to, let's say, add a persistent route to the destination 10.100.0.0 with the subnet mask 255.255.0.0 and the next-hop address 10.2.0.1, type **route -p add 10.100.0.0 mask 255.255.0.0 10.2.0.1**. If you want to delete the route to the destination 10.100.0.0 with the subnet mask 255.255.0.0, enter **route delete 10.100.0.0 mask 255.255.0.0**.
- And finally, if you want to change the next-hop address of a route with the destination 10.100.0.0 and the subnet mask 255.255.0.0 from 10.2.0.1 to 10.7.0.5, type **route change 10.100.0.0 mask 255.255.0.0 10.7.0.5**.

Let's move on to some other important Windows utilities.

Using the *nbtstat* Utility

Microsoft Windows uses an interface called Network Basic Input/Output System (NetBIOS), which relates names with workstations and is an upper-layer interface that requires a transport protocol—usually TCP/IP. But IPv6 can be used as well. Deploying the `nbtstat` utility will achieve these three important things:

- Track NetBIOS over TCP/IP statistics
- Show the details of incoming and outgoing NetBIOS over TCP/IP connections
- Resolve NetBIOS names

Understand that because NetBIOS name resolution is primarily a Windows network utility, the `nbtstat` command is available only in Windows-based operating systems.

To display a basic description of `nbtstat` and its associated options, type **nbtstat** at the command line. Then, use these options to get a display of information about NetBIOS over TCP/IP hosts. Here are some of the tools, or *switches*, you can use:

-a	-A
-c	-n
-r	-R
-S	-s

All nbtstat switches are case sensitive. Generally speaking, lowercase switches deal with NetBIOS names of hosts, and the uppercase ones deal with the TCP/IP addresses of hosts.

The –*a* Switch

Making use of the –a switch will get you a remote machine's NetBIOS name table consisting of a list of every NetBIOS name the machine from which you've deployed the switch knows of. The –a switch produced the output from server S1 shown in Figure 25.7.

So, using this switch arranges the NetBIOS name-table information in table form with output in four columns. The Name column displays the NetBIOS name entry for the remote host machine.

FIGURE 25.7   Sample output of the nbtstat –a command

```
C:\>nbtstat -a s1


    NetBIOS Remote Machine Name Table

    Name                Type       Status
    ------------------------------------------
    S1              <20> UNIQUE    Registered
    S1              <00> UNIQUE    Registered
    ACME            <00> GROUP     Registered
    ACME            <1C> GROUP     Registered
    ACME            <1B> UNIQUE    Registered
    S1              <03> UNIQUE    Registered
    ACME            <1E> GROUP     Registered
    ACME            <1D> UNIQUE    Registered
    .._MSBROWSE__.<01> GROUP       Registered
    INet~Services   <1C> GROUP     Registered
    IS~S1.............. <00> UNIQUE    Registered

    MAC Address = 00-A0-C9-D4-BC-DC
```

The next column gives you a unique two-digit hexadecimal identifier for the NetBIOS name. This identifier represents the last byte of the NetBIOS name depicted in the Name column, and it's important because the same name could actually be used several times for the same machine. Plus, it identifies the specific service on the particular host that the name is referencing. Table 25.5 and Table 25.6 list the hexadecimal identifiers for unique and group hostnames.

The Type column refers to (surprise) the type of NetBIOS name being referenced. Unique NetBIOS names refer to individual hosts, and group names refer to logical groupings of workstations—either domains or workgroups.

The Status column gives you information about the status of a host's NetBIOS even if it hasn't been registered with the rest of the network.

TABLE 25.5   Last-byte identifiers for unique names

Hex ID	Description
00	General name for the computer.
03	Messenger service ID used to send messages between a WINS server and a workstation. This is the ID registered with a WINS server.
06	Remote Access Server (RAS) server service ID.
20	File-serving service ID.
21	RAS client.
53	DNS.
123	Network Time Protocol (NTP).
1B	Domain master browser ID. A NetBIOS name with this ID indicates the domain master browser.
1F	Network Dynamic Data Exchange (NetDDE) service ID.
BE	Network monitor agent ID.
BF	Network monitor utility ID.

TABLE 25.6   Last-byte identifiers for group names

Hex ID	Description
01	Master browser for a domain to other master browsers.
20	Internet group name ID. This ID is registered with the WINS server to indicate which computers are used for administrative purposes.
1C	Domain group name ID.
1D	Master browser name.
1E	Normal group name.

The –*A* Switch

The -A switch works just like the -a switch and will give you the same output, but the syntax of the command is different. Obviously, you use an uppercase A instead of a lowercase one, and you also have to include the host's IP address instead of its NetBIOS name. To use it, type **nbtstat** followed by **-A** and finally the IP address of the specific host whose NetBIOS table you want to check out:

nbtstat -A 199.153.163.2

The –*c* Switch

Use the -c switch to display the local NetBIOS name cache on the workstation it's running on. Figure 25.8 shows sample output of the *nbtstat* -c command.

FIGURE 25.8   Sample output of the nbtstat -c command

```
Node IpAddress: [204.153.163.4] Scope Id: []

             NetBIOS Remote Cache Name Table

     Name               Type       Host Address    Life [sec]
    ----------------------------------------------------------
    S1              <00>  UNIQUE      204.153.163.2      420
```

Each entry in this display shows the NetBIOS name, the hex ID for the service that was accessed, the type of NetBIOS name (unique or group), the IP address that the name resolves to, and its life. The Life value shows how many seconds each entry will live in the cache. When this time expires, the entry will be deleted.

Sometimes, deploying nbtstat to display the cache will get you the response "No names in the cache" because all entries in the cache have expired. This is what happens if you don't regularly access machines or services with NetBIOS names.

The –*n* Switch

The -n switch will give you the local NetBIOS name table on a Windows device. Figure 25.9 shows output that's similar to the output of the -a switch except for one important thing: What you're seeing is the NetBIOS name table for the machine you're running the command on instead of that of another host. Check it out.

FIGURE 25.9   Sample output of the nbtstat −n command

```
C:\NBTSTAT -n

Node IpAddress: [204.153.163.4] Scope Id: []

           NetBIOS Local Name Table

   Name              Type        Status
---------------------------------------------
DEFAULT        <00>  UNIQUE      Registered
WORKGROUP      <00>  GROUP       Registered
DEFAULT        <03>  UNIQUE      Registered
DEFAULT        <20>  UNIQUE      Registered
WORKGROUP      <1E>  GROUP       Registered
WORKGROUP      <1D>  UNIQUE      Registered
..__MSBROWSE__.<01>  GROUP       Registered
ADMINISTRATOR  <03>  UNIQUE      Registered
```

The −r Switch

This switch is probably the one you'll use most often when you want to get a hold of
NetBIOS over TCP/IP (NBT) statistics because it tells you exactly how many NetBIOS
names have been resolved to TCP/IP addresses. Figure 25.10 shows sample output of the
nbtstat −r command.

What you can see here is that the statistics are divided into two categories. First, there
are the NetBIOS names resolution and registration statistics. This is how many names have
been resolved or registered either by broadcasts on the local segment or via lookup from a
DNS server.

Next you have the NetBIOS unique and group names and their associated hex IDs
that were resolved or registered. In Figure 25.10, you can see that there's a distinct lack of
information regarding names resolved by a name server. What this means is that the output
is telling you that there's no WINS server operating—instead, all NetBIOS names were
resolved by broadcast only.

FIGURE 25.10   Sample output of the nbtstat −r command

```
C:\>nbtstat -r


NetBIOS Names Resolution and Registration Statistics
------------------------------------------------------------

Resolved By Broadcast     = 2
Resolved By Name Server   = 0

Registered By Broadcast   = 12
Registered By Name Server = 0

    NetBIOS Names Resolved By Broadcast
------------------------------------------------------
     ACME             <1B>
     ACME             <00>
```

The –r switch comes in handy when you want to determine how a work-station is resolving DNS names and whether DNS is configured correctly. If DNS isn't configured correctly or it's simply not being used, the numbers in the Resolved By Name Server and Registered By Name Server categories will always be zero.

The –*R* Switch

Unlike the –a and –A switches, –r and –R use the same letter but do *not* have anything in common.

Here's an example. Let's say you have a bad name in the NetBIOS name cache but the right name is in the LMHOSTS file instead. (The LMHOSTS file contains NetBIOS names of stations and their associated IP addresses.) Because the cache is consulted before the LMHOSTS file is, that bad address will remain in the cache until it expires.

This command is used when you want to purge the NetBIOS name table cache and reload the LMHOSTS file into memory. You do that by using the nbtstat command with the –R switch, like so:

```
nbtstat -R
```

You can practice this nbtstat -R command on your host to purge the NBT remote cache table.

The –*S* Switch

Using the –S switch will display the NetBIOS sessions table that lists all NetBIOS sessions to and from the host from which you issued the command. The –S switch displays both work-station and server sessions but lists remote addresses by IP address only.

Figure 25.11 shows sample output of the nbtstat -S command.

FIGURE 25.11   Sample output of the nbtstat -S command

```
C:\NBTSTAT -S

                NetBIOS Connection Table
Local Name          State      In/Out  Remote Host        Input    Output
-------------------------------------------------------------------------
S1          <00>  Connected    Out     204.153.163.4      256B     432B
S1          <03>  Listening
```

Here you can see the NetBIOS name being displayed along with its hex ID and the status of each session. An entry in the In/Out column determines whether the connection has been initiated from the computer on which you're running nbtstat (outbound) or whether another computer has initiated the connection (inbound). The numbers in the Input and Output columns indicate in bytes the amount of data transferred between the stations.

The –s Switch

As with the –A and –a switches, the lowercase –s switch is similar to its uppercase sibling. The nbtstat -s command produces the same output as nbtstat -S except that it will also attempt to resolve remote-host IP addresses into hostnames. Figure 25.12 shows sample output from the nbtstat -s command.

FIGURE 25.12   Sample output of the nbtstat -s command

```
C:\NBTSTAT -s

           NetBIOS Connection Table

Local Name          State    In/Out  Remote Host          Input   Output
----------------------------------------------------------------------
S1         <00>  Connected  Out     DEFAULT     <20>    256B    432B
S1         <03>  Listening
```

Note the similarities between Figure 25.11 and Figure 25.12.

As with the netstat command, with the nbtstat command you can place a number for an interval at the end to direct it to deploy once every so many seconds until you press Ctrl+C.

Using the *netstat* Utility

Using netstat is a great way to check out the inbound and outbound TCP/IP connections on your machine. You can also use it to view packet statistics like how many packets have been sent and received, the number of errors, and so on.

When used without any options, netstat produces output similar to the following, which shows all the outbound TCP/IP connections. This utility is a great tool to use to determine the status of outbound web connections. Take a look:

```
C:\Users\tlammle>netstat


Active Connections

  Proto  Local Address          Foreign Address        State
  TCP    10.100.10.54:49545     gnt-exchange:epmap     TIME_WAIT
  TCP    10.100.10.54:49548     gnt-exchange:epmap     TIME_WAIT
  TCP    10.100.10.54:49551     gnt-exchange:1151      ESTABLISHED
  TCP    10.100.10.54:49557     gnt-exchange:1026      ESTABLISHED
  TCP    10.100.10.54:49590     gnt-exchange:epmap     TIME_WAIT
```

```
TCP    127.0.0.1:49174        globalnet-todd:62514    ESTABLISHED
TCP    127.0.0.1:62514        globalnet-todd:49174    ESTABLISHED
TCP    192.168.0.6:2492       blugro2relay:2492       ESTABLISHED
TCP    192.168.0.6:2492       blugro3relay:2492       ESTABLISHED
TCP    192.168.0.6:49170      64.12.25.26:5190        ESTABLISHED
TCP    192.168.0.6:49171      oam-d05c:5190           ESTABLISHED
TCP    192.168.0.6:49473      205.128.92.124:http     CLOSE_WAIT
TCP    192.168.0.6:49625      64-190-251-21:ftp       ESTABLISHED
TCP    192.168.0.6:49628      210-11:http             ESTABLISHED
TCP    192.168.0.6:49629      varp1:http              ESTABLISHED
TCP    192.168.0.6:49630      varp1:http              ESTABLISHED
TCP    192.168.0.6:49631      varp1:http              ESTABLISHED
TCP    192.168.0.6:49632      varp1:http              ESTABLISHED
TCP    192.168.0.6:49635      199.93.62.125:http      ESTABLISHED
TCP    192.168.0.6:49636      m1:http                 ESTABLISHED
TCP    192.168.0.6:49638      spe:http                ESTABLISHED
```

The Proto column lists the protocol being used. You can see that I'm connected to my Exchange server and an FTP server and that I have some HTTP sessions open; by the way, all of them use TCP at the Transport layer.

The Local Address column lists the source address and the source port (source socket). The Foreign Address column lists the address of the destination machine (the hostname if it's been resolved). If the destination port is known, it will show up as the well-known port. In the previous output, you see http instead of port 80 and ftp instead of port 21.

The State column indicates the status of each connection. This column shows statistics only for TCP connections because User Datagram Protocol (UDP) establishes no virtual circuit to the remote device. Usually, this column indicates ESTABLISHED when a TCP connection between your computer and the destination computer has been established. All sessions eventually time out and then close, and you can see that I have all of these listed in my netstat output.

> If the address of either your computer or the destination computer can be found in the hosts file on your computer, the destination computer's name, rather than the IP address, will show up in either the Local Address or Foreign Address column.

The output of the netstat utility depends on the switch. By using the netstat /? command, we can see the options available to us.

```
C:\Users\tlammle>netstat /?
```

All of the netstat switch options are listed in Table 25.7.

TABLE 25.7   netstat options

Option	Description
-a	Displays all connections and listening ports.
-b	Displays the executable involved in creating each connection or listening port. In some cases, well-known executables host multiple independent components, and in these cases the sequence of components involved in creating the connection or listening port is displayed. Note that this option can be time consuming and will fail unless you have sufficient permissions.
-e	Displays Ethernet statistics. This may be combined with the -s option.
-f	Displays fully qualified domain names (FQDNs) for foreign addresses.
-n	Displays addresses and port numbers in numerical form.
-o	Displays the owning process ID associated with each connection.
-p *proto*	Shows connections for the protocol specified by *proto*; *proto* may be TCP, UDP, TCPv6, or UDPv6. If used with the -s option to display per-protocol statistics, *proto* may be IP, IPv6, ICMP, ICMPv6, TCP, TCPv6, UDP, or UDPv6.
-r	Displays the routing table.
-s	Displays per-protocol statistics. By default, statistics are shown for IP, IPv6, ICMP, ICMPv6, TCP, TCPv6, UDP, and UDPv6; the -p option may be used to specify a subset of the default.
-t	Displays the current connection offload state. Redisplays selected statistics, pausing interval seconds between each display. Press Ctrl+C to stop redisplaying statistics. If -t is omitted, netstat will print the current configuration information once.

Simply type **netstat** followed by a space and then the particular switch you want to use. Some switches have options, but no matter what, the syntax is basically the same.

Note that with Unix-type switches, the hyphen absolutely must be included. This is common in Microsoft operating systems for TCP/IP utilities that originate from Unix systems. I'm not going to exhaustively go over each and every switch, but make sure you practice all of these on your own Windows machine.

The –*a* Switch

When you use the –a switch, the `netstat` utility displays all TCP/IP connections and all UDP connections. Figure 25.13 shows sample output produced by the `netstat` –a command.

FIGURE 25.13   Sample output of the `netstat` –a command

```
C:\ NETSTAT -a

Active Connections

Proto     Local Address        Foreign Address        State
TCP       default:1026         204.153.163.2:80       ESTABLISHED
TCP       default:1027         204.153.163.2:80       ESTABLISHED
TCP       default:1028         204.153.163.2:80       ESTABLISHED
TCP       default:1029         204.153.163.2:80       ESTABLISHED
UDP       default:nbname       *:*
UDP       default:nbdatagram   *:*
```

The last two entries in Figure 25.13 show that the protocol is UDP and give the source-port nicknames nbname and nbdatagram. These are the well-known port numbers of 137 and 138, respectively. These port numbers are commonly seen on networks that broadcast the NetBIOS name of a workstation on the TCP/IP network. You can tell that this is a broadcast because the destination address is listed as *:* (meaning "any address, any port").

> The State column in Figure 25.13 has no entry for the UDP rows because UDP is not a connection-oriented protocol and, therefore, has no connection state.

The most common use for the –a switch is to check the status of a TCP/IP connection that appears to be hung. You can determine if the connection is simply busy or is actually hung and no longer responding.

The –*e* Switch

The –e switch displays a summary of all the packets that have been sent over the Network Interface Card (NIC) as of an instance. The Received and Sent columns show packets coming in as well as being sent:

```
C:\Users\tlammle>netstat -e
Interface Statistics
```

	Received	Sent
Bytes	7426841	7226953
Unicast packets	25784	35006
Non-unicast packets	1115	12548
Discards	0	0

```
Errors                              0              71
Unknown protocols                   0
```

You can use the –e switch to display the following categories of statistics:

Bytes   The number of bytes transmitted or received since the computer was turned on. This statistic is useful for finding out if data is actually being transmitted and received or if the network interface isn't doing anything at all.

Unicast Packets   The number of packets sent from or received at this computer. To register in one of these columns, the packet must be addressed directly from one computer to another and the computer's address must be in either the source or destination address section of the packet.

Non-unicast Packets   The number of packets that weren't directly sent from one workstation to another. For example, a broadcast packet is a non-unicast packet. The number of non-unicast packets should be smaller than the number of unicast packets. If the number of non-unicast packets is as high as or higher than that of unicast packets, too many broadcast packets are being sent over your network. Definitely find the source of these packets and make any necessary adjustments to optimize performance.

Discards   The number of packets that were discarded by the NIC during either transmission or reception because they weren't assembled correctly.

Errors   The number of errors that occurred during transmission or reception. (These numbers may indicate problems with the network card.)

Unknown Protocols   The number of received packets that the Windows networking stack couldn't interpret. This statistic only shows up in the Received column because if the computer sent them, they wouldn't be unknown, right?

Unfortunately, statistics don't mean much unless they can be colored with time information. For example, if the Errors row shows 71 errors, is that a problem? It might be if the computer has been on for only a few minutes. But 71 errors could be par for the course if the computer has been operating for several days. Unfortunately, the netstat utility doesn't have a way of indicating how much time has elapsed for these statistics.

The –r Switch

You use the –r switch to display the current route table for a workstation so that you can see exactly how TCP/IP information is being routed. This will give you the same output as the route print command that we covered earlier in this chapter.

The –s Switch

Using the –s switch displays a variety of TCP, UDP, IP, and ICMP protocol statistics. But be warned—the output you'll get is really long, which may or may not be okay for you.

For this book, it's way too long for me to insert. With that in mind, we can add another modifier called the -p switch.

The –p Switch

Like the –n switch, the -p switch is a modifier that's usually used with the –s switch to specify which protocol statistics to list in the output (IP, TCP, UDP, or ICMP). For example, if you want to view only ICMP statistics, you use the -p switch like so:

```
netstat -s -p ICMP
```

The netstat utility then displays the ICMP statistics instead of the entire gamut of TCP/IP statistics that the –s switch will typically flood you with. For a different example, let's use the –s and -p switches to retrieve some IPv6 information:

```
C:\Users\tlammle>netstat -s -p IPV6

IPv6 Statistics

    Packets Received                 = 1400
    Received Header Errors           = 0
    Received Address Errors          = 6
    Datagrams Forwarded              = 0
    Unknown Protocols Received       = 0
    Received Packets Discarded       = 451
    Received Packets Delivered       = 10441
    Output Requests                  = 24349
    Routing Discards                 = 0
    Discarded Output Packets         = 3575
    Output Packet No Route           = 41
    Reassembly Required              = 0
    Reassembly Successful            = 0
    Reassembly Failures              = 0
    Datagrams Successfully Fragmented = 0
    Datagrams Failing Fragmentation  = 0
    Fragments Created                = 0

C:\Users\tlammle>
```

Nice! Gets right to the point. Now, let's see the TCP connections my host has:

```
C:\Users\tlammle>netstat -s -p tcp

TCP Statistics for IPv4
```

```
Active Opens                    = 7832
Passive Opens                   = 833
Failed Connection Attempts      = 1807
Reset Connections               = 2428
Current Connections             = 11
Segments Received               = 1391678
Segments Sent                   = 1340994
Segments Retransmitted          = 6246
```

Active Connections

```
Proto  Local Address          Foreign Address        State
TCP    10.100.10.54:54737     gnt-exchange:1151      ESTABLISHED
TCP    10.100.10.54:54955     gnt-exchange:1026      ESTABLISHED
TCP    10.100.10.54:55218     gnt-exchange:epmap     TIME_WAIT
TCP    127.0.0.1:2492         globalnet-todd:54840   ESTABLISHED
TCP    127.0.0.1:54516        globalnet-todd:62514   ESTABLISHED
TCP    127.0.0.1:54840        globalnet-todd:2492    ESTABLISHED
TCP    127.0.0.1:62514        globalnet-todd:54516   ESTABLISHED
TCP    192.168.0.6:2492       blugro2relay:2492      ESTABLISHED
TCP    192.168.0.6:2492       blugro3relay:2492      ESTABLISHED
TCP    192.168.0.6:54527      64.12.25.26:5190       ESTABLISHED
TCP    192.168.0.6:54531      oam-d05c:5190          ESTABLISHED
TCP    192.168.0.6:55163      207.123.44.123:http    CLOSE_WAIT
```

C:\Users\tlammle>

This kind of efficiency is exactly why it's good to use the -p modifier with the -s switch.

> Because the Network+ exam doesn't cover them, we won't go into detail about what all these statistics mean for most of these commands. You can probably figure out most of them—for instance, Packets Received. For more details, go to Microsoft's support website at https:// support.microsoft.com/en-us.

The –*n* Switch

The -n switch is a modifier for the other switches. When used with them, it reverses the natural tendency of netstat to use names instead of network addresses. In other words, when you use the -n switch, the output always displays network addresses instead of their associated network names. Following is output from the netstat command used with the `netstat -n` command. It's showing the same information but with IP addresses instead of names:

```
C:\Users\tlammle>netstat

Active Connections

  Proto  Local Address           Foreign Address         State
  TCP    10.100.10.54:54737      gnt-exchange:1151       ESTABLISHED
  TCP    10.100.10.54:54955      gnt-exchange:1026       ESTABLISHED
  TCP    127.0.0.1:2492          globalnet-todd:54840    ESTABLISHED
  TCP    127.0.0.1:54516         globalnet-todd:62514    ESTABLISHED
  TCP    127.0.0.1:54840         globalnet-todd:2492     ESTABLISHED
  TCP    127.0.0.1:62514         globalnet-todd:54516    ESTABLISHED
  TCP    192.168.0.6:2492        blugro2relay:2492       ESTABLISHED
  TCP    192.168.0.6:2492        blugro3relay:2492       ESTABLISHED
  TCP    192.168.0.6:54527       64.12.25.26:5190        ESTABLISHED
  TCP    192.168.0.6:54531       oam-d05c:5190           ESTABLISHED
  TCP    192.168.0.6:55163       207.123.44.123:http     CLOSE_WAIT

C:\Users\tlammle>netstat -n

Active Connections

  Proto  Local Address           Foreign Address         State
  TCP    10.100.10.54:54737      10.100.36.13:1151       ESTABLISHED
  TCP    10.100.10.54:54955      10.100.36.13:1026       ESTABLISHED
  TCP    127.0.0.1:2492          127.0.0.1:54840         ESTABLISHED
  TCP    127.0.0.1:54516         127.0.0.1:62514         ESTABLISHED
  TCP    127.0.0.1:54840         127.0.0.1:2492          ESTABLISHED
  TCP    127.0.0.1:62514         127.0.0.1:54516         ESTABLISHED
  TCP    192.168.0.6:2492        65.55.239.100:2492      ESTABLISHED
  TCP    192.168.0.6:2492        65.55.248.110:2492      ESTABLISHED
  TCP    192.168.0.6:54527       64.12.25.26:5190        ESTABLISHED
  TCP    192.168.0.6:54531       205.188.248.163:5190    ESTABLISHED
  TCP    192.168.0.6:55163       207.123.44.123:80       CLOSE_WAIT

C:\Users\tlammle>
```

> **⊕ Real World Scenario**
>
> ### Uses for *netstat*
>
> You might be saying to yourself, "Fine . . . I can use lots of cool switches with netstat, but really, what for?" I'm always finding uses for netstat. For instance, once I found a particularly nasty worm on my PC using netstat. I just happened to run netstat for giggles one day and noticed a very large number of outbound connections to various places on the Internet. My PC was sending out SYN packets to a large number of hosts (an indication that my computer was involved—unknowingly—in a large-scale denial of service attack). Upon further examination, I noticed that this activity would start shortly after bootup.
>
> I tried running netstat after bootup and noticed that the first outbound connection was to TCP port 6667, some Internet Relay Chat (IRC) server I'd never heard of—I didn't even have an IRC client on my machine at the time. The worm was particularly nasty to try to get rid of while active, so I turned off port 6667 on my firewall. That prevented the initial connection to the IRC server and, as I found out later, nicely prevented the worm from getting its instructions from the IRC server. I was then able to simply remap without netstat. Even my antivirus program missed it.

Using *tcpdump*

The tcpdump utility is used to read either packets captured live from a network or packets that have been saved to a file. Although there is a Windows version called windump, tcpdump only works on Unix-like operating systems.

Examples of Using *tcpdump*

Use this command to capture traffic on all interfaces:

```
# tcpdump -i any
```

Here is the command to capture traffic on a particular interface:

```
# tcpdump -i eth0
```

And to filter traffic by IP, whether it's the source or the destination, use this command:

```
# tcpdump host 192.168.5.5
```

Using the File Transfer Protocol

You already know that *File Transfer Protocol (FTP)* is a subset of TCP/IP and that FTP is used for the transfer of files. In recent years, FTP has become a truly cross-platform protocol for transferring files. Because Internet (and thus TCP/IP) use has skyrocketed, almost every client and server platform has implemented FTP. Windows is no exception. Its TCP/IP stack comes with a command-line `ftp` utility.

To start the `ftp` utility, enter **ftp** at a command prompt. The result is an `ftp` command prompt:

```
C:\Users\tlammle>ftp
ftp>
```

From this prompt, you can open a connection to an FTP server and upload and download files as well as change the way FTP operates. To display a list of all the commands you can use at the `ftp` command prompt, type **help** or **?** and press Enter. To get help on a specific command, type **help**, a space, and then the name of the command. Here is some output from the `help` command:

```
ftp>help
Commands may be abbreviated.  Commands are:

!               delete          literal         prompt          send
?               debug           ls              put             status
append          dir             mdelete         pwd             trace
ascii           disconnect      mdir            quit            type
bell            get             mget            quote           user
binary          glob            mkdir           recv            verbose
bye             hash            mls             remotehelp
cd              help            mput            rename
close           lcd             open            rmdir
ftp>
```

In the following sections, I'll give you an introduction to uploading and downloading files because every network technician and administrator positively needs to know how to do this. As they come up, I'll go over the specific commands necessary to perform those two operations as well as any commands that relate to those processes. But first, let's look at how to begin the process.

Third-party applications are available that provide a GUI interface for FTP, which is easier to use than a command line.

Starting FTP and Logging In to an FTP Server

Of the two FTP file operations (download and upload), the ability to download files is definitely the more crucial for you to have down as a network technician or sys admin. The reason it's so important for you to master is that network and client operating system drivers and patches are located on FTP servers all over the Internet.

The first steps in starting an FTP download session are to determine the address of the FTP site and start the `ftp` utility. The FTP site typically has the same name as the website except that the first three characters are `ftp` instead of www. For example, Microsoft's website is www.microsoft.com. Its FTP site, on the other hand, is ftp.microsoft.com. We'll use my personal FTP site as an example for the rest of this section because it works, so I can actually log in to it.

First, start the `ftp` utility as demonstrated earlier, and then follow these steps:

1. At the `ftp` command prompt, type **open**, a space, and the name of the FTP server, like this:

```
C:\Users\tlammle>ftp
ftp>open ftp.lammle.com
Connected to ftp.lammle.com.
220---------- Welcome to Pure-FTPd [TLS] ----------
220-You are user number 1 of 50 allowed.
220-Local time is now 11:45. Server port: 21.
220-IPv6 connections are also welcome on this server.
220 You will be disconnected after 15 minutes of inactivity.
User (ftp.lammle.com:(none)):enter
230 Anonymous user logged in
ftp>
```

As shown here, if the FTP server is available and running, you'll receive a response welcoming you to the server and asking you for a username. Right now, I just have *Anonymous* as the username (enabled by default on the FTP server), which means that anyone can log in to it. (By the way, don't bother trying this on my server because I disabled it for obvious reasons as soon as I finished writing this section.)

You can also start an FTP session by typing **ftp**, a space, and the address of the FTP server (for example, **ftp ftp.globalnettraining.com**). This allows you to start the `ftp` utility and open a connection in one step. Here's an example:

```
C:\Users\tlammle>ftp ftp.globalnettraining.com
Connected to ftp.globalnettraining.com.
220 Microsoft FTP Service
User (ftp.globalnettraining.com:(none)):todd
331 Password required for todd.
Password:not shown when typed
230 User todd logged in.
ftp>quit
```

2. Enter a valid username, and press Enter.
3. Enter your password, and press Enter. (The password won't show up when you type it.)

Most Internet web servers that allow just about anyone to download files also allow the username *anonymous*, as I demonstrated. In addition to *anonymous*, you can use the username *ftp* to gain access to a public FTP server. They are both anonymous usernames. Remember that FTP (and Unix) usernames are case sensitive.

All good, but if you want to access a private FTP server, as I'll demonstrate in a minute, you'll need to use the username and password given to you by the site's administrator. Oh, and sometimes you can use your email address as a password when accessing a public FTP server with a username like *anonymous*.

 You don't have to enter your entire email address to log in with the *anonymous* username. Most of the time, FTP server software doesn't actually verify the actual email address, only that it is, in fact, an email address. To do this, it checks for an @ sign and two words separated by a period. You just need to enter a very short email address to bypass the password (like u@me.com). This is especially helpful if you have a long email address, and it's a really good idea if you don't want to get a ton of junk email.

If you enter the wrong username and/or password, the server will tell you so by displaying the following and leaving you at the ftp command prompt:

```
530 Login Incorrect
Login failed.
```

This means you've got to try again and must start the login process over. If you're successful, the FTP server will welcome you and drop you back at the ftp command prompt. You're now ready to start uploading or downloading files.

Downloading Files

After you log in to the FTP server, you'll navigate to the directory that contains the files you want. Thankfully, the FTP command-line interface is similar to the DOS command-line interface. This is no surprise because DOS is based on Unix and FTP is a Unix utility. Table 25.8 lists and describes the common navigation commands for FTP. (Remember that these are also case sensitive.)

After you navigate to the directory and find the file you want to download, it's time to set the parameters for the type of file. Files come in two types:

- ASCII, which contains text
- Binary, which is all other files

If you set ftp to the wrong type, the file you download will contain gibberish. So if you're in doubt, set ftp to download files as binary files. Check out Table 25.8.

TABLE 25.8 Common FTP navigation commands

Command	Description
ls	Short for *list*. Displays a directory listing. Very similar to the DIR command in MS-DOS.
cd	Short for *change directory*. Works almost identically to the MS-DOS CD command. Use it to change to a different directory and navigate the server's directory structure.
pwd	Short for *print working directory*. Displays the current directory on the server. Useful if you forget where you are when changing to several locations on the server.
lcd	Short for *local change directory*. Displays and changes the current directory on the local machine. Useful when you are downloading a file and aren't in the directory where you want to put the file.

To set the file type to ASCII, type **ascii** at the ftp command prompt. ftp will respond by telling you that the file type has been set to A (ASCII):

```
ftp>ascii
Type set to A
```

To set the file type to binary, type **binary** at the ftp command prompt. ftp will respond by telling you that the file type has been set to I (binary):

```
ftp>binary
Type set to I
```

To download the file, just use the get command like this:

```
ftp>get lammlepress.exe
200 PORT command successful.
150 Opening BINARY mode data connection for 'scrsav.exe'
(567018 bytes).
```

The file will start downloading to your hard drive. Unfortunately, with its default settings, the ftp utility doesn't give you any indication of the progress of the transfer. When the file has downloaded, the ftp utility will display the following message and return you to the ftp command prompt:

```
226 Transfer complete.
567018 bytes received in 116.27 seconds (4.88 Kbytes/sec)
```

You can download multiple files by using the mget command. Simply type **mget**, a space, and then something known as a *wildcard* that specifies the files you want to get. For example, to download all the text files in a directory, type **mget *.txt**.

Uploading Files

To upload a file to an FTP server, you've got to have rights on that specific server. These rights are assigned on a directory-by-directory basis. To upload a file, log in and then follow these steps:

1. At the ftp command prompt, type **lcd** to navigate to the directory on the local machine where the file resides.

2. Type **cd** to navigate to the destination directory.

3. Set the file type to ASCII or binary.

4. Use the put command to upload the file.

   The syntax of the put command looks like this:

ftp>put local file destination file

Let's say you want to upload a file called 1.txt on the local server but you want it to be called my.txt on the destination server. To accomplish that, use the following command:

ftp>**put 1.txt my.txt**

You'll get the following response:

```
200 PORT command successful.
150 Opening BINARY mode data connection for collwin.zip
226 Transfer complete.
743622 bytes sent in 0.55 seconds (1352.04 Kbytes/sec)
```

You can upload multiple files using the mput command. Simply type **mput**, a space, and then a wildcard that specifies the files. For example, to upload all the text files in a directory, type **mput *.txt**.

When you're finished with the ftp utility, just type quit to return to the command prompt.

Using the Telnet Utility

Part of the TCP/IP protocol suite, *Telnet* is a virtual terminal protocol utility that allows you to make connections to remote devices, gather information, and run programs. Telnet was originally developed to open terminal sessions from remote Unix workstations to Unix servers. Although it's still used for that purpose, we now use it as a troubleshooting tool as well. Figure 25.14 shows the basic Telnet interface as it's being used to start a terminal session on a remote Unix host.

FIGURE 25.14   The Telnet utility

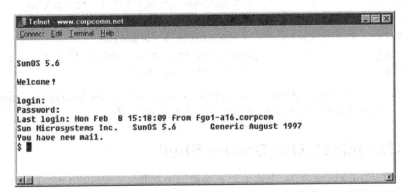

In today's Windows environments, Telnet is a basic command-line tool for testing TCP connections. You can telnet to any TCP port to see if it's responding—something that's especially useful when checking Simple Mail Transfer Protocol (SMTP) and HTTP (web) ports.

As you learned back in Chapter 6, "Introduction to the Internet Protocol," each upper-layer service in a TCP stack has a number for its address. And by default, each network service that uses a particular address will respond to a TCP request on that specific port.

How to Enable Telnet in Windows

Because most people have the Windows 10 operating system running on their PCs these days, it's good to know that, by default, this operating system installs without Telnet available. But there's a way around that one—if you really must have a Telnet client enabled in the Windows operating system, here's how to do it:

1. Open Control Panel.

2. Select Programs And Features.

3. In the left column, select Turn Windows Features On Or Off (get ready for the annoying User Account Control [UAC] prompt, and then enter your name and password).

4. Select the Telnet check box (and any other obscure services you may want enabled), and wait while Windows thinks for a while and then reboots.

Nice—now you can go to Start and then type **telnet** in the Start search box to get a Telnet window to open for you. You can also open a DOS prompt and just type **telnet** from there. Here are the options that Windows provides with Telnet:

```
Microsoft Telnet> ?
Commands may be abbreviated. Supported commands are:

c   - close                 close current connection
d   - display               display operating parameters
o   - open hostname [port]  connect to hostname (default port 23).
```

```
q   - quit                    exit telnet
set - set                     set options (type 'set ?' for a list)
sen - send                    send strings to server
st  - status                  print status information
u   - unset                   unset options (type 'unset ?' for a list)
?/h - help                    print help information
```

Now that we've finished talking about Telnet, my personal recommendation is that you never use it again. What? Yes, you read that right, and here's why.

Don't Use Telnet, Use Secure Shell

What? I just told you how to use Telnet, and now I am telling you not to use it. That's right, don't use Telnet! Telnet is totally insecure because it sends all data in crystal-clear text—including your name and password. And I'm pretty sure you know that's a really bad thing these days. If Microsoft doesn't even enable it on its latest OSs, then you know it really must be insecure.

So if you shouldn't use Telnet, what should you use instead? Secure Shell (SSH) is your answer. It provides the same options as Telnet, plus a lot more; but most important, it doesn't send any data in clear text. The thing is, your servers, routers, and other devices need to be enabled with SSH, and it's not configured by default on most devices.

Some configuration is usually necessary if you want things to work as they really should, and yes, sometimes it's a little painful to get everything running smoothly, but it's all worth it in the long run. Personally, I disable Telnet on all my routers and use SSH exclusively. No lie—I never use Telnet anymore if I can help it. Even so, you should still understand Telnet and get in some practice with it in case you do ever need it.

 In my Sybex book *The Cisco CCNA Study Guide*, I get into the details of how to configure SSH on all Cisco devices and use an SSH client.

Summary

In this chapter, you learned about many of the utilities for using and troubleshooting TCP/IP. These utilities include GUI tools like protocol analyzers, throughput testers, and connectivity software like Remote Desktop, and they include command-line utilities like tracert, ping, arp, netstat, nbtstat, ipconfig, ifconfig, and nslookup.

We discussed many of the tools that are used for troubleshooting wireless, wired copper, and optical networks. The commonly used command-line tools for both the Windows and Linux operating systems were introduced, including ping, ipconfig/ifconfig/ip, nslookup/dig, traceroute/tracert, arp, netstat, hostname, route, telnet/SSH, tcpdump par, and nmap.

You also learned how these utilities are used, including their various options and switches and how they all affect the use of the utilities. Finally, you learned about how these utilities work within the TCP/IP suite such as NetFlow analyzers, terminal emulators, and IP network scanners.

Exam Essentials

Describe some of the GUI tools available to assist in testing and troubleshooting.   These include protocol analyzers, bandwidth speed testers, and connectivity software. Understand each product's purpose and how to use it.

Know how to describe and use the troubleshooting information and statistics that arp and netstat provide for you.   The arp utility shows whether an IP address is being resolved to your MAC address (or someone else's, in case of conflicts). The netstat utility produces TCP/IP statistics.

Know how to diagnose a network by using TCP/IP's troubleshooting commands.   The ping command echoes back if a machine is alive and active on a network. The tracert command shows the path that the ping packets take from source to target. And telnet enables a user to participate in a remote text-based session.

Know what the tracert utility does.   The tracert utility finds the route from your computer to any computer on a network.

Know what the ping utility does.   The ping utility determines whether a particular IP host is responding.

Know what the ftp utility does.   The ftp utility allows you to reliably download and upload files from and to an FTP server across the Internet.

Know what the ipconfig and ifconfig utilities do.   The ipconfig utility displays TCP/IP configuration information for Windows NT and later operating systems. The ifconfig utility performs a similar function in Linux/Unix environments, in addition to performing certain interface-configuration tasks.

Know what the nslookup and dig utilities do.   The nslookup and dig utilities allow you to look up DNS resolution information.

Identify nmap and tcpdump.   While tcpdump is a command-line packet capture utility for Linux, nmap is a network reconnaissance tool that can identify live hosts, open ports, and the operating systems of devices.

Describe the use of the iptables utility.   Iptables is a firewall utility built for the Linux operating system. It is a command-line utility that uses what are called chains to allow or disallow traffic. When traffic arrives, iptables looks for a rule that addresses that traffic type, and if none exists, it will enforce the default rule.

Written Lab

You can find the answers to the written labs in Appendix A. Write the answers to the following questions about command-line tools:

1. What command can you type from a command prompt to see the hops a packet takes to get to a destination host?

2. What tool would you use to verify a complaint about a slow network?

3. You need your IP address, subnet mask, default gateway, and DNS information. What command will you type from a Windows command prompt?

4. You need to log in as a dumb terminal to a server or Unix host and run programs. What application will you use?

5. You need to add a route to your Windows server's routing table. What command will you use?

6. You want to log in to a server and transfer files. What application will you use?

7. You need to check your name-resolution information on your host. What command will you type from the command prompt?

8. You want to use netstat, but you want to see only the IP address, not the names of the hosts. Which modifier will you use?

9. You want the IP configuration on a Unix host. What command will you type at the command prompt?

10. Which Windows command will show you the routing table of your host or server?

Review Questions

You can find the answers to the review questions in Appendix B.

1. Which TCP/IP utility is most often used to test whether an IP host is up and functional?

   A. ftp

   B. telnet

   C. ping

   D. netstat

2. Which TCP/IP utility will produce the following result?

   ```
   Interface: 199.102.30.152
   Internet Address    Physical Address    Type
   199.102.30.152      A0-ee-00-5b-0e-ac   dynamic
   ```

   A. arp

   B. netstat

   C. tracert

   D. nbtstat

3. Which Windows utility can you use to connect to a machine 50 miles away to troubleshoot?

   A. Remote Desktop

   B. netstat

   C. arp

   D. Wireshark

4. Which TCP/IP utility might produce the following output?

   ```
   Reply from 204.153.163.2: bytes=32 time=1ms TTL=128
   Reply from 204.153.163.2: bytes=32 time=1ms TTL=128
   Reply from 204.153.163.2: bytes=32 time=1ms TTL=128
   Reply from 204.153.163.2: bytes=32 time<10ms TTL=128
   ```

   A. tracert

   B. ping

   C. WINS

   D. ipconfig

5. Which utility can you use to find the MAC and TCP/IP addresses of your Windows workstation?

   A. ping

   B. ipconfig

   C. ipconfig /all

   D. tracert

   E. telnet

6. Which ping commands will verify that your local TCP/IP interface is working? (Choose all that apply.)

   A. ping 204.153.163.2

   B. ping 127.0.0.1

   C. ping localif

   D. ping localhost

   E. ping iphost

7. Which new Linux command was added recently to configure IP and interface parameters?

   A. nbtstat

   B. ipconfig

   C. ip

   D. ifconfig

8. You need to find a NIC's specific MAC address and IP address. Which command-line tool can you use to find this information without physically going to the computer?

   A. ping

   B. nbtstat

   C. arp

   D. netstat

   E. ftp

9. Which netstat utility switch displays all connections and listening ports?

   A. -a

   B. -f

   C. -p

   D. -t

10. Wireshark is an example of a _____ .

    A. Throughput tester

    B. Protocol analyzer

    C. Remote connection tool

    D. IDS

11. Which utility produces output similar to the following?

```
1   110 ms   96 ms   107 ms fgo1.corpcomm.net [209.74.93.10]
2   96 ms   126 ms   95 ms someone.corpcomm.net [209.74.93.1]
3   113 ms   119 ms   112 ms Serial5-1-1.GW2.MSP1.alter.net
[157.130.100.185]
4   133 ms   123 ms   126 ms 152.ATM3-0.XR2.CHI6.ALTER.NET
[146.188.209.126]
5   176 ms   133 ms   129 ms 290.ATM2-0.TR2.CHI4.ALTER.NET   [146.188.209.10]
6   196 ms   184 ms   218 ms 106.ATM7-0.TR2.SCL1.ALTER.NET   [146.188.136.162]
7   182 ms   187 ms   187 ms 298.ATM7-0.XR2.SJC1.ALTER.NET   [146.188.146.61]
8   204 ms   176 ms   186 ms 192.ATM3-0-0.SAN-JOSE9- GW.ALTER.NET
[146.188.144.133]
9   202 ms   198 ms   212 ms atm3-0-622M.cr1.sjc.globalcenter.net
[206.57.16.17]
10 209 ms   202 ms   195 ms pos3-1-155M.br4.SJC.globalcenter.net
[206.132.150.98]
11 190 ms    *      191 ms pos0-0-0-155M.hr3.SNV.globalcenter.net
[206.251.5.93]
12 195 ms   188 ms   188 ms pos4-1-0-   155M.hr2.SNV.globalcenter.net
[206.132.150.206]
13 198 ms   202 ms   197 ms www10.yahoo.com [204.71.200.75]
```

A. arp

B. tracert

C. nbtstat

D. netstat

12. You are the network administrator. A user calls you complaining that the performance of the intranet web server is sluggish. When you try to ping the server, it takes several seconds for the server to respond. You suspect that the problem is related to a router that is seriously overloaded. Which workstation utility could you use to find out which router is causing this problem?

A. netstat

B. nbtstat

C. tracert

D. ping

E. arp

13. Which `ipconfig` switch will display the most complete listing of IP configuration information for a station?

    A. `/all`

    B. `/renew`

    C. `/release`

    D. `/?`

14. Which utility will display a list of all the routers that a packet passes through on the way to an IP destination?

    A. `netstat`

    B. `nbtstat`

    C. `tracert`

    D. `ping`

    E. `arp`

15. Which Windows TCP/IP utility could you use to find out whether a server is responding on TCP port 21?

    A. `tcp`

    B. `port`

    C. `ping`

    D. `netstat`

    E. `telnet`

16. Which `arp` command can you use to display the currently cached ARP entries?

    A. `arp`

    B. `arp -all`

    C. `arp -a`

    D. `ipconfig -arp`

    E. `arp -ipconfig`

17. Which command-line tool would best be used to verify DNS functionality in Linux?

    A. `netstat`

    B. `nbtstat`

    C. `dig`

    D. `icmp`

    E. `arp`

18. Which of the following arp utility switches perform the same function? (Choose all that apply.)

    A. -g

    B. -A

    C. -d

    D. -a

19. Which of the following is *not* a chain type used by iptables?

    A. Forward

    B. Backward

    C. Input

    D. Output

20. Which command captures traffic on all interfaces?

    A. tcpdump -i any

    B. tcpdump -i eth0

    C. tcpdump host 192.168.5.5

    D. tcpdump host all

Appendix

A

Answers to Written Labs

Chapter 1: Introduction to Networks

1. Bus, ring, and star
2. Multiprotocol Label Switching (MPLS)
3. Server
4. Client-server
5. Point-to-point
6. Hub or switch
7. Multiprotocol Label Switching (MPLS)
8. Wide area network
9. A segment
10. Bus

Chapter 2: The Open Systems Interconnection Specifications

1. The Application layer is responsible for finding the network resources broadcast from a server and adding flow control and error control (if the application developer chooses).
2. The Physical layer takes frames from the Data Link layer and encodes the 1s and 0s into a digital signal for transmission on the network medium.
3. The Network layer provides routing through an internetwork and logical addressing.
4. The Presentation layer makes sure that data is in a readable format for the Application layer.
5. The Session layer sets up, maintains, and terminates sessions between applications.
6. Protocol data units (PDUs) at the Data Link layer are called frames. As soon as you see the word *frame* and/or the term *physical addressing* in a question, you know the answer is always Data Link layer.
7. The Transport layer uses virtual circuits to create a reliable connection between two hosts.
8. The Network layer provides logical addressing, IP and/or IPv6 addressing, and routing.
9. The Physical layer is responsible for the electrical and mechanical connections between devices.
10. The Data Link layer is responsible for the framing of data packets.

Chapter 3: Networking Connectors and Wiring Standards

1. Category 6
2. Demarcation point, or demarc
3. Crossover
4. RG-6
5. Category 5e
6. Straight-through
7. To connect two CSU/DSUs
8. 1, 2, 3, and 6
9. 1 to 3 and 2 to 6
10. It is completely immune to EMI and RFI and can transmit up to 40 kilometers (about 25 miles).

Chapter 4: The Current Ethernet Specifications

1.

Decimal	128	64	32	16	8	4	2	1	Binary
192	1	1	0	0	0	0	0	0	11000000
168	1	0	1	0	1	0	0	0	10101000
10	0	0	0	0	1	0	1	0	00001010
15	0	0	0	0	1	1	1	1	00001111

2.

Decimal	128	64	32	16	8	4	2	1	Binary
172	1	0	1	0	1	1	0	0	10101100
16	0	0	0	1	0	0	0	0	00010000
20	0	0	0	1	0	1	0	0	00010100
55	0	0	1	1	0	1	1	1	00110111

3.

Decimal	128	64	32	16	8	4	2	1	Binary
10	0	0	0	0	1	0	1	0	00001010
11	0	0	0	0	1	0	1	1	00001011
12	0	0	0	0	1	1	0	0	00001100
99	0	1	1	0	0	0	1	1	01100011

4.

Binary	128	64	32	16	8	4	2	1	Decimal
11001100	1	1	0	0	1	1	0	0	204
00110011	0	0	1	1	0	0	1	1	51
10101010	1	0	1	0	1	0	1	0	170
01010101	0	1	0	1	0	1	0	1	85

5.

Binary	128	64	32	16	8	4	2	1	Decimal
11000110	1	1	0	0	0	1	1	0	198
11010011	1	1	0	1	0	0	1	1	211
00111001	0	0	1	1	1	0	0	1	57
11010001	1	1	0	1	0	0	0	1	209

6.

Binary	128	64	32	16	8	4	2	1	Decimal
10000100	1	0	0	0	0	1	0	0	132
11010010	1	1	0	1	0	0	1	0	210
10111000	1	0	1	1	1	0	0	0	184
10100110	1	0	1	0	0	1	1	0	166

7.

Binary	128	64	32	16	8	4	2	1	Hexadecimal
11011000	1	1	0	1	1	0	0	0	D8
00011011	0	0	0	1	1	0	1	1	1B
00111101	0	0	1	1	1	1	0	1	3D
01110110	0	1	1	1	0	1	1	0	76

8.

Binary	128	64	32	16	8	4	2	1	Hexadecimal
11001010	1	1	0	0	1	0	1	0	CA
11110101	1	1	1	1	0	1	0	1	F5
10000011	1	0	0	0	0	0	1	1	83
11101011	1	1	1	0	1	0	1	1	EB

9.

Binary	128	64	32	16	8	4	2	1	Hexadecimal
10000100	1	0	0	0	0	1	0	0	84
11010010	1	1	0	1	0	0	1	0	D2
01000011	0	1	0	0	0	0	1	1	43
10110011	1	0	1	1	0	0	1	1	B3

Chapter 5: Networking Devices

Description	Device or OSI layer
This device sends and receives information about the Network layer.	Router
This layer creates a virtual circuit before transmitting between two end stations.	Transport
A Layer 3 switch or multilayer switch.	Router

(continues)

(continued)

Description	Device or OSI layer
This device uses hardware addresses to filter a network.	Bridge or switch
Ethernet is defined at these layers.	Data Link and Physical
This layer supports flow control and sequencing.	Transport
This device can measure the distance to a remote network.	Router
Logical addressing is used at this layer.	Network
Hardware addresses are defined at this layer.	Data Link (MAC sublayer)
This device creates one big collision domain and one large broadcast domain.	Hub
This device creates many smaller collision domains, but the network is still one large broadcast domain.	Switch or bridge
This device can never run full-duplex.	Hub
This device breaks up collision domains and broadcast domains.	Router

Chapter 6: Introduction to the Internet Protocol

1. This would be a layer 2 broadcast, or FF:FF:FF:FF:FF:FF.

2. FTP uses both TCP ports 20 and 21 for the data channel and the control channel, respectively.

3. Both TCP and UDP! A DNS server uses TCP port 53 for zone transfers and UDP port 53 for name resolutions. Notice that DNS uses both TCP and UDP. Whether it opts for one or the other depends on what it's trying to do.

4. ICMP uses IP directly to build error-reporting packets that are transmitted back to the originating source host when issues arise during the delivery of data packets. ICMP is also used during Ping and some Traceroute operations.

5. Quite simply, the service might not be running currently on that server. Another possibility might be that a firewall between the client and the server has blocked the protocol in question from passing.

6. RDP uses port 3389.

7. MGCP uses ports 2427 and 2727.

8. ICMP is the protocol that the `ping` and `tracert` commands rely on. If you're having trouble getting pings and traceroutes through a router, you might need to check if ICMP is being allowed through.

9. TFTP servers respond to UDP messages sent to port 69.

10. SMTP uses TCP port 25, POP3 uses TCP port 110, RDP uses TCP port 3389, and IMAP4 uses TCP port 143.

Chapter 7: IP Addressing

Written Lab 7.1

1. The class C private range is 192.168.0.0 through 192.168.255.255.

2. IPv6 has the following characteristics, among others, that make it preferable to IPv4: more available addresses, simpler header, options for authentication, and other security.

3. Automatic Private IP Addressing (APIPA) is the technology that results in hosts automatically configuring themselves with addresses that begin with 169.254.

4. An IP address assigned to an interface, considered a one-to-one communication.

5. One-to-many address

6. A MAC address, sometimes called a hardware address or even a burned-in address

7. IPv6 has 128-bit (16-octet) addresses, compared to IPv4's 32-bit (4-octet) addresses, so 96 more bits than IPv4.

8. 172.16.0.0 through 172.31.255.255

9. 192–223, 110*xxxxx*

10. Loopback or diagnostics. Actually, the full range of 127.0.0.1 through 127.255.255.254 is referred to as the loopback address.

Written Lab 7.2

1. Unicast

2. Global unicast

3. Link-local

4. Unique local (used to be called site-local)

5. Multicast

6. Anycast

7. Anycast

8. ::1

9. FE80::/10

10. FC00::/7

Chapter 8: IP Subnetting, Troubleshooting IP, and Introduction to NAT

1. 192.168.100.25/30. A /30 is 255.255.255.252. The valid subnet is 192.168.100.24, broadcast is 192.168.100.27, and valid hosts are 192.168.100.25 and 26.

2. 192.168.100.37/28. A /28 is 255.255.255.240. The fourth octet is a block size of 16. Just count by 16s until you pass 37. 0, 16, 32, 48. The host is in the 32 subnet, with a broadcast address of 47. Valid hosts are 33–46.

3. 192.168.100.66/27. A /27 is 255.255.255.224. The fourth octet is a block size of 32. Count by 32s until you pass the host address of 66. 0, 32, 64. The host is in the 64 subnet, broadcast address of 95. The valid host range is 65–94.

4. 192.168.100.17/29. A /29 is 255.255.255.248. The fourth octet is a block size of 8. 0, 8, 16, 24. The host is in the 16 subnet, broadcast of 23. Valid hosts are 17–22.

5. 192.168.100.99/26. A /26 is 255.255.255.192. The fourth octet has a block size of 64. 0, 64, 128. The host is in the 64 subnet, broadcast of 127. Valid hosts are 65–126.

6. 192.168.100.99/25. A /25 is 255.255.255.128. The fourth octet is a block size of 128. 0, 128. The host is in the 0 subnet, broadcast of 127. Valid hosts are 1–126.

7. A default Class B is 255.255.0.0. A Class B 255.255.255.0 mask is 256 subnets, each with 254 hosts. We need fewer subnets. If we use 255.255.240.0, this provides 16 subnets. Let's add one more subnet bit. 255.255.248.0. This is 5 bits of subnetting, which provides 32 subnets. This is our best answer, a /21.

8. A /29 is 255.255.255.248. This is a block size of 8 in the fourth octet. 0, 8, 16. The host is in the 8 subnet, and broadcast is 15.

9. A /29 is 255.255.255.248, which is 5 subnet bits and 3 host bits. This is only 6 hosts per subnet.

10. A /23 is 255.255.254.0. The third octet is a block size of 2. Starting at 0, 2, 4. The host is in the 16.2.0 subnet; the broadcast address is 16.3.255.

Chapter 9: Introduction to IP Routing

1. False. RIP and RIPv2 are both distance-vector protocols.
2. False. RIP and RIPv2 are both distance-vector protocols.
3. False. EIGRP was created by Cisco as a proprietary routing protocol; however, it is no longer proprietary.
4. Autonomous system
5. RIP does not work well in large networks, so OSPF would be the best answer, and both RIP and OSPF are nonproprietary.
6. Static routing
7. The MAC address of your default gateway (router)
8. The IP address of the server
9. The MAC address of the router sending the frame to the server
10. The IP address of the server

Chapter 10: Routing Protocols

1. 120
2. 90
3. 120
4. 1
5. RIPng (Next Generation).
6. OSPFv3
7. EIGRPv6
8. When you need to connect two autonomous systems (ASs) together
9. When all your routers are Cisco routers and you want easy configuration
10. Distance vector

Chapter 11: Switching and Virtual LANs

1. Broadcast
2. Collision

3. Trunking allows you to send information about many or all VLANs through the same link. Access ports allow information about only one VLAN transmitted.

4. Power over Ethernet (PoE)

5. The VLAN port membership is set wrong.

6. Flood the frame out all ports except the port on which it was received.

7. Address learning, filtering, and loop avoidance

8. It will add the source MAC address to the forward/filter table.

9. Spanning Tree Protocol (STP)

10. Create a VLAN for contractors and another VLAN for guests.

Chapter 12: Wireless Networking

1. 11 Mbps

2. 54 Mbps

3. 54 Mbps

4. 2.4 GHz

5. 2.4 GHz

6. 5 GHz

7. 1 Gbps

8. The values of WPA keys can change dynamically while the system is being used.

9. The IEEE 802.11i standard has been sanctioned by WPA and is called WPA version 2.

10. Three

Chapter 13: Using Statistics and Sensors to Ensure Network Availability

Description	Term
The percentage of time the CPU spends executing a non-idle thread.	Processor\% Processor Time
The amount of physical memory in megabytes currently available.	Memory\Available Mbytes

Description	Term
The percentage of bandwidth the NIC is capable of that is currently being used.	Network Interface\Bytes Total/Sec
The delay typically incurred in the processing of network data.	Latency
Occurs when the data flow in a connection is not consistent; that is, it increases and decreases in no discernable pattern.	Jitter
Supports plaintext authentication with MD5 or SHA with no encryption but provides GET BULK.	SNMPv2
Sent by SNMP agents to the NMS if a problem occurs.	SNMP trap
Identifier mechanism standardized by the International Telecommunications Union (ITU) and ISO/IEC for naming any object, concept, or "thing" with a globally unambiguous persistent name.	Object identifiers (OIDs)
Hierarchical structure into which SNMP OIDs are organized.	Management information bases (MIBs)
Refers to the standard level of performance of a certain device or to the normal operating capacity for your whole network.	Baseline
Centralizes and stores log messages and can even time-stamp and sequence them.	Syslog
Provides real-time analysis of security alerts generated by network hardware and applications.	SIEM
Errors that mean packets have been damaged.	CRC errors

Chapter 14: Organizational Documents and Policies

Step	Plan
Utilization of three network interfaces on the DNS server	Business continuity plan

(continues)

(continued)

Step	Plan
Phased introductions of security patches	Change management plan
Degaussing of all discarded hard drives	System life cycle plan
Security issue escalation list	Incident response plan
System recovery priority chart	Disaster recovery plan

Chapter 15: High Availability and Disaster Recovery

Definition	Term
Technique used to spread work out to multiple computers, network links, or other devices	Load balancing
Allows multiple network interfaces to be placed into a team for the purposes of bandwidth aggregation	NIC teaming
Devices that can immediately supply power from a battery backup when a loss of power is detected	UPS
A leased facility that contains all the resources needed for full operation	Hot site
A Cisco proprietary FHRP	HSRP

Chapter 16: Common Security Concepts

Authentication Method	Term
Utilizes the connection-based TCP protocol.	TACACS+
When a user logs into the domain, the domain controller issues them an access token.	Single sign-on

Authentication Method	Term
The user's local account and password are verified with the local user database.	Local authentication
Defines a framework for centralized port-based authentication.	802.1X
Combines user authentication and authorization into one profile.	RADIUS

Chapter 17: Common Types of Attacks

Attack	Countermeasure
Shoulder surfing	Privacy filters
Piggybacking	Live guards
Tailgating	Access control vestibule/mantrap
Phishing	Security awareness training
Brute-force attack	Account lockout policy

Chapter 18: Network Hardening Techniques

Authentication Method	Term
Method of blocking rogue router advertisements	RA Guard
Can prevent many on-path/man-in-the-middle attacks	DAI
Can limit network access on a port to a single (or in the case of an IP phone, two) MAC address	Port security

(*continues*)

(continued)

Authentication Method	Term
Carries signaling traffic originating from or destined for a router	Control plane
Carries user traffic	Data plane

Chapter 19: Remote Access Security

Term	Definition
Clientless VPN	Requires only a browser that can perform SSL/TLS.
Full tunnel	All traffic goes through the VPN, including Internet traffic.
Site-to-site VPN	All traffic goes through the VPN tunnel.
Split tunnel	*Only* traffic to the office goes through the VPN. Internet traffic does not
Client-to-site VPN	*Only* the traffic between the user and the office will go through the tunnel.

Chapter 20: Physical Security

Term	Definition
Purging	Makes the data unreadable even with advanced forensic techniques.
Clearing	With this method, the data is only recoverable using special forensic techniques.
Destruction	Breaking the media apart or chemically altering it.
Overwriting	Writes data patterns over the entire media, thereby eliminating any trace data.

Chapter 21: Data Center Architecture and Cloud Concepts

1. Leaf, spine
2. East-West
3. Automation
4. Automation
5. Elasticity
6. A baseline
7. Crossover
8. Cloud computing
9. Virtual servers, virtual switches, virtual desktops, Software as a Service (SaaS), and Network as a Service (NaaS)
10. Infrastructure as Code (IaC)

Chapter 22: Ensuring Network Availability

1. CPU and memory
2. Baseline
3. Syslog
4. Duplex
5. Bits
6. FTP
7. CRC, or cyclic redundancy check
8. Giant
9. NetFlow
10. SNMP, or Simple Network Management Protocol

Chapter 23: Cable Connectivity Issues and Tools

1. True
2. True
3. True
4. True
5. False
6. Certifiers
7. False
8. Temperature monitor
9. Voltage event recorder
10. Crimper

Chapter 24: Network Troubleshooting Methodology

1. Test the theory to determine cause.
2. Document findings, actions, outcomes, and lessons learned.
3. By twisting the wire pairs together
4. IP addressing
5. Crossover
6. Attenuation
7. Establish a plan of action to resolve the problem and identify potential effects.
8. Implement the solution or escalate as necessary.
9. Routing problems
10. Incorrect pinout, transceiver mismatch, crosstalk, and attenuation

Chapter 25: Network Software Tools and Commands

1. `traceroute or tracert`
2. Throughput tester/bandwidth speed tester
3. `ipconfig /all`
4. Telnet
5. `route`
6. FTP
7. `nslookup`
8. `netstat -n`
9. `ifconfig`
10. `route print`

Appendix

B

Answers to Review Questions

Chapter 1: Introduction to Networks

1. C. A client-server logical topology allows you to have a centralized database of users so that authentication is provided in one place.

2. C. To install a physical topology that provides ease of scalability, use a star network. This is a hub or switch device, and this is the most common LAN network today.

3. D. Only a mesh physical topology has point-to-point connections to every device, so it has more connections and is not a popular LAN technology.

4. B. In a star topology, each workstation connects to a hub, switch, or similar central device but not to other workstations. The benefit is that when connectivity to the central device is lost, the rest of the network lives on.

5. C. Multiprotocol Label Switching has as many advantages as a LAN protocol. When labels are used, voice can have priority over basic data, for example.

6. B. A logical grouping of hosts is called a LAN, and you typically group them by connecting them to a hub or switch.

7. C. It is easy to relax about security in a peer-to-peer environment. Because of the trouble it takes to standardize authentication, a piecemeal approach involving users' personal preferences develops. There are no dedicated servers in a peer-to-peer network, and such a network can be created with as few as two computers.

8. A. When a central office, such as headquarters, needs to communicate directly with its branch offices but the branches do not require direct communication with one another, the point-to-multipoint model is applicable. The other scenarios tend to indicate the use of a point-to-point link between sites.

9. D. LANs generally have a geographic scope of a single building or smaller. They can range from simple (two hosts) to complex (with thousands of hosts).

10. B. The only disadvantage mentioned is the fact that there is a single point of failure in the network. However, this topology makes troubleshooting easier; if the entire network fails, you know where to look first. The central device also ensures that the loss of a single port and the addition of a new device to an available port do not disrupt the network for other stations attached to such a device.

11. D. A typical WAN connects two or more remote LANs together using someone else's network (your ISP's) and a router. Your local host and router see these networks as remote networks and not as local networks or local resources. Routers use proprietary serial connections for WANs.

12. D. Multiprotocol Label Switching provides logical links between sites, so branch offices can be easily and quickly added.

13. A. In a peer-to-peer network, all computers are considered equal. It is up to the computer that has the resource being requested to perform a security check for access rights to its resources.

14. D. In client-server networks, requests for resources go to a main server that responds by handling security and directing the client to the resource it wants instead of the request going directly to the machine with the desired resource (as in peer-to-peer).

15. A. The best answer to this question is an Ethernet switch, which uses a star physical topology with a logical bus technology.

16. D. Routers are used to connect different networks together.

17. D. In the mesh topology, there is a path from each connection to every other one in the network. A mesh topology is used mainly because of the robust fault tolerance it offers—if one connection goes on the blink, computers and other network devices can simply switch to one of the many redundant connections that are up and running.

18. A. As its name implies, in a point-to-point topology you have a direct connection between two routers, giving you one communication path. The routers in a point-to-point topology can either be linked by a serial cable, making it a physical network, or be far away and only connected by a circuit within a Frame Relay network, making it a logical network.

19. B. A hybrid topology is a combination of two or more types of physical or logical network topologies working together within the same network.

20. A, B, C, D. Each topology has its own set of pros and cons regarding implementation, so it's important to ask the right questions and consider cost, ease of installation, maintenance, and fault tolerance.

Chapter 2: The Open Systems Interconnection Specifications

1. C. A connection-oriented session is set up using what is called a three-way handshake. The transmitting host sends a SYN packet, the receiving host sends a SYN/ACK, and the transmitting host replies with the last ACK packet. The session is now set up.

2. D. TCP and UDP are Transport layer protocols. The Transport layer is layer 4 of the OSI model.

3. A. The top layer of the OSI model gives applications access to the services that allow network access.

4. A. If the remote server is busy or does not respond to your web browser request, this is an Application layer problem.

5. B. The Presentation layer makes data "presentable" for the Application layer.

6. C. Bridges, like switches, are Data Link layer devices. Hubs, like repeaters, are Physical layer devices. Routers are Network layer devices.

7. D. The Physical layer's job is to convert data into impulses that are designed for the wired or wireless medium being used on the attached segment.

8. D. A receiving host can control the transmitter by using flow control (TCP uses windowing by default). By decreasing the window size, the receiving host can slow down the transmitting host so the receiving host does not overflow its buffers.

9. C, D. Not that you really want to enlarge a single collision domain, but a hub (multiport repeater) will provide this functionality for you.

10. D. The Transport layer receives large data streams from the upper layers and breaks these up into smaller pieces called segments.

11. C. The encapsulation order is data, segment, packet, frame, bits.

12. B, C. Bridges and switches break up collision domains, which allows more bandwidth for users.

13. C. A reliable Transport layer connection uses acknowledgments to make sure all data is received reliably. A reliable connection is defined by the use of acknowledgments, sequencing, and flow control, which is characteristic of the Transport layer (layer 4).

14. A, C, D. When sequencing and acknowledgments are used, the segments delivered are acknowledged back to the sender upon their reception. At this point, any segments not acknowledged are retransmitted, and segments are sequenced back into their proper order upon arrival at their destination.

15. C. Flow control allows the receiving device to control the pace of the transmitting device so the receiving device's buffer does not overflow.

16. B. IP is a Network layer protocol. TCP is an example of a Transport layer protocol, Ethernet is an example of a Data Link layer protocol, and T1 can be considered a Physical layer protocol.

17. D. The Presentation layer is the sixth layer of the model. Only the Application layer is higher, but it is not listed. Session is layer 5, Transport is layer 4, and Network is layer 3.

18. C. A router is specified at the Network layer and a router routes packets. Routers can also be called layer 3 switches.

19. C. The phrase "Please Do Not Throw Sausage Pizza Away" contains the first letters of the layers in order, from layer 1 through layer 7. "All People Seem To Need Data Processing" works from the top down. The other options have all the right letters, just not in the right order.

20. B. The 802.3 standard, commonly associated with Ethernet, specifies the media-access method used by Ethernet, which is known as Carrier Sense Multiple Access with Collision Detection (CSMA/CD).

Chapter 3: Networking Connectors and Wiring Standards

1. B, C. Plenum-rated means that the cable's coating doesn't begin burning until a much higher temperature of heat, doesn't release as many toxic fumes as PVC when it does burn, and is rated for use in air plenums that carry breathable air, usually as nonenclosed fresh-air return pathways that share space with cabling.

2. D. UTP is commonly used in twisted-pair Ethernet like 10BaseT, 100BaseTX, 1000BaseTX, and so on.

3. D. Unshielded twisted-pair has standards from Category 2 through 8 for use on Ethernet networks. There is no Category 9 defined.

4. C. UTP usually connects with RJ-45. You use a crimper to attach an RJ connector to a cable.

5. A. Single-mode fiber allows for the maximum cable run distances.

6. B. You would use a straight-through cable to connect a host to a switch, and the typical pin-out is called T568A.

7. C. Fiber-optic cable transmits digital signals using light impulses rather than electricity; therefore, it is immune to EMI and RFI.

8. B. Remember that fiber-optic cable transmits a digital signal using light impulses. Light is carried on either a glass or a plastic core.

9. B. The difference between single-mode fibers and multimode fibers is in the number of light rays (and thus the number of signals) they can carry. Generally speaking, multimode fiber is used for shorter-distance applications and single-mode fiber for longer distances.

10. C. Standards limit UTP to a mere 100 meters. Different fiber-optic types have different maximum lengths, but fiber-optic is the only cable type that can extend well beyond 100 meters.

11. B, D, E. There are many different types of fiber-optic connectors. SC, ST, LC, and MT-RJ are some of the more typical connectors in use today.

12. B. To connect two devices for voice on a vertical connect, the minimum cable you can use is Category 5.

13. B. In half-duplex communication, a device can either send communication or receive communication, but it cannot do both at the same time.

14. B. Fiber-optic cable transmits only light (not electricity like UTP), so EMI has zero effect on it.

15. C. Full-duplex communication requires a point-to-point configuration between two directly connected devices because the collision-avoidance circuit is disabled.

16. B. 100BaseTX utilizes only pins 1, 2, 3, and 6.

17. D. All devices that are pinned the same for transmit and receive require a crossover cable to communicate directly. The current switches can autodetect the cable type.

18. A. A T1 cable uses pairs 1 and 2, so connecting two T1 CSU/DSU devices back-to-back requires a crossover cable that swaps these pairs. Specifically, pins 1, 2, 4, and 5 are connected to 4, 5, 1, and 2, respectively.

19. D. The demarcation point, or demarc, is the point at which the operational control or ownership changes from your company to a service provider. This is often at the MDF in relation to telephone connections and the CSU/DSU in regard to WAN connections.

20. B. Fast Ethernet is 100BaseTX and this type of cable uses two pairs of wires.

Chapter 4: The Current Ethernet Specifications

1. B. On an Ethernet network, the MAC address (hardware address) is used for one host to communicate with another.

2. B. 100BaseTX uses CAT 5e and can run 200 Mbps when using full-duplex.

3. D. When one device sends a packet out on a network segment, all other devices on the same physical network segment must wait and let it be transmitted.

4. E. 10Base2 was one of the very first Ethernet network physical mediums and is a thinnet coax.

5. B, E. Option B carrier sense multiple access with collision detection (CSMA/CD) helps packets that are transmitted simultaneously from different hosts share bandwidth evenly. You might think that CSMA/CD would be the only correct answer, but always think in terms of what is the best answer out of all the options, and B and E (CSMA/CA) are both correct. The exam will never have cut-and-dry answers.

6. B. A 10GBaseSR cable can have a maximum distance of 990 feet (302 meters).

7. B. With half-duplex, you are using only one wire pair at a time, with a digital signal either transmitting or receiving.

8. A. Full-duplex Ethernet uses two pairs of wires at the same time.

9. C. A 10GBaseLR implementation can go a distance of up to 6 miles.

10. B. Double up! You can get 20 Mbps with a 10 Mbps Ethernet running full-duplex or 200 Mbps for Fast Ethernet.

11. B. Full-duplex communication cannot be used with a hub because a hub is a half-duplex single communication device. A host, switch, and router have the ability to process traffic (frames), whereas a hub is a multiport repeater.

12. B. 11000000 is 192, 10101000 is 168, 00110000 is 48, and 11110000 is 240.

13. B. In February 2011, the IEEE finally published a standard for Broadband over Power Line (BPL) called IEEE 1901; this is also referred to as Power Line Communication (PLC) or even Power Line Digital Subscriber Line (PDSL).

14. C. Nibble values are 8 + 4 + 2 + 1, giving us a maximum value of 15. If we have a decimal value of 10, that means the 8 bit and the 2 bit are turned on.

15. D. The 128, 64, 32, and 8 bits are on, so just add the values: 128 + 64 + 32 + 8 = 232.

16. B. The first 10 hexadecimal digits (0–9) are the same values as the decimal values. We already know the binary value for the number 10 is 1010—in hex, the number 10 needs to be displayed as a single character. To display double-digit numbers as a single character, we substitute letters. In our example, 10 is A.

17. C. A MAC, or hardware, address is a 48-bit (6-byte) address written in hexadecimal format.

18. A. 100BaseT and 1000BaseT both have a maximum distance of 100 meters, or 328 feet.

19. B. The FCS can detect frames in the sequence by calculating the cyclic redundancy check (CRC), which verifies that all the bits in the frame are unchanged.

20. C. The 100 means 100 Mbps. The *Base* means *baseband*, which refers to baseband technology—a signaling method for communication on the network.

Chapter 5: Networking Devices

1. E. Intrusion detection and prevention systems are not a requirement for a SOHO Internet connection.

2. C. Like a hub, a switch connects multiple segments of a network together, with one important difference. Whereas a hub sends out anything it receives on one port to all the others, a switch recognizes frame boundaries and pays attention to the destination MAC address of the incoming frame as well as the port on which it was received.

3. B. When we say segment, we mean to create multiple collision or broadcast domains. Hubs don't segment a network; they just connect network segments together. Repeaters don't segment the network; they repeat a signal and allow the distance covered to be increased. So the only correct option is B, a switch.

4. A. The primary function of a bridge is to keep traffic separated on both sides of it, breaking up collision domains.

5. A. Hubs create one collision domain and one broadcast domain.

6. B. By allowing full-duplex operation on each port, a switch provides extra bandwidth to each port.

7. C. A switch is typically just a layer 2 device segmenting the network by using MAC addresses. However, some higher-end switches can provide layer 3 services.

8. D. Remember that DHCP servers assign IP addresses to hosts. Thus, DHCP allows easier administration than providing IP information to each host by hand (called static IP addressing).

9. B. Multilayer switches (also called layer 3 switches) don't have fewer features, less bandwidth, or fewer ports than a normal switch; they just allow routing functions between subnets.

10. B. A load balancer uses a little trickery and sends incoming packets to one or more machines that are hidden behind a single IP address. Modern load-balancing routers can use different rules to make decisions about where to route traffic, which can be based on least load, fastest response times, or simply balancing requests.

11. A. DNS translates human names to IP addresses for routing your packet through the Internet. Hosts can receive the IP address of this DNS server and then resolve hostnames to IP addresses.

12. C. Routers, switches, and bridges are all devices that help break up big networks into a number of smaller ones—also known as network segmentation. Hubs don't segment networks—they just connect network segments together.

13. A. Web cache, of course! Most proxy programs provide a means to deny access to certain URLs in a block list/blacklist, thus providing content filtering, usually in corporate environments.

14. D. Options A and C aid in boosting network performance. Option B is an advantage gained when segmenting the network. So the only option left is broadcast storms. Increased traffic will increase LAN congestion.

15. B. If the DHCP server has stopped functioning, it will not hand out IP addresses to hosts that are restarted. However, the hosts that were not shut down still have IP addresses because the lease time has not expired.

16. D. A proxy server can be used to prevent external traffic from reaching your internal network directly and can also be used to filter the sites to which your users are allowed to connect.

17. C. Switches create separate collision domains but a single broadcast domain. Remember that routers provide a separate broadcast domain for each interface.

18. A. Using appliances to offload functions such as encryption, content filtering, and VPN concentration can decrease the workload of other systems and add functionality that may be present in these dedicated devices.

19. C. A DNS server uses many types of records. An A record is a hostname–to–IP address record, and a pointer record is an IP address–to–hostname record.

20. D. A proxy server can provide many functions. A proxy server can use a caching engine so repeated access requests for web information would accelerate repeated access for users, and they can also limit the availability of websites.

Chapter 6: Introduction to the Internet Protocol

1. D. SMTP resides at the Application layer of the OSI and DoD models.

2. D. HTTPS, or Secure HTTP, uses port 443 by default.

3. C. Dynamic Host Configuration Protocol (DHCP) is used to provide IP information to hosts on your network. DHCP can provide a lot of information, but the most common is IP address, subnet mask, default gateway, and DNS information.

4. B. Address Resolution Protocol (ARP) is used to find the hardware address from a known IP address.

5. B. Secure Shell (SSH) allows you to remotely administer router, switches, and even servers securely.

6. C. The problem is with DNS, which uses both TCP and UDP port 53.

7. A, B. A client that sends out a DHCP Discover message in order to receive an IP address sends out a broadcast at both layer 2 and layer 3. The layer 2 broadcast is all *F*s in hex, or FF:FF:FF:FF:FF:FF. The layer 3 broadcast is 255.255.255.255, which means all networks and all hosts. DHCP is connectionless, which means it uses User Datagram Protocol (UDP) at the Transport layer, also called the Host-to-Host layer.

8. E. Telnet uses TCP at the Transport layer with a default port number of 23.

9. C, D. Internet Control Message Protocol (ICMP) is used to send error messages through the network, but ICMP does not work alone. Every segment or ICMP payload must be encapsulated within an IP datagram (or packet).

10. B, C, D, E. SMTP, SNMP, FTP, and HTTP are connection oriented and use TCP.

11. A, C, F. DHCP, SNMP, and TFTP use UDP. SMTP, FTP, and HTTP use TCP.

12. C, D, E. Telnet, File Transfer Protocol (FTP), and Trivial FTP (TFTP) are all Application layer protocols. IP is a Network layer protocol. Transmission Control Protocol (TCP) is a Transport layer protocol.

13. C. SMTP is used by a client to send mail to its server and by that server to send mail to another server. POP3 and IMAP are used by clients to retrieve their mail from the server that stores it until it is retrieved. HTTP is only used with web-based mail services.

14. C. Remote Desktop Protocol (RDP) allows you to connect to a remote computer and run programs, as Telnet does. However, the large advantage that RDP has over Telnet is that RDP allows you to have a GUI interface connection.

15. B. Simple Network Management Protocol is typically implemented using version 3, which allows for a connection-oriented service, authentication and secure polling of network devices, and alerts and reports on network devices.

16. D. File Transfer Protocol (FTP) can be used to transfer files between two systems.

17. B. The four layers of the IP stack (also called the DoD model) are Application/Process, Host-to-Host, Internet, and Network Access. The Host-to-Host layer is equivalent to the Transport layer of the OSI model.

18. C. Network Time Protocol will ensure a consistent time across network devices on the network.

19. A. Through the use of port numbers, TCP and UDP can establish multiple sessions between the same two hosts without creating any confusion. The sessions can be between the same or different applications, such as multiple web-browsing sessions or a web-browsing session and an FTP session.

20. D. DNS uses TCP for zone exchanges between servers and UDP when a client is trying to resolve a hostname to an IP address.

Chapter 7: IP Addressing

1. D. The addresses in the range 172.16.0.0 through 172.31.255.255 are all considered private, based on RFC 1918. Use of these addresses on the Internet is prohibited so that they can be used simultaneously in different administrative domains without concern for conflict. Some experts in the industry believe these addresses are not routable, which is not true.

2. B. APIPA uses the link-local private address range of 169.254.0.0 through 169.254.255.255 and a subnet mask of 255.255.0.0.

APIPA addresses are used by DHCP clients that cannot contact a DHCP server and have no static alternate configuration. These addresses are not Internet routable and cannot, by default, be used across routers on an internetwork.

3. C. Private IP addresses are not routable over the Internet, as either source or destination addresses. Because of that fact, any entity that wishes to use such addresses internally can do so without causing conflicts with other entities and without asking permission of any registrar or service provider. Despite not being allowed on the Internet, private IP addresses are fully routable on private intranets.

4. D. The Class A range is 1 through 126 in the first octet/byte, so only option D is a valid Class A address.

5. C. The Class B range is 128 through 191 in the first octet/byte. Only option C is a valid Class B address.

6. B. If you turned on all host bits (all of the host bits are 1s), this would be a broadcast address for that network.

7. B. A Layer 2 broadcast is also referred to as a MAC address broadcast, which is in hexadecimal and is FF.FF.FF.FF.FF.FF.

8. C. A default Class C subnet mask is 255.255.255.0, which means that the first three octets, or first 24 bits, are the network number.

9. A. Packets addressed to a unicast address are delivered to a single interface. For load balancing, multiple interfaces can use the same address.

10. C. I wonder how many of you picked APIPA address as your answer? An APIPA address is 169.254.*x*.*x*. The host address in this question is a public address. Somewhat of a tricky question if you did not read carefully.

11. B. An IPv6 address is 128 bits in size.

12. B. Packets addressed to a multicast address are delivered to all interfaces identified by the multicast address, the same as in IPv4. A multicast address is also called a one-to-many address. You can tell multicast addresses in IPv6 because they always start with *FF*.

13. C. Anycast addresses identify multiple interfaces, which is the same as multicast; however, the big difference is that the anycast packet is delivered to only one address: the first one it finds defined in terms of routing distance. This address can also be called one-to-one-of-many or one-to-nearest.

14. A, C. The loopback address with IPv4 is 127.0.0.1. With IPv6, that address is ::1.

15. B, D. In order to shorten the written length of an IPv6 address, successive fields of zeros may be replaced by double colons. In trying to shorten the address further, leading zeros may also be removed. Just as with IPv4, a single device's interface can have more than one address; with IPv6 there are more types of addresses and the same rule applies. There can be link-local, global unicast, and multicast addresses all assigned to the same interface.

16. C, D. IPv4 addresses are 32 bits long and are represented in decimal format. IPv6 addresses are 128 bits long and represented in hexadecimal format.

17. D. Only option D is in the Class C range of 192 through 224. It might look wrong because there is a 255 in the address, but this is not wrong—you can have a 255 in a network address, just not in the first octet.

18. C, E. The Class A private address range is 10.0.0.0 through 10.255.255.255. The Class B private address range is 172.16.0.0 through 172.31.255.255, and the Class C private address range is 192.168.0.0 through 192.168.255.255.

19. B. This can be a hard question if you don't remember to invert the 7th bit! Always look for the 7th bit when studying for the exam. The EUI-64 autoconfiguration inserts an FF:FE in the middle of the 48-bit MAC address to create a unique IPv6 address.

20. C. Option C is a multicast address and cannot be used to address hosts.

Chapter 8: IP Subnetting, Troubleshooting IP, and Introduction to NAT

1. D. A /27 (255.255.255.224) is 3 bits on and 5 bits off. This provides 8 subnets, each with 30 hosts. Does it matter if this mask is used with a Class A, B, or C network address? Not at all. The number of host bits would never change.

2. B. Don't freak because this is a Class A. What is your subnet mask? 255.255.255.128. Regardless of the class of address, this is a block size of 128 in the fourth octet. The subnets are 0 and 128. The 0 subnet host range is 1–126, with a broadcast address of 127. The 128 subnet host range is 129–254, with a broadcast address of 255. You need a router for these two hosts to communicate because they are in different subnets.

3. C. This is a pretty simple question. A /28 is 255.255.255.240, which means that our block size is 16 in the fourth octet (0, 16, 32, 48, 64, 80, and so on). The host is in the 64 subnet.

4. F. A CIDR address of /19 is 255.255.224.0. This is a Class B address, so that is only 3 subnet bits, but it provides 13 host bits, or 8 subnets, each with 8,190 hosts.

5. C. The host ID of 10.0.37.144 with a 255.255.254.0 mask is in the 10.0.36.0 subnet (yes, you need to be able to subnet in this exam!). Do not stress that this is a Class A; what we care about is that the third octet has a block size of 2, so the next subnet is 10.0.38.0, which makes the broadcast address 10.0.37.255. The default gateway address of 10.0.38.1 is not in the same subnet as the host. Even though this is a Class A address, you still should easily be able to subnet this because you look more at the subnet mask and find your interesting octet, which is the third octet in this question. 256 − 254 = 2. Your block size is 2.

6. D. A /30, regardless of the class of address, has a 252 in the fourth octet. This means we have a block size of 4 and our subnets are 0, 4, 8, 12, 16, and so on. Address 14 is obviously in the 12 subnet.

7. D. A point-to-point link uses only two hosts. A /30, or 255.255.255.252, mask provides two hosts per subnet.

8. C. Devices with layer 3 awareness, such as routers and firewalls, are the only ones that can manipulate the IP header in support of NAT.

9. A. A /29 (255.255.255.248), regardless of the class of address, has only 3 host bits. Six hosts is the maximum number of hosts on this LAN, including the router interface.

10. C. A computer should be configured with an IP address that is unique throughout the reachable internetwork. It should be configured with a subnet mask that matches those of all other devices on its local subnet, but not necessarily one that matches the mask used on any other subnet. It should also be configured with a default gateway that matches its local router's interface IP address.

11. A. A /29 (255.255.255.248) has a block size of 8 in the fourth octet. This means the subnets are 0, 8, 16, 24, and so on. 10 is in the 8 subnet. The next subnet is 16, so 15 is the broadcast address.

12. B. A 24-bit mask, or prefix length, indicates that the entire fourth octet is used for host identification. In a special case such as this, it is simpler to visualize the all-zeros value (172.16.1.0) and the all-ones value (172.16.1.255). The highest usable address, the last one before the all-ones value, is 172.16.1.254.

13. A, E. First, if you have two hosts directly connected, as shown in the graphic, then you need a crossover cable. A straight-through cable won't work for the exam objectives. Second, the hosts have different masks, which puts them in different subnets. The easy solution is just to set both masks to 255.255.255.0 (/24).

14. A. A /25 mask is 255.255.255.128. Used with a Class B network, the third and fourth octets are used for subnetting with a total of 9 subnet bits: 8 bits in the third octet and 1 bit in the fourth octet. Because there is only 1 bit in the fourth octet, the bit is either off or on—which is a value of 0 or 128. The host in the question is in the 0 subnet, which has a broadcast address of 127 because 128 is the next subnet.

15. A. A /28 is a 255.255.255.240 mask. Let's count to the ninth subnet (we need to find the broadcast address of the eighth subnet, so we need to count to the ninth subnet). We start at 16 (remember, the question stated that we will not use subnet 0, so we start at 16, not 0): 16, 32, 48, 64, 80, 96, 112, 128, 144. The eighth subnet is 128, and the next subnet is 144, so our broadcast address of the 128 subnet is 143. This makes the host range 129–142. 142 is the last valid host.

16. C. A /28 is a 255.255.255.240 mask. The first subnet is 16 (remember that the question stated not to use subnet 0), and the next subnet is 32, so our broadcast address is 31. This makes our host range 17–30. 30 is the last valid host.

17. A. The best method here is to check the configuration of devices that were using the old router as a gateway to the rest of the internetwork. Routers do not periodically cache their configurations to servers of any sort. You might have copied the old router's configuration to a TFTP server or the like, but failing that, you will have to rebuild the configuration from scratch, which might well be much more than interface addresses. Therefore, keeping a copy of the router's current configuration somewhere other than on the router is a wise choice. Routers don't auto-configure themselves; we wouldn't want them to.

18. E. A Class B network ID with a /22 mask is 255.255.252.0, with a block size of 4 in the third octet. The network address in the question is in subnet 172.16.16.0 with a broadcast address of 172.16.19.255. Only option E has the correct subnet mask listed, and 172.16.18.255 is a valid host.

19. D, E. The router's IP address on the E0 interface is 172.16.2.1/23, which is a 255.255.254.0. This makes the third octet a block size of 2. The router's interface is in the 2.0 subnet, and the broadcast address is 3.255 because the next subnet is 4.0. The valid host range is 2.1 through 3.254. The router is using the first valid host address in the range.

20. A. Network address translation can allow up to 65,000 hosts to get onto the Internet with one IP address by using port address translation (PAT).

Chapter 9: Introduction to IP Routing

1. C. Yep, you got it. RIP, RIPv2, and EIGRP are all examples of routing protocols; RIPv3 is nonexistent.

2. C. In dynamic routing, routers update each other about all the networks they know about and place this information into the routing table. This is possible because a protocol on one router communicates with the same protocol running on neighbor routers. If changes occur in the network, a dynamic routing protocol automatically informs all routers about the event.

3. D. Dynamic routing scales well in large networks and routes are automatically added into the routing table. Static routing is done by hand, one route at a time into each router.

4. B. Media Access Control (MAC) addresses are always local on the LAN and never go through and past a router.

5. C. Routing convergence is the time required by the routing protocols to update the routing tables (forwarding tables) on all routers in the network.

6. D. The arp -a command will show the ARP cache on your host.

7. D. Hope you answered D! A router will not send a broadcast looking for the remote network—the router will discard the packet.

8. C. RIPv1 and 2 and IGRP are all distance-vector (DV) protocols. Routers using a DV protocol send all or parts of their routing table in a routing-update message at a regular interval to each of their neighbor routers.

9. C, D. Open Shortest Path First (OSPF) and Intermediate System-to-Intermediate System (IS-IS) are link-state (LS) routing protocols.

10. B. The only protocol you could select is Enhanced Interior Gateway Routing Protocol (EIGRP).

11. A. Interior Gateway Routing Protocol is a distance-vector (DV) interior gateway protocol.

12. C. Border Gateway Protocol (BGP) is the most popular choice for ISPs or really large corporations.

13. A, C. Distance-vector (DV) and link-state (LS) are the two routing protocols to remember.

14. A, D. A frame uses a local MAC address (router) to send a packet on the LAN. The frame will take the packet to either a host on the LAN or a router's interface if the packet is destined for a remote network, which would be sent to the neighbor router.

15. A. I hope you said A! Packets specifically have to be carried to a router in order to be routed through a network.

16. C. Remember that the frame changes at each hop but that the packet is never changed in any way until it reaches the destination device.

17. D. When the routing tables are complete because they include information about all networks in the internetwork, they are considered converged.

18. A. This is step 6 in the IP routing process. If the hardware address isn't in the ARP cache of the host, an ARP broadcast is sent out onto the local network to search for the hardware address.

19. C. The best answer would be to reroute traffic using a temporary static route until the maintenance is complete on the router.

20. A. You are most likely to see a Request Timed Out message when (if) a packet is lost on the way back to the originating host for an unknown error. Remember, if the error occurs because of a known issue, you are likely to see a Destination Unreachable message.

Chapter 10: Routing Protocols

1. C, D, F. RIPv1 and IGRP are true distance-vector routing protocols and can't do much, really—except build and maintain routing tables and use a lot of bandwidth! RIPv2, EIGRP, and OSPF build and maintain routing tables, but they also provide classless routing, which allows for VLSM, summarization, and discontiguous networking.

2. B, C. RIP and RIPv2 are distance-vector routing protocols. OSPF and IS-IS are link state.

3. A, D. RIP and RIPv2 are distance-vector routing protocols. OSPF and IS-IS are link state.

4. B, E. RIP and RIPv2 are distance-vector routing protocols. OSPF and IS-IS are link state. EIGRP uses qualities from both distance vector and link state to create a hybrid routing protocol. BGP can be used as an EGP and IGP, so the objectives consider BGP a hybrid routing protocol.

5. C. Dynamic routing is typically used in today's networks because it scales to larger networks and takes less administrative work.

6. F. Hot Standby Router Protocol (HSRP) is Cisco's FHRP.

7. C. Static routes may be a good solution, but remember that they are not dynamic, and if a piece of equipment goes down, new routes to remote networks will not automatically update, so OSPF is the best answer. It dynamically will update the routing tables with faster convergence than RIP.

8. C. The administrative distance (AD) is a very important parameter in a routing protocol. The lower the AD, the more trusted the route. If you have IGRP and OSPF running, by default IGRP routes would be placed in the routing table because IGRP has a lower AD of 100. OSPF has an AD of 110. RIPv1 and RIPv2 both have an AD of 120, and EIGRP is the lowest at 90.

9. B. The routing protocols that have been upgraded to advertise IPv6 routes are RIPng, OSPFv3, and EIGRPv6. IS-IS can advertise IPv6 routes as well, but no upgrade was needed for IS-IS.

10. C. Dynamic routing protocols, like RIP, EIGRP and OSPF, automatically add route updates to the routing table. Static routes must be added by hand.

11. A. The distance-vector protocols RIPv1 and RIPv2 both have a maximum hop count of 15 (remember, 16 is unreachable). IGRP and EIGRP have a hop count of 255, and OSPF doesn't have a maximum hop count.

12. B. Routing convergence time is the time for all routers to update their routing tables (forwarding tables).

13. C. BGP is used to connect autonomous systems together on the Internet because of its ability to make classless routing and summarization possible. This helps to keep routing tables smaller and more efficient at the ISP core.

14. B. RIPv1 sends broadcasts every 30 seconds and has an AD of 120. RIPv2 sends multicasts (224.0.0.9) every 30 seconds and also has an AD of 120. RIPv2 sends subnet-mask information with the route updates, which allows it to support classless networks and non-contiguous networks. RIPv2 also supports authentication between routers; RIPv1 does not.

15. A, B. Both RIPv1 and RIPv2 have an AD of 120. EIGRP has an AD of 90 and OSPF is 110.

16. C. Border Gateway Protocol (BGP) attributes include the IP address to get to the next AS (the next-hop attribute) as well as an indication of how the networks at the end of the path were introduced into BGP (the origin code attribute). The AS path information is useful to construct a graph of loop-free autonomous systems and is used to identify routing policies so that restrictions on routing behavior can be enforced based on the AS path.

17. A. RIPng, which uses port 521, has many of the same features as RIPv2: It's a distance-vector protocol; it has a max hop count of 15; and it -uses split horizon, poison reverse, and other loop-avoidance mechanisms. And it still uses multicast to send its updates too, but in IPv6, it uses FF02::9 for the transport address. For RIPv2, the multicast address was 224.0.0.9, so the address still has a 9 at the end in the new IPv6 multicast range.

18. B, C. EIGRP holds three tables in RAM: neighbor, topology, and routing. The neighbor and topology tables are built and also maintained with the use of Hello packets.

19. D. A successor route (think "successful" rather than standby or backup) is used by EIGRP to forward traffic to a destination and is stored in the routing table. It is backed up by a feasible successor route that is stored in the topology table—if one is available. Remember that all routes are in the topology table.

20. A. RIP and RIPv2 use only hop count as a metric, with a maximum of 15 hops, to find the best path to a remote network.

Chapter 11: Switching and Virtual LANs

1. D. By creating and implementing VLANs in your switched network, you can break up broadcast domains at layer 2. For hosts on different VLANs to communicate, you must have a router or layer 3 switch.

2. B, D. Hosts are connected to a switch and are members of one VLAN. This is called an access port. Trunk links connect between switches and pass information about all VLANs.

3. C. Virtual LANs break up broadcast domains in layer 2 switched internetworks.

4. C, E. Both 802.1D and 802.1w are IEEE STP versions, with 802.1w being the latest and greatest version.

5. D, E. The best answers are that the VLAN membership for the port is configured incorrectly and that STP shut down the port.

6. B, C, F. VLANs break up broadcast domains in a switched layer 2 network, which means smaller broadcast domains. They allow configuration by logical function instead of physical location and can create some security if configured correctly.

7. B. The Spanning Tree Protocol is used to stop switching loops in a switched network with redundant paths.

8. A, E. Bridges break up collision domains, which would increase the number of collision domains in a network and also make smaller collision domains.

9. C. In order to see all frames that pass through the switch and read the packets with a network analyzer, you need to enable port mirroring on the port your diagnostic host is plugged into.

10. C. Trunking allows switches to pass information about many or all VLANs configured on the switches.

11. A, C, E. Layer 2 features include address learning, forwarding and filtering of the network, and loop avoidance.

12. B. Switches break up collision domains, and routers break up broadcast domains.

13. C. With the exception of the source port, switches flood all frames that have an unknown destination address. If a device answers the frame, the switch will update the MAC address table to reflect the location of the device.

14. C. Because the source MAC address is not in the MAC address table, the switch will add the source address and the port it is connected to into the MAC address table and then forward the frame to the outgoing port.

15. D. Virtual Trunk Protocol (VTP) is a Cisco proprietary method of having a single VLAN database advertised to all other switches in your network. This allows for ease of VLAN management in a larger network. Option C is not a possible configuration, by the way; I made that up.

16. A, B. The sequence of steps for STP convergence is, by default, blocking, listening, learning, forwarding, disabled. When all ports are in either the blocking or forwarding state, STP is converged.

17. C, D. In the blocking and listening states, the MAC address table is not learning. Only in the learning and forwarding states is the MAC address table learning MAC addresses and populating the MAC address table.

18. B. Switches break up collision domains by default, but the network is still one large broadcast domain. In order to break up broadcast domains in a layer 2 switched network, you need to create virtual LANs.

19. C. If you are configuring voice VLANs, you'll want to configure quality of service (QoS) on the switch ports to provide a higher precedence to voice traffic over data traffic to improve quality of the line.

20. B. Be careful when using port mirroring/spanning on a switch because it can cause a lot of overhead on the switch and possibly crash your network. It's therefore a good idea to use this feature at strategic times and only for short periods, if possible.

Chapter 12: Wireless Networking

1. C. It is imperative that a good site survey is completed before you install your wireless network. Trying various types of antennas and their placements is the key to covering the whole wireless area.

2. C. TLS provides really good wireless security, but it's hard to implement because you need to install a certificate on your server and also on all your clients. TTLS only uses a server-side certificate.

3. C. The IEEE 802.11b and IEEE 802.11g both run in the 2.4 GHz RF range.

4. B, D. If you are running 802.11b/g frequency, then you can receive interference from microwave ovens and cordless phones.

5. D. 802.11n uses channel bonding of both the 2.4 GHz range and the 5 GHz range to get increased bandwidth of over 100 Mbps.

6. D. Bluetooth works wirelessly to connect our phones, keyboards, and so on in small areas, also known as personal area networks (PANs).

7. B. The IEEE 802.11a standard provides up to 12 non-overlapping channels, or up to 23 if you add the 802.11h standard.

8. D. The IEEE 802.11a standard provides a maximum data rate of up to 54 Mbps.

9. C. If you have a large area to cover with wireless, you need to be concerned with channel overlap.

10. B. The IEEE 802.11b standard provides a maximum data rate of up to 11 Mbps.

11. B. If everything is correctly configured on the host, then MAC filtering would stop the host from connecting to the AP. If you try to connect and can't, check the AP's settings.

12. A. The IEEE 802.11i standard replaced Wired Equivalent Privacy (WEP) with a specific mode of the Advanced Encryption Standard (AES) known as the Counter Mode Cipher Block Chaining-Message Authentication Code (CBC-MAC) protocol. This allows AES-Counter Mode CBC-MAC Protocol (AES-CCMP) to provide both data confidentiality (encryption) and data integrity.

13. C. If you disable SSID broadcasting, which you should, then you must configure the SSID name on the clients that need to connect to the AP.

14. B. The IEEE 802.11b standard uses direct-sequence spread spectrum (DSSS). If you are running 802.11g, it uses orthogonal frequency-division multiplexing (OFDM).

15. B. If you are running an extended service set (meaning more than one AP with the same SSID), you need to overlap the cell coverage by 10 percent or more so clients will not drop out while roaming.

16. B. You need to use directional antennas, like a Yagi, to get the best signal between antennas.

17. A. Extended service set ID means that you have more than one access point, they all are set to the same SSID, and they are all connected together in the same VLAN or distribution system so users can roam.

18. D. WPA is cool because it is easy to configure and works great. Type in a passphrase (assuming you're using a pre-shared key) and you're done. Plus, you have great security because the keys change dynamically.

19. C. 802.11n uses two 20 MHz wide channels to create a 40 MHz wide channel, which provides over 100 Mbps wireless.

20. B. 802.11n MIMO sends multiple frames by several antennas over several paths. The frames are then recombined by another set of antennas to optimize throughput and multipath resistance. This is called spatial multiplexing.

Chapter 13: Using Statistics and Sensors to Ensure Network Availability

1. B. Four nines means 99.99 percent of the time.

2. C. Commonly used NetFlow flows include the following identifiers: source IP address, destination IP address, source port number, destination port number, layer 3 protocol field, Type of Service (ToS) marking, and input logical interface.

3. C. NetFlow statistics can analyze the traffic on your network by showing the major users of the network, meaning top talkers, top listeners, top protocols, and so on.

4. A. In networking, a baseline can refer to the standard level of performance of a certain device or to the normal operating capacity for your whole network.

5. B. When possible, server rooms and data centers should be located on upper floors. If not, raised floors should be deployed to help prevent water from reaching the equipment.

6. C. Putting a UPS in bypass mode removes the UPS from between the device and the wall output conceptually, without disconnecting it.

7. D. The capacity value assumes that all the attached devices are pulling the maximum amount of power, which they rarely do. As a rule of thumb, if you multiply the VA times .6, you will get a rough estimate of the maximum load your UPS may undergo at any particular time.

8. A. In most cases the software that came with the UPS will have the ability to report the current expected runtime based on the current state of the battery.

9. B. Many of today's enterprise-level UPS systems offer the ability to shut down a server to which they are attached when the power is lost. A proper shutdown is called a graceful shutdown.

10. D. Capacity is the maximum amount of power the UPS can supply at any moment in time. So if it has a capacity of 650 volt amperes (VA) and you attempt to pull 800 VA from the UPS, it will probably shut itself down.

11. C. Uninterruptable power supplies (UPSs) are designed to only provide short-term power to the devices, that is, a length of time sufficient to allow someone to gracefully shut down the devices.

12. B. High humidity cannot be tolerated because it leads to corrosion of electrical parts followed by shorts and other failures.

13. D. Low humidity sounds good on paper, but with it comes static electricity buildup in the air, which can fry computer parts if it reaches them.

14. A. Overheating causes system reboots and failures.

15. C. If it is too damp, connections start corroding and shorts begin to occur. A humidifying system should be used to maintain the level above 50 percent.

16. B. A failed encapsulation error message indicates that the router has a layer 3 packet to forward and is lacking some element of the layer 2 header that it needs to be able to forward the packet toward the next hop.

17. A. Giants are packets that are discarded because they exceed the maximum packet size of the medium.

18. C. Using a cable that is too long can result in late collisions rather than runts and giants.

19. D. CRC errors mean that packets have been damaged. This can be caused by a faulty port on the device or a bad Ethernet cable.

20. A. If you have a duplex mismatch, a telling sign is that the late collision counter will increment.

Chapter 14: Organizational Documents and Policies

1. C. For every policy on your network, there should be a credible related procedure that clearly dictates the steps to take in order to fulfill it.

2. C. Those making the changes should be completely briefed in these rollback procedures, and they should exhibit a clear understanding of them prior to implementing the changes.

3. B. A maintenance window is an amount of time a system will be down or unavailable during the implementation of changes.

4. B. An access control vestibule is an access control solution, not a device hardening technique.

5. D. Authentication period controls how long a user can remain logged in. If a user remains logged in for the specified period without activity, the user will be automatically logged out.

6. A. Bring your qwn device (BYOD) initiatives can be successful if implemented correctly. The key is to implement control over these personal mobile devices that leave the safety of your network and return later after potentially being exposed to environments that are out of your control.

7. C. Data loss prevention (DLP) software attempts to prevent data leakage. It does this by maintaining awareness of actions that can and cannot be taken with respect to a document.

8. B. The main distribution frame (MDF) connects equipment (inside plant) to cables and subscriber carrier equipment (outside plant). It also terminates cables that run to intermediate distribution frames (IDFs) distributed throughout the facility.

9. B. Verifying optimal distances between prospective AP locations is part of the Predeployment Site Survey step.

10. D. For networks and networked devices, baselines include information about four key components: processor, memory, hard-disk (or other storage) subsystem, and wired/wireless utilization.

Chapter 15: High Availability and Disaster Recovery

1. B. Backing up the system state backs up only the configuration of the server and not the data.

2. C. An RPO is a measurement of time from a failure, disaster, or comparable loss-causing event. RPOs measure back in time to when your data was preserved in a usable format, usually to the most recent backup.

3. B. Virtual Router Redundancy Protocol (VRRP) is an IEEE standard (RFC 2338) for router redundancy; Hot Standby Router Protocol (HSRP) is a Cisco proprietary protocol.

4. B. The hello timer is the defined interval during which each of the routers send out Hello messages. Their default interval is 3 seconds, and they identify the state that each router is in.

5. A. The last 8 bits (0a) are the only variable bits and represent the HSRP group number that you assign. In this case, the group number is 10 and converted to hexadecimal when placed in the MAC address, where it becomes the 0a that you see.

6. C. With three servers in an active/passive configuration with two on standby, only one is doing work. Therefore, it does not provide load balancing, only fault tolerance.

7. B. A cloud recovery site is an extension of the cloud backup services that have developed over the years. These are sites that while mimicking your on-premises network are totally virtual.

8. A. Deluge systems allow large amounts of water to be released into the room, which obviously makes this not a good choice where computing equipment will be located.

9. A. First-hop redundancy protocols (FHRPs) work by giving you a way to configure more than one physical router to appear as if they were only a single logical one. This makes client configuration and communication easier because you can simply configure a single default gateway and the host machine can use its standard protocols to communicate.

10. A. Switch stacking is the process of connecting multiple switches together (usually in a stack) that are managed as a single switch.

Chapter 16: Common Security Concepts

1. B. Role-based access control prescribes creating roles or sets of permissions required for various job roles and assigning those permissions to security groups. When a new employee is assigned that role, they are simply placed in the group and thus inherit all required permissions.

2. A. This concept prescribes that users should be given access only to resources required to do their job. So if Ralph's job only requires read permission to the Sales folder, that's all he should get even if you know he's completely trustworthy.

3. D. An exploit occurs when a threat agent takes advantage of a vulnerability and uses it to advance an attack. When a network attack takes advantage of a vulnerability, it is somewhat of an indictment of the network team as most vulnerabilities can be identified and mitigated.

4. B. This condition is known as a zero-day attack because it is the first day the virus has been released and therefore no known fix exists. This term may also be applied to an operating system bug that has not been corrected.

5. C. Common Vulnerabilities and Exposures (CVE)is a database of known vulnerabilities using this classification system. It is maintained by the MITRE Corporation and each entry describes a vulnerability in detail, using a number and letter system to describe what it endangers, the environment it requires to be successful, and in many cases, the proper mitigation.

6. A. An accidental file deletion by an employee is an example of an internal threat.

7. D. To ensure confidentiality, you must prevent the disclosure of data or information to unauthorized entities.

8. D. The Zero Trust concept supports least privilege. It prescribes that when a resource is created, the default permission should be No Access. It also means that when ACLs are configured on routers, all traffic should be blocked by default and only specific traffic allowed.

9. A. A defense-in-depth strategy refers to the practice of using multiple layers of security between data and the resources on which it resides and possible attackers.

10. A. Network Access Control (NAC) systems examine the state of a computer's operating system updates and antimalware updates before allowing access, and in some cases they can even remediate the devices prior to permitting access.

Chapter 17: Common Types of Attacks

1. C. Shoulder surfing is not a technology-based attack. It is a social engineering attack.

2. A. The command and control server is used to control the zombies in a botnet, which is a part of a DDoS attack.

3. B. Here's how a smurf attack works: The bad guy spoofs the intended victim's IP address and then sends a large number of pings (IP echo requests) to IP broadcast addresses. The receiving router responds by delivering the broadcast to all hosts in the subnet, and all the hosts respond with an IP echo reply—all of them at the same time.

4. D. In the SYN flood, the attacker sends a SYN, the victim sends back a SYN-ACK, and the attacker leaves the victim waiting for the final ACK. While the server is waiting for the response, a small part of memory is reserved for it. As the SYNs continue to arrive, memory is gradually consumed.

5. B. The attackers use the `monlist` command, a remote command in older versions of NTP, that sends the requester a list of the last 600 hosts who have connected to that server. This attack can be prevented by using at least NTP version 4.2.7 (which was released in 2010).

6. B. A man-in-the-middle attack (also known as an on-path attack) happens when someone intercepts packets intended for one computer and reads the data.

7. A. A VLAN hopping attack results in traffic from one VLAN being sent to the wrong VLAN. Normally, this is prevented by the trunking protocol placing a VLAN tag in the packet to identify the VLAN to which the traffic belongs. The attacker can circumvent this by a process called double tagging, which is placing a fake VLAN tag into the packet along with the real tag. When the frame goes through multiple switches, the real tag is taken off by the first switch, leaving the fake tag. When the frame reaches the second switch, the fake tag is read and the frame is sent to the VLAN to which the hacker intended the frame to go.

8. B. ARP spoofing is the process of adopting another system's MAC address for the purpose of receiving data meant for that system. It usually also entails ARP cache poisoning.

9. A. These are APs that have been connected to your wired infrastructure without your knowledge. The rogue may have been placed there by a determined hacker who snuck into your facility and put it in an out-of-the-way location or, more innocently, by an employee who just wants wireless access and doesn't get just how dangerous doing this is.

10. C. This ugly trick is achieved by placing their AP on a different channel from your legitimate APs and then setting its SSID in accordance with your SSID.

Chapter 18: Network Hardening Techniques

1. A. A captive portal web page may ask for network credentials, or in the case of a guest network, it may only ask for agreement to the usage policy of the guest network.

2. B. Geofencing is the process of defining the area in which an operation can be performed by using a global positioning system (GPS) or radio frequency identification (RFID) to define a geographic boundary.

3. **C.** IoT devices are easy recruits to a botnet, which is a group of systems that an attacker controls and directs to foist a DoS attack.

4. **D.** When enabled, guest network isolation creates two networks in one. One, the guest network, has client isolation in effect and has access only to the Internet. The second serves as the regular WLAN.

5. **A.** When you need to reshape the cell, you use antennas to accomplish this. For example, you may want to send the signal down a long hallway while not transmitting outside the hallway into the parking lot. That could be done with a directional antenna.

6. **B.** All MAC layer information must be sent in the clear—anyone equipped with a free wireless sniffer can just read the client packets sent to the access point and spoof their MAC address.

7. **C.** Using this approach, all traffic is denied unless it is specifically allowed by a rule. This is also called whitelisting or allow listing in that you are creating a whitelist or allow list of allowed traffic with the denial of all other traffic.

8. **A.** Role-based access control (RBAC) is commonly used in networks to simplify the process of assigning new users the permissions required to perform a job role. In this arrangement, users are organized by job role into security groups, which are then granted the rights and permissions required to perform that job.

9. **A.** You should not deny all public addresses. That would prevent all traffic from the Internet. When configuring ACLs between the Internet and your private network to mitigate security problems, it's a good idea to include these four conditions:
   - Deny any addresses from your internal networks.
   - Deny any local host addresses (127.0.0.0/8).
   - Deny any reserved private addresses.
   - Deny any addresses in the IP multicast address range (224.0.0.0/4).

10. **B.** You should always start your search on the website of the manufacturer. Drivers found elsewhere may be problematic and, in some cases, may introduce malware.

Chapter 19: Remote Access Security

1. **B.** Out-of-band management refers to any method of managing the server that does use the network. An example of this technology is Integrated Lights-Out, or iLO, a technology embedded into HP servers that allows for out-of-band management of the server.

2. **B.** The most effective way to control both authentication of remote users and the application of their permissions is to provision an AAA server, which can be either RADIUS or TACACS+.

3. B. A virtual desktop requires less computing power, especially if the applications are also delivered virtually and those applications are running in a VM in the cloud rather than in the local desktop eating up local resources.

4. C. VNC includes the following components:

    ▪ VNC server: Software that runs on the machine, sharing its screen

    ▪ VNC client (or viewer): Software on the machine that is remotely receiving the shared screen

    ▪ VNC protocol (RDP)

5. B. Secure Shell (SSH) creates a secure channel between the devices and provides confidentiality and integrity of the data transmission. It uses public-key cryptography to authenticate the remote computer and allow the remote computer to authenticate the user, if necessary.

6. B. You don't need to use a VPN. Using the SSL channel, RDP Gateway can tunnel directly to the remote server to increase the security of RDS.

7. B. Microsoft began calling all terminal services products Remote Desktop with Windows Server 2008 R2.

8. C. Remote Desktop Protocol (RDP) is a proprietary protocol developed by Microsoft. It allows you to connect to another computer and run programs. RDP operates somewhat like Telnet, except instead of getting a command-line prompt as you do with Telnet, you get the actual graphical user interface (GUI) of the remote computer.

9. D. A remote desktop connection gives one access to the desktop. SSH does not do that.

10. A. When a client-to-site VPN is created, it is possible to do so in two ways, split tunnel and full tunnel. The difference is whether the user use the VPN for connecting to the Internet as well as for connecting to the office.

Chapter 20: Physical Security

1. D. Training is considered a prevention method.

2. A. Passive infrared (PIR) systems operate by identifying changes in heat waves in an area. Because the presence of an intruder would raise the temperature of the surrounding air particles, the system alerts or sounds an alarm when this occurs.

3. B. These devices emit a magnetic field and monitor it. If the field is disrupted, which will occur when a person enters the area, the alarm will sound.

4. C. Tamper detection refers to any method that alerts you when a device or the enclosure in which it resides has been opened or an attempt has been made to open it. Another good example is chassis intrusion detection.

5. C. Security awareness training educates users about social engineering techniques and makes them less prone to fall for these attacks.

6. A. Biometric systems are designed to operate using characteristic and behavioral factors. While knowledge factors (password, PIN, or something you know) are the most common authentication factors used, characteristic factors represent something you are (fingerprint, iris scan), while behavioral factors represent something you do (signature analysis).

7. D. Multifactor required at least two factors of authentication derived from two different categories of factors. A USB fob and a smart card are both possession factors (something you have).

8. A. One of the issues with biometrics is the occurrence of false positives and false negatives. A false positive is when a user that should not be allowed access is indeed allowed access. A false negative, on the other hand, is when an authorized individual is denied passage by mistake.

9. B. An access control vestibule (previously known as a mantrap) is used to control access to the vestibule of a building. It is a series of two doors with a small room between them. The user is authenticated at the first door and then allowed into the room. At that point, additional verification will occur (such as a guard visually identifying the person) and then they are allowed through the second door.

10. B. Smart lockers include a new storage locker option born in the last decade. A smart lock is an electromechanical lock that is designed to perform locking and unlocking operations on a door when it receives such instructions from an authorized device using a wireless protocol and a cryptographic key to execute the authorization process. With smart locks, lockers can be assigned on-the-fly, reset, audited, and reassigned using simple desktop or mobile software.

Chapter 21: Data Center Architecture and Cloud Concepts

1. D. The core layer provides high-speed interconnections, the aggregation/distribution layer provides services and access switch connectivity, and the access layer is where devices such as servers connect to the network.

2. B. Straight-through cables, known as drop cables or patch cables will have the pins in the same order on both connectors.

3. B. On a crossover cable, one connector has flipped the wires. Specifically, pins 1 and 3 get switched as well as pins 2 and 6.

4. C. If you are going to make your own UTP cables (drop/patch cables) to customize length, you need to make sure that the right wires get to the right pins.

5. D. North-South data flow is traffic that remains in the data center between devices such as servers or storage systems.

6. C. Policies govern how the network is configured and operated as well as how people are expected to behave on the network, such as how users are able to access resources and which types of employees get network access.

7. B. A physical network diagram contains all the physical devices and connectivity paths on your network and should accurately picture how your network physically fits together in detail. This document will also have the firmware revisions on all the switches and access points in your network.

8. B. The software-defined networking controller provides the control plane for a SDN-based switching fabric.

9. B. Network monitoring can have several names, including load testing, connectivity testing, and throughput testing. You will also hear network monitors referred to as protocol analyzers.

10. C. The practice of creating infrastructure definitions in software is called Infrastructure as Code.

11. A. Those making the changes should be completely briefed in rollback procedures, and they should exhibit a clear understanding of them prior to implementing the changes.

12. B, C, D. You need to update the network configuration document.

13. B. There are many different service type offerings from the cloud providers, IaaS, or Infrastructure as a Service, is when the cloud vendor provides the hardware platform, and the company installs and manages its own operating systems.

14. B. If you add a new cable segment to the network, you need to update the wiring schematics document.

15. C. Machine to machine configuration interfaces are called application programming interfaces (APIs), and used to communicate with each other instead of human-based interfaces such as a GUI or the command line.

16. C. Multitenant clouds offer isolated space in the data centers to run services such as compute, storage, and databases. Think of this as your own private data center in the cloud.

17. A, C, D. Common cloud interconnect methods include Internet, VPN, and Direct Connect.

18. A, B, C, D. There are many bandwidth-intensive programs, like VoIP and video streaming. These are just a few of the reasons it's necessary to try to optimize network performance.

19. C. *Voice over Internet Protocol (VoIP)* is a general term that describes several technologies that are able to deliver voice communications over the Internet or other data networks.

20. B. A Type 2 hypervisor runs within a conventional operating system environment. With the hypervisor layer as a distinct second software level, guest operating systems run at the third level above the hardware.

Chapter 22: Ensuring Network Availability

1. C. The NetFlow standard provides session information including the source and destination addresses, applications, and traffic volume.

2. D. The Simple Network Management Protocol (SNMP) uses organizational identifiers (OIDs) and management information bases (MIBs) for the collection and organization of data.

3. B. An Ethernet frame below that standard size of 64 bytes is a runt.

4. C. Data traffic that transmits and receives in only one direction at a time is referred to as half-duplex.

5. D. A measurement is taken from network gear and servers to determine what is considered to be normal operations of a system.

6. A, C. When a system uses all available memory or CPU resources, it may become very unstable and fail. Devices must have available memory and CPU capacity available to be able to function.

7. C. A cyclic redundancy check, or CRC, is a mathematical calculation of a frame of data that is sent to the remote device where it is also calculated and compared to calculation it received. If the values match, the frame was error free.

8. D. The Simple Network Management Protocol (SNMP) is an application and protocol used to collect operational data from network devices.

9. A. An encapsulation error occurs when a software process fails to add or remove header data to a data frame.

10. A, C. Data centers monitor the temperature and humidity to ensure they are in safe operating ranges to protect the equipment and to make sure they are within their heat and humidity specifications.

11. E. A baseline can be taken on any metric that is considered to be critical for operations.

12. B, C. Utilization metrics include tracking both the uptime and downtime of applications, servers, and networking gear.

13. A. High availability is an architecture that enhances a device's ability to operate even if a component or software process fails.

14. A. Traffic that flows in both directions simultaneously is referred to as full-duplex.

15. A. The emergency syslog severity level is the most critical and means that a system may be down or unusable.

16. C. The syslog protocol provides a record of system events and is helpful in reviewing events over time.

17. C. SNMP version 2c added support for GET BULK, which greatly reduced network traffic. Instead of a network management station requesting objects one at a time, GET BULK allows for multiple objects to be fetched in one request.

18. A. When data arrives with delays that increase and decrease, there is jitter along the transmission path. This is very detrimental to jitter-sensitive applications such as voice and video.

19. C. Latency is the measurement of end-to-end delay.

20. A, D. Both high memory and CPU utilization can cause network equipment such as routers and switches to not have available resources to operate and they may therefore fail or reload.

Chapter 23: Cable Connectivity Issues and Tools

1. A, B, C. Yep, all of the above. The CompTIA Network+ objectives cover all three in regard to tools used to analyze today's networks.

2. C. The basic purpose of packet sniffers or network analyzers is to collect and analyze each individual packet that is captured on a specific network segment to determine whether problems are happening. You can also use them to see if there is too much traffic on a segment.

3. A. A toner probe sends a signal down a pair of wires so that the wires can be traced. Typically, a butt set is used to find this signal, but toner probe is the best answer to this question.

4. B. An optical time-domain reflectometer (OTDR) is an optoelectronic instrument used to give you the skinny on optical fibers. It works by putting out a series of optical pulses into the specific fiber you want to test and can tell you if a break in the fiber has occurred and where.

5. B. To create a patch cable (568A) to connect your host to a jack in the wall, you need to use a snip.

6. B. End-to-end loss is referred to as attenuation. If the loss is too great across a cable, the received signal may be too weak to be demodulated.

7. C. Hope you answered C! A port scanner is just a piece of software designed to search a network for open ports. Administrators of networks use port scanners to ensure security and bad guys use them to compromise it.

8. D. Wire-map testers are used to determine the cable pinouts from one end of a cable to the other. It can also identify open pins and shorts. By using a wire-map tester on an Ethernet cable, you can verify the cable is pinned correctly and has no open or shorted connections.

9. B. A time-domain reflectometer gives you very detailed information on the cable under test. It measures delay across the wire, and if there is a break in the cable, it can give you the approximate distance to where the break is.

10. B. A certifier connects to a cable and runs a bank of tests that can verify whether it meets the standards set by organizations such as ISO or TIA.

11. D. A packet sniffer captures and analyzes Ethernet frames on a network. The sniffer can be used for detailed troubleshooting of transmit and receive traffic on a LAN from the frame level to the Application layer.

12. C. A time-domain reflectometer is used to test Physical layer properties of a cable such as impedance characteristics, delay, cable lengths, splices, and cable breaks. It does not see application-level information such as unused services or any LAN information.

13. A. The trusty multimeter can be used to measure AC and DC levels and resistance.

14. D. A toner probe allows you to identify a cable that may be in a large bundle and hard to trace. At the remote end, a tone generator is attached to the cable and then at the probe can be used to find the cable at the other end.

15. A. Just as it is named, a punch-down tool is used to "punch" a wire into a cable block. Crimpers are used to put a jack onto the end of a cable, and snips and strippers are used to prepare the cable.

16. B. A crimper is the tool you would use to seat a RJ-45 connector to the end of a cable. Punch-down tools terminate a wire onto a cable block; snips and strippers are used to prepare the cable for the crimper operation.

17. C. Both 66 and 110 blocks are used for mass termination of wires. To insert the wire into the block connectors, you would use a punch-down tool.

18. D. To measure AC power levels to make sure they are within specifications, a surge protector is used. They can also mitigate overvoltage conditions to protect the connected equipment.

19. B. By using a loopback plug, you can connect the transmit signals to the receiver and test the condition of the connected port.

20. A. This is indication that when you plugged in the switch you exceeded the voltage available in the rack as all of the other equipment began to have issues.

Chapter 24: Network Troubleshooting Methodology

1. A, F. Rebooting servers and routers are not part of the troubleshooting model.

2. B. You need to check basic connectivity. The link light indicates that the network card is making a basic-level connection to the rest of the network. It is a very easy item to check, and if the link light is not lit, it is usually a very simple fix (like plugging in an unplugged cable).

3. B. When wireless users complain that the network is slow (latency) or that they are losing their connection to applications during a session, it is usually latency arising from a capacity issue.

4. B. Although all of these are good tests for network connectivity, checking the server console for user connections will tell you whether other users are able to log into the server. If they can, the problem is most likely related to one of those users' workstations. If they can't, the problem is either the server or network connection. This helps narrow down the problem.

5. B. Because of all the tests given and their results, you can narrow the problem down to the network connectivity of that workstation. And because no other users in this user's area are having the same problem, it can't be the hub or server. You can log in as the user from your workstation, so you know it isn't a rights issue or username/password issue. The only possible answer listed is a bad patch cable.

6. A. Because other users in the same area aren't having a problem, it can't be a downed server, network hub, or jabbering NIC. And because both you and the user can't log in, more than likely it's a problem specific to that workstation. The only one that would affect your ability to log in from that station is the Caps Lock key being pressed. That will cause the password to be in all uppercase (which most server operating systems treat as a different password), and thus it will probably be rejected.

7. D. Since this is a new connection, you need to start by troubleshooting and identify the symptoms and potential causes.

8. B. According to the Network+ troubleshooting model, the next step would be step 2, establishing the most probable cause.

9. C. After determining the affected area, you need to find out if any changes have taken place.

10. A. Because the user can't log in correctly from any machine, more than likely he is using the wrong procedure for logging in. Because no one else is having that problem (including yourself), the problem must be related to that user.

11. C. After you have implemented a solution, you need to test if the solution works and identify other effects it may have.

12. B. Because you cannot reach the web page that resides on the server, the problem is most likely related to your browser.

13. A, B, C. From a design standpoint, the physical environment for a server should be optimized for items such as placement, temperature, and humidity. When troubleshooting, don't forget to check the physical conditions under which the network device is operating. Check for problems such as those mentioned here as well as EMI/RFI problems, power problems, and unplugged cables.

14. D. Because most of today's networks still consist of large amounts of copper cable, networks can suffer from the physical issues that have plagued all networks since the very beginning of networking (and the answers here are not a complete list). Newer technologies and protocols have lessened these issues but have not resolved them completely.

15. A. Once you have determined that the switch or the configuration of the switch is the problem, you need to escalate the issue.

16. D. Because other people are experiencing the problem, most likely it is either network or server related. Because you can transfer files to and from another server, it can't be the network. Thus, the problem is related to the web server.

17. D. After investigating the problem thoroughly and successfully testing and resolving an issue, you need to document the solution.

18. B. Since users can get to the Internet, this means the DNS server is working and they have the correct default gateway. The intranet server is probably down.

19. C. Performance-monitoring tools can give you an idea of how busy the server and the rest of the network are. These tools use graphs to indicate how much traffic is going through the server.

20. C. Once you escalate the problem, you are done with the seven-step model. Meet with the escalation team to determine the next step.

Chapter 25: Network Software Tools and Commands

1. C. The program Packet Internet Groper (`ping`) is used to find out if a host has the IP stack initialized.

2. A. The `arp` utility is used to display the contents of the ARP cache, which tracks the resolution of IP addresses to physical (MAC) addresses and will produce the displayed output.

3. A. Microsoft has made what it calls Remote Desktop software available for free with Windows products since Windows NT. When this software is installed (installed by default in later versions) on both source and destination computers, a remote desktop connection can be made.

4. B. The purpose of the `ping` utility is to test the communications channel between two IP hosts as well as how long it takes the packets to get from one host to another.

5. C. The `ipconfig /all` utility will display the current configuration of TCP/IP on a given workstation—including the current IP address, DNS configuration, WINS configuration, and default gateway.

6. B, D. The address 127.0.0.1 is the special IP address designated for the local TCP/IP interface. The hostname localhost is the hostname given to the local interface. Therefore, pinging either the IP address or the hostname for the local interface will tell you whether the local interface is working.

7. C. The command `ip` was added to most Linux distributions and is replacing the depreciated `ifconfig` command.

8. C. The `arp` utility will show you the resolved MAC to IP address of all hosts on your network segment. Remember, this will work for only local hosts, not remote hosts.

9. A. Theo `netstat -a` command will display all connections and listening ports on the host computer. Remember that the `-a` must be lowercase and that it will not work correctly without the hyphen before it.

10. B. Commercial sniffers like Wireshark and Omnipeek can capture any packets because they set the NIC to operate in promiscuous mode, which means the NIC processes all packets that it sees.

11. B. The `tracert` utility will give you that output. The `tracert` command (or `trace` for short) traces the route from the source IP host to the destination host.

12. C. The `tracert` utility will tell you which router is having the performance problem and how long it takes to move between each host. `Tracert` can be used to locate problem areas in a network.

13. A. The `ipconfig /all` switch will display the most complete listing of TCP/IP configuration information, also displaying the MAC address, DHCP lease times, and the DNS addresses.

14. C. The `tracert` utility returns the names and addresses of all routers through which a packet passes on its way to a destination host.

15. E. The `telnet` utility can be used to test if a particular IP host is responding on a particular TCP port by running the `telnet` command and specifying a port number.

16. C. The `arp -a` command will display the current contents of the ARP cache on the local workstation.

17. C. `dig` is an old Unix command that will show you DNS server information.

18. A, D. The `arp` utility's –a and –g switches perform the same function. They both show the current ARP cache.

19. B. There are three different chain types:

Input: Controls behavior for incoming connections

Forward: Used for incoming connections that aren't being delivered locally (like a router would receive)

Output: Used for outgoing connections

20. A. To capture traffic on all interfaces, use the `any` keyword with the `-i` (interface) switch.

Appendix C

Subnetting Class A

Class A subnetting is not performed any differently than sub-netting with Classes B and C, but there are 24 bits to play with instead of the 16 in a Class B address and the 8 in a Class C address.

Let's start by listing all the Class A masks:

255.0.0.0	(/8)	255.255.240.0	(/20)
255.128.0.0	(/9)	255.255.248.0	(/21)
255.192.0.0	(/10)	255.255.252.0	(/22)
255.224.0.0	(/11)	255.255.254.0	(/23)
255.240.0.0	(/12)	255.255.255.0	(/24)
255.248.0.0	(/13)	255.255.255.128	(/25)
255.252.0.0	(/14)	255.255.255.192	(/26)
255.254.0.0	(/15)	255.255.255.224	(/27)
255.255.0.0	(/16)	255.255.255.240	(/28)
255.255.128.0	(/17)	255.255.255.248	(/29)
255.255.192.0	(/18)	255.255.255.252	(/30)
255.255.224.0	(/19)		

That's it. You must leave at least 2 bits for defining hosts. And I hope you can see the pattern by now. Remember, we're going to do this the same way as a Class B or C subnet. It's just that, again, we simply have more host bits, and we use the same subnet numbers we used with Class B and Class C, but we start using these numbers in the second octet.

Subnetting Practice Examples: Class A Addresses

When you look at an IP address and a subnet mask, you must be able to distinguish the bits used for subnets from the bits used for determining hosts. This is imperative. If you're still struggling with this concept, please reread Chapter 6, "Introduction to the Internet Protocol." It shows you how to determine the difference between the subnet and host bits and should help clear things up.

Practice Example #1A: 255.255.0.0 (/16)

Class A addresses use a default mask of 255.0.0.0, which leaves 22 bits for subnetting since you must leave 2 bits for host addressing. The 255.255.0.0 mask with a Class A address is using 8 subnet bits.

- *Subnets?* $2^8 = 256$.
- *Hosts?* $2^{16} - 2 = 65,534$.
- *Valid subnets?* What is the interesting octet? $256 - 255 = 1$. 0, 1, 2, 3, etc. (all in the second octet). The subnets would be 10.0.0.0, 10.1.0.0, 10.2.0.0, 10.3.0.0, etc., up to 10.255.0.0.
- *Broadcast address for each subnet?*
- *Valid hosts?*

The following table shows the first two and last two subnets, valid host range, and broadcast addresses for the private Class A 10.0.0.0 network:

Subnet	10.0.0.0	10.1.0.0	. . .	10.254.0.0	10.255.0.0
First host	10.0.0.1	10.1.0.1	. . .	10.254.0.1	10.255.0.1
Last host	10.0.255.254	10.1.255.254	. . .	10.254.255.254	10.255.255.254
Broadcast	10.0.255.255	10.1.255.255	. . .	10.254.255.255	10.255.255.255

Practice Example #2A: 255.255.240.0 (/20)

255.255.240.0 gives us 12 bits of subnetting and leaves us 12 bits for host addressing.

- *Subnets?* $2^{12} = 4096$.
- *Hosts?* $2^{12} - 2 = 4094$.
- *Valid subnets?* What is your interesting octet? $256 - 240 = 16$. The subnets in the second octet are a block size of 1 and the subnets in the third octet are 0, 16, 32, etc.
- *Broadcast address for each subnet?*
- *Valid hosts?*

The following table shows some examples of the host ranges—the first three and the last subnets:

Subnet	10.0.0.0	10.0.16.0	10.0.32.0	. . .	10.255.240.0
First host	10.0.0.1	10.0.16.1	10.0.32.1	. . .	10.255.240.1
Last host	10.0.15.254	10.0.31.254	10.0.47.254	. . .	10.255.255.254
Broadcast	10.0.15.255	10.0.31.255	10.0.47.255	. . .	10.255.255.255

Practice Example #3A: 255.255.255.192 (/26)

Let's do one more example using the second, third, and fourth octets for subnetting.

- *Subnets?* 2^{18} = 262,144.
- *Hosts?* $2^6 - 2$ = 62.
- *Valid subnets?* In the second and third octet, the block size is 1, and in the fourth octet, the block size is 64.
- *Broadcast address for each subnet?*
- *Valid hosts?*

The following table shows the first four subnets and their valid hosts and broadcast addresses in the Class A 255.255.255.192 mask:

Subnet	10.0.0.0	10.0.0.64	10.0.0.128	10.0.0.192
First host	10.0.0.1	10.0.0.65	10.0.0.129	10.0.0.193
Last host	10.0.0.62	10.0.0.126	10.0.0.190	10.0.0.254
Broadcast	10.0.0.63	10.0.0.127	10.0.0.191	10.0.0.255

The following table shows the last four subnets and their valid hosts and broadcast addresses:

Subnet	10.255.255.0	10.255.255.64	10.255.255.128	10.255.255.192
First host	10.255.255.1	10.255.255.65	10.255.255.129	10.255.255.193
Last host	10.255.255.62	10.255.255.126	10.255.255.190	10.255.255.254
Broadcast	10.255.255.63	10.255.255.127	10.255.255.191	10.255.255.255

Subnetting in Your Head: Class A Addresses

This sounds hard, but as with Class C and Class B, the numbers are the same; we just start in the second octet. What makes this easy? You only need to worry about the octet that has the largest block size (typically called the interesting octet; one that is something other than 0 or 255)—for example, 255.255.240.0 (/20) with a Class A network. The second octet has a block size of 1, so any number listed in that octet is a subnet. The third octet is a 240 mask, which means we have a block size of 16 in the third octet. If your host ID is 10.20.80.30, what is your subnet, broadcast address, and valid host range?

The subnet in the second octet is 20 with a block size of 1, but the third octet is in block sizes of 16, so we'll just count them out: 0, 16, 32, 48, 64, 80, 96 . . . voilà! (By the way, you can count by 16s by now, right?) This makes our subnet 10.20.80.0, with a broadcast of 10.20.95.255 because the next subnet is 10.20.96.0. The valid host range is 10.20.80.1

through 10.20.95.254. And yes, no lie! You really can do this in your head if you just get your block sizes nailed!

Okay, let's practice on one more, just for fun!

Host IP: 10.1.3.65/23

First, you can't answer this question if you don't know what a /23 is. It's 255.255.254.0. The interesting octet here is the third one: 256 – 254 = 2. Our subnets in the third octet are 0, 2, 4, 6, etc. The host in this question is in subnet 2.0, and the next subnet is 4.0, so that makes the broadcast address 3.255. And any address between 10.1.2.1 and 10.1.3.254 is considered a valid host.

Written Lab 1

Given a Class A network and the net bits identified (CIDR), complete the following table to identify the subnet mask and the number of host addresses possible for each mask.

Classful Address	Subnet Mask	Number of Hosts per Subnet (2x – 2)
/16		
/17		
/18		
/19		
/20		
/21		
/22		
/23		
/24		
/25		
/26		
/27		
/28		
/29		
/30		

Written Lab 2

Given the decimal IP address, write in the address class, number of subnet and host bits, number of subnets, and number of hosts for each IP address.

Decimal IP Address	Address Class	Number of Subnet and Host Bits	Number of Subnets (2x)	Number of Hosts (2x – 2)
10.25.66.154/23				
172.31.254.12/24				
192.168.20.123/28				
63.24.89.21/18				
128.1.1.254/20				
208.100.54.209/30				

Answers to Written Lab 1

Classful Address	Subnet Mask	Number of Hosts per Subnet (2x – 2)
/16	255.255.0.0	65,534
/17	255.255.128.0	32,766
/18	255.255.192.0	16,382
/19	255.255.224.0	8,190
/20	255.255.240.0	4,094
/21	255.255.248.0	2,046
/22	255.255.252.0	1,022

Classful Address	Subnet Mask	Number of Hosts per Subnet (2x – 2)
/23	255.255.254.0	510
/24	255.255.255.0	254
/25	255.255.255.128	126
/26	255.255.255.192	62
/27	255.255.255.224	30
/28	255.255.255.240	14
/29	255.255.255.248	6
/30	255.255.255.252	2

Answers to Written Lab 2

Decimal IP Address	Address Class	Number of Subnet and Host Bits	Number of Subnets (2x)	Number of Hosts (2x – 2)
10.25.66.154/23	A	15/9	32768	510
172.31.254.12/24	B	8/8	256	254
192.168.20.123/28	C	4/4	16	14
63.24.89.21/18	A	10/14	1,024	16,382
128.1.1.254/20	B	4/12	16	4094
208.100.54.209/30	C	6/2	64	2

Index

F

G

H

U

Y

Z

Online Test Bank

Register to gain one year of FREE access after activation to the online interactive test bank to help you study for your CompTIA Network+ certification exam—included with your purchase of this book! All of the chapter review questions and practice tests in this book are included in the online test bank so you can practice in a timed and graded setting.

Register and Access the Online Test Bank

To register your book and get access to the online test bank, follow these steps:

1. Go to www.wiley.com/go/sybextestprep.
2. Select your book from the list.
3. Complete the required registration information, including answering the security verification to prove book ownership. You will be emailed a pin code.
4. Follow the directions in the email or go to www.wiley.com/go/sybextestprep.
5. Find your book on that page and click the "Register or Login" link with it. Then enter the pin code you received and click the "Activate PIN" button.
6. On the Create an Account or Login page, enter your username and password, and click Login or, if you don't have an account already, create a new account.
7. At this point, you should be in the test bank site with your new test bank listed at the top of the page. If you do not see it there, please refresh the page or log out and log back in.